ALSO BY
DAVID GREENBERG

Republic of Spin: An Inside History
of the American Presidency

Calvin Coolidge

Nixon's Shadow:
The History of an Image

Alan Brinkley: A Life in History
(editor, with Moshik Temkin
and Mason B. Williams)

JOHN LEWIS

A LIFE

DAVID GREENBERG

SIMON & SCHUSTER
New York London Toronto
Sydney New Delhi

100 YEARS

SIMON &
SCHUSTER

1230 Avenue of the Americas
New York, NY 10020

First Simon & Schuster hardcover edition October 2024

SIMON & SCHUSTER and colophon are registered
trademarks of Simon & Schuster, LLC

Simon & Schuster: Celebrating 100 Years of Publishing in 2024

For information about special discounts for bulk purchases,
please contact Simon & Schuster Special Sales at
1-866-506-1949 or business@simonandschuster.com.

The Simon & Schuster Speakers Bureau can bring authors to
your live event. For more information or to book an event, contact
the Simon & Schuster Speakers Bureau at 1-866-248-3049
or visit our website at www.simonspeakers.com.

Interior design by Lewelin Polanco

Manufactured in the United States of America

1 3 5 7 9 10 8 6 4 2

Library of Congress Cataloging-in-Publication Data is available.

ISBN 978-1-9821-4299-5
ISBN 978-1-9821-4301-5 (ebook)

To Robert Greenberg (1934–2024),
who instilled in his children
a belief in equal rights for all;
to Suzanne, Leo, and Liza;
and to the men and women of
the civil rights movement

CONTENTS

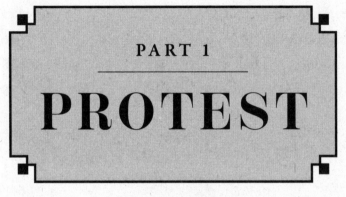

PART 1

PROTEST

1940–1968

Chapter One

THE BOY FROM TROY

■ ■

As a child, John Lewis stood out among his siblings for his love of reading. "He was always kind of a peculiar boy," his father, Eddie, said in a 1969 interview. "Now, you take a lot of times when the children would all be playing, he got some kind of book. And he would be messing with that book . . . reading, or doing something with it." One of John's sisters, Ethel Mae, known as Mimi, echoed her father's observations. "He mostly read and he loved to go to school," she said. "He'd pick up anything that he got to read. . . . Just a history book or something maybe my sister had when she was going to school." An uncle who was a school principal gave John volumes of Robert Louis Stevenson and Charles Dickens to read, along with biographies of famous Black figures like George Washington Carver and Joe Louis. Booker T. Washington was a favorite. In later years, Washington's reputation would suffer as his philosophy of Black self-improvement fell from favor among intellectuals. But Lewis remained an admirer. "After the Bible," he told a reporter in 1961, "my favorite book is *Up from Slavery*"—Washington's classic autobiography.[1]

Then there was poetry. "He had a poem" that he would recite, recalled Ethel Mae. "I don't know the name of it, but it began, 'Out of the night that covers me. . . .' When my momma and daddy would go to town or something and leave us all here, then he would start."

The poem was "Invictus," a Victorian verse by William Ernest Henley, whose words eerily presaged Lewis's trials later in life. John would recite its lines around the house:

Out of the night that covers me,
    Black as the pit from pole to pole,
I thank whatever gods may be
    For my unconquerable soul.

In the fell clutch of circumstance
    I have not winced nor cried aloud.
Under the bludgeonings of chance
    My head is bloody, but unbowed.

Beyond this place of wrath and tears
    Looms but the Horror of the shade,
And yet the menace of the years
    Finds and shall find me unafraid.

It matters not how strait the gate,
    How charged with punishments the scroll,
I am the master of my fate,
    I am the captain of my soul.[2]

John Lewis was born on February 21, 1940, in Pike County, a rural swatch of southeast Alabama, where his mother's family had lived for generations. His great-great-grandparents, Elizabeth (Betz or Betty) and Tobias (Tobe), had been slaves, owned by a man named Joel Carter. Many years later, Joel's granddaughter, Sarah Abernathy, wrote about the emancipation of Tobias and Elizabeth at the end of the Civil War:

Not being a secessionist at heart, Grandfather Carter didn't answer Jefferson Davis' call for cotton. He had expected his wealth to be grown in slaves; and too anxious for their health to allow his overseer to drive them, but allowed them to be worked enough to produce their upkeep and a little cotton which he stored. Before the onset of Federal Raiders, his negroes hid it among some difficult hills and gulches, all cotton grown by him after the Federal Blockade. His negroes were loyal to Old Marster. They refused to betray the place where they had cows, hogs, meat and lard hidden. Betz,

the cook, armed herself with ax and stood by the door and defied
the Yanks to pester Old Marster or the family, or to enter his home.
For her loyal and militant protection, with her freedom she and her
husband were given a piece of land, a cabin and supplies till they
could grow more. Said my grandfather, "They have grown old in my
service. My children are young and are able to get for themselves,
what Betz and Tobe are too old and feeble to earn for themselves."

Because Carter had given Tobias and Elizabeth a modest-sized plot, John
Lewis's ancestors possessed land of their own. Over the following decades
they bought more of it—76 acres here, 228 acres there. Eventually, though,
they were forced to sell the land, and when John was born, his parents were
working as tenant farmers for a white man named Josh Copeland.[3]

Besides claiming their own property when freedom came, the Carters,
then in their mid-forties, also claimed their right to marry—on December
16, 1865. Until then, the South's chattel slavery system had barred slaves
from legal unions, although many, like the Carters, were considered married
in the eyes of their communities. Even though slaveholders often broke up
families—selling a spouse or a child to a plantation or household far away—
they could not extinguish the human desire to wed. Black couples took wedding vows and performed rituals like "jumping the broomstick," a custom
long associated with extralegal unions. Informal marriage thrived even as
legal marriage was prohibited.[4]

When the Thirteenth Amendment, abolishing slavery, was ratified on
December 6, 1865, Black couples hurried to consecrate their bonds. Some
had children whom they wished to make "legitimate." Others wished to
qualify for soldiers' pensions or land allotments. Others simply wanted to
exercise their newly won rights. In some parts of the South, the demand for
nuptials was so great that mass weddings took place: as many as seventy couples tied the knot at once. Among the first to obtain a wedding certificate
were Tobias and Betty Carter.[5]

Alabama archives also document yet another step that Tobias Carter
took as a free man. In March 1867, three years before the Fifteenth Amendment was ratified, allowing Black men to vote, the U.S. Congress passed the
Reconstruction Act, which required Confederate states, as a condition for
rejoining the Union, to grant the vote to all men regardless of race. Under

military direction, boards of registrars enrolled voters. That summer, Tobias Carter registered.[6]

Within a generation, however, Tobias and other Black men across Alabama were systematically stripped of their rights. In 1874, white supremacist Democrats took control of the state government and established a Redeemer regime. Through new laws and extralegal violence, they disenfranchised Black citizens. Thus began the Jim Crow era and the long deferral of full freedom for Tobias and Betty and their progeny.

When John Lewis was born, Tobias and Betty Carter's son Frank—John's great-grandfather—was still alive. He had been emancipated as a small boy. John was impressed by his great-grandfather's reputation for immense strength; Frank was known to plow soil and pick crops as few men could. He was also a math whiz who performed financial calculations quickly, which he did on payday to make sure he wasn't cheated.

John also remembered the old man as "lighter than any other Black person I had ever seen" and having "remarkably straight hair." John's mother, Willie Mae, never talked about her grandfather's skin tone. The subject upset her. The implication was that Frank's biological father may have been white and may have raped Betty. The silence about the subject always made John uneasy.[7]

John held more vivid memories of Frank's wife, Betty Baxter Carter, or "Grandma Bessie," the matriarch of the extended Carter clan, who was the midwife at his birth. John would endear himself to Grandma Bessie on his family's Sunday visits to her house by shinnying up a chinaberry tree to retrieve eggs from a hollow where an eccentric hen would lay them.

Bessie and Frank lived near John in Pike County. So did John's grandparents Dink and Della Carter. So, too, did many other aunts, uncles, and cousins. The area was called "Carter's Quarters" because of all the family members that lived there. Holiday gatherings sometimes included hundreds of relatives, from Pike County and beyond.[8]

Although John grew up among Carters, his mother had become a Lewis. In 1931, at age sixteen, she met Eddie Lewis at the Macedonia Baptist Church. Nicknamed "Buddy" or "Shorty," Eddie was a compact, stocky young man five years her senior. His family had moved to Troy in 1904, although in the subsequent decades the Lewises shuttled around Georgia and Alabama before returning to Pike County in 1928. Eddie's grandfather, Carie Lewis, had been a sharecropper, and his father, Henry, had been a turpentine man, extracting pine resin from trees to make the solvent for construction projects. Eddie worked on bridges for several years before taking up farming.[9]

When she met Eddie, Willie Mae was smitten. "We just fell in love," she told her son. Married in 1932, the couple would have ten children: Ora, a girl; then Edward, who was deaf; and then—on a cold, rainy night in 1940—John Robert, whom they called Robert or Bob. Seven more children followed, with Henry Grant, the youngest, arriving in 1952. They all lived in a shotgun house: three rooms including the kitchen. John recalled that you could stand in one room and see almost all the way through the interior—or fire a shotgun's bullet from the front door straight through the back.[10]

All the Carters' homes were small and ramshackle. Once, when fifteen of the cousins were gathered at the house of one aunt, a fierce storm blew in, dislodging the tin roof. John's aunt had the children line up, clasp hands, and follow the wind from one room to another, so that each time the whipping blasts rocked the little house, the group would be there to provide ballast. "We just walked with the wind, backward and forward through the house until the storm was over," Lewis recounted.[11]

By the time John was four, Eddie had saved $700. With a loan of $100 from the Copelands, it was enough to buy his own place.* The plot Eddie purchased was 110 acres, set on a red-clay hill near a swamp off a dirt road: Route 5, Box 225. "It was a good deal," John reflected years later. "It was an unbelievable deal." But it was no ticket to middle-class comfort. The road to the house was steep and rugged. When it rained, cars would get stuck in the mud or slide into ditches. Years later, the county paved its roads, but only up to the point where the Black-owned properties began.[12]

John remembered the day the Lewises moved. Excitement filled the air as they loaded up a wagon and a borrowed pickup truck, carting everything

---

* John Lewis always said that his father bought the land for $300, but in a 1969 interview Eddie said it was $800.

down the road a few miles. John sat in the back seat, wedged between an old radio and his dog, Riley. His father drove. Even then, John understood that his family was graduating from being sharecroppers—a plight he would compare to slavery—to being farmers. The new house was hardly palatial, but it had two large front rooms, a kitchen, high ceilings, a fireplace, front and back porches, and a tin roof. Near the front porch were pecan trees and a covered well.[13]

Owning land marked a triumph for Eddie. The plot was in the heart of the Black Belt—the wide, curved swath of fertile land stretching from Virginia through Louisiana, named not for its concentration of African Americans but for the dark soil that made the terrain arable. The Lewises eked out a living growing cotton, corn, and peanuts. They had to go into debt to buy feed or fertilizer, and they always feared losing their land. Eddie took on extra work driving a truck, while Willie Mae did domestic work outside the house.[14]

Farming required the whole family's labor. When John was small, his mother would set out a blanket for him and his siblings in the field as she picked. Starting at age five or six, the children were expected to help. John despised the toil and decided at a young age that he wasn't meant for the farm. "You've got to catch up," his older brother, Edward, would say. "You're not pulling your load." John's father could pick three hundred pounds of cotton a day, his mother two hundred pounds. John criticized his parents for accepting the grueling demands of farming. "I've got to raise you all," his father replied. "I've got to do the best I can until I can do better." John pushed back. "Daddy, you're just working and you ain't getting it. I ain't going to do that. One day all of this is going to change."[15]

Luxuries were few. The Lewis house had no running water, electric wiring, insulation, or telephone. To bathe, they boiled water in a kettle and washed themselves in a zinc tub. Or they would take what John called a "bird bath," using a small basin. The outdoor toilets, noisome in the summer and frigid in the winter, were stocked with old newspapers, discarded Sears, Roebuck catalogs, or corncobs. Clothes were never thrown away, always patched up. Willie Mae could take two threadbare pairs of pants and fashion one good new pair. In later years, the Lewises' hard work brought about some modest improvements. By 1953, they had saved enough to tear down the ramshackle house and build a bigger one. A few years later, they wired it for electricity. They were able to buy a tractor. After John went to college, they would get a television.[16]

Despite his frugality, Eddie didn't want his children to feel deprived. He carried himself with poise and pride and wore crisp, clean shirts that were freshly ironed and starched. On Fridays and Saturdays, he bought fresh fish for dinner; he usually settled for mullet, the cheap fish, but he liked to splurge on red snapper when he could. "My father put a great deal of stress and emphasis on food," John said. "It was his philosophy that if we died, we would die with a full stomach. . . . That was his whole thing."

Eddie also resolved to keep his family safe, whether from the Ku Klux Klan or violent neighbors. "I grew up in a home with a shotgun over the door and a rifle in the corner," John said. He remembered Willie Mae once remonstrating with Eddie not to charge out of the house with the gun. She also warned her children to avoid the rowdy nightlife of Troy, especially around Love Street. "On a Saturday night, you heard where people were being shot, where people were being cut and killed," John recounted. It bred a hatred of violence. John avoided guns, even toy ones, and abstained from hunting. He never picked up a firearm until he was in his fifties.[17]

John also never played with—indeed, had no interaction with—white children. "The world I lived in was completely Black," he remembered of his earliest years. "I cannot even recall seeing somebody white." It was, he said, "two worlds—a Black world and a white world." The extended Carter family provided a bounty of playmates for John, even if he had to walk a mile or two to meet them. Siblings and cousins played marbles, dodgeball, jump rope, and Cowboys and Indians. Other pastimes were games of make-believe, like "house" or "church," where the only props needed were a few oak chairs from the house. John invested these games with his hopes for a better existence. One of his cousins, Della Mae, shared his fantasy life. "We had a dream," John recounted in the final weeks of his life. "We were going to cut down the large pine trees near my house and make a bus. And we were going to leave Alabama. We would use the round part of the trunk to make wheels, and we would travel to Buffalo." Two of Willie Mae's brothers had moved there during World War II, and in John's family, Buffalo had acquired a reputation as a faraway land of opportunity, a bustling big city of excitement and possibility. "We knew there was a better life," he said, "a better place."[18]

Another recreation was going into Troy on Saturdays to window-shop or see a movie. John enjoyed watching Superman, the Lone Ranger, Hopalong Cassidy, and Tarzan—during which he and his siblings would cheer for the African tribesmen. But at an early age, John realized that he and his family had to sit in the balcony because the theater was segregated. He felt humiliated. ("I don't go to many movies today because of that," he said decades later. "It's a shame.") He felt the same way at the segregated bathrooms and water fountains; or at Byrd's Drugs, where he and other Black kids had to drink their Cokes outside; or at the Pike County Fair, which they could attend only on "Colored Day." At first, John would mount little protests, drinking a lot of water before going into town so he wouldn't have to use the segregated fountains. But mostly, he said, "I stopped going."

Segregation intruded as well onto his favorite pursuit: reading. At a young age, he went to the county public library to check out some books, but was denied. The library, he was told, was for whites only. To protest, John gathered up some classmates to draft and sign a petition, but no one at the library ever replied to their request.

The steely determination that was evident in John from early on was always mixed with an unmistakable gentleness. The combination gave him his distinctive temperament. He could be insistent and stubborn when it came to boycotting the Jim Crow facilities in Troy or in resisting the toil of manual labor, but overall his family considered him a sweet and stoical child. Soft-spoken and even-tempered, he was, for all his vaunted courage later in life, easily frightened. The snakes he came across while farming scared him. So did a strange black fish that his mother once tossed his way while fishing. Thunder and lightning upset him so much that during rainstorms he would hide in a steamer trunk. He retained that fear his whole life.[19]

John's religious devotion reinforced his serene temperament. He inherited that devotion mainly from Willie Mae, a godly woman and relentless optimist who believed in prayer and salvation. She went to church "all the time," John said, and incorporated religious observance into the family's daily life. The children memorized Bible passages; at meals someone always said grace and recited a verse.[20]

The Lewises attended the Macedonia Baptist Church, in Troy. But because their preacher made the rounds among many congregations in the region, he was in Troy only on the third Sunday of each month. On other Sundays they went to Dunn's Chapel, a Methodist congregation near their farm, which also served as the children's elementary and Sunday school. John loved the singing, which was conducted without any musical instruments, and learned all the hymns and spirituals. The congregation, he said, exhibited "some of the best singing that I've heard in my life."

One evening in July 1949, John attended the church's annual revival meeting. The minister was beseeching the congregation to come to Jesus and be saved. John decided it was time. One of his older cousins, called "T-Baby," escorted him to the front. John and the minister clasped hands. At that moment the lights suddenly went out, filling John with a jolt of fear that he associated with accepting Christ as his savior. When the lights came back on a moment later, an old lady in the congregation hollered, "Thank you, Jesus!"[21]

As much as church services, Willie Mae recalled, "he loved the Bible." John remembered opening a Bible his uncle had given him as a present, and his mother reading him the words "In the beginning God created the heavens and the earth." He was reading by himself by age five, and perusing the Bible became his favorite pastime. Especially after he lost interest in the movies, he said, when others in the family went into Troy, "I would stay behind . . . reading the Bible someplace in a corner."[22]

Christianity also provided grounding for John's belief that race shouldn't affect how anyone was treated. "Very early in Sunday school, we discussed the fact that the whole question of color according to the Trinity is not relevant," he said. "If God is supposed to be the God of all Mankind and Jesus is the brother of all Mankind, color isn't an issue."[23]

His admiration for the church was not total. He saw that its strict moral codes could inculcate insensitivity or callousness. The church took a dim view of drinking, dancing, playing cards, going to the movies, and sex. Once, John remembered, T-Baby's little sister, a high school student, became pregnant and was excommunicated. She begged the church to come back, in vain. "Because of human nature," John sighed. "It was very sad. And I've never forgotten it."[24]

John's piety also led him to develop an unusual relationship with his family's chickens—a story he would recount his whole life. From a young age, he preached to the chickens on the farm as if he were a minister and they were, literally, his flock.

At about eight years old, John was put in charge of the five dozen chickens his family owned. Each morning he would step into the henhouse and whisper to them before providing them food. He tended to their nests and the fencing of the yards. He would mark the eggs with a pencil, to indicate which should be left to hatch. Because of his family's frugal habits, he also used a farmer's trick to get a hen to "set" on more eggs than she had actually laid, surreptitiously swapping in extra eggs under the hen. This method was unfair and even cruel to the hens; sitting on eggs was actually arduous work that caused the birds to lose weight and feathers. He felt guilty about it, and each month when the Sears, Roebuck catalog came in the mail—John and his siblings called it "the Wish Book"—he would linger longingly over the photographs of an $18.95 incubator. If only he could buy it, he wouldn't have to "cheat" the hens.[25]

Besides tending to the chickens, John also began preaching to them. For several years, with a Bible in hand, he would gather the fowl and settle them on their roosts before putting them into bed. He would read his favorite prayers or Bible verses as the chickens clucked and shook their heads. John gave each one a name—"Big Belle" or "Li'l Pullet"—and even baptized them. Once, he accidentally drowned a bird. The episode gave him nightmares, and one of his little brothers thereafter refused to be baptized. When a chicken died, John would hold a funeral, placing the bird in a lard can and rounding up his brothers and sisters by a pecan tree near a swing and benches. After John's eulogy they would march off to a little cemetery. John would say prayers and cover the grave with fertilizer, flowers, and a cross.[26]

Sometimes Eddie had to cook a bird for dinner. Or he might trade one for sugar or flour to the "rollin' store man," a dry-goods merchant who came by the house in his truck. The loss of a chicken caused John no end of distress.

He would become irate and refuse to eat or even to speak to anyone in the family for days. It was, he would later reflect, his first nonviolent protest.[27]

By age twelve, John had stopped preaching to the chickens. But by now his affinity for the ministry was obvious to all. Nicknamed "Preacher," he decided to enter the clergy. At sixteen, at Macedonia, he preached his first trial sermon. He wore his best suit, dark blue, with a white shirt and blue tie. He chose an Old Testament passage about Hannah, a woman past child-bearing age who prays for a son and is rewarded with Samuel, whose name in Hebrew means "God heard." It was a simple message, one of keeping faith in God despite long odds, and the congregation rejoiced in John's telling of it. Lewis later recalled that the *Montgomery Advertiser* ran a story about him, along with a picture of him in his Sunday suit, though no such story has been found.[28]

For the next two years John would preach at Methodist and Baptist churches around Pike County. In 1956, he was licensed as a minister and in 1957 was ordained—a higher honor that authorized him to perform weddings. He also began to teach at Sunday school and soon became its supervisor.[29]

Besides church, John's other great love was school. His parents, who never graduated high school, saw education as the route to a better life. "Go to school and get an education so you won't have to work as hard as we did," his mother would tell him.[30]

John's elementary school was at Dunn's Chapel. It had been built and funded by Julius Rosenwald, the Sears, Roebuck mogul who, with Booker T. Washington, created five thousand schools for Black children around the South. Although the Rosenwald schools were better than most Black schools, the education at Dunn's Chapel was mediocre. In one room, John recalled, students of all six grades massed together "like a herd," with the teacher unable to give much attention to anyone. The "old, shaggy building," John said, was beautiful in its simplicity, painted white with a green roof. A potbellied stove heated the school in winter, and kids would rest their lunches on top to heat them up. Drinking water was in another building. Each child had a glass with his name written on tape, and they had to take their own glass home now and then to wash them. "The glasses would stay there for a very, very long time," John remembered, "and get very, very dirty." Some of his happiest experiences were field trips, including one to the Tuskegee Institute, an hour north, to see where George Washington Carver had carried out his agricultural research.[31]

Just before seventh grade, in 1951, John's uncle Otis offered to drive him to visit their family in Buffalo for the summer. The trip would be John's first outside Alabama.

Early on a June morning, Otis pulled up to John's house. They packed the car with fried chicken, sandwiches, and pound cake so they wouldn't have to stop at restaurants in Alabama, Tennessee, or Kentucky. Neither John nor Otis had heard of the "Green Book," the guide for African American travelers, but Otis had made the trip before and knew the gas stations where they could safely stop.[32]

When he arrived in Buffalo, John was enchanted. The city offered a glimpse of the better world outside Pike County he had always envisioned: tall buildings, fancy clothes, busy streets and shiny cars, sidewalks thrumming with activity. His aunts took him to Sattler's, a department store, where John rode an escalator and took in the gleaming displays and candy counters. They went to Niagara Falls and to Crystal Beach in Canada.[33]

What struck John most was the simple fact of Blacks and whites living side by side. The North was hardly free of discrimination, but it was categorically different from the South. White neighbors lived next to the Carters, on both sides, without friction. Blacks and whites sat together at lunch counters, at the movies, and on city buses as if, John said, "it were the most natural thing in the world." He missed his family, and when he arrived back home at the end of the summer, he cried with joy. But after Buffalo, Pike County never felt the same again. It was his first taste of independence—and of something close to racial equality.[34]

Coming back to Pike County meant coming back to second-class status. In the seventh grade John began attending Banks Junior High School, ten miles away. The dilapidated secondhand buses struggled to get John and other Black students there because of the rutted roads, which became impassable when it rained. John might leave his house at seven in the morning and not reach school until noon. Or troubles might come on the ride home, causing John to arrive after nightfall.[35]

John did reasonably well at school and continued to read avidly, his interest encouraged by a teacher and librarian named Coreen Harvey. "Over and over again, she would say, 'Read, my child. Read.' . . . I tried to read everything," he recalled. He was also now following current events. His grandfather got the *Montgomery Advertiser* and would pass on day-old copies to the Lewises. John pored over the papers, especially a section called "Colored Events," written by a Black editor named E. P. Wallace.[36]

During harvest times—maybe twenty days a year—the Lewises would keep their children home from school, John said, "to pick cotton or pull corn or what we called 'shake the peanuts.'" John would pout and cry, begging to go to school. His mother would tell him he was needed in the field, but one of his younger brothers would take his side. "Just let him go, Mama," he would say. "All he's going to do is complain." John devised a ruse. He would dress for school and hide under the front porch with his books until the bus pulled up—and then dart aboard before his parents knew what was up.[37]

For high school, John went to the Pike County Training School in Brundidge, twenty minutes south by bus or car. The curriculum focused on vocational agriculture. John again spent his time in the school library, reading. He discovered racks of periodicals, including Black newspapers like the *Baltimore Afro-American*, the *Pittsburgh Courier*, and the *Chicago Defender* and the magazines *Ebony* and *Jet*.

John was too introverted and, in his word, "puritanical" to have any romantic life, though he went to the prom in eleventh and twelfth grades with dates. Once, he recounted, a girl wrote him a letter and another girl found it, leading them to fight over him on the bus ride home. But that was as exciting as his love life got. John chalked up his failure to date to his inability to drive (he didn't get his license until he was forty-two). "The girls I knew," he said, "lived halfway across the county." In truth, he was shy and serious and not yet ready for the amorous pursuits of a young man.[38]

John's teenage years coincided with the emerging civil rights movement, in which he took a special interest. The instinctive revulsion he felt toward the patent unfairness of the Jim Crow system fed that interest. So did the attitudes he learned from his parents, who taught John that there was goodness in people of all races—and meanness in people of all races, too. Over the years the Lewises had made some white friends, and if a Lewis family member died, white neighbors would come to pay their respects.

Notwithstanding their liberal beliefs, the Lewises were not especially political people. John remembered that his father admired Franklin Roosevelt for helping the poor, but there usually wasn't much discussion of politics around the house. When it came to the civil rights movement, Eddie and Willie Mae both worried about the consequences of challenging the system too aggressively. Activism, his mother would explain, was a recipe for "trouble." It was better to let white people do certain things than to "get in the way." Trouble could mean any number of things, from defying the strictures of segregation to venturing into violent spots like Love Street in downtown Troy. Once, a relative named Thomas Brewer, who was a leader in his local NAACP, was shot in cold blood in retaliation for his activism. The killer, who owned a store beneath Brewer's office, was never indicted.

As John got older, he concluded that his parents avoided trouble to protect their family and their livelihood. But he couldn't suppress the resentment he felt toward the "White Only" and "Colored Only" signs or the naked discrimination he faced at the library, movie theater, or ice cream parlor. He came to understand, too, that the shabbiness of his schools and buses and books was also a result of the Jim Crow system. He didn't need a judicial opinion to tell him that separate was inherently unequal.[39]

John was now following the national events that were starting to change life for African Americans around the South. He kept a scrapbook with clippings of Jackie Robinson, Ralph Bunche, and other Black heroes, and as his enthusiasm for politics grew, he would listen in on those occasions when the adults did talk about current affairs. He wrote to the NAACP, asking to become a "youth member." In May 1954, when the Supreme Court handed down its decision in *Brown v. Board of Education*, declaring segregated public schooling unconstitutional, John was elated. "It was like a day of jubilee," he said. He was convinced that his school would soon be desegregated or that he would go to a better school. He was crestfallen when nothing changed.

Nothing made a greater impact on John in his teenage years than the murder of Emmett Till. In 1955, white racists in Mississippi lynched Till, a fourteen-year-old Black boy from Chicago visiting relatives in the town of Money, for allegedly calling a young white woman "baby." For his supposed insolence, Till was pistol-whipped, shot, and thrown in the Tallahatchie River. A witness who saw the killers abduct Till testified at their trial, but the all-white jury acquitted the men. The story made national news, and John followed it through the *Advertiser* and the Black newspapers in his school library. He was very much aware that Till was just one year his junior.[40]

Equally important to John's growing awareness of civil rights activism was the time he happened upon Martin Luther King Jr. on the radio. The Lewis family usually kept the dial tuned to WRMA, a Montgomery-based soul station. "We listened to it every day, and we talked about what we heard," John said. One day, he remembered, "I heard this voice on the radio, and that changed my life."

The smooth, low, arresting voice was King's. He was delivering a sermon called "Paul's Letter to American Christians" in which he applied Jesus's precepts to the discrimination pervading the South. "Segregation," King declared, assuming the voice of Paul, "is a blatant denial of the unity which we all have in Christ." At the end of the broadcast, the announcer mentioned King as the minister who had just spoken. John remembered his name.[41]

Soon he was seeing it everywhere. In 1955, Black citizens of Montgomery launched their historic bus boycott, a collective refusal to ride public transportation until it was desegregated. The campaign resulted in a monumental victory one year later. John followed it all avidly. The boycott, he later said, "lifted me, gave me a sense of hope." It also spurred his own activism. His senior year, he initiated a drive to replace his school's broken-down buses, getting six hundred people to sign a petition to the county requesting new ones. A year later, after he graduated, the county agreed to provide them.[42]

King's sermons reinforced the tight connection Lewis saw between Christianity and the fight for racial equality. By his teenage years, he had come to see Jesus in modern terms, as "more or less simply another human personality who was so in love with people, . . . with what was right, and what was true." This quality, John concluded, was what "made him a powerful force for good." The Black freedom struggle stemmed from these same teachings. "What I saw in Montgomery during that period was the whole idea of a people . . . rising up," John remembered, "and saying . . . that they are going to take something from the heart of the Christian faith and make it real."

Finally, King offered Lewis a model of how he might spend his life. "Race was closely tied to my decision to become a minister," he said. "I wanted to use the emotional energy of the Black church to end segregation and gain freedom for Black people." He had dabbled with the thought of becoming a lawyer, helping his people "gain first-class citizenship," as he wrote in an early testament, "by fighting for them in the courts of Alabama." But he kept returning to King as his ideal and inspiration.[43]

Given his goals, John knew he should go to college. "My Uncle Otis, probably more than anyone," he recalled, "said, 'You've got to go to college. You've got to get an education.'" John had his eye on Morehouse College in Atlanta, King's alma mater, whose president, Benjamin Mays, was active in the movement, and he asked his homeroom teacher for an application. But Morehouse catered to the Black elite, and John concluded that a poor farm boy would never be admitted, nor be able to pay the tuition. Another option was Alabama State, a teachers college in Montgomery, but neither Otis nor John's high school teachers thought well of their experience there.

Then one day Willie Mae, who was cleaning in an orphanage, brought home a publication from the Southern Baptist Convention. In some accounts, John described it as a pamphlet or a conference program; in another, it was a magazine called *Baptist Home Mission*. The publication contained a notice about a Nashville seminary that boasted of "no tuition, room and board." On December 10, 1956, John sent away for an application, signing his name as "Rev. John R. Lewis." The academic dean wrote back, saying that he would "pray that it will be in God's plan for you to come and study with us." John, however, lost the application form.

Three months later he wrote to the school apologetically for another one. In April, he sent in his transcript, recommendation letters, and a medical report vouching for his "good physical condition" (although, the doctor added, "he needs to have some dental work done").[44]

He was accepted. John would be the first of Eddie and Willie Mae's ten children to earn a college degree.

In early September John hugged his brothers and sisters and watched his mother's eyes well up as he prepared to leave. Uncle Otis handed John a hundred-dollar bill. Eddie drove him to the Greyhound station in Troy, where they shook hands. From a seat in the back of the bus, Lewis pressed his face against the window, hoping for a final moment of eye contact.

His father had already driven away.[45]

Chapter Two

NASHVILLE

———— ▪ ▪ ————

Sunday, September 8, 1957. John Lewis stepped off a Greyhound coach in downtown Nashville. At seventeen, he was traveling alone for the first time. Stooping down to the bus's undercarriage, he retrieved his bulky wardrobe trunk, a gift from his uncle Otis, and peered around the station. He went outside and found a taxi with a Black driver—no white cabbie would drive him—climbed in the backseat, and rode north across the snaking Cumberland River, his footlocker tied to the roof with rope. After fifteen minutes, the driver dropped Lewis at a quiet cluster of small redbrick buildings on Whites Creek Pike.[1]

Lewis had arrived at American Baptist Theological Seminary, where he would study for the next four years. Perched near the riverbank on a knoll called Holy Hill, the fifty-three-acre college was an idyllic spot. An expansive, well-kept lawn sloped down from the road to the river. A thickly wooded grove of pine and oak trees stood off to the side. Lewis thought the campus looked beautiful in the September light—a world away from the red-clay and sandy-brown landscape of his rural Alabama.

Since its founding in 1924, the seminary had trained African Americans for the ministry. The all-white Southern Baptist Convention and the Black National Baptist Convention jointly funded the school; when it opened, the *Nashville Tennessean* expressed hope that it would lead to "the higher development of the Negroes of the nation through providing them with a better trained leadership in their preachers." In fact, the whites' motives were less than pure: in founding the school, Lewis later learned, they hoped "to keep

Black Baptists from going to the white seminary in Louisville," two hours to the north. Still, American Baptist built an interracial faculty and brought in both white and Black ministers to preach. By 1957, when Lewis arrived, it was home to seventy students—of whom he knew precisely none.[2]

Lewis walked over to Griggs Hall, a three-story brick dormitory that included offices, classrooms, and a basement with dining and recreational space. As he entered his second-floor dorm room, Lewis saw something he had never seen before: a bed of his own. Lewis had always shared a bed—or a floor—with one of his six brothers. He unpacked his trunk: khakis, blue jeans, some old suits, army underwear from Uncle Otis, long johns.

Lewis also met his roommate, a freshman named Ellis Toney, a G.I. from La Fayette, Illinois. Like most of the other boys at American Baptist, Toney was intent on becoming pastor of his local church. The school was, Lewis could see, a "highly religious place," full of young men bound for the ministry. A few had served in the army. A few others were married and lived by the river in cinder-block bungalows.

As a scholarship student, Lewis had to take a campus job. During his first year he worked in the dining hall, peeling potatoes and cracking eggs. Sometimes he set the tables or served breakfast. Worst of all, he had to wash the heavy, industrial-sized cast-iron pots and pans—an "awful sight," he would later recall, once the cooking was through. The pots were so big that if they were filled with water, Lewis—five foot six and 135 pounds—could hardly lift them. He would scrub the insides to scrape off the potatoes, eggs, and liver. Each night for the first few weeks of school he would collapse into bed, his strained muscles throbbing.[3]

One benefit of cafeteria work was that Lewis got to meet everyone. Still, he had trouble fitting in. Reticent by nature, Lewis spoke haltingly and with a mild speech impediment. He stumbled over or mispronounced words, and his thick rural Alabama accent was hard even for many Southerners to understand. Next to classmates from big cities like Cleveland, he felt unsophisticated. Bernard LaFayette of Tampa, Florida, who would arrive the next year and become one of Lewis's best friends, described Lewis as "pure hick."[4]

In his solitude, Lewis indulged his love of reading. "He was very committed to his academic work, very devoted," LaFayette said. "We all studied, but John really studied." His favorite subjects were history and philosophy, and his course syllabi included works by Plato, Aristotle, St. Augustine, and

Kant. Lewis found these texts demanding, full of arguments that made him think. His professors, too, seemed to be founts of knowledge. One teacher, John Lewis Powell, would dart around the classroom, scribbling on the blackboard as he held forth about Hegel. "Daring" and "courageous," in Lewis's telling, Powell was steeped in the work of Walter Rauschenbusch, who advocated a body of thought known as the social gospel: the application of Christian teachings to social problems. Powell used Hegel to illuminate the plight of Blacks in the South, putting an optimistic gloss on a dark history. Out of the struggle between segregation and its enemies, Powell argued, would emerge a synthesis of a harmonious, integrated nation. Lewis never mastered the finer points of Hegel, but he did, he later said, start believing in a "Spirit of History."[5]

The most important influence on Lewis at school was Kelly Miller Smith, the minister at First Colored Baptist Church, Nashville's largest African American congregation, and a local civil rights leader. Popular with students, Smith taught Lewis in homiletics. Smith could see that Lewis "had some rather rough problems in speaking" as well as a mediocre education; once, Smith recounted, Lewis turned in an assignment with "a lot of grammatical errors in it. . . . I marked it up quite a bit with red pencil, and he thanked me for it, thanked me for the comments." Despite his uneven prose, Lewis impressed Smith as "resourceful," "creative," and capable of "great thoughts." He had a first-rate intelligence, although it could be easy to miss.[6]

A fault line, Lewis discovered, ran through the faculty and student body. On one side were those strictly interested in the ministry, the boys like his roommate Ellis Toney who wanted to return home and save souls. They were called "whoopers," given to the emotional, evangelical style of the Black church. On the other side were those, like Powell and Smith, who preached the social gospel. These men brought current events into the classroom and raised questions about the relationship of theology to societal change. Smith taught a class on the theologian Howard Thurman, whose ideas synthesized Gandhian nonviolence and Christian activism. The divide was noticeable even outside the classroom. If Lewis was showering and a classmate in another stall was preaching—far from an uncommon occurrence at American Baptist—Lewis could instantly tell the man's approach to theology.[7]

Lewis himself was drawn to the social gospel. He had arrived on campus

already invested in the political fight for racial equality, which was continuing to shake up the South. That fall, the Little Rock Nine made national
headlines with their bid to enroll at the all-white Central High School in
Arkansas. Closer to home, a high school integration battle was underway
in Clinton, Tennessee. Nashville, too, had begun integrating its schools, but
at the slow-motion pace of one grade per year. Gradual though it was, the
Nashville plan sparked vehement opposition, including death threats to the
participating families. "We'll beat your little girl to death and string her up
by her toes," one father was warned. One night that year, white supremacists dynamited the Hattie Cotton Elementary School. Lewis was "very
conscious" of all these incidents, he said, following it all in the *Tennessean*,
Nashville's liberal paper.[8]

As the semester went on, Lewis later said, "going to class, meeting the
teachers, going to chapel like three times a week . . . it just didn't hit me." Before the term was out, he said, "I started sort of rebelling against the whole
idea of somebody going to chapel and preaching to me and singing and all
of that. I just couldn't take it." He began, he later said, to "drift away" and
"question for the first time the ritual, the ceremony, the creeds and beliefs
of the church" and sought out something else to "get involved in." He tried
to organize a campus chapter of the NAACP. But Maynard Turner, the college's president, quashed the idea. Turner explained to Lewis that the Southern Baptist Convention, the network of white churches that funded the
seminary, would never tolerate it.[9]

Instead, Lewis started going to meetings of an off-campus NAACP
chapter. He also began to explore Black Nashville, with its thriving civil
rights community, under the tutelage of an older student named Harold
Cox. Cox brought Lewis to events at Nashville's other Black colleges, such
as Fisk and Meharry Medical College. "It was just an eye-opener to go to
Fisk, to, say, a Christmas concert, and see the interracial climate," Lewis said.
Fisk had an exchange program under which white students from around
the country would come for a semester, make Black friends, and learn about
Black history and culture. In February 1958, Cox and Lewis attended a Lin-
coln's Birthday event where Lewis met Martin Luther King Sr. Over the next
few months, they heard talks from Thurgood Marshall, Roy Wilkins, Daisy
Bates, and Coretta Scott King, who had come in place of her husband after

an assailant stabbed him with a letter opener. One time Cox and Lewis saw W. E. B. Du Bois crossing the Fisk campus and hurried over to shake the old man's hand.[10]

Lewis's friendship with Cox was one of a few new relationships. On his first day in Griggs Hall, Lewis heard a booming voice echoing out of the bathroom. A balding, light-skinned man stepped into the hallway, Lewis recalled, "buck naked and dripping, not a trace of self-consciousness about him," asking, "Can you *preach*, boy?" This was James Bevel, a slightly older student who had been at American Baptist since the previous January. Confident, charismatic, and always chasing women, Bevel loved discussion, argument, and, Lewis said, "stirring the pot." A recurring argument between the two men centered on King. Bevel would ask Lewis, "Lewis, why are you always preaching this *social* gospel, and not the *Gospel* gospel?"

Bevel would also try—and fail—to enlist the straitlaced Lewis in his amorous pursuits. Sometimes Lewis went along because, he said, "there was a shortage of young ladies at American Baptist Seminary. A great shortage. Most of the parties that I attended were actually sort of Christian-oriented-type parties." But they were not his speed.[11]

Another Nashville student whom Lewis would soon befriend, Angeline Butler of Fisk, found Lewis's innocence in matters of the heart endearing. "I was fast with boys. I always had boyfriends around," she recalled. "John was always a bit baffled by this." Colia Clark, who would later marry Bernard LaFayette, said that Lewis didn't approach girls the way his friends did. "They were young men. They were chasing women. Some of them had a lot more experience, had been in the service. They were bent on finding women wherever they could find them," she said. "But John would report them to the dean." His prudishness led his friends to rib him and occasionally retaliate with a prank. One afternoon they tied Lewis to a small tree near the Cumberland River, told him that the Ku Klux Klan was coming, and ran off. A classmate dressed in a white sheet appeared in the distance. Lewis bolted, Clark said, pulling the sapling out by its roots as he scrambled to escape.[12]

Eventually Lewis found a female companion named Helen Johnson. They took walks by the river and shared thoughts about life, but the relationship remained platonic. It was the start of a pattern. Lewis's shyness and

sweetness would lead many girls to regard him with motherly protectiveness, but passionate romance was not in the cards.[13]

Anyway, he was more interested in the political ferment around Nashville.

Tennessee, a Jim Crow state, was not liberal in the common sense of the
word. But compared to other states of the old Confederacy, it had pronounced progressive leanings. During the Civil War, pro-Union loyalties
pervaded its eastern counties, and it was the last Southern state to secede.
Tennessee's citizens provided more regiments to the Union army than the
rest of the South combined. In 1956, the state's senators, Al Gore Sr. and
Estes Kefauver, refused to sign the "Southern Manifesto," in which other
Dixie legislators vowed to defy federal desegregation decrees in the wake of
the *Brown* decision.

Forty-three percent Black, Nashville was the most tolerant city in the
South. As the activist minister Cordy Tindell ("C.T.") Vivian said of Nashville's liberals, "They tried to set a tone far different than most cities. They
tried to set a tone of cultivation and of being civilized human beings. The
rest of the South didn't necessarily do so." Even so, Black Nashvillians endured second-class treatment, racist humiliations, and stunted opportunities. Northern whites who relocated to Nashville—like Marian and Nelson
Fuson, a Fisk faculty couple who hosted integrated salons for students to
discuss race relations—found the racism of Nashville shocking.[14]

In Nashville, these progressive and reactionary impulses jostled, resulting in a patchwork of selective prejudice. Nashville did not have separate
"white" and "colored" facilities in its state capitol; neither did it have racially
segregated lines at the post office, nor distinct seating areas in the courthouse, nor different ticket windows at the train station. On the other hand,
the same post office forbade Blacks from working the service window, con-
signing them to sort mail in the back room. Court officers expected Blacks
to keep their distance from whites. The railway station kept separate bath-
rooms and waiting rooms. Blacks had to sit in the back of the streetcars and
the balconies of theaters. Restaurants and hotels were segregated, and even
the Grand Ole Opry clung to the dictates of Jim Crow.[15]

The city's progressive tendencies were fostered by its many universities, home to some fifteen thousand students. Fisk, Meharry, American Baptist, and Tennessee A&I* were notable among the Black colleges; Vanderbilt, Scarritt, and the George Peabody College for Teachers among the white ones. The abundance of schools gave the city its nickname "the Athens of the South." The *Tennessean* also exerted a liberalizing force. It crusaded in favor of school desegregation and against the poll tax, and it hired young, open-minded reporters, among them a talented Harvard graduate named David Halberstam.†[16]

Nashville also nurtured a tradition of civil rights activism. One of its mid-century leaders was the sociologist Charles S. Johnson, the first African American president of Fisk, who made the school into a center of research on race. As early as the 1940s, Johnson was arguing that racial inequality "should no longer be viewed as a Negro problem but as a problem of American democracy," and he used his perch to elevate the issue. Also active in challenging the city's white supremacist laws was Z. Alexander Looby, a Black attorney from Antigua, who held degrees from Howard, Columbia, and New York University. Working with the NAACP Legal Defense Fund, Looby led successful fights to desegregate Nashville's airport, golf courses, and schools.[17]

In the 1940s and '50s, Blacks in Nashville began to pursue elective politics. Their votes proved decisive in the 1943 mayoral race, and after a coalition of Blacks and liberal whites enacted major voting reforms in 1950, Looby and attorney Robert Lillard won seats on the city council—the first Blacks elected in forty years. Black voters also played a key role in electing Mayor Ben West, who nudged the city toward egalitarian practices.[18]

Most important of all was a cadre of Black social gospel ministers, led by Kelly Miller Smith. Six foot one and dapper, with a stately demeanor, Smith had moved to Nashville from Mississippi in 1951 to lead the First Colored Baptist Church. He and his wife, Alice, appalled that their children had to attend segregated schools, joined Looby's successful lawsuit against

---

* In 1968 Tennessee A&I became Tennessee State.

† "David Halberstam was a very young, Jewish reporter at the Nashville Tennessean, very pro-movement," Lewis said in 1967. "He was really with us all the way. . . . He became very close to quite a few of us in the early days."

the Nashville Board of Education. Smith also led the local NAACP chapter. In 1954, *Ebony* magazine named him one of the country's "ten most out-standing Negro preachers."[19]

Close to Martin Luther King Jr., Smith helped found the Southern Christian Leadership Conference in 1957 and served on the SCLC's board. In Nashville, he organized an SCLC affiliate called the Nashville Christian Leadership Council. In January 1958 he wrote letters to Nashville's Black ministers, summoning them to a meeting to craft a civil rights agenda based on social gospel principles. Smith became the group's president, with Vivian assuming the vice presidency. Other ministers, both Black and white, who would be central to the group's efforts—Metz Rollins, Andrew White, Will Campbell—were also present at the founding.[20]

The group created a position called "social action leader." To this role they appointed James Lawson, a twenty-nine-year-old Vanderbilt divinity student. A Methodist from Massillon, Ohio, Lawson had worked for the Fellowship of Reconciliation with the pacifist A. J. Muste and was jailed for refusing to serve in the Korean War. Lawson then lived in India for three years where he studied satyagraha, Gandhi's nonviolent resistance philosophy. On coming home, he enrolled at Oberlin College for a master's degree.[21]

At Oberlin, in 1957, a campus chaplain, Harvey Cox, later a celebrated theologian, hosted a visit by Martin Luther King. Cox introduced King to Lawson. They bonded over their commitment to nonviolence. King told Lawson that he hoped to replicate the Montgomery bus boycott approach across the South. Lawson shared with King his plans to pursue a doctorate at Yale and then come south to work on racial issues. "Don't wait!" King replied. "Come now! We don't have any Negro leadership in the South that understands nonviolence." Lawson was persuaded. He got a job with the Fellowship of Reconciliation and transferred to Vanderbilt to complete his studies.[22]

Smith and Vivian allowed Lawson a strong hand in setting their new group's agenda. Lawson envisioned making Nashville into the center of a major nonviolent desegregation campaign, a showcase city, the way Montgomery had been with the bus boycott. With Glenn Smiley, a forty-seven-year-old white minister and veteran civil rights activist also with the Fellowship of Reconciliation, Lawson began offering workshops and lectures on nonviolence. The first ones were held as part of a three-day conference, March 26 to 28, 1958, at the Bethel AME Church.

Only about ten ministers attended. But it was a start.[23]

One day on the American Baptist campus in the fall of 1958, Kelly Miller Smith invited Lewis to services at his church. Lewis was honored to be asked. "Kelly Miller Smith was such an unbelievable, inspirational speaker and preacher," he said. "He had emerged as a leader in Nashville. He had these famous speakers come to his church." Lewis struck Smith as markedly different from any other student he had taught. Lewis didn't speak much, but he unfailingly chose his words with thought and care. They had a gravity and wisdom, Smith thought. "That young man is pure of heart," he would tell others. C. T. Vivian, who was a teaching assistant at American Baptist, felt the same way. "There is a kind of depth of sincerity, a profound sense of commitment and understanding," he said of Lewis, "not simply of issues but understanding of the human situation, that made Lewis a very real person to us all."[24]

Lewis had been attending services at the Spruce Street Baptist Church. But when he visited First Baptist, he found the services to be intellectually richer, more stimulating, more exciting. Black lawyers, doctors, and intellectuals from around Nashville—professors from Fisk and Meharry—populated the congregation. Mingling with these people made Lewis aware of the intelligence and distinction in Nashville's African American community. The worshippers never made Lewis feel like a poor kid from Alabama who didn't belong. From the pulpit, Smith would hold forth on politics, for which Lewis had an insatiable appetite. "He didn't talk about . . . pie in the sky when you die," Lewis said. "He didn't talk about Hell. But his gospel, his message, had some social relevance. He was concerned about the way people were living and being treated in Nashville." Smith opened First Baptist to evening meetings of the Nashville Christian Leadership Council, which were held in the basement. The church, Lewis noted, "became a rallying point, . . . a sort of haven where people could come on a Sunday evening at 6 o'clock and discuss social action, debate the question of segregation and social discrimination."[25]

Despite having found a home at First Baptist, in the middle of his soph-
omore year Lewis was missing his family. He had the idea that he should
transfer to a college closer to home, Troy State. He could live at home and
commute by bus. There was just one problem: Troy State was all white.[26]

Lewis didn't see this as an insurmountable challenge. On the contrary,
he was emboldened by the new mood taking hold in the South. Blacks
were testing segregation at public universities. In 1956, Autherine Lucy had
enrolled at the University of Alabama—only to face vicious harassment,
which gave the university an excuse to suspend her in the name of her own
safety. Though Lucy's story ended unhappily, other challenges seemed sure
to follow. Lewis sent his application materials to Troy State. But no reply
came.[27]

Lewis then wrote a letter to Martin Luther King. Since hearing King on
the radio in high school, Lewis had regarded the minister as a hero, an inspiration, and a role model. Before long, a return letter came from Fred Gray,
King's lawyer. Gray agreed to appeal to Troy State on Lewis's behalf and sent
the college a letter by registered mail. Still no answer came. Lewis also spoke
with Ralph Abernathy, King's lieutenant. Abernathy remembered the phone
call a decade later. "He said he was a Negro," Abernathy said, "and was a little
stammering in his speech. And he said, 'I want to enter Troy State Teachers
College.'" Abernathy and Gray invited Lewis to Montgomery. They would
pay his bus fare.[28]

Lewis made plans to visit once he was back in Troy. He told his parents
about his opportunity. Although Eddie wasn't enthusiastic, he agreed to let
Lewis go to Montgomery. On Saturday, June 13, 1959, they drove to downtown Troy in silence, and Lewis boarded the bus.

In Montgomery, Lewis walked the four blocks to Gray's Monroe Street
office. Gray greeted him in a spiffy suit, grabbed his briefcase, and drove
them to Abernathy's First Baptist Church, ten blocks away. Entering the
pastor's study in the church basement, Lewis was thrilled to see, sitting next
to Abernathy, Martin Luther King himself. The great minister was perched
behind a large desk, with Abernathy to the side. Gray and Lewis took chairs
facing them.[29]

"So you're John Lewis? The boy from Troy?" King asked in a jovial tone.
"Who is this young man who wants to desegregate Troy State?"

Lewis was tongue-tied. He could feel his heart beating. "Dr. King," he said deferentially, "I am John Robert Lewis." He did not know why he gave his full name.[30]

The three men talked with Lewis about a lawsuit. They were willing to file it, they said, and would cover Lewis's expenses. But it wouldn't be easy. Powerful men were determined to uphold segregation. "If you do this, something could happen to you," King warned, launching into a litany of possible harms. Lewis's parents could be targeted. "They could lose work, lose their jobs," King continued. "They could be assaulted. Your home could be attacked. The farm could be burned."[31]

In Alabama, King noted, anyone under twenty-one needed a guardian's permission to file a lawsuit. Lewis would have to talk it over with his parents and return to Montgomery with them. With that, they stood up and shook hands.[32]

Lewis had impressed his elders. "I just couldn't believe that this unimpressive-looking rural boy . . . could possess the courage to really want to go to Troy State Teachers College," Abernathy recalled. "I thought he was the bravest man that I had the privilege of meeting." Abernathy reached in his pocket and gave Lewis bus fare for the ride home.[33]

As Lewis rode back in the darkness, he couldn't stop telling himself that he had just met Martin Luther King. At the Troy bus station, Eddie was waiting. Father and son drove home together, again in silence.[34]

The next day John told his parents everything King had said. They could see his enthusiasm. But it became clear that they were afraid of what could happen—to their son, themselves, their friends, their neighbors. Whenever African Americans had sought equality in the South, they had faced retaliation, whether from the law, the Klan, the banks or shop owners to whom they owed money, or the employers on whom their livelihoods depended. Even though Eddie owned his land now, he was in debt to the bank for his tractor and machine tools, and he worried that the bank might call in his loan. Or that he might lose his bus-driving job, or jeopardize his credit at the feed-and-seed store. Willie Mae worried, too, about their friends and neighbors. Finally, they told their son that they wouldn't go along with a lawsuit.[35]

Lewis was heartbroken. But he wasn't about to cross his parents. He wrote to King, telling him that he would be returning to American Baptist in September after all.[36]

The fall of 1959 turned out to be a critical moment for Lewis and for many others in Nashville.

For months, the NCLC ministers had been debating what sort of campaign to wage. Should they prioritize voter registration? Police brutality? The paltry job opportunities for Blacks in Nashville? Lawson and Smith convinced their group to start with what would come to be called sit-ins to desegregate Nashville's downtown lunch counters. Lawson had been hearing from Black women who had no place to get a cup of coffee or a sandwich when they shopped downtown. It was degrading. In Harveys department store, one woman told him, white children rode on a gorgeous carousel while their mothers rested comfortably nearby. Black children were forbidden to ride.

A strategic calculation also lay behind this decision. "Our view was that the sit-ins would lend themselves to a kind of public presentation of the issue," Smith later said. Lunch-counter protests had the potential, like the Montgomery bus boycott, to get a great deal of attention and educate white Nashville about the blatant injustices Blacks faced.[37]

As they planned their campaign, Smith recalled, "at first there were no students involved anywhere." Then Lawson heard that the students at the Fusons' salons wanted to get involved.

"Can they participate?" he asked Smith.

"Yeah, why not?" Smith answered.[38]

When the colleges reopened that fall, the ministers began recruiting students. Smith invited Lewis to come hear Lawson speak one Sunday evening.[39]

It was a riveting performance, and Lewis was enchanted. In a small room at First Baptist Church, he recounted, Lawson projected "an aura of inner peace and wisdom that you could sense immediately upon simply seeing him." The minister spoke about the great religions of the world—Judaism, Christianity, Islam, Hinduism, Buddhism—and their shared belief in justice. Lawson told the group that he would be holding regular Tuesday night meetings, where they would explore questions of religion, justice, nonviolence, and social and racial progress.[40]

About fifteen or twenty students from Nashville's colleges began coming to these sessions, first held at Bethel AME, and then, as the numbers grew, at the Clark Memorial Methodist Church on the corner of Fourteenth Avenue and Phillips Street. "The students became very interested and outnumbered the adults, quickly and easily," Smith said. "And so it came to be known as a student movement, which we didn't particularly mind."[41]

Lewis never missed a session. Initially, they seemed unfocused. "For a long time it appeared to me that we were just theorizing," he said. Lawson taught the group about the theory and practice of nonviolent resistance. He spoke about nonviolence as a tool in history, from Jesus to Thoreau to King. Lawson discussed obscure chapters in the American past, like the abolitionist activism of Adin Ballou, a Rhode Island Unitarian who preached nonviolent resistance in the 1830s. The group talked about Jews who fought back against the Nazis and about Gandhi's quest for Indian independence. "Jim was really the thinker in this group," Lewis said. "We regarded him as our real teacher in nonviolence. I think he could have been the most important man in the civil rights movement, if he wanted." To Lewis, Lawson "came across as the embodiment, as the personification of the philosophy and the discipline of nonviolence. He was not just preaching a sermon. In a sense he was living it." C. T. Vivian dubbed Lawson their "guru of nonviolence."[42]

By the time Lawson began his workshops, two generations of Black leaders had been developing ideas about nonviolent resistance rooted in Gandhi. King was a devotee, but so were such movement figures as Bayard Rustin, James Farmer, Benjamin Mays, and even to some extent predecessors as disparate as W. E. B. Du Bois and Marcus Garvey.

The core principle was satyagraha, often translated as "soul force" or "truth force": the idea that a righteous movement, in challenging state policies or a governmental system, should abjure not only violent responses to oppression but the very feelings of anger and hatred that the oppression induced. In the hands of Black ministers like Howard Thurman—and, later, King, Smith, Lawson, and others—these Gandhian precepts mingled with the Christian social gospel teachings of Walter Rauschenbusch and his intellectual descendants. Lawson explained that the Christian Bible "infused all of my reading of Gandhi." Or as King said: "Christ furnished the spirit and motivation, while Gandhi furnished the method."[43]

According to this philosophy, only nonviolence could bring about what was called "the beloved community." That phrase, coined by the nineteenth-century philosopher Josiah Royce, a cofounder of the Fellowship of Reconciliation, referred to an ideal arrangement of human relationships, founded in love, that could transform a society, uniting former adversaries in peace and harmony. It envisioned a world that was racially integrated, rooted in equality, and capable of resolving conflicts without violence. "The aftermath of nonviolence," King explained in a 1957 speech, "is the creation of the beloved community."[44]

Coming from an intellectual powerhouse like Lawson, this was heady stuff. Yet not everyone who attended his classes was enthralled. Some, accustomed to a more flamboyant style, found Lawson cerebral, serene, and detached—more like a white college professor than a Black preacher. When he talked about oppression, some of his would-be disciples thought, it was as if these horrors were being inflicted on someone else, not their fellow Black Tennesseans.

But Lewis was hooked. "The whole idea of nonviolence was based on the love ethic of the New Testament," he explained. "We really accepted what the great teachers said: Turn the other cheek, and be willing to accept the beating, to suffer, because it's redemptive. It can change the oppressor, but it also can change you and help, in the process, to change the larger society."[45] Lewis also heard in Lawson's lectures echoes of King—more reason to take it seriously.

The workshops excited Lewis more than his college classes did. "Dr. King talked about the moment when the different parts of you come together, and this was it for me," Lewis said. "This was what I'd been waiting for. This was what I'd been called to do." For the rest of his life, Lewis would rank Lawson second only to King in the influence he had upon Lewis's young self.[46]

Lawson, for his part, saw Lewis as an apt pupil. "John Lewis was at the first workshop and went to all the workshops. Lewis was ripe. He knew the horror of segregation; he just needed to fasten on the philosophy and ideas and tactics. He was one of our keenest students." The wholehearted commitment was unmistakable from the start. "He realized," Lawson said, "that he was on the right path."[47]

Lawson was not alone in observing Lewis's intense affinity for Gandhi, King, and the social gospel. It was commonly remarked that Lewis was drawn to nonviolence as a way of life more completely than anyone else.

"John Lewis, perhaps as much as any man I've ever known, unless it'd be Jim Lawson, really *believes* in nonviolence," said Will Campbell, a white minister active in the NCLC. "I think you could kill him and he wouldn't resist. I don't think this is true of very many people."[48]

Eager to share his passion, Lewis recruited friends from American Baptist. At first, he said, "we had the most difficult time. People thought we were crazy, going down and encouraging people to attend the workshops. That we were going to have a big movement." But he found a few takers. Bernard LaFayette remembered dorm room discussions with Lewis about the conflicts percolating around the South. "This is what we talk about in the meetings!" Lewis told him with exasperation. LaFayette, who had protested that his schoolwork and jobs kept him too busy, finally relented. Soon Lewis was making the trip from American Baptist to Nashville's downtown with a small group of friends. Even Helen Johnson got involved.[49]

One holdout was Bevel. A self-described "chicken-eating, liquor-drinking, woman-chasing Baptist preacher" whose friends called him "Devil," Bevel fancied himself too cool for such virtuous work. Besides, he had a regular gig on Sundays preaching at a little church in Dickson. "He could not see the validity, the necessity, of being involved in the workshops," Lewis said. But Lewis kept asking, not least because Bevel possessed something valuable: a car. Lewis and LaFayette had been rising early to walk all the way to Lawson's sessions in town, so Lewis began to corral Bevel and beg him for a ride. But Bevel did not attend himself for many months.[50]

The numbers grew. "It was word of mouth, mostly," Lawson said. "I don't think we ever put up a poster." A white Fisk student named Paul LaPrad recruited friends from the Fusons' salons, including several other whites, creating a racially integrated group.[51]

The students resolved to make decisions by consensus—the "Quaker model," some called it. But leaders have a way of emerging. One woman whose initiative and skill became evident was a Chicagoan named Diane Nash. Having transferred that fall to Fisk from Howard University, Nash had never been to the South before. On an early date she was horrified to see "white" and "colored" signs at the Tennessee State Fair. She shared Lewis's steely determination, but also came across as polished, worldly, and commanding. Poised, even genteel, she had grown up in a middle-class Catholic family and once hoped to become a nun. She had also won a few beauty pageants. Many of her Nashville friends would comment on her looks before anything else. "The first time I saw her," said Rodney Powell, part of the student group, "it was like looking at Maria from *West Side Story*." Lewis called her "just about the most gorgeous woman any of us had seen." Some joked that the Nashville group grew so rapidly in the fall of 1959 because men were drawn to Nash. But it wasn't her beauty that made her the choice to lead the group. As Lewis put it, "She was dead serious about what we were doing each week, very calm, very deliberate, always straightforward and sincere."[52]

After the weeks of study came a phase that Lewis termed "sociodrama." Sitting in rows of folding chairs, the students practiced the techniques of nonviolent protest, with an eye toward staging sit-ins at Nashville's lunch counters. "We actually acted out roles," Lewis said, "trying to foresee the variety of possible alternatives, and how we could apply nonviolence to different situations." One student might play the part of a protester, learning to control his temper and mute his reactions, while someone else acted as a racist antagonist, yanking at the student's lapels, cursing him out, dumping drinks on him, spitting on him, or calling him "nigger" or, for a white student, "nigger lover." It was crucial, Lawson said, not to shy away from that hateful word; its cruel, totemic power had to be destroyed. During the sessions, a Black student might play the part of a white, or vice versa. The participants sought to dehumanize each other, break each other's spirits, and in so doing build up their own capacity to resist. "Jim was encouraging us to grow up, to dig deep inside us and let the true self, the best self, come out," Lewis said.[53]

"We'd try to stage it realistically," Lawson said. "I said, 'You have to cuss them out, call them bad names. Put yourself in that mood and act it.'" Lawson also taught them how to curl their bodies to protect their organs from kicks and blows, and how to keep eye contact with their assailant all the while. More important, he taught them, "You have to do more than just not hit back. You have to have no *desire* to hit back. You have to love that person who's hitting you."[54]

Even as the students' ranks swelled, Lewis stood out. Some friends, like Angeline Butler, noted how shy he was and how he spoke with difficulty. But she sensed something strong and good in his character. "John had this overwhelming sincerity," she recalled. "John never had an ego." To Smith, Lewis naturally "assumed kind of a position of leadership" rooted in "the quality of his fearlessness. He was always as steady as a rock. He was pretty clear what he was about."[55]

The Nashville students drew tighter. They ate together before the workshops and shared rides back to campus. Marian Fuson drove groups downtown, then waited for a call from the church secretary to pick them up. In informal moments, they opened up about their backgrounds and families. Lewis thought that the Nashville group was, in its own way, becoming a "beloved community unto itself."[56]

In late November 1959, the group planned some dry runs at the downtown department stores. The Nashville ministers had lobbied these establishments to desegregate voluntarily, without success. Now the idea was to stage a dress rehearsal—not to confront the store management yet, but simply to assess how aggressively the Jim Crow rules would be enforced. They would seek service at the lunch counters, but would not, for now, press the issue.[57]

On Saturday, November 28, Lawson, Smith, and a dozen students including Lewis met at First Baptist. Everyone dressed up: coats and ties for the men, blouses and skirts for the women. They wanted to show that they weren't an unruly mob, that they weren't intending anything violent. Lewis was excited but also suddenly felt scared. Since childhood he had seethed at being relegated to "colored" facilities yet had always complied. Now he would act differently.

The group walked from the church to Harveys department store downtown, where shoppers crowded the streets. Inside the store, Lewis bought a handkerchief—a gesture to signal that he was a legitimate customer. Then the group sat down at the Monkey Bar, which served hamburgers and fast food. A waitress took their orders. But after a minute or two she returned.

"I'm sorry," she said. "We can't serve you here."

Nash asked to see the manager. The waitress disappeared in the back. A middle-aged white man in a suit came out. "It is our policy not to serve colored people here," he said. Nash asked if their white companions could be served. No, the manager said, because they were part of an interracial group. Nash thanked him, and they filed out. Lewis was impressed with her equanimity. Only later did she tell him she was trembling inside. Back at the church, Lawson debriefed the students and praised them for their execution. On campus that afternoon, Lewis had a hard time containing his enthusiasm. Most of his classmates, however, remained uninterested, preferring to work on their sermons.[58]

The next week, Lewis and his friends repeated their exercise at Cain-Sloan, another department store. This time Lewis led the way, asking to talk to the manager and saying thank you when service was denied. Again, he went back to his dorm on a high, infused with a sense of anticipation. Though they had final exams to study for, he and LaFayette couldn't stop talking about what lay ahead.

When the semester ended, just before Christmas, the two friends boarded a Greyhound to Montgomery, where Lewis planned to transfer to a bus for Troy and LaFayette would continue on to Tampa. They took seats behind the driver.

The driver whirled around. "You can't sit there. You sit in the back," he ordered. The young men didn't flinch or budge. "I'm going to get off and go inside," the driver told them. "When I come back, you better be out of there."

Both worried about what might happen to them when they parted ways. "He was concerned something was going to happen to me," Lewis remembered. "I was concerned something was going to happen to him."[59]

But they stayed put. When the driver returned and saw them unmoved, he snarled. Clambering behind the wheel, he jammed the seat back—hard, as far back as it would go. Lewis and LaFayette rode to Alabama with their knees pushed up against their chins.[60]

Chapter Three

THE SIT-INS

———— ∎ ∎ ————

Before John Lewis returned to Nashville in January 1960, the ministers
of the Nashville Christian Leadership Council were already at work.
James Lawson and Kelly Miller Smith had reopened talks with department
store owners to persuade them to integrate. But the owners refused, and
Lawson said he wouldn't wait much longer. On January 5, the *Chicago Defender*,
the nation's leading Black newspaper, described the fruitless attempts
in November to obtain service at Harveys and Cain-Sloan. "The group plans
to continue the pursuit of the problem," the article noted matter-of-factly,
"until a morally defensible solution is discovered."[1]

After the holiday break, Angeline Butler felt a stirring, a coming to life,
as students returned to campus. "We were ready to seize the opportunity
and keep the story alive," she said. Lawson was planning sit-ins for late January,
but, busy with his own doctoral work, he procrastinated. The workshops
resumed, but there were no trips downtown.[2]

Then, before the Nashvillians could act, four freshmen at North Carolina
A&T in Greensboro stole their thunder. On February 1, the students
occupied a Woolworth's lunch counter and refused to leave. Activists before
them had attempted sit-ins (or "sit-downs," as they were also called) in sixteen
cities over the previous three years. But those demonstrations hadn't set
off tremors the way Greensboro did. Covered in the Black press and the national
media, the North Carolina students captured the imagination of the
country. In Harlem, Bob Moses, a high school math teacher, saw a picture

of the students and felt a calling. "These were kids my own age, and I knew this had something to do with my own life," he said. In Atlanta, a seventeen-year-old Spelman College undergraduate, Ruby Doris Smith, rushed home to watch a report about Greensboro on the evening news. In Orangeburg, South Carolina, Chuck McDew, a Black Ohioan who had converted to Judaism, thought about the words of the sage Hillel: "If I am not for myself, then who is for me?" In Birmingham, minister Fred Shuttlesworth, a King confidant, implored Ella Baker, executive director of SCLC, "You must tell Martin that we must get with this!"[3]

Word of mouth mattered as much as the press in spreading the news. "A brother may have been in school, let's say in Greensboro," Baker said, "and a sister was in school somewhere else. And he would write and tell her, 'Why shouldn't they do something?' This is the way it escalated." Students in Charlotte, Raleigh, and other cities began their own sit-ins.[4]

But just as the fable of Rosa Parks, the mild-mannered seamstress too weary to move to the back of the bus, omitted the backstory of the Montgomery community's long-standing work fighting segregation, so, too, the tale of the Greensboro students' spontaneous action left out the role of the veteran activists who had been preparing the ground. Those activists included Kelly Miller Smith, James Lawson, and the other Nashville ministers, as well as people like Douglas Moore, a Durham pastor active in the Fellowship of Reconciliation and SCLC. Moore called Lawson early in the morning on February 10. "What can the students in Nashville do to help the students in North Carolina?" he asked.[5]

When that phone call came, John Lewis asserted, "we were ready." The Nashville campuses were already humming with talk about North Carolina. Lawson summoned Lewis, Nash, and other student leaders to a meeting. The next day, seventy-five students showed up at a room in the Fisk University chemistry building. Some knew nothing about Gandhi or satyagraha, and when Lawson expounded in his raspy whisper about nonviolence, the newcomers laughed. That reaction disturbed Lawson and Smith, who considered postponing their sit-ins until they could train everyone properly. But Lewis and the students, now keen to strike, prevailed.[6]

On Friday night, February 12, two hundred students filled the pews at First Baptist. Lewis by now had come to share his mentors' concern that the neophytes wouldn't adhere to Lawson's methods. He worried about unleashing hundreds of untrained, keyed-up college students upon the five-and-dimes. An unruly crush of students would create a very different impression than a disciplined cadre pointedly exposing the injustice of segregation. The effort could fail or backfire.[7]

Under the solution they devised, Lewis said, "the people who had been attending the workshops were to be the leaders" and go first. Others would watch and learn. On Friday night, Lawson administered a crash course in satyagraha into the wee hours. "We tried to catch them up on the essentials," Lewis said. "They were instructed not to engage in any form of aggression or retaliation, to sit right up at the lunch counters and be quiet, literally to study, to do their homework." After midnight, Lawson told everyone that when they came the next morning, they should dress neatly, bring books, and be ready to go to jail.[8]

"Once Jim Lawson had spoken," Lewis said, "at that moment the way was clear. It was like he illuminated everything. . . . Our consciences had been activated, and there was no way you could then not act."[9]

When students gathered at the church on Saturday morning, a wintry light filled the skies and eight inches of snow coated the sidewalks. Lewis had never seen so much snow. Local churchwomen brought sandwiches and hot drinks. More than a hundred students streamed in, dressed in coats and ties, stockings and heels. Lewis, wearing a fine white shirt, print tie, and his high school graduation suit, felt as if he were going to Sunday services. Then the students set off two abreast for the Arcade, a covered passageway linking Fourth and Fifth Avenues downtown, for a rally. Afterward, they fanned out to Kress's, Woolworth's, and McLellan's. Each team mixed students from the different schools, to forge unity and to guard against cliques.[10]

Lewis led the Woolworth's contingent. As he walked in, he felt a knot in his stomach. But he became aware of an inner faith guiding him. It was, he said, a "faith that God would not allow his children to be punished for doing the right thing." Yet it was also a faith in much more—in Lawson, in Lewis's friends, in the justice of their cause, and in the conviction that Americans would respond well to their action. That faith prodded him to soldier on.[11]

Lewis drew on all he had learned in recent months. He and his friends bought notebooks and handkerchiefs to show that they were legitimate customers before sitting down at the counters. Then the room grew quiet.

"No one got up," Lewis remembered. "No one said anything." One waitress stopped "dead in her tracks" and pierced the silence with a racial slur.[12]

Lewis placed an order. The waitress refused him. He and his comrades then sat in place—for hours. As the clock ticked, they stayed on their best behavior, even brushing cigarette ashes from the countertop. Lewis immersed himself in a history of Greek philosophy. What Lawson called "a delusive calm" prevailed. The white patrons seemed less angry than confused. In the ladies' room, two Black students encountered a flustered white woman who blurted out, "Oh! Nigras, Nigras everywhere!" and ran away. Eventually the waitresses shut off the lights. But the store stayed open, and the students stayed put.[13]

Friends occupied the other stores. Lawson and a few of the adults moved "from place to place and kept our eyes on things," the minister recalled. "The police were orderly. The managers kept people from congregating without shopping." Plainclothes detectives monitored the scene. So did the movement's undercover white allies—"in case we needed witnesses," Lawson said. But apart from a minor incident at McLellan's, in which police came but arrested no one, there were no disturbances. If anything, Nash said, the day was intermittently comic. The waitresses were so nervous, she said, "they must have dropped two thousand dollars' worth of dishes."[14]

When Lewis and his friends got back to First Baptist, he recounted, it was "sheer euphoria, like a jubilee." People were "whooping, cheering, hugging, laughing, singing." Everyone wanted to do it again. They picked Thursday, February 18, to hold another round of sit-ins.

The students christened themselves the "Nashville Student Movement." Lewis and the most dedicated members formed a "central committee" to make decisions. They met before and after class, in the early morning and evening. They formed a finance committee, a publicity committee, and a work committee to paint signs and provide food.[15]

Outside Nashville, the sit-in movement also gained strength. Students from Norfolk to Tallahassee joined in. Ministers in other cities conducted workshops modeled on Lawson's. On Northern campuses, students raised funds and picketed in solidarity.

The sit-ins were front-page news. But the press misread the movement. It tended to portray the students as embodying a strain of protest different from Martin Luther King's or as posing a challenge to his leadership. Yet the sit-ins were a direct outgrowth of King's philosophy and strategy of non-violent direct action, guided by social gospel ministers affiliated with the SCLC. The sit-ins had only happened, Lawson argued, "because of King and the Montgomery boycott." Ministers "clustered around King," he said, "had emerged, preaching and teaching direct action and nonviolent action." Far from seeing the sit-ins as a threat, King endorsed them. "The demonstrations reveal that the Negro will no longer accept segregation in any form," he told the *New York Times*.[16]

In Nashville, the second set of sit-ins, held on February 18, made clear that the first foray had made an impact. Diane Nash now found herself a local celebrity, as well as a target. As she walked downtown, a gang of whites recognized her from a photograph in the *Tennessean*. "That's Diane Nash!" someone yelled. "She's the one to get!" The dime stores also changed their behavior. They blocked off their counters, unscrewed the barstools, or covered counters with wastebaskets and frying pans.[17]

The students came anyway. Two hundred students showed up for the second round of sit-ins; for the third round, on February 20, three hundred came. They expanded their sights to include W. T. Grant's, Walgreens, and Cain-Sloan. They also attracted more enemies. Young white provocateurs now hovered around the students, taunting them. The protesters sat politely and did their schoolwork. One *Tennessean* article mentioned "a ministerial student at American Baptist Theological Seminary," John Lewis, toiling on a sermon as he occupied the lunch counter.[18]

Late in February, white Nashville began to change its tune. Uncertain how long the disruptions would continue, the merchants lost patience. They asked the mayor to stop the students from entering their stores and to arrest them if they occupied closed-off counters. West waffled, afraid to alienate either the businessmen or the Black voters, whose support he also needed.[19]

Other local whites were also mobilizing. The menacing crowds at the sit-ins were growing. Bernard LaFayette and several other students met with Police Chief Douglas Hosse to ask him to restrain the mobs. Hosse claimed he lacked the manpower and urged the students to back down. "Is this all worth a twenty-five-cent hamburger?" he asked uncomprehendingly.

Around the South, other sit-in actions were met by rough tactics. In Chattanooga, demonstrators less well-trained than Lawson's legions were baited into a brawl, which police put down with fire hoses. As the third weekend of protests arrived, rumors circulated in Nashville about impending violence. The next sit-in, scheduled for February 27, was being dubbed "Big Saturday." Will Campbell, who would "mill around and hear what the cops were saying," warned the students not to go back to the shops that day. A friendly local woman whose husband worked at Harveys had told the ministers that Ben West had agreed to let the white hoodlums work their will for a few minutes while the cops would look the other way.[20]

Lewis worried again about maintaining discipline. If violence broke out, how many of the students would control themselves? The night before Big Saturday, the students and ministers gathered to decide how to proceed. Lewis volunteered to draft guidelines to hand out the next day. From King's *Stride Toward Freedom* book about the Montgomery campaign, Lewis adapted a list of rules to observe during nonviolent actions. Using keys to the American Baptist supply room (his dining hall duties having given way to janitorial ones), he and LaFayette pilfered a ream of mimeograph paper. A schoolmate's wife typed up the list. All night long, they printed and cut their leaflets to size. The instructions read:

DO NOT:

1. Strike back or curse if so abused.
2. Laugh out.
3. Hold conversations with floor walker.
4. Leave your seat until your leader has given permission to do so.
5. Block entrances to stores outside; nor the aisles inside.

DO:

1. Show yourself courteous and friendly at all times.
2. Sit straight; always face the counter.
3. Report all serious incidents to your leader.
4. Refer information seekers to your leader in a polite manner.
5. Remember the teachings of Jesus Christ, Mahatma Gandhi, and Martin Luther King. Love and non-violence is the way.

"MAY GOD BLESS EACH OF YOU."[21]

Early on Big Saturday, the ministers and the central committee leaders met at First Baptist. They gathered in the basement around what Kelly Miller Smith described as an "age-worn table in the Sunday School department." The adults advocated caution. "If you go downtown, you will probably be beaten," Campbell said. "There are a lot of young hoodlums on the streets. And you will probably be arrested." Lawson and Smith agreed. "Perhaps we will all be locked up before this thing is over," Smith said. He added that the NCLC lacked the funds to bail everyone out. According to its treasurer, the organization had only $87.50 left in its coffers. Nor had the ministers lined up the lawyers they would need in case of mass arrests.[22]

Cracks opened in the students' united front. "They may have a point," said Paul LaPrad. "If anybody else goes, I will probably go too, but I can see what they mean." Angeline Butler called it "a difficult moment for all of us." The students knew that they might end up with a criminal record, get expelled from school, face violence, or subject their families to retaliation.

Searching for consensus, they kept talking. Finally, an impassioned James Bevel—who only recently had begun coming to the meetings—seized the floor. "We woke up this morning with the roosters," he said. They had come ready to act and it would be wrong to delay. "If we wait until next week," he said, "we may be asked to wait until next month, and then the next month and on and on. Personally, I'm tired of this business of waiting."

Lewis nodded. Others now spoke up, too. They couldn't let the moment pass.

There was no point in continuing to argue, Smith realized. The adults gave in. "We are all in this together," he said. "When you go down to the stores, you will go with our full support."[23]

The students hurried upstairs to the sanctuary. It was now packed with around three hundred foot soldiers. God has spoken, LaFayette thought to himself. Lewis distributed his handouts. "You are to follow these instructions to the letter," Lawson commanded. "And remember this: Violence of the spirit is even worse than striking back."[24]

The students in the front pews set off first. If they were arrested and reinforcements were needed, the rows behind them would go next, and so on down through the rows. As they left the building, the students stopped by the church office and divested themselves of pocket knives, nail files, and anything that might taint their nonviolent image. Then, with what Smith described as the "casual haste" of young people hustling to a Saturday matinee or a football kickoff, the troops headed for their stores.[25]

When managers at Grant's and Cain-Sloan saw the wave of students coming, they closed up shop. Kress's had preemptively roped off its lunch counter. But thanks to the rumors of an impending showdown, Woolworth's, McLellan's, and Walgreens were all teeming with spectators, as were the sidewalks along Fifth Avenue.

The first incident occurred at McLellan's. LaPrad was the initial target; racist whites were often angriest at the white activists, whom they saw as betraying their race. LaPrad was sitting next to Maxine Walker and Peggi Alexander, both Black women, when several goons taunted him with the cry of "nigger lover." One seized LaPrad from behind, pulled him off his stool, and pummeled him with clenched fists. As he curled up on the floor, a wire service photographer took his picture, which ran in newspapers nationwide.[26]

At Woolworth's, when Lewis arrived, a crowd was waiting—almost 350 people, according to reporter David Halberstam's contemporaneous account, "all watching the counter like spectators at a boxing match." Reporters and photographers encamped on the mezzanine. The police stood outside. Lewis took a seat with his unit at a lunch counter upstairs, while a different faction claimed the downstairs bar.[27]

The altercation started downstairs. "Go home, nigger," jeered the hostile whites. "What's the matter, you chicken?" Name-calling escalated into spitting, slapping into punching. Lewis's group hurried down to join their friends. Some assailants threw merchandise. Others burned the students with cigarettes or stuffed butts down their collars. The white youths began yanking the sit-in students off their seats and hitting them. Someone slugged Lewis in the ribs, doubling him over. But no one fought back. Finally, Lewis stumbled out of Woolworth's into the daylight. At that point, he recalled, "I think we heard about the arrests at McLellan's and we walked there."

Police were keeping traffic off Fifth Avenue. Amid the mostly peaceful onlookers, a boisterous throng was hooting and yelling. "We walked to McLellan's and we got over the ropes," Lewis said. He found himself face-to-face with a cop. "You're under arrest," the policeman said. He frisked and handcuffed Lewis and others and led them into a paddy wagon. The crowd cheered.[28]

It was the first time Lewis had been arrested. He felt a twinge of fear. His mother's admonitions not to get into trouble with the law echoed in his head. But after a few moments he relaxed—and then realized that what he was feeling was exhilaration, even liberation. He had "crossed over," he later said, "from being afraid to feeling free." He took comfort in the camaraderie of his friends, the cosseting sense that "we have each other and we have our discipline and we know why we're there."[29]

As police vehicles drove the first round of students off to jail, new reinforcements claimed their seats. At McLellan's, Butler saw that after the beating of LaPrad, the manager was moving to lock the door; she rushed over to hold it open for the next wave of students. Word of the arrests filtered back to First Baptist, where the ministers dispatched more replacements. "We're going to fill their jails," Earl Mays, a Fisk student, excitedly told a reporter. "That's a promise." Students sang and rejoiced when they were arrested. Kelly Miller Smith was amused by the onlookers' bafflement. The police, faced with unfamiliar tactics, became belligerent. But the students maintained their poise. "We understand your problem and have nothing against you," one told a cop. "We know you're merely trying to do your duty. . . . We will not resist in any way."

By evening, Lewis and eighty companions were crammed into jail cells, segregated by race. Twenty people shared cells built for no more than four. None, so far as Lewis knew, had been in jail before. Yet the students were jubilant, cheering each batch of new arrivals at the lockup. Into the night, they sang and laughed. Eventually the police realized they had to stop arresting students. Professors from the colleges came to the jail to urge the students to let their bail be paid. But the students declined. The police, realizing it was in their interest to clear out the jails, cut bail from $100 to $5. Still, the students refused to pay. Finally, after 11:00 p.m., bail was waived and the students went home.[30]

The arrests galvanized the wider Black community. On Sunday, at six in the morning, eighty-five Black ministers met at Smith's church to take up the NCLC's demand for a meeting with the mayor. Lewis then went to an assembly in the Fisk chapel, where the university's president, Stephen Wright, pledged his solidarity to the students as well—"a great shot in the arm," Lewis said. Still later, the central committee gathered a thousand people for a rally.

Around the city, in barbershops and bridge clubs, sympathy for the students surged. Alexander Looby, the local Black lawyer, agreed to represent them in court with a team of twelve attorneys. Fifty thousand dollars in donations poured in to the NCLC.[31]

Two people who were not happy about Big Saturday were Eddie and Willie Mae Lewis. They learned about their son's arrest from a dean at American Baptist. Willie Mae wrote John a letter, repeating her old warnings about staying out of trouble. She told him to "get out of this mess," he recalled. "We send you off to get an education and we're terrified for what's going to happen to you. . . . You're going to get killed."

It bothered John that his mother was treating his arrest as though it were for public drunkenness. He tried to reassure her in a return letter. "Dear Mother," he wrote, "I'm doing fine. . . . I'm acting according to the dictates of my conscience and I'm only acting on what I think is God's will, and I can do no less."[32]

The Lewises weren't the only worried parents. C. T. Vivian recalled hysterical mothers and fathers phoning and writing college administrators. Bernard LaFayette's mother reproached him that the white friends of the LaFayettes who were paying for his schooling would frown on his activism. "Remember," she said, "God will straighten out everything if you give him time. You don't have to eat with the white people. . . . You're just making disturbance."

LaFayette, Bevel, and Lewis commiserated on the American Baptist campus near the Cumberland River. They had become a "trinity," LaFayette said. "Three people who had totally different kinds of personalities and also different kinds of theologies, but we were able to blend them together." As they sat, they repeated feelings about their parents that they had been sharing with one another. "I know she loves me," LaFayette said about his mother, "but she just don't understand." Ruptures like these were not easily healed. Lewis's conflict with his parents marked the start of several difficult years with his family—not an estrangement but a breach, a drift apart.[33]

Lewis now saw his friends in Nashville as something like a replacement family. In some respects he felt closer to them than to his family in Troy. Through the crucible of the last months, the movement had become Lewis's defining purpose, fueled by politics, faith, and his quest for personal dignity. As much as he wished to put his mother at ease, he could not desist from the struggle.[34]

Having been released from jail Saturday night, John and the other students still had to report to the city courthouse on Monday to face charges. A crowd of 2,500 gathered downtown, singing spirituals and freedom songs. Inside, Judge Andrew Doyle dismissed the loitering charges against the students, but not the charges of disturbing the peace, disorderly conduct, or sitting at a closed counter. Doyle then turned the proceedings over to a colleague, John I. Harris.

Harris was a crotchety, old-school judge who did little to conceal his biases. Surrounded by newspapermen, photographers, lawyers, defendants, witnesses, and spectators, he felt hard-pressed to control his courtroom. Representing the students, Looby asked that all eighty defendants be tried collectively, but Harris chose to try them in small bunches—dragging the proceedings out all week long. Overall, he treated Looby with disdain; at one point, the judge turned his back on the attorney midsentence. "What's the use?!" Looby cried. "You are so prejudiced," he told the judge, "that you can't rule on this case." Smith called the proceedings "farcical."[35]

The students were convicted of misdemeanors and fined $50 each. They refused to pay. "We feel that if we pay these fines," Nash explained, "we would be contributing to and supporting the injustice and immoral practices that have been performed in the arrest and conviction of the defendants." They would go to the city workhouse instead. Lewis and the men had to shovel snow. The women had to shine the courthouse marble.[36]

While this drama played out at the courthouse, Mayor Ben West was angling for a political solution. On Monday he met with the NCLC ministers and their new allies among the Nashville clergy at First Baptist. West sought forbearance. He was known never to judge people by their skin color, he reminded everyone. Yet as mayor he also had to uphold the laws. He added that he had instructed Hosse, the police chief, to prosecute the hooligans who had assaulted the students on Saturday.

James Lawson, sitting in the back of the church and quietly gesturing to his colleagues, emerged as the public face of the sit-ins. After West spoke,

Lawson pushed back vigorously. "Young men were there with indications of getting rough," he said of the scene on Saturday. "The police were there and then withdrew." What was more, Lawson added, closing the lunch counters in advance of the sit-in was a transparent "gimmick" intended to criminalize a legitimate protest. Under those circumstances, he said, he would keep counseling the students "to violate the law." When Lawson finished, his colleagues rose in an extended standing ovation.[37]

When the *Nashville Banner* reported Lawson's remarks, critics pounced. The newspaper's publisher, James Stahlman, who opposed integration, set out to demonize Lawson. "Leader Says He'll Advise Group to Break Law," the paper's inflammatory headline read. The editorial page labeled the mild-mannered clergyman an "agent of strife" and a "flannel-mouth agitator." The next day—even as C. T. Vivian oversaw more sit-ins, with adults from Nashville's Black community joining in—Lawson felt compelled to clarify his comments. He was neither advocating "lawlessness" nor seeking to incite a riot, he explained in a prepared statement, just encouraging defiance of unjust laws in keeping with the time-honored principles of civil disobedience. "When the Christian considers the concept of civil disobedience as an aspect of nonviolence," he said, "it is only within the context of a law or law-enforcement agency which has in reality ceased to be the law."[38]

But the *Banner*'s sensationalist framing gave the sit-ins' opponents ammunition. Stahlman and Cain-Sloan executive John Sloan, both members of Vanderbilt University's board of trustees, convinced the university's chancellor, Harvie Branscomb, to dismiss Lawson from his doctoral program. The expulsion letter cited the minister's "strong commitment to a planned campaign of civil disobedience." The police also arrested Lawson on the dubious charge of conspiracy to disrupt trade, which carried a potential sentence of almost a year in prison. Photographers snapped pictures as cops led Lawson down the front steps of Smith's church to a squad car. One image unintentionally delivered an ironic commentary, containing within its frame the church's marquee board, which read "Father, forgive them"—a reference to Luke 23:34 in the New Testament: "Father, forgive them, for they know not what they do."[39]

The persecution of Lawson backfired. Catapulted to national renown, the minister became a martyr in the eyes of civil rights advocates. Vanderbilt's divinity school dean and most of its faculty voiced solidarity. Other divinity school deans invited him to finish his degree at their universities. Students turned out on his behalf en masse, and national news coverage brought a flood of letters, donations, speaking requests, and words of encouragement to Nashville.[40]

West felt obliged to de-escalate the situation. He had Lewis and the other students freed from their court-ordered work assignments. District Attorney Harry Nichol suspended the other prosecutions. Coming back to campus, Lewis felt triumphant. West also convened what was called a "biracial committee" to negotiate a lasting solution, though Lewis was upset that the mayor had not named any of the NCLC clergymen to it. The students agreed to a brief moratorium while the new committee deliberated.[41]

When no progress was forthcoming, however, the students resumed their activities. On March 15, they expanded their sights to the lunch counters at the Greyhound and Trailways bus stations. They claimed a small victory when the Greyhound station dinette served coffee to two students encamped there; the proprietors acknowledged that a 1955 Interstate Commerce Commission ruling required them to do so. The next day, Diane Nash, Peggi Alexander, and two male companions returned to the station and were again served, although when a photojournalist tried to document the moment, a waitress charged him with a knife. A gang of white youths then beat the two Black male protesters, generating more headlines. Several days later, Lewis and others were again arrested and jailed for sitting at a Moon-McGrath drugstore counter.[42]

With each episode, Lewis's utterly serene style was distinguishing him even from his disciplined colleagues. "He always kept a level head," said Frankie Blakely, the executive secretary of the NCLC. "I never even saw him get angry." He not only stayed perpetually calm but kept others calm. "John, he stayed cool and would control them better than anyone," she recalled.[43]

On April 5, West's biracial committee produced a report. In an astonishing misjudgment, it recommended a ninety-day period in which the stores would allow Blacks to sit at their counters—yet also maintain separate Black and white sections. Lewis was stunned. It showed him how little those in power understood the students' demands or the very problem of segregation. The new plan was "separate but equal" all over again. Trying to be conciliatory, the students and NCLC ministers held a two-hour meeting and asked to meet with the store owners to "bridge the gap," as Smith put it. But when that meeting yielded no progress, the students rejected the committee's proposal. "Only a system based on integration is acceptable in a 20th century democratic society," they declared.[44]

Demonstrators also added another tactic to their campaign: a boycott of the downtown shopping area. With Easter shopping season approaching, Fisk University economist Vivian Henderson had argued for an "economic withdrawal," based on research he had done showing that Blacks constituted one-fourth of the stores' clientele and contributed $7 million annually to their revenues. "We realized that another way to get their attention was needed," C. T. Vivian said. "I knew that the business community would take us seriously if we stopped buying from them." Meanwhile, in an election for sheriff, Black votes were instrumental in defeating Ben West's preferred candidate. At a time when Blacks were deprived of the vote in much of the South, their effective use of the ballot in Nashville was another sign of their still-unrealized electoral power there.[45]

On April 6, amid sit-ins, boycotts, and the disappointing committee report, Thurgood Marshall of the NAACP, the famed lawyer who had argued *Brown v. Board of Education* and other landmark desegregation cases before the Supreme Court, arrived in Nashville for a speech. Some 4,500 people packed the Fisk gymnasium to hear the great litigator. Lewis and Nash spoke for the students; it was the biggest audience Lewis had ever addressed. He was still very much the country boy; Will Campbell, who later realized he had badly underestimated Lewis, thought that Lewis was "barely able to speak a whole sentence in the English language." But he was gaining confidence, and he delivered opening words that were passionate if anodyne.[46]

Marshall was not altogether popular with the student audience. Some younger activists considered his strategy of pursuing equal justice through the courts to be conservative and slow-moving. Marshall was also known to have disparaged the sit-ins, calling the youngsters "impatient." But on this night he made it clear that he and the NAACP fully backed the sit-ins, praising "these young people for exposing the whole hierarchy in the South." He added, "They are no more impatient than the people who threw the tea in the harbor at Boston." He pledged that the NAACP would assist any student who was arrested.[47]

Where Marshall differed with the students was over their policy of refusing bail. "Once you've been arrested," he said, "you've made your point."

Lewis thought that the comment showed that Marshall didn't understand the students after all. They were rebelling against more than racial discrimination; they were up against the "traditional Black leadership structure."[48]

More pressing at the moment, however, was the intransigence of the city's white segregationists. Violent incidents were still occurring downtown, and the grapevine carried stories about bomb scares and death threats. In recent years, hard-core white supremacists had planted bombs at the Hattie Cotton Elementary School and Nashville's Jewish Community Center, as well as elsewhere around the South. The new threats could not be written off as mere talk.

That possibility became reality on Tuesday, April 19. John Lewis was up early that morning when the phone in his dormitory hall rang. A friend told him that just before daybreak a motorist had flung a bomb at Alexander Looby's residence, destroying half the house. Lewis roused LaFayette and they hurried to Clark Memorial Methodist Church, where the students often met. Consternation reigned. Lewis learned the details of the blast, which was so powerful it shattered 147 windows at a Meharry Hospital building a block away. Yet somehow Looby and his wife, asleep in the back bedroom, were unhurt. "We lived every day in fear that something like this would happen," said Octavia Vivian, C.T.'s wife. "These were killers," a police inspector concluded. "You don't throw that much dynamite to scare someone."[49]

The students decided to march. They sent a telegram to Ben West asking him to meet them that afternoon at city hall. Everyone skipped class that day; high school students did, too. By one o'clock, a massive procession, between four and six thousand people strong, was snaking from the Tennessee A&I campus to city hall. The human train advanced in virtual silence. C. T. Vivian, at the front, realized that all he could hear was the sound of thousands of footsteps. Lewis judged the scene "stupendous." He had never seen anything like it.[50]

At the plaza, Guy Carawan, a white musician who worked at the nearby Highlander Folk School, a camp for political organizing, strummed his guitar and led everyone in an old labor song rooted in an earlier gospel tune, "We Shall Overcome." It soon became the civil rights movement's anthem. The voices of the students washed over the plaza. When the singing subsided, Ben West, standing on the building steps, pledged to bring the bomber to justice. But the crowd was not letting him off easy. Vivian read from a statement, denouncing the biracial committee's feeble proposal and faulting West for dragging his feet. He and the students peppered West with questions. Lewis, standing in front, heard every word.[51]

West declined to make any promises. "We are all Christians together," he said. "Let us pray together." To which one student called out, "How about eating together?"

"Is segregation moral?" Vivian asked the mayor.

"No," West conceded, "it is wrong and immoral to discriminate."

Diane Nash thought West was filibustering. She asked the mayor to use "the prestige of your office" to stop discrimination. When he said he would, she then asked about the lunch counters. "Little lady," he chided, "I stopped segregation seven years ago at the airport when I first took office and there has been no trouble since."

"Then, Mayor," she countered, going in for the kill, "do you recommend that the lunch counters be desegregated?"

West felt he had to be honest. "Yes," he said.

Lewis watched with astonishment and pride. He thought Nash's interrogation was brilliant, forcing West to plumb his innermost feelings and answer truthfully.

Then West backtracked. He added that he had to respect the merchants' rights. "I can't tell a man how to run his business," he said. This equivocation drew more questioning from Vivian and others.

Another student interjected. Had West, he wanted to know, "just recommended the end of eating facility segregation?"

"Right!" West said, reverting to his earlier declaration, as if wanting to be done with it all. "Right! That is absolutely right!" The thousands-strong crowd now let loose with a burst of applause that left him no more room to back out. The next day's headline in the *Tennessean* read: "Integrate Counter—Mayor."[52]

The next night, Kelly Miller Smith brought in Martin Luther King to speak. The segregationists were still promising violence. The original venue, the Nashville War Memorial Auditorium, canceled the speech, on the grounds that King was "controversial," but Fisk University offered its gymnasium. The event got underway at 7:45 p.m., with four thousand in attendance. Loudspeakers were set up for the spillover crowd outside. Carawan again led the assembled in "We Shall Overcome." Looby took the stage to cheers; he burst into tears. Next, King entered, escorted by Smith, Vivian, and Lawson.

Packed in among the multitude on the gym floor, Lewis felt a rush, thinking back to his visit with King in Montgomery. But before King could begin, Vivian took the microphone, announcing that there had been another bomb threat. The building was evacuated as policemen and firemen scoured the premises.[53]

Almost an hour later, with everyone back in the gym, King finally spoke. He used no notes. He praised the Nashville students as "the best organized and the best disciplined of all movements in the Southland today," singling out the depth of their understanding and commitment to the philosophy of nonviolence. "We will meet the capacity to inflict suffering with the capacity to endure suffering," he vowed.[54]

King's words thrilled the audience, but it was the mayor's commitment to lunch counter desegregation that convinced the merchants they had lost. It was a consequential declaration. On May 10, they began allowing Blacks to be served at their dinettes. Nashville thus became the first major city in the South to allow Blacks and whites to eat together in public places. By June 1, ten other Southern cities had also desegregated lunch counters. Over the next two years, two hundred more would do so.[55]

On May 13 and 14, the NCLC and the Nashville Student Movement held a two-day event—part celebration, part planning session—called "Where Do We Go from Here?" C. T. Vivian spoke on nonviolence and Vivian Henderson on the economics of Nashville. Lewis was selected to speak for the students. He chose the topic "Democracy as a Reality."[56]

The noted African American journalist Louis Lomax dubbed the sit-ins "the second major battle of the Negro revolt," the first having been Montgomery. The Greensboro undergraduates had sparked a wildfire that swept the South, but the Nashville students and ministers had shown how to harness the energy. "No group of Black people, . . . against the rapaciousness of a segregated system, ever thought about desegregating downtown, tearing down the signs, renovating the waiting rooms, taking the immoral signs off of drinking fountains," Lawson later reflected. In his view, moreover, "the Nashville scene perhaps more than any other single scene, with the possible exception of Montgomery in 1955–56, became . . . the most significant in terms of its ongoing effect across the country."[57]

Amid the celebrations, it was sometimes forgotten how limited the scope of the victory was. Only a handful of stores were desegregating their lunch counters. Most of Nashville's restaurants, hotels, theaters, swimming pools, and other accommodations continued to discriminate. Other forms of inequality—in jobs, income, education—persisted.

Still, for Lewis, the experience was profound. It turned some of his cohort into local or even national figures. It also taught them to be image-conscious, Lewis believed—to learn to deal with the media and to use the attention to serve their larger purposes. "He would always say, 'We must dramatize the issue,'" one friend of Lewis's recalled.[58]

The experience of facing down injustice on the front lines also gave these young people determination and confidence in their own strength. Ultimately, it made them aware of their power to affect the course of history. The media exaggerated the rift between the students and the older movement activists. In Nashville, attorneys, local NAACP allies, and middle-class families lent critical help. Lewis valued the support they got from the academic world, the local Jewish community, Church Women United, and the Unitarian churches. But the emergence of students as prime movers in the struggle for racial equality was a watershed. The Nashville sit-ins injected new urgency into the civil rights movement.[59]

The events of early 1960 also cemented Lewis's belief in the efficacy and righteousness of nonviolence as King and Lawson taught it. "Altogether it was a moving feeling within me that I was sitting there demanding a God-given right," Lewis said in an NBC documentary that year. "And my soul became satisfied that I was right in what I was doing. At the same time, it was something deep down within me moving me that I could no longer be satisfied of going along with an evil system that I had to be maladjusted to." Progress came to Nashville for several reasons, including the city's relatively liberal political class, not least a mayor who understood segregation to be fundamentally wrong. But important, too, were the organization of the ministers and the size, strength, and dedication of the student movement. Above all, the students' ability to endure suffering, to reject violence and anger as a response, had won over the merchants, politicians, and white citizens of Nashville. For all the hatred, violence, and injustice that Lewis faced, he reflected, "I have to keep loving the people who were denying me service, who stared at me."[60]

Chapter Four

SNCC

———— ▪ ▪ ————

The Nashville sit-ins brought about the desegregation of the city's downtown lunch counters. But an equally important consequence was to deepen the familial feelings and bonds of trust among John Lewis and his peers. Students and ministers in the Nashville campaign discovered that they were, along with thousands of others across the South, a movement. By one scholar's count, fifty thousand people participated in sit-in activities that spring. Hearing news from other cities bolstered the Nashvillians' sense of purpose and ignited an effort to coordinate the many local actions.

To that end, over the first three days of April 1960, Lewis, Nash, Bevel, LaFayette, Butler, and other Nashville students, ministers, and professors joined an interracial group of eighty-two sit-in activists from twenty colleges for a weekend retreat at the Highlander Folk School, a hub of civil rights activity ninety minutes away, in the Cumberland Hills.[1]

Founded as a labor-organizing school in 1932 by a white man named Myles Horton, Highlander ran on the Deweyan principle that disenfranchised people should identify and solve their own political problems. In Horton's conception, the teachers' role was not to indoctrinate but to midwife these citizens' political awakening and facilitate their problem-solving. Highlander also stood out for its interracial character. As early as 1934, the school flouted state laws barring Blacks and whites from eating together or sharing dorms, and in 1944 it initiated integrated workshops. Eventually Horton turned his institute into a training ground in nonviolent direct action for racial equality. Martin Luther King became so enamored of the two-hundred-acre retreat that he donned the role of publicist, touting to his networks, in the language of a tourism brochure, Highlander's "comfortable living quarters, excellent food, and ample classroom space. There is a fresh-water lake and beautiful scenic views from the mountaintop." Blacks and whites came away from the retreats convinced, sometimes for the first time, that they could trust people of the other race.[2]

Some Nashville activists, including Lewis, had been to Highlander before. It was there that Lewis had seen Blacks and whites not only dining together but cleaning up together, doing dishes together, playing volleyball together, bunking together. Especially inspiring was Septima Clark, a fifty-seven-year-old former NAACP official who set up "citizenship schools" with Horton to help African Americans beat the literacy tests that Southern states used to keep them from voting. Clark in turn discerned leadership qualities in Lewis. Many students who came to the retreats would pop off on any subject, but Lewis was neither "emotional nor aggressive," Clark said. "John Lewis, sitting in the workshops, was a rather reserved type of fellow." Whenever he answered a question, she added, "you could count on it as being well thought-out."[3]

For its left-wing ties, including to Communists, Highlander had drawn scrutiny over the years from various investigators. By 1960 it was being threatened with closure for illegally serving alcohol—a threat Horton took as a form of petty harassment. But it went forward with its annual college retreat and that April drew record attendance, from sit-in leaders across the South as well as sympathizers from Northern schools. Horton had the students name the conference. They called it "The New Generation Fights for Equality."[4]

On Friday night, April 1, Horton welcomed everyone. "This is the first time since these protests started that people from a variety of places have gotten together," he told them. "Something might come out of these discussions that will help further the thing you believe in." He encouraged them to take their destiny in their own hands.

Students reported on their various sit-in experiences. Discussion centered on whether to work with existing civil rights organizations. The Nashville students, who enjoyed a close relationship with the NCLC and their local community, praised the adults they worked with. But other students, lacking such tight relationships, wanted to chart their own course without direction from the established groups. They proposed, Clark wrote, "that a South-wide organization for promoting the student movement be considered." As Angeline Butler said, the idea of forging an alliance of the myriad local desegregation movements "was born at this weekend."[5]

Saturday began with a 7:30 a.m. breakfast, followed by remarks from Fisk professor Herman Long, who ran the university's Race Relations Institute. In the afternoon, participants split into clusters to discuss their philosophy, methods, communication strategies, and relations with the wider communities. Each unit hashed out its positions, took notes, and wrote up reports. The evening program featured a barbecue dinner, square dance, and talent show in which Bevel and LaFayette led a doo-wop quartet in their original anti-segregation compositions.[6]

On Sunday, Phil Schechter, a rabbi from Hebrew Union College, officiated at a worship service, and Horton conducted a Socratic dialogue with the students, playing the roles of the "average liberal white person" and the "average Negro businessman" to prod the students' thinking. Finally, the breakout groups shared their reports from the day before.

In these discussions, divisions emerged over the role of nonviolence. Lewis's group defended the philosophy and methods that they had learned from Lawson. Their commitment to nonviolence had a "religious motivation," they said, and it should be a "way of life." In the first remarks of his that were ever recorded and transcribed, Lewis distilled much of what he had learned in the last two years:

I think we are using nonviolence as a means of mass attack or mass assault on segregation. But at the same time, it is not only used as a weapon. In using it as a weapon, it will become a way of life for each of us, if we keep using it for a limited time. Getting to the point of this moral issue, we are using a moral principle, which is nonviolence. If we are going to use a moral principle, I think the issue should remain a moral issue. If you must care to be truthful, to carry love and nonviolence to the extreme, it means going to jail and staying in jail and refusing to pay the fine.

Within the Nashville group, this view enjoyed considerable purchase. But at Highlander, Lewis also met peers who hadn't undergone training like his or internalized the "soul force." For them, nonviolence was a tactic, good for mobilizing media attention and winning sympathy, but not a spiritual matter. They had no wish to try to love a racist shop owner, hoodlum, waitress, or cop. This debate would continue for months, as Lewis and the other sit-in leaders engaged in what he described as "a great deal of debate and a great deal of discussion and even verbal fights on the whole question of nonviolence. . . . Some people opposed the whole idea of basing the movement on the Judeo-Christian heritage—a belief in love and nonviolence." Surveying the attendees at Highlander, Septima Clark concluded that most of them "had not thought clearly through the implications of their own undertaking" the way the Nashvillians had. One breakout cluster said bluntly in its report: "We are using nonviolence as a method, but not necessarily as a total way of life. We believe it is practical."[7]

Usually at the end of a Highlander weekend, students without cars asked around for a ride home. But because Highlander was under investigation, Horton had warned the faculty that state troopers might stop any mixed-race cars. Alice Cobb, a white professor at Scarritt College, saw Lewis standing by the door, his suitcase packed. She explained to him why she couldn't drive him back to Nashville and apologized. He looked disappointed, she thought, as if he'd lost his last friend. She extended her hand, but he declined to shake it. Cobb drove off. Then, at the bottom of the hill, she turned around, went back, picked up Lewis, and drove with him to Nashville.[8]

Two weeks later, the Southern Christian Leadership Conference convened another gathering of the sit-in leaders. Months earlier, Ella Baker had asked James Lawson to oversee a "working conference," jointly run by SCLC and the Fellowship of Reconciliation, on nonviolent direct action. Events had overtaken those plans, and Baker was now hurrying to catch up. She visited Nashville and enlisted Lawson and the ministers, who combed newspaper articles from different college towns, tracked down the student sit-in leaders, and invited them to a gathering at Shaw University in Raleigh, North Carolina, Baker's alma mater. SCLC covered the costs.[9]

Held from April 15 to 17, Good Friday to Easter Sunday, the event drew

126 students from twelve states. Most colleges sent one or two students; Nashville sent sixteen. "We packed like sardines into cars" for the eight-hour drive east, Angeline Butler recalled, including someone's "tiny Fiat." Lewis didn't go, having volunteered to stay behind in busy Nashville. Julian Bond of Atlanta, the self-possessed, debonair son of a leading Black intellectual, was struck by the many young men in "preacher's uniforms"—dark suits, black shoes, knee-high black socks—looking like the "young up-to-date minister about town."[10]

King spoke on the opening night. "The youth," he declared, "must take the freedom struggle into every community in the South without exception." What mattered wasn't simply "nonviolence," but "reconciliation": "Our ultimate end must be the creation of the beloved community. The tactics of nonviolence without the spirit of nonviolence may become a new kind of violence." Students were awed to be in King's presence. But it was Lawson's keynote address that stole the show. Lawson posed a series of philosophical questions, which then served as the basis for small-group discussions on Saturday on topics such as interracial politics and "Jail Versus Bail." The rapturous reception he drew suggested that many students found nonviolence an exciting new means to their liberation.[11]

That sentiment was reflected, too, in the star power of the Nashville delegation. Among the many contingents, especially the three biggest ones—from Nashville, Atlanta, and Washington, D.C.—friendly rivalries emerged. "Everybody was jockeying, trying to get into something," according to Marion Barry, another Nashville leader. The Washington students, mainly from Howard University, called themselves the Nonviolent Action Group, but were the least religious or Gandhian in character. The Atlantans, reflecting their city's entrepreneurialism, talked a lot about economic boycotts. The churchy Nashvillians, in contrast—the only group in which whites as well as Blacks played key roles—wanted, in Julian Bond's words, "to love segregation to death."[12]

The Nashville students were conspicuous, too, for their self-assuredness, camaraderie, and philosophical sophistication. "Not a single place had the kind of workshop orientation that had preceded the sit-ins in Nashville," Baker noted. "They were with it in terms of the nonviolent concept." Chuck McDew, from South Carolina State in Orangeburg, admired their commitment to nonviolence, especially compared to his own group's merely tactical use of it. Although McDew talked for hours with Lawson that weekend, "we still didn't have the grasp of the concept as well as people from Nashville did." Although some students sneered that the Nashvillians were "addled by righteousness," others were impressed, as Bond said, by their "panache and confidence in each other."[13]

Nonetheless, the role of nonviolence remained subject to much debate. Only a fraction of the students in Raleigh believed in Lawson's vision as devoutly as Lewis and his friends did. The journalist Jeremy Larner, surveying sit-in participants for the *New Leader*, reported that "nine out of every ten students to whom I put the question replied that to them nonviolence was purely a matter of strategy." Even Marion Barry, a Nashvillian, conceded, "I never felt any real deep philosophical sense that we ought to do it this way, except that was the best way to do it at the time."[14]

Also still under debate was whether to affiliate with one of the existing civil rights organizations such as the Congress of Racial Equality (CORE), the NAACP, or, especially, SCLC. In a Saturday morning meeting at the Shaw University president's house, King and Baker discussed incorporating the students into a youth auxiliary. After all, the sit-ins' prime movers—men like Kelly Miller Smith—came from SCLC, as did the animating vision and philosophy. But Baker demanded that the students be independent, at one point storming out of the meeting, and she proceeded to lobby the students, practically one by one, to vote to stay separate. Lewis heard about her influential role. "She kept daring us to go further," he said. "She was much more radical than King . . . well to the movement's left. She did not want the students used by the SCLC or the NAACP."[15]

King was never bent on taking over the student groups. He also didn't need another fight with Baker, who was feuding with other SCLC colleagues and on the verge of being replaced. He agreed to let the students form an independent body, to which he and Lawson would be advisers. The students named themselves the Temporary Student Nonviolent Coordinating Committee. The word *temporary* proved to be temporary. Soon everyone just called them "SNCC"—which they pronounced "Snick."

Lawson wrote the group's mission statement:

We affirm the philosophical or religious ideal of nonviolence as the foundation of our purpose, the presupposition of our faith, and the manner of our action. Nonviolence as it grows from Judaic-Christian traditions seeks a social order of justice permeated by love. Integration of human endeavor represents the crucial first step towards such a society. Through nonviolence, courage displaces fear; love transforms hate. Acceptance dissipates prejudice; hope ends despair. Peace dominates war; faith reconciles doubt. Mutual regards cancel enmity. Justice for all overthrows injustice. The redemptive community supersedes systems of gross social immorality.

On Sunday morning, there was a vote for chair. Among the Nashvillians, Diane Nash was the obvious candidate, and when Lewis learned she wasn't chosen, he assumed that sexism had been at work. In fact, Nash had been late to the Sunday vote, and the group nominated Barry instead. Tall and handsome, Barry was "a good pol," in Bond's words, skilled at glad-handing from his fraternity days. "For whatever reason Diane was not there," Barry said, "and so the Nashville people knew that I was the second person."[16]

In exchange for Nashville winning the chairmanship, SNCC would make its headquarters in Atlanta. That meant working out of a corner of the SCLC offices. For all the fuss over its independence, the new organization would not be so distant from King after all.

Back in Nashville, victory on the courthouse steps had coincided with the end of the spring term. The students halted the sit-ins. Lewis and his comrades shifted their energies to projects like registering Blacks to vote. NCLC ministers worked with Ben West on getting Black policemen promoted. Lewis spent much of the summer in Buffalo, visiting relatives and attending the National Baptist Sunday School Congress, a fifty-four-year-old organization devoted to Black education. He also traveled to Chicago, Denver, and elsewhere to spread the gospel of nonviolent protest.[17]

SNCC plunged into presidential politics. The political parties were writing their platforms for the fall campaign, in which Black voters were poised to make a key difference. For decades after emancipation, Blacks had mostly voted Republican, when and where they were permitted to vote. But starting in 1932, they had gravitated toward the Democrats as the party came under the sway of Northern liberals. Blacks now constituted a powerful bloc in Illinois, Michigan, New York, Pennsylvania, and other swing states. But the GOP hoped to stay competitive. Dwight Eisenhower, despite largely neglecting Black concerns as president, had won 39 percent of the African American vote in 1956. In 1960, New York governor Nelson Rockefeller spoke for the many Republicans who wanted to preserve their reputation as the Party of Lincoln.[18]

The Democrats' presumed nominee in 1960, Massachusetts senator John F. Kennedy, though a liberal on racial issues, had never made civil rights a priority. During the 1960 campaign, however, his advisers prodded him to speak out. After "the apathy or inactivity and insensitivity of the Eisenhower administration," said James Farmer, the head of CORE, Kennedy was a breath of fresh air. "Kennedy was young. His rhetoric was good and seemed to hold some hope." In June, the candidate breakfasted with King and endorsed the sit-ins. "It is in the American tradition to stand up for one's rights," he said, "even if the new way to stand up for one's rights is to sit down." SNCC sent Kennedy a telegram praising his "clear appraisal of their peaceful protest against the denial of human rights." The Democratic platform committee also came out for the sit-ins and civil rights.[19]

Vice President Richard Nixon, the Republican nominee, was more equivocal. At first he acceded to Rockefeller and backed a strong liberal civil rights agenda, but his decision drew fury from the GOP's right wing. Retreating, Nixon waffled for the rest of the campaign over whether to court Black voters or segregationist white Southerners, ultimately disappointing both.[20]

In Nashville, Lewis followed the campaign closely. But he focused mainly on local activities. In the fall of 1960, the Nashville Student Movement was still a far more robust and viable organization than the fledgling SNCC. Lewis's leadership in the local movement had won him admiration not only among his fellow activists but throughout American Baptist—where he was elected student body president—and the community. "Even at that time, he'd built up a little reputation for getting arrested and getting hit in the head and all that kind of stuff," according to one local politician active in the movement.[21]

SNCC held its next meeting in Atlanta on October 14 to 16. This time Lewis attended. By now, students at other colleges knew who he was. At the October meeting, according to Lewis, "SNCC really took on a new direction, became more of a stable or permanent organization." Lawson again held forth on nonviolence. Nash outlined the Nashville group's plans to re-start the sit-ins to desegregate restaurants and movie theaters.

King spoke again, too. After his speech, the students persuaded him to join a sit-in for the first time. They had planned one for later that week in At-lanta. King's participation would have far-reaching consequences. Along with fifty students, he was arrested, and, following SNCC practice, refused bail. To make an example of him, Georgia authorities charged him with violating a probation order—he had been convicted of driving without a proper license, having recently moved from Alabama. For that minor offense, the judge gave King a draconian sentence of four months' hard labor at a maximum-security prison.[22]

At the urging of his top civil rights aides, Kennedy called Coretta Scott King during a free moment at Chicago's O'Hare airport. "Hello, Mrs. King, this is Senator Kennedy," he said, in her recollection. "I'm calling because I wanted to let you know I was thinking about you. How are you? I understand you are expecting your third child." Mrs. King was impressed that Kennedy knew about her situation. "I'm thinking about you and your husband, and I know this must be very difficult for you," Kennedy continued. "If there is anything I can do to be of help, I want you to please feel free to call on me."

Nixon displayed no such compassion. When asked about Kennedy's call, the Republican could muster only a wan "No comment," leading Mar-tin Luther King to judge him a "moral coward."

As important as Kennedy's phone call was the reaction of his brother Robert, his campaign manager and closest adviser. Though Robert Ken-nedy was at first upset when he learned of his brother's call to Mrs. King, a briefing changed his perspective. He then placed his own call, to the judge, urging him to release King. The judge complied, and the campaign claimed credit. Kennedy's team distributed leaflets in Black communities nation-wide contrasting Kennedy's show of concern with Nixon's "No comment."[23]

On Election Day, John Kennedy won the ballots of Black Americans by a 70–30 margin—and with them the presidency.

In Nashville that day, Lawson was holding a workshop on the continued importance of nonviolence. "What is the need for direct mass action in Nashville?" he jotted in a note to himself.[24]

Since May, the downtown lunch counters had been integrated. Some 112 Southern cities had integrated theirs as well. But the hoopla over the spring victory masked the fact that no progress had come to Nashville's cafeterias, grills, fast-food joints, or fine-dining restaurants. These establishments' owners rebuffed quiet overtures from the NCLC. The sit-ins thus resumed, targeting a number of short-order franchises with names like Krystal, Tic Toc, and Candyland.[25]

Two days after Kennedy's victory, Lawson led a series of actions at seven eateries around Nashville. Krystal, a Chattanooga-based chain known for its square hamburgers, had a restaurant on Church Street downtown. That afternoon, LaFayette and two Fisk women ordered sandwiches at the window. After receiving their food, they tried to sit down, but were told to leave. When they refused, a waitress doused them with water and poured detergent down their backs. She then hosed them down with cold water and cranked up the air-conditioning. "She went wild," one of the women told a reporter. The other waitresses "just stood around and laughed."[26]

At the First Baptist Church, Lewis and Bevel heard about what was happening. They hustled over to Krystal, four blocks away, and replaced their soaking-wet friends. "I'm closed," the manager lied. "You'll have to leave." Lewis and Bevel stood fast. An employee then locked the front door, while others filed out a back exit. The manager followed them, pausing at an electrical panel to flip a switch.[27]

It was a fumigator. A billow of toxic gas—"this huge foam," as Lewis described it—filled the restaurant. Lewis couldn't unlock the front door. He tried the back door; it was also locked. Lewis dampened his handkerchief, but it provided little relief from the sickening chemical taste. (It didn't occur to him to try to turn off the machine.) Bevel, his eyes closed, began preaching fervently from the book of Daniel, warning about a "burning fiery furnace" and the children who God saved from perishing. Lewis wondered if he was going to die. But he told himself, "No, the man couldn't let us die in here. He wouldn't do that."

After half an hour, fire trucks pulled up. As firemen readied to shatter the windows, the manager unlocked the front door. Gasping for air, Lewis and Bevel staggered outside.[28]

The incident showed how much resistance to integration remained. Over the following days, more nastiness arose at other establishments:

students were muscled out of a Mickey's restaurant; a Tic Toc owner chased sit-inners out with a rifle; rowdy crowds of whites made clear they were ready to pick up where they had left off in the spring. Establishments hired guards to bar students from entering. In early December, LaFayette was roughed up at a Trailways dinette by a taxi driver. The cabbie was arrested and jailed, but so was LaFayette.[29]

Although the fall events in Nashville generated fewer headlines than the spring's, the students were coalescing more tightly. Some drifted away, but those who remained redoubled their commitment to one another. "We would sleep under the same sheets and blankets," Butler said, "laughing and talking into the night." Lewis, Bevel, and LaFayette became a happy threesome. "If Bernard's mother sent a care package, we shared it," Lewis recalled. "If mine sent a care package, we shared it." As Butler saw it, "Bernard had the great legal mind. John could recruit people. That was his great strength. Bevel, his skill was strategy." Diane Nash, she added, was "the administrator."[30]

The Nashville group was also gaining a margin of celebrity. Guy Carawan, the Highlander song leader, enlisted Folkways Records executive Moses Asch to produce *The Nashville Sit-In Story*, an LP of songs sung by movement participants (including Bevel and LaFayette's doo-wop quartet). Interspersed with the music were speeches and re-creations of events like the "Jail Sequence" and "Scene on Mayor's Steps" and a track of Lewis recounting how he joined the movement. The album introduced many listeners to the voices—and even the names—of Lewis, Nash, Barry, and the other Nashville students. Lewis gave his family a copy. His sister Rosa Mae enjoyed listening to him sing, in his incorrigibly off-key register, as she looked at the accompanying pictures of him in jail.[31]

Other Americans were introducd to Lewis in December, when NBC aired an hour-long prime-time documentary about Nashville called "Sit-In," part of its *White Paper* series. The program, directed by Robert Young and narrated by Chet Huntley, combined interviews, re-creations, and actual news footage, including previously unseen film that Young found in cabinets at the local NBC affiliate, and culminated with the April confrontation with Mayor West. Lewis was featured prominently. The film opened by showing him, in jacket and tie, walking down a Nashville street as he recounted the first sit-in of February 13. "Sit-In" also contained affecting footage of Lewis, LaFayette, and Bevel lazing on the American Baptist greensward, with LaFayette reading a letter from his own mother questioning his political activities.[32]

Some stations in the South refused to air "Sit-In," and racial conservatives like the Richmond journalist James J. Kilpatrick griped that the producers had showcased the stupidest whites they could find. But where the show ran, it was met with positive reviews. Its broadcast in December 1960 even stirred some viewers to action. Andrew Young, a Louisiana-born minister who had recently moved to New York City, watched "Sit-In" with his wife, Jean, from the living room of a house they had just bought in Queens. As they watched the show, she declared, "It's time for us to go home."[33]

"We are home," Young said.

"No," she replied, "this is not my home." Young saw that she was right. The couple quit their jobs, sold their house, and moved to Atlanta. "John," Young later reflected, "was a big influence in my moving back to the South."[34]

February 1, 1961, marked the first anniversary of the Greensboro sit-ins. SNCC and the Nashville movement labeled it "Freedom Day" and issued a call to target movie theaters. In Nashville and other cities, Blacks had to sit in the balconies, in some cases by climbing a fire escape.[35]

Borrowing a tactic from students at the University of Texas, Lewis and his friends undertook a series of "stand-ins." Ten to fifteen students would line up at the box office window. On reaching the counter, Black students would ask to buy a ticket in the white seating area. When denied, they would move to the end of the line to try again, or go to another theater and do the same. White students, on reaching the window, would ask if the theater was integrated; on being told no, they would voice their disapproval and cycle through the line. Scores of participants would travel from theater to theater on a given night. The point was to tie up the lines. "We set our watches so that every ten minutes this one would move to the second and the next one would move to the third," Lewis remembered. At one point, he said, there were fourteen different lines at various cinemas. The protest made the salespeople painfully aware of their discrimination, while impeding their sales. Some theaters closed rather than face the hassle. At Loew's, an employee posted a sign saying "No, we are not integrated."[36]

After a few quiet nights, local white youths, some reportedly as young as ten, began showing up to harass the picketers. Taunts escalated into spitting, then into throwing eggs, tomatoes, or snowballs, sometimes into hurling bricks and bottles. The police rarely intervened.[37]

By now, Lewis's self-discipline was famous. "I noticed at the movie demonstrations," said Frankie Blakely of the NCLC, "they would throw tomato catsup and eggs and things and some of them would really . . . have a reaction toward it. But John would always remind them of the nonviolent method." On the first night, Nelson Fuson, the Fisk professor, was roughed up. "This is the colored people's fight and eventually they are going to win anyway," his assailant said, "so they don't need no help from the white people." Another time, Jim Zwerg, a white Fisk student who had, in his own words, "come down there not knowing anything," was knocked out by one of the hooligans. Lewis made it his mission to look out for the white students, making sure they knew what they were getting into.[38]

Overall, the violence was worse than what the students had endured the year before. Once, a policeman's nightstick broke the rib of Fred Leonard, an A&I student. "A general scuffle followed," the *Tennessean* reported about another altercation, "but none of the Negroes hit back." In a replay of the previous year's Big Saturday deliberations, Kelly Miller Smith convened a meeting one evening to argue for a cooling-off period. Lewis sat quietly as Bevel and LaFayette pushed back. Will Campbell asked for Lewis's opinion.

"We're going to march," Lewis said.

"John," Campbell said, "I think that you agree with what we're saying. You know that there's very apt to be violence, serious violence, tonight if there's another demonstration. And I can only conclude that it's just a matter of pride with you, and bullheadedness. You're refusing to agree with us because of your own pride and because of your own sin."

"OK," Lewis replied with a smile. "I'm a sinner. But we're going to march."[39]

Campbell thought the moment represented a passing of the generational torch. The adults realized that they should let the children lead them. The stand-ins resumed. Lewis and his friends restarted their picketing. On February 20, on a snowy night, several of them were arrested for blocking the entrance to Loew's. Refusing to post bail, Lewis spent his twenty-first birthday in jail. He spent his days practicing his senior sermon, the capstone assignment at American Baptist, which he was supposed to present to his professors. But was still behind bars when his exam date came. He wrote the following lines:

> On this day in which I am scheduled to preach my Senior Sermon and also the day of my twenty-first birthday, I find myself behind bars with 27 other hungry Freedom Fighters for the 5th time in less than a year for acting as a free man in an un-redeemed society. I am fully convinced that the true way to bear witness to the Truth is to preach through action also and not by faith alone.
>
> I definitely feel that if the historical Jesus were here today, He would be in this jail cell with us for the same cause, the cause of justice and righteousness. Since He is not here, we must do what He would do.

Lewis's professors took it all in stride. No one was surprised by now that he was missing schoolwork to protest.[40]

In May, Nashville's movie theaters agreed to integrate. The city's dramatic stages, ballet, and drive-ins followed. It was the first instance of theater desegregation in the South.[41]

Lewis took pride in the results. But he knew there was much more work to do.

Chapter Five

THE FREEDOM RIDES

—— ■ ■ ——

I would like to become a teacher in a seminary or school of religion," John Lewis wrote in his application to Fisk University. "I feel that I could do a better job in serving humanity by transferring some of those truths that have been given to me to someone else." In February 1961, with the end of his senior year at American Baptist in view, Lewis was looking to stay in Nashville—to continue his work with the movement and remain within a community that had become a second family. He and Bernard LaFayette both applied to Fisk to continue their studies.

Lewis's application—his handwriting alternating between a rickety print and a messy cursive—captured his thinking at age twenty-one. His favorite subjects in school, he recorded, were "English Lit, History, Economics": the former because it "expresses ideas and ideas of people," the latter two because "I have always been concerned about world affairs, past and present." His least favorite subjects: physics, agricultural chemistry, and algebra, because "I didn't see the value for me . . . when my ambition was to become a teacher and minister of religion." Asked to name the books ("not school books") he'd read in the last two years, he listed Martin Luther King's *Stride Toward Freedom*, biographies of Nixon and Kennedy, "Karl Marx's Manifestoes," and "The life and work of Gandhi." Lewis also acknowledged that preaching from the pulpit had lost its appeal. "I felt that God had something else for me to do," he wrote. "As time pass [*sic*], I saw the need for training of Negro Baptist ministers who would be prepared to lead the mass of Negroes into the acknowledgement that the Christian religion has something that would end racial injustice and segregation, if they would only put their Christian faith into action."[1]

Putting his own faith into action, Lewis came up with the idea of trying to integrate Southern bus stations—starting in Birmingham, Alabama. A bastion of white supremacism, Birmingham was controlled by its notorious "commissioner of public safety," Eugene "Bull" Connor. Lewis proposed the idea to Fred Shuttlesworth, the city's charismatic minister and civil rights leader. Shuttlesworth discouraged him. As an out-of-towner, he said, Lewis might be jailed on any number of charges. Shuttlesworth added, "It would probably be all right for you to ride in and sit in the station, for we have a court ruling on that." Lewis dropped the idea.[2]

Coincidentally, the Congress of Racial Equality was planning something similar. In 1942, members of the Fellowship of Reconciliation, including James Farmer and Bayard Rustin, had founded CORE to apply Gandhian principles to the desegregation struggle. In 1946, a Supreme Court decision decreed separate seating on interstate buses to be unconstitutional, and the next year CORE sent an interracial band of riders through the South on a "Journey of Reconciliation" to test the ruling. Nobly conceived and coura- geously executed, the trip drew considerable attention. But it ended grimly. A North Carolina judge sentenced the riders to time on a chain gang, and no federal intervention or public outcry came to their rescue.

Under Eisenhower, enforcement of the court's desegregation rulings languished. But in 1960, another high court verdict, *Boynton v. Virginia*, desegregated bus terminals as a whole—meaning also the lunch counters, waiting rooms, and surrounding facilities. Farmer, now president of CORE, decided to reprise the 1947 campaign, this time calling the trips "Freedom Rides." He envisioned "a sit-in on wheels."[3]

CORE contacted friendly ministers to find volunteers. Metz Rollins, a leader in the Nashville movement, showed Lewis an ad in the SNCC *Stu- dent Voice*:

Freedom Ride, 1961, sponsored by CORE, will be a dramatic move to complete the integration of bus service and accommodations in the deep South. The ride will begin in Washington, DC, about May 1 and end in New Orleans on May 17. Traveling via Greyhound and Trailways, the Ride will test the recent Supreme Court decision banning segregation of interstate passengers in lunch room facilities operated as an integral part of a bus terminal. . . . For further information write Gordon R. Carey, Field Director, Congress of Racial Equality, 38 Park Row, New York, N.Y.

Lewis needed no persuading. He wrote to CORE, explaining that while he hoped to graduate in June, the mission of the Freedom Rides mattered more to him than even his education. "This is [the] most important decision in my life," he wrote without hyperbole, "to decide to give up all if necessary for the Freedom Ride, that Justice and Freedom might come to the Deep South." Days later, CORE welcomed Lewis with a bus ticket from Nashville to Washington. LaFayette was also accepted. But he was shy of twenty-one, and his father wouldn't let him go. "I'm not going to sign my son's death warrant," he said. Rollins also signed up, but then had to withdraw. Lewis alone would represent the Nashville movement.[4]

Some friends thought Lewis was crazy for setting off just weeks before graduation. But LaFayette and Bevel cheered him on and on April 30 drove him to the bus station. The young men missed the bus, however, and in a mild panic they sped down the highway and flagged it down in the next town. Lewis headed off into the night and to Washington, D.C.[5]

Walking out of Union Station in the morning light, an awestruck Lewis took in the majestic Capitol dome. It was his first time in the nation's capital. A taxi drove him to a Victorian row house at 945 L Street NW, owned by the Fellowship of Reconciliation. Fellowship House, as it was called, had one room after another, each chockablock with art, posters, books, furniture. The other riders were all there when Lewis walked in: Black and white, old and young, Northern and Southern, male and female. At twenty-one, he was one of the youngest. James Farmer—a tall, broad-framed man with a deep, commanding voice—welcomed them all.[6]

Before they hit the road, Farmer held three days of nonviolent workshops. Lewis's new comrades noted his moral seriousness. "John's demeanor was granite, fixed, immovable," remembered Charles Person, the youngest rider. "It was hard to see John's teeth, his lips always pursed."

On the last night, Farmer took everyone out for dinner in nearby Chinatown. To Lewis, who had never eaten Chinese food before, the meal was a revelation. The spectacle dazzled him. A maître d' ushered the party to a huge circular table, where waiters in suits scurried about, bringing a stream of bright silver platters and bowls piled high with strange foods. Lewis marveled at the unusual tastes and the efficiency of the operation. The excitement was punctured when one rider called attention to the peril ahead. "We'd better eat well," he said, "because this may be our last supper."[7]

On Thursday, May 4, the riders set off. A small press contingent— reporter Simeon Booker and photographer Ted Gaffney from *Ebony* and *Jet*, Moses Newson of the *Baltimore Afro-American*, and freelance writer and CORE activist Charlotte Devree—joined them. Their route wended through seven states, starting in Virginia, down into the Carolinas, and then west across the Cotton Belt, to end in New Orleans. Between legs, the riders would visit colleges and churches and stay with boosters. Singing "We Shall Overcome" as they boarded, the riders split into two groups, one Greyhound, one Trailways. On each bus, pairs of white and Black riders were interspersed. On the Greyhound, Lewis sat by the window next to Albert Bigelow, a fifty-five-year-old architect and former navy commander from Cos Cob, Connecticut. Lewis's bag held his Bible, a book by the Trappist monk and philosopher Thomas Merton, and a third book, on Gandhi. He also carried a toothbrush and toothpaste in case of arrest.[8]

The early days passed uneventfully. The riders suffered nothing worse than chilly stares and a few truculent waiters. In one town, Lewis preached at an old Black church with a patched carpet and old high-backed brown chairs. "Give us the courage and spirit to be willing to turn our world, our nation, and especially the Southland upside down," he said, "until freedom becomes a reality for all men." The congregation passed the hat for the riders.[9]

At first the trip was jolly. Seatmates James Farmer and James Peck, veterans of the 1947 Journey of Reconciliation, passed a bottle of brandy back and forth. Lewis formed a friendship with Hank Thomas, a Howard student, sit-in veteran, and SNCC member. At one point Lewis remarked matter-of-factly that they all had to be prepared to die. His voice lacked even a smidgen of bravado. Thomas was amazed by his sangfroid.[10]

An early incident occurred on May 8, in Charlotte, when Joe Perkins, a Black twenty-seven-year-old, was arrested for trying to get a shoeshine in a whites-only terminal barbershop and spent two nights in jail. More significant trouble came at the next stop, Rock Hill, South Carolina, a cotton-mill town known to be especially unwelcoming to Blacks. Earlier that year, ten sit-in students had been arrested and sentenced to hard labor. In one of SNCC's first concerted actions, supporters from across the South had gone to Rock Hill as reinforcement, only to be given hard labor as well. Now the locals greeted the Freedom Riders in the same spirit.[11]

Lewis sensed trouble as soon as he stepped off the bus. But he knew his mission was to test *Boynton*. Followed by Bigelow, he walked into the station's white waiting room. A gang of leather-jacketed young men stood by the pinball machines, smoking, their sport shirts untucked.

"Other side, nigger," one growled.

"I have a right to go in there," Lewis said calmly, "on the grounds of the Supreme Court decision in the *Boynton* case." Thomas watched with incredulity as Lewis carried on without fear. Farmer said he exuded "ministerial dignity."[12]

The white kids—at least one of whom, Elwin Wilson, was in the Klan— were unimpressed. "Shit on that," said one. Then, in Bigelow's account, "one man rushed forward and he started slugging John Lewis as hard as he could." Three others joined in until Lewis collapsed. The warm, salty taste of blood filled his mouth. The gang circled him, delivering kicks on all sides as blood pooled around his head.

Bigelow, a hockey player in his Harvard days, stepped between Lewis and his assailants. The men then set upon Bigelow with "these haymakers, round-house punches," knocking him to one knee. A third rider, Genevieve Hughes, approached next; she, too, was shoved to the ground. The manhandling of a slender, twenty-eight-year-old white woman spurred the policemen on the scene to intervene. A police captain offered to take a report, but Lewis and Bigelow declined to press charges. Lewis said that he held no grudge against the assailants. They, too, were victims of a racist system. The riders' goal was to make the South obey the law of the land.[13]

Lewis was badly hurt, with bruised ribs and cuts across his face. His lips, always sensitive, kept bleeding. He felt woozy, with pain throbbing above his eyes. But he collected himself and walked over to the lunch counter to claim a hard-won cup of coffee. As Lewis and Bigelow nursed their wounds, Lewis said wryly, "You know, the trouble with having a black skin is that those bruises all show on *your* face, but mine don't show at all. You'll go to the mass meeting tonight in Rock Hill . . . in the church, and everybody will say, 'Gee, that guy really took a beating.' And they don't know that I had a worse beating than you did." Not until later that evening did someone find a first aid kit to bandage Lewis's wounds.[14]

That night, at a junior college where the riders were staying, Lewis was handed a telegram from the American Friends Service Committee, the pacifist Quaker organization. He was a finalist for an overseas fellowship—the same one on which James Lawson had once studied in India. The Friends invited Lewis to come to Philadelphia right away for an interview. Lewis tossed and turned all night, unsure what to do. In the morning he decided to accept the interview and rejoin the Freedom Rides a few days later in Birmingham. He said his goodbyes, and a student drove him to the airport.[15]

In Philadelphia, Lewis aced his interview and won the fellowship. He had been hoping to go to Tanganyika but was offered a position in India.* Still, he was excited to follow in the footsteps of his mentor.

On Saturday, May 13, Lewis flew back to Nashville. His friends had planned a picnic for the next day, Mother's Day, to celebrate the city movie theaters' pledge to integrate. Afterward, Lewis would meet his bus in Alabama. But the riders were about to undergo a dramatic change of plans.[16]

After Lewis's departure for Philadelphia, the Freedom Riders had run into more trouble in Winnsboro, South Carolina, when three of them were arrested and harassed by police. When the group arrived in Atlanta on Saturday, they still felt good about their progress. That night they dined with Martin Luther King on Auburn Avenue, enjoying their first restaurant meal since the Chinatown outing. Most of the riders, meeting King for the first time, were starstruck. The minister's enthusiasm for their project prompted speculation that he might join the ride. But he didn't. (To Farmer's annoyance, he also didn't pick up the check.) King explained that, in Alabama, the ride could turn deadly.[17]

King's assessment was widely shared. After dinner, Farmer steeled the group for what he called "the most ominous leg of the journey"—a sobering

---

* Tanganyika, on the African mainland, together with the island of Zanzibar, became the independent nation of Tanzania in 1962.

reminder that gave way to lusty verses of "We Shall Overcome." Later that night, however, at the Atlanta University dorms, Farmer was awakened by a phone call: his father had just died. He left to attend the funeral. He asked Joe Perkins to helm the Greyhound group and James Peck the Trailways group.[18]

Sunday morning, May 14—Mother's Day—as Lewis was readying for his Nashville picnic, the diminished ranks of Freedom Riders left for Birmingham. The Greyhound took off first, at 11:00 a.m. Midway through its journey, the driver told Perkins that bus drivers heading the other way were cautioning him about a mob lying in wait in Anniston, east of Birmingham.

When the Greyhound reached Anniston at 1:00 p.m., fifty Klansmen and hard-core white supremacists (some estimates said two hundred) swarmed the bus. Armed with pipes, bricks, bats, and knives, they smashed windows, slashed tires, and tried to force open the doors. At this point, two highway patrolmen who had been riding undercover on the bus revealed their identities and pulled their guns to keep the mob at bay. A long twenty minutes passed. "To us," said Hank Thomas, "it seemed like an hour." Local police finally cleared the crowd and escorted the bus back to Highway 202. No one was arrested.[19]

But the danger was just beginning. After a few miles, the slashed tires forced the driver to pull over. The mob—which had been following in a frenzied caravan—resumed its attack. Their numbers had grown with the arrival of families coming from church, relishing a massacre the way their parents used to turn out for lynchings. Someone smashed the bus windows with an axe. Someone else hurled a gasoline-filled soda bottle through one of the holes. It exploded on impact. Flames coursed through the bus; thick black smoke saturated the interior. Rioters blocked the door from the outside. "Burn them alive!" the mob screamed. "Fry the goddamn niggers!"[20]

In a flash, the riders had to decide, as Thomas said, "Do I go outside and this mob is going to kill me, beat me to death? Or do I stay here and burn on the bus?" Thomas found himself thinking about the courage of his new friend John Lewis. Eventually, his physical need to get away from the smoke took over, and he and other riders crawled out the windows. Bigelow, the former navy commander, barked at the riders to evacuate the bus, while one of the patrolmen, wielding his revolver, forced the pack to let him open the bus doors before the gas tank exploded. But no sooner had the riders escaped immolation than they were set upon with boots, fists, and bats. Eventually, more troopers showed up, firing guns in the air, prompting the aggressors to fall away.[21]

The Anniston carnage turned out to be just the start of a long day of bloodletting. The Trailways bus also contained undercover riders—not patrolmen, in this case, but Klansmen. Having boarded in Atlanta, they menaced the riders once the bus reached the highway. As this second bus neared Anniston, the driver notified his passengers about the earlier attack. To avoid more violence, he said, the Black riders should move to the back of the bus. The riders refused. Their adamancy enraged the Klansmen, who punched and kicked them, beating two of the men into unconsciousness. The assailants dumped the wounded riders' bodies in the back of the bus. The driver chugged on to Birmingham.[22]

Incredibly, still more brutality lay in store. In Birmingham, when the Trailways bus arrived, Bull Connor's police force was nowhere to be seen. Armed Klansmen were waiting. When two riders stepped off the bus to test *Boynton*, the locals unleashed another whirlwind of violence, beating up anyone they could find. Some riders escaped harm by slipping onto city buses or into taxis. But others were battered—including the already-bloodied James Peck (whose head would need fifty-three stitches), a local newspaper photographer, a radio reporter, several innocent bystanders, and, in an ironic case of mistaken identity, a Klansman who emerged from the men's room at the wrong moment.[23]

By evening, the wounded, shaken riders—some having been hospitalized—reunited in Birmingham, where Fred Shuttlesworth rebuffed Connor's calls to hand them over to the police. Reports and images of the day's butchery had hit the wire services and radio waves, horrifying Americans and Kennedy administration officials. For most of their journey, the riders had been disappointed by the sparse news coverage. Now that all changed. In Anniston, photographer Joseph Postiglione took dramatic pictures of the burning bus that landed on front pages across the country. Witnessing the Birmingham violence, CBS newsman Howard K. Smith went on the radio every hour for the rest of Mother's Day, comparing the carnage to something out of Nazi Germany. Later in the day, a hospitalized James

Peck, his head swathed, whispered his way through a widely covered press conference.[24]

In Nashville, Lewis and his friends were eating and drinking in the springtime sun. Bevel was preaching—performing, really—about the movie theater stand-ins, his remarks laced with biblical references. Over a transistor radio came reports of the bloodshed in Alabama. Lewis felt a chill, realizing immediately that he could have been hurt or hospitalized. Suppressing pangs of guilt, he wanted to act. The now-silent group folded up their picnic and hurried to the First Baptist Church.[25]

On Monday, the Freedom Riders, having slept at Shuttlesworth's Birmingham parsonage, voted to soldier on. From Washington, Attorney General Robert Kennedy promised them a police escort. But when the riders tried to board a Montgomery-bound bus that afternoon, Governor John Patterson reneged on his guarantee of safe passage, necessitating a delay. In a series of phone calls, Kennedy chewed out Patterson, but the governor wouldn't budge. Late Monday night, at last, they settled on a face-saving plan. Joined at the local airport by Justice Department aide John Seigenthaler (until recently a *Tennessean* reporter), the riders agreed to fly straight to New Orleans, their journey's ultimate destination, and declare victory. Landing in New Orleans around midnight, the riders rejoiced.[26]

But Lewis was disappointed. Earlier on Monday—even before the decision to fly to New Orleans—he and the other Nashville students had heard that CORE might discontinue the rides. He believed they had to go on. To abandon them would not only look bad; it would violate the tenets of satyagraha. And it would signal to the segregationists that intimidation worked. Lewis argued for pressing ahead. "John," LaFayette later said, "was responsible for the Freedom Rides continuing."[27]

The others agreed. They decided to complete the unfinished journey. "The Nashville movement," said Diane Nash, "since one of our own was taking part in the Freedom Ride, had a personal stake in how the Freedom Ride went." Lewis tracked down James Lawson in Ohio, who agreed to participate. Lawson instructed Nash to tell Farmer, King, and the Justice Department about the Nashvillians' plan.[28]

Nash called Farmer. At first, he wasn't sure who this self-assured twenty-three-year-old woman was. "Would you have any objections to members of the Nashville Student Movement," she asked, ". . . going in taking up the ride where CORE left off?"

Farmer was stunned. "You realize it may be suicide."

"We fully realize that," she said. "But we can't let them stop us with violence. If we do, the movement is dead." By the end of the call, Farmer had promised to rejoin the ride himself.[29]

The Nashville students busied themselves with plans to send a new platoon of riders to Alabama. Among the Nashville ministers, Lawson, C. T. Vivian, and Metz Rollins backed the idea. But others hesitated. "I think some of you are going to die if you go ahead," said Kelly Miller Smith. "I want you to think about it more."

At a Tuesday night meeting of the NCLC leadership, Lewis assured the ministers that they understood the risks and were even prepared to die. Looking over at Smith, Lewis realized that the minister saw the students as his own children and genuinely feared for their lives. But the ministers came around, voting 9–1 to buy the students bus tickets. Nash called Shuttlesworth in Birmingham to tell him to expect reinforcements.[30]

Lewis was appointed the leader. Nash stayed behind to run the operation. Two American Baptist students, William Barbee and Paul Brooks, signed up as riders, as did five from Tennessee A&I. Two white undergraduates, Mary Salynn McCollum and Jim Zwerg, also volunteered, ensuring an integrated group.

The students told their professors that they might not finish the semester. Lewis felt no ambivalence. It was a crisis, and he needed to act.[31]

The bus left Nashville at 6:30 a.m. on Wednesday. Lewis took note of the date, May 17—the anniversary of the 1954 *Brown* decision. As the students boarded, several of them handed Nash sealed envelopes containing their last wills and testaments. Paul Brooks thought the back of the bus looked crowded, so he and Zwerg sat in front. The students read or slept.

Near Birmingham, police stopped and boarded the bus. Seeing Brooks and Zwerg sitting together, they arrested the interracial pair. The bus was allowed to finish its trip, but at Birmingham, Bull Connor's men stormed the vehicle. Connor ordered the windows and windshield covered with news-paper and cardboard—to keep journalists from seeing in, Lewis thought. Lewis protested their confinement, but when he stood up, a cop poked his baton into Lewis's stomach. Outside, a hostile crowd gathered.[32]

After several hours, Connor, concluding that he didn't want another bloodbath, let the riders off the bus. They claimed a small victory by heading for the whites-only restrooms. But then Connor reversed himself again and arrested them. At the Birmingham lockup, Lewis, who had been jailed many times, was struck by the dungeon-like cells. There were no bed frames or mattresses, chairs or benches, just a concrete floor. The riders refused food and belted out freedom songs. They remained in jail overnight.[33]

Political pressure built on Connor to free the riders. On Thursday night, CBS aired an hour-long news special casting a harsh light on Birmingham's entrenched racism. The bad press convinced Connor he was better off with-out the riders around. "You people came in here from Tennessee on a bus," he announced at the jailhouse late that night. "I'm taking you back to Ten-nessee in five minutes under police protection." Lewis led the group in going limp, forcing the officers to carry them into police cruisers. Asked why he changed his mind, Connor sneered, "I just couldn't stand their singing."*[34]

Sitting in a police car, Lewis was puzzled to see Connor himself climb behind the wheel. The lawman further surprised Lewis by venturing some friendly chitchat as he drove his charges toward Nashville. At one point he rambled on about the 1948 Democratic presidential convention, when he had led the Alabama delegation's walkout to protest Harry Truman's sup-port for civil rights. Lewis tried to teach him about the students' philosophy of love and nonviolence. Rider Catherine Burks invited him to join them for breakfast at the Fisk student union when they reached Nashville.

The relaxed mood dissipated abruptly at four o'clock in the morning, when Connor stopped the cars at the state line in a town called Ardmore,

---

* Brooks and Zwerg, having been arrested separately, remained in jail. Salynn McCol-lum, whom the original dragnet had missed, had by now been released to her unsym-pathetic father, who had flown down from Buffalo.

forced the students out, and unloaded their luggage. With a nasty laugh he pointed to the railroad tracks, telling them to catch the next train. "Or," he added, "maybe a bus." Thinking of old cowboy movies, Burks shot back, "We'll be back in Birmingham by noon." Connor waved. They waved back.[35]

Lewis was afraid. This was Klan territory. Had Connor left them to be ambushed and lynched? "What are we going to do?" he asked Bill Harbour, one of his Nashville companions.

"If we walk down this railroad track," said Harbour, "I can just about identify a Black family house."

"How are you going to know?"

Harbour said he used to play basketball in similar towns and learned to tell the Black and white homes apart.[36]

They wandered, talking in whispers, not even lighting a match for a cigarette. Eventually, they spied a run-down house across the tracks. With some trepidation, Lewis knocked on the door. "We're the Freedom Riders," he said. "Please let us in." An older Black man refused to admit them. "Can't come in," he said.

An idea came to Burks. Her mother had once told her that if she ever needed help, she should talk to the lady of the house. "Let's talk loud and wake up his wife," Burks said. Soon, they heard a woman's voice saying, "Let them children in here." Locks clicked. The door opened.[37]

The students shuffled in. The couple had heard about the Freedom Rides. They led their guests to a back room with a few chairs and a cot. The students washed themselves in a tin tub. At his wife's urging, the man hopped in his truck to fetch some breakfast; the students hadn't eaten in a day. So as not to arouse suspicions, he went to several different stores, buying a few items at each—cheese, baloney, cinnamon buns. "If anyone asks," he told the riders, "say you're my cousins from Nashville."

Lewis phoned Nash. She told him that another wave of riders was already en route to Birmingham. But she promised to send a car. Lewis said his group wanted to return to Birmingham, too. Connor's treatment of them had only fortified their resolve.[38]

In Nashville, their friend Leo Lillard borrowed a tan Studebaker and covered the ninety miles to Ardmore in an hour. By late Friday morning he had found the house. Amid joyful smiles, Lewis and his crew piled into the Studebaker and set off for Birmingham. Before long they were at

Shuttlesworth's parsonage, sweaty and exhausted, enjoying a fried-chicken lunch. Lewis spoke again to Nash, who said to get the Freedom Riders back on the buses as soon as possible.[39]

Everyone reunited at the Birmingham station. Lewis was delighted to see Bernard LaFayette, his best friend, sporting his floppy Irish cap. Lewis had never liked the goofy hat, but now he smiled at the sight of it. The second busload of Nashville riders was also there. So were Paul Brooks and Jim Zwerg, freed from jail.[40]

The combined Nashville contingent waited anxiously to depart. Greyhound suddenly canceled the midafternoon Montgomery bus. No driver was willing to make the run. Then it canceled another bus. At the station, angry whites gathered. Among them were Imperial Wizard Robert Shelton and other Klansmen wearing their fearsome black "Night Hawk" cloaks. Some swaggered through the waiting room. Lewis preached and led rounds of "We Shall Overcome," but the tension remained thick. The riders didn't even go to the bathroom alone. After police cleared the room of everyone but the riders, Lewis watched through the windows and glass doors as the vigilantes outside raved and gesticulated. Occasionally someone would hurl a brick or a rock. For news, the riders relied on a few friendly reporters, including Herb Kaplow of NBC and Calvin Trillin of *Time* magazine.[41]

In Washington that Friday, administration officials, though annoyed that the riders were persisting with their plans, felt bound to ensure their safety. The Kennedys were even more angry with Alabama officials, especially Patterson. The governor had been hiding from the president and attorney general all day, pretending to be out fishing. After many hours, Robert Kennedy told the governor's staff that if their boss didn't cooperate, he would send in federal troops. Patterson finally surfaced and agreed to meet with Seigenthaler.

At the meeting, on Friday evening, Patterson harangued the Justice Department aide for an hour. He made endless excuses for being unable to protect the riders. At length, Floyd Mann, who ran the highway patrol, spoke up and contradicted his boss, affirming that he could ensure the riders' safe passage to Montgomery. Boxed in, Patterson acquiesced.[42]

The departure was now set for Saturday. The riders slept on benches in the bus station. But in the morning another driver walked off the job. An exasperated Robert Kennedy phoned George Cruit, the Greyhound superintendent in Birmingham. "Do you know how to drive a bus?" the attorney general asked sarcastically, in a call that Cruit surreptitiously recorded. "I think you should . . . get in touch with Mr. Greyhound, or whoever Greyhound is," he said. "The government is going to be very much upset if this group does not get to continue their trip. . . . Under the law, they are entitled to transportation provided by Greyhound. . . . Somebody better get in the damn bus."

A bit later, Connor marched the original driver back to the bus's berth to carry out his assignment. Trailed by a cavalcade of state troopers, FBI agents, news reporters, and even a highway patrol plane, the Greyhound now sped to Montgomery. Most of the Freedom Riders, having barely napped in days, fell fast asleep. Lewis gazed at the patrol cars out the window and the plane buzzing overhead.[43]

The bus pulled into its bay in the Montgomery station just before 10:30 a.m. on Saturday. Lewis knew this station well; he changed buses there going to and from Troy. Now it was eerily silent. The police escort had vanished. "Bill, it doesn't look good," Lewis said to Harbour. "We should have had a point person here. We should have had some people from the Montgomery movement here, waiting on us. And nobody's here." Lewis saw only a couple of taxi drivers, some reporters, and a dozen or so white men standing by the doorway. There were no police officers in sight. Lewis stepped off the bus to speak to reporters.[44]

Floyd Mann, having ensured the riders' security on the highway route, had handed off that responsibility to Montgomery public safety commissioner Louis Sullivan, whose jurisdiction began at the city limits. Mann had reminded Sullivan about the guarantee of safe passage. Sullivan, an unregenerate segregationist, had other ideas.

Near the bus, Norman Ritter of *Life* magazine asked Lewis a question. "We just got out of Birmingham," Lewis began. "We got to Montgomery . . ." He got no further. A ferocious mob set upon the riders and newsmen. They brandished pipes, bats, tire irons, and, Lewis later wrote, "even garden tools—hoes and rakes." Anything that might inflict pain served as a weapon. First the crowd roughed up the journalists, destroying their cameras and sound equipment. Then they moved on to the riders. Harbour was horrified as a "little old lady," with children in tow, hollered repeatedly, "Kill them niggers! . . . Just kill them!" Lewis counseled nonviolence. "Do not run," he told his group. "Let's stand here together."[45]

It was no use. Some riders, seeing no other exit, leaped over a low wall overlooking a parking lot, hoping to reach Ralph Abernathy's church, to which Lewis began shouting directions. Lewis tried to make sure the women got into taxis. A white cabbie insisted he was forbidden to drive an inter-racial group of women, leading Catherine Burks to order him aside so she could take the wheel. But a mob encircled the taxi, yanked out the driver, and beat the women. In the meantime, Seigenthaler had arrived and tried to help another woman being assaulted. "Get back," he shouted at the seething crowd. "I'm a federal man." A rioter clubbed the Kennedy aide with a metal pipe, knocking him unconscious. Others kicked him on all sides, breaking ribs. They rolled his inert body under a parked car.[46]

Back on the platform, Lewis and Zwerg were cornered. Zwerg, nicely dressed in a suit, white shirt, and thin white tie, drew the mob's ire first. Crying "nigger lover" and "filthy Communist," the vigilantes knocked him over. Zwerg prayed for the strength to follow his nonviolent methods. The crowd surged, swallowing him up; Lewis, standing right next to him, could see only his friend's legs. The locals kicked Zwerg in the back, cracking three vertebrae. They smashed his head with his own suitcase. One man pinned Zwerg's head between his knees while others took turns pounding their im-mobilized quarry in the face, knocking out his teeth. Blood gushed all over his suit. Women and children clawed Zwerg's face with their fingernails. Fel-low rider Lucretia Collins, having reached the safety of an idling taxicab, had to avert her eyes.[47]

After Zwerg, the next to fall was William Barbee. One swing of a base-ball bat into his skull knocked him to the pavement. He extended his hand to his assailant and said, "I love you, brother." After he blacked out, thugs stomped on his head and shoulders.[48]

It was now Lewis's turn. Someone lunged for his briefcase, which he had been gripping the whole time. It was ripped from his fingers. Then he felt a sudden heavy crash against his skull. One of the assailants had smashed him over the head with a wooden Coca-Cola bottle crate. Lewis's knees buck-led. He tottered. He saw nothing but a white field. Thinking he was dying, he wondered if his own final act on earth would be to have witnessed Jim

Zwerg's murder. At least they were dying for a cause, he told himself. Then Lewis, too, was unconscious, blood streaming out of his mouth.[49]

As the melee raged, Floyd Mann fired shots in the air and enlisted state patrolmen to restore order. Lewis, fading in and out of consciousness, heard him yell, "There will be no killing here today!" But the local police, under Sullivan's direction, either actively helped the vigilantes or looked the other way. The arrival of state judge Walter B. Jones and the state attorney general seemed to bode well, but the officials blithely ignored the raging mob and walked over to Lewis, still prostrate on the ground, his clothes drenched in blood. Hovering over the bleary-eyed student, Jones cleared his throat and read an injunction forbidding the Freedom Riders from testing segregation laws within the state. Lewis was on notice that he and the riders were in contempt of court.[50]

Lewis struggled to his feet. "Good God," he thought to himself, "is it possible for me to lose this much blood?" Barbee was also now rousing himself. Despite their injuries, they were most alarmed by Zwerg's condition. He was so badly disfigured, his lips and eyes so swollen, that for a moment Lewis didn't recognize him. His blond hair was caked with dried blood and grime. As he came to, Lewis gave Zwerg his handkerchief—completely inadequate for stanching any bleeding, but a gesture Zwerg remembered long afterward. Lewis tried to find a cab, but no one would help. First, a white driver refused. Then Lewis found a willing Black driver, but policemen stopped him. Lewis saw Stuart Loory of the *New York Herald Tribune* nearby. "Can't you do something to get him out of here?" he asked. Loory sought help from a policeman, who said, simply, "He's free to go." Eventually, Mann—seemingly the only Alabama official concerned about the riders' lives—ordered a trooper to take Zwerg to a hospital, where he would remain for five days. Barbee was also hospitalized.[51]

Lewis found his way to the office of Roman Adair, a Black Montgomery doctor and friend of the movement. Adair shaved a patch of Lewis's head, cleaned the gash, stitched it up, and covered it with adhesive tape, forming a bright white X that Lewis thought looked like the Red Cross symbol. The bandage would identify Lewis in photos for days to come.[52]

The riders, reporters, and Seigenthaler had by now all found their way to doctors, hospitals, churches, or private homes. A few took refuge in the back rooms of the post office. Still, the mayhem downtown continued. Assailants burned the Freedom Riders' luggage in a bonfire and even began assaulting bystanders. Talking to the press that afternoon, Sullivan shrugged. "I really don't know what happened," he professed. "When I got here all I saw were three men lying in the street. There was two niggers and a white man."[53]

Robert Kennedy realized too late that he had to do much more. Men like Patterson and Sullivan were not going to keep their word. Kennedy handed the ball to Byron "Whizzer" White, the college football star turned deputy attorney general. White mobilized federal marshals to provide the security that state officials would not. Some of these men worked full-time for the U.S. Marshals Service, the agency, founded in 1789, that protects judges and enforces court orders; others were employees of other federal agencies and had to be deputized as marshals. Meanwhile, Justice officials obtained stronger court orders for the riders' defense. President Kennedy, too, now issued a fierce rebuke to Alabama officials—although, still worried about holding on to his Southern support, he also admonished the riders not to "provoke further outbreaks."[54]

The riders regrouped Saturday at the home of Solomon "S. S." Seay, a prominent SCLC minister and activist. From Nashville, Nash briefed national civil rights leaders including Farmer, Shuttlesworth, and King, who cut short a trip to Chicago to come to Montgomery. King agreed to speak at a mass meeting at Abernathy's church on Sunday night, one full week after the Mother's Day carnage.[55]

Arriving in Montgomery, King met with Lewis, LaFayette, and Nash, who had just come down from Nashville herself. Aware that he was still at risk of arrest, Lewis then headed to Abernathy's church and hid out in the basement library—the same room where, just two years before, as an aspiring applicant to Troy State, he had first met King and Abernathy. Shuttlesworth was coming from Birmingham, Farmer from Washington. Eventually, Lewis and the other riders took seats in the choir loft, hoping to blend in with the singers. Lewis wore a cap, but his big white bandage made him easy to spot.[56]

As the size of the population inside the church climbed, so did that of the white mob outside. Seay opened the night's program, praising the riders and the Nashville students and introducing Nash. Down in Abernathy's library, King and his advisers debated how to handle the rioters. Federal marshals were on hand, but many were untrained, and they were already telling Byron White—working from a nearby air force base—that they needed help. King and some aides stepped outside, surveying the scene as the crowd bayed and threw projectiles.

King went back inside and took the pulpit briefly, but it was too chaotic for him to speak at length. Outside, the mob hurled stones, stink bombs, and Molotov cocktails. Some rioters overturned and torched a car. A brick shattered one of the church's stained glass windows, spewing shards and injuring one man. Inexperienced marshals threw tear gas against the wind, causing it to drift back the wrong way and waft inside. King now spoke to Robert Kennedy, laying out the urgency. When the attorney general promised more help "very soon," King replied: "If they don't get here immediately, we're going to have a bloody confrontation. Because they're at the door now." The outnumbered marshals eventually managed to drive the crowd back. Abernathy's deacons fastened shut the church windows, raising the temperature inside along with the sense of panic.[57]

Around ten o'clock, Patterson relented and sent in the Alabama National Guard. The sight of the white-helmeted guardsmen brought a sense of relief and King finally went forward with his speech. But when the rally finished and the audience tried to leave, they saw that the guardsmen were now facing toward the church, their bayonets pointed—and ordering everyone to stay inside. The general in charge, Henry V. Graham, informed the assembled that they might have to stay in the church overnight. Grandparents took grandchildren to the basement. Soon President Kennedy and Patterson were on the phone yelling at each other again. Only at 4:30 a.m. did National Guard jeeps begin carrying the rally-goers to sleep and safety.[58]

Most of the riders bunked at the home of Richard and Vera Harris, friends of King. Their three-story, eighteen-room redbrick house, across from King's old parsonage on South Jackson Street, became an informal headquarters. On Monday and Tuesday, a who's who of movement leaders arrived there: Farmer and King; Lawson, Vivian, and Bevel from Nashville; Ed King and Lonnie King, two young SNCC leaders; and various CORE activists. Lewis was especially happy to see Hank Thomas, his friend from the first half of the trip. Vera Harris cooked meals as the depleted riders relaxed and strategized after their harrowing weekend. Lewis, who grew up being taught that drinking was sinful, had his first beer.[59]

Amid the good feeling, however, personal and institutional rivalries created strains. Lewis, Nash, and the Nashville movement had engineered the rides' revival, but now CORE, SCLC, and SNCC were all claiming credit. CORE sent a few staff members to Montgomery to join the rides for their resumption as Farmer trumpeted his sponsorship of the project. "I thought Farmer was arrogant, egotistical, self-centered, somewhat false," Lewis said. "Maybe my problem, but . . . he was really trying to use the ride . . . to keep CORE's involvement, to build CORE." Ed King of SNCC also touted his organization's role, but Lewis thought it obvious that "SNCC's role during those early days of the Freedom Rides was very, very small." The Nashville students at this point still thought of themselves mainly as members of the Nashville movement. "In 1961," said Jim Zwerg, SNCC still wasn't well known. "I don't ever recall hearing the term 'Snick' mentioned," he recalled. "The Nashville people became the vanguard," agreed Chuck McDew, "although I doubt there's very much credit given to them. . . . Without the Nashville people picking up the Freedom Rides at that point, it would have just died out." Even James Forman, soon to be SNCC's executive secretary, concurred: "It was the Nashville Movement"—not SNCC—"that had continued the Freedom Rides."[60]

King, too, came under heat from the students, who again asked him to join the Freedom Rides. His example would elevate their cause, raise the stakes, and add luster to the movement. But the SCLC staff balked, citing the risk to King's life, the need for him to negotiate with the Kennedys, and even the old traffic arrest that had landed him in jail in October 1960. The students scoffed. "I'm on probation, and I'm going," one volunteered. "Me, too," another chimed in. Lewis, who remained loyal to King, was bothered by his peers' insolence. He reminded them that according to Gandhian precepts, no one should be pressured to do more than he was comfortable doing. But when King proudly asserted his right "to choose the time and place of my Golgotha"—in effect comparing himself to Jesus at his crucifixion—one of the young skeptics coined a sardonic nickname for the great man that would endure. They began to call King "De Lawd."[61]

As the sole passenger on both legs of the Freedom Rides, Lewis was now thrust into the national spotlight. A *New York Times* article on Monday noted his crucial role: "A Negro divinity student in Nashville, Tenn., was the direct link between the original 'Freedom Riders' and those now at the center of the Alabama race dispute. He was identified yesterday as John Lewis of Troy, Ala., a student at the American Baptist Theological Institute." Lewis, who hadn't even told his parents about the rides, now called home. To his relief, Eddie Lewis wasn't upset. On the contrary, he said that around Troy he had been telling people, "You hear about this Freedom Rider John Lewis? That's my boy Robert."[62]

Lewis also served as the riders' spokesman in court that Monday as they sought to dismiss the injunction against the rides. The presiding judge was Frank M. Johnson of the U.S. District Court, who had struck down Montgomery's segregated bus ordinance in 1956. Lewis shook as he surveyed the courtroom's lofty ceilings, arched windows, mammoth doors, and oak benches. In a trembling voice, he explained that he and his fellow students were seeking recognition of their constitutional rights. Johnson lifted the order.[63]

On Tuesday, May 23, Lewis and Nash joined Farmer, King, and Abernathy for a press conference at Abernathy's house. Although Robert Kennedy was now calling for a "cooling-off period," and other civil rights leaders urged the riders to desist, the men announced that the rides would proceed. Lawson would hold a nonviolence workshop for any new riders, and then they would head for Jackson, Mississippi.

"The ride must continue in order to accomplish a goal," Lewis said solemnly, sitting directly to King's left, "to fulfill and uphold the Supreme Court decisions that people can travel from one part of the United States to another without being discriminated against." Having been twice beaten so far, he acknowledged the prospect of more violence. "If I had any fear, it left me. I love life, I don't want to die. But at the same time, if I must, this is the price I have to pay."[64]

Kennedy administration officials were divided. In 1961, asking the federal government—whether marshals or a federalized National Guard—to enforce law and order at the local level struck most Americans as an extraordinary step. After much deliberation Robert Kennedy cut a deal with Mississippi and Alabama officials. They would crack down on the Klan and any other vigilantism, but the riders would, on arrival in Jackson, face arrest under local ordinances.

Kennedy would come to regret the compromise. But at first it seemed to work. Early Wednesday, May 24, when the riders left the Harrises' home for the Montgomery station, an armed escort accompanied them. Several in their party, including Martin Luther King, ordered coffee and rolls from the bus station's white concession, reminding their swelling audience, including the journalists, that they still intended to see federal law enforced.

The reenergized riders boarded two Jackson-bound buses, the first one in the early morning, the second at eleven thirty.[65]

Lewis rode on the second bus. Out the window, he could see locals gathered in the small towns along the way. Some threw rocks, shook their fists, or jeered. Lawson complained that the presence of the National Guard, by removing any true threat of violence, turned the trip into a charade. "We would rather risk violence and be able to travel like ordinary passengers," he explained. "We will accept the violence and the hate, absorb it without returning it."[66]

Any debate over Lawson's position, however, never got far. When the buses reached Jackson and the riders tried to test *Boynton*, they were arrested and taken to the Jackson city jail. Lewis was apprehended while at a urinal in the white men's bathroom.

"Just a minute," he told the cop. "Can't you see what I'm doing?"

"I said, 'Move!'" replied the officer.[67]

Meanwhile, a cadre of new arrivals led by Yale University chaplain William Sloane Coffin independently appeared in Montgomery on Wednesday. Scion of a wealthy New York family and a member of Yale's Skull and Bones secret society, Coffin had a reputation for seeking the limelight. He had never undergone training in nonviolence, and his group's sudden appearance alarmed both political officials and civil rights leaders. But volunteers around the nation were now clamoring to join the rides in a show of support, and although Coffin would soon head back to Yale, the idea of dispatching additional reinforcements to Mississippi took hold.[68]

Robert Kennedy was upset. Having battled for days on behalf of the riders' right to finish their journey, Kennedy was now concerned that a new influx of riders would only prolong the conflict. The riders, it seemed, were refusing to take yes for an answer. Public opinion polls also showed that a majority of Americans, though sympathetic to the riders' goals, wanted them to end their campaign. Liberal voices, including the *New York Times* editorial page and NBC newsman David Brinkley, expressed similar views.

Yet Kennedy's position was evolving. He took seriously a suggestion from King to have the Interstate Commerce Commission make unambiguous the rights of interstate travelers to be free of discrimination. By the end of May, Kennedy set the Justice Department to the task. His staff spent the summer researching arguments, drafting documents, and lobbying the ICC to put its full weight behind the integration of buses and terminals.[69]

In Jackson, the first batch of arrested riders was tried on Friday. The judge gave them suspended sentences of sixty days in jail or a $200 fine. According to Mississippi's laws, prisoners who did not post bond within forty days of conviction would forsake any right to appeal—which would mean serving the full term behind bars. Most decided, for the time being, to forswear bail in the hope of filling the jails and putting pressure on state officials—the old sit-in tactic.[70]

Lewis and other riders were transferred to the Hinds County Detention Center across the street from the city jail. Two days later, they were moved again, to the Hinds County Prison Farm, eighteen miles outside Jackson. The men, segregated by race, filled the lower-floor cell block. Overcrowded cells forced them to sleep on the floor, on benches, or under tables. Guards were racist and violent. Rider Frank Holloway called them "the meanest looking tobacco-chewing lawmen I have ever seen." The superintendent bloodied C. T. Vivian with a blackjack for failing to call him "sir" and knocked to the floor a female CORE activist who weighed only ninety pounds. These acts of abuse set off a protest, leading to the riders' return to the Hinds County jail.[71]

Those who had been to jail before took their incarceration in stride. They sang freedom songs and mounted a hunger strike. Bevel preached with his typical fervor—so much so that Farmer, unused to the young man's manic style, thought he might be having a nervous breakdown.[72]

As the days went by, a few riders chose to pay bail. Some wanted to graduate with their classes. But Lewis didn't mind missing his commencement, which passed while he was behind bars. All the while, busloads of reinforcements kept arriving in Jackson. The first few groups of riders consisted of Nashville students, but in time people from around the country joined them: white and Black, old and young, students and professors, clergymen and politicians. Some, lacking training in nonviolence, had a hard time coping. In one instance, Lewis and the other veteran activists in jail lobbied movement leaders to bail out one particularly ill-adapted newcomer, for everyone's benefit.[73]

Morale among the prisoners remained strong, but there were some squabbles between newcomers and veterans, Northerners and Southerners, religious riders and secular ones. Some of the Howard University students would abstain from prayers, preferring to talk politics. Howard freshman Stokely Carmichael, an early June arrival, was scornful of the Southerners' churchiness. He irritated Lewis and the Nashvillians with his contempt for Gandhi and his general quarrelsomeness. Still, Lewis came to like Carmichael for his wit, charm, and candor. He had many qualities of a natural leader.[74]

Notwithstanding the departures, the ranks of the incarcerated kept growing. Lewis helped organize them into a community. Volunteers led the group each day in prayers, calisthenics, and cleaning up. At night they sang. Lewis thought that after a few days the guards came to see the prisoners as "intelligent and loving human beings" and softened their attitudes. Farmer was pleasantly surprised when he heard one white prisoner yell from across the cell block, "I am for integration one hundred percent. Sing some more songs, Freedom Riders!"[75]

Things took a turn for the worse on June 15. Late that night, guards marched into the riders' cell block and ushered Lewis and the men into trailers without windows or seats, slamming the doors shut to seal them in pitch-blackness. They were being handled, Lewis thought, like cattle. The bodies of the human cargo swayed and bumped against one another as the drivers sped over rutted roads and swerved heedlessly around curves. Their destination was the notoriously wretched Mississippi State Penitentiary, a compound ringed by watchtowers and barbed wire, colloquially known as Parchman Farm. On their arrival, they were forced to strip naked. Two men who refused were shocked with an electric cattle prod. The guards, Farmer said, "cackled with laughter and obscene comments," displaying a "fixation" with the prisoners' genitals.[76]

After an hour of standing around naked, the men were taken to an open shower. Men with beards and mustaches had to shave them off. For Lewis, it brought to mind the Nazi concentration camps. "This was 1961 in America,

92 JOHN LEWIS

yet here we were treated like animals," he recounted. They were given no socks or shoes, just T-shirts and boxers. "The big guys got tiny little undershorts, and the little guys had huge undershorts," Farmer recalled—the better to humiliate them. Bevel tried to stop the complaining. "What's this hang-up about clothes?" he chided. "Gandhi wrapped a rag around his balls and brought the whole British Empire to its knees!"[77]

Lewis found the miseries and indignities nearly intolerable. The design of the cell block kept the riders isolated from one another, and they were forbidden from going outside even to exercise. The jailers kept the lights on at night. Some days they closed the windows, turning the cells into ovens. Lewis and his comrades were allowed to shower only twice a week. They could write and receive only two letters a week; Lewis used one to tell the registrar at American Baptist why he and his friends would be missing graduation. Receiving packages or visitors was forbidden. Worst of all for an inveterate reader, Lewis had no access to any books except a small Salvation Army Bible. White prisoners were given a racist tract to read by the segregationist businessman Carleton Putnam.[78]

At the best moments, however, it was like a university or a seminary. Among themselves, they discussed Gandhi and Thoreau, Jesus and Martin Luther King. Several rabbis were now amid their ranks along with the ministers, and everyone taught and learned from one another. They also drew up a code of conduct for themselves:

Having, after due consideration, chosen to follow without reservation the principles of nonviolence, we resolve while in any prison:

to practice nonviolence of speech and thought as well as action;
to treat even those who may be our captors as brothers;
to engage in a continual process of cleansing of the mind and body in rededication to our wholesome cause;
to intensify our search for orderly living even when in the midst of seeming chaos.

They also sang, infuriating their jailers.

One conflict arose when a guard confiscated the riders' mattresses, forcing them to sleep on the concrete floors. Lewis and others stoically adjusted, but Stokely Carmichael and his cellmate, Fred Leonard, refused to accept the punishment. Leonard clung to his mattress so ferociously that the guards enlisted a beefy Black inmate to beat him until he let go.[79]

Female Freedom Riders were also taken to Parchman, placed in a different wing. They, too, had their mattresses confiscated and endured sexual humiliations. Male guards leered as they undressed and showered, and they were subjected to intrusive bodily examinations. Carol Ruth Silver, a white woman who kept a diary, recorded that guards asked her about sex with "Negro boys." After Ruby Doris Smith refused once to shower, she was handcuffed, shoved under the water jets, and forcibly scrubbed. Many were denied medical care. One female prisoner, Janice Rogers, suffered a miscarriage.[80]

Outside Parchman, however, the Freedom Riders' campaign was still drawing attention and getting results. It no longer led the nightly news or the front pages, as it had in May. But activists rallied on their behalf and prominent newspaper columnists like Walter Lippmann defended them in print.* In a victory for the riders, Greyhound announced that it would obey the law and removed the "colored" and "white" waiting room signs in Montgomery. The Kennedy administration not only pushed the ICC to take a stronger stand on enforcement—which paid off in September with an order banning segregation in interstate terminals—but also launched a new voting rights initiative for Blacks in the South.[81]

By July, Lewis concluded that staying in jail had served its purpose. He and the other remaining original prisoners decided to post bond. He felt triumphant for having survived. During his six weeks behind bars, moreover, he had reflected on his future. As exciting as it would be to travel to India, he decided, he wanted to stay in Nashville. The fight against segregation there was just beginning.[82]

---

* Right-wing critics accused the rides of being run by Communists, but the rides' organizers were anti-Communist. On the application form for new riders they asked, "Are you in sympathy with any Communist movement in or outside of the United States of America, advocating the over-throw of the United States government?"

Chapter Six

OPEN CITY

———— ▪▪ ————

The Freedom Riders left Parchman conquering heroes. Lewis found himself a minor celebrity. In July he spoke at a "Freedom Jubilee" at Forbes Field in Pittsburgh, where a crowd of twelve thousand watched as Martin Luther King sermonized, Count Basie performed, and Lewis was honored for his courage with an award. He accepted it with his usual unfeigned humility. Despite the beatings he had taken in Rock Hill and Montgomery, he said in acknowledging the tribute, "I feel as if I have done nothing."[1]

The Freedom Rides also redounded to the glory of the Nashville movement. The city in the summer of 1961 became a hive of activity, with conferences, discussions, and protests. Many of those who would become SNCC's key players traveled to Nashville, where they forged close relationships. The summer, however, also revealed differences of temperament and philosophy, some of which would shadow the movement for years.

Fisk University, where Lewis was to start his new degree program, hosted the summer's first gathering, over two weeks in June and July. More than a hundred participants came, from thirty-three states as well as India, South Africa, and Rhodesia. The Nashville students were again recognized. "We used to tell these kids what we were going to do in the next year," one senior speaker said. "Now they tell us what they're going to do in the next week." Thurgood Marshall came and sang the Freedom Riders' praises. From the audience, Lewis—who still had to appeal his

Mississippi conviction—told the litigator that he and his friends still needed legal guidance. "If you need help, here is my telephone number," Marshall replied as the crowd roared. "Many students feel that older organizations seek to control their efforts. We don't. . . . Remove this fear from your mind." Where the students led, the establishment was now following.[2]

A second Nashville symposium, a three-week student leadership seminar, kicked off at the end of July, convened by Tim Jenkins of the National Student Association. Lewis participated, as did Nash, Bevel, LaFayette, Barry, and other Nashvillians. From out of town came Chuck McDew, who had succeeded Barry as SNCC chairman, and other SNCC members. National luminaries like psychologist Kenneth Clark and sociologist E. Franklin Frazier gave talks. John Doar and Harris Wofford represented the Kennedy administration.[3]

Doar and Wofford came to prod the students to take up the cause of registering Southern Blacks to vote. Earlier that summer, Robert Kennedy had met with Freedom Ride leaders to outline an undertaking called the Voter Education Project. Several philanthropies had agreed to provide tax-free funding to civil rights groups to conduct registration work. Despite the prospective windfall, some of the students balked, believing it a ploy to divert them from more confrontational tactics. They doubted Kennedy's sincerity, remembering his call for a "cooling-off period" during the Freedom Rides in May. Yet others favored the plan, which would help SNCC obtain the funding that was otherwise going to the bigger, better-known entities.[4]

In Nashville, these differences blew up into arguments about SNCC's future. Tim Jenkins and Chuck McDew argued that Kennedy's voter registration plan would increase the students' political power. But the Nashvillians, including Lewis, wanted to stick with fighting desegregation through direct action. That work had given their group cohesion and vitality and produced striking gains in a short time.

The debate came to a head when SNCC's executive committee gathered at Highlander Folk School from August 11 to 13. The arguments grew testy. Many people thought SNCC was about to fracture. But Ella Baker brokered a compromise under which the group would establish two wings, one for direct action and one for voter registration. In October, SNCC formalized the arrangement and created a new executive committee.[5]

Amid the seminars and debates, there was also time for protesting. Desegregating Nashville remained an unfinished task. There were other fronts, too, on which to fight. In August, the visiting legions joined a demonstration against H. G. Hill supermarkets for its discrimination in hiring. The protest generated a strong turnout, but Lewis was troubled. Students from outside Nashville weren't dressing respectfully or were too quick to taunt, curse, or fight with provocateurs. Worse still, they didn't seem interested in learning the nonviolent ways.[6]

One flash point came on Saturday night, August 5. Forty students were picketing the supermarket when a gang of white teenagers set upon them, throwing eggs, tomatoes, and a few punches. Some of the out-of-towners, among them Stokely Carmichael, rose to the bait. That summer Carmichael had already rubbed the Nashvillians the wrong way with his impulsivity and braggadocio. Outside H. G. Hill, he got into a scuffle and either kicked in or (depending on the account) was thrown into a storefront window, shattering the sheet glass. Lewis chewed him out, just before all of them were arrested.

The next day, James Lawson convened an "emergency mass meeting" at First Baptist. He underscored the need to follow the prescribed rules. Lewis again chided Carmichael for his belligerence, adding that those unwilling to remain peaceful should stay home. Hearing this rebuke as a threat of expulsion, Carmichael despaired that his short-lived activist career was over. But Fred Leonard, Carmichael's Parchman cellmate, spoke in his defense. By the meeting's end Carmichael suspected that the future of the movement might lie with him, not Lawson and Lewis.[7]

Another visitor to Nashville that summer was James Forman, a teacher and organizer from Chicago a decade older than the students. Forman had been working in Fayette County, Tennessee, helping Black sharecroppers thrown off their land for trying to register to vote. He arrived in town on July 20. At Tim Jenkins's seminar, he met the student leaders. He also joined the H. G. Hill picket. But as he marched, Forman struggled to summon the equanimity of Lewis and his Nashville peers. He found his blood pressure rising after a fairly mild hazing—getting heckled and sprayed in the face with Coca-Cola. Each time, Forman had to steel himself not to lash out.[8]

It was Lewis's first time meeting Forman. He found the older man opaque and calculating. He seemed to harbor unspoken agendas and lacked the warmth and openness of the Nashville ministers. Lewis also noted Forman's skepticism about passive resistance. As the summer went on, Lewis realized he was observing an emerging split within the movement much more significant than the one between direct action and voter registration. The deeper rift lay between those who placed the principles of King and Lawson at the heart of their vision and those who never quite accepted Gandhian precepts and were ready to try other methods. Astutely, Lewis also recognized that the differences were in part regional in nature. Lawson's approach resonated with Blacks from the South, who were literally fighting for their freedom; Blacks from Northern cities tended to downplay desegregation as merely "fighting for a hamburger" and instead emphasized addressing deep-seated economic inequalities.[9]

Lawson was also concerned about this schism. "In recent weeks there is real indication in some student circles that nonviolence is nothing more than a handy gimmick," he wrote to McDew. "I am not sure that this trend can very easily or properly shape SNCC's present and future role." Lawson warned that the fledgling organization was "in real jeopardy of not being what it could be and ought to be in a nonviolent struggle."[10]

Martin Luther King, too, stayed true to the path. King had gotten to know Lewis much better over the summer as they spent time together during the Montgomery church siege in May, the Forbes Field rally in July, and SCLC's annual September conference, held at Nashville's Ryman Auditorium. At that event, SCLC bestowed $500 scholarships on ten Freedom Riders, including Lewis. He needed it badly. "Money was a real, real problem," he said. "It was very difficult in terms of getting books and the necessary school supplies." He had never received a gift as big as the scholarship check. Even more gratifying was getting the award from King.

King had a high opinion of Lewis, whom he continued, endearingly, to call "the boy from Troy." He considered Lewis to be Lawson's purest disciple, the one who embraced nonviolence most fully, incorporated it into his being most completely. King also knew that SCLC had to maintain the loyalty of the younger generation and asked Lewis to come work for him. But Lewis was now chairman of the Nashville Student Movement and also felt committed to SNCC. Hard as it was, he said no to King.[11]

Compared to the thriving Nashville movement, SNCC in the fall of 1961 remained embryonic. Its executive secretary, Ed King, who left that fall for graduate school, wrote a farewell memo urging a move from Atlanta to Nashville. "Since Nashville, Tennessee, has, in actuality, been the strongest of the student groups, and gained an image as the center of student activity," King proposed, "Nashville would logically be the place. . . . Nashville has best assimilated a real philosophy and has produced therefore people who are well grounded in its philosophy and developed some real leadership capacities." But Forman, who succeeded King, rejected the advice.[12]

Lewis, for his part, prioritized the Nashville movement's goals over SNCC's. "In Atlanta there was a SNCC group and there was an SCLC group," said Archie Allen, a Scarritt College student activist who would become one of Lewis's closest friends. "But here it was all just 'the Nashville Movement.'" Focused on local issues, they launched a campaign called Operation Open City. The goals were desegregation and equality in hiring. The prime targets remained the dining establishments: Cross Keys, Tic Toc, Candyland, Wilson-Quick, and others. In November, sit-ins resumed.[13]

The press now had mostly gone away, and few students were rushing to get involved. But Lewis persisted. One afternoon in November, Andrew Young was in town, crossing the Fisk campus. He noticed scores of students "jumping up and down, acting foolish." Fraternity brothers were scampering about wearing dog collars and barking. Then Young saw, as he put it, "one little group of about twelve to fifteen people, formally dressed, setting off in the opposite direction." Who were they? he asked a companion. "That's John Lewis's group," came the reply. "There are a couple of restaurants that still haven't desegregated."[14]

Lewis knew that it was more than a couple. And he didn't find his classmates' frivolity funny. For all his gentleness, Lewis could be fiercely moralistic, and he was indignant at his Fisk classmates' indifference to the continuing struggle. Many came from the Black upper class, but they showed no inclination to lead on social issues. He found it ironic that more white exchange students were picketing with him than Black Fisk men.[15]

The subdued mood was understandable. People were burned out. Many drifted away or went to graduate school. C. T. Vivian accepted a pastorate in Chattanooga, Lawson a ministry in Alabama. Others headed to Mississippi, where SNCC was mobilizing. Robert Parris Moses, the math teacher from New York, was heading up a voter registration project in the state. Nash, Bevel, and LaFayette were running SNCC's direct-action campaign there. Some were starting families. To the surprise of friends, Nash and Bevel got married. Freedom Riders Catherine Burks and Paul Brooks also left Nashville for Jackson—and also got married.[16]

To replace his dispersed comrades, Lewis assembled a new, interracial cohort: Fred Leonard, Lester McKinnie, siblings Bill and Elizabeth Harbour, and two Fisk students, David Thompson, who was Black, and Rick Momeyer, who was white. This core group called itself the "Horrible Seven." Others were intermittently involved. On a good day, Lewis might get twenty people for a rally; on rare occasion, forty. Although he was frustrated at the lack of a mass movement, he took solace in the industry of the seven. They carried on out of principle and duty despite receiving little attention. If you believe in fighting segregation, Lewis would say, you do it not only when the cameras are there but also when they aren't.

For months, the Horrible Seven kept staging protests and kept the movement alive. Lewis chose the sites, coordinated the strategy, and rounded up the volunteers every weekend. He also developed a talent for recruiting. "He knew exactly what he was doing and he could get other young people involved," said Harriet Tanzman, who went to work for SNCC. "He was a beautiful guy. He was full of spirit."[17]

Momeyer was a typical recruit. He met Lewis at a picnic on his third day in Nashville in the spring 1962 semester. Lewis and LaFayette then dropped by his dorm room, kindling his interest in the freedom struggle. He started attending workshops, which Lawson still occasionally conducted. But Momeyer knew that he had missed the heady days of 1960 and 1961 and wondered if the sit-in movement had already seen its best days.[18]

If the Nashville movement's ranks had thinned, however, the tasks before them had multiplied. By January 1962, the NCLC had established a half dozen different committees: one to pressure the restaurants and another to go after the drive-ins; one to lobby Vanderbilt University to admit Black undergraduates, another to get downtown merchants to hire Black workers; one to deal with real estate discrimination, another to desegregate the YMCA. Besides the sit-ins and stand-ins, they were also now waging "sleep-ins" (at hotels), "kneel-ins" (at churches), and "drop-ins" (where women would seek service at a restaurant and, if denied, leave the manager a disapproving note).

Progress came slowly and unevenly. The drive-in theater campaign worked. Vanderbilt agreed to admit Black students. But there were also defeats, delays, and dispiriting standoffs.[19]

Lewis and his happy warriors were picketing and sitting in on almost every weekend and sometimes on weekdays, too. Momeyer thought of the Horrible Seven as scrappy guerrillas, waging quick strikes against one establishment, then moving on to another, then a third. Sometimes they would be thrown out, sometimes arrested. One time a waitress poured scalding-hot water on them. Another time, a grill manager locked Fred Leonard inside his store.[20]

One typically frustrating campaign was directed at Cross Keys, an upscale restaurant with fancy silverware and fine tablecloths. One February day Lewis had Momeyer and Peter Schwartz, another white student, make reservations. After they took their seats, Lewis and two Blacks students then joined them. In a flash, the busboys cleared the table, seizing even the tablecloth. Lewis and his friends then spread out over three tables, removed their schoolbooks, and began to read. Policemen came to arrest them.[21]

The Cross Keys incident also kept Lewis returning to another familiar place: the courtroom. In March, a grand jury indicted the Cross Keys sit-inners for "unlawful conspiracy" and provoking riotous conduct—charges much more severe than the usual count of disturbing the peace. The district attorney, Harry Nichol, a liberal, claimed he wanted to test and perhaps overturn three long-standing statewide segregation laws. "I carefully picked this case just to test the validity of some state laws," Nichol said. "I tried not to be prejudicial." Lewis took Nichol at his word. He even found some excitement in the prospect that their case might go to the U.S. Supreme Court. But he didn't let up. In mid-April, Lewis, Momeyer, and Thompson went back to Cross Keys with more friends, only to be arrested again.[22]

As the conspiracy case dragged on into May, Lewis and Momeyer drafted a form letter for people to sign avowing solidarity with the "Nashville Five." "Since I am a supporter of the movement for desegregation, equality of opportunity, and the elimination of racial discrimination," the letter read, "... then I, too, am guilty of 'unlawful conspiracy. You must do your duty and have me arrested." CORE and SNCC circulated it, and more than two hundred people sent signed copies to Nichol. Their appeal also brought in contributions. In May, when Martin Luther King came to Fisk to give a speech, Lewis visited with him beforehand in a makeshift greenroom, bringing along Momeyer. Fishing from his pocket $68 that his own schoolmates had raised, Momeyer handed it to King, who, though appreciative, was a little unsure what to make of this oddly solicitous young white man.[23]

Ten days later, a judge threw out the conspiracy cases. The Nashville Five were free. But Cross Keys continued to discriminate.[24]

As Lewis was fighting Jim Crow in Nashville, SNCC under Jim Forman was expanding its sights. It was now undertaking projects based not in college towns but rural counties, notably in Mississippi and Georgia. In the spring of 1962 Forman and McDew agreed that SNCC could no longer be called a "coordinating committee" of discrete campus units. McDew wrote to Lewis telling him that "the question of the relation of SNCC to local chapters of the action has been on the minds of many of us." McDew said he wanted to "rethink its purposes, its existing and potential functions." He invited Lewis to a meeting in Atlanta. "This will be an extremely important session."[25]

It was all part of Forman's effort to bring order to this ill-defined network. Paul Brooks, Lewis's classmate who had recruited Forman for the job, had told the older man that SNCC needed "a dictator to organize and pull the strings and tell us what to do." Whether or not Forman lived up to that description, the onetime air force serviceman was imposing discipline on a horde of independent-minded young people. Lewis compared him to a "general who saw the big picture."[26]

Forman was good at his job. Before SNCC's second-anniversary conference in April 1962, some students feared that SNCC was unraveling, that they wouldn't even be able to pull off another conference. But the event, held April 27 to 29 in Atlanta, dispelled everyone's qualms. Two hundred sixty participants came, including Lewis and a large Nashville contingent. SNCC adopted a new constitution that reinvented the executive committee, which would now include three "at-large" student members (Lewis was one). With the 1962 conference, Forman boasted, "SNCC became more than just a name and an office, or a staff person who happened to be placed in their community.... The personal relationships established at the conference will carry over."[27]

Lewis presided that weekend over a Saturday morning plenary session in which Chuck McDew and Marion Barry talked about SNCC's history and its future. Lewis also detected more signs of the organization's changing character. SNCC still described itself as a body of "student sit-in leaders" and spotlighted its direct-action training sessions. But Lewis now heard less talk of nonviolence and more talk of "self-defense," less talk of integration and more of "revolution." Significantly, neither King nor Lawson attended.

The question of Communist involvement also reared its head. The ministers and most of the students who founded SNCC were either hostile toward or unconcerned with Communism. Marxist theory was seldom discussed. Martin Luther King, even as he grappled with reports that his close adviser Stanley Levison was maintaining ties to Moscow, forcefully denounced Communism as rooted in "ethical relativism, a metaphysical materialism, a crippling totalitarianism, and a denial of freedom which I could never accept." But many young people in SNCC distrusted any expression of alarm about Communist influence as crude red-baiting, or as political rhetoric whipped off by Southern segregationists to discredit the movement—which indeed it sometimes was.[28]

Though he read a lot of political philosophy, including Marx, Lewis was never drawn to Marxism. He was more often found reading Gandhi, Thoreau, Thomas Merton, or King. King especially—without whose inspiration, Lewis believed, he would not have entered the movement—was a lodestar. Many of Lewis's friends thought he admired the man all out of proportion, even trying to talk and walk like him. Lewis never so much as criticized King.

Lewis maintained this reverence despite a fight between SNCC and

SCLC in the winter of 1961–62 about the Albany campaign. Having initiated the direct-action campaign there, SNCC members resented King and
SCLC for coming in and taking over. In the wake of that infighting, the
SCLC board, newly concerned about losing the younger generation, proposed hiring new field secretaries, with Lewis's name floated. They hired
Bevel instead, but a few months later King asked Lewis to join the SCLC
board. SNCC might fancy itself a vanguard, but Lewis would stay true to
the philosophy of nonviolence and its most esteemed exponent.[29]

By mid-1962, Lewis was spending so much time on movement activities
that some of his classmates and professors thought he was simply using
the college as a base of operations. But Lewis was still hungry to learn. His
years at American Baptist hadn't given him the liberal arts education he had
wanted. Fisk, a wealthier institution steeped in Black history (his dorm was
called Du Bois Hall), had more to offer. A philosophy and religion major,
Lewis struggled in physics and in German but did well in his other classes.
One classmate, June Fair, described him participating avidly and knowledge-
ably in a seminar on existentialism. Though the movement was his top priority, Lewis cared about his studies and vowed to make the dean's list. "You
ranked about no. 19," he wrote teasingly to Rick Momeyer. "Very good. . . . I
am going to really study. . . . I am sure I can do it."[30]

Lewis also still worried about money. He was perpetually petitioning
civil rights and church groups for scholarships, or just $10 or $25 for expenses. Some adults in the movement worried when they saw the holes
in his shoe soles; he bought his coats and suits at thrift stores and pawn-
shops. In summer, when school was out and the dining halls were closed, he
would skip meals. Katherine Jones, who worked at the Tennessee Council
on Human Relations, a state agency, was attentive to Lewis's deprivation.
When her agency hosted a meeting with catered food, she would stuff leftovers in his pockets, knowing he wouldn't take them on his own. Once, she
demanded that he accept a gift of some cash in an envelope.[31]

Lewis still returned to Troy from time to time, for a few weeks in the
summer or at Christmas, but he didn't talk to his parents much about his activities. "When I'd come home and preach civil rights," Lewis recalled, "my
mother would say, 'Preach the Bible, preach the Scripture.' She'd talk about

my 'call,' and I'd say, 'Mama, if I'm called by God, why can't I listen to what He tells me to preach?'"

With his siblings, there was less strain. They took pride in his independence and fame. Ora, the oldest of the girls, expressed interest in following him to Fisk. Rosa Mae would hear from her schoolteacher that Lewis was doing great things for Black people. Rosa also liked to ask her brother how many times he had gone to jail. When Lewis came back to the farm, he could slip back into a loving relationship. He would hide from his little siblings and, when they discovered him, he'd pretend to be someone else, saying, "This isn't Robert. This is John Rousseau," a pseudonym likely inspired by his philosophy classes. But after a day or two in Troy, Lewis would find himself bored to tears. His thoughts would be in Nashville.[32]

In June 1962, the semester over, Lewis went back to the family farm. He had just spent a few days in Atlanta at a SNCC meeting and was already feeling restless in Troy. He reached out to Forman and McDew. "Look, fellows," he wrote, "I want to make it clear that I am at your disposal this summer. If I can be useful for anything, let me know. . . . Yours For Freedom, John Lewis."[33]

Forman had an idea. A spirited desegregation campaign was underway in Cairo, Illinois, a small town at the state's southern tip. Situated on a peninsula where the Ohio and Mississippi Rivers met, wedged between Kentucky and Missouri, the town of ten thousand was one-third Black, Southern in character, and rigidly segregated. Even the pronunciation of its name, KAY-ro, was Southern.

The city was home to a small nonviolent movement led by Blaine Ramsey, a social gospel minister, and a sixteen-year-old named Charles Koen. Salynn McCollum, one of the Nashville Freedom Riders, was now studying at nearby Southern Illinois University and helping out. Ramsey had asked SNCC for more help. After McCollum was slashed across the thigh at a June 27 sit-in at a segregated barbecue joint, Forman decided to send reinforcements. Armed with a letter of introduction from Forman and McDew, Lewis set off for what was technically SNCC's first campaign in a Northern state.[34]

Lewis arrived early on Sunday morning, July 8. He stayed with McCollum at the home of an elderly Black couple. Lewis bunked with the man,

McCollum with the woman. Several other Nashville students were in town to train the locals, help build their movement, and mount actions against segregated institutions. Emulating Nashville, they launched their own Operation Open City, demanding the desegregation of restaurants, hotels, barbershops, swimming pools, bowling alleys, and theaters.[35]

The Cairo operation was much smaller in scope than the SNCC campaigns underway in Mississippi and Georgia. But it still demanded intense work. Lewis led workshops in the basement of Ward Chapel. He and McCollum recruited Southern Illinois University students. They held sit-ins at restaurants and stand-ins at the swimming pool. They presented the mayor with an eleven-point plan for equality in housing, employment, medical care, and public accommodations. They got beaten up and arrested. They forswore bail, went to jail, and mounted hunger strikes. They organized a prayer vigil at city hall. They picketed at supermarkets for fair employment practices. They sang "We Shall Overcome." Lewis arranged for a telegram from Martin Luther King, who pledged the "full support of the Southern Christian Leadership Conference."[36]

It all made a difference. By mid-July, the restaurants agreed to desegregate and the Cairo group turned to the swimming pools and roller rink. Attending one of the swimming pool events was Danny Lyon, a photographer and University of Chicago student who had come to town when a classmate of his was arrested. That morning, he heard Lewis speak at a church meeting, and in the afternoon, after leaving the pool, he saw Lewis and others kneeling in prayer in front of a brick wall. Some white youths were shouting slurs from a distance, but Lewis remained untroubled. Lyon thought the tableau had a holy aura. He took some pictures. One of the most stirring images, of Lewis and his colleagues kneeling in front of the wall, was later given the caption "Come Let Us Build a New World Together" and turned into SNCC posters that would sell thousands of copies.

The peaceful moment, however, was fleeting. Immediately after the prayers, several students walked into the empty street to sing. Down the road came a man in a blue pickup truck, driving fast and showing no signs of braking. Lewis hurried to the side of the road. But one thirteen-year-old girl held her ground. The driver slowed but didn't stop. His bumper clipped her, knocking her to the pavement.[37]

The summer saw other violent incidents. The bloodiest came on

August 17. At 8:30 p.m., Lewis and forty comrades targeted the segregated T-Wood Roller Bowl, owned by a man named William Thistle-
wood. In anticipation of the protest, a mob had gathered, hooting and
yelling. Other locals jumped out of cars and set upon the protesters with
tire chains, sticks, pipes, and iron rods wrapped in barbed wire. One hoo-
ligan swatted Charles Koen on the head with a blackjack, leaving a bloody
gash. Another demonstrator, Ronnie Hale, was clubbed in the stomach
with a pipe; he was found doubled over, vomiting. Debbie Flowers, twelve,
was whipped with a bicycle chain. In all, a half dozen people were taken
to the hospital. According to the Associated Press, sheriff's deputies were
"parked in cars a few hundred yards from the scene," but failed to intervene. Several officers stood by and laughed. For much of the night, officers
declined to pursue the white assailants even to take reports, though by the
end of the night two men were arrested.[38]

The incident drew national media coverage, galvanized the community,
and forced political action. The state NAACP organized a march on the
state capitol in Springfield. Governor Otto Kerner met with the group for
two hours and promised an investigation. Within a month, under state pressure, Cairo's segregationist proprietors, including the roller rink, agreed to
desegregate.[39]

Throughout it all, Lewis was indefatigable. At twenty-two, he was now a
veteran organizer, sharing his knowledge and methods with the young Cairo
activists. While in jail that July, Charles Koen said, Lewis "taught me how to
fast." (Momeyer teased Lewis that whenever he was jailed, he would immediately say, "Let's have a hunger strike!") To the high school kids, Lewis was
a mentor, a model, and a pillar of resolve.[40]

He was also burning out. Writing to Forman on August 13, Lewis explained that he was "giving serious consideration to . . . being less active in
the fight for the time being, but not less concern or interest." (Lewis sometimes dropped the -ed from his participles.) "Since the spring of 1960 during
both the school year and the summer I have been active in the movement. I
have had little times for rest or relaxation or to spend any length of time with
my family. For the last few months I have been under a great deal of mental
stress and sometime physically exalted [sic]." He explained that "to be fresh
for the new school-year I must slow down. I hate to do this but I must. The
spirit is willing but the body is weak." He asked for bus fare back to Troy.[41]

Except he didn't go home.

First he had trials to attend. One was in Charleston, Missouri, just across the river from Cairo, where Lewis faced charges of trespassing and obstructing a sidewalk. The drama had begun the day after he wrote Forman, when he visited the town to lead a workshop for local activists. Lewis was accompanied that day by a new acquaintance, a nineteen-year-old white Shimer College student named Nick Kundra. Kundra had been hitchhiking throughout the Midwest learning folk songs when he met Lewis, who persuaded him to join the Cairo campaign. As the two pulled into the Charleston bus terminal on Tuesday, August 14, Lewis said, "Let's find out what is doing at the restaurant," called Watkins Café.

Signs saying "We Reserve the Right to Choose Our Customers" made clear that the place was segregated. But Lewis knew that, as part of an interstate bus terminal, it was violating federal laws. He and Kundra took seats. Before long, the proprietors, Vern and Eula Watkins, demanded that they leave. "We don't serve colored people," Vern said. Eula called the police. Lewis and Kundra went to jail. Lewis could tell his little sister that it was his seventeenth time.

For the next ten days, Lewis traveled back and forth between Charleston and Cairo, rotating among protests, courtrooms, and jail cells. By now he was run ragged. "As soon as the trial is over," he wrote to Momeyer, "I am going to some place and get a decent meal, then get my clothes together for Green Lake."

All summer long, Lewis had been writing to Momeyer, LaFayette, and other friends about a retreat to be held by the American Baptist Assembly in early September in Green Lake, Wisconsin. "Man, we must make it," he wrote to Momeyer. "This will be the last real break before school begins. . . . It will be a grand opportunity for a Methodist student (you) to get to know some of the wild Baptist students." In letter after letter that summer, the phrase "Green Lake" recurred—Lewis's own personal Shangri-La.[42]

Lewis made it to Green Lake eventually, and before returning to Fisk he also spent ten days in Troy. There, two FBI agents showed up at the door, conducting an investigation of the incident at the Watkins Café in Charleston, which Chuck McDew had reported to the Justice Department's Civil

Rights Division. The agents spoke to Lewis for two hours and he prepared an affidavit. In December, the FBI would conclude it had insufficient evidence to prosecute, but it was a sign that SNCC, at least to some extent, now had the Justice Department's ear.[43]

Shortly after Lewis's return to Fisk, the fight against segregation in the South heated up again with a bid to integrate the University of Mississippi by James Meredith, a twenty-nine-year-old Black air force veteran. Even more than Alabama, the Magnolia State was Jim Crow's most formidable redoubt. The murder of one of Bob Moses's associates, Herbert Lee, in broad daylight, as well as other acts of violence against SNCC volunteers, had led President Kennedy to pledge federal protection for the Mississippi voter registration drive. The Justice Department promised to ensure that Meredith could enroll safely at "Ole Miss."[44]

Mississippi governor Ross Barnett, however, was implacable. Neither pressure from President Kennedy nor the dispatch of federal marshals to the campus prevented two thousand white students and outsiders from gathering to resist Meredith's enrollment. On September 30, under the protection of armed lawmen, Meredith managed to register. But that evening the mob let loose in a fifteen-hour orgy of destruction. A lynch mob failed to find Meredith, but in the rioting hundreds of people were injured and two—a French reporter and a jukebox repairman—were killed. Kennedy had to send in U.S. Army units to put down the unrest.

Despite the death and destruction, Lewis saw great importance in the Kennedys' determination to uphold the law of the land. "This is [the] best steps that the Federal Government has taken since the Civil War," he wrote to Momeyer. "The whole affair is no longer the question of getting a Negro into Ole Miss, but the real question is the order of the Federal Courts must be obeyed and carried out."[45]

Lewis was also following Nashville politics attentively. During the summer, voters had approved a new charter to combine the city and county governments into a consolidated "Metro" government. Consolidation was supposed to bring efficiency and financial stability to the city and its near suburbs. A new mayoral election pitted Ben West against Beverly Briley, a county judge, and Clifford Allen, a prominent liberal politician. Lewis favored Allen. "If we can get the Negroes to block vote, with labor, liberal white businessmen and others, Allen will win," Lewis told Momeyer. "I am along with others going to work hard in this race."[46]

Lewis also agreed to chair the Nashville Student Movement—or "what was left of it," as he remarked—for another year. The idea of a central committee with a nominal chair had given way to an acknowledgment of Lewis's indispensability.

Forman and McDew also asked Lewis to organize a SNCC conference in Nashville in November. Lewis believed that an influx of bodies into the city would be "a shot in the arm" to his local efforts as well as a boon for SNCC. On the weekend of November 23 to 25, more than two hundred students poured into Nashville. Friday featured reports from the field about the Georgia and Mississippi projects. Saturday morning was given over to workshops and discussions about voter registration and direct action.[47]

For Saturday afternoon, Lewis planned a mass protest. Attendees would split up and target Nashville's segregated eateries and the YMCA. The Nashville ministers distributed seven thousand leaflets on the city's campuses, calling on students to make their presence felt. "For over two years we have sought to negotiate with the major business establishments, the Chamber of Commerce, the restaurant association, and individual owners and managers," the flyer said. "We have no choice but to again witness in dramatic but loving fashion that segregation is an evil we cannot and will not support."[48]

The turnout showed that direct action could still command a large following. About 150 students crowded into First Baptist, where they met with NCLC leaders and heard Lewis speak. Singing "We Shall Overcome," they paraded downtown and fanned out to their targets. "We feel there is a very serious moral question involved here in denying service to anyone on anything as superficial as the color of his skin," Rick Momeyer, who had returned to Nashville for the occasion, told the *Tennessean*. The establishments were unyielding, and in a few places students were punched, slapped, and elbowed. The scene at Tic Toc was especially ugly. Outside, SNCC staffer Sam Block was punched in the groin and stabbed with a ballpoint pen. Inside, manager Herschel Ewing sprayed the sit-inners with a fire extinguisher and Lewis was roughed up. Forman proclaimed the day a success. Whatever his private doubts, he declared that "nonviolence has produced a social revolution in the South." The weekend also brought many new young

people into the Nashville movement, including Vencen Horsley of Tennessee A&I and David Kotelchuck, a young physics professor at Vanderbilt,
both of whom would join Lewis's merry band.[49]

Nonetheless, Lewis also witnessed more disdain for nonviolent methods
of the sort he had first seen at the H. G. Hill supermarket pickets in 1961.
Some participants were indifferent or hostile to rules like dressing nicely and
forming neat lines. They seemed to think they could come in and behave
however they pleased. During Saturday's pickets, Lewis roamed about, asking people to put out a cigarette, tuck in a shirt, or stand up straight.

Not everyone took kindly to the lecturing. Stanley Wise of Washington,
meeting Lewis for the first time, grew annoyed when Lewis told everyone
to hold hands and be quiet. Wise, who later became Lewis's close friend,
thought the admonitions were "nonsense. . . . He was talking that foolish-
ness about holding hands and being quiet and walking orderly. Don't smoke
cigarettes. What in the hell was this?" At one point, Wise, having ignored
the briefings in the church, was mocking the formality of it all, when Lewis
chided him. "Young man!" Lewis said. "I don't know what your name is,
but on these demonstrations we are silent. And we obey our leaders. If you
cannot obey, then get out of this line."

"Wow!" Wise said. "Thank you." Wise could see Lewis's seriousness. He
fell silent. After that, he began following instructions. Over time he came
to admire the way that Lewis could stand there and take a beating, or a cigarette burn, or an egg broken on his shoulder. He had never seen such restraint among his friends in Washington.[50]

Lewis's distress over the diminishing faith in nonviolence was noted
by the Nashville ministers. They felt compelled to reassure him. C. T. Vivian, now working for SCLC, found himself trying to persuade Lewis that
the popularity of James Baldwin's recent New Yorker essay "The Fire Next
Time"—a bleak warning about the depth of racial division in America—
didn't augur an abandonment of nonviolence. But Lewis was worried.[51]

Lewis was also feeling lonely. He had served as best man at LaFayette's
wedding, but was disappointed that his best friend hadn't returned to Fisk.
He wrote to Momeyer that his friends Joy Reagon and Freddie Leonard had
also gotten married. Everyone was paired up. "I guess Liz and I will be next,
according to some of my friends," he added, referring to Elizabeth Harbour,
who had taken a shine to Lewis. But it was not a romantic relationship.

"Nothing happening there," Lewis told Momeyer frankly. "To be true, I am trying to find some nice young lady who would be fool enough to marry me since all of my friends are getting tied up." For now he was, as he liked to say, married to the movement.[52]

The spring semester at Fisk saw no letup in Lewis's activity. In recognition of his leadership, he was made a member of the NCLC—a symbolic graduation from the ranks of the students to the company of the ministers. He also continued to chair the Nashville Student Movement.

As 1963 opened, District Attorney Harry Nichol remained determined to test Tennessee's nineteenth-century segregation laws. After a sit-in at B&W in October, Nichol had charged Lewis and three others with "conspiracy to obstruct trade and business," counts similar to those he had brought in the Cross Keys case. Then, on January 19, Lewis led the first big sit-in of the new term, at the YMCA, leading to his arrest and more conspiracy charges. Weeks later, an all-white jury found Lewis and the others guilty. Their sentence was exceedingly harsh: ninety days in the workhouse and $50 fines.

If Nichol had hoped to see the courts strike down these laws, his strategy failed. He came under fire as the harsh penalties elicited widespread indignation. "We are deeply disturbed that young people of our community have been sentenced to jail for attempting to eat in a public place," exclaimed an interfaith group of Nashville clergymen. They called the ruling "not only a denial of our democratic way of life but of the moral and ethical principles on which the laws of our nation are founded."[53]

The verdicts also spurred the Nashville students and ministers to redouble their energies. Kelly Miller Smith told Lewis that too much time had passed since a major victory. They drew up a plan of action to "enlarge and step up the direct action phase of 'Operation Open City,'" enlisting help from political and business leaders, newspaper publishers, and clergy. The NCLC invited "every Nashville Leader and interested citizen" to kick things off at a mass meeting at the Mount Zion Baptist Church on March 19.[54]

Finally, things started moving again. "We got the Nashville Movement organized on a massive scale again," Lewis said. On March 21, five hundred Nashvillians jammed into the courtroom for Lewis's trial following another sit-in arrest, stemming from yet another confrontation at Cross Keys. The show of strength persuaded the judge to throw out the charges.[55]

Lewis kept up the drumbeat the following Saturday with a march from the A&I campus to the downtown shopping area. Carrying signs, eighty-five people stopped in front of the B&W, Cross Keys, Krystal, Tic Toc, Wilson-Quick, and other holdout restaurants. Workers inside rushed to block or bolt the doors. A group of local whites pelted Lewis and his crew with eggs. But Lewis and his friends now believed the wind was at their backs.

The hostile mobs got bigger, too. "There would be hundreds of kids coming out of school, white kids, and the street would be lined, literally, with hundreds of people," according to Archie Allen. The whites would pick fights, throw rocks, or follow the protesters back to First Baptist. But the revitalized Nashville movement kept marching and meeting. On March 26, four hundred community members showed up and voted unanimously to boycott the downtown establishments. The goal was to get Beverly Briley, who had won the mayoral election and was to take office April 1, to convene a "biracial committee" like the one that had led to the lunch counter desegregation of three years earlier. To Lewis, it felt like 1960. "The city of Nashville is on the move again," he wrote to Momeyer. "The community is coming together once more to destroy the system of segregation."[56]

Even more important than the conspiracy trials in boosting the Nashville movement in the spring of 1963 were the historic events unfolding 180 miles to the south, in Birmingham. There, Martin Luther King and Fred Shuttlesworth were waging a high-profile drive to break the back of segregation in Bull Connor's stronghold. Although the national media's focus on Alabama diverted attention from Nashville, the excitement sparked by King's campaign reignited Nashville's own activism. On April 12, Good Friday, Alabama officials sent King to solitary confinement for violating an injunction against protesting; in Nashville, on the same day, Metz Rollins led a vigil on the Davidson County Courthouse steps. Nashville was keeping pace with Birmingham, action for action.

Although Birmingham was garnering the headlines, activists in both cities were drawing inspiration from each other. In Birmingham, Andy Young reminded the SCLC staff that back in April 1960 four thousand Nashvillians had marched on city hall after the Looby bombing, leading to their first breakthrough. "We would like to have that many here in Birmingham," Young said. Bevel, also now working for SCLC, screened the 1960 NBC "Sit-In" documentary for his Birmingham recruits. He also conscripted high school students, despite doubts from King about the wisdom of the tactic. Yet here, too, Nashville provided a precedent: in 1960, high schools had emptied out, bolstering the huge April procession that produced Ben West's historic concessions.

High school students were getting involved again in Nashville in 1963 as well. Some people thought it was a mistake. "Somebody's going to get hurt," Vanderbilt professor David Kotelchuck told Lewis. "Violence will break out, John." Lewis acknowledged to Vencen Horsley that some of the kids taking part looked as though they belonged in day care. But Horsley wanted to keep them involved. "They're coming anyway," he said. "There's no way we can prevent that. The only thing we can do is to teach them to be nonviolent."[57]

In Birmingham, the showdown came on Thursday, May 2. Thousands of students rallied that day, leading to so many arrests that the police ran out of paddy wagons and had to take them to jail on school buses. The next day, with the jails full, Bull Connor ordered firemen to douse the children with high-pressure fire hoses. Officers sicced German shepherds on the protesters, beat them pitilessly, and assaulted them with water jets so intense that their force sent Fred Shuttlesworth to the hospital. The news reports and gruesome images shocked people the world over. The Kennedy administration demanded that Birmingham's political and business leaders sit down and negotiate. Within days, on May 10, Shuttlesworth and King announced a stunning victory: a promise to desegregate the city's public accommodations and to cease discriminating against Blacks seeking to work in Birmingham stores.[58]

All that week in Nashville, Lewis watched the evening news and read the papers. He clipped articles, pasted them onto poster board, and tacked them to trees by the Fisk student union and chapel. If Birmingham was standing up to fire hoses and police dogs, so could Nashville.[59]

In the events of the next weeks, Lewis played as important a role as anyone. Kelly Miller Smith, Metz Rollins, and Will Campbell remained

important leaders and spokesmen, but Lewis had now joined the ministers'
ranks in those roles.

They launched their big push on Tuesday, May 7. That night, James
Lawson addressed a mass meeting, urging everyone to come out the next
day in solidarity with Birmingham. NCLC activists, college students, and
high schoolers heeded the call. On Wednesday morning, nearly one thousand people attended a rally at First Baptist, followed by a short workshop in
nonviolence. They divided into groups of twenty or twenty-five, and Lewis
assigned each one to a different store downtown. Three thousand whites
were there waiting, some as onlookers, others to heckle and harass. Scuffles
broke out, and the violence, though limited, led the local news.[60]

Thursday and Friday saw more of the same. Physical altercations continued. The Black students sang, picketed, and staged sit-ins, while disorderly
whites threw bottles and rocks. In one prolonged incident, Metz Rollins was
struck in the head by a rock and two Black teenage girls were injured. The
Banner, Nashville's conservative paper, headlined its story "Negroes Attack
Police Here." The more liberal *Tennessean* reported that "some of the Negroes returned the fire."[61]

After three days of conflict, Mayor Briley intervened. On Friday night,
May 10, he met for three hours with Kelly Miller Smith, Will Campbell, and
Lewis and largely gave in to their demands. He announced the next day that
the three of them would be part of a negotiating committee to pursue the
total desegregation of Nashville's restaurants, hotels, and businesses.

In return, Lewis and the ministers agreed to a two-day moratorium on
assemblies. Smith instructed students to steer clear of downtown, saying
that those who ignored the moratorium would "betray by that very act the
sufferings of those who have gone before them." The irony was not lost on
Lewis. Having struggled for two years to drum up volunteers, he now found
himself telling people to stay home.[62]

The weekend was quiet as the parties negotiated. To keep the pressure on,
Lewis said on Sunday that marches would resume the next day "unless some
concrete steps are taken to end segregation here. . . . We want something besides progress reports from committees." On Monday, with the moratorium
over and progress wanting, Lewis led a new march of 250 people from the
church to downtown. White vigilantes resumed their rock throwing. This
time, however, a significant number of Black youths responded in kind. One

round of fighting, described in the press as a "pitched battle," lasted an hour and a half, as "bands of youths and adults of both races roamed the streets at times uncontrolled." At one point several Black marchers pulled two white hecklers from the crowd and beat them on the pavement. Six people were arrested.

It was a difficult moment for Lewis, who was realizing how unrealistic his expectation of complete adherence to nonviolence could be. He and the other NCLC leaders condemned the misbehavior on their own side and reiterated their nonviolent principles, pleading with the demonstrators not to get into fights. In the streets, the peacefully inclined marchers impressed their views on the journalists at the scene. "We don't want any of you who just want to fight," one Black student declared to "an intoxicated Negro who brandished a knife," reported the *Tennessean*. Others sang "We Shall Overcome" and "America the Beautiful."[63]

On Monday night the mood grew ominous. At around 11:00 p.m., a vigilante hurled a rock from a car—thought at first to be a shotgun blast—while driving past the house of an NCLC minister. It knocked out a window and nearly hit the minister's wife. Nashville seemed poised to explode. The chamber of commerce executive who was leading the negotiations threatened to end them, citing "flagrant and unwarranted riots."*[64]

The fighting rekindled Lewis's old worries. The youngsters weren't hostile to nonviolence, but he observed in them a "greater degree of militancy…a greater sense of defiance." Even so, he tried to prove that nonviolent methods were not a thing of the past. Speaking to the press, he maintained an upbeat message, saying on Monday that the negotiations would soon render additional street actions unnecessary.[65]

On Tuesday, prospects brightened considerably. The negotiating committee met in Briley's office for two hours. On behalf of the NCLC, Lewis spoke again to reporters, even more upbeat than the day before. He said that the Nashville movement was on the cusp of seeing its three-year-old demands satisfied. "There are definite signs we are moving into the beloved

---

* There was also a turn toward violence in Birmingham. The day after the historic May 10 settlement, white supremacists bombed the hotel where King was staying and the home of his brother, A.D. Riots then erupted in the Black community.

community. In order to show our faith, to purge ourselves of our sins, we have called off the demonstrations for the night." He noted that "for three years we have been fighting. . . . Now we are in an area of real progress. The mayor is doing as much as any mayor in the South can do."[66]

That night, Lewis spoke at the Lee Chapel AME church, a "neat red brick building," a visiting journalist wrote, "topped by a white frame spire," sitting "stolidly on a small rise of ground several paces back from the sidewalk." Five hundred people filled the mahogany-colored pews, many of them students, no more than one-tenth of them white. "We have been involved in a very real revolution, a revolution for elementary democracy, in the last few days, since last Wednesday," Lewis began. "We admit that the discipline of some hasn't been up to par. But you must understand the process of a revolution. People grow weary of the slow progress and their militancy bursts the bounds of our prescribed forms for the struggle. . . . We don't want violence. No," he asserted. "But . . . our community as a whole now is restless and will not be denied. Yes, we will counsel our brothers in our tactics of our struggle, but we understand them. We will save our wrath for those who continue the crimes of racism against our people."[67]

Afterward, Lewis took the journalist, James E. Jackson, back to his "small bedroom-study," as Jackson described it, in the Fisk dorms. "It was approaching midnight and John Lewis's roommate was already asleep in one of the single beds. Although it was hot in the room, the lad had his pillow over his head in a practiced technique to block out the noise and light simultaneously. I sat on the edge of the other bed. Lewis was seated in an arm chair at one of the two desks." Lewis talked to Jackson about his life, the history of the Nashville movement, and the state of America and the world. Lewis, the writer concluded, "is not only a man of action but a man of ideas and a serious student of philosophy."[68]

Mayor Briley took the major step of creating a permanent biracial committee. Named the Metropolitan Human Relations Commission, the entity was tasked with charting a course toward citywide desegregation and equal-opportunity hiring. An auspicious sign was the appointment of five NCLC ministers. "I think that the downtown businesses not integrated will do so," Briley told the press. Lewis agreed. "There are signs of real progress."[69]

The mayor's timing was shrewd. Briley cast his city in a flattering light just before the arrival of a notable visitor. On Saturday, May 18, President Kennedy came to Nashville to mark the thirtieth anniversary of the Tennessee Valley Authority and the ninetieth anniversary of Vanderbilt University. In his speech he praised the city's steps toward desegregation as significant progress toward a society in which "all Americans enjoy equal opportunity and liberty under law." It was perhaps the strongest call for racial equality that any president had ever delivered south of the Mason-Dixon Line.[70]

Two days later came more good news. Ruling on a series of sit-in cases, the Supreme Court held that in segregated states and localities, Blacks couldn't be prosecuted for seeking service in segregated stores. In other words, a state, by practicing segregation, was nudging its stores to discriminate, and so the stores couldn't be said to be acting in a private capacity. The ruling vacated thirty-one convictions and pushed the court closer to a broad holding that segregation in hotels and restaurants was unconstitutional.[71]

Buoyed by the progress, Lewis saw no reason to relent. As his spring semester ended, he and several of his friends met, Archie Allen said, "to have one last night together before the summer vacation." They drove to the airport to pick up Catherine Burks-Brooks, now teaching school in Chicago, who was coming back to see her husband, Paul. Driving back to town, the interracial party stopped for dinner at a Shoney's restaurant, only to be denied service. Lewis refused to leave. The manager proceeded to clear out the entire restaurant and lock up the store. The friends continued on to a Howard Johnson's—where again they were refused service. The impromptu testing of restaurants continued, but Catherine was tired and Paul wanted to take her home. They ended up at a Burger Boy Drive-In, where, Allen was happy to note, "we were served by a white waitress with excellent and courteous service." The denial of service earned a brief write-up in the *Tennessean*. For Lewis, no night of celebration was complete without a few sit-ins.[72]

Victory came on June 11. The Human Relations Commission announced that the city's restaurants, hotels, and motels would now cater to Blacks alongside whites. ("The only one we didn't get," said Joseph Lowery, an NCLC minister, with slight exaggeration, "was Morrison's. We could not get Morrison's to budge.") Lewis had played a key part in this breakthrough. The Nashville movement's 1963 offensive—culminating three years of persistent, often lonely work—had secured desegregation on a much wider scale than the celebrated but limited victories of 1960 and 1961.

Some establishments continued to discriminate, and Blacks would still face prejudice in areas like employment and housing. But after the spring of 1963, most businesses acted with impressive speed. Kelly Miller Smith cheered the "substantial progress" that followed from the Open City campaign. Lewis proclaimed the agreement with the restaurateurs "a great victory for the nonviolent movement." *Jet* magazine named Nashville the "Best City in the South for Negroes," calling it "the city with the most comprehensive and diverse integration achievements." The *Tennessean* declared that progress "can be seen everywhere . . . at a movie on the weekend, on a shopping trip during the week, even during a hospital visit."[73]

Lewis had reason to be proud. Of all the students who had been there at the beginning, in Kelly Miller Smith's church in 1959, he was the one who had fought segregation in Nashville most unrelentingly. Many brave and dedicated activists had done their part. But, Dave Kotelchuck said, "he was the one who kept the movement going and alive and fighting."[74]

A bittersweet marker of the progress was the sudden exodus of many of Nashville's Black leaders following the 1963 victory. Smith accepted a pastorate in Cleveland and Metz Rollins moved to New York City. Lawson, who had been only an infrequent Nashville presence for some time, resigned from the NCLC. Fisk professors Vivian Henderson and Herman Long, both active in the movement, took positions at universities elsewhere. But if the departures were a blow to the Nashville movement, they also demonstrated that the leaders considered their recent gains to be substantial enough that they could now move on.[75]

One question nagged at Lewis. Although he considered the spring accords to be validation of the nonviolent approach, some of his friends argued with his logic. Kotelchuck told Lewis that without the street brawling and the threat that widescale violence might flare up, the spring marches might not have been so consequential. "John," Kotelchuck said, "you say that this shows that nonviolence works. But you've demonstrated that the *fear* of violence is effective in making change. When you have mass demonstrations with violence as possible, things will happen. That's not the success of nonviolence."

"No, Dave," Lewis said, refusing to entertain the argument. He maintained that the overwhelmingly peaceful nature of the marches had made the difference. He said as much publicly. "It is this reality of purpose," he declared, that "I believe our young people need in order to rededicate their lives and their sacred honor. Our aim is to desegregate all public places in Nashville. That will enable us to move from desegregation to integration. Through disciplined action, we can transform this community."[76]

Chapter Seven

THE MARCH ON WASHINGTON

——— ▪ ▪ ———

The weeks after Nashville's historic breakthrough saw John Lewis doing what one would expect: leading more protests. Despite the promise of citywide desegregation, Lewis's mission wasn't yet accomplished. After his semester ended, he got back to work, staging a swim-in at the segregated Cascade Plunge pool (which wasn't covered by the latest agreement) and picketing the H. G. Hill supermarket (which was still lagging in hiring Blacks).

At the supermarket, Lewis and his friends debuted a novel technique: forming a human barricade to keep customers from entering the store. They would remain nonviolent, Lewis promised. But if shoppers wanted in, he said, "they'll have to push their way in." The blockade held for five hours before Lewis and the others were arrested.[1]

A local news article cast this technique as a break from the movement's tried-and-true methods. "Negroes Changing Tactics," read the headline. But the Nashville movement hadn't revised its philosophy. The framing of the story reflected, rather, an emerging focus throughout the news media on what was being called the "new militance."

In the ten weeks since Birmingham, racial protests had erupted in two hundred cities. Some were nonviolent and drew reprisals from law enforcement or white vigilantes. Others were little more than riots, untethered from any political program. Still others were a mix—marches alongside mayhem. In Cambridge, Maryland, demonstrations spilled into ugly nighttime clashes as the main thoroughfare became a battle zone. In Winona, Mississippi, and Danville, Virginia, SNCC staffers endured vicious beatings by jailers or police officers. SNCC's activities also made headlines in Jackson, Atlanta, Greensboro, Knoxville, Raleigh, and Savannah. Did this ferment represent a triumph for the Gandhian philosophy? Or was nonviolence losing its purchase?[2]

What the ferment did signal, unmistakably, was a shift—though what was "militant" about that shift depended on how the word was used. Sometimes the term was applied to the raw, disorderly acts of revolt that were threatening to replace the nonviolent methods Lewis held dear. After Birmingham, Adam Clayton Powell and Malcolm X threatened that chaos would overtake America's cities if the federal government didn't act on civil rights. Here *militancy* meant a rejection of nonviolence. But elsewhere it suggested something milder: an intensification of protest, the adoption of a defiant edge, born of impatience with the lugubrious pace of change.[3]

Whatever it was, the new militancy prodded the Kennedy administration. In early June, the president ordered his staff to draft a bill that would, among its provisions, bar racial discrimination in public accommodations and take steps to protect the right to vote—striking at two key pillars of white supremacy in Dixie.

The final straw was a showdown at the University of Alabama, where the state's demagogic governor, George C. Wallace, refused to let two Black students register for classes. His resistance raised the specter of a disaster like the Ole Miss riot of 1962. This time the White House cut a deal that let Wallace save face by grandstanding on camera before yielding to federal marshals.

On June 11, as that saga played out in Tuscaloosa, the president finally introduced his bill—on television, that night. From the Oval Office, Kennedy gave a strong, stirring speech that labeled equality for Black Americans a "moral issue . . . as old as the Scriptures and . . . as clear as the American Constitution." His language was unequivocal: "One hundred years of delay have passed since President Lincoln freed the slaves, yet their heirs, their grandsons, are not fully free."[4]

Reactionary forces struck back. Hours later, Byron De La Beckwith of the Mississippi White Citizens Council shot and killed thirty-seven-year-old Medgar Evers, an NAACP official who was leading the local desegregation campaign. The next day brought more violence. Bernard LaFayette, who was in Selma, Alabama, launching a SNCC voter registration push, was ambushed and nearly killed outside his apartment. Kennedy's address, welcome as it was, neither sated Black demands nor deterred retaliatory violence. In the week after his speech, the country teetered on the brink.[5]

In Nashville, John Lewis had been planning to take a paid summer position with the NCLC. The ministers had created a new role for their protégé so he could tide himself over until school resumed. He was also looking forward to his first trip abroad, to Germany, to participate in church workshops.[6]

Then came a telegram from SNCC chairman Chuck McDew, inviting Lewis to an emergency meeting in Atlanta on June 14 to 15. Lewis wasn't clued in to the office politics, but McDew, though just elected to a new term, was about to quit. He and James Forman were at odds: Forman thought McDew spent too much time courting donors; McDew resented that his fundraising wasn't appreciated. He was also having health problems and wanted to return to his studies.

Lewis was the ideal replacement. He was known throughout the civil rights world for his courage, his faith in nonviolence, and his considerable accomplishments. He would be the perfect symbol, the epitome of the student movement's highest virtues. As a skilled recruiter and mentor, Lewis could also nurture local movements around the South. Then, too, one friend noted, "His purity made him appear more militant politically than he actually was"—a quality that made him broadly acceptable.

Lewis knew none of this when he opened McDew's telegram. "I had no thoughts, ever, of being the chairman of SNCC or any southwide or national organization, nothing like that," he insisted. "It was out of the blue."[7]

A few friends drove with him to Atlanta. Sue Thrasher, a Nashville activist, offered up her parents' 1957 Pontiac. Lester McKinnie drove. Also along were David Kotelchuck and 1960 sit-in veteran Paul LaPrad.

As they drove, rain fell, and outside Murfreesboro the roads got slick. Rounding a bend, McKinnie lost control of the car. It veered off the road and tumbled into a drainage ditch. Flipped upside down, the five passengers were silent. The car doors, blocked by the culvert walls, wouldn't open. The car began to smoke. Frantically, they escaped through the windows. They tossed wet grass onto the car, trying to douse the flames.

McKinnie and Thrasher flagged down a motorist, who happened to have a fire extinguisher. Two men, both white, began to quench the fire. "Where's the other car?" one of the men asked. They assumed that white and Black passengers must be riding separately. "It's just us," replied Kotelchuck. The men stopped helping and drove away.

A state trooper arrived next. He put out the fire and took Lewis's group to the police station. They tracked down a friend to fetch them. Thrasher returned to Nashville to tell her parents about the wrecked vehicle. Lewis went on to Atlanta. For years after, whenever Lewis pondered whether he should learn to drive, he thought about the accident and put it off.[8]

In Atlanta, Lewis heard whispers about the prospect of his becoming chair. Charles Sherrod's name was also floated. A churchgoer and believer in nonviolence, Sherrod had joined early sit-ins in Richmond, attended SNCC's founding conference, and led SNCC's Albany campaign. But when the Friday night meeting began, with Marion Barry chairing in place of McDew, no one nominated Sherrod. On Saturday, Lewis was elected unanimously. After dinner and a round of "We Shall Overcome," the new chairman closed the meeting by leading a prayer.[9]

The statement that SNCC gave to the press reflected the handiwork of a new public relations bureau. Julian Bond, a talented writer whom Lewis had befriended at the October 1960 conference, was chosen to run it. A work of some negotiation, the press release reflected the new militancy. "There is a great possibility of race riots and violence this summer unless the demands of the whole Negro community, North and South, are met," it quoted Lewis as saying, in words that didn't quite sound like him. "We do not want violence and we do not advocate it, but we will not slow down because of the possibility. Violence represents the frustration of the Negro community and the slow pace of progress in achieving real democracy; the only way to avoid this is to show tangible proof to American Negroes that his life is getting better—and this must be done with deeds, not promises." That weekend, when a *New York Times* reporter asked Forman about SNCC's new chairman, Forman said bluntly, "It means more action."[10]

Lewis was ambivalent about the statement's aggressive tone, which he thought reflected the influence of Forman and other Northerners. Lewis wanted to topple Jim Crow as urgently as anyone, but he also wanted SNCC's rhetoric to hew to its Gandhian and Christian principles. "Redemptive love was the heart of the movement, the appeal to the best instincts of human beings," Lewis said. "Redemptive love came naturally to Negro Southerners. The role and place of the Negro church was the idea of salvation. Many Negroes, young and old, were involved in the movement out of a strong moral, religious feeling, conviction." Even as he assumed the SNCC chairmanship, Lewis was concerned that not everyone in the organization appreciated these ideas.[11]

Accepting the chairmanship brought major changes to Lewis's life: moving to Atlanta, suspending his studies, resigning from the Nashville movement. "With regret I must resign as coordinator and chairman of the Student Central Committee," he wrote to the NCLC. "This is necessary for I have been elected National Chairman of the Student Nonviolent Coordinating Committee. . . . It is not that I am leaving you, but rather joining you in a fuller sense. The contribution which you and the entire Nashville community have made to my life is immeasurable. For this I am most grateful."[12]

Given Lewis's spartan lifestyle, moving didn't require much. He had six shirts, two suits, and a small library of books. In Atlanta, he found a second-floor apartment in a brick walk-up on Gordon Road, in a Black neighborhood, a fifteen-minute bus ride from the SNCC offices. SNCC would cover the $54-a-month rent. The apartment was sparsely furnished, with a couple of paintings on the walls, bookshelves, and a couch with rickety legs. The alcove kitchen had a small stove and fridge. Lewis was soon joined by two roommates: Danny Lyon, the photographer he had met in Cairo, and Sam Shirah, a white Troy native.[13]

Lewis was assuming control of a body in the midst of change. "The organization," he noted, "was becoming less and less a student-based organization. Most of its emphasis was shifting from the college campus to the community," especially rural areas where Blacks were most immiserated. Instead of a resource for campus-based projects, it was a regional entity with a new agenda. The turn toward rural Southern hamlets also meant focusing on voting and economics more than desegregation. SNCC's growth also brought new members, many with backgrounds and philosophies different from the founders'.

Some SNCC members were also growing irritated about their organization's place in the civil rights firmament. Time and again, they felt, their foot soldiers would endure dangerous challenges, only to see SCLC or the NAACP reap the credit—and the money. One reason Forman had favored Lewis as chairman was that Lewis's gentleness, sincerity, and goodness made him an attractive, compelling figure in the eyes of the media and donors.[14]

Lewis was self-aware enough to see that he was a perfect symbol for SNCC's purposes: a son of the poor, rural South; trained for the ministry; radicalized in the student movement; preternaturally brave; arrested and beaten repeatedly; and supremely devoted to nonviolence and love. Forman and Barry urged Lewis to be more visible, to court the press and place himself at the center of group photographs. It didn't come easily to Lewis, but he learned to handle the increasing media attention.

In the early summer, Lewis recounted, he went "from city to city in the South, from project to project, trying to find out what was going on, and also speaking at fundraising benefits, talking to people, speaking at cocktail parties." He visited cities and towns where SNCC had projects underway, from Selma, Alabama, to Cambridge, Maryland, to Danville, Virginia. In Greenwood, Mississippi, Lewis spoke at a SNCC folk festival featuring the Freedom Singers and twenty-two-year-old Bob Dylan, "the first time in the history of the Delta," Lewis said, "that Black and white are standing and singing together."

"I was more or less a guy from the local movement," Lewis later said. "In a matter of months, I was taken out of it and settled down in Atlanta. Then it became my responsibility to keep up with what was going on." Bond taught him about dealing with the press, sometimes joining him on his travels, sometimes keeping in touch by phone. Bond or Mary King, his deputy, would write the quotations attributed to Lewis in press releases. Sometimes reporters looking for a comment from the chairman would simply go to Bond.[15]

Lewis's travels kept him in motion all summer. But soon his attention would be drawn away from the South, toward a big rally, scheduled for late August, to take place in Washington, D.C.

The idea of a march on Washington had been percolating for months. After a SNCC meeting in June 1962, Lewis had written to Momeyer about "a mass demonstration in Washington for around Jan. 1 or 2, 1963"—the hundredth anniversary of the Emancipation Proclamation. That idea never came off, but others were thinking along the same lines—notably, A. Philip Randolph and Bayard Rustin.[16]

Randolph, seventy-four, was the grand old man of the movement. A lifelong socialist and stalwart anti-Communist, he had led the Brotherhood of Sleeping Car Porters, the premier African American labor union. (He now led a new group called the Negro American Labor Council.) Tall and slender, with tufts of white hair framing a bald dome, Randolph had a regal presence. Rustin, fifty-one, an early acolyte of nonviolence, was a longtime Randolph ally and also staunchly anti-Communist. A gay man who had once been arrested for performing sex acts in a parked car, Rustin was kept at arm's length by King for a time lest scandal taint the movement. Yet Randolph stood by him. "If the fact is, he is homosexual, maybe we need more of them," Randolph had said. "He's so talented."[17]

Just as the 1961 Freedom Rides had been modeled on the 1947 Journey of Reconciliation, so the March on Washington took inspiration from Randolph's idea of a rally in the capital in 1941. Back then, Franklin Roosevelt, afraid to spotlight America's racial shortcomings with world war looming, pressured Randolph to scotch the plan. Randolph agreed in return for a promise to create a Fair Employment Practices Committee—one of FDR's boldest steps to promote civil rights.*

In December 1962, in Randolph's Harlem office, he and Rustin hatched the idea of a new march focused on jobs and employment. Rustin, an organizational wizard, took control. "He could get five people on the telephone, five chairmen of five different organizations, and at the end of the day have them all agree to get twenty-seven buses to a given spot," said Rachelle Horowitz, a junior aide. "But he also always had his eye on the next project . . . and where the movement should be going." Rustin believed that Black Americans, who could never win change on their own, had to forge

---

* In 1957, Randolph, Rustin, and other civil rights leaders had organized a "Prayer Pilgrimage for Freedom" at the Lincoln Memorial, drawing twenty-five thousand people.

alliances. For the march, he assembled a coalition of partners, from civil rights, labor, Christian, and Jewish groups.[18]

Some key figures rebuffed him at first. Martin Luther King, busy with Birmingham, paid the march little mind. Many at SNCC were skeptical, expecting the march would be, Lewis said, "a lame event, organized by the cautious, conservative traditional power structure of Black America." Forman said that SNCC would participate only if the march were a "forum from which we articulated to the nation a militancy not heard before from civil rights organizations."[19]

To entice SNCC, Rustin and his aides concocted a range of theatrical stunts of civil disobedience, such as having two thousand ministers and rabbis ring the Capitol in a massive prayer vigil. A proposal they drafted talked about flooding "all Congressmen with a staggered series of labor, church, and civil rights delegations . . . so that they would be unable to conduct business." This imaginative plan attested to a willingness to be confrontational. In April, Julian Bond wrote Randolph to pledge SNCC's participation. James Farmer and CORE signed on as well.[20]

King's involvement would be crucial. His aide Clarence Jones allowed King's name to be listed on the organizing materials. Yet not until after Birmingham did King turn his full attention to the march. On June 1, he told Jones that he wanted in and instructed him to reach out to Randolph.[21]

The quickening of protests and spikes of violence in June, along with Kennedy's unveiling of his civil rights bill, solidified King's commitment. Expecting Southerners to filibuster Kennedy's legislation, King argued that any protest should target Congress, not the White House. But the sponsors differed about how militant a posture to strike. Without clearing his remarks with King, George Lawrence, SCLC's man in New York, threatened at a press conference on June 11—the same day as the University of Alabama showdown and Kennedy's historic speech—to stage a "massive, militant, and monumental sit-in" in the Capitol. "We will tie up public transportation," he blustered, "by laying our bodies prostrate on the runways of airports, across railroad tracks, and in bus depots." Blindsided by Lawrence's freelancing, King deemed the comments "unauthorized" and walked them back a few days later.[22]

Still, Lawrence's comments—and the provocative ideas Rustin had floated in his earlier memo—alarmed Washington. One senator warned that

Capitol police would quash any protest inside the Capitol building. The White House, rather than arguing publicly with the civil rights leaders, invited them to meet with President Kennedy on Saturday, June 22.[23]

A few days beforehand, the civil rights chiefs met to find common ground among themselves. On June 18, at Randolph's New York office, Rustin and King held a small planning discussion that included Freedom Rider Bill Mahoney, who was running SNCC's small New York office. The participants agreed that the march, combining Randolph's Northern emphasis on employment and King's Southern focus on liberation, would be billed as a rally "for jobs and freedom." Rustin instructed each participating group to name one principal to represent it at future meetings. He also said he still hoped to bring the NAACP and other groups on board.

The following day, many of the same men met at the posh Carlyle Hotel on the Upper East Side at what was a far grander affair: a breakfast hosted by Stephen Currier, president of the Taconic Foundation, a generous but reclusive movement funder. Since February, Currier had been caucusing monthly with six major movement leaders: King, Farmer, Whitney Young of the National Urban League, Dorothy Height of the National Council of Negro Women, Roy Wilkins of the NAACP, and Jack Greenberg of the NAACP Legal Defense Fund (technically a separate body). For the June breakfast, Currier also invited a hundred wealthy donors. SNCC, seen as a second-tier organization, wasn't included.

The fraught national mood loosened the donors' purse strings. Collectively, their pledges that morning totaled $800,000. Currier also proposed forming an umbrella group to serve as a clearinghouse for the donations, which, to minimize internecine competition, would be divvied up according to a formula. When the breakfast ended, Currier picked up the $1,062.85 tab.[24]

Two days later, George Lawrence of SCLC and Cleveland Robinson of the Negro American Labor Council* formally announced the march. SNCC and CORE would also be cosponsoring it. They said they hoped to attract one hundred thousand people to Washington in late August. They made no mention of tying up the airports or train tracks.[25]

---

* Later named the Council for United Civil Rights Leadership, or CUCRL.

Before the June meetings in New York, SNCC had been only tangentially involved—just "a few telephone calls," Lewis said. Lewis himself knew little about the plans. But when word came of the invitation to the White House on June 22, SNCC had to decide how to respond.[26]

The staff was divided. Some argued for abstaining altogether. Jim Forman, according to Lewis, was "very cold" to the idea. Others still wanted to undertake militant nonviolent actions, such as lying in on the airport tarmac, encamping on the White House lawn, or occupying congressional offices. Executive committee member Courtland Cox argued that the march would be a big event, worthy of SNCC's participation; as a result of his enthusiasm, he was assigned to help. Lewis also wanted to be a part of whatever took place. His Nashville experiences had made him, he said, "action-oriented." "Anytime, when you can get a large group of people together, whether it's marching or a prayer vigil or sitting in," he explained, it was smart "to point up the issue, to educate the people."

Given their respective attitudes, Forman agreed that Lewis should represent SNCC at the White House meeting. It would be his first time in the executive mansion and his first time meeting a president. Thirty civil rights bigwigs would be there.[27]

On Saturday, hours before the meeting, Kennedy had a private meeting with King. They walked out to the Rose Garden, where the president pled with the civil rights leader to ditch Stanley Levison and Jack O'Dell, both men with Communist ties. Their Communist activities, Kennedy said, were hurting the movement and the cause. King knew about Levison's Communist past, but the attorney had distanced himself from the party some time ago, and King was ignorant of the full extent of Levison's continuing ties. He recoiled at believing the worst about his close friend and trusted adviser, even after the president assured him that the intelligence on Levison was solid. Eventually, King agreed. Days later he demanded that O'Dell resign. Levison formally left SCLC as well, though he continued to communicate with King through side channels.[28]

Meanwhile, the other leaders—including Lewis—were arriving at the White House. They were greeted at the North Portico by Preston Bruce, a Black doorman. A few of the visitors asked Bruce if Kennedy was sincere about civil rights. Bruce said that the president indeed "cared heart and soul about justice for Black people."

From there they filed into the Cabinet Room. Joining them from the administration were Robert Kennedy, Vice President Johnson, Labor Secretary Willard Wirtz, and the historian and presidential adviser Arthur Schlesinger Jr. Guests jockeyed for seats close to the president's chair. Farmer quipped that he should have brought shoulder pads and a helmet. Lewis, who could barely believe he was in the White House, took no notice. He remembered only the sight of President Kennedy striding in, confident and smiling, offering a rapid fire of hellos as he shook hands around the table. He seemed in a hurry, Lewis thought. In fact, the president was departing for Europe that evening.[29]

Kennedy's advisers had prepared a sheet of talking points. "Consider carefully the negative impact of a march on Congress," read one. His strategy was to present the White House as their ally, not their antagonist, and he mostly talked up his civil rights bill. He described them all as partners in a shared enterprise. Then he laid out the obstacle course of challenges the bill would face en route to passage, explaining how it could be sidelined by committees, individuals, or the dreaded Senate filibuster. Robert Kennedy added a few short words. Then hands around the room shot up.

Roy Wilkins of the NAACP spoke first. One of Kennedy's closest allies, Wilkins ingratiated himself with the president, pledging support for the bill. Next, Whitney Young of the Urban League brought up the march. Like Franklin Roosevelt two decades earlier, Kennedy hoped to avoid a huge, unpredictable event in the streets of Washington, especially given the recent violence in other cities. Kennedy now expressed his worry that the march would backfire, emboldening Southerners to tie up his bill. But he chose his words carefully. "We want success in Congress," he said, "not a big show on the Capitol. Some of these people are looking for an excuse to be against us. I don't want to give any of them a chance to say, 'Yes, I'm for the bill but I'm damned if I'll vote for it at the point of a gun.' It seemed to me a great mistake to announce a march on Washington before the bill was even in committee. The only effect is to create an atmosphere of intimidation—and this may give some members of Congress an out."

Randolph pushed back. A Shakespearean actor in his youth, he could transfix an audience with his low, resonant voice and refined accent. Lewis was in awe. As a boy, he had clipped Randolph's picture from the newspapers, where it would run alongside his syndicated column. Lewis regarded Randolph as a figure like Frederick Douglass, someone who, in a different age, could have been a senator, ambassador, or president. When Randolph spoke, the room hushed.

"There will be a march," Randolph said softly. Protesters were already in the streets, he said; the question was whether they would choose violence. Offering up a big Washington march as an outlet for their energies would fend off trouble.

Lewis watched Kennedy squirm in his chair. His body language said he didn't like what he heard. But he was listening.

Lyndon Johnson reiterated that the march could complicate the administration's delicate strategy. He listed the senators who were for and against the bill. But James Farmer reminded his hosts that the civil rights heads had political considerations, too: if they scuttled the march and then Kennedy's bill failed, "frustration would grow into violence and would demand new leadership."

Martin Luther King, who had been keeping his counsel, now weighed in. "This could serve as a means through which a people with legitimate discontents could channel their grievances under disciplined nonviolent leadership," he said. "It could also serve as a means of dramatizing the issue and mobilizing support in parts of the country which don't know the problems at first hand." He continued: "It may seem ill-timed. Frankly, I have never engaged in a direct-action movement that did not seem ill-timed. Some people thought that Birmingham was ill-timed."

"Including the attorney general," Kennedy interrupted. The president was ribbing his brother, but he might as well have been pointing to himself. In any case, his joke contained a tacit admission: sometimes the movement had to disregard the White House's wishes.

Kennedy made a final play. With a flourish, he pulled from his pocket a slip of paper. "I have just seen the new Gallup poll," he said. "National approval of the administration has fallen from 60 to 47 percent." Actually, Gallup's latest poll showed him down only three points, from 64 to 61 percent, in the last month. Further, Thursday's weekly mail count had tallied

2,364 letters approving of JFK's civil rights speech versus 398 against. The president was bluffing. "I may lose the next election because of this," Kennedy said. "I don't care." That, too, was a bluff.[30]

By now almost two hours had passed. Kennedy no longer held hope of aborting the march. Now he was just explaining himself. "He came across to me," Lewis said, "as a guy who was interested in learning, and he did listen well." He had a sense of fairness that Lewis hadn't expected. His concluding remarks were half-resigned, half-apologetic. "You have problems, I have problems," the president said. "We all have problems." Reeling off a welter of global challenges he faced, he put forth his bottom line: "I can't have riots."

Randolph promised that the march would be orderly. But, he repeated, the Black masses were restless—elongating the word, *MAAH-ses*, Lewis recalled, in his basso profundo. Kennedy ended on a note of cooperation, saying he wanted to "keep in touch."

The youngest person in the room, Lewis had been silent throughout. He never pretended to know more than he did; even at SNCC meetings, if discussion moved to subjects he didn't understand, he would sit and listen. Around a table with Kennedy and King and Randolph, he felt no need to pipe up.

The president exited into the Oval Office, then out through the French doors to the White House lawn, where he and his family boarded a helicopter for Camp David. Lyndon Johnson and Robert Kennedy continued the discussion a little longer. Then the participants all filtered out to meet with reporters. Wilkins said that he was "not involved at the present moment" in the march, but King said that the march was going forward and that President Kennedy was not standing in the way.

Lewis felt thrilled to be there. "It's a long way from Pike County," he told himself.[31]

Ten days later, Lewis and Forman flew to New York City for more face time with the movement brass. Forman was concerned that the new chairman—"young, inexperienced, from a small Southern town"—would be eaten alive by the skilled infighters around the table. He decided to come along.[32]

It was Lewis's first trip to New York City. In Harlem, where Rustin had set up the march headquarters, Lewis was struck by the "sea of blackness"—so many African Americans living together, cheek by jowl, with few whites in their midst. Lewis also noted the despair and anger; he was put off by a street-corner orator ranting and raving about "whitey." It reinforced his belief in the differences between Northern and Southern Blacks. The latter, he believed, despite having endured slavery and Jim Crow, tended to display an optimistic spirit of a kind that was not visible to him on the streets of Harlem.[33]

The leadership meetings took place at the Roosevelt Hotel in Midtown Manhattan on July 2. For the first meeting, a luncheon, fifteen officials gathered in the hotel dining room. At the start, Roy Wilkins imperiously reminded everyone that only one person per group could be present. The march was now officially a joint venture of six entities: the Negro American Labor Council, SCLC, SNCC, and CORE, plus the NAACP and the Urban League, both now on board, constituting what would be called the "Big Six." These groups' principals alone could attend; everyone else had to leave the room. Humiliated, eminences like Rustin and Fred Shuttlesworth trooped out. Wilkins's demeaning treatment of them enraged Lewis. Some people speculated that Wilkins was hoping to kill the march.[34]

Wilkins actually was ready to forge ahead, but on his own terms. The first issue to settle was who should be in charge of operations. Randolph proposed Rustin, who was already running things. Wilkins countered that he would be discredited over his sexuality or his brief stint as a Communist. After some jousting, which struck Lewis as "petty politics," they agreed that Randolph would serve as titular chief and Rustin as his deputy. The compromise would give Rustin the responsibility, while shielding him from the spotlight.* The assembled also settled upon August 28 as the event's date—a Wednesday, so that clergymen wouldn't miss a turn at the pulpit. They agreed, too, to forgo the radical forms of civil disobedience: no sit-ins in the halls of Congress, no tying up traffic. Lewis again said little. At twenty-three, he was still unsure of himself, mindful of his junior status, grateful just to be at the table.[35]

---

* During the summer, Senator Strom Thurmond of South Carolina went after Rustin from the Senate floor over both his brief membership in the Young Communist League and his sexuality.

After the luncheon, Lewis joined a larger meeting of the Leadership Conference, an alliance of fifty-two civic, labor, women's, fraternal, and religious groups. Their numbers were buttressed by still other participants, about one hundred in all. Walter Reuther of the United Auto Workers presided over the sprawling session, pledging that his union—large and always flush—would furnish planning space in Washington. Everyone promised to back the march and the president's bill, whatever its flaws.[36]

Lewis saw SNCC's inclusion in the formal leadership team as evidence that their ragtag band had arrived. Stephen Currier even invited SNCC to join his fund-sharing council. Lewis didn't like the council's formula for allocating money, which was based on each group's existing budget—which meant that SNCC, the tiniest group, would get the fewest dollars. But the cash infusion did wonders for SNCC. Lewis believed that the council structure gave the movement a "sense of unity and focus that it needed during that time."[37]

Rustin now got to work. He and his staff operated out of a weather-beaten stucco walk-up on 170 West 130th Street in Harlem, dubbed "Utopia House." Owned by a friendly church, the building normally served as a community center for neighborhood children. Outside, kids cruised by on scooters, transistor radios blared, and men played bridge and dominoes. Between the third- and second-story windows, staffers hung a banner that ran the width of the building. "National Headquarters: March on Washington for Jobs and Freedom," it read—now the event's official title. The rooms bustled with harried staffers, ringing telephones, clattering typewriters, and spirited conversations. Visitors and volunteers navigated mazes of workstations, bookcases, folding chairs, and an old upright piano. Rustin, his gray shock of hair visible across the room, presided over it all with a cigarette glued to his lips, writing notes or doodling energetically.

Rustin cast a spell over Lewis. Lewis was charmed by the meticulous care with which the otherwise frenetic workhorse disposed of his cigarette butts, admiring Rustin's fastidiousness of style. Even more, Lewis admired Rustin's command of detail. "He was so smart, so brilliant," Lewis said. "He was concerned with things like people having some place to eat, and everybody on the stage having a chair, . . . and the microphones and people getting in and out, how many buses, how many trains. . . . At one point, he said, 'How many toilets? We can't have any disorganized pissing in Washington.'" Rustin's team would arrange for 292 outdoor toilets, twenty-one water fountains, and twenty-two first aid stations in anticipation of the crush.[38]

While Courtland Cox and Dorie Ladner of SNCC dealt with logistics for the march, Lewis continued his visits to SNCC field operations around the South. On July 15, he visited Bernard and Colia LaFayette in Selma and headlined a rally at Brown Chapel on behalf of the voting rights movement they were building with the local Dallas County Voters League. Lewis had to limit his Selma speech to ten minutes, however, because he was immediately summoned away to Cambridge, Maryland, where rioting had forced the governor to call in the National Guard. President Kennedy used the chaos in Cambridge to stake out a moderate position, formally endorsing the March on Washington while warning about the dangers of violence. "In Cambridge, Maryland," Kennedy said, ". . . they have almost lost sight of what the demonstration is about." With violence, he added, "I think the cause of advancing equal opportunities only loses."[39]

Lewis disapproved of the street violence in Cambridge, but he resented Kennedy's castigation of the protests. "Kennedy doesn't understand the depth of the movement and doesn't realize the true problem," Lewis told a reporter. He reaffirmed that SNCC has "always deplored violence, and we have always conducted our demonstrations nonviolently." But, he explained, "the instances of violence in Cambridge have been the result of constant frustration and have been provoked by whites shooting at us and marching on our community."[40]

To resolve the Cambridge conflict, Robert Kennedy invited Lewis and Gloria Richardson, a forty-one-year-old activist spearheading the local campaign, to Washington on the evening of July 22. State and local officials were also there. The attorney general brokered a temporary truce, but what struck Lewis was the clear evolution in Kennedy's attitudes. After the discussions, some of the guests stayed behind. A heavyweight prizefight between Sonny Liston and Floyd Patterson was on the radio. Kennedy was rooting for

Patterson, who was knocked out in two minutes. Afterward, Kennedy surprised Lewis with some candid, personal remarks. "I want to thank you," he said—his "you," Lewis thought, referring not to Lewis personally but to the student movement. "All of that helped me a great deal. You have educated me. You have helped me."[41]

As plans for the march proceeded, many SNCC staffers grumbled that the White House and the mainstream civil rights bodies had coopted the event. The president's endorsement yoked the march to his bill. What SNCC had envisioned as an anti-government action now seemed like a Kennedy campaign rally. Groans greeted news of each concession that Rustin made. The comedian Dick Gregory, who was close to several people in SNCC, joked to Burke Marshall of the Justice Department that the event that had once frightened official Washington was now destined to be "a great big Sunday school picnic."[42]

Lewis found it all exciting. SNCC was now part of the leadership, and Lewis was counted among the Big Six. It was lofty company for a twenty-three-year-old. "Behind the scenes, there was some grumbling that this young upstart was even included with the rest of them," said Paul Anthony of the Atlanta-based Southern Regional Council, another civil rights group. Lewis himself regularly marveled that he was sitting among such giants.

The organizational leaders kept jockeying. Jack Greenberg and Dorothy Height were dropped from the official list of organizers. Height's exclusion was especially inexcusable given her extensive role in the planning. Eventually the objections of several women persuaded the march's leaders to include on the program a "Tribute to Negro Women Fighters for Freedom" that collectively recognized Height, Rosa Parks, Diane Nash, Gloria Richardson, and others—a far from equitable remedy. Meanwhile, Rustin expanded the roster of march leaders still further to include Walter Reuther and a trio of clergymen: Joachim Prinz of the American Jewish Congress, Mathew Ahmann of the National Catholic Council, and Eugene Carson Blake of the Presbyterian Church. The Big Six had become the Big Ten: white and Black, Jewish and Christian, but still all male.[43]

Lewis also had a speech to write. He began composing it in SNCC's offices, a cramped, shabby cluster of rooms at 6 Raymond Street in Atlanta, upstairs from a tailor shop, in a run-down mint-green building. Lewis was convinced he owed his opportunity not to who he was but to what SNCC symbolized: the younger generation. "I was just there as a representative of SNCC," he said, "without any talents or skills or anything." Accordingly, he wanted his remarks to express the organization's views, not simply his own. He felt obliged to convey his colleagues' lukewarm feelings about the march and about Kennedy's civil rights bill. He also wanted to speak about what SNCC members were seeing in their campaigns around the South. Most recently, in Americus, Georgia, police had roughed up a group of SNCC voter registration workers, who were then held without bail and charged, outrageously, with insurrection, a capital offense. Lewis recounted these and other horrors as he jotted down his ideas.[44]

Once he had finished a draft, he showed it to Nancy Stearns, a new staffer who worked on the floor just below him. "Nancy," he said, "listen to this!" Stearns loved it. She provided some comments and offered to be his typist. Over several days, they refined the draft, with other SNCC staffers including Forman and Bond offering input.[45]

Lewis's upcoming star turn excited his Nashville friends. "I'm really glad for you," wrote Joy Reagon when he was named SNCC chairman. "I can't think of anyone who deserves it more. . . . I know you're working real hard. Too bad I can't be there to help. You must need a secretary (smile)." She said that she and her husband, Fred Leonard, hoped to come to the march, and signed off, "Take care of yourself, Chairman." Gerald Davis, Lewis's roommate at Fisk, also wrote, giddy about his friend's sudden stature. Davis reported meeting Robert Kennedy and John Seigenthaler who, "when he found out that I was from Fisk and had known you . . . became most congenial, . . . and asked me to say 'Hi' to you whenever I should have the opportunity." The NCLC organized buses to send Nashvillians to the march.[46]

In August, Lewis visited New York City again. Rustin took a liking to him, finding him a reliable ally in Big Six meetings. "Get John on the phone and see when he can make it," Rustin would say to Rachelle Horowitz. Of the Big Six, Lewis was always the most diligent about attendance. He was also a natural ambassador for the march, exuding an unaffected excitement when talking to the press. "Everything we've done so far has been preliminary, almost a rehearsal," he told one visitor to Utopia House, the journalist Harvey Swados. "On August 28, the curtain goes up on the first act of the revolution."[47]

Horowitz and Rustin had apartments in a union cooperative in the West Twenties called Penn South. Throughout the summer, Horowitz's one-bedroom flat served as a makeshift hostel for young activists passing through. Lewis stayed on her couch. Things sometimes got crowded. Joyce Ladner of SNCC also bunked at Horowitz's, and one night came back to find Bob Dylan on her bed, picking out songs on his guitar, romancing her sister, Dorie. The activists jelled socially, sometimes joined by a group of socialist twenty-somethings in Rustin's circle.[48]

The weekend before the march, Lewis made a final trip to New York, where Harlem's Apollo Theater was hosting a benefit concert for the march featuring Thelonious Monk, Quincy Jones, Tony Bennett, and Stevie Wonder. Lewis stayed with Horowitz again. He shared the living room with the Ladner sisters, while Horowitz and Yale law student Eleanor Holmes* took the bedroom.

Believing his speech draft to be "representative of the feelings of the people in SNCC," he showed it again to his friends. Its unsparing tone reflected the adversarial stance that SNCC wanted to express. Lewis said plainly that his organization "cannot support the administration's civil rights bill," calling it "too little, too late." He blasted Kennedy for "trying to take the revolution out of the street and put it in the courts" and assailed the Justice Department for bringing charges against the SNCC workers in Georgia, while failing to indict police officers who had brutalized a local activist there and his pregnant sister-in-law. If the Kennedy administration was hoping to co-opt the march, Lewis refused to go along.[49]

Lewis had never faced an audience of a hundred thousand people. He remained self-conscious about his speaking style, his accent, and his tendency to stumble over certain words. ("Register," one friend noted, always came out as "reddisher.") Over the weekend, at Penn South, he rehearsed his remarks constantly, with Horowitz and others providing a sounding board. Courtland Cox and Rustin disciple Tom Kahn wanted to give Lewis's draft

---

* Later Eleanor Holmes Norton.

an even sharper edge. In one place, Lewis had knocked both political parties for harboring enemies of civil rights. "The party of Kennedy is also the party of Eastland. The party of Javits is also the party of Goldwater," Lewis had written. Cox added a pointed question: "Where is *our* party?" Kahn added a line that invoked Civil War general William Tecumseh Sherman's notorious "March to the Sea," from Atlanta to Savannah, in which Union forces had laid waste to rail lines, houses, farms, and whatever else lay in their path. "We will march through the South, through the heart of Dixie, the way Sherman did," the Brooklyn-reared Kahn wrote. "We shall pursue our own 'scorched earth' policy and burn Jim Crow to the ground." Then, as if grasping the contradiction between his incendiary words and Lewis's actual beliefs, he added: "nonviolently!"[50]

Lewis made one other change. Reading the newspaper that weekend, he saw a photograph of women in Northern Rhodesia (soon renamed Zambia), which had announced plans for its first elections under a new constitution. The women held a sign bearing the slogan "One man, one vote"—a phrase also associated with a recent U.S. Supreme Court ruling. Lewis added a reference. "'One man, one vote' is the African cry," he wrote. "It is ours, too. It must be ours."[51]

Lewis was happy with this version. He was even happier to have it completed. He showed it to Rustin. "It's actually terrific," Rustin said. "Now fold this up, John, and keep it in your pocket."[52]

On Sunday, the hard work done, the twenty-somethings went to Westchester County, where Horowitz's friend Debbie Meier's family had a backyard swimming pool. As they were horsing around, Paul Feldman tossed Lewis into the water. Lewis began to sink. "I don't swim," he calmly announced. Penn Kemble jumped in and pulled him out. Someone offered Lewis an inflatable chair so he could float about, with a gin and tonic nestled in an armrest notch. They ribbed the SNCC chairman as he drifted, pretending he was an executive or plutocrat living the high life. Then a phone call from Mississippi came for Lewis. No one could figure out how to get him onto terra firma. "We finally got him out with a net," Horowitz recalled, as someone hooked the raft with the long-handled cleaning tool and towed Lewis in.[53]

On Monday, Lewis spoke at a fundraising event at the Polo Grounds in Upper Manhattan before heading to Washington, where the organizers

had rooms at the Statler Hilton* near the White House. On Tuesday morning, he went to the hotel lobby, only to run into Malcolm X. They spoke
briefly. No one had thought to include Malcolm or his Nation of Islam in
the march; Lewis didn't even consider Malcolm a civil rights leader. In any
case, the Nation of Islam minister had been noisily belittling the march for
weeks, calling it "the Farce on Washington." Yet here was Malcolm in the
Hilton lobby, commanding press attention. He confided to some SNCC
members that he couldn't imagine missing it.[54]

Tuesday was filled with meetings, phone calls, press events, and a Bob
Moses–led picket line at the Justice Department to protest the indictment
of the Georgia civil rights workers. Over at the Statler Hilton, Courtland
Cox saw copies of Whitney Young's speech on the press table and decided
to put Lewis's there as well. Why should SNCC be denied equal exposure?
He and Bond mimeographed a pile of copies of Lewis's address for passersby
to pick up. When Rustin and Horowitz saw them preparing the copies, they
objected. "What are you doing that for?" Rustin asked. "No one is seeing
King's speech." Cox insisted that Lewis and SNCC get their share of the
limelight.[55]

Lewis was oblivious to the exchange until that night, when he returned
to his hotel room, where Danny Lyon was crashing on the floor. A note from
Rustin was waiting for him. "John," it read, "come downstairs. Must see you
at once." Then the phone rang. It was Rustin. "We have a problem," he said.[56]

"A problem? What problem?" Lewis asked.

"It's your speech. Some people are very concerned about some of the
things you're going to say in your speech. You need to get down here. We
need to talk."

Lewis went to Rustin's room. Several others were there. They explained
to Lewis that an associate of Archbishop Patrick O'Boyle of Washington,
who was to deliver the invocation the next day, had shown the clergyman
the speech. O'Boyle was refusing to participate if Lewis delivered the speech
as written. He had shared his objections with Burke Marshall of the Justice
Department and labor boss Walter Reuther, who also wanted alterations.
Rustin had promised to try.

---

* The Statler was renamed the Capital Hilton in 1977.

As Rustin and Lewis spoke, Rustin said he thought O'Boyle might be appeased with one fix. A line in Lewis's speech spurned counsels of "patience," calling it "a dirty and nasty word."

"This is offensive to the Catholic Church," Rustin said.

"Why?" Lewis asked.

"*Payyy . . . tience.*" Rustin dramatically articulated the word. "Catholics believe in the word 'patience.'" It was a theological tenet, cited throughout the Bible and by thinkers like St. Augustine.

Lewis relented. It was an insignificant change. Rustin was pleased. He added that there might be more edits to make the next day. But Lewis should get to bed.

Back in his room, Lewis paced, fuming over the prospect of additional edits. He was, he said, "angry that someone would tell me what to say and what should be deleted."

When Danny Lyon woke up Wednesday morning, Lewis was long gone. The organizers were up early. It was going to be a hot Washington summer day, maybe eighty-four degrees—"the kind of day that reminds you why anyone who can afford to leaves Washington in August," recalled Andrew Young. Only a strong breeze made the heat tolerable.

The early hours were quiet. The rush-hour traffic that normally clogged the Virginia bridges and the avenues to Maryland was absent. Some 160,000 federal and city employees stayed home from work. Liquor stores were closed. The Washington police force canceled leaves for its officers; the National Guard and U.S. Army troops stood by. Rustin's staff double-checked plans for the musical program, the speakers, parking, foot traffic, celebrity management, and food. (Volunteers had assembled eighty thousand cheese sandwiches.) At eight in the morning, Cox and Rustin went out to a desolate Mall. "Is anybody going to be out here?" Rustin wondered.[57]

With actors Ossie Davis and Ruby Dee emceeing, a morning preprogram included performances from Peter, Paul and Mary, Odetta, Joan Baez, and the SNCC Freedom Singers. Dylan played his new song about Medgar Evers, "Only a Pawn in Their Game." CBS suspended regular programming to provide coverage; the other networks aired intermittent reports and evening wrap-ups. The new Telstar satellite beamed the proceedings around the globe. Television cameras homed in on celebrities, including Sidney Poitier, Diahann Carroll, Jackie Robinson, Marlon Brando, and Josephine Baker, who had flown in from Paris. During breaks, the crowd chanted, "Pass the bill! Pass the bill!" which must have brought the White House satisfaction.[58]

As the crowd swelled, Rustin brought the leaders to Capitol Hill to lobby lawmakers. One of the Big Ten was not there: James Farmer, having been arrested for protesting in Plaquemines Parish, Louisiana, was languishing in jail. Floyd McKissick, his number two, had come instead. As Lewis made the rounds on the Hill, he thought the meetings were mostly theater, although a few politicians, including Senators Hubert Humphrey and Jacob Javits, offered strong and heartfelt support.

When the leaders left the Capitol, the once-sleepy streets were teeming. Wave after wave of human beings was emanating from Union Station, from the avenues, from the side streets. Black and white marchers mingled easily. Freedom songs filled the air. The men who had intended to lead the march were caught in the middle of it.

By midday estimates pegged the crowd size at 250,000, more than twice the organizers' goal. Perhaps one-quarter was white. Congress canceled business because too many members would be attending. Organizers issued 1,655 special press passes on top of the 1,200 held by regular Washington correspondents.[59]

With the formal program soon to begin, a row broke out at the Lincoln Memorial over Lewis's speech. As Forman reached the top step of the memorial, Matthew Jones and Chuck Neblett of SNCC's Freedom Singers accosted him.

"Hey, man. Did you hear what they did to John's speech?"

"What do you mean?" Forman asked. "What are you talking about?"

"They don't want Lewis to give his speech," they said, not quite accurately.

Forman began to smolder. Ralph Abernathy intervened. "We're going to work it out. Just stay calm, Jim."

It had been naive of Lewis and others—a reflection of their inexperience in national politics—to suppose that a speech opposing the civil rights bill, calling for revolution, and striking a defiant tone could have been allowed to go forward with only a single edit. Earlier that morning, in a car to Capitol Hill, Roy Wilkins had made clear there would be more objections, describing Lewis's lack of support for the Kennedy bill as a "double cross." Now, at the memorial, Rustin was spelling out other necessary changes.[60]

O'Boyle, it turned out, hadn't been fully appeased by the excision of the "patience" line. He—and others—also could not abide the line about Sherman. The Kennedy officials and Walter Reuther wanted SNCC to endorse the civil rights bill. Burke Marshall, who had been working on a new draft himself, brought it over via police motorcycle sidecar. But Lewis, Forman, and Cox stood firm. "No way," Cox told Rustin. "Over our dead bodies."

Rustin gathered everyone in an anteroom behind Daniel Chester French's colossal Lincoln statue. Randolph, Wilkins, King, and others came and went. An irate Forman lectured the older men on the importance of Lewis's passages about the suffering and deprivation of rights of Blacks across the South. Wilkins in turn berated the SNCC kids, saying they "always wanted to be different."

Wilkins's condescension annoyed Lewis. "I'm not just speaking for myself," he told Wilkins earnestly. "I'm speaking for my colleagues at SNCC, and for the people in the Delta and the Black Belt. You haven't been there, Mr. Wilkins. You don't understand."

Wilkins replied that Lewis's obstreperousness would sabotage the bill.

"We're not here to support a civil rights bill," Lewis countered. "This march is much broader than that." He remained soft-spoken, never screaming or shouting.

With the program about to start, O'Boyle agreed to give the invocation. Rustin promised to show him Lewis's final remarks. If the speech didn't pass muster, O'Boyle warned, he would walk off the stage. At 1:15 p.m., the proceedings began.

Negotiations and rewriting continued. Passages were softened. Eugene Carson Blake of the Presbyterian Church, President Eisenhower's pastor, wanted Lewis to strike the words "masses" and "revolution," which smacked of Marxism. "There's nothing wrong with the use of the word 'the Black masses,'" Randolph countered. "I use it myself." In one instance, the word "social" was inserted before "revolution," to dispel any possible Communist associations. In another, it was changed to "the unfinished revolution of 1776."[61]

A bigger argument broke out over Lewis's non-endorsement of the

Kennedy bill. At one point the parties agreed that Lewis would simply say that he couldn't back the bill "wholeheartedly." But Blake now objected to that formulation. More wordsmithing followed. It was agreed that Lewis would say that he and SNCC supported the bill, but "with reservations," which he would then spell out. These included the omission of a Fair Employment Practices Committee to ensure job opportunities for Blacks and a section called Title III that would empower the U.S. attorney general to sue local officials over police abuses.*

The final conflict centered on the Sherman sentence. Martin Luther King reasoned with Lewis. "John, I know who you are," he said. "I think I know you well. I don't think this sounds like you." King was right. The passage had been Tom Kahn's. Its whole sensibility was alien to Lewis's thinking. He had liked its confrontational thrust, but it simply didn't make sense.

Randolph ultimately appealed to Lewis's compassion and pragmatism. "Would you accommodate an old man?" he asked the SNCC trio. "I've waited twenty-two years for this opportunity. Please don't ruin it." To Lewis, he added, "John, we've come this far together. Will you make these changes? We need to stay together."

The trio caucused. Lewis was angry, but his instinct for accommodation prevailed. The speech still said most of what he wished to say. He wanted to maintain the day's unity. And he realized that the episode could yield an incidental benefit: it would bring SNCC "to the attention of the people and the press."[62]

In his dense handwriting, Cox entered the changes on the script, with Lewis looking on. Forman typed it up on a portable typewriter. Lewis was now concerned less about the substance than about his delivery. For all his rehearsing, he now had to read from a revised text for the first time, in front of 250,000 people. From over Forman's shoulder he implored his colleague, "Don't change too much! Don't change too much!" The final draft was less shrill, but still powerfully conveyed SNCC's demand for a stronger bill and more rapid change.[63]

---

* The White House did add Title III to its bill, but it did not survive into the version passed in 1964. Not until the comprehensive crime legislation of 1994 did a version of it become federal law.

When Ahmann showed the final draft to O'Boyle, the archbishop asked his opinion. "It's fine," Ahmann said. O'Boyle didn't even bother to read it.

Amid a throng of reporters at the speakers' platform, Bond handed out copies of the original text, without Lewis's knowledge. He told everyone to note the differences.[64]

Suddenly, Lewis heard Randolph's voice echoing over the public address system. "I have the pleasure to present to this great audience," he began, "young John Lewis, national chairman, Student Nonviolent Coordinating Committee. Brother John Lewis!" As Lewis stepped through the clusters of people on the steps, Rustin grabbed his hand to help him to the podium, conveying him on to Randolph.

A roar of applause followed. Lewis settled himself behind the podium, outfitted with at least seven microphones. Along the Reflecting Pool and far beyond stood row upon row of listeners. Lewis could see intrepid youths on the tree branches; they had shinnied up for a better view. The crowd estimates of 250,000 had to be undercounts, he thought. From the steps he could see his SNCC friends vaguely in his peripheral vision and hear them cheering him on.

His anger and anxiety dissipated. Lewis began, first at a hurried pace, then slower, with measured cadences and graceful pauses and no indication that he was seeing some of these lines for the first time:

> We march today for jobs and freedom, but we have nothing to be proud of. For hundreds and thousands of our brothers are not here. For they are receiving starvation wages, or no wages at all. While we stand here, there are sharecroppers in the Delta of Mississippi who are out in the fields working for less than three dollars a day, twelve hours a day. While we stand here there are students in jail on trumped-up charges. Our brother James Farmer, along with many others, is also in jail. We come here today with a great sense of misgiving.

Lewis was reading, not reciting, but he looked up often at the vast blanket of people before him. Randolph reached in to bend the necks of the microphones. Lewis took on the Kennedy legislation.

It is true that we support the administration's civil rights bill. We support it with great reservations, however. Unless Title III is put in this bill, there is nothing to protect the young children and old women who must face police dogs and fire hoses in the South while they engage in peaceful demonstrations. In its present form, this bill will not protect the citizens of Danville, Virginia, who must live in constant fear of a police state. It will not protect the hundreds and thousands of people that have been arrested on trumped charges. What about the three young men, SNCC field secretaries in Americus, Georgia, who face the death penalty for engaging in peaceful protest?

As it stands now, the voting section of this bill will not help the thousands of Black people who want to vote. It will not help the citizens of Mississippi, of Alabama and Georgia, who are qualified to vote, but lack a sixth-grade education. "One man, one vote" is the African cry. It is ours too. It must be ours!

We must have legislation that will protect the Mississippi share-cropper who is put off of his farm because he dares to register to vote. We need a bill that will provide for the homeless and starving people of this nation. We need a bill that will ensure the equality of a maid who earns five dollars a week in a home of a family whose total income is $100,000 a year. We must have a good FEPC bill.

He waited for the applause to subside and pivoted to a larger critique:

My friends, let us not forget that we are involved in a serious so-cial revolution. By and large, American politics is dominated by politicians who build their careers on immoral compromises and ally themselves with open forms of political, economic, and social exploitation. There are exceptions, of course. We salute those. But what political leader can stand up and say, "My party is the party of principles"? For the party of Kennedy is also the party of East-land. The party of Javits is also the party of Goldwater. Where is our party? Where is the political party that will make it unnecessary to march on Washington?

Where is the political party that will make it unnecessary to march in the streets of Birmingham? Where is the political party that will protect the citizens of Albany, Georgia? Do you know that in Albany, Georgia, nine of our leaders have been indicted, not by the Dixiecrats, but by the federal government for peaceful protest? But what did the federal government do when Albany's deputy sheriff beat attorney C. B. King and left him half-dead? What did the federal government do when local police officials kicked and assaulted the pregnant wife of Slater King, and she lost her baby?

Lewis's voice rose in volume and in pitch, and a tremor crept into his voice. Behind him, Rustin puffed a cigarette. The next line, delivered with preacherly thrusts of his arm as he looked out at the audience, drew the most applause of any in the speech.

To those who have said, "Be patient and wait," we have long said that we cannot be patient. We do not want our freedom gradually, but we want to be free now!

We are tired. We are tired of being beaten by policemen. We are tired of seeing our people locked up in jail over and over again. And then you holler, "Be patient." How long can we be patient? We want our freedom and we want it now. We do not want to go to jail. But we will go to jail if this is the price we must pay for love, brotherhood, and true peace.

I appeal to all of you to get into this great revolution that is sweeping this nation. Get in and stay in the streets of every city, every village and hamlet of this nation until true freedom comes, until the revolution of 1776 is complete.

He now was hitting his stride—gesturing more, looking down less, modulating his voice.

We must get in this revolution and complete the revolution. For in the Delta in Mississippi, in southwest Georgia, in the Black Belt of Alabama, in Harlem, in Chicago, Detroit, Philadelphia, and all over this nation, the Black masses are on the march for jobs and freedom.

They're talking about slow down and stop. We will not stop. All of the forces of Eastland, Barnett, Wallace, and Thurmond will not stop this revolution. If we do not get meaningful legislation out of this Congress, the time will come when we will not confine our marching to Washington. We will march through the South, through the streets of Jackson, through the streets of Danville, through the streets of Cambridge, through the streets of Birmingham.

More applause—a fourteenth burst—erupted. Lewis waited for it to pass.

But we will march with the spirit of love and with the spirit of dignity that we have shown here today. By the force of our demands, our determination, and our numbers, we shall splinter the segregated South into a thousand pieces and put them together in the image of God and democracy. We must say: "Wake up America! Wake up!" For we cannot stop, and we will not and cannot be patient.[65]

All of a sudden, he was done. The speech, in the end, reflected the new militancy within SNCC and the radicalism of the rising generation. It struck a markedly different note from the day's other addresses. But Lewis's words also reflected his abiding belief in nonviolence and love as a healing force.

Lewis returned to his seat. Mahalia Jackson sang, and more speeches followed. King closed out the program. Carried live on all the networks, his magisterial speech left the audience euphoric. His stirring vision of an America in which "little Black boys and Black girls will be able to join hands with little white boys and white girls as sisters and brothers" would ascend to canonical status. In the White House, watching the thirty-four-year-old minister, Kennedy told his aides: "He's damn good."

Lewis, too, was enthralled. As different as King's oratory was from his own, he thrilled to its message of hope for the arrival of the beloved community.

Final words followed from Randolph and Rustin, then a benediction from Benjamin Mays of Morehouse College. As loudspeakers played "We Shall Overcome," the pilgrims, depleted from the heat, emotionally drained by King's speech, buoyed by the day's success, returned to their buses and trains, hotels and homes. From the White House solarium, Kennedy listened to the crowd through an open window, telling Preston Bruce, "I wish I were out there with them." The leaders hastened to their five o'clock White House meeting.[66]

Relief prevailed as the guests arrived. Lewis was struck by how happy and proud Kennedy seemed. He was beaming. "I saw you," he said warmly as he greeted Lewis. "I heard you. You did a good job." The march would be a boon for the movement, his bill, his presidency, and the country.[67]

"Mr. President," a visibly exhausted Randolph asked Kennedy, "I wonder if I could just have a glass of milk." The president called for milk and other refreshments: drinks, sandwiches, cherry cobbler.[68]

Kennedy and Johnson talked with their guests for more than an hour. Recorded by the White House, the discussion ranged over the day's events, but focused on the legislation. Lewis again kept silent as Wilkins, Randolph, and others dominated. But his influence was felt. One leader after another pressed the president to include a new Fair Employment Practices Committee and Title III, precisely as Lewis had demanded in his speech.

Reluctant to commit, Kennedy read off lists of senators and congressmen, noting who would be for and against the bill. He leaned on the leaders to pressure Republicans to make the bill a bipartisan cause. Winning over House Minority Leader Charlie Halleck would be crucial. "I think when you go out," Kennedy said in closing, "it would be a good time to indicate, Mr. Randolph, your strong judgment that *both* parties will be supporting the right thing." He added, "And I think [if] you could start that theme, it would be very useful. And maybe we'll get this thing so bipartisan that we get Mr. Halleck." Everyone laughed. Outside, Randolph addressed reporters, with Lewis behind his left shoulder. "History," the old man pronounced, "was written today."[69]

Limousines drove Lewis and the other leaders to the WTTG television studios on Wisconsin Avenue, near the Maryland border. There they taped an hour-long program with the Metropolitan Broadcasting Television network, to air the next night. Host Jay Richard Kennedy posed questions to each man.

He asked Lewis what the movement could offer to "white youth." In reply, Lewis sounded more like a King acolyte than an uncompromising militant. "Just looking at the crowd and looking at the people marching," he said, "what raised my heart . . . was to see hundreds and thousands of young white people walking the streets hand in hand with young Negroes." He compared the civil rights movement to the Peace Corps—a vehicle for idealistic youth "to get involved with something that would help to create a real democratic society. In our own organization we like to talk about the beloved community, the community of love, community of brotherhood. And the only way this can be done is people together, both Black and white."[70]

Lewis called his parents in Pike County. They hadn't watched the speech. But they were excited about how many people had heard him speak, and they were especially happy that he shared the program with King. His mother told him that if he was with Dr. King, she knew he was okay.[71]

Washington was calm again Thursday. The good feeling lingered. The press coverage had a celebratory tone, with accounts noting the event's size, majesty, and upbeat atmosphere—a far cry from the dangerous melee that some had forecast. Large swaths of the public now regarded the movement as righteous, even necessary. Rustin believed that the march had broadened the base of the movement, cementing a coalition of citizens—Black and white, Jewish and Christian, professional and working-class—behind its goals.[72]

Lewis's speech, even in revised form, stood out for its critical edge. "Nashville Leader Raps Kennedy, Both Parties" was the *Banner*'s headline. Articles described him as "militant," "radical," "fiery," "aggressive," "violent," and the "harshest of all." SNCC had leaked an account of the behind-the-scenes drama over the excisions to the media. Newspapers and newsmagazines devoted paragraphs or sidebars to O'Boyle's demands and published the excised phrases. It all redounded to SNCC's benefit. Later that fall, wherever he went, Lewis would hear people express more interest in SNCC than ever before—identifying with it, donating money, requesting its officers to come to speak. "For this," he told his colleagues, "we can thank our good brethren Archbishop O'Boyle, Messrs. Wilkins, King, Young, and Randolph."[73]

At Christmas, Lewis sent O'Boyle a holiday card. The archbishop received the gesture magnanimously.[74]

Chapter Eight

ONE MAN, ONE VOTE

—— ▪ ▪ ——

The stopped clock on the wall told the time it happened: 10:22 a.m. Birmingham's Sixteenth Street Baptist Church, a spired brick sanctuary built in 1911, sat catty-corner from Kelly Ingram Park, the site of the city's historic April protests. On September 15, 1963, in a basement restroom, four girls in fancy white dresses were primping and knotting their sashes before serving as ushers in the eleven o'clock service. A blast of dynamite, planted by local Klansmen, killed them instantly. One girl was decapitated. The explosion blew out the church's stained glass windows, loosed rafters from the ceiling, collapsed a skylight, obliterated the rear stairwell, and left a gaping seven-foot hole in the exterior wall. Cars outside crumpled like soda cans. As wailing ambulances arrived for the injured, church deacon M. W. Pippen heaved away concrete chunks and reached for a white shoe. It belonged to eleven-year-old Denise McNair, his granddaughter. "She's dead, baby," he told his daughter, Denise's mother. "I've got one of her shoes."[1]

In John Lewis's adult life, white supremacists in Nashville had bombed the Hattie Cotton Elementary School, the Jewish Community Center, and Alexander Looby's house. In May they had blown up the Birmingham motel where King stayed and the house where his brother, A.D., lived. "Bombingham," as it was morbidly called, had seen three more blasts in September and nearly fifty over the last fifteen years. Murder was a commonplace tool of Jim Crow's most fanatical guardians. That these tactics turned people of goodwill against segregation did little to deter their perpetrators. After the church bombing, President Kennedy dispatched FBI agents to the city. The civil rights leadership mobilized.

Lewis was visiting his family in Troy. The radio brought news of the bombing. Within minutes Forman called from Atlanta, summoning Lewis to the scene of the crime. John's uncle Otis drove him to the bus station. Because Lewis's parents were afraid that the killers would target their son, Otis avoided the Troy and Montgomery stations and, in an act of misdirection, drove south to Dothan, where Lewis boarded a bus back north to Birmingham. He arrived at the same terminal where he and the Freedom Riders had two years earlier spent a long night of anxious waiting.[2]

Lewis met up with Bond and other SNCC colleagues. He also saw Nash and Bevel, now working for King. They all felt "a sense of outrage and righteous indignation," Lewis said. "They wanted to demonstrate; they wanted to march; they wanted to do something."[3]

Reporters swarmed the city. Lewis and Nash talked to Wallace Terry, a twenty-five-year-old Black *Washington Post* correspondent. Frustrated and angry, they bandied about ideas for spectacular acts of civil disobedience that would drive home the urgency of the civil rights agenda. One was a mass pilgrimage to Montgomery that would culminate by encircling the capitol. Another was to halt all transportation with lie-ins on runways, highways, and railroads, as had been proposed for the March on Washington.[4]

To reconcile the dictates of nonviolence with the rising demand for spectacular action was difficult. The dilemma loomed especially large for Lewis, since he was now both the public face of young Negro militancy and the purest incarnation of the movement's rarefied Gandhian precepts. He embodied the very tensions afflicting the movement.[5]

Nash typed up the plan. She called for the mobilization of a civil rights "army," with a standard uniform (black clothing, denim overalls) and a flag, armband, or other insignia. She envisioned reviving the old workshops and drills to teach nonviolent methods to tens of thousands of recruits. Tactics included blockading the Alabama capitol and transport routes, tying up statehouse telephone lines, and arranging a mass refusal to pay state taxes. Her plan would conclude with a political campaign against George Wallace and his administration—forcing him, in a fanciful imagined climax, to abdicate the governor's chair.[6]

Nash was hopeful when she shared her memo with Fred Shuttlesworth.

But he responded coolly. He questioned whether her bold tactics could really be defended as nonviolent; besides, the whole thing was ill-timed. "A funeral is not the time to do what you're talking about," he said. Undeterred, Nash, Bevel, and Lewis met with Martin Luther King and others in his hotel room the next night, after a funeral for three of the girls. Nash argued that the civil rights leadership needed now to offer Black citizens a path forward, a channel for their pent-up emotions.[7]

Lewis agreed with her. But King rebuffed the idea, at one point failing to stifle a condescending laugh. For months, SCLC had resisted the siren song of militancy. King wasn't going to change course now. He and Shuttlesworth were due in Washington to meet with Kennedy the next day.[8]

To many in SNCC, King's demurral confirmed his knee-jerk moderation. But King's political judgment may have been more finely tuned than that of his protégés. Others echoed his caution. When news of Nash's plan appeared, Gerald Davis wrote to Lewis, warning that he was "endangering the hopes and dreams and achievements of millions of people" by embarking on "hasty, irrational actions." He continued: "You have the Whites of America in your hand; they are willing to write letters to their congressmen; they are willing to listen to your demands." After the March on Washington, support for racial equality was at an all-time high. A stunt like a "lay-in in the streets of Montgomery" would squander their goodwill and betray the Blacks who counted on his leadership. "John, you are no longer the angry youthful leader of the NCLC. . . . You are a sophisticate, an intelligent and dynamic leader. . . . You are representing all of the people who have contributed to the idea of constructive, dynamic Passive Resistance."[9]

Those who had known Lewis since Nashville knew that "passive resistance" and the "beloved community" remained his watchwords. Anne Braden, a left-wing radical from the Southern Conference Educational Fund, interviewed Lewis for a perceptive newspaper profile. Media portrayals of the SNCC chairman as a "firebrand," she wrote, were flat wrong. His "militance" was "the kind that keeps a man going at 6 a.m. to a picket line over a period of months when no more than five or six persons are willing to follow him." It resided in his ability "to walk calmly into an angry mob" and remain stoical. "There is a distinctly gentle quality about him."[10]

Braden sent Lewis a draft of the profile in early October, telling him he could change anything he didn't like. He didn't respond. She sent a copy to

Bond, who handled Lewis's press. "I don't think John will mind the 'Gentle Revolutionary,'" Bond wrote back. "He'll like it, in fact."

Bond explained that he was replying on Lewis's behalf because "John is still behind bars."[11]

After the Birmingham funeral, Lewis had gone to Selma, where SNCC's voter registration work was running up against intransigent opposition. Bernard and Colia LaFayette, having worked with the Dallas County Voters League for eighteen months, had left at the summer's end. SNCC sent in Worth Long and Prathia Hall to work with Amelia Boynton, a fifty-two-year-old local activist whose son Bruce's 1960 Supreme Court victory had inspired the Freedom Rides.[12]

Located on the bluffs of the Alabama River, fifty miles west of Montgomery, Selma was the seat of Dallas County. About 58 percent of its twenty-eight thousand citizens were Black. But less than 1 percent of eligible Black residents were on the voting rolls, compared to 54 percent of eligible whites. Fear and intimidation dissuaded most Blacks from even trying to register, and those who did faced the infamous "literacy tests," composed of ridiculously obscure or impossibly broad civic questions like "Summarize the Constitution of the United States." Answers were judged according to the whims of racist registrars. The Justice Department had sued to stop these discriminatory practices, but two and a half years later the case was still tied up in court.[13]

To keep dissident Blacks in line, the county's paunchy, swaggering sheriff, Jim Clark, assembled a three-hundred-man posse that surveilled and suppressed any stirrings. Lewis considered Clark a textbook villain. "He was vicious. Some of the things that he did"—the way he treated children—"I don't know how any human being could do it." Lewis thought the sheriff must have been emotionally troubled; he compensated for his insecurity by making himself as intimidating as possible. "He looked at you and you felt his contempt," Lewis said. Clark conveyed through his gaze that "you were below him, that you were subhuman." When needed, the sheriff could also count on additional manpower from Colonel Al Lingo, a Wallace henchman who ran the state police with a ruthlessness that rivaled Clark's.[14]

The September dynamiting of Birmingham's Sixteenth Street Baptist

Church led two Selma high school students to renew their agitation. On September 16, ninety Selma marchers were arrested during a protest. The next day the police detained twelve more. The city bristled with tension. "Selma is in a state of siege," Worth Long reported to SNCC headquarters. "Everywhere you look you can see state patrolmen or members of the special posse brandishing clubs and cattle prods."[15]

On Monday night, September 23, Lewis arrived at Selma's First Baptist Church for an enormous rally. He took the stage at 9:50 p.m., energizing the crowd of 1,400 with a barn burner of a speech. Denouncing Wallace as "sick" and Lingo and his "goons," Lewis asserted that Blacks would wait no longer for their freedom. Nonviolence was the route to liberation, he preached; the people of Selma would "turn the town upside down" with sit-ins and peaceful demonstrations until, he added in a King-like touch, "justice would roll in Selma." The crowd chanted, "Two, four, six, eight, we want to integrate."[16]

Outside, fifty of Lingo's men ringed the church wielding carbines. Another sixty-five men from Clark's posse sat on buses. Remembering the Freedom Rides, Lewis feared that the lawmen would lock the audience inside the church. When the meeting ended at 11:00 p.m., however, the assembled were allowed to leave unharmed—although, an FBI report noted, "while Negroes were filing out of the church, Sheriff Clark called in the state troopers to drive around the church in caravan style in a show of force." Rallygoers heading to their cars or homes traversed a gantlet of automatic rifles jutting out of car windows, aimed skyward.[17]

Lewis's Monday night exhortations sparked another week of protests. On Wednesday, Lewis was out marching with a group, carrying a homemade sign reading "One Man, One Vote"—a phrase SNCC adopted as its motto after Lewis's March on Washington speech. Clark and his posse charged at them. "You are all under arrest," the sheriff snarled. Lewis fled, knowing that Clark's men liked to swing their electric cattle prods near protesters' genitals. He evaded the weapons but was forced with others onto a bus and driven to jail. "Officers were not aware they had arrested Lewis," the *Selma Times-Journal* reported, "until he identified himself at the booking at the Dallas County Jail several hours later."[18]

Lewis was jailed for a week, given a 180-day sentence, and moved to a prison farm. Filthy and neglected, it reminded him of a chicken coop. His cell had a toilet, a sink, and an old dirty mattress on the floor—and nothing else. When food came on trays, Lewis ate it standing up.[19]

Selma's voter drive continued with Lewis in jail. The main event was to be a "Freedom Day," scheduled for Monday, October 7. SNCC was planning to bring hundreds of disenfranchised citizens to the courthouse to register. To publicize the drive, Forman invited Dick Gregory and James Baldwin. Historian and SNCC adviser Howard Zinn chronicled the day for the *New Republic*. At a Saturday night rally, Forman urged the crowd to recruit more participants. "Go through the phone book. You'll know who's Negro because they won't have Mr. or Mrs. in front of their names. You got to get to the phone tonight and call these people and tell them to come down to the courthouse [on] Freedom Day."[20]

Although Lewis later remembered otherwise, when Freedom Day came he was still in jail. The drive proceeded without him. By 9:30 a.m., a line of well-dressed men and women snaked down the steps of the green stone courthouse and alongside the building. By ten o'clock, the procession stretched around the corner. Clark and his henchmen, outfitted with helmets, batons, and prods, prowled the scene. Inside, registrars conducted their business with excruciating slowness, processing only a few voters each hour—even as three hundred were queued up outside. When two SNCC workers tried to bring sandwiches and water to those in the queue, they were roughed up and arrested. Reporters and photographers were manhandled. "This is the most rabid racism I've seen," Baldwin pronounced.[21]

Lewis posted bail on Thursday, October 10. He was out long enough to engage in a second round of voter registration on October 15 and to hear King speak at First Baptist. Lewis proudly reported to colleagues that King "called SNCC a sister organization and said it was doing a fine job." But Lewis would return to the Selma jail before the month was out. "I was granted a two-week vacation at the expense of Dallas County," he joked. "I rested at the Dallas County Manor, and shuttled back and forth between Camps Selma and Cameda [Camden]. All in all, what with trials, etc., I spent about three weeks as a guest of the State of Alabama."

Still, Lewis was heartened to see Selma come alive. "I think SNCC did a very good job, really putting the community together, laying the groundwork, making people conscious of their power," he said. In the larger sweep of history, that first Freedom Day was "a turning point in the right to vote," Lewis concluded. "Selma was perhaps the first case of a voter drive being turned into a massive public action campaign." Over the next two years, Selma's activists would keep pushing against the county authorities like a battering ram. SNCC also began mounting other Freedom Days—in Hattiesburg and Greenwood, Mississippi, and southwest Georgia. The goal of securing the vote was no longer deemed secondary to direct action; they were fully fused. "One thing we can learn from Selma," Lewis wrote to SNCC colleagues, "is that we can effectively have a positive program of Direct Action centered around Voter Registration."[22]

For the rest of the fall, Lewis was on the move. After Selma, he led a rally at the Greenwood Freedom Day. Then he traveled to campuses in Vermont, Michigan, Illinois, and Pennsylvania. There was a SNCC conference in Washington, D.C., planned for the end of November. In early December he would embark on a West Coast college tour and fundraising swing.

On Wednesday, November 20, Lewis visited his old Fisk friends Rick Momeyer and June Fair at Allegheny College in northwestern Pennsylvania for two days of lectures on nonviolence. He and Momeyer woke up at four o'clock on Friday morning to drive to the Cleveland airport, two hours away, for an early flight to Nashville, where he had to appeal an old sit-in conviction.[23]

The Friday hearing was brief. Lester McKinnie was about to drive Lewis back to the Nashville airport when a bulletin on the car radio interrupted the programming. President Kennedy had been shot. McKinnie stopped the car on Seventeenth Street, by the Fisk campus, where the two men listened to the news. Students gravitated to the car, their ears turned to the vehicle.

At the airport, Lewis learned that the president had died. He cried, and then called Atlanta. He was due in Detroit, where a labor union was honoring him. Lewis wanted to skip the event, but everyone at SNCC thought he should go, so he boarded his plane. Not normally much of a drinker, Lewis had two drinks and turned his speech into a eulogy. He called Momeyer, talked about how Kennedy had made them all hopeful about the future, and cried some more. From there it was on to more speaking gigs in Ann Arbor, Champaign-Urbana, and Cincinnati—when all he wanted was to go back to his apartment. Late Sunday night Lewis arrived at home, exhausted and depressed.[24]

Lewis knew that Kennedy had been slow to act on racial equality, and he hadn't been shy about saying so. But he also believed that the president listened, learned, and grew. Kennedy had come to be, Lewis felt, "a friend to the movement and . . . a friend to young people in particular." Students and activists took from him a sense of hope and possibility. "People could tend to identify with him," Lewis said. "He spoke their language."[25]

The African American community felt similarly. Knocks on Kennedy's moderation were scarcely heard amid the cascade of grief, love, and gratitude. Black leaders and editorialists described him as a second Great Emancipator who had done more to advance equality than any president in a century. "His place in history will be next to Abraham Lincoln," said A. Philip Randolph. "It would be impossible to speak of the Negro revolt," said Fred Shuttlesworth, "without saluting our martyred president, John Fitzgerald Kennedy, whose understanding, skill, and determination of purpose" helped bring about so much change. A parishioner at Harlem's Abyssinian Baptist Church told a *New York Times* reporter: "We needed him to lead us to freedom. What are we going to do?"[26]

SNCC met at Howard University's Rankin Chapel for a previously scheduled three-day conference starting November 29, the day after Thanksgiving. The program booklet was revised to feature a black-bordered picture of the late president. A formal statement extolled Kennedy as "deeply committed to the idea of Justice and Democracy in safety and peace for all Americans." Internally, however, SNCC members quarreled. When news of the assassination had reached the Atlanta office, comments around the table had been unsentimental, focused on the implications for SNCC.[27]

Members debated holding a vigil at the Lincoln Memorial. "Some people wanted to have a sort of silent memorial march in memory of President Kennedy," Lewis recalled. It would include a pilgrimage to his grave at Arlington National Cemetery. But Forman, Carmichael, and others objected, betraying, Lewis said, "an edge of greater bitterness." In public remarks, Forman stingily described the assassination as "a very unfortunate incident." The idea of a gravesite visit to Kennedy's tomb as well as Medgar Evers's was also voted down. "It was sort of a schizo position," Lewis said. "Even then in 1963 SNCC as an organization on one hand was struggling to get people involved in the political process but at the same time . . . didn't want to get too close to the political system."[28]

Opinions about the new president, Lyndon Johnson, were also mixed. On Wednesday, November 27, LBJ had spoken to the nation, resoundingly endorsing Kennedy's civil rights bill. "We have talked long enough in this country about equal rights. We have talked for a hundred years or more," Johnson said. "It is time now . . . to enact a civil rights law so that we can move forward to eliminate from this nation every trace of discrimination and oppression that is based upon race or color." Almost everyone cheered the speech, but within SNCC distrust of Johnson—a white Southerner— lingered. Ever the optimist, Lewis told reporters he hoped Johnson would fill Kennedy's shoes "but make larger footprints."[29]

At one point in the conference, Lewis took a walk around the Howard campus with SNCC friends Courtland Cox, Ivanhoe Donaldson, Charlie Cobb, and Danny Lyon. They came across a Black nationalist gathering and went to check it out. The registration table was covered with pamphlets and flyers. Some featured Lyon's photographs. As they tried to enter, one of the men manning the table said of Lyon, "He can't come in." Lyon protested, explaining that those were his photographs on the table. But he was told again—referred to in the third person—"He can't come in."

Cox, Donaldson, and Cobb went in. Lewis turned on his heel and walked away with Lyon. He said he knew what it felt like to be excluded because of his skin color.[30]

Lewis closed out the SNCC conference with a speech. He began by joking that he would be giving the talk that "the archbishop and other persons stopped me from giving" in August. In language he had been using for months, Lewis acknowledged that patience with nonviolence was wearing thin, and he called on his colleagues to develop "a program to satisfy the needs and aspirations of these people." He also mentioned discontent in the North. "Let's get a real nationwide movement going this time," he implored. "We want freedom, justice, and equality now, not tomorrow." The audience rose in a sustained ovation.[31]

———

"*At home, as far back* as I can remember, they used my middle name, Robert, and they called me Robert. When I went away to school in Nashville . . . most of the students on the seminary campus called me Lewis. . . . But most of the people in the movement started calling me John. Part of a movement thing. People that I got to know and became my friends called me John."

"Outside of Pike County, Alabama, I am John Lewis. But in Troy, in Pike County, my home, my family, my parents, my brothers and sisters, I'm John Robert, but I'm really just Robert."

"Robert is a barefooted boy who likes to raise chickens, likes to plant trees and flowers and grass. He is lazy. I never liked to work in the fields."

"Robert is the preacher. Lewis is the student. And John is the participant in the movement."

"John is the sincere guy who is interested in bringing about justice. Detests violence with a passion. He hates war and wants to see an open society, a community at peace with itself. John is also a guy who loves the scene of action. Wants to be involved in the action, whether it's social action or political action. . . . I'm not really sure who or what John is."[32]

At twenty-three, John Lewis was still figuring out who he was—a preacher, a student, an activist, and now the head of a major civil rights organization at a time of tumultuous change. His job sent him on the road continually, and when he did stay put for a few days, he had to adjust to his new city. Nashville, the student movement, Kelly Miller Smith's church, the American Baptist and Fisk campuses—all had anchored him. Atlanta was different. The last mayor, William Hartsfield, called the city "too busy to hate," a phrase that became its motto, and next to Birmingham or Mississippi, it was a paragon of tolerance. But on desegregation, Lewis believed, "Atlanta was far, far behind Nashville." On a personal level, he still considered Atlanta "a strange scene. I didn't know the downtown area, and I didn't drive, so I had to know how to get around . . . go downtown and get a haircut, or whatever."[33]

An important companion was his roommate, Danny Lyon—an energetic, talkative, caustic, funny New Yorker. The two became close. Lewis's main problem with his roommate was that he had converted their bathroom into a darkroom, and when Lewis would get up at night for a drink, he was afraid he would imbibe some toxic chemicals. One time he mistook the chemicals for shampoo.[34]

Lewis didn't cook much and often dropped by an apartment building where a half dozen SNCC staffers including William Porter, Stanley Wise, and Muriel Tillinghast lived. Porter and Tillinghast were good cooks and would throw meals together. Lewis would come by for the food and conversation.[35]

He made two other close friends in Julian Bond and Don Harris. Both had grown up middle-class. Bond's father, Horace Mann Bond, was a prominent Black scholar of education and a university president. Harris, from Brooklyn, had attended the tony Ethical Culture Fieldston School in New York City—one of three Blacks in his class—and Rutgers University. He had been one of the men jailed in Americus, Georgia, over the summer.

Lewis was self-conscious about his poor, rural upbringing and was sensitive when people from worldlier backgrounds condescended to him. Harris and Bond helped him gain confidence. Hanging out with them, Lewis learned how to act in social situations—what to order at a nice restaurant, what alcoholic beverages to drink. Harris liked scotch and water, so Lewis began drinking scotch and water. From another friend he discovered gin and tonics, which he liked because they tasted almost like soda.

Bond and Harris would gently tease Lewis, calling him "Mr. Chairman." Bond sometimes played a game with Lewis to get his friend to loosen up. The two men would pretend to be prosecutor and witness. "Do you know the aforementioned Miss Smith?" Bond might ask about someone in SNCC. If Lewis said yes, Bond would follow up, "And do you know her carnally?" Lewis, painfully shy about sexual matters, would get flustered.[36]

Sometimes they were joined by Nancy Stearns, a refugee from a graduate program at Berkeley. Stearns was amazed by Lewis's energy, his packed schedule, his exclusive focus on the movement. Other SNCC staffers were dating or coupling up. Some, like Bond and Marion Barry, were known to be ladies' men. But romance played no major part in Lewis's life. Women were drawn to his sweetness, sincerity, and quiet leadership, but it went unrequited.[37]

As Lewis evolved into a national leader, he taught himself to overcome certain ingrained personality traits. His inner intensity, the relentless pace of his schedule, the passion with which he believed in the cause—all made it hard for him to relax. With close friends, he tried to loosen up. He had a comically low tolerance for alcohol. Bond said that if you emptied a glass of beer and then filled it with water, Lewis would get drunk from the water. But Bond and Harris showed him that it was okay to drink and let loose.

On one trip to New York on a snowy winter day, Lewis told Harris that he worried that if he had even one beer, he wouldn't be able to find his way back to where he was staying. Harris assured him that he could relax and enjoy his beer and things would be all right.

He also loosened up on the dance floor. He knew he didn't have the best moves. But his readiness to join in became the subject of affectionate teasing. "John wasn't the best dancer, but he got out there," Cox remembered. "Everybody appreciated it." Archie Allen, from Nashville, recalled him trying to square dance. "He was incompetent, always going the wrong way, but he was game." Matthew Jones said his style was simply that "he would jump around. . . . He'd dance until he fell out."

Once, Danny Lyon took some photos of Lewis close dancing with Casey Hayden, a twenty-six-year-old blond Texan with a lustrous smile. In the photos, Lewis's face radiated ease and joy. On another occasion, the actress Shirley MacLaine came to a party in Atlanta at someone's apartment, where R&B music was playing. "One of the guys on the floor caught my eye and began to sway and bump his hips toward me," she remembered. ". . . He was John Lewis. His dancing was laced with mischief. We grooved to the center of the floor and in two minutes were putting on a show. I had never met him before, but I felt I had known him all my life. Up and down, around and in and out we jerked and undulated and tripped out. I could see the others grin and nod as they watched us, lost in the movement."[38]

SNCC friends in Atlanta turned into a family, much the way Lewis's Nashville friends had. "They worked, ate, socialized, and slept together," said Cleveland Sellers, a longtime SNCC leader. "They read the same books and wore the same kind of clothing." Forman frequently described SNCC as "a band of brothers, a circle of trust," a phrase everyone came to use. Conferences were especially attractive, noted Penny Patch, a white Georgia field organizer, because they "gave us the opportunity to all party together."[39]

In December, Atlanta itself became a priority for SNCC's activism. With other civil rights organizations, SNCC had formed an "Atlanta Summit Leadership Conference" to push for desegregation of public accommodations and for progress in voting, education, and hiring. They forced city and business leaders to engage in talks. But when the board of aldermen rejected a desegregation proposal, SNCC took to the streets. For a mid-December "Pilgrimage for Democracy," which the *New York Times* called "the first major civil rights demonstration in the South since President Kennedy's assassination," the Atlanta alliance brought out their biggest name—Martin Luther King—who denounced the city's paltry integration record before a crowd of three thousand and called for an escalation of direct action.[40]

A local campaign offered advantages. Headquarters was full of staffers bogged down with administrative work and itching to see the front lines. On Saturday, December 21, a delegation from Kenya, including government minister Oginga Odinga, visited with Lewis and the Atlanta staff at Peachtree Manor, one of the city's few integrated hotels. The activists were growing mindful of the links between their cause and African independence movements, and they found the session transformative. The SNCC group sang freedom songs; Odinga recited poetry. Together they chanted, "Uhuru," Swahili for "freedom."

Toward the end, a few emboldened staffers went next door to the segregated Toddle House restaurant for an impromptu sit-in. When they were denied service, a messenger reported back to the Peachtree group. Reinforcements hurried over; seventeen people were arrested. The next day, Lewis led another sit-in. He, too, was arrested. From the SNCC office, Bond rushed out a special edition of the *Student Voice* with a banner headline reading "Christmas in Jail" and a picture of a smartly dressed Lewis being carried away by three policemen. Odinga, asked about U.S. race relations, called them "very pitiful."[41]

For all his traveling, Lewis had spent every Christmas for twenty-two years with his family. In 1963 he was in the Fulton County Jail. "It was a strange and funny feeling to be in jail [on] Christmas," he later said. "I was locked in a cage of humiliation. But, you know, I felt that maybe there was no other place to be but in jail during that period of the year. Maybe there was something wrong in Atlanta and someone had to protest against it and try to correct it." His parents were unfazed. No longer did Lewis's prison sentences seem remarkable.

In prison, there were no presents—only some cigarettes, apples, and candy that the sheriff handed out. Lewis was free after a couple of days.[42]

In January, SNCC launched its own "Open City" campaign. Lewis was in his element. One day he was leading a procession of high school students to the mayor's office; another day he was sitting-in at a diner or a hotel. Some of Lewis's colleagues had their first view of a consummate practitioner of nonviolence in action. "John Lewis's commitment to nonviolence was not mindless," Mary King wrote. "I could often see him working in a form of meditation to achieve his strength and the peace of mind he required for nonviolence." When he faced police brutality, he didn't flinch. She explained: "I had seen John kneel and look his adversary in the eye, it seemed without blinking, as billy sticks crashed down on his forehead, breaking the skin and sometimes blinding him with his own blood. . . . Again and again he would be thrust forward by a group to lead a demonstration because of his inner determination and tranquility under adversity. I don't think it was possible to frighten John. . . . John was not naïve but he made no claim to political shrewdness. What he had was character and courage, which he gave with raw, uncalculating largess."[43]

The Atlanta Open City campaign struggled to win hearts and minds. Tactics were now more confrontational, if still nonviolent: lying down in front of police cars, parading to the mayor's house, and, in one instance, taunting robed Klansmen, who were, perversely, occupying a Krystal to forestall a SNCC protest: a sit-in to stop a sit-in. Whereas the 1960 sit-ins had created a clear-cut moral dynamic that generated broad sympathy, the new methods met with fretful clucking from senior leaders, who believed that negotiations with the city were progressing nicely and provocations would backfire. The new approach also alienated politicians and journalists. Instead of its usual positive TV coverage, SNCC was now cast in a Walter Cronkite documentary as the movement's enfant terrible. Still, it claimed victories. In December, under threat of a holiday-season boycott, the department stores agreed to hire more Black workers. In January, several hotels and restaurants including the Toddle House desegregated. Mayor Ivan Allen endorsed the public accommodations provision of the national civil rights bill. Atlanta was coming around.[44]

By early 1964, John Lewis—like most of SNCC—was focused on Mississippi.

Since the fall, Bob Moses had been urging SNCC to ramp up its voter registration campaign there. As a first step, on Election Day 1963, SNCC and its partner organizations in the state had held mock elections. More than eighty thousand people cast symbolic ballots. For governor, they voted for Aaron Henry, a Black druggist and local NAACP leader. For lieutenant governor, they chose Ed King, a white college chaplain. Though entirely symbolic, the large turnout made vivid the demand of Black Mississippians to be free to vote.

The next step—well in the offing—was to challenge Mississippi's all-white delegation at the Democrats' national convention in August 1964. Moses hoped to import as many as a thousand college students into the state for a "Freedom Summer" of voter registration. He lobbied Forman to relocate SNCC's headquarters to Mississippi for the summer: its administrative apparatus, the press office, the Wide Area Telephone Service (WATS) line, for making long-distance phone calls. An all-hands-on-deck campaign would highlight the wretched dispossession of Blacks in the state. The Freedom Summer plan also acknowledged a racist reality: any violence against the visiting white students would command far more attention than violence against Blacks, which often failed to make a blip in the national media.[45]

SNCC was divided about Moses's plan. Lewis, now fully committed to the voting rights cause, argued for it. While on his December West Coast tour, he told a San Francisco audience that SNCC hoped to "saturate" Mississippi that summer with volunteers. If mass arrests followed, he said, there could be "75,000 people crowding the Mississippi jails," forcing the federal government to "take over the state." Then, he said, "out of this conflict, this division and chaos, will come something positive."[46]

Lewis was not blind to the dangers. Flooding the state with Northern white students from elite schools could introduce tensions. The SNCC staff was now about 20 percent white, and while the racial mingling had produced interracial friendships, romances, and even marriages, it also led to conflicts. SNCC field-workers in Mississippi worried that an influx of white college students risked undermining the sense of empowerment that Moses and his team had cultivated among Black Mississippians over three years. One solution was to circumscribe the roles that whites could assume—although that idea came with obvious problems of its own.

The division within SNCC pained Lewis, who hated to see bickering and acrimony. Eventually the commitment to interracial politics won out. Limiting someone's role because of his "whiteness," Moses declared, "is no argument. That's an irrational, racist statement. That's what we're fighting."

Fannie Lou Hamer, a forty-six-year-old sharecropper from Ruleville who had gotten involved with SNCC, explained: "If we're trying to break down this barrier of segregation, we can't segregate ourselves." Hamer and other Mississippians made it clear that they wanted whatever help, of whatever color, they could get.

Lewis saw interracial cooperation as a good in itself. He touted Freedom Summer as a Peace Corps for Mississippi. He envisioned the volunteers modeling what it meant to overcome racial barriers. He also thought that the presence of white students could show local Blacks that "all white people are not alike."[47]

Another question that provoked soul-searching discussions within SNCC was the viability of Gandhian techniques in their Mississippi work. Lewis had come to see that passive resistance was a hard sell to many poor Black families. "In Alabama and Mississippi, the Negro is pushed to the wall," he explained to a reporter. "He is not so sympathetic to nonviolence." Older residents could remember when, not so long ago, lynching was commonplace. During the short time that SNCC had been working in Mississippi, they had seen the killings of Herbert Lee in 1961, Medgar Evers in 1963, and Louis Allen in January 1964—shot dead for having witnessed Lee's murder. Many Black Southerners relied on guns to defend themselves. Given that reality, many SNCC staffers thought it wrong or at best questionable to be preaching nonviolence.[48]

Lewis remained uncertain how confrontational a posture to strike. He was still searching for a synthesis that would allow him to stay true to his philosophy while maintaining SNCC's position at the vanguard of the movement. He gave voice to his thoughts in an interview with a college newspaper that spring. He rejected terms like "radical, militant, and oppressive" for SNCC, yet he conceded that the organization's tactics were changing. He used the phrase "aggressive nonviolent action" to describe SNCC's new position. "You no longer walk quietly to paddy wagons and happily and willingly to jail," he explained. But he was ambivalent about this approach, which tended to repel rather than win over potential allies.[49]

These questions came to the fore in the spring of 1964 when a Brooklyn chapter of CORE announced a "stall-in" to disrupt an upcoming World's Fair exhibition in Queens by tying up traffic on the highways leading to the fairgrounds. CORE's chairman, James Farmer, proclaimed the idea "harebrained." At a newspaper editors convention, Farmer and Roy Wilkins prevailed on the other civil rights leaders present—including Lewis—to repudiate the stall-in. Lewis hadn't given the question much thought, and he signed Farmer's statement in a spirit of unity. But he immediately caught flak from Forman and others at SNCC, and the next day he rescinded his support, evasively stating that "we have not as yet carefully studied the plans." In the end, the controversy was moot. The Brooklyn CORE chapter failed to muster more than a smattering of drivers, and the much-hyped stall-in never materialized. For Lewis, however, the dilemmas remained unresolved.[50]

Another conundrum was whether SNCC should work with Communists. By 1964, the Communist Party in the United States was a joke. Yet FBI director J. Edgar Hoover persisted in the delusion that Martin Luther King operated under Communist sway, even after he let go of O'Dell and Levison. Southern segregationists slapped the red label on anyone with integrationist views. This red-baiting had the perverse effect of seeding in younger activists a disdain for even the most reasonable forms of anti-Communism. Defiantly, they refused to see any problem in aligning with Communists.

The issue blew up in November 1963, when the journalist Theodore H. White, in *Life*, grossly distorted the nature of SNCC's militancy by insinuating Communist connections. White wrote breathlessly of the group's "penetration" by "agents" who had tried "to convert a peaceful march into a violent Putsch on government offices." Preposterously, he described Diane Nash's September action memo as "one of the most chilling documents this writer has seen." White acknowledged that the "lunatics and aliens" within SNCC remained only "irritants" and hadn't taken over. This was true. While books of Marxian theory might be found on SNCC bookshelves, and some members eventually adopted extreme left-wing beliefs, "in fact, there was no role for communism in SNCC," wrote Mary King. "We were not educated in it." Still, White's piece fed negative impressions that SNCC had to dispel.[51]

SNCC was also asked to assist a campaign to abolish the House Un-American Activities Committee—an effort, the young activists almost certainly didn't realize, that was being led by a secret Communist, Frank Wilkinson, although it was also backed by anti-Communist liberals like

King and Eleanor Roosevelt. SNCC's executive committee debated what its position should be toward Communist front groups, arriving at what Lewis called an "open door" policy, or one of "non-alignment, or no political test for members." SNCC signed on to the anti-HUAC campaign. This posture, though rooted in principles of toleration, would have repercussions down the road.[52]

Amid the Freedom Summer preparations in the spring of 1964, SNCC had turned for legal help to the National Lawyers Guild, a Communist front. SNCC's liberal allies, both Black and white, strenuously objected. Collaborating with the guild would taint SNCC's image. Those with long memories knew how in the past the Communists had exploited the naïveté or tolerance of liberals and non-Communist leftists, infiltrating and hijacking their labor unions or public interest groups. But the young SNCC activists saw any policy of exclusion not as a prudent act of self-preservation but as a form of McCarthyite fearmongering. They declined to revise their policy.[53]

Lewis had no compunctions about denouncing Communism, which he did from time to time. But he considered red-baiting a greater threat than Communist co-optation. In April, columnist Joseph Alsop wrote that while "the infiltration is spotty as yet . . . known Communists have also begun to play a certain role in SNICK." ("John Lewis," he wrote, in another wild distortion, "though not a Communist, quite frankly believes in quasi-insurrectionary activities.") On April 22, the House released testimony from Hoover alleging a Communist presence in the movement. Lewis slammed the FBI director, saying he was playing into the hands of segregationists. Lewis had also come to believe that civil rights and civil liberties were intertwined. "We weren't going to judge people nor organizations on the basis of philosophy or ideology," Lewis said of SNCC, "but we would judge people and individuals on the basis of what they did, how they supported us, and how they worked with us in the time of trouble." He cited the New Testament: "Whosoever will, let him come."[54]

At SNCC's spring conference in Atlanta over Easter weekend, Lewis's colleagues showed their confidence in him by reelecting him chairman. He then resumed his punishing schedule—recruiting students, drumming up financial contributions, and serving as SNCC's public face around the country. Bill Hansen, a SNCC field organizer in Arkansas, remembered Lewis showing him his air travel card, a credit card that let him buy tickets at any airline office or airport counter. Hansen had never seen such a thing; Lewis, the frequent flyer, carried it in his wallet.[55]

The unforgiving pace of Lewis's travel worried colleagues. In December, SNCC volunteer Penny Bartlett had sent a memo to the leadership warning that "John Robert Lewis is <u>Tired</u> and that he needs a Rest." In April, Jimmy Bolton, a factotum in the Atlanta office, told the staff that the toll on Lewis was getting worse. "Since June of last year," he wrote, "John has also managed to travel over 100,000 miles, making personal appearances, for fund raising and presenting SNCC to the general public." Making matters worse, he usually traveled alone. "There have been many times when John needed company, someone from SNCC . . . moments when John was put into or forced into tight spots wherein he needed someone to call the Atlanta office . . . [or] needed someone to help him write and type his speeches . . . [or] to keep an accurate schedule for him. John simply needs someone to travel with him." No assistant was assigned.[56]

Lewis plugged away. One recurring stop that spring was Nashville. Since he had moved to Atlanta, his Nashville friends had continued picketing the few local establishments that refused to integrate. Despite the historic gains of 1963, he said at a February rally, Nashville was "not yet free, not yet an open city." In April, when the Nashville movement sprang alive again with huge protests and the police responded with extreme force, Lewis flew down from New York to lead a trek of several hundred to Morrison's, the most adamant of the holdouts. He assiduously kept the lines of demonstrators moving, in keeping with city ordinances. He was arrested anyway—for the thirty-second time, according to SNCC's newspaper—along with seventy-five others. The Nashville papers put him on their front pages again after a white counterprotester at a Tic Toc slugged him in the mouth, splitting his lip. Only mildly hurt, Lewis went to have dinner at the Fisk cafeteria late that afternoon when he saw a paperboy selling the afternoon *Banner*. The headline said "Race Scuffle Hurts Lewis." Lewis was flattered that his injury was considered headline news. But he thought the paper was poorly serving its readers "by suggesting that I was hurt in an interracial scuffle. I was only hit on the lip."[57]

The Nashville protests continued into May. Lewis welcomed back

Martin Luther King on May 3, when they both addressed a two-thousand-person rally at Fisk. Mayor Beverly Briley cut short a trip to Washington, convening the Human Relations Committee for new negotiations. Tic Toc and Candyland, two of the holdouts, finally agreed to serve Black patrons. What *Newsweek* called "the last vestiges of formal segregation in public places" were being swept away.[58]

As Lewis was having a last hurrah in Nashville, Freedom Summer plans were speeding along. "By February or March," Lewis recalled, "I think we had the structure. We had the organization." On March 15, it was announced that Moses would be the summer project director, with CORE's Dave Dennis as his number two. They planned to field candidates in the June state primary, including Fannie Lou Hamer, who was running for the Second District U.S. congressional seat held by the segregationist Jamie Whitten. Six weeks later was the founding convention of the Mississippi Freedom Democratic Party, which would become the vehicle for their convention challenge.[59]

In bringing word of Freedom Summer to the wider world, Lewis could wax evangelical. "We feel that what happens in Mississippi this summer could determine the civil rights struggle across the country," he said in an interview. Whites were afraid to let Blacks vote, he said, because they feared Blacks would "take over and rule." Those fears, he argued, were groundless. Blacks were perfectly willing to get behind white candidates with liberal politics, as happened recently in Nashville and Atlanta, he pointed out. Interracial coalitions could bring about "decent and liberal legislation for the benefit of all people."[60]

Others, however, saw dark clouds approaching. A. Philip Randolph wrote to Lewis that spring about several looming threats to the movement. These included Malcolm X's growing appeal, "left-totalitarian influence in a number of protest groups," and, on the opposite flank, an "organized Right" that was "separating many previously committed white people from our movement." Evidence of the last of these trends appeared in George Wallace's strong showings in the Wisconsin and Maryland presidential primaries that spring, which revealed a backlash to civil rights outside Dixie more intense than anyone suspected. All the same, the civil rights bill was advancing through Congress, with proponents determined to surmount what had become the longest filibuster in Senate history.[61]

Before moving to Greenwood, Mississippi, for the summer, SNCC held a final three-day staff meeting in Atlanta, at Frazier's Cafe Society and the Gammon Theological Seminary. Heated disputes again centered on the legitimacy of violence. Should SNCC staffers, as they entered the lion's den, arm themselves? What about local Mississippi activists who already kept guns? Greenwood activist Laura McGhee's house was "almost bombed," reported Mississippi staffer Sam Block. "She has guns and has been able to stop some violence. What are we to say to her?" Tempers rose. Shouting broke out. Ella Baker, who as an adviser usually abstained from the debate, tipped her cards, confessing her disdain for nonviolence. "I thought the meeting might shatter like a piece of glass," said Mary King.

Amid the many voices, Lewis declined to weigh in. He didn't have to: everyone knew his beliefs. If anything, it was more persuasive when others, like Courtland Cox, made the case for adhering to nonviolence. "Self-defense can only maintain the status quo," Cox explained. "It can't change the existing situation."

A consensus emerged. No guns would be allowed. SNCC would remain nonviolent. But it would be a loose rule. Staffers were free to look the other way if local allies followed a different code.[62]

In the end, everyone came together to reaffirm their common purpose. Standing in a large circle at Gammon, their arms draped on their neighbors, they sang "We Shall Overcome." Staughton Lynd, a young history professor, recalled that, after running through all the verses, they started to hum—a musical backdrop for an impromptu Lewis speech. Lewis recounted the story of the Freedom Rides, how he and his Nashville friends had gone into Birmingham after the Anniston bombing, how they had been arrested, how Bull Connor had driven them back to the state line. "We knew one thing," Lewis said. "We had to start back to Birmingham."[63]

People cried and hugged. The next day, Lewis and others left for the Western College for Women in Oxford, Ohio, where the first waves of volunteers were arriving for their training. "It's going to be," Lewis had been saying for months, "a long, hot summer in Mississippi."[64]

Chapter Nine

FREEDOM SUMMER

——————— ▪ ▪ ———————

I n early June, the Western College for Women in Oxford, Ohio, opened its doors to hundreds of students. They came to learn what was in store during Freedom Summer. More male than female, more white than Black, the volunteers came from thirty-seven states and a range of backgrounds, from churchgoing Midwesterners to Jewish New Yorkers. Some dressed in the natty collegiate style of the early 1960s, wearing khakis, Brooks Brothers shirts, and horn-rimmed glasses. Others sported goatees, denim skirts, or sandals—earning them the moniker "beatnik," a term later superseded in the mass media by "hippie."

Each group trained for a week. Lewis was at Oxford for the first week, sometimes lingering on the perimeter of a room where a discussion was taking place. "His hands were lost behind him, resting in the rear pockets of his jeans," wrote the journalist Tracy Sugarman, observing Lewis one day. "His shoulders rested against the wall and his neat bullet head was tipped forward, his chin resting in the V of his open work shirt. . . . His upper lip was heavy, overhanging the lower, and it added to the image of a somnolent beaver."[1]

The training was much like what John had experienced five years earlier in Nashville. Role-playing exercises had the students act out awkward and dangerous situations. Moses lectured them about the Mississippi operation. Fannie Lou Hamer taught them freedom songs. Historian Vincent Harding warned them about exoticizing the much-anticipated interracial romantic fling. "Using people sexually is no different from using them politically or economically," he chided. Bayard Rustin expounded on the power of nonviolence. "All mankind is my community," he told the students. "When I say I love [James] Eastland," he added, referring to the racist Mississippi senator, "it sounds preposterous—a man who brutalizes people. But *you* love him or you wouldn't be here. . . . You love Eastland in your desire to create conditions which will redeem his children."[2]

The students were told to expect violence. "I may be killed," Forman warned. "You may be killed." Geoff Cowan, a volunteer, wrote to his sister that the gathering at Western College, with reporters everywhere, was already a big story. "And when one of us gets killed," he added, "the story will be even bigger."[3]

Discordant notes punctured the camp-like atmosphere. A screening of a CBS documentary that showed an obese county registrar spewing racist nonsense provoked derisive laughter from the volunteers, but Black SNCC workers, who had seen these ruthless enforcers of segregation up close, took umbrage. Conflict also arose after talks by Rustin and Lawson on nonviolence, when Stokely Carmichael rose in rebuttal, arguing that the Gandhian way had run its course. Moses intervened. "In Mississippi, we have two ground rules," he said, laying down the law. "One: No weapons are to be carried or kept in your room. Two: If you feel tempted to retaliate, please leave." Also tense was a visit by the Justice Department's John Doar, who stressed the limits of the federal government's power within state borders to protect the students. The audience booed. But these moments of friction had value, as they drove home the harsh reality of what lay ahead.[4]

Lewis was pleased with the training. The students were enthusiastic. SNCC was working amicably with CORE, its main partner in the summer project. Late in the first week, when he went home to Troy for a funeral, he felt that the Oxford training was in good hands.

While in Alabama, Lewis heard good news. On June 19, one year after Kennedy had introduced the Civil Rights Bill, the Senate overwhelmingly passed it. Only twenty-one Democrats and six Republicans voted nay. Although the House still had to approve the Senate's revisions, the bill's passage was now assured.

Two days later came more news—disturbing news. Freedom Summer had barely begun, and already three workers in Neshoba County were missing.[5]

"Mississippi Tense over Voter Drive," read a headline in the *New York Times* on Sunday, June 21. "The average citizen," the story said, "has been led to believe that this will be an 'invasion' to make Mississippi the battle-ground for Federal intervention in behalf of Negro rights." The Ku Klux Klan and other white supremacist groups had been drawing thousands of white Mississippians to their ranks and were encouraging them to take up arms.[6]

That same morning, before sunrise, Mickey Schwerner, James Chaney, and Andrew Goodman climbed into a blue Ford station wagon to go to Longdale, Mississippi, near Philadelphia, to investigate the burning of a church being used for voter registration. Chaney, twenty-one, a Black Mississippian, and Schwerner, twenty-four, a Jew from Pelham, New York, both CORE activists, had worked together for months and become friends. Schwerner had recruited Goodman, a twenty-year-old Queens College anthropology major, to the summer project.[7]

After their visit to Longdale, the men were driving home, when Cecil Price, a Neshoba County deputy, pulled them over. He claimed they were speeding and locked them up at the county jail, allowing them no phone calls. After many hours, their SNCC and CORE colleagues grew worried because they hadn't heard from the men. They called the jail, but were told nothing. At 10:30 p.m., the county released Schwerner, Chaney, and Goodman, who headed back toward Meridian, their home base, an hour away.

They never made it home. Through the night, phone calls went out to colleagues, family members, reporters, FBI offices, congressmen, even the White House. By midday Monday, the men's disappearance was national news. At the Neshoba County Jail and sheriff's office, reporters demanded answers. Price and Sheriff Lawrence Rainey claimed to know nothing.

Lewis arrived in Meridian on Tuesday. The city was teeming with police, troopers, and federal agents, who were conducting searches alongside local law enforcement officers. On Tuesday, they found the men's car, stripped and charred, plunged into Bogue Chitto Creek near Philadelphia. There was still no sign of the men.

Lewis checked into a hotel. James Farmer, also newly arrived, had the room next door. Farmer brought a security guard. He had also called Dick Gregory, a friend, who flew in from Chicago.[8]

Lewis, Farmer, and Gregory felt obliged to be on hand, but there was little they could do. Joined by George Raymond, CORE's Mississippi field director, they drove to Philadelphia with a thirty-five-person reconnaissance team. Sheriff Rainey, backed by a squadron of cruisers, stopped their motorcade, stipulating he would let only a single car through. Lewis's group of four was chosen to drive past the checkpoint to meet with Rainey and Price.

In the meeting, the officers continued to plead ignorance. "From the outset, I saw them as liars," Lewis said. "They were lying." Their racism was ill-concealed. "They had a great deal of hatred, for Black people in particular, but perhaps more for white people who sympathized with Black people." After a fruitless day, Farmer told the press that Schwerner, Chaney, and Goodman should be presumed dead.[9]

Lewis was still in shock. "How could it happen in our country?" he kept wondering. "How could three young Americans be killed in America for only wanting to register other Americans to vote?"[10]

In Jackson, Lewis held a press conference. The small ramshackle offices where he spoke, in the Black part of town, could barely handle the crush of reporters and the heat of the camera lights. Lyndon Johnson, consumed by the men's disappearance, was taking steps each day: dispatching navy servicemen to the search, sending in former CIA director Allen Dulles as a special emissary, meeting with Goodman's and Schwerner's parents. (Chaney's parents couldn't afford the trip to Washington.)

But the cocky impunity with which state officials conducted themselves told Lewis that the federal government had to do more. The Freedom Summer staff were living in mortal fear, moving around like fugitives—installing two-way radios in their cars, driving on back roads, checking over their shoulders. It was good that the Justice Department was working overtime, but the staff needed more protection.

Lewis also broached an ugly reality. "It is a shame that national concern is aroused only after two white boys are missing," he said at the press conference. Mississippi had seen dozens of instances of anti-Black violence recently: bombings, church burnings, beatings, shootings. Herbert Lee and Louis Allen had been shot and killed in cold blood. None of these incidents received a sliver of the attention being given to Schwerner, Chaney, and Goodman.[11]

Tuesday night, Lewis joined Moses and a few other SNCC friends on a haphazard rescue expedition. The crew drove out to Bogue Chitto Creek and walked around in the dirt and scrub grass, looking in vain for a clue—"a very SNCC thing to do," Moses later said. Lewis knew the mission was useless. Given the dangers, it was also foolhardy. But it was better than sitting around. FBI agents and state policemen dragged the Pearl River, aided by a navy helicopter and a hundred sailors, finding nothing. Futility set in.[12]

Most Americans recoiled at the barbarism. Yet some ostensible champions of racial equality were remarkably unsympathetic, implying that the murdered men had invited their fate. Columnist Joseph Alsop, once considered a liberal but increasingly given to reactionary screeds, twisted Lewis's words from earlier in the year to vilify SNCC. "Provoking the military occupation of Mississippi and other recalcitrant regions of the South is, in fact, the avowed aim of John Lewis," Alsop wrote. "No one in his senses ought to want what John Lewis so obviously wants."[13]

Alsop's column displayed his ignorance of Lewis's temperament and ideology. But Lewis felt responsible. In the fall, he had endorsed Moses's plan to bring white students into Mississippi to direct attention to the state's violent suppression of its Black population. "If white people are intimidated and harassed and abused," Lewis later said, explaining his thinking, "then maybe this country would say something. So Mississippi Summer was a gimmick, but a good gimmick."[14]

Now he was seeing the worst outcome of that gamble. "I had a sense of guilt," he later admitted. "I had gone out there, I had recruited people, I had gone to Queens and Columbia, those colleges, and I had a sense of guilt." Moses felt similarly. But they didn't talk about their burdens.[15]

On Thursday, July 2, with gloom and fear still rife in Mississippi, the House passed the revised Civil Rights Act, sending it to Johnson's desk. The White House had invited Lewis to the signing ceremony, but he declined to go. He wanted to stay in Mississippi.

When Johnson signed the bill, Lewis was in Greenwood for a voter registration canvass, sitting in a Black community playground, surrounded by kids and Freedom Summer volunteers. His public statement was positive, yet muted. "The passage of the civil rights bill is a victory for the forces of good will and the legislative processes of this nation," Lewis said. "It is my hope that both the executive and judicial branches of government will not only enforce the new law but already existing civil rights laws. . . . In spite of the new law, the situation ahead for voter registration workers in Mississippi and those who attempt to register to vote will be one of constant fear, terror, and violence." The next day, at a rally in Ruleville, introducing three U.S. congressmen who had flown to Mississippi in a show of solidarity, Lewis declared, "The Civil Rights Bill is not the end, just the beginning. Just as the ICC regulations became meaningful only with the bodies of the Freedom Riders, it will still take our bodies and our efforts to make this civil rights bill meaningful."[16]

The sober pragmatism of Lewis's comments masked the joy he took in the bill's passage. "It was like manna from heaven," he later said. "It was very exciting, and it was a day that people had been praying for and worked toward and wishing for—*and it happened!*" The law would instantly improve the lives of millions of people, and he felt personal pride that his actions had played a direct role in bringing it about. Lewis also believed that the bill's passage showed something good about America. While the country would always need more prodding, the goal of racial equality now commanded broad popularity. "All across the South," he recalled, "there was this sense of openness, the sense of 'We can do it now.'" At the Greenwood Holiday Inn, he was served without incident.[17]

Lewis returned to Mississippi often that summer, including for a late July tour of the state with Farmer and King. On some trips, he gave speeches; on others, he knocked on doors, urging locals to register. All the while, terror shadowed him. Lewis saw and heard about SNCC workers getting harassed, roughed up, or arrested. It would be the most violent summer in Mississippi since Reconstruction. He watched as his friends taught each other how to drive fast, how to drive without headlights, and what to do when followed. Lewis became convinced he would die in an auto accident. In Greenwood, he usually stayed with a Black family named Greene, sharing a room with Carmichael. (They got along famously and, despite their different heights, even shared clothes.) At night, vigilantes would sometimes shoot at the Greenes' house. Every time a car went by, Lewis would leap out of bed. He had to train himself not to become paralyzed by his fear, to move forward in spite of it.[18]

The Civil Rights Act emboldened African Americans across the South to mount fresh challenges to Jim Crow. In Selma, Black residents decided on the day after the law's passage to visit an all-white movie theater—now required to integrate—bringing on the wrath of Sheriff Clark. Protests in Selma escalated, leading Lewis to make a return visit.

On Monday, July 6, Lewis brought several dozen local citizens to the Dallas County Courthouse to try to register to vote, as they had the previous fall. Implacable, Clark and his posse steered Lewis and the other marchers into a backstreet passageway. The lawmen wielded their cattle prods, sticking them under women's skirts. They marched the protesters five blocks to jail as freedom songs filled the air. Days later, a segregationist judge, James Hare, a Clark ally, issued a sweeping injunction prohibiting gatherings of more than three people. It was a naked bid to shut down the organizing. Badly constrained, the local activists pressed on.[19]

The next week Lewis went to San Francisco for the Republican National Convention. In 1960, both parties had courted the Black vote. By 1964, however, the Republican Party was rallying behind the conservative Arizona senator Barry Goldwater, who had voted against the Civil Rights Act. The designation of a right-wing standard-bearer heralded a change for the GOP, which, since the 1940s, had picked moderately conservative presidential nominees. But the racial backlash coursing through the electorate had boosted Goldwater over liberal rivals like Nelson Rockefeller. Republicans were gambling that they could trade the votes of Black Northerners for those of white Southerners, whose age-old fealty to the Democratic Party was being severed.

On Sunday, July 12, the day before the Republican convention, Lewis joined a huge "human rights march" to sound the alarm over Goldwater's takeover. The procession included Rockefeller and other white liberals as well as Black leaders like Farmer, Randolph, and Abernathy. To the strains of the "Battle Hymn of the Republic," thousands paraded down Market Street to city hall. Jackie Robinson—an Eisenhower Republican who had endorsed Nixon in 1960—told the crowd that if Goldwater were nominated, he would pull the lever for Johnson.[20]

Standing before the majestic Beaux-Arts city hall, Lewis delivered a long, rousing speech. He told the crowd on Civic Center Plaza about "the devastating acts of brutality and intimidation" he had seen that summer. "Mississippi is more than a police state," he said. "The conditions that exist in this state amount to those of a totalitarian and fascist state." Goldwater's claim to oppose the Civil Rights Act in the name of "states' rights" rang hollow. "No political party can expect to survive that nominates a man like Barry Goldwater for the presidency of the United States," Lewis said. "Goldwater would leave the fate of the Negroes of Alabama and Mississippi in the hands of Governor Wallace, Governor [Paul] Johnson, the Ku Klux Klan, the White Citizens Council, and the John Birch Society. Do we want a candidate for president who will place states' rights over human rights?" It was a choice, Lewis declared, "between freedom and tyranny."[21]

All week long, moderates fought to preserve the GOP's reputation as the Party of Lincoln. CORE staged demonstrations on the convention floor. But Goldwater proved unstoppable. States that once hosted integrated delegations now seated lily-white slates, resulting in the fewest Black delegates in the party's history. "The Great Purge of Negroes," lamented *Jet* magazine. The Goldwaterites' rage could be frightening. "I now believe I know how it felt," Jackie Robinson said, "to be a Jew in Hitler's Germany." The selection of an extremist raised the stakes of the fall election, stirring apprehension that a Republican triumph would set back the hard-won civil rights gains of recent years.[22]

Scrambling the calculus further were the riots that shook Harlem as the convention drew to a close. On July 16, Thomas Gilligan, an off-duty white policeman, shot and killed a fifteen-year-old Black summer school student, James Powell, after the boy slashed the officer with a knife. Powell's classmates congregated to protest. Over the next days, as tempers and temperatures soared, crowds formed nightly and turned lawless. The police cracked down, sometimes brutally. Beginning in Harlem, the mayhem jumped to Brooklyn's Bedford-Stuyvesant neighborhood and then to other cities.

Though also an excuse for hooliganism, the Harlem unrest was widely inter-preted as an outgrowth of long-simmering grievances against police miscon-duct, exploitative merchants, pervasive racism, and economic immiseration. Democrats and civil rights activists feared that more summer violence would feed the white backlash and abet Goldwater's chances.[23]

Roy Wilkins convened the Big Six to declare a joint moratorium on demonstrations through election season. He sent the others a telegram on July 22 arguing that the Harlem riots, George Wallace's strong primary showings, and Goldwater's ascendancy "were all linked," and that Goldwa-ter's election must be avoided at all costs. Rustin—who had gone to Harlem to preach calm during the riots, only to be jeered and spat upon—broached the notion of a moratorium with Randolph, persuading the older man of its wisdom.[24]

Lewis flew to New York for what Wilkins called "a difficult meeting" at NAACP headquarters on July 29. Lewis was joined by Courtland Cox, perhaps sent by Forman to keep an eye on Lewis after his stall-in blunder in April. Having rudely booted Rustin from a Big Six meeting one year earlier, Wilkins this time included him happily, knowing he would be an ally.[25]

Wilkins stage-managed the opening. He spoke first, stressing the need to keep Goldwater out of the White House. He then called on Randolph, who cautioned that unruly demonstrations could whip up reactionary forces. Rustin went next, producing a written statement declaring a moratorium and pressing the case with his customary dexterity.

Then James Farmer spoke. Farmer had been struggling to control CORE as his organization, like SNCC, grew more militant. Surprising his colleagues, he declared that he couldn't go along. "For CORE to give up its demonstrations, even for six months, would be to give up its genius, its rai-son d'être," he said. "It might sound our death knell."[26]

Lewis didn't want to do anything to damage LBJ's election prospects. But he also didn't think SNCC should subordinate its principles to the short-term goal of an election outcome. "I felt that . . . we would be giving up one of our basic rights—to raise certain questions, to raise certain issues," he later said. Rustin's statement also lumped together protests and riots. Lewis suggested that in the proposed statement, "demonstrations shouldn't be mentioned, that the emphasis should be placed on voter registration." His suggestion failed. He decided not to sign the final document.[27]

Whitney Young did sign on. So, to Lewis's surprise, did King. That was all Wilkins needed in order to announce that "most of us agreed" to the moratorium. The final language called for "a broad curtailment if not total moratorium of all mass marches, mass picketing, and mass demonstrations until after Election Day, next November 3." Justifying the extraordinary step, the leaders explained, "We see the whole climate of liberal democracy in the United States . . . threatened."[28]

The leaders also entertained a second statement in which they would "go on record as strongly opposing looting, vandalism, or any type of criminal activities." This one Farmer agreed to. But Lewis again refrained—alone—saying that he needed to run it by SNCC.

At a jam-packed press conference, Wilkins read both statements aloud. Lewis stood by quietly, "in the interests of unity," he later explained. Bond's press office later told the *New York Times* evasively, "it is not the policy of SNCC to publicly discuss situations in individual Negro communities"— an obviously untrue claim. But Lewis felt comfortable knowing that he was acting in line with SNCC's wishes. "People in SNCC and particularly in this area, they supported me almost 100 percent, right down the line," he said. Unlike with the stall-in, "I didn't have any problem, any difficulty."[29]

Lewis elaborated his position days later. He explained that SNCC was busy leading voter drives in Alabama, Arkansas, Georgia, and Mississippi, which he couldn't suspend. "Demonstrations must continue," he said. "The pressure must be kept on. Demonstrations must be played by ear. If we need to, we will demonstrate in connection with voter registration."[30]

In August, Lewis's focus shifted to Atlantic City, where the Democrats would be holding their convention on August 24.

Freedom Summer had more than one objective. Adding Black voters to the rolls was the ostensible purpose, although everyone expected, given the state's entrenched racist practices, to make only modest gains. By summer's end, of the 17,000 Blacks who attempted to register, only 1,600 had their applications accepted. But that poor yield helped to advance other goals, such as drawing national attention to the plight of Blacks in Mississippi. The organizing itself also bolstered the local movements that SNCC hoped would outlast the summer volunteers. Finally, the expected rejection of so many aspiring voters would justify Moses's other plan: to field an alternative delegation to represent Mississippi at the Democrats' convention.

By mid-July, the last of these goals emerged as the focus of Freedom Summer. "Everyone," Moses demanded in an urgent July 19 directive, ". . . must devote all their time to organizing the convention challenge" if it were to stand a chance of succeeding.

Moses's strategy was to first try to win representation for Black Mississippians in the official Mississippi state delegation. It was all but certain that they would be denied. They would then have grounds to challenge the legitimacy of the state's all-white slate and request that the national party seat their own Mississippi Freedom Democratic Party delegation in Atlantic City instead.[31]

The multitiered process began in June. First at the precinct level and then at the county, district, and state conventions, white party regulars systematically excluded Blacks trying to participate—turning them away at the door or changing a meeting site without telling them. The party regulars then appointed an all-white slate. Ironically, most of these racially conservative Democrats preferred Goldwater over Johnson.

Shut out, the Freedom Democrats conducted their own conventions, culminating in a state convention on August 6 in Jackson.[32]

Two days before that conclave, FBI agents, acting on a tip from a paid informant, arrived at the Neshoba farm of a man named Olen Burrage. "At approximately 2:50 p.m., the pungent odor of decaying flesh was clearly discernible," their report said. "Numerous vultures or buzzards were observed reconnoitering." Minutes later they found the bodies of Schwerner, Chaney, and Goodman under an earthen dam. Autopsies showed the three men had been shot and killed and their bodies bulldozed into the ground. Chaney had been castrated. Eventually, the investigation would reveal that Deputy Cecil Price, after releasing the trio from jail, notified a gang of Klansmen, who went in pursuit of the men. The gang had stopped and murdered the three men.[33]

The confirmation of the men's killing made national news. Lewis issued a statement. "Now we know without a doubt that Mickey Schwerner, James Chaney, and Andrew Goodman—three brave and courageous freedom fighters—have been murdered by sick men who are victims of a vicious and evil system," he said. "America is burning its own cross on the graves of its children."[34]

The Freedom Democrats soldiered on with their plans. On August 6, Lewis joined 2,500 Mississippians at the Masonic Temple on Lynch Street in Jackson for the MFDP convention. Carrying brown-bag lunches and church-issue hand fans, they sorted themselves by county under hand-drawn poster boards. A large American flag over the stage marked where speakers should stand.

In the course of the day, the delegates chose sixty-eight representatives to go to Atlantic City. Most seats went to the local Mississippians—sharecroppers, day laborers, housemaids—whom SNCC referred to as "indigenous," such as Aaron Henry, elected chairman, and Fannie Lou Hamer, vice chair. They had lived their lives under the boot of Mississippi's white supremacism, coming to political action only recently. Four seats went to whites; it was important that the delegation be integrated. Convention-goers adopted a platform endorsing anti-poverty programs and a foreign policy that backed the United Nations and called for an end to tyranny in Soviet bloc countries and undemocratic African regimes.

Lewis gave a speech at the convention. But the critical remarks came from Joseph Rauh, the Freedom Democrats' attorney. Since his work on A. Philip Randolph's 1941 March on Washington, Rauh had functioned as a liaison between liberal activists and the Washington establishment. With Clarence Mitchell of the NAACP, he had run the lobbying campaign for the Civil Rights Act. Rauh also had convention experience: in 1948, with Minnesota senator Hubert Humphrey, he had engineered the Democrats' approval of their historic civil rights plank. Lewis thought highly of Rauh, considering him canny about strategy, respectful of the Black activists, and passionate about human rights.[35]

In Jackson, with his shirtsleeves rolled up in the stifling heat, the bow-tied, bespectacled lawyer presented a plan for Atlantic City. The national party's 108-person Credentials Committee, on which Rauh sat, probably would not accept the MFDP's petition. But a rule allowed as few as eleven committee members to issue a minority report and, with the endorsement of just eight state delegations, take that minority report to a roll-call vote on the convention floor. Rauh said that this "eleven-and-eight" strategy would have "a very good chance."[36]

Moses remained skeptical. He told the delegates that they should count on getting a hearing, but that President Johnson would be afraid to further

antagonize the South. Still, even if they lost in Atlantic City, Moses maintained, they had created in the MFDP a "permanent institution" that could
carry on the fight in the future. Organizing wasn't just about getting what
you wanted in the short term; it was about building a movement that could
endure over the long term.[37]

Following the high of the convention, Lewis went to Meridian, where
James Chaney's funeral was being held at a Baptist church. It was the first of
three funerals Lewis would attend that week. Schwerner's parents wanted
Mickey to be interred next to Chaney, but Mississippi law forbade it. So
after Chaney's burial, Lewis traveled to New York City. Goodman's funeral
was next, on Monday, at the Ethical Culture Society on Central Park West
and West Sixty-Fourth Street in Manhattan. Schwerner's was across town, at
the Unitarian Community Church on East Thirty-Fifth Street that night.
Lewis spoke at the latter. He urged the audience to forswear feelings of vin-
dictiveness and to recommit themselves to the path of love. Even as he spoke,
he knew that feelings of rage and impatience were rampant. He wondered
how many hearts he was able to reach.[38]

The discovery of the three corpses in Mississippi drove home the justness
and urgency of the Freedom Democrats' cause. Rauh's optimism appeared
justified. By mid-August, nine state delegations had endorsed the Freedom
Democrats, along with an array of prominent liberals. Lewis hit the road
again, meeting with key Democrats to line up more votes.[39]

Privately, Lyndon Johnson sympathized with the Freedom Democrats.
The all-white regular delegation, he said, "oughtn't to be seated. [They]
wouldn't let those Nigras vote. And that's not right." But he was convinced
that the challenge would harm him in November. Although he held a commanding lead over Goldwater in the polls, the Harlem riots were feeding
talk of a backlash, and the president's insecurity nagged at him. He brooded
that his hoped-for coronation would be clouded by walkouts, disruptions,
or bad press. "The only thing that can really screw us good," he told Walter
Reuther, "is to seat that group of challengers from Mississippi."[40]

Johnson resolved to stop the Freedom Democrats. J. Edgar Hoover,
surveilling the civil rights leaders, fed the president overblown reports of
Communist influence in the movement's ranks. "I would say out of the

twenty-five top ones," Johnson remarked as the convention approached, "twenty of them are Communists." At other moments, the president fantasized that his longtime nemesis Robert Kennedy was masterminding the Mississippi crusade.[41]

To thwart the Freedom Democrats, Johnson enlisted the toadyish Reuther, for whose union Rauh served as counsel, and Humphrey, a longtime Rauh ally whose precarious place atop Johnson's vice presidential short list was an open secret. A week before the convention, the president invited the Big Six to the White House for a meeting on Wednesday, August 19. Lewis hustled to Washington. He joined Randolph, Wilkins, and Farmer—King and Young were absent—for a 10:30 a.m. session that Johnson put under wraps. He didn't want other Black leaders to think that they might also get his ear. Nor did he want Southern Democrats "all upset that we're having some special deal."[42]

Johnson windily dominated the meeting. He spoke for almost the full hour about his accomplishments and future plans. Randolph later pronounced the meeting a "fiasco." Lewis, having anticipated that he might not get to speak, had written a two-page letter that he gave the president at the end. His letter described a litany of violent incidents in Mississippi that summer, including eight unsolved killings, and beseeched the president "for increased federal action" in the state. Lewis also told Johnson that hundreds of Freedom Summer volunteers had now decided to stay in the state that fall and would need continued protection. The letter closed with a plea. "Without the seating of the Mississippi Freedom Democratic Party, and without strong preventive and protective action by the federal government . . . the Democratic Party and the federal government can never become the instruments of justice for all citizens that they claim to be." The next day, aide Lee White replied with a polite, bureaucratic letter that made clear Johnson was not giving ground.[43]

Word of the meeting leaked. Asked by press secretary George Reedy what to say about it, LBJ dictated a response: "I gave them a little report on progress, what had happened in the civil rights field in Mississippi and Georgia. . . . We didn't discuss anything connected with the party or the convention." Publicly, Reedy denied that the issue of the contending Mississippi delegations had come up. Wilkins and Farmer went before the Democratic Party platform committee to plead the Freedom Democrats' case. King released a telegram he sent to LBJ urging the same.[44]

On Thursday, August 20, the Mississippi Freedom Democrats boarded coach buses at Tougaloo College for the thirty-hour drive to the Jersey Shore. Lewis made his way separately. Amid radiant sun and a brisk breeze that snapped the boardwalk flags, he reunited with SNCC friends and the newly arrived Mississippians—some having ventured out of state for the first time in their lives—greeting one another with hugs and hearty clasps. Laughter and animated conversation revealed a high-spirited confidence among the delegates. Although some SNCC leaders, including Moses, remained doubtful of victory, Lewis was excited, even elated—optimistic that this intrepid crew would pull off a historic achievement.[45]

Lewis lodged at the inexpensive, run-down Gem Hotel on Pacific Avenue, just off the boardwalk and a mile from Convention Hall. But he spent very little time there. He had work to do before Monday's opening gavel. Moses and the staff had mimeographed lists of state delegates and Credentials Committee members to be lobbied. "I was there talking to and speaking before delegates to the convention, buttonholing individuals, congressmen, labor leaders, religious leaders from some of the key states, student groups," Lewis recalled, "to get them to put pressure on the delegates from their states."

At two o'clock on Saturday afternoon, August 22, Lewis crammed into an overflow room to watch on closed-circuit TV as the Credentials Committee heard testimony from the rival Mississippi delegations. Aaron Henry and Ed King spoke powerfully, but it was Fannie Lou Hamer—heavyset, weary-looking, the twentieth child of sharecroppers and a survivor of childhood polio—who riveted the nation. Wearing a cotton print dress borrowed from her best friend, she spoke in church-like cadences no less lucid because of her untutored syntax. Relying on no notes, she told of being forced from her home of eighteen years for trying to vote. She recounted vigilante snipers shooting at her friends and neighbors. She described being beaten in the Winona jail in 1963. "All of this is on account we want to register, to become first-class citizens," she said, sweat beading on her face under the television lights. "And if the Freedom Democratic Party is not seated now, I question America."[46]

Hamer's searing account, received with a spontaneous ovation, provided high drama. It was the rare public speech that could change minds on the spot. Lewis called it "a stunning moment. . . . Who could help being moved by this woman and these words?" Desperate to shut her down, Johnson called a spur-of-the-moment press conference to commandeer the television cameras. News organizations, dying to learn his vice presidential selection, assumed the announcement was at hand and cut away from Hamer's remarks. Johnson then recited brief, generic remarks before repairing to a meeting with governors in the East Room. Still, Hamer had made her mark. If anyone missed it, the news programs reran her electrifying testimony that night.[47]

More speakers addressed the Credentials Committee that afternoon, including King, Farmer, Wilkins, and Rita Schwerner, Mickey's widow. "Are you going to throw out of here the people who want to work for Lyndon Johnson, who are willing to be beaten and shot and thrown in jail to work for Lyndon Johnson?" Rauh asked the committee in closing. "Are we the oppressor or the oppressed?"[48]

Letters, telegrams, and phone calls backing the Freedom Democrats flooded in to the White House and party headquarters. Rauh now had seventeen commitments from Credentials Committee members, more than enough to pursue his eleven-and-eight strategy. The Freedom Democrats, he said, wouldn't settle for any "second-rate compromises." "We had momentum now," Lewis said. "It was working."[49]

Rauh did agree to one modification. The minority report of the Credentials Committee would call for seating *both* Mississippi delegations, with each representative getting half a vote. This method had been used to resolve convention disputes before. Everyone expected that the white Mississippi regulars would bolt in disapproval, leaving the Freedom Democrats as the seated delegation.

Over the next two days, Lewis stayed out of the negotiations, deferring to Moses, Henry, and others. Instead, he spoke at a Sunday afternoon rally and joined a sit-in outside Convention Hall. But he still heard about the strong-arm tactics Johnson and his allies were using to scuttle the compromise. One Credentials Committee member was warned that her support of the Freedom Democrats would cost her husband a judgeship. "They were under a tremendous amount of pressure," Lewis recalled.[50]

On Tuesday, the negotiations were cut short when Reuther and Humphrey presented the Freedom Democrats with their own Johnson-approved compromise. First, all official delegates would have to endorse the party's nominee. This provision would force the regular Mississippi delegates—who favored Goldwater—to either fall in line or relinquish their seats. Second, all future delegations would be integrated—a huge historic step, but without an immediate payoff. Third, two Freedom Party delegates, Aaron Henry and Ed King, would be seated, while the others would be welcomed as nonvoting guests. It was the best they were going to get.

At the Union Temple Baptist Church, the unofficial Freedom Party headquarters, Moses, the Mississippians, and their allies gathered to discuss their options. Lewis came over from the vigil outside Convention Hall. Recriminations flew. Rauh shared the delegates' indignation at the short-circuiting of the process but argued for accepting the deal anyway. So did Henry, the delegation chairman. Several SNCC leaders argued for rejecting it.

Lewis decided to weigh in. He could see both sides of the argument, finding merit in Rauh's pragmatism, yet unable to swallow the insulting offer. "John was caught between our practical, Southern view," Andrew Young said, "and what I considered to be the purely ideological position of Jim Forman and Stokely Carmichael."

Lewis came down against the deal. "We have shed too much blood in Mississippi to accept a compromise," he said. "That is the problem with the civil rights bill; it doesn't protect us. It was open season on us in Mississippi this summer. People were murdered in Philadelphia and there is no punishment. When we try to register to vote, we get sent to jail, we are beaten, we are threatened. We can't back down. We've come too far."[51]

The Freedom Democrats agreed. They rejected the compromise.

That night, the convention approved the Johnson compromise on a voice vote. In an ironic twist, the white Mississippi delegates also spurned the compromise, refusing to swear fealty to Johnson, and walked out. With their chairs empty, twenty Freedom Democrats, using borrowed credentials, occupied the Mississippi section of the floor in what they termed, appropriately enough, a "walk-in." Lewis watched from the nosebleed seats, both proud and disappointed.[52]

On Wednesday morning at ten o'clock, again at the Union Temple Baptist Church, Rauh and Henry tried one last time to sell the deal. They lined up heavyweights, including King, Rustin, and Farmer, to make their case. "When you enter the arena of politics," Rustin argued astutely, "you've entered the arena of compromise." But the Freedom Democrats remained opposed. Hamer repeated what she had said to a reporter the day before: "We didn't come all this way for no two seats." They voted down the deal again.[53]

Later that day, Johnson named Humphrey as his running mate. On Thursday, which was also the president's fifty-sixth birthday, Johnson accepted his party's nomination.[54]

Commentators were almost unanimous in holding that the Freedom Democrats had spurned what had actually been a big victory for them—the result of their own courage and the nobility of their cause. Having opened the nation's eyes to the injustice of the South's racially exclusive politics, the MFDP had made it impossible for the Democratic Party to ignore segregation in its own midst. By adopting the proposal, the party guaranteed that it would never again seat segregated delegations.

But few commentators outside the Black press showed an appreciation of the betrayal and hurt felt by the Mississippians and their partners. As Lewis had said, they had come too far to accept such a paltry deal. Within SNCC's militant faction, bitterness ran high. Forman denounced the moral bankruptcy of LBJ, the Democratic Party, and the "liberal-labor establishment" consisting of groups like ADA, the NAACP, and the UAW, and even of anti-Communist socialists like Bayard Rustin. Many in SNCC stopped thinking of electoral politics as a legitimate vehicle for effecting change.[55]

The Freedom Democrats themselves, interestingly, viewed the outcome differently. For all their disappointment, they took great pride in what they had achieved. In the fall they worked hard to elect Johnson and continued afterward to build inclusive political institutions in their state. "We changed the rules of the national Democratic Party convention system," said Leslie McLemore, one of the delegates. "And that changed the body politic of this country." Victoria Gray, another delegate, insisted, "I never say the 1964 exploration was a lost cause, although many other people did." That fall, when a Freedom Party representative thanked Lewis, she called the Atlantic City challenge a "great victory."[56]

Lewis, however, was devastated. "I realized how naïve I had been to believe we could walk in there and be given those seats," he said. It was "a stunning blow." It was made worse by his grief over the murders of Schwerner, Chaney, and Goodman. He had learned, he said, "that when you play the game and go by the rules, you can still lose."[57]

Lewis refused to blame Rauh, who he thought unfairly bore the brunt of his SNCC colleagues' acrimony—wrongly cast as "a villain, a traitor, a back-stabber." Lewis also regretted the erosion of respect within SNCC for King and Rustin. Most surprisingly, Lewis showed empathy for LBJ and admitted a certain respect for his political skills and methods. "I really don't have any bitter feelings toward anyone, any hostile feelings toward him today," he said of the president a few years later. "If you know anything about that guy at all, he's a wheeler and a dealer out of this world. He believes in pressuring and pushing people all the way. If he wants something, he's going to get something. It matters not, in a sense, how it hurts or whom it hurts." Lewis concluded that Johnson had been inflexible simply "because he's a politician. . . . It doesn't have too much to do with Southern loyalties. You learn the tricks and trades of politics and you use them. You use them well."[58]

Most unfortunate in Lewis's view was the "crippling" toll that Freedom Summer took on "the morale of SNCC." Although he got over his own anger, "I could feel myself outnumbered by friends and colleagues who felt different. . . . This disaster at Atlantic City was like a knockout punch." SNCC had dealt with internal conflicts before, but after the convention, Lewis noted, "people began turning on each other. The movement started turning on itself."[59]

Chapter Ten

AFRICA

———— ▪ ▪ ————

"Hello, Robert," Willie Mae Lewis wrote to her son in September. "I haven't heard from you in a long time? What you doing these days?... Robert, when you come home?"

Willie Mae's letter to her son was short—just one page. She told him that his father had been sick but was now okay, that his brothers and sisters sent regards, that they were all busy "digging peanuts," and that they had had "a good singing Sunday."[1]

Lewis did call home that September to tell his parents some exciting news: he was going to Africa. They did not share his enthusiasm. "Boy, what are you doing going over there?" they asked. "That's too far for you to go."[2]

Lewis had wanted to visit Africa for a while. He knew nothing about his family's roots, not even where his ancestors had lived. But since his time in Nashville and Highlander he had taken an interest in the African students he met. He followed news from Africa and thought about the resemblances between the anti-colonial movements there and the racial struggle at home. He wrote to Bayard Rustin about it early in the summer. "For some time it has been my hope to visit Africa," Lewis wrote. "I have now decided to put some effort into making the trip. I think that such a trip would be good for SNCC and for me personally." He asked Rustin to suggest possible patrons.[3]

One person who stepped up was Harry Belafonte. Belafonte had pledged $60,000 to the Freedom Summer project, $10,000 of which hadn't been spent. Seeing so many SNCC members exhausted and despondent after

Atlantic City, he offered to bankroll a group excursion to Guinea, whose president, Sékou Touré, had become a friend, and where the young Americans might meet with contemporaries in the West African movements, known as *La Jeunesse*. Touré, a charismatic leader in Guinea's 1958 independence drive, agreed to host a SNCC contingent at a seaside villa in the capital city of Conakry. Lewis and his friend Don Harris—who had relatives in Africa and had visited the continent before—lined up another $250 apiece through a small foundation recommended by Rustin, to continue their travels afterward.[4]

On September 10, Lewis flew from Atlanta to New York, where he stayed with Nancy Stearns. That first evening he had dinner with SNCC Arkansas project leader Bill Hansen, Don Harris, and Kate Clark, Harris's girlfriend and future wife. Stearns drove Lewis and Harris to Kennedy Airport the next day. Lewis, she said, "could barely contain himself. . . . He was just like an excited little kid, and who can blame him? Don was, too, but a bit more sophisticated."

At JFK, Pan Am told the SNCC group that the flight was overbooked and wanted to bump them onto another flight. The group deliberated. They were reluctant to delay their anticipated journey. Finally, Ruby Doris Smith Robinson took matters into her own hands by staging a one-woman sit-in on the jetway. Pan Am let the SNCC group fly. Lewis boarded the plane along with Hansen, Harris, Robinson, James Forman, Julian Bond, Matt Jones, and Fannie Lou Hamer, as well as Bob Moses and his new wife, Dona Richards, and Harry and Julie Belafonte.* "I was very, very excited," Lewis said. "It was my first time out of the country, going abroad. . . . I wanted to see. I wanted to learn."[5]

Lewis was "petrified of flying," according to Bill Hansen, who sat next to him and would hold his hand whenever the plane lurched. "He thought every time the plane bumped it was going to go down." But the mood lightened. On board were several Peace Corps members, close in age to the

---

* Kate Clark was the daughter of psychologist Kenneth Clark. Bill Hansen was the SNCC delegation's only white member (not counting Julie Belafonte). Prathia Hall missed the flight and joined the group a day later.

SNCC group, and they all mingled and talked. "It was a big party, really, over the Atlantic Ocean," in Lewis's account. "We spent most of our time . . . drinking and eating. We were walking in the aisles, falling in the aisles of the plane. It was really a glorious time."[6]

"Welcome, SNCC," said the signs that greeted them at Senegal's Dakar airport. As soon as they got off the plane, Hamer knelt and kissed the ground. "It was a great feeling, not just for her, but for all of us," Lewis said—a sense of "pride and dignity. . . . We were returning home." They refreshed with banana and grapefruit juice and then took a connecting Air Guinea flight to Conakry. Lewis was happily surprised to see that the pilot and stewardesses were Black, and throughout his Africa stay he took pleasure in seeing Black people in roles—bank managers, customs officials, traffic cops—that they rarely if ever held in the American South.[7]

At the Conakry airport Lewis and the group were met by the American ambassador, James Loeb, a Hubert Humphrey confidant, along with Guinean officials. Chauffeured sedans took them to the Villa Sily, the old French governor's residence. ("Who the hell had been in a motorcade before?" Don Harris asked with amazement years later.) Lewis and Bond shared a three-room suite decorated in beautiful tile. The compound boasted a wide-open courtyard, elegant rooms and bungalows, and a grand T-shaped marble veranda with dazzling ocean views. Each night for two weeks, Touré feted the SNCC delegation with lavish spreads of food and drink. Since the trip fell during Guinea's annual cultural festival, the meals were followed nightly by elaborate entertainments.[8]

"Each day we gathered around this big table, and Harry Belafonte would be at the head of the table, like he was the king," Lewis recalled. An enormous broiled fish sat regally in the middle of the banquet table. "It looked like it was still alive," Lewis said, "but it was well cooked. . . . You [would] just get your hunk, pull a large piece out" and eat it with peas and potatoes. More extravagant still was the liquor, poured generously at every meal. Afterward, in their rooms, the SNCC guests found more libations including premium whiskey, rum, and scotch. "There was a new bottle of Johnnie Walker in the room every day," Don Harris remembered. "If you drank a third of it, the next day you still got a brand-new bottle." Lewis thought it was quite an abundance for a religiously observant Muslim country. "We had wine, going and coming. Beer, plenty of beer." Bond, Harris, and Hansen, the biggest drinkers, "stayed pretty high," Lewis said, with their steady intake. "I had my part of wine. But one day I made up my mind that I would go off, I wouldn't drink for a week. . . . I was checking myself."

A couple of times, Touré dropped by the villa unannounced. In one instance, he found Harry Belafonte asleep and Julie "with her hair down and in a housecoat." In another case, Hamer was soaking in the tub when she was summoned to meet the president. "I'm having a bath!" she yelled through the door. "I'm definitely not ready to meet no president." When she did see Touré, smiling broadly in his white fez and linen robes, she "threw her arms around him," Belafonte later wrote, "buried her face in his chest, and wept."[9]

After dinner came hours of performances: ballets and folk dances, bands and orchestras, drummers and choirs and dramatic plays. "We saw the National Ballet of Guinea perform at night, outside, under the stars," Harris said, "spectacular stuff that you keep forever in your head." Lewis considered the artistic displays to be a form of national identity-building. "They put a great deal of emphasis on culture, on the arts and dance," he said.[10]

Daytimes were given over to consultations with government ministers, sightseeing trips, and downtime spent wandering the streets or relaxing at Villa Sily. Forman read and debated socialist literature and typed up an aide-mémoire from the compound's veranda. Bob Moses and Dona Richards would peel off from the group, sometimes joined by Hamer, who liked to stop in the marketplace and strike up conversations with strangers, despite the language barrier; Moses would pry her away. Hamer also delighted in noting the "little common things" the Guineans did that her family had also done—"like they boil peanuts with salt when they're real green."[11]

The vacation afforded a respite from the drumbeat pressures of work. As Forman said, "there were no sheriffs to dread, no Klan breathing down your neck." But not everyone considered Guinea a lost homeland. What struck Matt Jones was that "we learned how American we were. . . . When we walked around and saw the Blacks who looked just like us, culturally, we had nothing in common." He said he felt a greater affinity with Hansen, the one white SNCC member, than the Guineans. The gap—"wider than the Atlantic Ocean," Jones said—was driven home when a man on the street sneered, "Look, man, my great-grandfather sold three million of you all."[12]

To Guinean politicians, Lewis found himself dispelling misconceptions about the U.S. Tourism minister Diallo Alpha assumed that African Americans were all partisans of either Martin Luther King or Malcolm X. The SNCC delegates smiled at his simple binary, explaining the movement's many strands. Someone drew a vector from left to right and mapped out the positions of various groups and their ideas along the line.

Lewis was impressed with Touré, the hero of the anti-colonial struggle who had built one of sub-Saharan Africa's first independent nations. Admiration for his devotion to his people's autonomy eclipsed concerns about his repressive measures, which, already in evidence, would become notorious. In a SNCC report, Forman wrote nonjudgmentally about Guinea's one-party political system and the state-run media's censorship. "No articles are written in the paper which is [sic] contrary to the line of the Democratic Party of Guinea. . . . Only articles which are constructive are permitted. . . . No scandals are printed. No news of thefts, fraud, et cetera."[13]

Toward the end of the three-week stay, Forman heard from Atlanta that SNCC was in chaos. He was needed back home. Lewis let Forman tackle the crisis. Forman was the better administrator, the stricter disciplinarian. With six more weeks of travel planned, Lewis was happy to steer clear of debilitating office politics. Instead, he and Harris hopscotched the continent, meeting with students, activists, and journalists, learning about political movements in each region.[14]

After leaving Guinea, Lewis and Harris first went to nearby Liberia— the oldest continuously independent African nation, founded in 1848 by Black American expatriates. With a flag and constitution modeled on America's, the nation, Lewis reflected, seemed like "a little United States. They copy the United States all over." Lewis and Harris gave interviews to the major newspapers, the local radio stations, and the Voice of America, but next to the royal reception they received in Guinea, they wrote, "most of the people seemed pretty unimpressed." They in turn encountered little political activity—unsurprisingly for a country that had undergone its throes of revolution more than a century before.[15]

It was also in Liberia, Harris said, that he got "caught up in a currency exchange scam. I knew it was a scam, but I thought I could beat it." In exchanging money in the street, he wound up with some coinage that "whatever the hell it was, wasn't worth a subway token." So when he and Lewis left

Liberia, "we only had about $20 or $25 between us. We had weeks to go. In some ways not having the money made it a good trip because it had to be shoestring, scrappy. We had to meet people, talk to people."

Their next stop was Ghana, on October 9, where Harris had relatives, including a cousin who worked for Mobil Oil. In contrast to sleepy Liberia, Ghana under President Kwame Nkrumah was abuzz with radical pursuits. Lewis and Harris spent time with Julian Mayfield, an expatriate American journalist, and Shirley Graham Du Bois, the sixty-seven-year-old widow of W. E. B. Du Bois, herself a prominent writer, composer, and activist. They visited Du Bois's grave, where Lewis reminisced about shaking the old man's hand on the Fisk campus. Political discussion was constant. Ghanaians quizzed them about the plight of Blacks back home and asked their positions on a host of international issues—"Cuba, Vietnam, the Congo, Red China, and the U.N." Many waxed romantic about Malcolm X (who was simultaneously traveling on the continent), scoffing that in comparison to Malcolm, SNCC's politics were woefully bourgeois.[16]

After stops in Khartoum and Addis Ababa, Lewis and Harris landed in Nairobi, where they expected little more than a quick glimpse. But their next flight, to Lusaka, was canceled, and the airline lodged them for three days at the New Stanley Hotel—"a very beautiful, modern hotel," Lewis said, "one of the finest hotels in Africa." On their first day, they were sitting in a restaurant courtyard sipping coffee when, out of nowhere, up strolled Malcolm X. Lewis had previously met Malcolm only briefly, at the March on Washington, but the Nation of Islam leader recognized the SNCC chairman. "Hello," Malcolm said. "What are you doing here?" Malcolm had just flown in from Cairo, where he had spoken at a meeting of the Organization of African Unity, a newly formed congress of independent states. He was staying on the same floor of the same hotel as Lewis and Harris.

It was Lewis's first opportunity to take the measure of the controversial leader. One quality in Malcolm that Lewis immediately noticed was his constant sense of fear—not quite paranoia, but a jitteriness. Months earlier he had broken with Elijah Muhammad and the Nation of Islam and was afraid of retaliation. He believed he was being watched. Lewis noticed that whenever they sat down in his hotel suite or at a restaurant, Malcolm would position his back against a wall so he could survey the whole room. He said he did this wherever he went.[17]

Over the next two days, Malcolm shared his plans to persuade African nations to bring the situation of Blacks in the United States before the UN—a move that American civil rights organizations had opposed. He also shared his impressions of various African leaders, his thoughts on SNCC's future, and his desire to build bridges between movements in the U.S. and Africa. Malcolm also said that he was leaving behind the polarizing racial doctrines for which he was known. Lewis noted that when Malcolm talked about the people he had met in Cairo, he emphasized that they "were not dark. They were not black, but were light. And he felt that the whole problem . . . was not on the basis of race or color, but had to do also with class." When Malcolm expressed admiration for SNCC—not a position he would have taken a few months earlier—Lewis concluded he was "becoming a changed person, a changed man." Harris formed the same impression. "He talked about where he was," Harris said. "Which was changing from hard Black Muslim dogma to 'We have to internationalize. We have to globalize. Freedom movements are connected. They must be inclusive, rather than exclusive.'" The sojourn in Africa was affecting them all, Lewis thought—broadening the frame of reference through which they looked at their own freedom struggle.[18]

Setting off the next day for Zambia, Lewis and Harris reported, they had only $2.81 remaining. They also learned that all the hotels in Lusaka were full. But at the airport they ran into an acquaintance of Harris's, who knew an Indian family with a spare room. It was a big chamber with two double beds. The friend's mother doted on her guests—she "ultimately tried to adopt us," Harris said—and fed them well. The only rub, Lewis said, was that "the food was so hot. It was terribly hot. . . . Even the thing that was supposed to be sweet was hot." They took to squirreling the food away, "because we didn't want the lady to think we weren't eating her food. We would put it in our pockets and destroy it."

English was Zambia's official language. Its population was racially mixed—Black, white, Indian, and colored, a designation for people of blended heritage. Lewis found Zambia to be "very much like America" in many ways. People knew American pop songs; hot dogs and hamburgers were served along with Indian cuisine and indigenous African dishes. Young adults went to parties and nightclubs, where new acquaintances tried to educate Lewis and Harris about such topics as "the practicality of different kinds of daggers" and "where the best women on the continent were." Lewis was surprised to see how much the nightlife revolved around "go-go shows and burlesque shows, where they did strip-tease and all this stuff"—a new experience for him. "I'm not one of these guys that have been around that much," he said a few years later. "I had not seen similar entertainment in the U.S."

The Zambian independence ceremonies were the trip's highlight. Long a British protectorate called Northern Rhodesia, the new nation was formally recognized as Zambia, under President Kenneth Kaunda, on October 24. Over several days, the Zambians told Lewis and Harris how grateful they were to be with leaders of the American civil rights struggle. "We were given tickets for the ceremonies," Lewis and Harris reported, along with "auto passes (of course we had no car), invitations to some of the receptions, as well as press cards."

The night of October 23, 175,000 people flooded into Lusaka for the festivities, which included, they wrote, "parades, marches, native dancing, singing, acrobats, planes flying overhead, bands, military exhibitions, everything." A few minutes before midnight, all the lights went off but two spotlights trained on parallel flagpoles. Standing among "hundreds of people on a hill," Lewis and Harris waited in silent anticipation. "We were there to see the British flag come tumbling down and the Zambia flag go up," Lewis said. "God Save the Queen" wafted from the loudspeakers as the Union Jack was lowered; then, slowly, the new green Zambian standard climbed the opposite pole. "The roar crescendoed for the full minute," they reported, "and as it hit the top the sky broke with fireworks." Lewis was overcome by the emotion around him. "There was a great sense of joy and happiness . . . and freedom," he said. "And it was a great thing for us to see. We saw there a whole country of Black people, of brown people, of colored people, being freed and liberated while we were still fighting for the right to vote in America. . . . It was quite inspiring. It gave me a great sense of hope, a great sense of belief that something can be done."[19]

Lewis and Harris stuck around for a few more days before flying back north. Kaunda happened to be on their flight, and thousands of Zambians assembled at the airport to send him off. They spent another stopover in Addis Ababa, where Lewis listened to the American election returns on Voice of America radio. He wasn't surprised to learn that Johnson routed Goldwater, or that Robert Kennedy had unseated Republican Kenneth Keating in his bid for a New York Senate seat. Lewis did feel bad that he had missed his first chance to cast a ballot for president.

Lewis's final stop in Africa was Egypt. Cairo was bewildering to Harris and Lewis—"a big, crowded, hustling metropolis," they wrote, in which they got lost en route to their first rendezvous. "After some three hours of carrying our suitcases all over the city, from place to place, not understanding people and they not understanding us, being followed around by junk jewelers, shoeshine boys, pimps, beggars, and an array of various kinds of hustlers," they found David Du Bois, Shirley Graham's son, an American writer and activist. Du Bois arranged for them to address the African Association, a congress of various Pan-African and liberation movements. For several hours they spoke to and took questions from a gathering that included representatives of fourteen different bodies. "They gave us credit for more than we deserved," Lewis said.

Lewis and Harris concluded their African journey with a bus trip to the Great Pyramids and the Sphinx at Giza. They arrived late in the afternoon to avoid the blazing heat. "The desert sand was white and brilliant, and the dunes were rolling, almost sensual, with strange zig-zag lines formed by the wind," they wrote. Camels carried them from the parking lot out to the pyramids. "Dusk fell," they chronicled, "and the loudest noise was the breathing of the camels." Short visits to Rome and Paris followed, where they relaxed at the nightclubs, "eating and drinking it up." They touched down in New York City just before Thanksgiving.[20]

In New York, Lewis attended a ceremony at Harlem's National Guard Armory for King, who had just won the Nobel Peace Prize. Governor Nelson Rockefeller and Mayor Robert Wagner were there, along with other civil rights leaders. In his remarks, King praised Lewis by name. "He mentioned me in his speech and everything," Lewis remembered years later. "It was wonderful, really."[21]

A few weeks later, Lewis wrote to Harris, who had decided to leave

SNCC, get married, and go back to school. Lewis divulged what their trip and their friendship meant to him:

> *Since you will be leaving SNCC and the South in a few days, it is fitting for me to say a few things that come from both the essence of my soul and my heart, which is from John, and not from John Lewis, chairman of SNCC. . . . I feel like I am losing a FRIEND AND BROTHER when you leave.*
>
> *I will never forget the early days in January when I really had a chance to get to know you better. The time that I spent in New York at your home, when all the snow was on the ground, was a turning point in my life. By no means can I forget the trip, the many wonderful and bitter moments we shared together in Africa, Rome, and Paris (you teaching me to swim, the arguments, fights, and the drinking, etc.)*
>
> *I have grown to the point where I like or love, admire, trust, and respect you as a FRIEND AND BROTHER. To be FRANK AND HONEST, I cannot say this about any other person outside of my family.*
>
> *During the past years, I have tried to journey through life alone, that is not to become closely attach to any person, for to otherwise I thought would invite heartbreak; maybe this is one of the risks in every man's life.*
>
> *It is very difficult for me to write these notes for they are unusual and not of the ordinary. . . . It is my most sincere and deepest hope that we will continue our friendship for years to come. . . .*
>
> *A FRIEND,*
> *John*[22]

Lewis's two months in Africa had been unlike any experience he had had. The exposure to different peoples, cultures, and ideas forged in him a personal connection to the freedom movements across the continent and convinced him that the American movement was part of a worldwide upheaval. He came back wanting SNCC to undertake collaborative projects with partners in as many of these countries as possible.

First, though, SNCC had some urgent challenges to confront. While Lewis was away, the organization had experienced considerable turmoil—so much so that, Forman concluded, "the trip to Guinea had been a mistake." Harris was thankful that he and Lewis had missed it all, although he noticed that his friend had been "somewhat preoccupied by the fact that he's SNCC chairman and he's eight thousand miles away from where he's supposed to be."[23]

The problems SNCC was facing were complicated. Allies who stood together on one issue might disagree on another. Some problems were the perennial philosophical debates about which goals to prioritize—desegregation, voting rights, movement building, political equality, economic equality. Members still split over how militant they should be and how closely they should hew to nonviolence. In the wake of Atlantic City, they debated whether or how much to work with the political and civil rights establishments.

But new issues, too, arose, stemming from SNCC's stupendous recent growth. With roughly 170 staffers now and an annual budget in the hundreds of thousands of dollars, SNCC faced unprecedented organizational challenges. Members clashed over whether the organization needed more direction from above, as Forman believed, or whether the field secretaries should have freedom to tackle local needs as they saw fit, as Bob Moses wished. Some people argued for disbanding the Atlanta office and letting different roles rotate among the membership. Since Nashville, Lewis had always believed in democratized group decision-making, but he now agreed with Forman that SNCC needed "a certain amount of structure" or it would become dysfunctional.[24]

Freedom Summer introduced still other challenges. SNCC had always been an interracial association. But the influx of white volunteers, scores of whom sought to remain on staff even after the summer, threatened to transform the organization. Some veterans feared SNCC would lose its character as a Black-led movement. Others, in contrast, were troubled by the elevation of racial difference into a first principle. Lewis was aware of the surge in Black consciousness among his peers—what he called "a radical change in our people since 1960, the way they dress, the music they listen to, their natural hairdos." That consciousness was now colliding with a fear that hundreds of white students were wanting to make SNCC their own.[25]

Finally, there was the simple fact that this was a motley group of very young adults, mostly in their twenties, with varying degrees of maturity and wisdom. Over many months had come stories of petty office theft, sexual harassment and the mistreatment of women, negligence on the job. But no one was ever fired. Many people were disillusioned after Atlantic City and burned out from years of relentless work. Forman was having health problems. Ruby Doris Smith Robinson, overwhelmed in her duties, had bouts of despair. "People were wandering in and out of the organization," Marion Barry said. "Some worked, some didn't work."[26]

In early November, with Lewis still overseas, Forman convened a weeklong retreat in Waveland, Mississippi. Forty staffers drafted position papers on the full gamut of subjects roiling the organization. But these papers and the conversations they provoked failed to create any consensus in favor of the increased professionalization that Forman sought for SNCC. One of the most talked-about papers came from Mary King and Casey Hayden, which they presented anonymously, about systemic sexism in SNCC. It occasioned both soul-searching and resistance among the staff, with Carmichael infamously remarking that the "the only position for women in the movement is prone." (Several people maintained that Carmichael made the remark in jest; King said she "collapsed with hilarity" when he said it. But other women, such as Ruby Doris Smith Robinson, were not amused.*) In the near term, King and Hayden's paper led to no reforms within SNCC, though later would be credited with helping to launch the women's liberation movement.[27]

Overall, the Waveland retreat did little to resolve SNCC's myriad problems. If anything, it aggravated a welter of personal and political conflicts and served mainly to fracture the "band of brothers" and "circle of trust" that Forman fervently wanted SNCC once again to be.

For Lewis, the most consequential issue that emerged from Waveland was a plan to restructure SNCC that was informally adopted toward the end

---

* Mike Thelwell, also presumably intending to be funny, said Carmichael had meant to say that the position of women in SNCC was not *prone* but *supine*. Fastidious lexicologists know that the words, though often confused, technically have different meanings, prone meaning lying face down, supine meaning face up.

of the week. "While we are away," Harris said, "there's the beginning rum-
blings of 'Listen, John's been a little too passive. We need to start thinking
about getting a new chairman.' His chairmanship was shaky." Some people
resented his absence. "John was not a leader," said Joan Browning, a white
SNCC member who later fell out with Lewis. "He wasn't even there at a
time of crisis."[28]

His chairmanship, it turned out, was not only shaky; it was at risk of
being eliminated. A memo from two dozen staffers including Forman was
hammered out late in the week after most people had left Waveland. "John
Lewis has been very frustrated in a non-functional job," it claimed on his
behalf, "having to speak for SNCC yet not having daily organizational contact." This was an exaggeration. Although Lewis experienced frustrations,
he had thrived in his role as SNCC's public face and carried out his functions as a speaker, recruiter, fundraiser, and liaison to outside constituencies
extremely well. But the memo's signatories showed no compunctions about
speaking in their colleague's name. They argued that the chairman's roles
could be passed on to a new "speaker's bureau." The memo even outlined
steps to implement this new structure. In the end, Forman never carried
out those steps. But it was clear that the demand for significant structural
change was strong.[29]

The proposed revisions to SNCC's structure did not spring from personal animus toward Lewis. "It was not about John," said Courtland Cox. "It
was about what SNCC was going to look like and who was going to make
decisions after Mississippi and Atlantic City." The organization was finding
its way toward a less centralized system of decision-making. But that wasn't
clear to Lewis when he returned from Africa. He hadn't been back long before friends like Bond, Hansen, and Charles Sherrod filled him in, providing
murky and contradictory accounts. Some chided him for having been away
too long. Others hyperbolically, but not altogether baselessly, described the
Waveland restructuring proposal as a "coup." As Lewis saw it, "the staff was
just disintegrating."

Feeling "as close to desperate as I've ever felt," Lewis moved to avert a
schism. "I tried to mend as many fences as possible," he said, "and push the
idea of some form of structure to keep SNCC together." In mid-December,
he wrote a letter to the staff, stating that he, Forman, and Moses were all still
in their same roles. (In practice, the disaffected Moses was not running the

Mississippi project anymore, although he hadn't formally relinquished his role.) Lewis assured the staff that there had been no "coup." He also shot down other rumors that he was planning to leave SNCC and go back to school.

His letter also addressed new external attacks on SNCC as having been taken over by Communists. Reports by hostile columnists, especially Rowland Evans and Robert Novak, were raising hackles among SNCC's liberal allies. Lewis said that both the rumors of Communism in SNCC and the whispers of an internal shake-up needed to be rebutted. He asked Bond and the communications team to do so.[30]

SNCC's politics were coming to resemble a Catiline conspiracy, but Lewis had little appetite for the infighting. His prominence was drawing him into other national issues. He spoke before labor groups, anti-poverty groups, and Zionist groups; he received invitations from the Homophile Society, the Conference on Soviet Jewry, and groups protesting the war in Vietnam. One cause he backed heartily was the Free Speech Movement at Berkeley. On the University of California campus, two Freedom Summer veterans led an uprising over constraints on student expression, which fast became a cause célèbre. Lewis believed civil liberties and civil rights to be intertwined. "We know well the attempts by administrators on the campuses of Southern Negro colleges to break the civil rights movement by not allowing students to meet and advocate ideas on the campus," he said. "Now university administrators in the North are borrowing these same tactics. Such denial of students rights—North or South—is an affront to the ideals of American democracy."[31]

As sought-after as Lewis was around the country, however, his position in SNCC had weakened further. Mary King told him that his December letter hadn't helped. Forman had made up his mind to oppose Lewis's re-election at the next SNCC meeting, believing that "the position of chairman had been reduced to nothing more than spokesman" and that "John himself had not done a great deal personally to extend his role." Lewis also heard that Carmichael and another SNCC member, Lafayette Surney, would seek the chairmanship. "I think there was a feeling in SNCC, on the part of some of the people, like Stokely and others, that they needed someone who would be Blacker, in a sense, who would not preach interracial effort, preach integration."[32]

The question came to a head at a February 1965 staff meeting. At

Atlanta's Gammon Theological Seminary during the week of February 12, the organization tried once more to resolve its festering problems. A huge segment of SNCC's 250-person staff attended, some days filling the pews of the chapel. Casey Hayden described the week as "a sort of thrashing about, with occasional impassioned and sometimes incomprehensible speeches relieving an otherwise cold experience." In the meeting's most dramatic development, Bob Moses declared to a dumbstruck room that he would thereafter be known as Robert Parris—his middle name—to escape the unwanted cult-hero status he had attained. Moses also said to Lewis—as well as to Forman, Carmichael, Robinson, and other SNCC leaders—"It's time for you to leave." Bad blood, he suggested, had so poisoned the organization that a transfusion was necessary. Moses then walked out, never to attend another SNCC meeting. His departure, Lewis said, "left an unbelievable void."[33]

Lewis had his own future to worry about. Even some friends were whispering that he should step down. Although he didn't speak much at the Gammon meeting, he seemed anxious, taking pains to make sure tempers remained calm and the conversation civil. Taking the minutes, Mary King recorded, "During entire mtg., John Lewis called for 'Order' [at] every sound!!"

In preparation, Lewis read all the Waveland position papers and reviewed minutes from the meetings he had missed. He arrived with a speech designed to reassure the rank and file that he remained in tune with their thinking. "I felt that I was being challenged in SNCC—my leadership, my stewardship, was being challenged," he said. "That speech was an attempt to rise to the occasion."

Lewis's statement was influenced by the Atlantic City ordeal, which drove home the unreliability of establishment allies, as well as by his trip to Africa, which led him to see the American movement as part of the global "liberation of Black people." His language differed from his usual invocations of the beloved community. "Too many of us are busy telling white people that we are now ready to be integrated into their society," he said, in words that might have sounded strange to the leader of the 1960 sit-ins. "The fact that a Negro sits down next to a white woman at a lunch counter and orders a Coke and a hamburger is still short of revolution."

Lewis also talked bluntly, as he seldom had before, about the hostility that many whites felt toward Blacks. "I am convinced that this country is a racist country," he said. "The majority of the population is white, and most whites still hold to a master-slave mentality." He emphasized divergences in how the races saw the world, invoking the novel *A Different Drummer* by William Melvin Kelley. "The Negro hears a drummer with a totally different beat," Lewis said, "one which the white man is not yet capable of understanding." He maintained that the movement should be, as he put it, "Black-controlled, dominated, and led," although he still insisted that SNCC and the movement should be open to people of all races. He used the word "nonviolent" only when he spoke his organization's name, and he took shots at the civil rights establishment and liberal allies who had let down the Freedom Democrats the past summer.

Lewis's speech still contained a few echoes of his usual rhetoric, with references to Thoreau and Thomas Merton. His peroration, too, expressed a hopeful note, appealing "to all of us . . . the silent staff, the intellectuals, Southerners and Northerners, to move forward" together. But all in all, Lewis had never given such a radical speech before.

The emphasis Lewis placed in February on racial differences over commonalities, and the dim view he took of onetime allies, rarely if ever resurfaced in his rhetoric. This led to speculation that he was striking a posture to hold on to his chairmanship; more charitably, it could be said that he was selectively voicing those beliefs of his that he thought would resonate in the moment, as politicians do. Of the general push toward a more race-conscious sensibility in SNCC, Lewis later conceded, "Too many of our Black SNCC members were demanding it, and I could understand why. I didn't share that feeling, but I had to respect it and respond to it."

Whatever his motivation, Lewis's remarks helped quash any serious challenge to his chairmanship. "I reversed my position" on eliminating the job, Forman said flatly, concluding that SNCC needed continuity. When it came time to vote, several people besides Lewis were nominated, but no one garnered much of a following. SNCC was moving in new directions, becoming less a creature of the Atlanta office, but Lewis would remain, for the time being, its leader.[34]

Chapter Eleven

SELMA

——— ▪ ▪ ———

W hile SNCC was meeting at the Gammon seminary in mid-February, a major new campaign in the fight for voting rights was gaining traction two hundred miles away, in Selma, Alabama.

Since July, when Judge James Hare's draconian order forbade gatherings of more than three people, activism in Selma had languished. But in December 1964, Amelia Boynton and the Dallas County Voters League appealed to Martin Luther King for help. Newly crowned as a Nobel laureate, King agreed to visit the Alabama city. He viewed Sheriff Jim Clark as a perfect foil—Andrew Young called him a "near madman"—whose overreactions to peaceful demonstrations could be counted on to gin up attention and sympathy. King planned to use Selma to launch a drive for a federal voting rights measure, something the Johnson administration was planning to introduce, but balked at bringing to Congress so soon after the 1964 Civil Rights Act.[1]

King's imminent arrival angered the SNCC field-workers in Selma. Again, they felt, they had nurtured a local movement, only for "De Lawd" to sweep in and steal the credit. They worried, too, that SCLC's modus operandi—instigating short-term, high-profile confrontations to achieve political goals—would undercut their own long-term, Mississippi-style movement building. "There was this real animosity toward the SCLC organization," Mark Suckle of SNCC said. "Running in, stirring up the community, and running out again."[2]

As usual, Lewis felt differently. "John was the soul of SNCC," said Frank Smith, his friend and colleague in the organization. "He was a bridge

between the SNCC style and the SCLC style. He had all the fiery nature
of SNCC, but was like a preacher from SCLC." Lewis's esteem for King
remained undimmed; he remained on SCLC's board; he welcomed SCLC's
participation. The town's residents had invited King, and it wasn't SNCC's
place to object. Anyway, they had no choice: King was coming.[3]

Judge Hare's injunction remained in force on January 2, 1965, when
King, resplendent in a sleek black suit and tie, arrived at Brown Chapel. The
Romanesque brick church, trimmed in white stone with matching cupolaed
towers, served as the local movement's headquarters. Seven hundred citizens
packed its interior, filling its three balconies, to hear King. Confident and
defiant, he announced what he called "a determined, organized, mobilized
campaign to get the right to vote everywhere in Alabama."[4]

Two days later, on January 4, Lyndon Johnson delivered his State of the
Union message to Congress. Lewis awaited some comment about guaranteeing the vote. Although the 1964 Civil Rights Act contained voting rights
provisions, they were acknowledged to be weak, and civil rights advocates
were pushing for stronger medicine. Many legislators who had backed the
1964 bill, however, needed a breather; they expected, the *Washington Post*
reported, that "no further legislation would be asked until the effectiveness
of the 1964 Civil Rights Act had been thoroughly tested." Caught in the
middle, LBJ vowed to "eliminate every remaining obstacle to the right and
the opportunity to vote," but provided no details or timetable. The Selma
campaign would try to force his hand.[5]

SNCC and SCLC leaders spent January organizing. Lewis was happy
to be reunited with Bevel and Nash. Bevel had emerged after Birmingham
as an influential, charismatic leader in his own right, eccentrically wearing
a yarmulke in tribute to the Hebrew prophets and prodding King to adopt
creative new tactics. Completing the reunion was Bernard LaFayette, who
returned to help bridge the SCLC-SNCC divide. Seeking unity, the two
groups coupled up their staffers, each pair working in tandem to survey a
different ward of the county. Joint staff meetings each morning dissipated
tension and dispelled suspicions.[6]

After two weeks, Lewis and King together headlined a rally on Sunday, January 17, announcing more Freedom Days. Prospective voters would
queue up at the Dallas County Courthouse starting Monday, January 18.
They would repeat as needed.[7]

On Monday, Lewis and King led four hundred locals from Brown Chapel to the green marble courthouse steps. Clark and his henchmen lay in wait. But Clark did not have the same unfettered power he had had a few months before. Selma had just elected a new mayor, Joe Smitherman, who had appointed a new public safety director, Wilson Baker. Both men were moderates by Deep South standards and wanted to avoid the violence—and negative publicity—that Clark was keen to instigate. "We hope this is going to be the most disappointing trip of your life," Baker joked to the reporters who had descended on Selma. On Monday, he kept the cocksure sheriff and his paramilitary posse in check.[8]

The lack of drama didn't trouble Lewis, who knew that this attempt would be just the first of many. At the day's end, he walked with King to the Hotel Albert, Selma's poshest guesthouse, which now, because of the Civil Rights Act, was obliged to desegregate. King would be its first Black guest.

As King was signing in at the front desk, Jimmie Robinson, a wiry twenty-six-year-old white supremacist, approached the minister, saying, "I'd like to see you a minute." Robinson lunged at King, fists flying, knocking him to the floor and overturning a lamp, then kicking his fallen victim.[9]

On impulse, Lewis seized Robinson in a bear hug, pinning his arms to his sides. Wilson Baker wrested the assailant away and into a patrol car.

Lewis scolded himself. His reaction had fallen short of nonviolent behavior by using physical force against the attacker. Lewis chalked up his failure of discipline to his reverence for King. "That moment," he reflected, "pushed me as close as I've ever been to the limits of my nonviolent commitments."[10]

The assault garnered front-page stories, including in the *New York Times*. Reporters realized that Selma was shaping up as another major civil rights saga. On Tuesday, Clark gave them more to work with when, unprovoked, he manhandled the fifty-three-year-old Amelia Boynton, shoving her down the sidewalk as photographers clicked away. Clark's men arrested seventy others that day, including Lewis and SCLC's Hosea Williams, when they failed to line up in the courthouse's back alley, as ordered.[11]

Lewis was in and out of jail quickly enough to lead a third day of protests on Wednesday. At one point that afternoon, he was trying to keep the weary Selma foot soldiers in an orderly line. He reminded them that even if they didn't succeed in registering—and so far no one had—their patient determination would drive home their point. As Lewis tended the line, Clark sauntered up and ordered the petitioners to the back alley. Lewis refused.

Clark exploded. "You are here to cause trouble, and that's what you are doing," he yelled. "You're nothing but an outside agitator. And an agitator is the lowest form of humanity." Clark's body was trembling with rage as he dressed Lewis down.

"Sheriff," Lewis said calmly, "I may be an agitator, but I'm not an outsider. I grew up ninety miles from here. And we're going to stay here until these people are allowed to register to vote."

"If you do not disperse in one minute or go in as I have directed you," Clark hissed, "you will be under arrest for unlawful assembly." Lewis remained impassive. Then, Lewis recalled, "we all got arrested again."[12]

The same pattern recurred day after day. "In less than two weeks," Lewis said, "I think I went to jail about five times in Selma. It was a very bad scene. . . . Hundreds and thousands of people would go down there each day trying to register."[13]

After Lewis left jail in late January, he flew to the West Coast to raise money for SNCC. The Selma campaign continued in full swing without him, with the Dallas County Voters League and SCLC in command. Again and again, they lined up; again and again, they got arrested—thousands in all, including a contingent of schoolteachers one day and hundreds of schoolchildren another. Reliably belligerent, Clark's men overreacted and kept Selma in the headlines.

On Monday, February 1, King and Ralph Abernathy set off on another short march from Brown Chapel to the courthouse. This time they intended to go to jail. For the last two weeks, Wilson Baker had broken their processions into clusters of three—a charade that both sides observed to evade the judge's injunction. But King deliberately asserted the marchers' right to gather, and Baker felt obliged to arrest all 250, including King and Abernathy. At the day's end, they were released, except the two ministers who, in order to escalate the conflict, refused bail.

On Thursday, the men's wives, Coretta and Juanita, spoke in their stead at another Brown Chapel rally. Lewis was still out west. They were joined by James Bevel and Fred Shuttlesworth, crowd-pleasing orators, and, unexpectedly, Malcolm X, whom two SNCC staffers had met the night before in Tuskegee and invited to speak. Their freelancing angered the SCLC brass, who hadn't forgiven Malcolm's disparagement of King. The two organizations' representatives caucused feverishly, arguing over whether to give Malcolm the stage. Ultimately they let him speak.

To everyone's relief, Malcolm steered clear of inflammatory rhetoric, winning applause and, with his caustic humor, provoking bursts of laughter. Afterward, while sitting on the platform, he leaned over and whispered to Coretta King that he wanted to help and not undermine her husband. Having considered Malcolm "a really violent-type person," Coretta was surprised and intrigued. Then, as the program closed, Malcolm darted off for Montgomery, three hours after coming to town. "There was no great impact on the people of Selma by Malcolm," C. T. Vivian said about his visit. "They hardly knew Malcolm in the first place."[14]

King used his incarceration to alert the nation about the abysmal situation of Blacks in Selma. He penned a "Letter from a Selma Jail," meant to echo his 1963 Birmingham letter, though the document was little more than a fundraising appeal to run in the *New York Times*. "*This is Selma, Alabama*," King wrote. "There are more Negroes in jail with me than there are on the voting rolls." The statement called on "decent Americans . . . lulled into complacency" by the passage of the Civil Rights Act to realize that the fight for voting rights remained "unfinished business in the South."[15]

Lewis retuned to Selma on Friday. King and Abernathy posted bail. Together the three men escorted an interracial delegation of fifteen U.S. congressmen around Selma—a publicity move designed to show Governor Wallace that Washington and the nation were watching. On Saturday, more confirmation came that Selma's reverberations were being felt at the highest levels when White House press secretary George Reedy disclosed that the president would introduce a voting rights measure before the year was out. Then, on Tuesday, King met with LBJ, who went further, promising to send a bill to Congress "very soon."[16]

If movement was visible in Washington, however, in Selma things looked much the same. Lewis found himself disgusted anew by Clark's cruelty. On Wednesday, February 10, 160 Selma teenagers gathered for a protest. "You want to march so bad, now you can march," one of his deputies yelled. The posse forced the kids, under threat of clubs and cattle prods, to jog for two miles on a country road. Bystanders were pushed away.

Appalled, Lewis scrawled a denunciation of Clark, which SNCC issued as a press release. "Sheriff Jim Clark proved today beyond a shadow of a doubt that he is basically no different from a Gestapo officer during the Fascist rape of the Jews," Lewis said. ("Rape" was changed to "slaughter" before the release went out.) "This is but one more example of the inhuman, animal-like treatment of the Negro people of Selma, Alabama. This nation has always come to the aid of people in foreign lands who are gripped by a reign of tyranny. Can this nation do less for the people of Selma?"[17]

That night, Lewis spoke extemporaneously at a mass meeting that was recorded for posterity. Passion and pain resounded in his voice. "My fellow freedom fighters," he began, as he often did, "we're involved in a serious struggle." He continued:

> We're involved in a revolution. We're fighting a war. We're winning battles, but we've got to win the war. We have a long ways to go. Tonight, I know some of us are angry and some of us are bitter. We have reason to be angry and we have reason to be bitter on behalf of more than 200 students. . . . Jim Clark and the members of the posse that forced people to run down the streets of Selma and three or four miles outside the city down that highway with their electric cattle prods and their clubs, knocking people down and hurting people.
>
> Something is wrong. Something is wrong. . . . It's time for all of you that are here in this day, in this city, it's time to rise up in a nonviolent fashion and say, we're going to put an end to it.

The crowd let loose a burst of cheers and applause. Lewis went on.

> The United States government will send troops to South Vietnam. We can intervene in the Congo. Well, why [can't] the federal government intervene in Selma, Alabama? We can protect people around the world. We can put the whole United States Army—not only the Army but the Air Force, the Marines, all the other areas of the Department of Defense—to protect citizens abroad and protect

foreign land and foreign soil, and cannot provide protection for the
Black people of Selma, Alabama. I know something is wrong.

More vigorous applause.

> Tonight, we must make it clear. . . . There will be no peace, there will
> be no tranquility in this city, in this county, until all of us can walk
> the streets of Selma and walk together.
>
> I'll be frank and honest with you. I'm angry. I've seen peo-
> ple beaten too many times. I've seen people harassed too many
> times. . . . Right here in the state of Alabama. We are living in a police
> state where people do not have the freedom to walk down the street,
> to march, to protest, to assemble. . . . All of us must rise up together
> and say, "Mr. Clark and your posse, you're not just asking for a battle.
> You demand all-out war, and we will give it to you." That's what we
> must have.[18]

Nightly mass meetings and speeches testified that the voter drive was coming alive. Now they were pushing into Perry County to the north, Lowndes
County to the east, Wilcox County to the south.

On Thursday, February 18—when Lewis and the SNCC executive
committee were meeting in Atlanta—the tension boiled over. Early in the
day, rumors had circulated of a Klan plot to lynch an SCLC employee who
was in jail in Marion, Alabama. C. T. Vivian came to Marion, where he gave
a tour de force of a speech, firing up the locals. He then led a walk to the
courthouse.

Scarcely had the marchers set off when state troopers surrounded them.
After shutting off the streetlights, Al Lingo, the head of the Alabama Highway Patrol, gave his men license to run riot, bloodying and injuring dozens.
Richard Valeriani of NBC News, hit with an axe handle, was hospitalized
with a head wound. Two UPI photographers were roughed up, their cameras destroyed.

Jimmie Lee Jackson, a twenty-six-year-old millworker, saw police maul-
ing his eighty-two-year-old grandfather. Jackson spied a café that could
provide haven and shooed the old man and other family members inside.
Lingo's troopers chased them, their billy clubs swinging—smashing lights,

upending tables, shattering dishes. After a trooper swatted Jackson's mother, Jimmie Lee shielded her, only to be hurled against a cigarette machine. Another trooper shot Jackson twice in the stomach. Bolting out of the café, bleeding profusely, the young man was hunted down, drubbed into unconsciousness, and then ambulanced to the hospital.

Lewis learned about the bloodbath from Friday's newspaper. He felt dread. If Jackson died, then people would snap. The steadfast nonviolence of the Selma project might give way. Over the next days, as Jackson clung to life, Lewis monitored events closely.

Sunday, February 21, was his twenty-fifth birthday. While riding in a car, listening to the radio, he heard a news bulletin—not from Selma but from New York. Malcolm X, speaking at the Audubon Ballroom in Washington Heights, had been shot and killed, reportedly by Nation of Islam members.

Lewis was stunned. He regretted that he had been out west when Malcolm visited Selma. He thought about their encounter in Nairobi and his belief that Malcolm had turned over a new leaf. Despite his unwavering belief in nonviolence and in the oneness of people of all races, Lewis respected Malcolm as an important force in American and African American life. "More than anyone else on the American scene, Malcolm was able to articulate the deep feelings of the Negro masses in the Delta and rural areas of the South and the slums and ghettoes of the North," Lewis said in a statement on behalf of SNCC. Lewis believed that to some degree, though he later revised it to say that Malcolm best articulated African Americans' "bitterness and frustration"—not *all* their feelings. And while Malcolm had a following in the cities, Lewis knew that he was less popular in the Southern countryside. Lewis's truest sentiments came through in the next sentence: "His wide travels throughout Africa helped to cement the bonds between the liberation movement in Africa and the civil rights struggle in America."[19]

Lewis would attend Malcolm's funeral the next Saturday in New York. In the meantime he remained in Selma. With King and Abernathy, he visited Jimmie Lee Jackson in the hospital, and he continued to meet with SNCC and SCLC leaders to maintain harmony. It became clear to Lewis that Andrew Young, Hosea Williams, and James Bevel were calling the shots. Some of his SNCC colleagues groused about being cut out.[20]

Things got worse on Friday, February 26, when Jackson died in his hospital bed. A grief-stricken Bevel seized on an idea floated by local activist Marie Foster that they march on Montgomery. Bevel told LaFayette that they should walk the fifty miles from Selma to Montgomery as a response to Jackson's killing—to deliver a message to Governor Wallace. America's attention still wasn't focused on Selma or disenfranchisement. The walk, he said, would give them "the five or six days we need to address the nation."

"I'll walk with you," LaFayette said, "for protection and for companionship."

That evening, six hundred people packed Brown Chapel. Bevel was electric. "The blood of Jackson will be on our hands if we don't march," he shouted. "Be prepared to walk to Montgomery. Be prepared to sleep on the highways." He put the question to the audience: "How many of you are willing to walk with me?"

Everybody stood.

"I guess," Bevel said, turning to LaFayette, "we've got ourselves a march."[21]

Slate-gray skies and a cold rain greeted mourners on Wednesday, March 3, for Jimmie Lee Jackson's funeral in Marion. Lewis sat glumly as King repurposed his eulogy for the Birmingham girls killed in September 1963. Then King, Lewis, and a train of hundreds, trailing the hearse by foot, trudged three miles along a muddy road to Jackson's burial site as the rain drenched their clothes. When it was over, Bevel announced the Selma-to-Montgomery pilgrimage, telling reporters that it would start on Sunday, March 7. King would head the procession.

Made without SNCC's consent, the announcement reopened the rift between the groups. SNCC's staff in Selma complained that it would be a pointless stunt, endangering lives and livelihoods. But Lewis thought the idea was inspired. ("I remember he used to get drunk and wander through the streets with us," SNCC's Harriet Tanzman said, "and talk about how great an idea the march was.") In his view, publicity had always been the movement's "friend." As he later put it, "Without the media, there never would have been a civil rights movement." Publicity from the "Walk for Freedom," as it was now being called, would increase the pressure on George Wallace and Lyndon Johnson. Conceding the value of a march, the SNCC staff agreed to furnish cars, medical services, and the use of its long-distance telephone line, although they declined to join the march themselves.[22]

Before the Sunday march, Lewis returned to Atlanta for a two-day SNCC meeting. Over Friday and Saturday, at Frazier's Cafe Society, the executive committee plowed through a sprawling agenda: field reports from around the South, assessments of the unraveling Mississippi voting-rights project, more of the usual debates over structure and procedure. But the urgent business of the Walk for Freedom kept resurfacing.

Silas Norman, SNCC's newest Selma point man, spelled out the understanding he had reached with SCLC. A slew of logistical questions followed. Would there be portable toilets for the pilgrims? Blankets and tents at the roadside farms along the way? What was SNCC's financial commitment?

Discussion proceeded haltingly. People repeatedly returned to the question of whether SNCC should participate at all. For some, it was about sticking with community organizing over direct action. For others, it was about conflicts with King and SCLC. For still others, it was about the danger of bloodshed.

On Saturday morning, Wallace raised the stakes by declaring that his troopers would do everything in their power to stop the protest. He seemed to confirm that violence lay in store. SNCC hard-liners again argued against risking their lives for an SCLC undertaking. Forman, Carmichael, and Cox were all "adamantly against the march," Lewis recalled. They argued that SCLC was "just using the people," that "a lot of people are going to get hurt," that "we shouldn't be a part of it."[23]

The conversation at Frazier's went around in circles. The minutes recorded a free-for-all without a clear purpose or direction, as members continued to question the march's goals and even to ask whether SNCC should continue to work in Selma, in Alabama, with King, or with SCLC. It was eventually agreed that SNCC would send King a letter, but even the contents of that document became grist for protracted debate.

The final version dripped with hostility. It accused SCLC of breaking agreements, citing "a serious unwillingness on the part of key SCLC staff . . . to deal honestly with SNCC." The unilateral announcement of the Walk for Freedom had been the final straw. SNCC would "live up to [only] those minimal commitments to which we have already agreed," the letter vowed, such as providing cars, medical help, and ancillary support. "Hereafter," it concluded, "we will maintain and develop our programs and we feel it necessary that we maintain separate offices."[24]

Lewis didn't like the letter. But he allowed it to carry his signature, alongside Norman's. It wasn't the first time that SNCC had issued a statement in his name he didn't fully agree with. He felt obliged to represent the dominant sentiment in the group even when it diverged from his own.

The harder decision was whether to march. Lewis wanted to be a part of the event. But as the second day of deliberations wore on, he could see he was virtually alone. Even some allies who had previously defended the march now opposed taking part. "Some of us tried to warn John not to march," Cox later said. "But his experience with James Lawson gave him a bravery that some of us did not understand, that I didn't understand. It had to do with John's religious faith."[25]

Lewis was aware of the split. His closest allies from Nashville days—Bevel, Nash, LaFayette, Vivian—were now at SCLC, not SNCC, and they all favored the march. Most of his SNCC colleagues stood opposed. Here was more evidence of SNCC's continuing evolution away from its roots in the Southern Black church and the Gandhian teachings of King and Lawson. It was moving toward the kind of Northern, urban radicalism that was distrustful of interracial alliances, contemptuous of politics, and open in its disdain for King.

"I grew up in Alabama," he said to his colleagues at Frazier's. "I feel a deep kinship with the people there on a lot of levels. You know, I've been to Selma many, many times. I've been arrested there. I've been jailed there. If these people want to march, I'm going to march with them. You decide what you want to do, but I'm going to march."[26]

No one could deny Lewis's sincerity or the legitimacy of his wish. His cri de coeur wrung a concession from the executive committee. Any SNCC member who wished to take part in the march, they agreed, could do so—as a private individual.

Lewis wasn't entirely alone. Two colleagues, Bob Mants and Wilson Brown, also wanted to march. Shortly after midnight, Lewis said, "We left the meeting, different factions and different groups left the meeting, and we all went our separate ways." Lewis, Mants, and Brown climbed into Brown's white Dodge for the three-hour drive to Selma.[27]

Sometime before daybreak on March 7, Brown pulled up at the "Freedom House" that SNCC operated in Selma—a weather-beaten edifice where transient workers would crash for a few days. Lewis unfurled his sleeping bag and found a spot on the floor.

He woke up after a few hours, showered, and dressed: suit, tie, trench coat. He filled his backpack with an apple, an orange, a toothbrush and toothpaste, and two books: Thomas Merton's *The Seven Storey Mountain* and Richard Hofstadter's *The American Political Tradition*. He left for Brown Chapel.[28]

A crowd was milling about in the playgrounds of the George Washington Carver Homes. People had come from surrounding counties. Some wore their Sunday best, expecting a short walk; others, with bedrolls and knapsacks, looked ready for days of hiking. Medical volunteers were setting up. SCLC staffers were holding quickie nonviolence training sessions. James Bevel, Andrew Young, and Hosea Williams of SCLC huddled off to one side. Lewis walked up.

Young shared with him the news: King wasn't coming. He had been away from his pulpit for too many Sundays, he said, and decided to stay in Atlanta. King later repeated this same explanation. But when Young spoke to reporters that day, he gave a different reason, saying that King had changed his strategy as the prospect of violence increased; he now hoped to postpone the march. This story was mostly accurate, but it omitted a fact that no one wanted to disclose: the FBI had learned of credible threats to King's life, and Attorney General Nicholas Katzenbach urged him to stay home.[29]

With news of King's absence, many of the SNCC people became enraged all over again. Some nursed resentments decades later. "I was done with King after Selma," said Maria Varela, a SNCC staffer active in the campaign. "I wasn't even that impressed with him before. He was supposed to be there and he didn't show." But Lewis would not criticize his hero.[30]

King had hoped to postpone the Walk for Freedom and participate another day. But when Young saw the huge turnout at Brown Chapel that Sunday, he told King he couldn't send the pilgrims home. King agreed. Young, Bevel, and Williams drew straws to see who would take his place. Williams drew the short straw. He would march at the head of the column, next to Lewis, who would be representing—yet not representing—SNCC.

Around three o'clock, Lewis and Young read statements to the press. Young raised his arm to deliver a prayer as Lewis, Williams, Amelia Boynton, and others knelt, bent their heads, and prayed.

Then, two abreast, orderly and resolute, six hundred people set off southward down Sylvan Street, turned west, and continued marching parallel to the Alabama River. Five blocks later, the column reached Broad Street, which became Route 80 as it led out of town. The plan was to turn left and cross the river via the Edmund Pettus Bridge—an unhandsome 1,200-foot, high-arched, steel-and-concrete crossing named for a former Confederate general and Klansman, built in 1940, the year Lewis was born.[31]

At first there was singing and chanting. Onlookers cheered. But soon a hush descended, leaving rhythmic footfalls as the only sound. "We just walked in twos, like we were on our way, on a journey," Lewis recalled, imagining it to be like Gandhi's 1930 March to the Sea protesting British rule. Wallace's warning instilled a frisson of trepidation. But no one knew what to expect. "We had no idea," Lewis said, "what force he would use or what he would do to prevent the march."[32]

Rounding the corner onto Broad Street, turning to face the bridge, Lewis saw a bulging crowd held back by Clark's khaki-clad posse. Lewis and Williams pushed on, leading the procession up the slope of the Pettus Bridge. Although the road was empty of cars, they stuck to the sidewalk. It was a steep ascent—so steep that Lewis and Williams couldn't see the other side. Near the apex, a breeze brushed Lewis's trench coat and skimmed the water below. Then, as they reached the top, they stopped short.

A few hundred yards away stood a phalanx of blue helmets and blue uniforms—Lingo's state police. The lawmen were massed in line after line, several dozen strong. Behind them, on foot and on horseback, were more men from Clark's posse.[33]

Williams looked down at the Alabama River. He turned to Lewis. "Can you swim?" he asked.

"No," Lewis said.

"Neither can I. But we might have to."

Turning back was not an option. The two men stepped forward slowly, toward the lawmen.

Major John Cloud, the officer in command, held a bullhorn to his mouth. "This is an unlawful assembly," he shouted. "Your march is not conducive to the public safety. You are ordered to go back to your church and to your homes."

Williams asked to have a word with Cloud.

"There is no word to be had," Cloud said through the bullhorn. "You have two minutes to turn around and go back to your church."

"We should kneel and pray," Lewis said. But before they could do so, Cloud ordered his troopers to advance.

"They advanced right into us," Lewis remembered. The troopers swept forward all at once. Lewis was poked with a baton, then turned around as the lawmen kept moving into the column. Those on foot swung their clubs. Those on horseback flailed at the protesters with whips and ropes. Men and women fell to the ground. "It was like dominoes going backward," Lewis said, "and all started falling backwards and they're hitting us and kicking us and swinging at us."

Lewis was one of the first to go down. He saw a blur of bodies. He heard the thump of boots and the clip-clop of hooves, shouts of pain and whoops from the crowd. "Get the niggers!" someone yelled. It was, "without question," he later said, the most frightening moment of his life.[34]

A trooper's club knocked him hard on the left side of his skull—the same spot where he'd been bludgeoned during the Freedom Rides. Blood ran down his head. The world began to spin.

It was now about 3:15. Lewis was fading from consciousness. He might have passed out, but suddenly his nose and lungs came alive with the acrid smell of tear gas. Before he knew it, he was choking on the fumes. He vomited.

Lewis believed he was going to die, just as he had at the Montgomery bus station in 1961. As before, he realized that he did not fear death. A feeling of peace and serenity—even lucidity—came over him. "How odd to die in your own country when you are orderly," he remembered thinking, "when you are only wanting to bring justice to people. How odd to die while exercising your constitutional rights."[35]

SNCC staffer Lafayette Surney, observing it all from a street corner, manned a public pay phone and filed detailed reports with the Atlanta office. He described cops herding the protesters into back alleys, people "running, crying, telling what's happening." Five minutes later, Surney reported that "white hoodlums" had entered the fray, busting out of the sidelines to maul fleeing demonstrators. Fay Bellamy, who took Surney's call, could hear through the telephone "the screams and the sirens. . . . It was just horrendous." Journalists, photographers, and cameramen captured the carnage in word and image.[36]

After a spell—he had no idea how long—Lewis staggered to his feet. His head was exploding with pain. The thick yellow gas prevented him from seeing much. Everywhere, people were fleeing and falling as the troopers and deputies pressed their assault. Lewis noticed Amelia Boynton and other women lying on the pavement. A teenage boy sat with blood gushing from his head. Someone else was vomiting. "People were crying," Lewis said, "and old women were hollering and left lying in the street."[37]

With the help of Bob Mants, Lewis wobbled back to Brown Chapel, stanching the blood from his head with a handkerchief. As he walked, he saw Clark's possemen make their horses rear up behind the marchers, then hit them with their bullwhips, yelling, "Go on, nigger. Go on, nigger."

At the church, bedlam reigned. Everyone was asking about missing friends and loved ones. Young and Bevel talked down angry Selma residents, trying to stop them from hurling bricks at their tormentors or grabbing guns from their homes.[38]

Bloodied and disoriented, Lewis telephoned SNCC's Atlanta offices. He recounted his beating and said that the possemen, whips and ropes in hand, were chasing everyone back to the chapel. "I've never seen anything like it in my life," he said.[39]

A SNCC worker told Lewis he had "a small hole in his head." He refused any help. He went inside the church sanctuary, now teeming with people, to speak. "I think John was out of his head for a moment," said P. H. Lewis, the pastor of Brown Chapel, who watched Lewis gather himself. What amazed John—what made this brush with death different from the previous one—was who had attacked him. "It was carried out not by the Klan or some group that decided to take the law into their own hands," he later reflected, "but it was carried out with the sanction of the state government."[40]

Lewis realized that the only force strong enough to rein in George Wallace was the federal government. He focused his remarks on that point, using words he had been saying at rallies for weeks. "I don't see how President

Johnson can send troops to Vietnam," he began. "I don't see how he can send troops to the Congo. I don't see how he can send troops to Africa and can't send troops to Selma, Alabama, to protect people whose only desire is to register to vote." People in the church cheered. "Next time we march," he continued, "we may have to keep going when we get to Montgomery. We may have to go on to Washington."[41]

Eventually it dawned on Lewis that he was in bad shape. He walked over to the church parsonage, now a triage unit with doctors and nurses. "I need to go to the hospital," he said to no one in particular. Someone led him to an ambulance on Sylvan Street. By six o'clock he was at Good Samaritan, diagnosed with a fractured skull. His injury, one of six broken skulls diagnosed that day, was one of the most serious the medical staff saw all afternoon as they ministered to bruises, cuts, gashes, broken bones, and symptoms caused by inhaling chemical gas. Lewis's wound was cleaned and dressed, his head x-rayed. He was given painkillers and admitted overnight.[42]

A film crew from Reuters came to his hospital bed. He lay covered in a sheet, staring straight up at the ceiling as he answered their questions. "It was just a vicious attack, I think, on all of us," he said. "The march to Montgomery that we started today should have continued. Because I see the march as a legitimate form of nonviolent protest. To dramatize to this country and to the world the desperate plight of the Negro people in this part of Alabama."[43]

In the meantime, the television crews who had filmed the day's atrocities had escaped the police with their footage intact, taking back roads to evade the troopers blocking the highway. Given the era's technology, airing their film that night required developing it in Montgomery, then flying it to network headquarters in New York. The CBS and NBC evening news shows featured segments about the confrontation, while ABC had the inspired idea to interrupt its popular Sunday night movie—*Judgment at Nuremberg*, about the complicity of the German people in unspeakable evil. Anchor Frank Reynolds delivered a lead-in and showed fifteen minutes of the massacre. Viewers could not fail to make the connection.[44]

The next morning's news coverage further galvanized the nation. A photograph of an Alabama trooper bludgeoning a helpless Lewis—on his knees on the grassy median, in his trench coat, his right hand desperately trying to shield his head—was plastered across front pages everywhere.

The photograph showed a dozen helmeted troopers in the background, a woman also on her knees, and, in the distance, a huge sign for Haisten's Mattress and Awning Company. The headlines did not soft-pedal the violence.

"Negro Marchers Gassed, Beaten," said the *Boston Globe*.

"Alabama Police Use Gas and Clubs to Rout Negroes," said the *New York Times*.

"Melee in Selma," blared the *Los Angeles Times*.

In Washington, calls for action emanated from Capitol Hill and beyond. The Justice Department dispatched more FBI agents. Indignant congressmen denounced Wallace, Clark, and their legions and demanded a voting rights bill. "Sunday's outrage in Selma, Alabama, makes passage of legislation to guarantee Southern Negroes the right to vote an absolute imperative," said the junior senator from Minnesota, Walter Mondale.[45]

On Monday, King and Abernathy returned to Selma. They paid a call on Lewis at the hospital. "We'll make it to Montgomery," King promised. "They're not going to stop us now." John Doar came by, promising federal action. Two FBI agents (one of whom had himself been assaulted on Sunday) also showed up, to interview Lewis. But no one from SNCC visited except for Lafayette Surney—and he did so because he needed a photo of Lewis for a press release. Lewis told himself that his friends and colleagues were probably just busy, but he was disappointed and alienated from the organization he still ostensibly led.[46]

Meanwhile, strangers who had seen his picture in their hometown papers sent telegrams, flowers, and gifts. Others staged rallies, mounted petition drives, or phoned their representatives. "In a sense," Lewis said, "the violence in Selma that day represented a low point in modern America, but also—for the civil rights movement and for the liberal community in America and for people of goodwill, I think that it represented the finest hour. The reaction and response was unbelievable. . . . I'd never witnessed or seen anything like this."[47]

Lewis came away fortified in his commitment to nonviolence. "It may sound strange," he later said, "but I think someplace along the way I made up my mind that I would not become bitter or hostile. I think that's part of the whole philosophy of nonviolence. When you let the nonviolent discipline or philosophy become a way of life, it will control all aspects of your life."[48]

King, guilt-ridden over having skipped the march, resolved to atone. On Sunday night he had telegrammed clergy nationwide—Black and white, Jewish and Christian—asking them to come to Selma. Nearly five hundred did so, as did assorted other volunteers, moved by images of what became known as "Bloody Sunday." King promised to lead a new crossing of the Pettus Bridge on Tuesday. To minimize the chances of violence, SCLC petitioned Frank M. Johnson—the federal judge who had struck down Montgomery's segregated bus seating in 1956 and supported the Freedom Riders in 1961—to keep Wallace from halting this second attempt. Johnson scheduled a hearing on SCLC's filing for later in the week, but ordered that no march proceed until he considered the case.[49]

SNCC, too, reversed course. With their chairman hospitalized, and with millions rallying behind the Selma campaign, Lewis's colleagues could hardly wallow in doctrinal fights, tactical quibbles, or personal grudges. Dozens of SNCC staffers, including Forman, sped to Selma.

Ironically, the two organizations' positions were now switched. Suddenly Forman, who had opposed the Sunday march, demanded that they march on Tuesday. In contrast, King talked of postponing again, confident that Judge Johnson would soon approve a march.[50]

By Monday night King seemed ready to go forward. But the next morning Katzenbach awakened him with a phone call saying that LBJ wanted absolutely no marching until Judge Johnson ruled. Yet the people of Selma and neighboring towns, their ranks swelled by clergymen descending on Alabama, were massing again at Brown Chapel Tuesday morning. They were not likely to go home quietly.

Unable to stay away from the action, Lewis hurried out of Good Samaritan Hospital Tuesday morning, despite his doctors' misgivings. (At the end of the month, he would spend several days at Massachusetts General Hospital in Boston, for a lumbar puncture, a brain scan, and other tests.) He felt strong enough to speak at noontime at Brown Chapel, which was fuller than reporters had ever seen it. Lewis mounted the rostrum with his head swathed in so much gauze that he looked to Arlie Schardt of *Time* magazine as if he were wearing a football helmet. Hearty yells and cheers greeted his arrival. His head still ached, but he gave what Schardt judged "one of his best speeches in months; his eyes blazed and his gestures became violent as he moved to his climactic point."

"Sunday afternoon, I was beaten by a state trooper and knocked down," Lewis said. "I was in a hospital until an hour ago. Right now I feel exhausted and sick. Quite a few other people are still in the hospital with broken legs and broken arms, fractures of the skull and other injuries.... We saw George Wallace at his best, a vicious system at work. . . . All of us must do it for our sisters and brothers. Let us do it with a sense of dignity. . . . We *must* march."[51]

As Lewis spoke, Martin Luther King strode into the sanctuary, provoking more cheers and hollers. Privately, King was still wavering. He did not want to violate a court order. He had even discussed—but not committed to—a deal with Wallace. Yet when he spoke at the chapel, he hid his ambivalence. He talked of marching along the highways to Montgomery as if he intended for the show to go on.

Tuesday afternoon, with King in the front, fifteen hundred protesters retraced Sunday's path to the bridge. Lewis, in no condition to risk another beating, stayed behind. When King reached the foot of the bridge, a federal marshal read him the judge's injunction, and then let the column continue on—a signal, or so it appeared, that they would be allowed to advance. They continued over the bridge, as Lewis and Williams had on Sunday—until King, too, ran into John Cloud and his troopers.

This time the script went differently.

Confronting Cloud, King asserted the demonstrators' right to march. Cloud contradicted him, citing the injunction. But when King asked to pray, Cloud consented. "You can have your prayer and return to your church if you so desire," he said. Clergymen then led the prayers: Abernathy, then Methodist minister John Wesley Lord, then Rabbi Israel Dresner. After a round of "We Shall Overcome," Major Cloud—to everyone's amazement—withdrew his men, clearing the path ahead.[52]

This was the deal floated earlier that King had entertained but never explicitly accepted: *both sides* turning around to save face. King took a moment, as if to decide what to do. After a pregnant pause, he wheeled around and led his warriors back in the direction whence they had come.

What was going on? No one knew. Some marchers followed King dutifully. Others thanked God for sparing them violence. Others were confused, disbelieving, or angry. One cluster of SNCC workers belted out a sarcastic chorus of "Ain't Gonna Let Nobody Turn Me 'Round" as they trudged back to Sylvan Street.

At Brown Chapel, King insisted that reaching the point of Sunday's confrontation amounted to a symbolic victory. The crowd was skeptical. From the pews came hostile questions. One marcher asked King why he hadn't just staged a sit-in on the highway until the judge lifted the injunction. Forman piped up that the day's march was spared violence only because, unlike on Bloody Sunday, whites were among the marchers' ranks. That wasn't true; from the sit-ins to Freedom Summer, whites had often suffered violence when fighting alongside Blacks. Even so, a local Black woman rebuked Forman: Yes, perhaps the presence of whites had forestalled violence, she said—and if so, that was to be celebrated. "Don't let these white people feel we don't appreciate their coming," she said, winning applause. Forman, unappeased, would fume for years about King's "trickery." He labeled the day "Turnaround Tuesday."[53]

Lewis, typically, was more forgiving. He believed that under the principles of nonviolence retreating was an honorable course. He shared King's expectation that Judge Johnson would soon permit the Walk for Freedom. But King's behavior over Bloody Sunday and Turnaround Tuesday deepened the conflict between SCLC and SNCC. So did King's decision to run an ad for SCLC in Wednesday's *New York Times* with a picture of Lewis being beaten. "That just burned us up," Julian Bond said. "It was *our* chairman who was leading the march." Some SNCC members aired their grievances. When news stories hyped the rift between the organizations, Lewis tried to patch things up. He made sure that his reporter friends—Arlie Schardt of *Time*, Paul Good of the *Washington Post*, Don McKee of the Associated Press—quoted him, downplaying the split. "There have been normal disagreements in tactics, but no split," he told Schardt. "SCLC is not the enemy. George Wallace and segregation are the enemy."[54]

The clergy who had come to Alabama to march gave King the benefit of the doubt. They stuck around for the next attempt, whenever it might occur. Selma took on the unwonted feel of a tourist town, with newcomers prowling around for restaurants and lodgings. On Tuesday night, hours after the turnaround, three ministers were heading home from dinner when vigilantes brutally savaged them. "Here's how it feels to be a nigger down here!" one assailant yelled, swinging a club and knocking one of them, James Reeb, unconscious. The other ministers were also beaten up. Reeb was rushed to the hospital. Two days later he died.

His murder reignited protests. At the White House, a dozen students, having posed as tourists to gain entrance, plunked themselves down on the floor near the library for an hours-long sit-in. In Judge Frank Johnson's courtroom in Montgomery, Lewis testified about his beating. Then, remarkably, he made a quick trip to Harlem for a rally in support of Selma.

The accumulated pressure led President Johnson to accelerate the unveiling of his voting rights bill. The White House announced a speech to Congress on Monday, March 15. Lewis and King were invited to sit in the galleries, but that afternoon there was a memorial service for Reeb in Brown Chapel. Lewis and King stayed in Selma for the service. They would watch the address on TV.[55]

That night, King gathered with friends at the home of his friends Sullivan and Richie Jean Jackson. Andy Young, C. T. Vivian, and others crammed into the Jacksons' modest-sized living room. "Every seat was taken," Jean Jackson recalled, "and even the floor was full. I was sitting on the floor at Martin's feet." King occupied an armchair pulled close to the TV set.[56]

The living room fell silent when the president began speaking. Johnson framed his cause in grand historical terms, comparing the battles of Selma to those of Lexington and Concord and Appomattox, all turning points in "man's unending search for freedom." The right to vote could not be compromised. "It is not just Negroes, but really it is all of us who must overcome the crippling legacy of bigotry and injustice," Johnson said. "And we shall overcome."

Hearing an American president—a Southerner no less—invoke that proud, hopeful refrain, the Jacksons' guests let out a collective cheer. In his armchair, King was quiet. A tear rolled down his cheek.*

Lewis was watching elsewhere. He felt a shudder of emotion. "I knew that the battle was over," he said. "I knew that we had won."[57]

Johnson closed in the same vein. He praised the Selma protesters. Although he spoke generically of "the Negro," his language could have been drafted with Lewis in mind. "His actions and protests," LBJ said somberly, "his courage to risk safety and even to risk his life, have awakened the conscience of this nation." Johnson pledged to introduce a voting rights bill to Congress. To those around him, King said, "We'll write it for him."[58]

Lewis called the speech "historic, eloquent, and more than inspiring"— indeed, he thought, it was one of the most moving he had ever heard.[59]

More good news came Wednesday. In his courtroom, Frank Johnson had watched television footage of Lewis's beating, which NAACP attorney Jack Greenberg had subpoenaed from CBS. "He literally pulled up his robe and just shook his head," Lewis said, "and he was disgusted when he saw it. He came back out and said, in effect, that the relief that we had been asking for was granted. Just like that." The Walk for Freedom could proceed.

"The right to assemble, demonstrate, and march peaceably along the highways and streets in an orderly manner," Johnson wrote in his opinion, "should be commensurate with the enormity of the wrongs that are being protested and petitioned against. In this case, the wrongs are enormous." Lewis's faith in the judge was vindicated. "It seems safe to say," Lewis later

---

* Lewis's memory worsened over time. In a 1973 interview he said, "I understand that Dr. King, who was also in Selma at the time, shed tears when Lyndon Johnson said, 'We shall overcome.'" In 1979, when Lewis recalled watching the speech, he said, "I am sure that I was in Selma," but he didn't place himself at the Jacksons' house and he again implied that he wasn't with King, saying, "I understood that Dr. King cried." As early as 1983, however, in an interview with William Beardslee, as well as in a 1995 interview with David Halberstam and in his memoir, he describes himself as having been "sitting with King" at the Jacksons'. In one interview, he said incorrectly that they were all at the home of Selma activist Marie Foster.

wrote, "that the wrongs of that time were matched blow for blow by the rights upheld by Judge Frank Johnson."[60]

Johnson asked SCLC to provide a plan for their march. Lewis joined Hosea Williams, Andrew Young, and Jack Greenberg at the Albert Pick Motel in Montgomery to draft one. They chose Sunday, March 21—four days away—for the starting date.

SNCC was now committed to the march. Yet some members still grumbled. Especially obstreperous was Forman, whom King suspected of trying to sabotage the campaign. Privately, Bayard Rustin was urging King to cut ties with SNCC once the march was over. "The SNCC leadership tried very hard to undermine the march," said Metz Rollins, the NCLC minister who was among the many clergymen who heeded King's call to come to Selma. "But John's affection and John's feeling for Dr. King remained staunch."

Amid this strife, Lewis and Ivanhoe Donaldson, who was overseeing the march's logistics for SNCC, labored to keep the peace. "We joined because it was our only option," Cleve Sellers said. "We still believed, however, that the march was a gigantic waste: in terms of money, human resources, and human lives." Other SNCC members skipped the event—notably Silas Norman, who let it be known that he would be spending Sunday shellacking the floors of the organization's Selma offices.[61]

Scheduled for 10:00 a.m. on Sunday, the march got underway more than two hours later. The first row of marchers—its configuration the product of much haggling—featured King and Lewis, along with Coretta Scott King, Ralph and Juanita Abernathy, Hosea Williams, Andy Young, and Forman, who at least for now grasped the wisdom of burying the hatchet with King. Crowding the front, too, were newly arrived luminaries A. Philip Randolph, Ralph Bunche, Dick Gregory, NAACP attorney Constance Baker Motley, Rabbi Abraham Joshua Heschel of the Jewish Theological Seminary, and the eighty-two-year-old Cager Lee, grandfather of the slain Jimmie Lee Jackson. Many wore Hawaiian leis, sent in bulk by Reverend Abraham Akaka of Honolulu, as a symbol of *aloha*, or peace.

Retracing the route of their unfinished marches, they walked without fear, knowing that federalized National Guardsmen were there on the president's orders. As Lewis went over the Pettus Bridge—completing the crossing for the first time—he couldn't help noticing "the representatives of the Old South, Jim Clark and his posse, . . . the state troopers . . .

they just stood in silence. Because you had the full protection and the full power of the commander in chief of the United States Army behind you." No longer confined to the narrow sidewalk, Lewis and his compatriots spilled into the vehicular traffic lanes as they paraded over the river, down Route 80, and out of town. Military helicopters flew overhead. Guardsmen cased out bridges, stopped suspicious motorists, and pointed their guns into the trees when the marchers neared wooded areas.

A "festive humor" took hold among the marchers, the *New York Times* reported. It was, Lewis would long recall, "a fantastic feeling"—of elation, triumph, power. The weather was glorious, their spirits were high, and, he remembered, "there was a sense of victory in the air . . . almost like a movie."

Over the next five days, the protesters advanced from town to town, trekking seven miles Sunday, sixteen Monday, eleven Tuesday. That was the most grueling leg of the journey, as a cold rain pelted the determined marchers. Lewis's friends protected his injured head during the rain, covering him with an umbrella; at one point, King gently placed his green trapper's hat on the crown of his protégé. "I don't like getting wet," Lewis said, "but during the march from Selma to Montgomery . . . on that particular day, it was like it was part of the cause. . . . It renewed the spirit."[62]

Many pilgrims spent the night under tents in campsites, on land offered by patrons like hotelier A. G. Gaston. Tuesday evening was especially challenging, since the rainfall had turned their resting place into a muddy pit. Lewis, like many others, rode back to indoor quarters at the end of each day, rejoining the procession the next morning. "I won't lie," he later said. "I did walk the fifty miles, but I didn't stay in a tent. Not a single night. You know, I had suffered head injuries—that's true—but for some reason I wanted to go back and each night I went back and stayed in Selma."[63]

On Tuesday night, at the campsite, Lewis was interviewed by a reporter for a socialist newspaper. The joy he felt on hearing Lyndon Johnson's speech the week before was still palpable. "It's unbelievable," Lewis said. "I have been amazed by President Johnson's stand and believe it indicates that even Johnson will respond to public pressure. . . . Johnson made it clear that he would not permit a repetition of last Sunday's beatings. I think he has responded to the mandate given him in the presidential election."[64]

After another day of hiking, the pilgrims on Wednesday night reached the thirty-six-acre grounds of the City of St. Jude's campus, a Catholic school and hospital outside Montgomery. There they took in a star-studded slate of performances. Organized by Harry Belafonte, two dozen singers, comics, actors, and musicians—Mahalia Jackson and Nina Simone, Nipsey Russell and Nichols and May, Joan Baez and Leonard Bernstein—performed on a makeshift outdoor stage. The raucous program concluded around 2:00 a.m., when performers retired to rooms at Montgomery's Greystone Hotel and the exhausted marchers bedded down to rest for their final day.[65]

When Thursday dawned, sunshine and dry air greeted the crowd at St. Jude's. Thirty thousand strong, they joyfully began their final six miles. Before long they were streaming into Montgomery, past the Dexter Avenue Baptist Church where King had preached, toward the capitol. Lewis, according to Mark Suckle, was enjoying "being out in front, arm in arm, leading people, in a showman kind of way. . . . That's the kind of thing that John was best at."

"I felt like, I guess, a general," Lewis said, "maybe just a lieutenant . . . maybe just a plain foot soldier who had been involved in a great battle, a long battle. . . . We were on the edge of victory."[66]

Jubilation was in the air. "There was never a march like this one before," Lewis later said, "and there hasn't been one since." As the demonstrators swarmed through the city streets, local Black citizens cheered them on, while a few angry young white men jeered and flipped their middle fingers. No one was rattled. "It seemed like nothing could stop that surge of people coming into the heart of downtown Montgomery," Lewis said. "It seemed like the streets of Montgomery were too narrow. They were not wide enough to hold the people as we came through."[67]

Near the capitol, on a flatbed truck, the organizers had set up a podium. Lewis joined Abernathy, Shuttlesworth, Bevel, Rustin, Rosa Parks, and others in taking a turn at the microphone. King spoke last, delivering what Lewis called "one of the most important speeches of his life."

"How long will it take?" King asked rhetorically. ". . . Not long," he answered himself, quoting the abolitionist Theodore Parker, "because the arc of the moral universe is long but it bends toward justice."[68]

The voting rights drive was on the verge of triumph. But the forces of hate did not surrender easily. On Thursday night, Viola Liuzzo, a thirty-nine-year-old white Detroit woman, was driving along Route 80 with Leroy Moton, a Black SCLC worker, after ferrying marchers home to Selma. A carful of Klansmen, who had been tailing the interracial pair, pulled even with her Oldsmobile and shot her dead. Moton feigned death until the killers left the scene. They were arrested the next day. One man in the car, Gary Thomas Rowe Jr., was working as an FBI informant.[69]

Liuzzo joined Jimmie Lee Jackson and James Reeb as a martyr in the Selma struggle. Lewis was staying at the Ben Moore Hotel in Montgomery on Friday when he heard about her killing. He flew to Detroit for the funeral on Tuesday, joining King, Farmer, and Wilkins. None of them gave a eulogy. "It was a service where people sat in quiet and simple dignity." As the mourners filed out of Immaculate Heart of Mary Catholic Church, they somberly sang "We Shall Overcome."

Inconspicuously, John left his pew, glancing back before exiting. Not until years later would Liuzzo's family even know he had been there.[70]

Chapter Twelve

REVOLT AT
KINGSTON SPRINGS

■ ■

I n May 1965, the byline of John Robert Lewis appeared above an essay
in the *New York Herald Tribune*, the organ of moderate Republicanism.
At this point, a voting rights bill seemed destined to pass Congress, and activists were asking, as a headnote to Lewis's article put it, "what direction is
next for the civil rights movement."

Lewis offered an answer. "The movement," he began, "must become politically oriented." Recently, Bayard Rustin had published an article in *Commentary* titled "From Protest to Politics" that called for tackling deep-seated
racial and economic issues—inequalities in jobs, education, housing, and
health care—through political power. This power had to be won, Rustin argued, in concert with "the coalition that staged the March on Washington,
passed the Civil Rights Act, and laid the basis for the Johnson landslide—
Negroes, trade unionists, liberals, and religious groups." Lewis put forward
similar ideas.

Lewis's essay began by recounting some forgotten American history. He
cited an 1871 law called the Third Enforcement Act that established "federal
supervisory power over congressional elections." He also noted that it had
long been illegal to deprive citizens of their constitutional rights on account
of race. But these laws had gone unenforced. The main reason, Lewis argued, was that Blacks lacked political power. Economic disparities between
the races persisted for the same reason. Only the entry of African Americans into public office would force change. "The Negro must . . . remain

the conscience of both political parties." Lewis added that whites must wage this fight, too. "Only when all Americans see the relevance of these issues to their lives will meaningful political activities contribute to their own political well-being."[1]

Others in SNCC agreed about the need for Blacks to gain political power. But they were pursuing it in different ways. In Lowndes County, Alabama—situated between Selma and Montgomery—Stokely Carmichael, Bob Mants, and Judy Richardson were getting local Blacks registered to vote. In Mississippi, the Freedom Democratic Party launched a campaign to have Congress reject the state's regular House members—segregationists all—and instead seat Fannie Lou Hamer and other members of their organization.

The most dramatic SNCC bid for elective office was Julian Bond's campaign for the Georgia legislature. After a court ruling forced Georgia to redraw its districts, creating eight that were mainly Black, the state scheduled special elections for June. Bond declared for the Fulton County seat. Some in SNCC were unhappy, rejecting any cooperation with "the system." Others quarreled with Bond's choice to run as a Democrat. But Lewis was thrilled that his good friend might win office. "I felt," he said, "it was important that in a city like Atlanta, somebody who had been involved in the height of the student movement transfer some of this energy, some of the understanding, to the political arena. . . . I thought the Atlanta community needed Julian and also that his leadership would inspire other people." Lewis knocked on doors and visited barbershops and beauty shops on Bond's behalf. On May 5, Bond won his primary and then coasted to victory over his Republican opponent in the June 16 general election.[2]

Lewis thought that Bond's victory heralded change. Despite his belief in democratic decision-making, Lewis appreciated the importance of individual leadership, too. When colleagues griped about Martin Luther King's high-handedness, Lewis thought they failed to grasp the value of a heroic figure at the movement's helm. "We had to be strong Black men and women standing in leadership positions within the civil rights movement, for several reasons," Lewis said. "One was to give Black people symbols, to develop Black heroes, to develop some visible personalities who could verbalize the feelings and aspirations of Black people. . . . In any mass movement there is a need for a strong, visible symbol. You need somebody to personify, to be the essence, to embody the idea, the wholeness, the totality of it all." King was such a symbol. Lewis thought Bond might become one, too.

Lewis was also aware that he himself was now being called a "symbol" and a "hero." The encomiums left him with mixed feelings. "I had no desire as a person to become a symbol, to become the essence of a leader," he said. "I didn't think about leadership, about becoming a symbol, a hero. But the American media, the American press, the American community—you become a hero. I'm not saying that I was a hero, but on several occasions I was described as a hero. It made me feel good, but I did not see myself as a hero . . . and I may blush when someone says it. But my primary concern at that time was to accomplish a goal."[3]

One major goal was achieved when, on August 4, the Senate passed the landmark Voting Rights Act, 79–18. The law outlawed literacy tests and made it hard for states to impose poll taxes in state and local elections. White House aide Larry O'Brien invited Lewis to Washington for the signing and a presidential parley beforehand. Lewis brought along Cleve Sellers and Marion Barry, the latter of whom was now serving as SNCC's man in Washington.

On the morning of August 6, the three men and James Farmer met with LBJ and Hugh Robinson, a Black military attaché, in a small study near the Oval Office. The guests squeezed onto a sofa against the wall, while the rangy Johnson leaned in close—an elbow on each knee, his fingers jutting outward—creating an intimacy Lewis hadn't experienced on other presidential visits. Always animated, Johnson would pull back as if to lie down on his side, Lewis recalled—"leaning over in an awkward position, just leaning over," with his gangly legs bent and his feet perched on an ottoman.[4]

As usual, Johnson dominated. "He was very happy" about the bill, Lewis said, "and so were we." Johnson explained that after it became law, "we've got to go out and get all these people registered." He made clear "that he was really going to need the votes in the upcoming election. . . . You couldn't say much, but I recall saying, 'You're going to need a lot of help, Mr. President, in seeing that people get out and get registered, and in seeing that the law is enforced.' And we had a chat about making the law real."[5]

LBJ also flashed his incorrigible crudeness. "Now, John," he said, "you've got to go back and get all those folks registered. You've got to go back and get those boys by the balls," he said. "Just like a bull gets on top of a cow. You've got to get 'em by the balls and you've got to squeeze, squeeze 'em till they hurt." Though unprepared for the vulgarity, Lewis found himself charmed by the president he had been denouncing just a few months ago at Selma. "I was impressed with him," Lewis confessed. "I got a sense of commitment, a deep sense of commitment from him, a feeling that he understood the problems of Black people, of poor people, the downtrodden, and he was very, very sympathetic toward the movement."[6]

In the afternoon, Lewis joined a larger crowd of congressmen, senators, and civil rights leaders in the President's Room of the Capitol. LBJ used fistfuls of pens—Roy Wilkins guessed one hundred—to sign the bill, one stroke at a time, doling them out to the guests, Lewis included. "That was a fantastic thing," Lewis said. "We could see some of our dreams and hopes coming true." From SNCC's Washington office, Lewis called Atlanta with jubilation in his voice. He sent the president a thank-you note praising his "timely and wise leadership" and calling the day a "milestone in the progress of American democracy . . . every bit as momentous and significant as the Emancipation Proclamation or the 1954 Supreme Court decision." Within days, Attorney General Nicholas Katzenbach sent federal registrars to the South, including to Dallas County, Alabama, to ensure Black voters could get on the rolls.[7]

For all Lewis's optimism, he knew that the law would work only if it were aggressively enforced. SNCC had to make sure it was. "We shouted 'Hallelujah,'" Lewis said after the law passed, but they also "urged people to intensify their efforts to get people registered. We had Freedom Days where people went to courthouses all across the South."[8]

Things didn't go smoothly everywhere. On August 8, Lewis was in Americus, Georgia, where two summers before Don Harris and others had been roughed up and jailed. Lewis was now there to protest the use of separate white and Black lines for voter registration—a brazen violation of the new law. While in Americus, Lewis and others also tried to integrate two all-white churches (which were exempted from the Civil Rights Act). He led his group in a kneel-in, only to be arrested for trespassing. It was, said the *Atlanta Constitution*, Lewis's thirty-eighth arrest.[9]

But there were also victories. In Pike County, Alabama, two residents went to their county courthouse that month and put their names on the rolls. For the first time in their lives, Eddie and Willie Mae Lewis were registered voters.[10]

As hope was taking hold in the South, frustration and despair were rising in Black urban communities nationwide. The previous summer had seen the Harlem riots, and, days after the Voting Rights Act passed, an even worse explosion of violence rocked the Watts neighborhood of Los Angeles. Following a Black motorist's altercation with police officers, the area was consumed by six days of destruction, leaving thirty-four people dead. Other cities, too—Chicago, Cleveland, Jacksonville—suffered violent uprisings.

Lewis sympathized with the rioters' grievances. When asked about the uprising's causes, he cited "police brutality, economic and social discrimination, and the failure and refusal of men with power to meet the needs of an oppressed people." But he stoutly refused to excuse the violence. Temperamentally, he recoiled at the undisciplined, wanton nature of the outbursts; intellectually, he considered it lacking in strategic purpose. "It is a mistake," he said years later, "for people to consider disorganized action, mayhem, and attacks on other people and property as an extension of any kind of movement."[11]

Watts revealed how much the fight for Black equality was about to change. The passage of the Civil Rights and Voting Rights Acts meant, as Rustin wrote, that "the legal foundations of racism in America were destroyed." James Bevel declared, "There is no more civil rights movement. President Johnson signed it out of existence when he signed the voting rights bill." These claims may have sounded hyperbolic, but they pointed to a historic transformation. Unlike Jim Crow and disenfranchisement, the economic problems facing African Americans weren't confined to the South and brooked no simple solutions. In that sense, Lewis mused, "something died at Selma. . . . From 1955 to 1965 there was a particular period, and it was concentrated primarily in the Deep South." Now, he believed, "it's a new movement, and the emphasis has shifted primarily from the South to the North."

What was needed, Lewis contended, was "the will on the part of the government, of the administration that happens to be in power, to spend more energy and resources, more money, on the problems at home . . . around school and around employment." He cautioned against the triumphalism he heard in Rustin's and Bevel's assessments. "It may appear," he wrote to the SNCC staff, that "the struggle . . . is over and there is 'nothing left to do.'" But the people taking that position, he gibed, "are a little misinformed."[12]

On this point, LBJ agreed with Lewis. Even before Watts, in a June speech at Howard University, the president had outlined an ambitious agenda for Black Americans. "You do not take a person who for years has been hobbled by chains and liberate him, bring him up to the starting line of a race and then say, 'You are free to compete with all the others,'" Johnson said, calling for a battery of social programs to ensure "not just equality as a right and a theory but equality as a fact and equality as a result." He announced a White House Conference on Civil Rights for the following spring, with a preliminary symposium to be held in November.[13]

Lewis and Marion Barry came to the November meetings. So did two hundred other policy experts, civil rights leaders, academics, and activists. Held at the Washington Hilton north of Dupont Circle, the panels addressed a panoply of socioeconomic issues facing the Black community. Much discussion focused on an opening-night call by A. Philip Randolph, the conference's honorary chairman, for a $100 billion "Freedom Budget." Debated, too, was the recent report by Labor Department official Daniel Patrick Moynihan (who had since decamped for academia) that sought to explain the plight of inner-city African Americans as related to the high proportion of Black families headed by single mothers.

Lewis—who, according to one account, "spent more time lobbying than conferring"—participated in several sessions, including one on voting. He argued that the government wasn't doing enough to enforce the Voting Rights Act, noting that federal registrars still hadn't been sent, for example, to Georgia or North Carolina. SNCC and other private civil rights groups, he added, shouldn't be burdened with mounting costly enrollment drives. "In a sense the federal government should be doing for civil rights what the civil rights organizations are doing," Lewis said at the conference. "The civil rights organizations do not have the money and the resources. . . . The government has money and the resources."

Katzenbach half-heartedly defended his department. He could only dispatch registrars where state officials were derelict, he said. And the federal government could not launch voter drives. But he added that if he were in Lewis's shoes, "I would be kicking the hell out of the Attorney General."

Lewis replied with a friendly warning that Black people were beginning to doubt whether "the Justice Department at this time is prepared to protect the right of the people to register and vote."[14]

The November conference drew mostly sour reviews. Coverage emphasized the participants' failure to coalesce around any agenda. Conflict had overwhelmed consensus. With two SNCC colleagues, Lewis set down his thoughts in a letter sent both to Randolph and to the White House. He opened in an adversarial tenor, asserting that the spring White House conference would be "meaningless" unless yoked to purposeful action. Before the spring conference got underway, he argued, the administration must aggressively enforce Title VI of the Civil Rights Act and the Voting Rights Act.[15]

After this opening salvo, however, Lewis struck a more agreeable tone. Over five pages the letter proposed constructive recommendations about format, participants, and procedure. It called for a more open, diverse, and wide-ranging conference—less academic in character and more inclusive of "civil rights activists, community organizers, poor people, and Negroes." SNCC, Lewis and his colleagues made clear, was still open to participating in the spring event.[16]

The rocky launch of the White House conference hinted at the obstacles the Johnson White House—and America—would face in uniting behind an agenda for Black America. SNCC was also struggling in the new climate to identify its goals and projects. Internal divisions persisted. SNCC's financial situation, moreover, had become "critical and serious," Lewis told the staff, with debt piling up. The young staff was impatient or burned-out. Lewis himself was exhausted. But there emerged, too, a new problem for SNCC, and for the freedom struggle broadly: the war in Vietnam.

Until 1965, James Forman wrote, "most of us—including myself—had considered the war not irrelevant but simply remote." Early in the year, however, LBJ had buttressed the American troop presence in Southeast Asia. Activists, including in SNCC, had begun confronting the issue. Lewis, who years before had registered as a conscientious objector to military service, spoke out against America's escalating involvement. He signed anti-war statements and proposed leaves of absence for SNCC staff wanting to do anti-war work. He told the *New York Times* in August 1965 that SNCC believed that "the issues of freedom in the South and freedom in the world are inextricably entwined."[17]

Yet into the fall some old hands at SNCC counseled against taking a formal anti-war stand. Doing so, they argued, would hurt fundraising, backfire politically, and divert energies from civil rights work. Only at its November 1965 executive committee meeting, where Lewis pushed for an anti-war statement, did SNCC decide to issue one. Even then, the process of drafting, circulating, and revising it stretched into the new year.[18]

Lewis unveiled SNCC's declaration to a roomful of reporters at SNCC's Atlanta headquarters—now located at 360 Nelson Street SW, a mile from its old digs—at 1:30 p.m., on Thursday, January 6, 1966. The statement pulled no punches. Days earlier, a white man had shot and killed Sammy Younge, a Tuskegee Institute student working with SNCC. The murder directed attention anew to the persistence of white supremacist violence in the South. Lewis's remarks drew parallels between Younge's murder and the killing of Vietnamese. He also implied that he supported draft evasion, though he hedged his words. "We are in sympathy with and support the men in this country who are unwilling to respond to a military draft which would compel them to contribute their lives to United States aggression in Vietnam in the name of the 'freedom' we find so false in this country," Lewis said. He proposed a creative solution: "We believe that work in the civil rights movement and other human relations organizations is a valid alternative to the draft. We urge all Americans to seek this alternative, knowing full well that it may cost them their lives—as painfully as in Vietnam."[19]

As he read the statement to the press, Lewis was struck by the "stunned looks on their faces." Fielding hostile questions, he clarified that neither he nor SNCC was endorsing draft dodging. Rather, he said, he wanted the government to consider work in the Peace Corps or the civil rights movement as valid alternatives to combat service. Lewis added that he himself was not a draft dodger but a conscientious objector, legally permitted to avoid service owing to his religious beliefs. Everyone had to choose what course to follow, he said, based on "the individual's conscience."[20]

Lewis's press conference was rough going, but things went even worse for Bond. He was in a meeting during Lewis's press conference, and when he got back to his office a pile of messages awaited. The first person he spoke to was Ed Spivia of WGST radio, who asked Bond if he agreed with Lewis's statements. "I concur fully," Bond said. He added that while he himself wouldn't do so, "I would admire the courage of anyone who burns his draft card." As soon as Bond's statement got around, colleagues in the Georgia statehouse began talking of denying him his seat when legislators were sworn in for the new term.

The brouhaha exploded. On returning to Atlanta from a speech in Virginia, Lewis glimpsed a copy of the *Atlanta Journal* at an airport newsstand with a headline blaring that Bond faced a "loyalty challenge." On Monday, he watched in anger from the statehouse gallery as the legislators jousted over whether to seat Bond. The frenzied session, which went on past midnight, included prolonged shouting, the playing of a tape of Bond's comments to Spivia, and even, wrote the *Atlanta Constitution*, "fisticuffs in the corridors."[21]

Late at night, the body voted 184–12 not to seat Bond. The young assemblyman fought back tears, but the vote hardly ended the fight. When the legislature reconvened on Tuesday, Lewis and Forman held an impromptu press conference on the capitol steps, where Lewis assailed "the fact that the 136th House District is unrepresented in the Georgia Legislature." Lewis also spoke to an audience of a thousand at Atlanta University. Soon, Martin Luther King entered the fray, and Bond's case became a cause célèbre, endorsed by liberal editorialists and celebrities like Harry Belafonte, Woody Allen, and Joseph Heller. A lawsuit set the case on a path toward adjudication at the Supreme Court.[22]

Lewis felt bad. It was his statement that had landed Bond in trouble. "For a long time I felt sort of guilty," Lewis said, "responsible that I had played a part in his ousting. I kept saying to myself, 'If only the statement had been read a week later, he would have been seated.'"[23]

As Bond was fighting for his Atlanta seat, electoral politics were also heating up in Lowndes County, Alabama. Stokely Carmichael had ripened into a skilled organizer. The lanky New Yorker, with his bright smile and bristling charisma, had emerged as an influential player in SNCC. Since August, he had been urging Black Lowndes County voters to boycott the Democratic Party, controlled as it was by unrepentant racists, and to run independent candidates. By late 1965, he and SNCC had helped birth a Lowndes County Freedom Organization to field candidates for office. Because the state Democratic Party used a logo proclaiming "white supremacy," featuring a white rooster, Carmichael chose a black panther, inspired by the mascot of Atlanta's Clark University, for the new party. At a January 1966 meeting with SCLC representatives, he unveiled the plan to much contention.[24]

Controversy centered on the gubernatorial race. Term limits barred George Wallace from serving again, but his wife, Lurleen, was running in a naked ploy to continue his reign. The best hope to stop them lay in winning the May Democratic primary. Attorney General Richmond Flowers, a progressive on race, was courting the newly empowered Black vote. Flowers sang "We Shall Overcome" at campaign events and pledged to appoint Black state officials. King and the Black establishment endorsed him.[25]

Lewis campaigned with King in Alabama. His support for Flowers pitted him against Carmichael and other SNCC hard-liners, who wanted nothing to do with the Democratic Party in Alabama. "After that," Carmichael said, "I wanted his blood." Lewis again found himself out of sync with many of his colleagues. Lewis still commanded respect and affection, but to some his conviction now looked like ossified thinking and his perseverance like arrogance. As important, the ideas he valued—nonviolence, interracial democracy, the beloved community—were falling from favor. Meanwhile, Carmichael was exciting young African Americans with his Black Panther Party, offering a vision for Black political success that wasn't reliant on white support.

In early May, Lurleen Wallace won her primary. Although the Alabama Black electorate had doubled in size over the last year, few whites were willing to entertain even modest change. Yet Lewis remained hopeful. "I think in the long run in the South we are going to have more of an integrated community than we have in the North," he told a pair of interviewers. "Because of the increase in Negro registration, the whole political structure, just because of mere numbers, is going to become interracial."[26]

Lewis continued traveling, speaking, fundraising, and protesting through the early months of 1966. In February, he found himself red-baited again, when a North Carolina college, in accordance with a 1963 state ban, demanded that Lewis "prove" that he wasn't a Communist before letting him give a scheduled speech. At his January press conference, Lewis had stubbornly refused to deny any Communist affiliation (even though he had done so in the past), as if he no longer wished to dignify such scurrilous questions. Naively, he had also spoken to the National Council of American-Soviet Friendship, a Communist front group. Those statements together rekindled attacks from the right that SNCC was under Communist sway. But Lewis stood his ground, the college relented, and he delivered his speech. He took the occasion to denounce the state's speaker ban and extol freedom of expression.[27]

March found Lewis, along with Marion Barry, back at the White House, in anticipation of the June civil rights conference. Presidential aides considered him easier to work with than most of his colleagues. But Lewis left the March meeting with the president irritated. LBJ had wanted to talk only about the midterm elections, not about his agenda for African Americans. "He kept saying, 'I need your help, you have to help me,'" Lewis said. "It was embarrassing."[28]

Lewis's activities also took on an international cast. In April, he accepted a pair of invitations to Europe. One came from the War Resisters' International, a leftist peace group, to its triennial conference, on the theme of "Non-Violence and Politics," at La Domus Pacis, a villa near the Vatican. Accompanied by his SNCC friend Stanley Wise, Lewis arrived in Rome during Holy Week. Some 120 participants from nineteen countries attended, he recalled, listening to "some of the great thinkers and scholars who had studied peace and nonviolence." Discussion centered on Vietnam. "It was really gratifying to me and very educational." In his remarks, Lewis gave no hint of SNCC's diminishing interest in King, Gandhi, and nonviolence; he touted, according to one account, "the nonviolent revolution SNCC was carrying out in the Deep South." One night during the conference, near an arch in the Aurelian Walls, as rain fell, Lewis led a raggedy, joyfully wet band of 150 conference-goers in singing "We Shall Overcome."[29]

Lewis and Stanley Wise went to see the pope at the Vatican. Lewis was dazzled by the beauty of St. Peter's—"the buildings, the statues, the works of art." Having always loved the pageantry of the Catholic Church, he said, he "felt at home and really at ease."

The night of April 8, Good Friday, Lewis and Wise dined on Via degli Annibaldi near the Colosseum—one of many nights full of "a lot of good wine, good Italian food," Lewis said. Joining them were Paul Good of the *Washington Post*, who had followed Lewis's career since Nashville, and journalists Thomas Powers and Robert Kaiser and their wives. At dinner, they debated Vietnam. Some people were resolutely against the war and others "not there yet," Powers said. Lewis mostly listened.[30]

When talk turned to SNCC, Wise told their companions that Lewis was "being squeezed out of the group." Differences between Lewis and other members were growing: over interracial cooperation, nonviolence, working with King and with the White House, and more. Fundamentally, Lewis saw the movement as King and Lawson had, primarily as a "moral crusade," whereas many of his colleagues regarded it as a political struggle, over power. Lewis was even considering stepping down as chair. Paul Good questioned Lewis. "John," he said, "you've devoted your life to nonviolent struggle for political rights and have gotten your head beaten in for your efforts, over and over again. How do you keep going? What makes you think anything might ever change?"

"Paul," Lewis replied, "you can't let them take away your faith and belief that it will make a difference." Powers, who was meeting Lewis for the first time, was struck by his "rock-like strength in sticking to what he thought mattered."[31]

After dinner, Good recorded, in a lengthy unpublished draft of a profile, "Lewis and Wise stood with thousands outside the floodlit walls of the Colosseum while Pope Paul, carrying a wooden cross, said the stations of the cross over ground Roman legionnaires have trod. The Pope spoke of how all Christians should 'shoulder their own crosses.'"

"That's just what I mean, Stanley," Lewis said to Wise. "You have to carry the cross in the nonviolent spirit. It's the only way."

"We've been carrying that cross long enough, John," Wise replied.[32]

Lewis was aware of the changes underfoot at SNCC. "I said this in Rome in April 1966: 'I may very possibly be replaced in the future. We are having a meeting in May and if most people in SNCC decide to end the nonviolence, then that's the way it will be. I wouldn't want to see it happen. . . . But what else can you try to live by?'" It was then, he later said, that he began "thinking of leaving the movement"—as hard as that would be "with all the years put in, all the time and energy."[33]

After Rome, Lewis continued to Norway, Sweden, Denmark, England, and France. His Africa journey had taught him the pleasures of travel and meeting people from foreign cultures, and he took pleasure in sizing up each of his stops. The rain in London and the "flat" food "without any taste" disappointed him, he said, but he had fun speaking to an Afro-Caribbean group called the Cards and sampling chicken and lamb curry. In Paris, he spoke to a "Friends of SNCC" group, as he had in 1964, and to students at a U.S. Information Agency center. An especially warm welcome came in Stavanger, Norway, he said, where "they treated me like a king. They brought gifts. A guy brought me a sweater." In Copenhagen, he joined with hundreds of students in a big debate in a beer hall. Everywhere, he spoke to the media.[34]

As in 1964, Lewis's absence gave rise to scheming and skulduggery back home. While abroad, he received a letter from a friend "saying there was turmoil and chaos in SNCC and that I should get back as soon as possible because of the things that were happening." A clique in Atlanta was embracing Black separatism and now "wanted to exclude all white people from the meetings, wanted all white people off the projects." Lewis headed home with foreboding.[35]

Arriving in early May, he learned that Carmichael planned to challenge him for the chairmanship. Forman—who suffered from bleeding ulcers and a heart ailment—was stepping down as executive secretary. Forman urged Lewis to step down as well. "I suggested we both give up our titles," Forman recounted, "and to give some of the younger staff members a chance to acquire the experience." Lewis had considered moving on, but he now realized he wanted to fight SNCC's drift toward separatism and Black nationalism. SNCC would have its first true contested race for chairman.[36]

SNCC's May meeting opened on a warm, sunny Sunday, at a church-based retreat center called Bethany Hills in the rustic town of Kingston Springs, Tennessee. In attendance were 130 members. For a week, they bunked in spare dormitories and took meals in an airy mess hall, a simple longhouse with pine walls and floors. Upstairs was a spacious meeting room with wood paneling and big windows looking out onto the surrounding woodlands. "It was a typical staff meeting in many ways," Lewis said. "People singing and preaching, having a lot of fun, telling a lot of jokes and lies and sharing war stories and some of their accomplishments and some of their defeats. It was a reunion for some people who hadn't seen each other for some time." They played volleyball, swam in the lake, and took strolls in the woods.[37]

Yet the week also saw its share of discord. People argued about Vietnam, electoral politics, finances, organization, and agendas. Group exercises subjected members to labored introspection; in one drill, everyone volunteered mistaken "assumptions" they had made. Lewis volunteered: "We assumed we have a monopoly on truth and that we are per se the best organizers."

Unresolved issues from SNCC's earliest days resurfaced, including over nonviolence. Matthew Jones asked sarcastically if SNCC should make room for "violent personnel" interested in a "liberation front." Someone else said, more sincerely, that they should drop the word "nonviolent" from their name. Others questioned whether they should still pursue what Lewis called "redemptive suffering" or whether his Christian ideas were passé. Still others looked to the future. Lewis pushed the idea of expanding SNCC's international footprint, talking up planned trips to the Soviet Union, the Dominican Republic, Israel, and Japan.[38]

The most fraught debates centered on the role of whites in SNCC. Especially since Freedom Summer, the group's racial makeup had engendered painful discussions. The Atlanta faction's turn toward explicit separatism heightened the tension. Many Blacks warmed to the idea that they should more actively embrace Blackness as a political identity to guide their work. Forman shared a position paper about the burgeoning enthusiasm for Black nationalism, seeking to reassess what positions and functions whites should perform within SNCC. Some suggested minimizing or eliminating altogether the participation of whites.

Lewis insisted that SNCC remain open to all. His formative experiences in Nashville had convinced him that Blacks and whites had to fight for equality together. That principle was fundamental to SNCC's character. The group's logo featured a Black hand clasping a white hand; its anthem, "We Shall Overcome," included the line "Black and white together." "Some of us felt," Lewis recalled, "that the only real and true integration that existed in American society was within the civil rights movement itself." Besides, Lewis considered the group a family, its white members as much as its Black members. Philosophically, he couldn't abide excluding anyone on the basis of race.[39]

A compromise emerged. Whites would remain in SNCC but were encouraged to work in white communities. This arrangement wasn't much different from SNCC's original vision. It could be understood as pragmatic, not separatist: putting staffers to work where they would be most effective.

Yet it still seemed to Lewis and other SNCC old-timers an inauspicious omen.

All the while, the matter of elections loomed. On Friday morning, Carmichael told Lewis of his plans. "John," he said, "I just want you to know that I'm running for the chairmanship." He said it simply, without hostility. Lewis was sportsmanlike. "I've heard," he said. "Congratulations. Let's have a good race."[40]

That evening, everyone gathered in a rough semicircle in the large meeting room. People stood, sat on the floor, or took chairs. Forman said that they would evaluate the candidates in a frank discussion before any vote. Discomfort was evident.[41]

As SNCC members discussed the candidates, many people voiced their admiration for Lewis. They said, he recalled, "that I had been a good chairperson and had been fair and that sort of thing." But as the conversation went on, it took a negative turn, and grievances tumbled forth: Lewis traveled to too many white campuses, some said. He sided with King over SNCC. He had supported Richmond Flowers. Some said Lewis's Christian orientation, as Jack Minnis, a white Marxist, later put it, wasn't "what the times required"—a sentiment Lewis took as an aspersion on his faith. Others judged Lewis too friendly to the establishment, pointing to his desire to take part in the White House conference. "Every time LBJ called," Fay Bellamy later remarked, "he'd rush his clothes to the cleaners and be on the next plane to Washington. You had to wonder where his head really was."[42]

For others, it was a matter of admiring what Carmichael had to offer. "Stokely had just come out of Lowndes," recalled Courtland Cox. "He had a lot more energy than John. He probably reflected the mood of the Black community and a lot of younger people in SNCC. And I think John held on to the ways that he knew and his views of how things should be."[43]

The tone became nasty and vulgar. Carmichael said SNCC needed a leader who could grab LBJ "by his balls and tell him to kiss our ass," adding, "And John Lewis won't say that to Lyndon Johnson." Said another person: "We need someone to tell Martin Luther King to go to hell." The contrast between Lewis's soft-spoken sweetness and Carmichael's confrontational bravado was pronounced. It was clear who was more likely to deal bluntly

with King and Johnson. "You must remember," Carmichael later said, "John
Lewis came off the SCLC executive committee to become chairman of
SNCC. So you can see his close ties to SCLC and his total refusal to fight
Dr. King on any issue." Lewis remembered that some people talked about
"who was the blackest." He was even criticized for how he spoke.[44]

For all the criticism of Lewis, however, most people in the room didn't
participate. "The people who spoke out were very loud, but the vast majority
simply listened," Lewis said. "It was hard to tell what they were thinking."[45]

Around midnight it came time to vote. Cleve Sellers was reelected as program secretary. Ruby Doris Smith Robinson, the unheralded mainspring of
the Atlanta office, replaced Forman as executive secretary. For chairman—in
a surprise to anyone listening to the fusillade of negativity leveled at Lewis—
the vote broke overwhelmingly in Lewis's favor, 60–22. He was reelected.[46]

The tension lifted. "Well," Carmichael said to Sellers, "sentiment won.
But it's OK. I'm not going to fight Lewis. This was useful. The issues have
been clarified." People went back to their cabins. They were leaving that
night or the next day and needed to pack or sleep. Others milled about.[47]

Before the room emptied out completely, however, Worth Long—who
had spent time in the Selma jail with Lewis, but had since quit the SNCC
staff—entered the room. When Long heard about Lewis's reelection, according to Sellers, "he hit the ceiling."

"John Lewis?" he spat. "How'd y'all do that? You can't do that." Minnis,
who had urged Carmichael to run in the first place, said that the time for objections had passed. "Sorry about that, boss white man," Long shot back. He
claimed that the procedures hadn't been followed. "I challenge this election!"[48]

Pandemonium ensued. No one knew if Long had standing to issue such
a challenge. Nor was the basis of his complaint clear, since SNCC had never
followed its bylaws. But no one had the presence of mind to consider the
legitimacy of the motion. "People were just completely baffled," said Lynn
Wells, a newer SNCC member. "A third of the people had just gone out—
gotten drunk or gone to sleep."[49]

Emotions now poured forth. Where the early evening had been impassioned but orderly, the late-night debate was rowdy and belligerent. "People just started jumping up and screaming and yelling how they didn't want
John," said Julius Lester, a newcomer to SNCC. To Lewis, the crowd had become a mob. At a certain point, he stopped rebutting the salvos that critics

launched from various corners of the room. Many of his friends and allies had retired for the night: Charles Sherrod and the Georgia group, Bill Hansen and the Arkansas project, friends from around Mississippi. His white allies remained silent, he noted, "immobilized from participating." His opponents sprinted off to the cabins to roust their sympathizers, but Lewis's friends seemed dumbstruck. Stanley Wise, though a close friend, believed a change of direction was needed and spoke against him. No one defended him.[50]

Minnis pulled Carmichael, Sellers, Ralph Featherstone, and some others into a huddle. His idea, Sellers later wrote, was that "we could get Stokely elected if we were shrewd enough." They hatched a plan for Carmichael to stay quiet while Sellers laid the groundwork for a new vote. Returning to the discussion, Sellers struck a fair-minded pose. "There seems to be some question in the minds of some as to whether or not the vote just taken was legitimate," he proposed. "For that reason, I submit my resignation so that another vote can be taken." Robinson did likewise. Forman, too, endorsed the plan.

Lewis refused to legitimize the ploy. Visibly unnerved, he rose and declared that he was the rightfully elected chairman. He fumed, in Sellers's recollection, that he wasn't going "to allow a group of troublemaking Northerners to take the office from him." Lewis cast the conflict as one of North versus South, arguing that SNCC should stay true to its Southern roots and orientation. According to Carmichael, Lewis implied that he would quit SNCC altogether if the revote went forward.[51]

In the past, Lewis's righteous streak had won him respect even from critics, who admired his principle and resolve. This time, his adamancy backfired. People thought he seemed to think he was entitled to be chairman in perpetuity.

Denunciations followed. Fay Bellamy, recalled Willie Ricks, "lit into John like a duck on a June bug." Lewis, she said, "was a nice enough person and all that. But in some important ways he didn't seem like he had a clue. . . . He may have represented SCLC. Or Dr. King. Maybe he was representing himself. But he sure wasn't representing us." Her tirade was the coup de grâce. "It was after that they decided to vote everything over again," Ricks said.[52]

It was near dawn. The crowd had long since thinned. A fraction of the original participants remained. They voted again. Carmichael was elected.

Lewis felt betrayed and hurt. With the sun coming up, he collapsed into bed, stunned and exhausted. At breakfast, he broke the news to friends who had missed the drama. "I woke up the next morning and they said the election had been held," said Marion Barry, who had slept through the whole thing, "and Stokely was the new chairman." Some friends of Lewis's said that if he left SNCC, they would leave, too. Others cried and "got very sick over it," he remembered. It was "painful, painful," said Jennifer Lawson. Jo-anne Grant wrote that she was "incensed" by the revote, which she called "a non-democratic ploy." Charlie Cobb, who had also gone to bed early, called it "unfair and suspicious." Staughton Lynd compared it to the way the Communist Party operated: "You wait till you have the room, then you call for a revote."[53]

Matthew Jones, who had been in the Nashville Student Movement in 1960, was still emotional when recounting the night forty years later: "People came in—I might as well put it on tape—and, *coup d'etat*, took his chairmanship away after he had won it. I sat there and watched him win the chairmanship one night and for people to come in later at night and have another election when everybody from the South had gone back home and took John's chairmanship away. Fraudulently. I will never forget when that happened. I was right there when it happened. I was hurt. John was our leader."[54]

Others defended the chicanery. Maria Varela thought it was "a bogus vote," but ultimately justified because "John was not in touch with what was going on at the ground level. I supported the new direction. I supported Stokely as chair." Another of Lewis's opponents said that Long, Sellers, and Carmichael had done "a bad thing," but added: "Ideologically, they were right. Everybody loved John. We voted for him out of loyalty. We had nothing against him. But his politics were zilch." It was hard to deny that Carmichael better reflected the thinking of young Black radicals or the political zeitgeist.[55]

Though wounded, Lewis tried, he said, to stay "cool and calm." He suspected, without firm foundation, that Forman had orchestrated the revolt. Acrimony between them had been worsening. Lewis found Forman to be obsessed with control and more than a little Machiavellian, while Forman was fed up with what he called Lewis's "growing conservatism." Lewis usually made it a practice to overcome his feelings of bitterness, but this time he found it hard to do so, given what seemed to him a clear-cut "miscarriage of justice and fair play." According to Varela, "John took it very personally. It is hard to take rejection, especially when you were there at the beginning." The trauma would stay with him for a long time. "The pain of that experience," he said years later, "is something I will never forget."[56]

For Lewis it was, he admitted, "a serious blow, a personal thing." But he also knew that the ordeal at Kingston Springs had consequences beyond his own fate. It would lead, he feared, to "the death of SNCC, of the movement. We had had a diverse group, reaching into all parts of the country. It had all been very new and hopeful." Though SNCC had been evolving for a long time, now it had chosen a starkly different course.[57]

Back in Atlanta, Lewis spoke to friends. He called Arlie Schardt, who covered the movement for *Time*. "Would you mind if I came over for a while?" Lewis asked. It was a beautiful spring night, with flowers blooming. Lewis found Schardt on his back porch on Rockhaven Circle, in Atlanta's Pine Hills neighborhood, where he was working on an article on his Smith-Corona typewriter, his reading light on. "We talked for two hours out on that screen porch," Schardt said. "I was commiserating. We talked about what it all meant. It was a melancholy, sad conversation."[58]

Lewis heard from others, too. "The crazies are taking over," Julian Bond told him.[59]

Over the next few days, Lewis dutifully attended the meetings of SNCC's executive committee—now renamed the central committee—where members followed up on the plans made at Kingston Springs. Despite Lewis's shellacking, affection for him remained. Many people hoped to keep him from leaving SNCC. They named him to lead a new bureau of "international relations"—the creation of which he had been recommending since his Africa trip. But the job was a minor one, the appointment a sop. Some intimations of SNCC's new direction became clear when the committee green-lighted a planned trip to the Soviet Union but not one to Israel, with Featherstone warning that they "must take into account exploitation of Negro by Jew." Committee minutes stipulated that "John Lewis and James Forman will be at the Atlanta press conference to avoid any interpretation of there being a split in the organization."[60]

Lewis tried to be a team player. The media recognized the changing of the guard as a huge story. Coverage focused on Carmichael's militancy, often relayed in sensationalized tones. Jack Nelson of the *Los Angeles Times* described him as "one of the more radical leaders of SNCC," while Bill Shipp of the *Atlanta Constitution* said the group would become "more oriented toward the philosophy of Black nationalism." King and other mainstream Black leaders voiced concern and criticism.[61]

Bond gamely played it all down. He told Gene Roberts of the *New York Times* that there was no "major bitterness." To Shipp he called the shake-up "just a normal organizational change." Of reports of a "schism," Lewis gave his own statement to the wire services, insisting, "Nothing could be further from the truth. The new officers of SNCC have my support and cooperation." These bits of spin fooled no one. To Roberts, who described Lewis as "obviously shaken by his defeat," the former chairman confessed: "I'm here today and I'll be here tomorrow, and that's all I can say."[62]

To mollify nervous SNCC supporters and donors, Lewis came to the Atlanta press conference on Monday, May 23. He and Forman sat far apart, on either end of a row of chairs, with the new leaders in the middle. Lewis read the statement he'd given to the Associated Press days before, denying any "schism," with all the sincerity of a hostage in a captivity video. Otherwise he stayed silent. When the *Washington Post's* Nicholas von Hoffman came by the SNCC offices later that day, he noted colleagues constantly popping in on Lewis, "checking up on what he might be saying to a visitor." "You're not supposed to be talking!" Lewis was reproached. "Don't say anything!" Lewis felt distrusted. "People were very suspicious of me while I was there," he said.[63]

Days later Lewis joined Carmichael at a Washington fundraiser at a predominantly Black club. He let the new chairman run the show but felt himself swallowing his dignity by standing by in tacit approval. In the meantime, Ruby Doris Smith Robinson announced, almost gloating, that SNCC would boycott the upcoming White House conference on civil rights. "We cannot be a party to attempts by the White House to use Black Americans to recoup a loss of prestige internationally," her statement said. Lewis put his signature to it. As the bickering raged, Bond announced he was taking a hiatus from SNCC to write a book, hinting that he might not return.[64]

Lewis tried to reconcile himself to his new role. To quit SNCC would seem petty. He wanted to abide by his ideals of charity and forgiveness.

In early June, James Meredith, who had integrated the University of Mississippi five years earlier, was shot and badly wounded on a solo protest walk across the state. The assault led Carmichael and others to head to Mississippi to take up Meredith's journey. King and Floyd McKissick, CORE's new head, joined as well. These were uneasy alliances. Some of the marchers' chants sounded radically different from the old freedom songs. "Jingle bells, shotgun shells, freedom all the way," went one. "Oh what fun it is to blast a trooper man away." When whites joined the march, King welcomed them. McKissick thanked them, while stipulating that they take a backseat role. Carmichael told them to go home.[65]

In Atlanta, a few days into the resumption of the march, Lewis overheard Sellers talking to Carmichael. It sounded to him as if his friends were scheming to trick King and the SCLC people into getting arrested so that Carmichael could take control of the march. "This was too much," Lewis said. "I could never be a party to anything that involved deviousness or deceit." That afternoon, at a central committee meeting, Lewis said he would be quitting the organization, though he agreed not to go public yet with the news.[66]

On June 17, at a Meredith March rally in Greenwood, during a call-and-response with the audience, Carmichael began using the phrase "Black Power." Hosea Williams, disliking the separatist connotations he heard in the chant, tried with SCLC colleagues to substitute the phrase "Freedom Now," but to no avail. The snippet of Carmichael's defiant refrain, captured by cameras, was broadcast widely, and instantly became the focus of controversy.[67]

A week later, in Canton, Lewis showed up, still trying to be a good soldier. When the time for speeches came, Lewis mounted a rickety soapbox and reminded the crowd—who had just endured brutal police treatment—of the virtues of nonviolence. "The whole man must say no nonviolently, his entire Christian spirit must say no to this evil and vicious spirit," he began. But, reported Paul Good, "even as he spoke, people sloshed away." This audience wasn't in the mood. "I felt like an uninvited guest," Lewis said. "It wasn't the same anymore. Something was missing."[68]

What people were talking about was "Black Power." At the time, and for decades afterward, the phrase polarized Americans. No phrase so widely used could possibly have only one correct meaning. It stood to reason that different audiences would attach different interpretations to it. Some African American audiences found it inspiring or thrilling—a frank recognition of their decision to seize control of their own destiny. Others argued that it was less radical than the media claimed, that it implied only what integrationists like Lewis and Rustin had long urged: the attainment of political power by Black Americans to ensure progress. And some interpreted the slogan as a direct renunciation of interracial collaboration. Especially when paired with the news of whites' newly circumscribed role in SNCC, or with Carmichael's other inflammatory gibes, "Black Power" could evoke separatism or hostility to whites. Carmichael didn't help matters by giving shifting explanations of what he meant, sometimes speaking contemptuously of whites as a class, but at other times asserting that a Black American simply wanted, as he told one interviewer, "to build something of his own, something that he builds with his own hands. And that is not anti-white."[69]

Moderate civil rights leaders renounced the phrase. Roy Wilkins and Whitney Young repudiated Carmichael. "No matter how endlessly they try to explain it," Wilkins said, "the term 'Black Power' means anti-white power." Rustin pointed out that making "Black Power" a guiding slogan "isolates the Negro community, and it encourages the growth of anti-Negro forces." Even King—who hoped to preserve a working relationship with SNCC—called it "an unfortunate choice of words." As he explained, "It gives the impression that we are calling for exclusive power and a kind of Black nationalism that does not involve a coalition with whites."[70]

Lewis felt no need to weigh in. He understood the phrase's layers of meaning and believed that, at least for Carmichael, "it had more to do with self-reliance than with Black supremacy, though that distinction was hard to see." Yet before the month was out, Lewis revealed his thinking to the media. Covering the Meredith March, Don McKee of the Associated Press questioned Lewis on his view of "Black Power." Lewis reaffirmed the importance of Blacks holding power, but added that the slogan, without a fully developed argument behind it, would scare people. "As an organization, we don't believe in sloganeering," he told McKee. "We believe in programs."

Writing up his interview for the next day's papers, McKee reported that Lewis "disagrees" with the slogan and that he "refused to use" it in his

Canton speech. More important, McKee reported for the first time that Lewis had submitted his resignation to SNCC. His article quoted Lewis: "I have spent almost six years working full time in SNCC. I feel there are other things I could do or would like to do. I will continue to be active in the civil rights movement. I hope to study and do some writing."

The next day's headlines stripped away the nuance. "Ex-Leader Quits, Hits 'Black Power' Slogan," said the *Washington Star*, one of many papers that ran McKee's story.[71]

Cut off from the organization that had been his community since he was twenty, Lewis toyed with writing a memoir, "putting down my involvement, my experiences in the movement." Evan Thomas, an editor at Harper & Row, expressed interest. On an undated piece of paper, Lewis started an outline, seemingly of the chapters of his life. It began:

1. Boy Preacher on the Farm
2. Days of Nashville
3. Ride for Freedom

For the fourth entry, he wrote "MA," but left the rest of the line blank, as if planning to return to it later. He repeated the same letters on the next line and continued:

5. March on Washington
6. Journey to Africa
7. Battle of Selma

Lines 8, 9, and 10 were left blank.[72]

Lewis would have to write the remaining chapters of his story. But he had little sense of what they would include. He found himself, at age twenty-six, with no job, unmarried, and unsure what to do with his life. The movement to which he had devoted his adult life was veering away from the ideals that had animated it. To remain in the struggle, he would have to find another path.

Chapter Thirteen

LOST IN NEW YORK

———— ▪▪ ————

Stokely Carmichael did a great deal to promote the values of Black pride and self-reliance and to articulate a systemic critique of racism in America. But his ascent at SNCC had devastating consequences for its future. Donors, mostly white, deluged the Atlanta offices with letters expressing pain and confusion and disgust. The tone ranged from polite ("I regret to say that . . . I no longer feel in tune with your cause") to nasty ("I support Many Liberal Causes—BUT Stokely Carmichael is a bigot. He is a liar"), from curt ("Please take me off your mailing list since I do not intend to contribute to your 'Black Power' philosophy") to racist ("Go to Hell, you Black Bastard—KKK"). Carmichael's responses dispensed with the customary tact. "Thank you for your letter," began one. "I would like to inform you that *Time* magazine has lied. . . ." Funds dried up.[1]

Carmichael tried to stanch the bleeding. Intellectually dexterous, he would explain thoughtfully in interviews and essays how everyone was misconstruing his words. But then, unable to resist a provocation, he would shock audiences anew. "When you talk of 'Black Power,' you talk of bringing this country to its knees," he said at a CORE conference that summer. "When you talk of 'Black Power,' you talk of building a movement that will smash everything Western civilization has created."

Lewis watched the train wreck from afar. "Stokely," he sighed, "likes to scare the hell out of the white folks."[2]

Press coverage didn't help. Journalists usually wrote about Black Power as a doctrine of separatism or violence or both. They played up the contrast between Lewis—not long ago cast as a truculent militant but now invariably deemed "soft-spoken," "likable," and "moderate"—and his flamboyant, hot-headed successor. All summer long stories detailed the turmoil.

Key SNCC personnel followed Lewis out the door: Bond, Moses, Sherrod, Hansen. "Within a matter of two to three months, a large number of people left," Lewis said. Freedom Singer Matthew Jones, a nonviolence devotee since Nashville, was plaintive. "I said, 'This can't be the SNCC I know,'" he recounted. "We believed in love and in all races of people." Kingston Springs, said Lewis's friend Frank Smith, who had voted for his reelection, "was the end of SNCC. I've always said that that was the end of SNCC."[3]

With so many resignations, field operations cratered. Within SNCC, fractiousness reigned. Even hard-liners grew impatient with Carmichael's pursuit of celebrity. Worse, he was unilaterally setting policy for SNCC—which, Ruby Doris Smith Robinson tersely noted, did not actually favor "the destruction of Western civilization." Things hit bottom in September, when an Atlanta policeman shot a Black man fleeing arrest for auto theft and Carmichael incited a crowd to "tear this place up." An hours-long riot ensued, with sixteen people hospitalized. Carmichael and other SNCC workers were indicted. More dire headlines followed.[4]

Still smarting from his ouster, Lewis indiscreetly shared his grievances with reporters. To Jack Nelson of the *Los Angeles Times*, he fretted that whites once sympathetic to the movement would now cast their lot with those frightened by the new rhetoric. "In the past the movement had been conveyed as well-disciplined and nonviolent," Lewis explained, "and it appealed to millions in this country and around the world. It was dignified, peaceful, and orderly, and it exposed the demagogues." But now, he worried, "elements in the movement" were themselves "using the methods of demagogues." Lewis blamed Forman, who he said "could cut off 'Black Power' like that," as he snapped his fingers.

A second stinging piece followed, in the *New York Times*, in which Gene Roberts claimed, with Lewis as a source, that the racial separatism that the breakaway Atlanta Project promoted had furnished the blueprint for Carmichael's Black Power agenda. This wasn't quite accurate; both developments, it would be fairer to say, stemmed from a rising impulse to assert Black autonomy. A rumor took hold that Lewis had leaked the Atlanta group's memo to Roberts, even though he hadn't.[5]

Lewis's interviews antagonized old colleagues. "The bad thing he did," said Julius Lester, "was when he went out to California and gave this interview saying that—well, he made like it was a vendetta of Forman's against him." Lewis explained to Elizabeth Sutherland, who ran the New York Friends of SNCC, that Roberts had already obtained the memo when he contacted Lewis. Lewis added, in a classic dodge, that he thought his comments to Nelson had been off the record. Sutherland passed Lewis's protestations on to Forman, who came to New York to forge a truce. Lewis agreed not to criticize SNCC publicly anymore, but the distrust remained. Lewis's comments, Lester said, "really created a bad feeling . . . a bitter feeling, which I think still exists, from people within the organization toward John." Sutherland drafted a point-by-point rebuttal of press errors, taking potshots at "former" SNCC friends in the media like *The New Republic* and Ted Poston of the *New York Post*, a Black reporter.[6]

In time, Lewis came to analyze his ouster with a margin of dispassion. "I was too pious," he said. "I was pious, not hip. I believed in an interracial democracy and I believed in the beloved community. And I was not modern, verbal. I was never used to the sniping that went on, and I couldn't snipe at Martin King and I wasn't in any of the cliques." Ironically, his actions in Selma—which would later become the cornerstone of his heroic reputation—hurt him within SNCC. "I had gone ahead and marched, and that worked against me."[7]

Lewis needed time to heal. He also needed a job. At twenty-six, he had never earned more than $40 a week. "I wasn't married," he recalled. "I just didn't have any outside life." A job offer came from Leslie Dunbar, a forty-four-year-old white activist who had run the Southern Regional Council. "Les Dunbar absolutely loved John," said Vernon Jordan, then a young Atlanta attorney who worked at the council. Dunbar would enlist Lewis to brief journalists, foreign leaders, funders, and others passing through town. In 1965 Dunbar had moved to New York to lead the Marshall Field Foundation and wanted Lewis as his associate director. "That was really the only offer that I received," Lewis said, "and that's what saved me." He interviewed with Dunbar in Washington on July 18, received and accepted the job almost immediately, and agreed to start August 1.[8]

Lewis took a long train ride from Atlanta to New York. He was now earning a tidy $10,000 annually, five times his SNCC salary. He found a walk-up studio for $110 a month, at 343 West Twenty-First Street, #4A, between Eighth and Ninth Avenues, in Chelsea. He hung one of Danny Lyon's photos on the wall—a black-and-white picture of segregated drinking fountains in Albany, Georgia—but left the place mostly unfurnished. A short subway ride took him to Times Square, where he would transfer to the crosstown shuttle and walk to his Park Avenue office. "The worst thing you can do to a country boy from the rural South," he later said, "is to drop him in Grand Central Station at rush hour."[9]

His work involved reviewing funding proposals and making recommendations to Dunbar and the board. Dunbar brought him to lunches and dinners with foundation heavyweights, "people who helped to broaden my own outlook and educate me to that whole world," Lewis said. He also sent Lewis back to the South to check out the projects that the foundation was bankrolling. And Lewis continued to speak on campuses, still talking up nonviolence and interracial democracy. "The movement must become more than just a movement of the concerns of the Negro people," he told a Yale audience that fall, maintaining that the "Black Power" philosophy didn't appeal to most African Americans. "I think it's tragic that in Mississippi the movement still only thinks in terms of the Negro's rights," he said, rather than that of all Americans.[10]

He spent most of his time at Field's offices. The boy from Troy cut an incongruous figure amid the high-powered suits of Midtown. Visitors noted how uncomfortable and lost he seemed away from the movement's front lines. "The poor guy was sitting behind a desk like it was the last place he wanted to be," said Staughton Lynd, who came by to petition for funding. "He looked as though someone had set him up with this job. He hadn't a clue what to do with that job." His work kept him in contact with various former colleagues. Once, Senator Robert Kennedy dropped by, seeking help with the Bedford-Stuyvesant Restoration Corporation, a public-private partnership for reviving the distressed Brooklyn community. Another time, Martin Luther King and Andrew Young showed up to discuss an SCLC project—which, Lewis said, "felt odd, to say the least."[11]

Lewis also wanted to complete his Fisk degree, which he had abandoned when he became SNCC chairman in 1963. Over the years he had intermittently kept in touch with his professors, assuring them that he was keeping up with his studies. (In one letter he noted he was in the middle of reading Sartre's *To Freedom Condemned*.) In 1966, Oswald Schrag, his department chair, informed Lewis that he had received an "unsatisfactory" grade on his comprehensive exams but said the requirement could be fulfilled through independent study. During the fall, Lewis took courses in political thought and political history at the New School in Manhattan and completed an independent thesis. He showed a draft to his Nashville friend Archie Allen, who had begun doing some political speechwriting, including for the governor of Kentucky. "The thesis was very solid, but it needed some editing," according to Allen. "Maybe I did the typing, too."[12]

At thirty-five pages, "The Impact of the Civil Rights Movement on Organized Religion in America" dealt with the two key institutions in Lewis's life. It rebutted the idea, popular among journalists, that the Black student movement was disconnected from or even hostile to the Black church. As Lewis explained, "I saw the civil rights movement as an extension of the church, . . . as a real attempt to make organized religion relevant." The churches, he maintained, were central not only to avowedly Christian groups like SCLC but also to superficially secular outfits like SNCC. "The people in SNCC who went to organize people in small towns and rural areas," Lewis said, "worked through local church groups, community organizations, and the minister. . . . The church was the only place where Negroes could come together." Later that year, in June, his thesis completed and accepted, Lewis would return to Nashville to don cap and gown and collect his degree with 229 other graduates.[13]

Despite finding these outlets for his intellectual energies in New York, Lewis remained profoundly lonely. He had a few friends in town, including his old roommate Mark Suckle, and occasionally he'd see one of his sisters, who lived on Long Island. He spoke and exchanged letters with Bond, who kept him apprised of doings in Atlanta. "The SNCCers, it seems to me, are getting harder and harder," Bond wrote. "I spent about an hour at the office today, and except for Stanley and Cleve, it was like talking to foreigners." Bond also ribbed Lewis for not writing more. "I don't know why I write you letters, since you obviously have developed paralysis in both your hands." Don Harris, attending Harvard Law School, would spend time with Lewis when visiting New York to see family. Archie Allen also visited. But mostly Lewis kept to himself. "I didn't go out that much. On weekends, when I was in New York, I would spend a great deal of time walking. Some days I would walk all the way from Central Park down to the Village, down Fifth Avenue or Avenue of the Americas." On Saturday nights, he would buy the early edition of the Sunday *New York Times* and a ninety-nine-cent six-pack of Carling Black Label or Rheingold and lie on the floor of his apartment, reading the paper from front to back.[14]

He occasionally saw his old companions from the summer of 1963, in the days before the March on Washington, many of whom clustered around the socialist magazine *Dissent*: Tom Kahn, Rachelle Horowitz, and especially Bayard Rustin. One day in 1967, Lewis sat for a long discussion with *Dissent* founder Irving Howe, one of America's leading intellectuals and essayists. Howe took notes for an article.

"Right now John Lewis is a homeless man," Howe began his account, which took up the dispersal of those he called "the first SNCC generation": "They work for the poverty program, they go to school, or they simply drift." He and Lewis discussed the history of the student movement, going back to Lawson's Nashville workshops, finally coming to Howe's question, "What went wrong and did it have to go wrong?" Howe described the scene:

This was the last question I asked Lewis after we had been talking for several hours, and as I asked it there occurred perhaps the most vivid event of the evening. About an hour earlier Bayard Rustin had dropped in at the apartment where we were talking. Rustin sat quietly, not saying a word. But as I asked this final question and Lewis clearly indicated that this indeed was the key problem but one about which he could not yet speak with assurance, Rustin asked permission to break in. Lewis quickly, humorously agreed: "Sure, tell us."

Rustin, more confident than Lewis in his big-picture analysis, had become an important mentor to the younger man. He told Howe that troubles like SNCC's were intrinsic to all youth movements. But, he added, the college-educated SNCC activists, in adopting their radically democratic, anti-leadership philosophy, had denied their own elite status within the Black population; they thus failed to reckon with differences in values that might separate them from the people they hoped to work with. As a result, they were "further and further cutting themselves off from the masses of Negro people." The revolutionary politics, the militant rhetoric, the remorselessly ideological analyses—these could never sustain a popular Black following of the sort King or Randolph had attained.

Lewis listened, Howe wrote, "with complete absorption." Howe asked him if he agreed.

"Lewis smiled," Howe continued, "and said, 'There's a lot to what the man says.'"[15]

As Lewis reflected on his future, SNCC continued to court controversy. At a November 1966 meeting at the upstate New York home of the tap dancer Clayton "Peg Leg" Bates, its diminished corps voted to do what they had wrongly been reported to have done at Kingston Springs: expel the remaining whites from the organization. The separatist faction triumphed with only nineteen votes—a fraction of the total attendees. The decision predictably brought about more negative press, fundraising challenges, internecine warfare, and grave doubts from Forman and other elders about SNCC's viability. Lewis followed SNCC's decline with sorrow and disgust.

Anti-war activism was siphoning away energies from the civil rights cause. Liberals and radicals alike were now judging the Vietnam War to be wrongheaded if not immoral and joining movements to hasten its end. Desperate to stop the war, activists seldom appreciated that every hour spent on an anti-war rally, petition, or campus chapter meant one less hour devoted to the Black freedom struggle. When James Bevel visited Lewis in his Chelsea apartment in 1967, he talked animatedly about Vietnam, explaining that he hoped to send an SCLC delegation to stage a sit-in at the Mekong Delta. However creative or noble such a gesture, it marked a stark departure from Bevel's unwavering focus on toppling the barriers for Black Americans at home.[16]

The conflict between the two causes was generally overlooked because the prevailing wisdom in left-liberal circles held that they were intertwined. The war promoted violence, diverted resources and sent young African Americans to die for freedoms they lacked at home. Lewis had expressed those ideas in 1966. And by early 1967, Martin Luther King—who had been criticizing the war for two years yet never prioritized the issue—finally chose to take a bold anti-war stand. He scheduled a speech for April 4 at Manhattan's Riverside Church, the storied home of social gospel pastors.

On a temperate Tuesday evening, Lewis rode the subway up from his Chelsea apartment to Morningside Heights, joining a crowd of three thousand at the august neo-Gothic church. He took a seat in the pews. Then, he said, "the religious leaders filed in: the priests, rabbis, nuns, ministers." They listened as King delivered a scathing denunciation of the war, rooted in his Christian and nonviolent beliefs, but also incorporating stark anti-imperialist rhetoric. While conceding "the ambiguity of the total situation" and taking care not to apologize for the National Liberation Front or the Communist forces, King nonetheless spoke in a radical idiom. He warned that, as "the shirtless and barefoot people of the land are rising up as never before" around the globe, the United States, once the font of "so much of the revolutionary spirit of the modern world," had become "the arch antirevolutionaries." For America, ending the war and getting right with the emerging nations of the world was a precondition for salvation.

Lewis was astonished by King's indictment. "I heard him speak so many times. I still think this is probably the best," he later said. Afterward, Lewis "just had the opportunity to say, 'Hello, Dr. King. Good to see you. Thank you for a wonderful address.'" Still, he found the experience exhilarating. "The climate, the environment, the setting"—the exquisite masonry of the church, the multicolored stained glass windows behind the pulpit, the eight-story-high ceiling—"it was so right. Seeing all of these unbelievable people . . . dressed in ministerial robes and people wearing collars. And I see the nuns, the rabbis, the bishops, the priests, the ministers, and just everyday people," he said. It underscored the moral core of King's message. "I came away from that evening inspired," believing that despite all the setbacks of the last year, Lewis said, "we were continuing to move in the direction we should."

Most Americans disagreed. Editorial opinion was critical, arguing both that King's rebuke was too harsh and that plunging into anti-war politics would diminish his influence in civil rights. But Lewis believed King had done the right thing. He was following his conscience.[17]

In August, Lewis, still on the SCLC board, traveled to Atlanta for the body's annual convention. With his room at the Regency Hotel covered, Lewis offered his second bed and floor space to younger friends, including Charles S. Johnson III, a grandson of the famed Fisk president, who had gotten to know Lewis while interning for Kenneth Clark in New York. In Atlanta, Lewis took Johnson to the SNCC offices, where he caught up with old colleagues. The officers elected at Kingston Springs in 1966 had not lasted long. H. "Rap" Brown had now replaced Carmichael as chairman, Stanley Wise assumed Forman's old job, and Ralph Featherstone was the new program secretary. Lewis was still dismayed by SNCC's politics, but he was capable of preserving friendships despite ideological differences.[18]

On the second night of the SCLC conference, August 15, Lewis invited Wise and Willie Ricks back to his hotel room for drinks and conversation. That morning, the *New York Times* had run a front-page story about a SNCC newsletter that, in the wake of the June Six-Day War between Israel and its Arab neighbors, had for the first time waded into the thorny Middle East conflict. The SNCC newsletter had adopted a strong anti-Israel stance—breaking with mainstream, pro-Israel Black leaders like King, Randolph, and Rustin. Worse, it had done so with inflammatory and classically anti-Semitic language and imagery, calling Israel an "illegal" state and trotting out hoary conspiracy theories about the Rothschilds. Crude cartoons by SNCC's Kofi Bailey showed Israeli general Moshe Dayan with dollar signs on his military epaulets. "It might have been an Arab propaganda sheet," reported *Newsweek*. Politicians, labor leaders, Jewish leaders, and many Black leaders—Randolph, Rustin, Belafonte, Whitney Young— denounced the newsletter. To contain the damage, Johnny Wilson, a new SNCC spokesman, stated, not quite truthfully, that the items were the sole handiwork of another newcomer, Ethel Minor, and didn't reflect the organization's positions. Yet in Atlanta, Featherstone, with Wise and Minor by his side, doubled down on the article's ugly claims, likening Israelis to Nazis and calling the Jewish state a "tool" of Western powers. Longtime Jewish SNCC supporters, such as folk singer Theo Bikel and writer Harry Golden, publicly disassociated themselves from the new regime.[19]

Such was the backdrop for a "hot and heavy" argument in Lewis's hotel room that Tuesday night. "John and Wise got into a real hot thing," Charles Johnson recounted. Lewis didn't share SNCC's new hostility to Israel, but his argument to Wise was chiefly pragmatic: "Why is it necessary to alienate people?" he wondered. As Johnson said, "He'd seen the newsletter and they had gotten that reaction on television and everywhere." Lewis stressed the importance of sustaining interracial coalitions. Wise pushed back that SNCC, in its new guise, was forging partnerships with international "revolutionary" movements. "SNCC is now in such a position," Wise said, that "we've formed such alliances outside the country that we don't need to woo white, Jewish liberals." In Johnson's recounting, "Wise was giving this theory of international revolution and John couldn't take it."

The evening ended amicably. But a few days later, by chance, the same players found themselves together again in New York. Johnson was hanging out at Lewis's Chelsea apartment when Wise and Featherstone, in town to raise money, called from the Port Authority bus station and "came on over to the place." Discussion veered back to the question of SNCC's politics, and soon, Johnson said, "John and Stanley were in the bathroom and shouting at each other for the rest of the night. We didn't see them again."[20]

By September, Lewis was ready to go back south. He looked into applying to law school at Columbia University but decided that one year in Manhattan was enough. "New York was too big. To me, it was just hopeless," he said. He was starting to think, too, about a career in politics. He told Mark Suckle that he envied Julian Bond's political success. (After the Supreme Court ruled in December 1966 that the Georgia legislature had to seat Bond, his career was back on track.) "John was thinking about [going] back down to the South," Suckle said, "and setting up a base of operation where he could finally get elected someplace. He felt very strongly that the South should be led by Black people and that he should be one of them."[21]

Lewis talked to Paul Anthony, who had replaced Les Dunbar at the Atlanta-based Southern Regional Council. Anthony discerned beneath Lewis's unprepossessing exterior an almost preternatural greatness. "John was once an extremely influential person in American life," he said in 1969, "and he is destined to be again."[22]

Anthony asked Lewis to run his group's Community Organization Project, which provided seed money to African Americans in poor communities to set up credit unions or cooperatives. The idea was to cultivate business opportunities and income while relieving their dependence on mercenary or racist lenders. Lewis was formally hired in October. At the council, Lewis had only a simple desk in a big open room in a nondescript downtown building—nothing like the chic grandeur of the Field Foundation's Manhattan offices. But Lewis had never been at ease on Park Avenue anyway, and compared to SNCC's dilapidated quarters, the council's offices were luxurious. His salary was $11,000 a year, amounting to a 10 percent raise.[23]

Lewis found an apartment—again on Gordon Road—and resumed his busy pace. After his years of chairing SNCC, crisscrossing the country to visit campuses, funders, projects, and protest sites, Lewis had become a creature of the road, able to travel lightly and on short notice, at ease before all audiences. At the Southern Regional Council, he partnered with a white civil rights veteran, Al Ulmer; they went to villages and farming communities, helping them to coordinate their efforts, pool their financial resources, and collaborate in selling their crops or goods. Even small contributions could do wonders. "We helped a group called the Freedom Quilting Bee," Lewis said. "I remember giving them a two-hundred-and-fifty-dollar contribution. These were Black women in the Black Belt of Alabama. In these communities [and] cooperatives emerged unbelievable leaders, small farmers, people having a sweet potato cooperative, raising chickens, hogs, goats, to try to improve their economic conditions."[24]

In southwest Georgia, Charles Sherrod—who had also quit SNCC—was doing similar work. He and Slater King, a stalwart of the 1961 Albany campaign, believed that Black poverty in the region was worsened by the retaliation by white landlords, who were known to kick Black sharecroppers off their land if they availed themselves of their right to vote. In 1968 Sherrod and King led a delegation to Israel to visit the kibbutzim and moshavim—the collective farms that had become vital to the young nation. Blacks in the

South, they saw, could similarly collectivize to buy farmland and achieve some independence from white landowners.

"Charles Sherrod discussed his trip to Israel, and it was fascinating, very moving," Lewis said. "At that time, I had never traveled to the state of Israel, but years later I had an opportunity to go and visit and see exactly what Charles was talking about. People latched on to it, this new wave of cooperative land ownership. Not just an individual but a community where people live as equal participants and happen to build a better way. It was in keeping with this idea of the beloved community."

In 1969, with Lewis among the advisers, Sherrod would raise funds to buy 5,700 acres outside Albany, the largest Black-owned tract of land in the country, and establish New Communities, Inc., the first community land trust. Black families owned and farmed it for many years thereafter.[25]

Not long into Lewis's tenure at the Southern Regional Council, Bernard LaFayette—back in Atlanta, working for SCLC—invited him to a New Year's Eve dinner, hosted by Xernona Clayton, a journalist and SCLC officer. At twenty-eight, Lewis had never allowed himself much time for romance; if Atlanta was too busy to hate, Lewis was too busy to date. "My work was my religion, my entire life," he said. But LaFayette told him about a young woman who would be at the party. "You'll like this young lady. She's very pretty. And," he added pointedly, "she can drive."

The guest was Lillian Miles, a librarian at Atlanta University. A Southern California native, one year older than Lewis, she was the daughter of a contractor and grew up middle-class. She had majored in English at Cal State Los Angeles and earned a master's degree in librarianship at USC. She had worked in Operation Crossroads Africa and in the Peace Corps in Nigeria. In Atlanta, she had been attending Ebenezer Baptist Church.

At Clayton's place, she and Lewis passed an enjoyable evening. Lillian was highly cultured, an avid reader, and a connoisseur of art. She was lively and intelligent and held her own in conversation. But Lewis didn't swoon. "I'm not sure I have that in me," he later wrote.

Still, he invited her to his birthday party in February. He prepared plates of chicken wings—the only recipe in his repertoire, which he had learned from his sister Ora. Lillian came wearing a green dress adorned with peace symbols. Lewis was pleased to see this indication of a political sensibility, only to discover that Lillian didn't know what the symbol meant. Yet she was far from apolitical. She held strong opinions about issues that mattered to Lewis and had closely followed his career. "I was attracted to him before I knew him," Lillian later said. "Every day and every night on the news was something about what was happening in the civil rights movement, so I felt like I knew him."

They began dating.[26]

Chapter Fourteen

RFK

— ∎ ∎ —

In March 1968, John Lewis was at a convention at the Mount Beulah Missionary Baptist Church near Jackson, Mississippi, with two old SNCC friends, Connie Curry and Joan Browning, when Robert Kennedy announced that he would challenge Lyndon Johnson for the Democratic presidential nomination. Watching the news in Curry's room at the Holiday Inn, the three friends danced and rejoiced. For months Kennedy had resisted calls to run, even as Johnson's standing among Democrats plummeted over his prosecution of the Vietnam War. But a strong second-place showing in the New Hampshire primary by another challenger, Minnesota senator Eugene McCarthy, had exposed Johnson's vulnerability, and Kennedy sensed an opportunity.[1]

McCarthy fans were furious. They saw Kennedy's decision as opportunistic—and, given his star power, a likely death blow to their candidate's hopes. LBJ, too, discerned a threat; by month's end, he would stun the nation by dropping out of the race. But for Americans upset with Johnson's war policy yet dubious about McCarthy's fitness to be president, Kennedy's candidacy was cause for celebration.

That camp included Lewis. Years before, during the Freedom Rides, he had considered the attorney general too fainthearted, insufficiently committed to bringing about the end of Jim Crow. But since their meeting during the 1963 Cambridge, Maryland, crisis—when Kennedy credited Lewis and the student movement with having "educated" him—Lewis had seen the man "grow and change," he later said. Kennedy came to believe in the civil rights struggle and in the broader fight against poverty and injustice. Lewis thought that "after being elected to the Senate and making those trips to Mississippi, to the Delta, going to the Southwest, and Appalachia, and speaking on college and university campuses," Kennedy "became a different human being." By 1968 Lewis concluded that Kennedy was uniquely poised to rescue America. "If there was one politician, one person I thought could hold the community together and continue to give Black people and poor people in the country a sense of hope," Lewis said, "that was Robert Kennedy."[2]

From the Holiday Inn, Lewis sent the campaign a telegram. "Senator Kennedy," it said, "if I can be of any help, let me know." Kennedy staffers had been trying to hire a well-known Black leader like Vernon Jordan, then running the Voter Education Project, to build support within the Black community. But the heavy hitters hesitated to cross Johnson. Instead, Kennedy was relying on Earl Graves, an African American Senate staffer, who was able and industrious but not especially well-connected. It was Graves who fielded Lewis's telegram and invited him to join the campaign. Lewis took a leave from his Southern Regional Council job.[3]

Black voters were key to Kennedy's hopes. Though college students and white professionals swooned over McCarthy, few African Americans did, and McCarthy pridefully refused to court them. On the other hand, Black voters retained great affection for JFK; families showcased photographs of the late president on their mantels. Early signs suggested that his younger brother might benefit from that esteem. "Black Voters Say They 'Dig' Kennedy," read a spring headline in the *Chicago Defender*.[4]

In 1968, before structural reforms would transform the nomination process, few states held presidential primaries. Governors or local sachems ruled their state delegations and decided whom to support. A presidential aspirant could prove his vote-getting prowess by besting the competition in a few hard-fought state contests and bring around the all-important bosses. Indiana's May 7 primary loomed as the first face-off between Kennedy and McCarthy. Lewis relocated to Indianapolis to get to work.

Kennedy aides scheduled a kickoff rally in a downtown Black neighborhood for Thursday, April 4, at 7:30 p.m. All day long, through the city's Black precincts, Lewis rode around in a green Ford Mustang with loudspeakers affixed to the roof, announcing the evening's event. Late in the afternoon, he arrived at a vacant lot in what campaign staffer Walter Sheridan called "the worst section of the Black community." The choice of venue was deliberate. "The mere fact that Kennedy will come into the heart of the ghetto," said local activist Charles Hendricks, "will pull the whole Black vote." The staff set up tables to register voters and paid neighborhood teens to tidy up the trash-strewn square. By early evening, a large crowd had formed—six hundred people, the newspapers said, but closer to a thousand, Lewis guessed. Most were African American.[5]

At about 6:30, Sheridan ran up to Lewis, visibly distraught. "John," he said, "we just got word that Dr. King has been shot in Memphis."

Lewis went into a state of shock, "obliterated," he said—"blown beyond any sensations whatsoever." Mayor Richard Lugar argued that Kennedy should cancel his speech. The staff debated whether to do so. Lewis was one of those who insisted the show must go on. "You can't have a crowd like this come and something like this happen, and send them home without anything at all," he said. "Kennedy has to speak, for his own sake and for the sake of these people."

Kennedy landed at the local airport. He contacted his advance team through a two-way radio in a staffer's car. He asked to speak to Lewis—the campaign staffer who was personally the closest to King. By now his death had been confirmed. "I'm sorry, John," Kennedy said to Lewis. "You've lost a leader." He paused and corrected himself. "*We've* lost a leader."[6]

There was no time to draft new remarks. In any case, Kennedy preferred to extemporize. "He didn't have a manuscript or a written statement," Lewis said. "He had a little piece of paper." By the time Kennedy approached the microphone, the night had turned cold and blustery. He asked an aide if the crowd had heard the news. Most had not. Kennedy would have to tell them.[7]

The candidate began in an even-keeled tone. "I have some very sad news for all of you," he said, "and I think sad news for all of our fellow citizens, and people who love peace all over the world. . . . And that is that Martin Luther King was shot and was killed tonight in Memphis."

Shrieks and gasps filled the air. Kennedy ran a hand through his mop of hair and waited a beat. He had to hold the crowd's attention, subdue their anger, channel their grief. By now he wasn't even glancing at his paper, just absently grasping it, furled up, in his hands. After praising King, he directed his remarks without any glimmer of awkwardness to "those of you who are

Black and are tempted to be filled with hatred and mistrust of the injustice of such an act, against all white people." He went on: ". . . I would only say that I can also feel in my own heart the same kind of feeling. I had a member of my family killed," before adding, a bit opaquely, "but he was killed by a white man."

From memory, Kennedy recited a line from Aeschylus: "In our sleep, pain which cannot forget falls drop by drop upon the heart until, in our own despair, against our will, comes wisdom through the awful grace of God." He concluded by reminding his audience that "the vast majority of white people and the vast majority of Black people in this country want to live together, want to improve the quality of our life, and want justice for all human beings that abide in our land."

Lewis thought it was a magnificent performance. "He did such a fine job, so sensitive, so fine," he said. "I saw his campaign as an extension of the movement, as another step after the March on Washington, after Selma. Martin's death made it all the more important for me to work in Bobby's campaign, and I was able to transfer my loyalty to him."[8]

Dozens of cities that night, and in the days following, experienced destructive rioting. Indianapolis was spared.

Back at the hotel, Kennedy flopped down on a bed and cried. He called Coretta Scott King and asked how he could help her. She had a request: arranging the transportation of Martin's body to Atlanta. The task was assigned to Lewis and Graves, who, unable to find a commercial flight, chartered a plane for $800, to Kennedy's irritation. But he followed through.

There remained a meeting that night between Kennedy and fourteen local Black leaders. The Indiana Black establishment wasn't ready to abandon Lyndon Johnson, despite his withdrawal from the race. Hubert Humphrey stood to inherit the president's support, and Humphrey was a known friend to Black Americans. In the meantime, Indiana governor Roger Branigin was running as a favorite son—someone who might win the state's delegates and then play kingmaker at the August convention. With such scenarios in play, the African Americans in Indianapolis who were ready to deal with Kennedy were younger, less experienced, and more radical. Some of them, Earl Graves believed, weren't really leaders at all. They had no profiles outside their communities. They were small-time operatives, in his view, "trying to get some money out of the campaign."[9]

Their meeting with Kennedy began badly. The activists, Lewis said, simmered with "hostility and bitterness." "Our leader is dead tonight," one said to Kennedy, "and when we need you, we can't find you." Others charged that the candidate had no interest in helping them beyond getting their votes. Kennedy pushed back, and after the angry words subsided, the activists agreed to drive voters to the polls on Kennedy's behalf. In return, Graves complained, "they got a huge pile of money from that meeting." This was politics of a crudely transactional sort. On the night of King's murder, it was not what Kennedy had wanted.[10]

Lewis could see that Graves—who was handling outreach to the Black community but had been out of town when this particular meeting was arranged—was displeased. Making matters worse, some of Kennedy's aides now set up Graves as a scapegoat. Lewis, who knew the botched meeting wasn't Graves's fault, took it upon himself to set Kennedy straight. After the parley ended, he stopped RFK in the hallway to explain what had happened. Graves watched from a distance. "You know, you had a meeting tonight with some Black people who are not 'good' Black people," Lewis said, in Graves's recollection. Lewis meant that they weren't people with Kennedy's or even their own communities' best interests at heart. "And you had some advice today," Lewis continued, "from some white people who do not know what they are doing in terms of dealing with the Black community."

Kennedy listened. "Well," he said, "let's talk about it a little bit." He took Lewis on a stroll down the corridor, outside the earshot of Graves. When they returned, Kennedy apologized to Graves. "If there was some misunderstanding," he said, "then we'll straighten it out." Graves concluded then that Lewis was a "very fine fellow" who didn't hesitate to jeopardize his own standing for the sake of fairness. He had done so, moreover, on a night when, more than anyone else on the staff, he was burdened with unbearable grief.[11]

King's funeral wouldn't be held until the next Tuesday, but Lewis left right away for Atlanta. He craved the comfort of home. The SCLC board was also meeting, with much to discuss. A few days later, Kennedy came to town, and Lewis escorted him to the King household to meet Coretta. On Monday, April 8, the night before the funeral, Lewis joined a large gathering of civil rights leaders in the senator's Hyatt Regency suite.

Many of the Black leaders present reacted to King's assassination with cynicism. Why should they work to elect an ambitious white senator, some asked, when the forces of reaction could so easily derail the movement's progress? Even Kennedy's friends were impatient. John Conyers, the Detroit congressman, was angry; Harry Belafonte sulked. But Lewis wasn't giving up. In politics, he had come to understand, you could play only your given hand. For now, that was Kennedy's candidacy. Ralph Abernathy agreed: the Black community should remain with their candidate, for all the acrimony and anger. At the end of the session Abernathy stood up and hugged Kennedy, hoping to dispel the feelings of mistrust.[12]

Since its arrival from Memphis, King's body had lain in repose at the Spelman College chapel. Tens of thousands of people had paid their respects over the weekend. Now, on Monday night, it was lying at Ebenezer Baptist Church, awaiting the next day's rites. Kennedy had asked for a private visitation, and so in the wee hours Lewis and Graves met the senator and his wife at the church. Apart from an honor guard and a security detail, the interior was empty and dark, lit only by flickering candles. Footsteps were enough to break the silence.

The Kennedys prayed at the open mahogany casket by the pulpit. Then Lewis said his farewell. Ever since he had heard King on WRMA as a teenager, he had loved the man—as teacher, mentor, friend, leader, and symbol. But casting his gaze on King's lifeless body unsettled Lewis. He could see where the morticians had reconstructed the slab of King's face that James Earl Ray's bullet had blasted away. The corpse didn't look like the man he had known. "It was not him anymore," Lewis later said. "This was just a shell, his body. *He* was dead."[13]

After a short sleep, Lewis attended another SCLC meeting, where the board chose Abernathy as president. Lewis then hurried to the funeral. Over the last few days, movement leaders, political big shots, and Hollywood celebrities—along with platoons of soldiers to keep the peace and planeloads of journalists to record it all—had descended on Atlanta. Citizens clogged the streets. For all the controversy King had provoked in life, death confirmed him as a singular hero for his times. The rites unfolded in stages: first a service at Ebenezer, where Abernathy spoke; then a three-mile procession in the sweltering sun to Morehouse College, where Benjamin Mays gave a eulogy; and finally, the burial at South-View Cemetery.[14]

As Lewis was taking in the remarks at Morehouse, standing alone in a shady spot on the greensward, Lillian Miles and Xernona Clayton walked over. They offered him a ride to the cemetery, where together they watched the casket lowered into the earth. Afterward, they ate at Paschal's, the gathering place of Atlanta's Black political class. Lewis went home alone.[15]

After the hiatus, Lewis returned to the Indiana campaign trail. On May 7, primary day, Kennedy romped with 42 percent of the vote. Roger Branigin, the favorite son, placed a distant second, with McCarthy a third. Strengthening his hand, Kennedy performed well with both Black voters and blue-collar whites. Although a long fight remained ahead, winning the nomination now seemed plausible. The energy that suddenly infused the campaign fortified Lewis's resolve. In a time of despair, when the movement was divided and the country adrift, Kennedy alone, he believed, could recapture the sense of progress and achievement of the early 1960s. Kennedy had inherited King's mantle.

Lewis's next posting was Nebraska, another proving ground, whose primary was on May 14. A Republican state, it had shown little love for JFK in elections past or for Easterners in general. Lewis was sent to Lincoln, a college town, where he spoke at a University of Nebraska rally in tribute to King. In Omaha, which had a modest-sized Black community, he and Graves and a team of Black volunteers fanned out to visit about thirty churches on the Sunday before the vote. On Monday, despite a downpour, Kennedy rode on a flatbed truck through the Black neighborhoods—a rare visit from a white politician of national stature—stopping at stores, restaurants, and beauty parlors, where, Graves observed, "women were just ecstatic." The campaign also benefited from the political machine of former lieutenant governor Phil Sorensen, brother of JFK's trusted aide Ted, who was now a part of Bobby's retinue. Kennedy ended up trouncing McCarthy. The win, said *Time*, "crushed the argument that his appeal is restricted to city dwellers, the Black, and the poor."[16]

From Nebraska, it was on to Oregon, whose primary was two weeks later. Lewis canvassed, spoke at rallies, and introduced Kennedy at a campus event. But with its abundance of upscale white progressives and paucity of minority voters, the state was tailor-made for McCarthy, who won by six points. The loss was Kennedy's first and the first by any Kennedy seeking office. McCarthy's win revived his wheezing campaign. Now California, with its June 4 primary, would determine which man would go to Chicago as the challenger to Humphrey—who, despite having entered no primaries, was still the odds-on favorite.

Lewis threw himself into the California contest. He teamed up with labor activist Cesar Chavez, holding rallies in Black and Mexican American neighborhoods by day and speaking at ritzy West Los Angeles parties at night. Lewis also partnered with Steve Isenberg, a young "whiz kid" on loan from the administration of New York mayor John Lindsay; Lewis would deliver Kennedy's civil rights message, while Isenberg spoke about youth and Vietnam. Sometimes Isenberg would simply step aside, deferring to Lewis's star power. "I remember we came to a party at the screenwriter Budd Schulberg's house," Isenberg said. "I told him, 'Just let John speak. Nobody needs to convince you guys on the Vietnam War.'" Graves, seeing the reception Lewis got everywhere, thought him a natural campaigner. "Going around the country . . . he was excellent," Graves said. "He was well identified and going into the synagogues and so forth, he was fantastic."[17]

On Memorial Day weekend, Isenberg invited Lewis to his parents' home in tony Mar Vista. In their dining room, his mother set out a generous deli spread typical for a Jewish family's Sunday brunch. Isenberg's father, Jerry, asked Lewis to say grace, which he did, and Lewis loaded up his plate. Jerry, eyeing Lewis's sandwich, gently suggested that the lox and corned beef might taste better if consumed separately.

Lewis recounted his visit to a Black church that morning and the frustration he saw in the young people there. "Thank God they're still going to church," he said. "They're out of patience. They really don't want to hear the way I describe the world and what we ought to do." Lewis knew that the temper had been changing since before he left SNCC. But now, after King's assassination, everything was more dire. "I've got to think through what Black leadership is going to do, what the rest of us should be doing," he said. "Because it's not just that they're brokenhearted over Martin and everything else. The tides are shifting here."[18]

Still, Lewis was having fun campaigning. The staff had become like a "community" to him, he said, "people caught up in the cause," providing the

cocoon of belonging he had once found in Nashville and SNCC. The good
feeling extended into their crowds. During the motorcades, throngs would
surround Kennedy, cheering, grasping to touch his outstretched arm. People
hoisted their children up high to see him or shake his hand. "I haven't seen
anything like it since," Lewis said. "People turned out in the streets by the
hundreds and by the thousands, pulling for Robert Kennedy, especially in
the African-American community and the Hispanic community."[19]

On the day before the primary, Lewis rode across Los Angeles in a
motorcade, with loudspeakers again jury-rigged to the vehicle roofs. They
drove through Watts, Compton, and Venice. "You felt it in the air—he was
going to win," Lewis recalled. But the crush of humanity was also frightening; Lewis sensed danger in the crowds' fanaticism. "This is just too much
for Senator Kennedy to be traveling around like this," Lewis told others on
the campaign. He worried that "somebody would try to take his life."[20]

On primary day, June 4, Lewis got out the vote, checking in with headquarters about which precincts were showing up at the polls. That night,
in a suite at the Ambassador Hotel downtown, family and campaign aides
gathered: Jean Kennedy Smith, the candidate's sister; civil rights activist
Charles Evers, brother to Medgar; journalists Jack Newfield and Theodore
White. "We were sure he had the victory sewn up," Lewis later remembered.
"And everybody was in high spirits." Kennedy joked with Lewis. "John, you
let me down," he said. "More Mexican Americans turned out to vote than
Negroes."

On his way to a five-percentage-point victory, Kennedy left the suite to
address thousands of ebullient supporters in the main ballroom. Lewis and
others waited upstairs. Before he headed down, Kennedy told Lewis, "I hope
to see you in New York. Come to New York."[21]

"We were watching TV when it happened," Lewis said. After the candidate's victory remarks, as he walked from the dais through a kitchen passageway to a planned press conference, Sirhan Sirhan, a deranged Palestinian
American angry about Kennedy's support for Israel, shot him in the head
with a .22-caliber pistol.

"We just fell to the floor and started crying," Lewis said. "To me that was
the darkest, saddest moment." "Why? Why? Why?" he asked himself, over
and over.[22]

Finally, Lewis got up and went to the ballroom, but there was nothing there for him to do. He went outside, wandered to the campaign offices, then came back to the Ambassador. At a late hour, he caught a few hours of sleep.[23]

On the flight home, he could not fall asleep. He looked down at the snowcapped peaks of the Rockies, bright white in June, and asked himself, "What is happening in America?" First King, then Kennedy. "It was the loneliest, just the longest flight of my life," he later said. "I had traveled a great deal all across this country from 1964 on. I traveled, speaking for SNCC, and I'd been on many, many planes, long trips, from California to Atlanta . . . but this flight was the longest, the most depressing and the saddest flight in my life. . . . I would cry a little; I had to cry coming back on this flight. I felt all alone, just completely alone."

The Kennedy family invited Lewis to the funeral at St. Patrick's Cathedral in New York. Lewis took a rotation as part of an honor guard, standing with Abernathy beside the casket for an hour as mourners walked past. Then he joined a twenty-one-car funeral train that ferried Kennedy's coffin to Washington, D.C., where the senator would be buried near his brother at Arlington National Cemetery. As with all things Kennedy, media coverage of the cortege was overwhelmed by excitement about the celebrities on board—luminaries from the worlds of politics, journalism, literature, and film. Lewis spent the ride grieving alongside old friends including Julian Bond and Ivanhoe Donaldson, Ralph Abernathy and Coretta King. Kennedy's coffin rested in the trailing car, perched on red velvet chairs at window level so that well-wishers could glimpse it as the train rolled by. A rotating honor guard again stood watch.[24]

As the train chugged southward, past cities, farms, and fields, a million Americans came out to the trackside. In some towns a brass band or a bugler would play, or a chorus would sing the "Battle Hymn of the Republic," one of Kennedy's favorites. Elsewhere, mourners quietly waved placards and flags. The trip, normally four hours, took eight. John Seigenthaler joked that had it taken any longer, the famously impatient Kennedy would've been "kicking the box." On board, Joseph Alsop remarked, the scene was a "ludicrous mixture of heartbreak and how to get your sandwiches." By the end, the food, ice, and alcohol were gone. Lewis passed the time catching up with Bond—whom he had asked to campaign with him in California and who now regretted having declined. Lewis also spoke with Senator George McGovern of South Dakota, who wondered if he should pick up Kennedy's fallen standard. Mostly Lewis looked out the window. "The people who really came out and poured out their love, and showed it for Senator Kennedy. I think most of us, we just couldn't believe it, we couldn't believe that we were on this train ride. And we didn't want the ride to come to an end. Just wanted it to continue and continue."[25]

In Atlanta, Lewis fell into another funk. The situation was beyond bleak. "There were great hopes and expectations in 1963," he told Jack Nelson, "but with a reactionary Congress, and with the assassinations and the riots and the whole bit, the hope now seems shattered, and there seems to be a feeling that the light is going out." Compounding his problems, he felt badly fatigued—as in those days when SNCC staffers had had to circulate memos warning of his exhaustion. Some friends believed he was clinically depressed. His physician said he needed some enforced relaxation and admitted him for three days to the Holy Family Hospital. From his bed, Lewis watched the Republican convention as Richard Nixon was nominated for president—another depressing event in the annus horribilis of 1968.

One bright spot was that Lillian Miles came to visit each day, bringing his mail and the morning newspaper. Theirs had not exactly been a whirlwind romance; Lewis had been traveling with the campaign and he was anything but a skilled romancer of women. But she brought stability to his life and made him feel confident.

Lillian believed she had caught Lewis at a moment of vulnerability, when he desperately needed someone. One day, while lying in his bed, he said to her, "Why don't we get married?" It was far from the most sentimental proposal, but Lillian accepted.[26]

No sooner was Lewis discharged, however, than romance again took a backseat to politics. Earlier in the summer, he had agreed to lend a hand to a political insurgency that, in the spirit of the 1964 Mississippi Freedom Democrats, hoped to go to the Democratic National Convention in Chicago to challenge the regular Georgia delegation, which was led by the segregationist governor Lester Maddox. Although Maddox's group included a few token African Americans and was thus technically integrated, it also included allies of George Wallace. Just as troubling, Maddox had violated new Democratic Party rules aimed at making the delegate-selection process transparent. Deeming the Maddox group illegitimate, Atlanta labor activist Al Kehrer formed a group called the Georgia Democratic Party Forum, which scheduled its own state convention in Macon to nominate a rival slate to go to Chicago and petition to be seated instead.[27]

Internecine warfare stymied Kehrer's plans. Although a Humphrey supporter, Kehrer wanted the Macon delegation to be neutral between Humphrey and McCarthy; his purpose was to block the Maddox group. But McCarthy's backers eyed an opportunity. Two "Clean for Gene" University of North Carolina students, Parker Hudson and Taylor Branch, spent July rounding up Democrats to come to Macon. McCarthy's headquarters dispatched staffers to help, even retaining the legal services of a man versed in convention challenges: onetime Humphrey confidant Joe Rauh.[28]

Lewis was not taken with McCarthy. But Ivanhoe Donaldson, now working for the candidate, persuaded him. "I called John Lewis, and I talked John into going down there," Donaldson remembered, "and the rest started to roll." They brought Bond on board as well.[29]

On Saturday, August 10, Lewis and Bond drove to Macon. Six hundred other Georgia Democrats converged on the Dempsey Hotel—a "dateless" building, Parker Hudson noted, "neither particularly old nor particularly new," with low ceilings and walls painted "an institutional pale yellow." Taylor Branch was struck by the "sea of intrigue"; McCarthy staffer David Mixner described feverish action: "Ministers in clerical collars leaned over into the rows of chairs, arguing for this point or that. Black students in dashikis walked around with lists, counting the votes." Having bused in droves of supporters, the McCarthy group had gained the upper hand by late afternoon. Kehrer, his project hijacked, resigned as convention chairman. The McCarthy faction elected Bond as delegation cochairman and Lewis as a delegate. They called themselves the "Georgia Loyal National Democrats."[30]

Bond made the Loyalists' case before the credentials committee in Chicago. Lewis helped arrange transportation for the delegates, many of whom, like their 1964 Mississippi counterparts, had never left their state before. Getting everyone from O'Hare airport to the Del Prado Hotel, twenty minutes south of the convention site—and then carting them around the city all week—proved difficult, since all the coach buses in Chicago had long since been booked. Lewis rented a dilapidated yellow school bus, which the Loyalists adopted as a symbol of their scrappy underdog status. Riding to the convention hall on Monday, August 26, they sang freedom songs, with two of the delegates providing harmonica accompaniment.[31]

On their arrival at the International Amphitheatre, however, the delegates' mood soured. Their seats, they discovered, were in the balcony, while the Maddox delegates had coveted floor spots. The snub echoed the spurned 1964 proposal to the Mississippi Freedom Democrats, which Aaron Henry had acidly compared to the Jim Crow seating of Southern movie houses. After much hell-raising, however, the Loyalists got their demand, and by ten o'clock were streaming out of their upper-deck seats, flashing the V-for-victory sign, and claiming chairs on the floor. The galleries broke out in applause.[32]

Lewis had spent Monday with Bond, pleading their case before different delegations. Where once Lewis would have been the featured speaker, now Bond claimed the starring role. Slender, smartly dressed, quick-witted, and dashingly handsome, he fast became a media darling. Magazine profiles told the story of the shift: in 1967, Lewis had been the subject of a lengthy, admiring *New York Times Magazine* profile; soon after the convention, the same publication showcased Bond with his own multipage spread. Lewis was untroubled by his friend's celebrityhood. Indeed, he rhapsodized about Bond when talking to the press. "With the death of Martin Luther King and Senator Robert F. Kennedy," Lewis told one reporter, "I think Julian has real potential to emerge as the symbol that can bring together certain elements within the old civil rights movement."[33]

Yet Bond, who was new to national politics, misplayed his cards. Over the weekend he tentatively accepted a compromise that would seat one-half of each Georgia delegation. The arrangement disappointed his fellow Loyalists. They secured a floor vote on a motion to seat them alone. Although their motion failed, the whole episode elevated Bond's profile. Raucous cries of "Julian Bond! Julian Bond!" echoed through the hall as the delegates voted on the motion.

The next day, the convention passed the compromise. The Loyalists glumly accepted it. But it still amounted to a victory—especially because twenty of the Maddox delegates walked out. And just as the 1964 Mississippi challenge had brought about integrated delegations in 1968, the Georgia challenge spurred another round of reforms that would make caucuses and primaries all but mandatory in the future. The short-term loss would prove to be a long-term victory.[34]

All week long, amid this jockeying, anti-war protests had been raging in Chicago's streets and parks, leading to violent clashes with the police. Lewis judged the city to be "in a state of near war," as the odors of "tear gas and stink bombs and marijuana" and "the thumping of helicopters overhead" filled the air. Arguments and fights broke out on the convention floor.[35]

Wednesday night brought the balloting for presidential nominees. Lewis caught wind of a "Draft Ted" boomlet to nominate Senator Edward M. Kennedy of Massachusetts. On the convention floor, Lewis pigeonholed Ted Sorensen, a New York delegate, who gave Lewis a green light to pursue the draft. Excitement surged when Fannie Lou Hamer—triumphantly present in Chicago as a full-fledged Mississippi delegate—agreed to make the nominating speech for the surviving Kennedy. But as Taylor Branch led Hamer to the speaker's platform, Kennedy brother-in-law Stephen Smith sent word that Teddy was nixing the draft. Hamer folded up her speech.[36]

Most of the Georgians defaulted back to McCarthy. Bond gave a speech seconding McCarthy's nomination, although it was now clear that Humphrey had victory in hand. In the balloting, the Loyalists cast 13½ votes for McCarthy, 2½ for Humphrey, and the rest for assorted others. Lewis cast his half vote for Ted Kennedy, in tribute to his late brother.

When the proceedings adjourned, the streets were still rowdy with protesters and police. Lewis and the delegation decided to go downtown to join a peaceful protest in Grant Park. To show solidarity, they rode in their yellow bus to Michigan Avenue. Given the police violence against the protesters, it was clear that even orderly demonstrators could get hurt. On the bus, Lewis "gave a very serious talk" on nonviolence, according to Parker Hudson, teaching everyone how to curl their bodies and protect their heads and vital organs from police blows. When they arrived at the protest site, they lit candles and sang "We Shall Overcome." Lewis had come a long way and America had changed much since the 1960 sit-ins, but the influence of the Nashville movement was still making itself felt.[37]

PART 2

POLITICS

1969–2020

Chapter Fifteen

THE VOTER EDUCATION PROJECT

■ ■

Politically, 1968 ended on a grim note for John Lewis, with Richard Nixon winning the White House. The former vice president had allied with Dixiecrat leader Strom Thurmond and other racial reactionaries during his campaign, and he had both stoked and profited from a backlash against rising crime, urban riots, and anti-war militancy. Although Nixon professed a commitment to civil rights, what Lewis and other African Americans took note of were his hands-off approach to school desegregation, his use of school busing as a wedge issue, and his promise to name conservative judges to the federal bench. It was clear that under Nixon the fertile, historic period of civil rights legislation and liberal Supreme Court rulings would be coming to an end.

But if November brought gloomy headlines, it also brought Lewis happy personal news. "Ex-SNCC Leader Plans Another March—to the Altar," announced *Jet* magazine, as society pages in the Black press and a few white outlets noted John and Lillian's imminent nuptials. Marriage had been a long time coming for Lewis, now twenty-eight. Virtually all of his friends had wed in their early twenties; some were divorced by now. Lewis had never pursued women much, although in his memoir he would feel compelled to state, awkwardly, that when he married he was not without sexual experience. Still, he was innocent enough that his engagement stunned his friends and family. "Robert getting married—I didn't think he would ever get married," one of his sisters said at the time. "He had girlfriends, but getting married—I didn't think he would." Said another: "We'd say, 'Robert, nobody's going to marry you. You're not going to slow down that long.' . . . Everybody was surprised because, really, everybody around here thought Robert would never get married."[1]

The wedding was held on December 21, at 3:30 p.m., at Ebenezer Baptist Church. Martin Luther King Sr. officiated. Don Harris served as best man. Xernona Clayton did the planning. Archie Allen took photos. Associates from SNCC, SCLC, and Atlanta attended, as did Lillian's family, who flew in from Los Angeles. Lewis's father, Eddie, however, didn't make the drive from Pike County, nor did several of John's siblings. Eddie explained that owing to the unrelenting demands of the farm, he couldn't take time off. John accepted his father's decision with equanimity. Willie Mae did travel to Atlanta—her first time—as did John's siblings Henry and Rosa Mae. The Lewises felt a bit out of place amid this worldly and well-traveled crowd, though Willie Mae was pleased to meet and talk to "Daddy" King. Lewis for his part "was all giddy all day," recalled his friend Tom Houck, and "Lillian was on her best behavior."[2]

Following the reception, there was an after-party at Paschal's. Lewis was "wiped out," Houck said, after two gin and tonics. At the evening's end, everyone gathered around Lillian's Plymouth Valiant to send off the newlyweds—only to watch Lillian, amid the excitement, back the car into the restaurant wall with a loud boom. The Bonds drove John and Lillian to the Peachtree Plaza hotel downtown for their first night of matrimony.[3]

The Lewises were still working at their same jobs: John at the Southern Regional Council, Lillian as a university librarian. They rented a house near Emory University, in Druid Hills, a white section of town. A new federal civil rights act—a final, unsung achievement of Johnson's Great Society—barred racial discrimination in housing, and the Lewises were among the first Black couples to move into the neighborhood. Lewis liked it so much he wanted to buy a house nearby, but Lillian insisted on living in a Black part of town. Months later, they bought a place on Pinehurst Drive in Cascade Heights, in southwest Atlanta, where they would remain for three and a half decades. In the backyard garden Lewis liked to tend to the flowers or just sit by the fountain and reflect.[4]

Lillian's devotion to her husband was immediately apparent. Neither she nor Lewis was given to public displays of affection or the moony-eyed

THE VOTER EDUCATION PROJECT

romantic behavior common among newlyweds. "I did not see any sign of affection between John and Lillian at the wedding," Archie Allen said, "and I never have." "It wasn't a relationship where you would see them kiss and hug, and hold hands," said Carol Dove, a longtime friend of Lillian's. "It was in their soul." Lillian's devotion often took the form of a fierce protectiveness. At one party thrown before the wedding, Connie Curry, an old SNCC friend, showed up at the door. Lewis greeted her with one of his big hugs, to Lillian's evident displeasure. Later, when Curry and Lillian were alone in the kitchen, Lillian, who was chopping vegetables, flashed her knife, warning her guest, "Don't you ever put your hands on my fiancé again."[5]

Lillian was often uncomfortable with the affection that her husband showed to others. Before the wedding, Allen was visiting John in his old apartment. Boxes were stacked everywhere—in closets, in the back of the room. Some contained valuable memorabilia like letters from the White House or Martin Luther King. Allen began sorting through the materials to save the valuable mementos. Lillian flew into a rage, insisting that he not touch a thing.

Allen and his wife, Bonnie, received an even chillier reception one night after the wedding. Returning to Atlanta on a wintry night to show the newlyweds the wedding photos, the Allens ran into an ice storm, which knocked out the power at the Holiday Inn. Having eaten only snacks from the hotel vending machine, they arrived at the Lewises' famished. John asked Lillian to go to the kitchen and fix something for their guests. Lillian reemerged minutes later holding two popsicles.[6]

Although some of Lewis's friends found his new wife's prickliness off-putting, others fought past it. During a contentious dinner discussion at the home of Ed Elson, an Atlanta businessman active in civil rights, Lillian called her host a racist. Elson pushed back. "Lillian, you've got two choices," he said. "Go to the bar, get yourself another drink, and be my friend. Or go to the door and go home." She fixed a drink, talked through their disagreement, and became a good friend of Elson's.[7]

Two months after the wedding, Lewis returned to Selma for the first time since 1965. It was the fourth anniversary of Bloody Sunday. There was no formal commemoration. Lewis was accompanied only by Pat Watters, a civil rights journalist, now a colleague at the Southern Regional Council. They strolled about in a ruminative mood, with Lewis "murmuring to himself," Watters wrote, and explaining the significance of each spot they visited. "We were here," Lewis told Watters. ". . . This is where the march formed. . . . I can remember Martin standing up there on the steps, with that Greek archbishop with the beard beside him." They ran into locals who had fought in the struggle. The children were "clamoring around John, remembering him," Watters recorded. Lewis, who always loved talking to children, told Watters that he hoped to see a whole generation come of age touched by the spirit of Martin Luther King.[8]

Lewis and Watters made their way to the apartment of a Black family with ten children, who, despite their number, had always found room to host Lewis and other activists visiting Selma. Lewis and the woman of the house reminisced. Watters didn't report her name; Lewis described her as "one of those little people who would emerge in the movement, enduring, and with endless energy, ready to do any work, take on any responsibility, make any sacrifice." Two of her sons were at home at the time, and she photographed Lewis with his arms draped over their shoulders. Her other children were out canvassing the neighborhood, she said, collecting signatures on a petition for a holiday in honor of King.

She told Lewis that she remembered seeing him on the ground on Bloody Sunday and fearing he was dead. But as dreadful as those times had been, she and other Selma residents now viewed them nostalgically, talking about 1965 as "those good old days" and recalling the spirit of hope and change. Turning to Lewis, the woman asked, "Do you think, John, it will ever come back?"[9]

As the 1960s drew to a close, the movement's future was on everyone's minds. For SNCC veterans, the moment was bittersweet, with major goals having been achieved but the organization a spent force. Newspaper articles carried headlines like "'Success Killed Us,' SNCC Worker Says." Some activists blamed the FBI, which, disturbed by SNCC's espousal of violence and revolutionary rhetoric, targeted Black radicals as part of its counterintelligence program. But even without the FBI's undermining, SNCC had been bound for irrelevancy since 1966, when it embraced an ideology that alienated a large bulk of its supporters, white and Black, and went on to expel whites from the organization.[10]

Whatever antagonism Lewis harbored toward certain SNCC colleagues, he was gracious when reporters interviewed him. In 1970, he told the *Washington Post*'s Carl Bernstein that although SNCC's civil rights work was all but dead, "a spirit cannot be destroyed, and the SNCC spirit still exists." The assessment was generous. In fact, none of the other key figures from SNCC's heyday remained active. Forman, who had for years held his militant impulses in check to serve the group's greater interest, gave himself over to an apocalyptic politics. Changing his name to Kwame Ture, Carmichael moved to Guinea in 1969. Ruby Doris Smith Robinson developed lymphosarcoma, a rare blood cancer, and died in 1967 at age twenty-five. In 1968, Cleve Sellers was tried for draft evasion; although he had helped engineer the coup at Kingston Springs, Lewis testified as a character witness on his behalf. (Sellers would serve prison time for his role in the Orangeburg Massacre, in which police killed three student protesters; he was later pardoned.) Another premature death was that of Ralph Featherstone, whose car blew up as he was driving to see SNCC chairman Rap Brown, then on trial for trafficking firearms. Federal investigators concluded that Featherstone had been transporting a homemade bomb, which had accidentally detonated. Brown became a fugitive; after being caught and convicted of armed robbery, he converted to Islam and changed his name to Jamil Abdullah Al-Amin. Though Lewis never knew Brown well, he testified on his behalf, too.[11]

For Lewis, the saddest story was that of James Bevel. Unlike some SNCC friends, Bevel had always stayed true to the way of nonviolence. Yet he was beset by psychological troubles. His philandering led Diane Nash to divorce him, and after King's murder he became unhinged. In 1970, he sequestered himself for days in a suite at Paschal's—which included a motel alongside its restaurant—with a group of Spelman College students, to whom he preached in his fervent style. Fashioning himself a prophet, Bevel was more like a cult leader, demanding fealty from the women and at one point making them drink his urine. Word of the bizarre session spread, and Andrew Young and Joseph Lowery of SCLC intervened to break it up. Despite Lewis's pleas for compassion, SCLC forced Bevel to resign. The incident was hushed up, and Bevel drifted away from the movement.[12]

For all these sorry tales, the turn of the decade was not altogether bleak. Even as some movement veterans struggled, other African American leaders were charting a new course in elective politics. Democrats John Conyers of Detroit, Louis Stokes of Cleveland, Bill Clay of St. Louis, and Shirley Chisholm of Brooklyn all entered Congress in the 1960s; Ed Brooke of Massachusetts, a liberal Republican, became the first Black senator since Reconstruction. Black mayors came to power in Cleveland and Gary, Indiana, and would soon take office in Detroit, Los Angeles, and Washington, D.C. In Atlanta, the maverick Maynard Jackson was elected vice mayor in 1969; he would win the mayoralty four years later.

Lewis believed that electing Black politicians was the key to progress. "The new leaders of the movement are the politicians, the elected officials, without question," he argued. "People who came up through the Civil Rights Movement," Lewis said, were winning office, from alderman and sheriff to mayor and congressman. He wanted to help them. With Bond, he formed an organization called the Southern Elections Fund. Backed by activists and politicians including Conyers, Chisholm, Harvard professor Martin Peretz, and Connecticut politico Anne Wexler, the fund aimed to boost candidates for state and local office—white and Black—committed to a liberal racial agenda.[13]

No city held more promise for Black politicians than Atlanta. Both the white and Black communities had their "power structures" or "establishments"—networks of business and civic leaders who conferred with one another about the city's interests and brokered deals. These elites were committed to interracial comity and helped give Atlanta its reputation as a dynamic, cosmopolitan hub where the races collaborated. The city enjoyed booming job growth, an influx of Fortune 500 businesses, a soaring skyline, new major-league sports teams, and a swelling population of young people and professionals.[14]

Among the burgeoning African American political class, talk turned in the late 1960s to running a Black candidate for the House of Representatives. Believing that Bond was the obvious choice, Lewis pressed his friend to run. In November 1969, over lunch at Paschal's, he handed Bond a letter he'd written spelling out why Bond should seek the Fifth District seat. But Bond demurred. Finally, after many months of his equivocation,

Andrew Young expressed his own interest in the seat, and Bond stepped aside.

Young lost his race to the Republican incumbent. But his nomination had broken a color line, and two years later, in 1972, he would run again and win, becoming Georgia's first Black congressman. Barriers were tumbling.[15]

Although Lewis had enthusiastically backed Young's congressional bid, he had done so privately. The reason was that, in early 1970, Lewis had taken a job that required him to be nonpartisan. The job had him working on the issue that had been dear to his heart since Selma: voting. For the next seven years, Lewis's labor on behalf of voter registration fortified his belief in the power of the ballot, a belief that would become his lifelong trademark.

The opportunity arose in January 1970, when Atlanta attorney Vernon Jordan announced he was stepping down as executive director of the Voter Education Project. A unit of the Southern Regional Council, the VEP had been formed in 1961 when the Justice Department, together with philanthropists and activists, sought a way to direct foundation monies into registration activities. Back then, Lewis had worried that Robert Kennedy's proposal was meant to blunt the sharp edge of direct-action campaigns like the Freedom Rides. But Lewis had long ago abandoned those concerns, and at least since his March on Washington speech, voting rights had been a cause dear to his heart. He was an obvious choice to replace Jordan. The VEP announced his appointment in February 1970; the board of directors approved it on March 21. His salary would be over $20,000.[16]

Lewis was taking over an institution that, the *Atlanta Constitution* wrote, "may have done as much as any single political organization to shape the patterns of the South in the last decade." The VEP's drives, the paper noted, "have meant the registration of nearly one and one-half million new Southern voters, almost all of them black. While there are few parts of the South where the new black voters are decisive in any election, there are also today few sections in the South were black voters can be safely ignored."[17]

Still, Lewis had his work cut out for him. Even with the Voting Rights Act in place, Black registration in the South lagged. Many African Americans weren't politically minded, or they refrained from registering out of a learned passivity. "Black voters who have been kept out of the political process, they have been excluded," Lewis said. "And some people are registering and voting for the first time and they have got to get into the habit of voting and the habit of participating." Despite the toppling of white supremacism, Lewis and Archie Allen wrote in a law review article, it would for years "continue to dominate the psyche of an oppressed people even after the barriers to full participation had been removed."[18]

Many impediments remained. "Whites who control jobs, homes, welfare checks, Social Security, food stamps, Medicare, and mortgages have a very real weapon with which to threaten Blacks who would 'step out of line' and register to vote," Lewis told a House subcommittee in 1971. In virulently racist areas, like southwest Georgia, Pat Watters reported, for a Black person to try to get on the rolls "is still to take your life in your own hands." When Blacks did summon the courage to try, they faced "harassment and hostility . . . in offices of local registrars," Lewis and Allen wrote. Old-fashioned practices such as "opening late . . . and closing early, taking prolonged lunch breaks, and keeping blacks waiting in line are commonly reported."[19]

In 1965 the burden had been to change the laws. Now, Lewis said, the need was to change the culture. "When I took over as executive director of the Voter Education Project," he later said, "we felt and truly believed that we had to create a real movement to dramatize the need for people to get registered and have an opportunity to cast a vote." He argued his case constantly, whether talking to the press or to donors. "The goal of a truly representative government is still distant," he explained. "If we fail to realize how incomplete the movement is now and do not attend to the remaining needs, the accomplishment thus far may turn out to be empty achievements."[20]

Two particular challenges loomed. First was the fact that Richard Nixon was president. Nixon's political strategy relied on courting white votes in the South. "In the minds of Blacks in the South," Lewis told Congress in 1971, "the federal government is no longer seen as an advocate for equal opportunity. . . . The current administration has earned an image of seeking to woo white political support and of seeking to tone down civil rights enforcement." Over time, Lewis would find that the career civil rights attorneys at the Justice Department provided a counterweight to Nixon and his political team. But the VEP still had to hound the federal government to send registrars and observers to the South to enforce the law.[21]

The second, more specific obstacle was the bipartisan Tax Reform Act of 1969, which Nixon signed at the end of his first year in office. One provision of the new law took direct aim at the VEP: it stipulated that nonprofit voter-registration organizations could receive no more than 25 percent of their budgets from any single philanthropy. Because VEP was, at the time, part of the Southern Regional Council, the law meant that the council—which had subsisted on grants from a few big foundations—would be burdened by this onerous requirement. Paul Anthony of the Southern Regional Council decided to spin off the VEP as a distinct organization and make it responsible for its own fundraising—shifting the new law's burden from the council to the VEP. "There was a great deal of concern on the board of SRC and the lawyers, the legal counsel, that it could be the end," according to Lewis. He would have to return to his old SNCC role of supplicant, working overtime to diversify the VEP's funding streams and assuming responsibility for the organization's very survival.[22]

Complying with the law consumed Lewis during his first year. Only in June 1970 was the "Voter Education Project, Inc." incorporated as an independent body. But even with its financial future uncertain, Lewis took the occasion of its incorporation to announce bold new plans. "Our major area of involvement and interest," he said, would remain enrolling African Americans across the South. But he now also pledged to expand the VEP's purview to include other minority groups, including Mexican Americans, American Indians, and poor whites. "Our whole idea is to do what we can to increase participation of minorities and make the political arena much more democratic," Lewis told the *New York Times*.[23]

By 1971, Lewis believed his organization was on sound footing. "It was not until about September that all our problems, including the receipt of sufficient foundation funds, were ironed out, and full-scale operations were resumed," he wrote in an internal report. "Some programs continued throughout the year, but others—particularly voter registration—were curtailed during much of the year." He secured contributions from a mix of donors—seven major foundations and five smaller civil and religious groups. The largest donor, the Ford Foundation, had had to slice its original pledge of $125,000 to $73,000 so as not to surpass a quarter of the VEP's budget.[24]

Though freighted with these administrative burdens, Lewis's first year in office also brought some decidedly good news. In June 1970, Congress renewed the Voting Rights Act for five more years. The measure kept alive key parts of the landmark law that had been set to expire, including the all-important "preclearance" requirement of Section 5, which required states to obtain advance approval from the federal government for any changes they wished to make to their voting laws. Bundled into the bill, too, was the establishment of a national right to vote at age eighteen—a nod to the growing activism among the young.

The bill's passage represented a major victory over Nixon and his allies, who had tried to strip out the preclearance provisions. At one point, Nixon threatened to veto the bill, arguing that lowering the voting age could be achieved only by constitutional amendment. In the end, however, the president grasped that to terminate the 1965 law would have been politically disastrous. Churlishly, he signed the renewal in his Old Executive Office Building hideaway office, with just one aide present, eschewing the pomp and ceremony of LBJ's signing ceremony five years before.[25]

Lewis's first years at VEP were also spent building a staff. Gradually he brought in people of his own choosing, increasing the staff from twelve to forty. Some were old SNCC friends, like Stanley Wise and Bob Mants. Others were part of the larger civil rights family, like Julian Bond's brother-in-law Claude Clopton and Harry Belafonte's half sister Shirley Cooks.[26]

One important addition was Archie Allen. Allen had first joined the Nashville movement after hearing Lewis talk to his class at Scarritt College, and since 1967 he had occasionally written speeches for John. He had also begun a full-scale biography of Lewis, interviewing dozens of colleagues, friends, and relatives. Not long after Lewis took the VEP reins, Allen came aboard, first as research director and then as communications director, responsible for speechwriting, press releases, and media relations.[27]

Also assuming a vital role was Julian Bond. Bond joined VEP's board of directors and became Lewis's joined-at-the-hip sidekick in his travels and media appearances. For many years, the two had mingled their personal and professional lives, working together in SNCC's Atlanta offices, quitting the organization when it embraced Black Power, collaborating in the 1968 Democratic convention challenge, and cultivating a Black political class in Atlanta. At VEP they were nearly inseparable, traveling the South together, going on TV together, lunching together, celebrating their birth-days together. "People used to call them the Civil Rights Twins," according to Michael Bond, Julian's oldest son.[28]

Alice Bond and Lillian also became close. After dinner at one of their homes, the couples would stay up late talking or playing Scrabble. The Lew-ises became godparents to Michael. They took trips together, including to Zambia.[29]

Bond became Lewis's dedicated partner in a traveling VEP road show. Under Vernon Jordan, the VEP had doled out grants to local organizations around the South that would carry out the on-the-ground labor of enrolling voters. The grant-making continued under Lewis, but he also took to vis-iting the towns where Black registration lagged. Touring became the heart of his work, as it had been at SNCC. It was of a piece with Lewis's lifelong attraction to life on the road. He was an itinerant preacher, spreading the good news of voting. He called his trips Voter Registration Tours.[30]

One of the first was to Mississippi in June 1971. Earlier that year, two dozen Mississippi counties had announced brazen plans to purge their voter rolls and require everyone to reregister before the fall elections. State officials disingenuously claimed these steps were necessary after the recent redistrict-ing, and the Nixon Justice Department okayed the plans. Lewis denounced the move as a ruse to disenfranchise Black voters. The ploy was all the more galling, he added, because some two hundred Black candidates were seek-ing office in Mississippi, including Charles Evers, running for governor, and Aaron Henry and Fannie Lou Hamer, trying for seats in the legislature.[31]

Lewis sent an urgent telegram to Attorney General John Mitchell, as-sailing the Mississippi plan for "violat[ing] the letter and the spirit of the 1965 and 1970 Voting Rights Act." But the Justice Department never re-plied, and on June 10, Lewis sounded the alarm before a House subcommit-tee. In his testimony, he denounced the plan—and a similar one proposed in Alabama—as "tactics of continued harassment and intimidation . . . serving no purpose other than to possibly roll back the advances which Black voters have made in recent years." Across the South, he said, Voting Rights Act violations were rampant, and he called for more federal registrars, observers, and FBI agents to halt "the serious forms of intimidation and harassment of the voter registration workers in Mississippi at this time."[32]

Months later, the Justice Department would cede to pressure and issue guidelines to prevent such mischief. But as of June 1971, the Mississippi counties' reregistration scheme stood. That meant that voters would have to reenroll by July 2 in order to cast a ballot in the upcoming elections. Lewis and Bond decided to barnstorm the state to bring the news to the poor communities that were not plugged in to local political happenings. "No large-scale public announcements were made about the action," Lewis explained to *Ebony*, "and Bond and I knew that if we couldn't reach some of those people affected, particularly the ones living in rural areas, Black candidates for office would lose a considerable number of Black votes in the elections."[33]

Lewis and the VEP staff put in twelve-hour days, making thirty-seven stops in twenty-five counties. "It was almost like a political campaign," Lewis said, "just trying to convince people to come together and get out, and organize, mobilize, and get people registered." Lewis and Bond were a classic odd couple: the tall, lithe Bond dapper in his tailored suits; the short, thickset Lewis, looking earnest if rumpled. Comfortable companions, they fell into an easy banter. "Are you ready, Dr. Bond?" Lewis would call from a bathroom as he washed up before a talk. "Ready, Dr. Lewis," Bond would reply. "John had his Baptist minister delivery, and Julian had his Chet Huntley delivery," Archie Allen said, "and they would joke about it with each other" with a locker room repartee—the two young men asking each other if they had "got it up" with the audience.[34]

Across the state, Lewis and Bond held news conferences and rallies. They visited homes, pool halls, schools, campuses, churches, plantations, clubs, and courthouses. Crowds of one hundred showed up at almost every event. The Mississippi swing transported Lewis back to Freedom Summer as he sweated through the muggy weather, shouting his message at gatherings of farmers and workers. "The progress we have made . . . is in danger of being reversed," he warned. During one stretch Fannie Lou Hamer accompanied the two men, and on their final day of stumping, they brought in Coretta Scott King and Ralph Abernathy for a monster rally at the Tallahatchie Courthouse—the county of Emmett Till's 1955 lynching—before some five hundred Mississippians. "We're finally getting ourselves together," one inspired sixty-year-old farmer told a reporter. "And I believe there's going to be some change in these parts before I die."[35]

Lewis could see the change happening. "There is a different feeling when you go into those places now," he explained. "You don't think about what might happen to you—if you're killed. That time has passed. Now there are other concerns." In towns where law enforcement officers had once harassed or arrested them, Lewis and Bond now enjoyed police escorts or a mayoral welcome. In Belzoni—where in 1955 white supremacists had killed local NAACP leader George Lee for registering to vote—Henry Gantz, the white mayor, bounded into the Green Cove Missionary Baptist Church and took Lewis and Bond by the hands. "Welcome to Belzoni!" he said. "You two are doing wonderful work. You're fighting bigotry and injustice. You're a credit to your race." White sheriffs likewise showed their support in former segregationist strongholds like Amite County.[36]

Lewis knew that these professions of esteem did not spell the end of racist practices. "Local Black people told us time and again," Lewis said of the Mississippi trip, ". . . of physical abuse, hostile registrars, economic reprisals, and of the senseless difficulties caused by re-registration." In some counties, whites could reregister by mail while Blacks had to go to the courthouse. Lewis also knew that elected officials like Gantz were welcoming them because they now depended on Black votes. That dependency only underlined the need for Blacks to exercise political power everywhere.[37]

Buoyed by their Mississippi swing, Lewis and Bond made Voter Registration Tours a central part of their activities. That summer alone, they visited Louisiana, Florida, and Mississippi for a second time, and in the next few years they made dozens of additional trips to all eleven states of the old Confederacy. Lewis was in constant motion, crisscrossing the South, usually with Bond, often, too, with other politicians such as Shirley Chisholm and Virginia state senator Douglas Wilder, or civil rights leaders and spokesmen such as Hosea Williams, Fred Gray, and James Baldwin. "One day, you'd go from town to town," as Lewis described the routine. "Sometimes there would be a staff person from the Voter Education Project, or some staffers we would borrow or use from other groups that would do the advance work. And we would be jumping in the car or van, . . . going from town to town. It was very meaningful."

Tom Houck served as an advance man, staking out churches and venues for rallies and contacting local officials or organizations. Publicity became an important goal; Allen learned the ropes from Bond, who at SNCC had mastered the art of placing stories in the papers. Bond taught Allen how to write press releases, which, he explained, might be reprinted verbatim, especially by the resource-strapped African American papers. "And if we got them into the Sunday papers," Allen said, "that was twelve to sixteen million readers." Allen and others also took photographs. Rural tableaus—Lewis and Bond chatting with Mississippians on a rickety front porch, or standing with Louisianans in an overgrown sugarcane field—went out over the wires.[38]

One exciting trip for Lewis, in March and April 1972, began with a homecoming to Nashville. Flying in amid a fearsome lightning storm on Tuesday night, March 28, Lewis, Bond, Allen, and Wise rose the next morning for a packed day: a 7:00 a.m. local television call-in show, speeches at Fisk's Gothic chapel, a visit to Meharry Medical College to see an ailing Fannie Lou Hamer, a second TV taping at Tennessee State University, and then a third TV appearance, before doubling back to meet with students at the Tennessee State cafeteria. The Nashville leg ended with the four men climbing into their rental car, way behind schedule, and speeding toward a Black church in Jackson, Tennessee, two hours to the southwest, where as an undergraduate Lewis had once taught Bible school. En route, in the backseat, Lewis gabbed animatedly with Wise, while an exhausted Bond fell asleep.[39]

After Jackson, the group stopped in Somerville, a onetime hotbed of Klan activity. In 1960, hundreds of Black tenant farmers had formed a tent encampment there after being evicted from their homes for trying to vote. Traversing Fayette County's roads in darkness, Lewis and his friends noticed a headlight trailing them and feared hostile troopers or Klansmen—only to see the car eventually veer off the thoroughfare. Finally, recalled Boyd Lewis, a journalist who was covering the trip, "John takes us in to a beat-up house. I asked, 'Where are we going?' He said, 'I've got some good friends in here.' The door swung open. It was John and Viola McFerren"—the couple who had led the voting fight there twelve years earlier. "They were greeting John as a brother. He was respected, revered."[40]

So it went, day in, day out. In Memphis they reunited with James Lawson, who was pastoring the Centenary Methodist Church. Lewis's speech thrilled the congregation, who interrupted six times with applause; Bond was introduced as a future president. After Memphis they went on to Shreveport, Louisiana, and then to Texarkana, Houston, and San Antonio.

Wolfing down their meals—cheeseburgers and chess pies in Jackson, enchiladas and Mexican beer in San Antonio—they concluded the tour at the Stardust Ballroom in Corpus Christi for yet another rally. On Sunday morning, on the flight home, Bond perused *The Age of Paranoia*, an anthology of *Rolling Stone* reportage, while Lewis napped. Exhausting as the travel was, Lewis said, he had never enjoyed a job more than this one.[41]

Though the road beckoned, Lewis also logged hours at the VEP's offices at 5 Forsyth Street NW in downtown Atlanta. Located across the street from the *Atlanta Journal* and *Constitution*, the run-down five-story edifice also housed the Southern Regional Council, the American Civil Liberties Union, and other liberal organizations—"a sanctuary," said the *Constitution*'s Ralph McGill, "for renegades who insist on telling the truth." Lester Maddox thought differently: "The whole place is crawling with subversives," he said. "It ought to be torn down and paved over." When the old hulk was slated for demolition in 1971 (for downtown development, not out of political spite), VEP and the other tenants moved five blocks away to a fancier redbrick building at 52 Fairlie Street NW. Working from this new perch, on the third floor, Lewis could drop in on the ACLU's Chuck Morgan or Norman Siegel, voting rights attorneys, or Tom Houck and James Bond, Julian's brother, at the Youth Citizenship Fund. Lewis was often found lunching at Paschal's or Emile's French Cafe ("French for Atlanta"), a popular rendezvous for judges, lawyers, politicians, and reporters. Lewis's lunches embedded him in Atlanta's elite networks, although his "fondness for hot buttered cornbread and other Southern delicacies," *Ebony* reported, forced him "to go on periodic diets."[42]

Lewis's work at VEP became intertwined with his standing in local politics. His registration work boosted the fortunes of Black politicians, while his political connections aided his VEP work. He was, said David Morrison, a reporter at the *Constitution*, "a key operative in all of this. . . . Voter registration was the key to everything. That was John's job." Lewis joined "Leadership Atlanta," a group started by the Atlanta Chamber of Commerce to develop civic leaders, and he spoke at political societies like the Hungry Club. "People would see me out and around so much," he later wrote, "they'd tease me, saying, 'John, are you running for something?'"[43]

In the office, Lewis won regard from his staff, who tolerated his struggles with punctuality. "At almost every meeting, he would arrive late, saying, 'I'm so sorry. I'm so sorry I'm late,'" said Cherie Murdock, his administrative assistant. "He was not the most organized person in the world. But he managed to get things done. I sat opposite him, and I was always trying to keep him on time. I was always trying to impose more order on the office." Organization wasn't Lewis's strong suit, and some people wondered how this unassuming man in his early thirties—gentle-mannered, modest, inclined to listen before he spoke—could run such a big operation. But Lewis had developed a strong sense of his own strengths and weaknesses. With help from a talented staff, an engaged board, allies at friendly organizations, and Lillian as a sounding board on his big decisions, Lewis steered VEP away from the precipice of insolvency. Budget problems never disappeared; staff would share memos on how to pare xeroxing, printing, and telephone costs. But the VEP developed into an efficient machine. Lewis earned annual raises that eventually took his salary up to $35,000.*[44]

He enlarged the board to include national leaders in politics, civil society, and the arts—people like Theodore Hesburgh, president of Notre Dame; the journalist Hodding Carter; Atlanta insurance executive Jesse Hill; and Vivian Henderson, now president of Clark University. The fundraising operation grew to include direct-mail campaigns, outreach to corporations and unions, and benefit dinners feting marquee names including Senators Ted Kennedy and Jacob Javits. (Lewis alternated between Democrats and Republicans because of the VEP's tax-exempt status.) Bond pushed Lewis to strengthen its publicity operation, and under Archie Allen's direction, the VEP began publishing the *V.E.P. News* and issuing slick brochures, mailers, and reports. One popular poster, designed by Kofi Bailey (who had inked the infamous anti-Semitic cartoons for SNCC in 1967), showed a pair of Black hands, one grasping a cotton boll, the other a slip of paper, above the slogan "Hands that pick cotton . . . now can pick our public officials." Another poster featured a 1965 photograph of Lewis being bludgeoned by troopers at Selma. There were radio and TV commercials, too. One year, sitcom king Norman Lear directed public-service spots using actors from

---

* About $180,000 in 2024.

All in the Family, *Maude*, and *Chico and the Man*, urging everyone to take advantage of the right to vote.[45]

The publicity was in the service of VEP's mission of getting people to seize their newly won franchise. That mission, though centered on African Americans, now came to include Hispanics, Native Americans, and young voters—especially after the 1971 ratification of the Twenty-Sixth Amendment, granting the vote to eighteen-year-olds. "We did work especially in Texas with the Latino population," Lewis recalled, "and out of the VEP something emerged called the Southwest Voter Education Project"—a spin-off Hispanic-oriented group that Lewis, working with the Mexican American activist Willie Velasquez, would establish in seven states from Texas to California. College tours, aimed at eighteen- to twenty-one-year-olds, would attract hundreds or even thousands of students, with registrars on hand, one VEP report noted, "so that people could be registered on the spot."[46]

Nor was this the sum of Lewis's activities. His work included monitoring and reporting voting rights infractions, holding seminars and workshops, testifying to Congress, providing assistance to novice Black officeholders, and more. "It was not just putting out money," Lewis said, "but we had educational programs to help newly elected officials. We had workshops. We had people to come in and provide leadership training for them to go back to their local communities."[47]

Well into the mid-1970s, resistance to Black voting remained strong in some parts of the South. Bob Mants described flagrantly illegal situations in rural areas. "One fellow had the polling place on his front porch and no voting booth and no privacy," he said, "and as you approached the house, there was a big barking Dalmatian dog." Mostly, however, explicit intimidation had given way to subtler methods. "You see very little direct violence," Lewis said in 1976. "It's not physical and overt and open. But at several of the meetings and rallies in Mississippi, we heard people saying the boss man told them they didn't need to vote, they didn't need to register. People on the farms, the plantations are afraid to come in and register." There were new cynical schemes to suppress registration, such as a "long form" in Mississippi that required prospective voters to furnish all kinds of irrelevant information that was likely to deter newer and poorer voters, and hence Black voters.[48]

Despite these methods, the mountains of research that the VEP produced showed the numbers of Black voters climbing across the South by roughly 1.5 million, reaching nearly 4 million during Lewis's tenure at VEP. With those gains came a corresponding rise in the number of Black elected officials. In 1965, only seventy-two African Americans held elective office of any kind in the South; a decade later there were 1,588 Black officeholders. Lewis took immense pride in these gains. "People who were sharecroppers and tenant farmers are now running for office," Lewis said in 1972. "Someone like John Hulett. When Courtland and Stokely went into Lowndes County, Alabama, in 1965, he was not even a registered voter. But today he is the sheriff of the county."[49]

One dramatic case Lewis liked to highlight was that of the charmingly named Waterproof, Louisiana, a river town with 1,500 residents, 900 of them Black. When Lewis and Bond visited in August 1971, they held a meeting at the Good Samaritan Hall—"an old building, almost like a shotgun house," as Lewis described it—and sized up a grim situation: in the previous election, all but one of the African American candidates for town council had lost, owing to low Black turnout. The Black population simply wasn't engaged. "Our problem," said Harold Turner, the lone Black councilman, "is that we have people who don't know Black politics can bring real change to their lives." White employers would tell Black domestic workers or farmhands that voting was a waste of time, and government officials would withhold food stamps (illegally) from those who tried. After Lewis and Bond's motivational visit, however, Waterproof's registration numbers climbed, and when Lewis returned three years later, the mayor and half the city council were Black.[50]

Lewis partook of the optimistic talk of a "new South" in which discrimination and bigotry were yielding to racial cooperation. Whites, he argued, were voting for Blacks as never before. And Blacks, too, were setting racial solidarity aside to elect white liberals. "People just have to move beyond that element of race," Lewis said. Doing so would bring about change.[51]

In his optimism, Lewis stood at one pole of a broad spectrum of opinion. Many others focused on the endurance of racially separatist impulses. "Today," wrote Paul Delaney, a Black *New York Times* reporter, in 1973, "blacks snicker at the refrain 'black and white together' from the theme song of the movement, 'We Shall Overcome.'" The last decade had seen tremendous strides in wealth accumulation, political representation, political freedom, and other indices. But African Americans, Delaney reported, had grown disillusioned with the reluctance of whites to join the new political battles, which were centered on social problems like impoverished ghettos and de facto school segregation that admitted no simple moral answers. "Our problems are harder to identify now," Coretta King said. "Segregation barriers have been replaced with economic barriers."[52]

As reporters, academics, and politicians discussed the gains and losses of the 1970s, they increasingly sought out Lewis's opinion. Archie Allen assiduously marketed Lewis as a spokesman on civil rights, race, and voting. "I was promoting him and quoting him all the time," Allen said. Bond sent Lewis memos full of media advice, while telling prominent Black reporters, like Charlayne Hunter of the *New York Times*, that Lewis "needs to establish some on-going relationships with key Black media people, print and electronic." When Lewis learned about Burrelle's Press Clipping Bureau, a private firm that monitored and collected media mentions, Allen said, "we subscribed for all those years at VEP and followed all the clippings about John."[53]

Lewis showed up on local and national news shows, sometimes interviewed alongside the more voluble Bond. In 1972, the pair appeared on the syndicated Washington-based show *Black on White*, hosted by Cliff Alexander, a prominent Black Kennedy and Johnson official. In January 1974, the duo faced a more hostile interlocutor when William F. Buckley came to Atlanta with his public television program, *Firing Line*. The onetime enfant terrible of the postwar right had fashioned himself into the country's leading conservative intellectual, editing *National Review* and hosting the talk show, on which he sparred with liberal guests. Witty, highly mannered, and more than a little pretentious, Buckley relished snaring his guests in intellectual traps like the college debater he used to be. Sitting with Lewis on Buckley's set, Bond did most of the jousting with Buckley over policy issues like community policing and public housing. Lewis unostentatiously stuck to describing the concrete changes happening in the South. "Because of Black people's involvement and the changes on the part of white people," he told Buckley, "we do see a new breed of public officials, both Black and white. . . . People who were hostile to Black people during the early Sixties are now going out and actually campaigning for the Black vote." Unexpectedly speechless, Buckley changed the topic to whether the minimum wage killed jobs.[54]

Reporters were now calling Lewis to weigh in on a widening array of issues, from the 1972 revelation of the Tuskegee experiments (in which Black men in the 1930s and '40s were injected with syphilis and left untreated for research purposes) to the burgeoning Watergate scandal, which Lewis said "eroded the faith of the people in the democratic process and the electoral system." But Lewis had to be careful not to jeopardize the VEP's tax-exempt status. "We were very, very mindful not to get involved in political campaigns, not to do anything that was partisan," he said. "We really wanted both the Democrats and Republicans to be in position to compete or at least campaign for the African American vote."[55]

Occasionally that led him into contortions. In an interview at the 1972 Republican convention, Lewis derided the thousands of young conservatives smugly cheerleading for Nixon—part of a Republican push for the newly empowered youth vote. "I attended the Democratic convention as an observer, and the breed of young people that I saw at the Democratic convention was altogether a different breed," Lewis told interviewer Maureen Orth. "This breed seemed to be a sort of, a paid and hired-hand group. . . . It's just sad to me to see a group of young people get so caught up and to support something that is so out of date and obsolete. It just made me feel very bad for my country." Orth then asked whether he held this opinion simply "because you're liberal Democrats." Lewis pushed back. "Well, I consider myself more or less an independent voter," he said, a bit disingenuously. "I just think there comes a time in the life of a country and the life of a people, that you stand for something. And you don't stand for it because of a party or because of a particular man, but because it's right." Lewis later got into a spot of trouble in April 1974 before the Alabama gubernatorial primary, in which George Wallace was seeking reelection, claiming to have turned over a new leaf. Alarmed that some Black officials had endorsed Wallace, Lewis told a Selma audience that "a vote for George Wallace was a traitorous step backward." Those comments prompted a rebuke from the Ford Foundation, though no serious consequences followed. Far more troubling to Lewis was that Wallace won reelection.[56]

Lewis's 1974 trip to Selma was one of many he was now taking to the scene of his historic confrontation. Over the years, the media had been spotlighting the anniversaries of many historic episodes of the civil rights struggle. On the tenth anniversary of the Freedom Rides, Lewis had given a keynote address in Nashville; on the tenth anniversary of the March on Washington, he tried (unsuccessfully) to persuade A. Philip Randolph and Bayard Rustin to reassemble the surviving leaders. And where his 1969 Selma visit with Pat Watters had been a private affair, in 1972 he began using marches over the Edmund Pettus Bridge to gain attention for the VEP's work. A planned April 1972 pilgrimage might have gone unnoticed, but Mayor Joe Smitherman foolishly sought to block it; the VEP then won a court order allowing it to march and garnering national headlines.[57]

Thereafter, Lewis never failed to commemorate Bloody Sunday with a visit to Selma. Early in 1975, as the tenth anniversary approached, Lewis held a televised press conference to announce a march over the Pettus Bridge to lobby for the renewal of the Voting Rights Act, which was again set to expire. A march, he said, would "dramatize to people in Washington, particularly officials of the Justice Department, that they need to do a great deal more to implement and to enforce the present act and to make the act a permanent and lasting act." Lewis also testified before a House subcommittee, and on March 8, along with Coretta King and Frederick Reese of the original Selma campaign, he led some five thousand marchers across the bridge.[58]

These media events were designed to renew the Voting Rights Act and raise the VEP's visibility. But they also elevated Lewis's own profile. Naked self-promotion didn't come easily to him, but in an age when advertising, public relations, and image-making had become indispensable to politics and issue advocacy, no leader could afford to shun these tools. Bond implored Lewis to check his modesty and "blow your horn as loudly as you can." Lewis must, he implored, find ways to "keep you in place as the authority on Southern Black voting behavior and remind the reading world of the role you have and will play in this area. You don't like to operate by press release, but you do have to pursue an aggressive posture." Bond reeled off a dozen profile-raising ideas: sharing his speeches with journalists; having Archie Allen ("a good writer, when he writes") profile recipients of VEP grants for the Black press; enlisting Tom Houck ("the rotund Rasputin, the maniacal Machiavelli") to drum up coverage in cities he visits; getting on the local

"'Black' show" on every trip ("each station has one"); cultivating the editors at *Jet*; even writing a book about his work. "I could go on and on," Bond said, "but won't. Keep on pushing and keep on blowing that horn."[59]

Lewis's public relations campaign bore fruit in late 1975, when *Time* magazine ran a piece titled "Saints Among Us." Gracing the newsweekly's cover was sixty-five-year-old Mother Teresa, the Albanian nun who ministered to the destitute in Calcutta. But the article also cited a dozen other clergymen, doctors, and do-gooders whose work *Time* deemed holy—including Lewis. The tone was, fittingly, hagiographic:

> The U.S. has its own civil rights heroes. John Lewis, 35, the young apostle of nonviolence in the '60s, was arrested more than 40 times in civil rights demonstrations, and his skull was fractured at Selma in 1965. Since 1970 he has headed the Voter Education Project in Atlanta and helped register some 3.5 million blacks. As a Baptist seminarian, Lewis was kidded for talking up the Social Gospel, but he insists that some "immutable principles" must be at the base of the "Beloved Society" [*sic*] he envisions, and nonviolence is one of them. If a compassionate world is the end, he argues, "then the means we use must be consistent with it."

Lewis, no doubt, had his saintly qualities: the unerring commitment to racial justice, the capacity for self-sacrifice, the ability to inspire people with his mere presence. But no man is a saint, and Lewis didn't think of himself as exceptional. As much as he took pride and pleasure in the laurels, he winced at the gentle mockery that followed. When he showed up at Christmas parties that December, friends chanted, "Here comes the saint!"[60]

Lewis's beatification was a deserved recognition of his years of selfless activism. But it was also, inevitably, a function of his self-promotion. Winning attention for himself and his work was a necessary part of Lewis's job. That meant he would have to live with both the ego gratifications and the discomforts of being the subject of modern media hype.

As 1976 opened, Lewis could take pride in not only admiring press coverage but also his tangible accomplishments. Starting in 1974, as the United

States entered a long spell of economic hardship, he had had to lay off staff members and scale back programs. But he pressed on. In the summer of 1975, he had played a key role in renewing the Voting Rights Act. Although Lewis had hoped to make the act permanent, he considered the terms of the renewal—for seven years instead of five—a triumph. Congress extended the preclearance provisions of Section 5 to certain Hispanic areas, including parts of Texas. The new law also required that communities with heavy foreign-language populations provide election material in the relevant tongues. Lewis had pushed hard to include Hispanics under the new law. "It would be a mockery of the whole Voting Rights Act effort during the past ten years," he said before a Senate committee, "if we leave the Voting Rights Act as it is and not cover the other minorities in this country." In August 1975, ten years to the day after Johnson signed the original act, President Gerald Ford held a Rose Garden ceremony to mark its renewal. Lewis was again present for the signing.[61]

Ford's presidency, Lewis believed, had been a significant improvement over Nixon's. But in 1976 Lewis also found himself rooting—hesitantly—for Ford's opponent in the presidential race, former Georgia governor Jimmy Carter. When in 1970 Carter had first run for governor, Lewis hadn't known a thing about him, other than that he had sat out the civil rights movement. Carter "never spoke up or spoke about what his Black neighbors were going through," Lewis said. Yet on taking office Carter had boldly proclaimed, "I say to you quite frankly, the time for discrimination is over." He hung Martin Luther King's portrait in the statehouse and governed as a racial liberal.[62]

Many Black Americans were unsure whether to believe Carter's conversion. In 1976, Wallace was running again for president, and some saw Carter as, at the least, a bulwark against their old nemesis. "Carter's support in the Black community is relatively soft and shifting," an ambivalent Lewis told *Time* magazine at the time of the Florida primary in April. "It's more of a vote against Wallace than it is a vote for Carter."

Carter worked hard for Black votes, even as he also tried to placate conservative whites. He secured endorsements from Andrew Young and Daddy King, visited Black churches, and praised the Voting Rights Act as "the best thing that ever happened to the South." Despite competition from liberal candidates with stronger civil rights records—Morris Udall, Henry Jackson,

Sargent Shriver—Carter netted large majorities of the Black vote in state after state.[63]

On the other hand, in attempting this tightrope act, Carter sometimes stumbled—or fell. In April, he defended a role for the federal government in fighting housing discrimination, but then saw fit to pay respect to white communities seeking to preserve their ethnic or racial character. "I have nothing against a community that's made up of people who are Polish or Czechoslovakian or French⬚Canadian, or Blacks," Carter said, "who are trying to maintain the ethnic purity of their neighborhoods." The sentiment was dubious; the phrase "ethnic purity" was catastrophic. After a delay, Carter apologized. Julian Bond, who had sought the Democratic nomination himself, was unforgiving, denouncing Carter in print and on the *Today* show. But Lewis—more forgiving, more political—didn't write Carter off. Lewis told Bond he was "torn between Carter's almost intuitive appeal to Blacks and revulsion against his anti-issue campaign and its success."[64]

Shortly before Carter sewed up the nomination in June, boosted by Black votes, Lewis got on board. "Of all the candidates, Jimmy Carter has been able to project himself as able to relate to and understand Black people," he told the *New York Times*. He invited Carter to keynote the VEP's annual $100-a-plate gala at the Hyatt Regency Hotel in Atlanta that summer. Lewis took Carter's acceptance as a thank-you for the VEP's work. Some 1,500 guests attended. Carter joked that he wanted to "put John Lewis out of business" by passing a law to automatically register every American on his eighteenth birthday. The dinner raised $70,000—"our best fundraising dinner ever," Lewis exulted. It also gave Lewis his first chance to talk to Carter one-on-one.[65]

During the fall, Lewis, while formally neutral between Ford and Carter, worked to drum up November turnout. News outlets profiled him as a professional voting advocate. ("Apathy Irks Man Who Fought for Vote," read a *Los Angeles Times* headline. "Southern Black Risked Life, Now Must Urge People to Use Right.") On Election Day, Carter eked out a narrow victory, winning by less than 2 million ballots nationally and 57 Electoral College votes. Taking 95 percent of the Southern Black vote, he swept the states of the Old Confederacy except Virginia. Watching the returns, Lewis thought about King. "I wish—Lord, how I wish—Martin were still alive today," he

THE VOTER EDUCATION PROJECT

said. "He would be very, very happy. Through it all, the lunch counter sit-ins, the bus strike, the marches and everything, the bottom line was voting."[66]

As Lewis teared up that night, Lillian reacted with surprise. She knew, Lewis said, "I wasn't *that* crazy about Carter." What made him weep wasn't any great personal affection for the new president but what his election revealed. As the VEP's year-end report put it, "The Black vote in the South on November 2, 1976, was the largest and most decisive exercise of minority political power in this century. Almost uniformly across the South, the Black vote provided the winning margin for Jimmy Carter and was also crucial for the victories of several southern Congressional candidates and state and local office-holders." The hands that once picked cotton, as Lewis liked to say, had now picked a president.[67]

If Black empowerment was a central goal of Lewis's work at VEP, it was also about something even bigger. From his home in Paris, the writer James Baldwin wrote to Lewis about his dogged voter registration work. "The truth is that you are involved in a very difficult and important endeavor," Baldwin wrote, in his inimitable prose, "—and this on a level which has less to do with the stated aims of VEP, though these are real enough, as it has to do with the possible creation of a viable America." The full integration of African Americans into the electorate, was necessary not just to afford them power but to make the nation whole—not for their sake alone, but for America's. Few people were suited for such a mission. But Baldwin made clear that he believed Lewis to be among those few. "I'll take this opportunity to say something which I'm always too shy to be able to articulate adequately in person," he wrote, "and that is that I love and admire you very much, stocky little brother, and it's a gas to be associated with you. You're a survivor, and a very honest man."[68]

Chapter Sixteen

THE FIRST RACE

■ ■

J immy Carter's election shook up Atlanta politics. In December 1976, immediately after his victory, Carter named Andrew Young—who had just won another term representing Georgia's Fifth District—as ambassador to the United Nations. Young's appointment set off a scramble for his seat. Two Georgia assemblymen jumped in the race. Ralph Abernathy and Joseph Lowery both signaled interest. John Lewis, too, was an obvious candidate— though at first, when asked, he allowed only that he would "give serious thought" to the idea and urged Young to remain in Congress. If he entered the administration, Lewis explained, Young would risk leaving the Deep South without an African American congressman—a setback for Black political progress.[1]

But Young wanted to advance his career, and so did Lewis. Lewis had done yeoman's work at the VEP over seven years, and he and Lillian now enjoyed a comfortable middle-class lifestyle and a busy social calendar. They also now had a family. In May, an adoption agency had introduced them to a newborn, whom they instantly adored. They knew little about the boy's parents, only that his mother was an unmarried schoolteacher. In August they adopted the child, naming him John-Miles. Xernona Clayton threw them a shower in the park.[2]

For all their comforts, however, Lillian believed that her husband was destined for greater things. Her ambition for him was indeed limitless. She believed he had the ability to become congressman, senator, and perhaps even president; she talked about nominating him for the Nobel Peace Prize. Even as she advanced in her career as a librarian at Atlanta University,* she had become immersed in politics and taken an active role in his career. Friends described the couple as "teammates," "best friends," and full partners in charting his path. "Their political conversations were intense," said Sharon Adams, a friend and political adviser, concerned with "not just immediate but long-term goals and prospects."[3]

Lillian's strengths complemented her husband's. Where he was sensitive, she was steely; where he indulged in long conversations, she was brisk and businesslike, with one eye on the clock. Her efficiency backstopped John's easygoing ways. "Anything that John has ever done," said Tom Houck, "Lillian had to sign off on." In late 1976, Lillian argued emphatically that he shouldn't pass up a shot at a seat in Congress. "Let's do it," she said. "Let's go for it."[4]

Lewis knew his skills and deficiencies as a candidate. He didn't consider himself handsome or articulate, but he worked as hard as anyone. The main question mark for Lewis was whether Julian Bond, now a state senator, was interested in the seat. Bond had flirted with running in the past but had always pulled back, believing the odds too long in a white-majority district. Young had disproved that hypothesis, but when Lewis asked Bond about seeking the seat, Bond said, "No, Mr. Chairman, I'm not going to. But why don't you?" Lewis resigned from VEP, effective January 15, and began organizing a campaign.[5]

Both the white and Black power structures in Atlanta held Lewis in high esteem. He had an unimpeachable reputation for courage and principle and moved comfortably among different racial and ethnic groups. And while the years since King's death had seen nasty infighting within SCLC, Lewis remained apart from it—earning respect, the *Constitution* noted, for "his lack of political enemies in the black community."

In short order, Black Atlantans including Daddy King, Benjamin Mays, minister William Holmes Borders, and insurance executive Jesse Hill

---

* Atlanta University and Clark College merged in 1988 to form Clark Atlanta University.

anointed Lewis the heir apparent. At a mass meeting at Paschal's on December 18, Young told 150 local leaders of his decision to take the UN job, formally pledging to stay neutral in the race to succeed him. "All my friends are running," he said. "I'm really trying to stay out of it." But he not-so-quietly lent Lewis his support, as well as his Houston Street headquarters.[6]

Three days later, Lewis declared his candidacy at the American Motor Hotel downtown. A biracial gallery of Atlanta's political players turned out. Julian and James Bond were there. Coretta Scott King put in an appearance. Young stayed away, but his sentiments were clear from the presence of his wife, Jean, and several top aides. Georgia's forty-four-year-old lieutenant governor, Zell Miller, showed up, as did leaders in the local women's and labor movements. Daddy King, the honorary campaign chairman, put his name on a campaign mailer titled "Let's send Congress our best."[7]

At the hotel, Lewis turned his lifelong themes into political slogans. "For the past nineteen years," he avowed, "I have worked to build what I like to call a Beloved Community—a community of justice, a community of love, a community at peace with itself. . . . This campaign is one of hope and optimism, a continuation of my life's work to create a new order in the South . . . of hope and harmony." A message of racial inclusion and toleration, Lewis expected, would resonate in the city too busy to hate.[8]

But while his message had appeal, Lewis lacked a clear path to office. Some years before, to make it harder for Black candidates to win office, Georgia had created an idiosyncratic election system that required candidates to win an outright majority of the votes cast, which usually entailed a runoff between the top two contenders. Thus the Fifth District special election would begin with a first vote on March 15, open to all comers from either party—a "bedsheet ballot" that soon would grow to include a dozen candidates. If no candidate earned an outright majority, the top two finishers would face off three weeks later.

According to the polls, Lewis was not the front-runner. That mantle went to Wyche Fowler, the white city council president. Relatively liberal in his politics, Fowler was the same age as Lewis, thirty-six, and enjoyed the backing of the white power structure. He was coming off a strong but unsuccessful challenge to Young in the 1976 Democratic primary. As city council president, he appeared on the evening news programs so often that he had rented an apartment near the studios. In addition to Fowler, an outside threat to win the seat came from Republican Paul Coverdell, who was wagering that with the Democratic vote splintered, he might gain a runoff berth.[9]

With appealing Black and white competitors in the mix, the Fifth District contest raised new and difficult questions about race and representation. The district was 60 percent white. In a city only now burying its white supremacism, it had taken Young two attempts to win the seat. Even after his 1972 victory, moreover, Young had won over white Atlantans only incrementally. How many of these voters would line up behind a different Black candidate—untested in office—remained uncertain. At the same time, many Black Atlantans thought it vital to elect another African American. Young had made the Fifth District, Julian Bond explained, a "showcase Black district in the public mind," and for the seat to revert to a white politician would suggest that Black attainments might be ephemeral. Others feared that the calls to maintain Black representation at all costs would exacerbate racial strife and undermine the city's progress.[10]

As a lens onto the nation's evolving racial politics, the Fifth District race attracted media attention well beyond Atlanta. Syndicated columnists, including David Broder and the team of Jack Germond and Jules Witcover, wrote about it. So did *The New Republic*, the *Nation*, and *National Review*. The Washington pundits treated the race as a test case for the racial dynamics of the post–civil rights era. Everyone agreed that after centuries of exclusion, it was important for Blacks to hold elective offices. But should an elected official's color matter more than his positions? Must heavily Black districts have Black representatives? What about a mixed district like the Fifth, which had already proven itself by electing a Black congressman— would choosing a white successor signify backsliding, or only that voters now felt at ease relying on other criteria? "What is significant about this campaign," Germond and Witcover wrote, "is that the racial lines are being drawn so much more sharply than they have been in the past."[11]

For Lewis, it would be an uphill battle. For starters, he didn't have much of a staff. Lillian, who had administrative skills that he lacked, was his "closest adviser," he said, and served as de facto campaign manager. "She was the power behind the campaign," said Nick Taylor, a *Constitution* reporter who came aboard as press secretary. Bond gave advice unofficially, and Lonnie King, an old friend of Bond's from SNCC days, was a top aide. Sharon Adams, a dean at Emory College and Zell Miller confidante, signed up as well. None of them drew a salary. At the campaign offices on Houston Street, near the old civic center, furnishings were so sparse that when volunteers arrived to stuff envelopes, they had to sit on the floor.[12]

Another problem was that Lewis had never run for office before. At first he struggled to connect with voters. "Lewis has yet to find the oratorical smoothness some voters expect of a man who once addressed 250,000 in the civil rights March on Washington," lamented a *Constitution* reporter. "His handshake is still a little stiff." To Ken Bode of *The New Republic*, Lewis seemed "an uncharismatic and ineffective campaigner." *In These Times*, a left-wing monthly, derided his "mumbling speaking style" and the campaign's "amateurism and poor decision making." Lewis couldn't resist chatting with anyone who approached him, lingering in conversations and blowing his schedule to smithereens. Lillian ordered Nick Taylor to tug on her husband's sleeve and make sure he got to his appointments on time. Taylor also did a lot of the driving, since Lewis still didn't have his license.[13]

The campaign's inexperience showed up in other ways as well. One controversy arose when Lillian decided that her husband should throw a "press party" for Black reporters. Lewis hesitated, given his beliefs about racial inclusion, but then relented. "Lillian thought John would be more relaxed, that it would have an informal vibe," Taylor said. "But it was just a bad idea. You get pegged as saying one thing to one group, another thing to another group." Held on the evening of February 15 at campaign headquarters, the event bombed. "Lewis Has a Party; 3 Show Up," the *Constitution*'s headline mocked. "It wasn't intended to be a big deal," Taylor awkwardly explained to the press, adding that "any white journalists who had come to the affair would have been admitted." A white photographer hanging around the headquarters did stick around for the press event. It wasn't clear whether he was counted among the three guests.[14]

Lewis also struggled to raise money. He used his networks to line up events in Washington, New York, and Boston, but local donors claimed to be tapped out after the Carter campaign. Staff members lent money to the campaign with no guarantee of reimbursement. In mid-January, Massachusetts senator Ted Kennedy headlined a breakfast fundraiser at Lewis's Cascade Heights home. To the guests squeezed into the living room, Kennedy enumerated Lewis's impeccable personal qualities. He told them that, in 1968, Lewis had become a trustee of the Robert F. Kennedy Memorial Foundation, a low-profile role that brought no glory or remuneration but to which he committed himself wholeheartedly. "He takes the time and has never missed a meeting," Kennedy enthused. "He attends meetings that aren't publicized and works to carry on the interests of Robert Kennedy in a variety of areas—particularly for the poor, for the disadvantaged, and for young people. . . . It is important that we hear John's voice in the Congress of the United States." Even with connections like Kennedy, however, Lewis's fundraising lagged. When the candidates filed their reports at the end of February, he had just $515 on hand, compared to $19,675 for Fowler and $8,411 for Coverdell.[15]

And then there was racism. Overt expressions of bigotry were less common than they had been a decade before, but old prejudices died hard. Taylor described campaigning at the Atlantic Steel company during a shift change, when workers were coming and going. Taylor was handing out flyers as Lewis shook hands. "John was doing what he usually does," Taylor said, "which is talk to people and listening to people." One white steelworker, shuffling past the factory gates, eyed Taylor scornfully. "How can a white guy," he asked with disgust, "be working for a nigger?" Sharon Adams had a similar experience. She and Zell Miller were leafletting near Young Harris College, which Miller and other notable Georgians had attended, when they recognized a member of the board. The man was appalled that Miller was working for a Black candidate. "This guy's never going to be on our board," he declared for Miller to hear. "I think he even used the n-word," Adams said.[16]

Where racism wasn't explicit, it could operate subtly. "Atlanta proved it was ready for the urbane son of a New Orleans dentist," one Lewis supporter told Ken Bode, referring to Andrew Young. "How about the son of an Alabama sharecropper?" Compared to Young, Lewis was less experienced in elective office and spoke less gracefully—leading voters to underestimate his intelligence and competence. To ascend in a white environment, Blacks often found, required comporting themselves in ways that whites would not read as "Black."[17]

Even as Lewis faced old-fashioned racism from unreconstructed bigots, moreover, he also drew fire on racial grounds from his Black rivals. Considering Lewis a softer target than Fowler, several of them calculated that by wounding Lewis, they could overtake him among Black voters and make the runoff. Some accused Lewis of being a puppet of the Black establishment, handpicked in a secret meeting at Paschal's. Ralph Abernathy, who had entered the race and was furious at Young and the King family for backing Lewis, denigrated his younger rival as a "Johnny-come-lately" to civil rights work. "I had the privilege of bringing John into the movement," Abernathy asserted. The claim contained perhaps a smidgen of truth, if Abernathy was referring to his encounter with the eighteen-year-old student who wanted to integrate Troy State in 1958. But it was a lame gibe, given that Lewis could scarcely have begun his activism any younger. Lewis took the high road. He had "too much respect for the Rev. Abernathy," he said, to respond in kind. "The people know my record. I've spent the best years of my life trying to create an interracial democracy."[18]

Another potshot came from Hosea Williams. Twelve years earlier Williams had walked alongside Lewis over the Pettus Bridge. Now, even though he wasn't running, he resented his old comrade's favored status. Grandiosely, Williams convened what he called the "Coalition to Save Atlanta," urging Blacks to unite behind a single contender. But Williams's event fizzled; the only candidates who showed up were Abernathy, state representative Henrietta Canty, and Clennon King, a gadfly who had won notice in 1976 for trying to desegregate Jimmy Carter's all-white church in Plains.[19]

Still more brutal was Billy McKinney. A former policeman who ran as a maverick hybrid—part law-and-order populist, part militant race man— he was, a *Constitution* reporter wrote, "the campaign's rascal-in-residence, complete with wisecrack." Taking aim at the "King Klan" (an audaciously distasteful spelling), he mocked "little John" as a creature of the old guard, a simpleton and stooge for the Black establishment, who relied on out-of-state money and speechwriters' words, spelled out on cue cards. McKinney called Lewis "not smart enough to be congressman" and derided Lewis's work at the VEP, criticizing his $35,000 salary. "The real heroes of the voter registration drive are the volunteer voter registrars," McKinney said. "They didn't get paid a dime."[20]

Lewis kept his head down. Yet the attacks underscored the difficulty of his racial balancing act. The election was shaping up as a two-track contest, split into racial lanes. Fowler led the white lane, Lewis the Black lane. Since the rifts over Black Power and racial separatism a decade before, some African Americans had regarded Lewis as insufficiently radical—"not Black enough," in a common (and insulting) shorthand. He now faced pressure to prove that he was concerned specifically with problems afflicting Black voters. At the same time, Lewis had always proclaimed that progress would come when a politician's race mattered less than his positions, that progress could take the form of Blacks voting for liberal whites. As a practical matter, too, Lewis knew that he couldn't afford to be seen as "the Black candidate," because if he reached the runoff, white voters would need to believe that he would be every bit as much their champion as well.

Lewis's solution was to cleave to his racially inclusive message. Apart from its tactical value, it had the virtue of reflecting his true beliefs. "I would like to see a continuation of the racial harmony that has existed here," Lewis told David Nordan of the *Constitution*, who joined him one night to watch the hit miniseries *Roots* in Lewis's den. "I think I have the capability and ability to represent both the neighborhoods" (a euphemism for the Black communities) "and the unincorporated areas of the city" (a euphemism for the white ones). Before labor groups and community groups, he outlined a transracial message with appeal across classes. "One of the great needs of this country is to put our people back to work," he said to the United Auto Workers. "Too many people, Black and white, and particularly the young people, are out of work and have almost lost hope." The young and the aged were a special focus of his concern. He called for expanded, high-quality day care facilities and programs for the elderly to "be able to live with dignity and pride."[21]

To address the campaign's weaknesses, Lewis and Lillian made concrete changes. They hired Marvin Chernoff, a high-profile campaign consultant who had helped elect Carl Stokes mayor of Cleveland. Chernoff and Lewis were given space to work in a separate office off the main room of their headquarters, near the Xerox machine. But there was little privacy; even when Chernoff closed the door, people would barge in. One day he posted a sign that said "Knock first." A couple of days later, Chernoff spied Lewis walking toward the office, seeing the sign, and meekly knocking on the door. "John," Chernoff said, "I don't think this sign applies to you."[22]

Chernoff did more than teach Lewis to act like the boss. He placed ads on television and radio. And although Lewis spurned advice to "cultivate a Carter-like 'peanut smile'" (as one journalist put it), he did loosen up, making jokes and toning down his congenital earnestness. Lillian joined him more often, spirited and acerbic, and far less reluctant than her husband to mix it up with his detractors. When Billy McKinney taunted Lewis by saying, "Well, Lillian Lewis is actually the candidate here," John kept to the high road, but Lillian punched back, publicly calling McKinney a "buffoon."[23]

As Lillian used her voice, Lewis found his. Qualities that had seemed like political liabilities—his kindheartedness, his concern with principle, his lack of guile—came to be appreciated as virtues. "When Lewis first announced his candidacy," wrote Charles King in the *Atlanta Voice*, "I was astounded. Not our gentle John. John doesn't look like a congressman, talk like a congressman. . . . He will be slaughtered out there on a fast track, crowded with the know-it-alls, the strategists, the wheelers and dealers." But, the columnist confessed, this suspicion was misplaced. "Not only did John Lewis survive, but the plain decency of his approach and efforts proved that we were wrong."[24]

Lewis portrayed himself as both an agent of and a testament to the egalitarianism that made Atlanta prosper. "It wasn't so long ago here in the South people like us couldn't get together like this. We couldn't get together to discuss our political views with one another—it was against the law," one speech began. "I'm proud because that day is gone and because I believe that in some small way I helped bring that about. We live in a new day now, in a new South. . . . The nation looks at Atlanta and the Fifth District and sees a model of harmony, people working together toward common goals." Lewis talked about his childhood on the farm, his years in the movement, his work registering voters, his wife and baby son. "For the past nineteen years—all of my adult life—I have been working to build what I like to call an interracial democracy here in the South, a place where people can be viewed as people, not by race or color but as human beings."[25]

Most important was his work ethic. Lewis had always poured all his energy into his causes—marching, speaking, organizing, day after day, month after month. In the cold winter mornings of early 1977, he began an arduous daily routine, rising before dawn, hustling downtown by 5:30 a.m. to reach the house cleaners and laborers boarding buses for the suburbs. He would then get to the factories when they opened at seven o'clock. Taking care of John-Miles at home, Lillian would set up appointments and provide Nick Taylor with the day's itinerary, warning him, "Do not miss an event." Taylor and Lewis would run from one engagement to the next, getting in and out of the car, with Taylor badgering him to stay punctual. One day's printed schedule had John canvassing from 10:00 a.m. until 5:30 p.m. in twelve different neighborhoods, followed by a 5:45 event at the St. Paul AME Church, a 6:10 meeting with the Grant Park Area Council, a 7:30 event with the Alpha Pi Chi sorority, and a 9:00 p.m. fundraiser with "Tom Houck and Company."[26]

Support began breaking his way. Women's groups, newly influential at a time of heightened feminist consciousness, got behind him. So did the unions. So did Atlanta's Jewish community, which appreciated Lewis's support for Israel and the emigration of Soviet Jews.[27]

On March 4, Andrew Young—having all but endorsed Lewis—did so officially in an effusive twenty-minute testimonial at the Empire Realty Board's banquet. "It is important for Atlanta to have a Black congressman from the Fifth District," Young told the crowd of one thousand. "But we are not going to have a Black congressman unless we can develop a consensus around one person who we can support and trust and who also has support and trust in the white community." Marvin Chernoff had the remarks recorded and repackaged as radio spots for broadcast in the days before the runoff.[28]

Columnists and editorialists, too, now lined up behind Lewis's campaign. Political writers took to reminding voters of his leadership in the sit-ins, the Freedom Rides, the March on Washington, the Selma campaign; the beatings and the nights he spent in jail; his years at the VEP. The passion and sincerity that Lewis had displayed since his youth now showed up in newspaper stories in the form of a cute anecdote that would become a hardy staple of John Lewis profiles: he was, one *Atlanta Constitution* headline put it, the "Man Who Preached to Chickens."[29]

Then came the endorsements. The city's three Black papers—the *Voice*, the *Daily World*, and the *Inquirer*—all came out for Lewis. So did Atlanta's biggest paper, the *Constitution*, which published a robust five-paragraph testament on March 10, followed by a paean three times as long on March 14, the day before the election. Titled "John the Unknown," the second piece asked why, despite Lewis's historic achievements, he remained a mere name to so many voters. The answer, the editorial argued, was that his "mouth does less work than his mind," that he "gain[s] more satisfaction from accomplishing deeds than in speaking of them." The endorsement also echoed Lewis's nuanced position on the role that race should play in the election. "The fact is, blacks *are* desperately underrepresented" in Georgia politics, it asserted, holding only 3 percent of public offices, while forming 25 percent of the state's population. "That's a good argument for electing John Lewis, a black man, a man who understands the problems and concerns of blacks." Nonetheless, the editorial continued, "the seat is *not* a black seat. Voters demand someone who is recommended by something more than race. John Lewis is."[30]

On March 15, Lewis's campaign staff arrived early at headquarters to find that the office had been burglarized. Someone had cut the phone lines and stolen the lists of drivers who were to take people to the polls. But his turnout specialist, Ella Mae Brayboy—known for her genius at coordinating fleets of vans and station wagons—was undeterred, delivering streams of Black Lewis partisans to their polling places.[31]

As Lewis had hoped, the Black community propelled him to a second-place finish in the initial vote. He won almost 29 percent of the overall vote—which included, according to one calculation, 75 percent of the Black vote and 10 percent of the white vote. Fowler finished first with 40 percent, and Coverdell came in third with 22 percent.[32]

Lewis had his own work at the VEP to thank, in part, given the large number of Black Atlantans now registered. Some signs suggested that Lewis might yet consolidate the other candidates' support before the runoff. Abernathy and Hosea Williams set aside their grudges and backed Lewis. He won the endorsement of the Atlanta Baptist Ministers Union, which had previously favored Abernathy. But the new endorsements only went so far. As strong as Black turnout had been, white turnout had been stronger— and the district was 60 percent white. This left a challenge, the *Constitution* pointed out, "akin to a political Mt. Everest." To prevail in the runoff, Lewis would have to pry a large number of white voters away from Fowler in a matter of three weeks.[33]

Lewis's long days of knocking on doors resumed. Pitching in now were many of John's old friends. Don Harris arrived with his son, Scott. They rented a Chevy Caprice and drove around knocking on doors and passing out flyers. Bond and his children pitched in, too. "My dad would lend us, farm us out, to different campaigns every summer," Michael Bond remembered. Lewis received help from a posse of SNCC allies, including some who had been on the opposite side of the Black Power debate in 1966. In particular, a station wagon full of Washingtonians—Marion Barry, Courtland Cox, Sharlene Kranz, Reggie Robinson, Frank Smith—drove through the night to spend a week in Atlanta helping out. Kranz stayed in the Lewises' guest room, while the men bunked in the basement rec room. Lillian fed them cheese grits each morning before they hit the streets. Joined by SNCC veterans Stanley Wise and Muriel Tillinghast, both now living in Atlanta, the crew fanned out across the city to canvass or to join the occasional motorcade that would snake through Black neighborhoods with loudspeakers blaring dance music and segments of Lewis's speeches. "John really was an amazing campaigner," Smith said. "He liked campaigning. He would talk to anyone he saw." At the end of the day, everyone would gather at headquarters, stuffing envelopes and licking stamps—and on one day, Kranz recalled, enjoying foot massages from a volunteer that were positively "blissful."[34]

Cold arithmetic dictated that some voters' minds had to be changed. Reluctantly Lewis concluded that he had to go negative against the affable Fowler. As the underdog, he bore the burden of drawing contrasts that might sway wavering voters. There were not many. Lewis had long called for a national health care plan, while Fowler preferred expanding medical coverage incrementally. Lewis, a labor ally, opposed "right to work" laws that let workers opt out of unions; Fowler supported them. Both men endorsed a new package of voting reforms floated by President Carter, but where Lewis favored only modest penalties for voter fraud—fearing that steep sanctions would scare legitimate voters away from the polls—Fowler said it was necessary to crack down hard on any possibility of ballot-box mischief.[35]

At joint forums, Lewis called attention to these policy differences, wrapping them in the broad claim that he alone would speak for the dispossessed. At a televised debate six days after the initial vote, Lewis declared that he was

running to represent "that segment of the population that has been left behind . . . both white and black," and blasted Fowler as cozy with business. But
hard-knuckled campaigning went against Lewis's nature, and his gentleness
led him to soften his blows. "I don't think he understands the problems of
the people," Lewis said in the debate. "I think Mr. Fowler is representative of
those people who've got lobbyists, who've got money, who've got lawyers in
Congress." In the annals of negative campaigning, this was mild stuff. When
asked afterward about the jabs, Lewis shrugged. "I tried to do it nonviolently," he said.[36]

Lewis also eschewed appeals to racial solidarity. Appearing together on
a radio show on Wednesday, March 30, he and Fowler both disavowed any
support based on skin color. "I have worked too hard to create a biracial society to try at this time to be a part of something that is segregated," Lewis said.
Fowler took a similar stand. As an *Atlanta Constitution* columnist noted,
Lewis and Fowler had "built their entire public careers on the bedrock belief
that white and black Americans can work together, can overcome prejudice
and even the scars of history, and can participate in a greater community not
marred by the blinders of racial discrimination (in either direction, white or
black)." Neither wanted to make the campaign about race.[37]

Yet there was a big difference. As the white candidate and front-runner,
Fowler had an easier position to defend. He could point to the district's election of Young to suggest that most Fifth District voters were unconcerned
with race, even as he banked on the loyalty of most whites. Lewis, in contrast, couldn't ignore the fact that, as the columnist David Broder noted, the
Fifth District was the only congressional district east of Memphis and south
of Philadelphia to have elected a Black congressman; he had to make clear,
in other words, that for the district to choose another African American
representative was no small thing. So Lewis walked a fine line, emphasizing
issues that he hoped would mobilize Black voters—federal aid to cities, jobs,
health care, day care—but in a manner calculated not to come across as racially divisive.[38]

Some of Lewis's positions might have helped him gain ground, but
on one big issue his sympathy for the underdog played poorly. During the
campaign, Atlanta's 1,024 garbagemen, most of them Black, went on strike.
They demanded fifty-cent-an-hour raises—money that the cash-strapped

municipal government lacked. They also wanted the formal recognition of an informal rule that let them stay home whenever the temperature fell below twenty-five degrees. Maynard Jackson, eager to show that the city's first Black mayor was fiscally disciplined, deemed the strike illegal. Most Atlantans, annoyed by the piles of garbage, agreed. So did the Black press, many local unions, and the Atlanta chapters of the NAACP and Urban League. Even Daddy King urged Jackson to "fire the hell out of the striking workers."[39]

On April 1, days before the runoff, Jackson fired the garbagemen. He blamed the union leadership for forcing the issue.

Almost alone, Lewis stood with the workers. "John spent time with them and sympathized with them," said Nick Taylor—even neglecting other commitments. On the Sunday before the election, Taylor recounted, "We were there at the headquarters. He was talking to garbage workers, and he's listening to their stories. . . . John was a listener, and he embraced the concerns of these people who were not making enough money." But he was due at Phipps Plaza, a shopping center in well-to-do Buckhead in northern Atlanta, for a televised appearance with Fowler. It would be his last chance to draw direct contrasts. "On a good day with not much traffic, the Phipps Plaza is fifteen or twenty minutes away and more if there's traffic," Taylor said. "So we were late to this event."[40]

The debate went badly. The garbage dispute loomed large, with the candidates on opposite sides. Lewis defended the demand for raises. "What we have here is an emergency," he said, criticizing Jackson and calling on the federal government to cover the cost. Fowler dismissed Lewis's plan, noting that the city "got in trouble six years ago" for using federal monies to pay firefighters' salaries; it would be wrong to try again. Fowler thought that Lewis still had a lot to learn about being a politician. Though principled, Lewis's stand was imprudent. "In the midst of an unpopular strike," wrote Jim Merriner of the *Constitution*, "Lewis was for it and Fowler was against it."[41]

On Election Day, Fowler cruised with more than 60 percent of the vote. Though probably destined to lose, Lewis had hurt his chances by defending the garbagemen. Some twenty-eight precincts held their balloting at sites that had been deemed drop-off points for household refuse. Atlanta voters, in other words, were showing up to vote and encountering putrid reminders of the candidates' contrasting positions.[42]

Lewis took his loss in stride. He had been realistic about his chances all along and had calculated, as Sharon Adams said, "even if it doesn't work out, it's going to work out." Running a good race still left him well placed, at thirty-seven, to claim more opportunities in the future. He gave an upbeat concession speech, telling his followers not to be disappointed, that they had acquitted themselves well. "We came as far as we could," he said, "and I'll be heard from again."[43]

Chapter Seventeen

ACTION

———— ▪▪ ————

Thejob offer had come in April. Although Jimmy Carter—part Southern populist, part technocrat—was the first Democratic president since Grover Cleveland who couldn't be called a liberal, he placed liberals and even radicals in key administration posts. Arnie Miller, Carter's personnel chief, made a point of hiring women, African Americans, and people from nontraditional backgrounds, including lots of 1960s activists and organizers. Sam Brown, a former Eugene McCarthy aide and anti-war advocate, was tapped to run ACTION, an umbrella agency comprising the Peace Corps, VISTA, and other volunteer programs. Mary King from SNCC was his deputy. Miller, Brown, and King all agreed that Lewis, having lost his congressional bid, would be a good candidate to be ACTION's associate director for domestic operations.[1]

Lewis had few other options. He was still musing about writing a memoir of his civil rights days. Or, he told a reporter, "I may go fishing."[2]

The ACTION job had a lot to recommend it. During his brief campaign, Lewis had gotten excited about moving to Washington. The job also carried a handsome salary of $48,600—more than a congressman's. Above all, Lewis thought the job would allow him to "carry on my life's work," as he said, "to build a community based on love, a community at peace with itself." He accepted the offer.[3]

A few weeks later, Eddie Lewis died at the age of sixty-eight. He had recently suffered a stroke and stopped working. Lewis believed that his father's idleness hastened his death. All of Pike County turned out for the funeral at the Antioch Baptist Church. John delivered a eulogy and the family buried him on a hillside near the church grounds.[4]

Lewis's Senate confirmation hearings were in July. By now he was a pro before congressional panels, familiar with the routines and even the repartee. (Grilled about his many board memberships, Lewis deadpanned, "I see this appointment as a way of getting off some of the boards.") In a sign of how much America had changed in the last decade, Georgia senator Herman Talmadge—a onetime segregationist who had opposed the Civil Rights and Voting Rights Acts—introduced Lewis as "eminently qualified" and "a credit to both Georgia and the nation."

To the Senate committee, Lewis said that he wanted ACTION to carry out on a national scale the sort of community work he had done in SNCC. "An agency like ACTION, through VISTA volunteers," Lewis said, could start "going in and creating neighborhood organizations, community groups, to give people a sense of involvement, to give people a role, to let people know somebody cares." As he told a reporter, "I see the job as a continuation of my work. . . . In the past I've been on the outside fighting for change. I'm still fighting, but now it's from the inside."[5]

Confirmation went smoothly. By August Lewis was working in a tenth-floor office at 806 Connecticut Avenue, off Lafayette Square, with a view of the White House. The atmosphere was bustling. Under Sam Brown, a reporter wrote, ACTION's headquarters had been transformed into "a time warp into the Sixties . . . lots of boots, Levi's, wire-rimmed glasses on un-pretentious faces, laughter, telephones on floors, Styrofoam coffee cups and very long arguments over certain principles." One August afternoon, while sorting through job applications, Lewis fielded a congratulatory call from a surprising source. "I wish you the greatest success and I'm looking forward to working with you on behalf of the good Black people of South Carolina," said the state's senior senator, Strom Thurmond.[6]

After briefly renting an apartment at the Imperial House, on New Hampshire Avenue off Dupont Circle, Lewis bought a townhouse on Logan Circle, a mile north of his office. The $99,000 price tag struck him as outrageous for a building in a run-down, high-crime neighborhood rife with prostitutes and drug dealers. Although Lewis had been to Washington many times by now, he still displayed a boyish wonder at the big city—not unlike when he had moved to New York City a decade earlier or Nashville before that. "He is really a country boy," one profile noted, "on his way to conquer the big city."[7]

Lillian and John-Miles stayed behind in Atlanta. They visited Washington frequently, and when in town Lillian would sometimes dine with John and other couples. "We would double-date," Sharlene Kranz of SNCC recalled. "Lillian was effervescent, warm, totally with it." More often, though, Lewis hit the social scene by himself. "You didn't expect her at social functions," according to Sam Brown. "You didn't say, 'Oh, there are the Lewises.' He would come alone." Lewis's unceasing travels at VEP had accustomed the couple to frequent nights apart. Now John-Miles, rambunctious and needy, demanded Lillian's attention. Eventually, in August 1979, she took leave from her job so the family could be together in Washington.[8]

To compensate, Lewis made a family of his staff, re-creating the close-knit communities he had cherished in Nashville and SNCC. "John built a family out of that group, not just a bunch of colleagues," said John Podesta, an attorney at ACTION. "We were a group of friends relatively the same age, in our early thirties. We all became tight." Lewis was popular with the staff. "John was one of the most humane people I met in my entire life," said his colleague Karen Paget. "And one of the most kind."[9]

As he readily admitted, he wasn't a skilled manager. "I don't see my role as being an administrator," Lewis told a reporter, "but to get out there and inspire and mobilize, literally to help create a sense of community." He promoted Paget, a field director, to be his deputy. She remembered that "John traveled 80 percent of the time, and he was happy to have me doing the details." Lewis convinced his longtime right hand, Archie Allen, to resume the role he had played at VEP: speechwriter, publicist, alter ego. "He was with John at ACTION as a sort of factotum," said Paget, "totally dedicated to John and to keeping him in the public eye, to manage his public image."[10]

Lewis and Allen turned the ACTION job into one like those John had held at SNCC and VEP. With the agency's volunteer programs scattered across the country, Lewis would traverse two hundred thousand miles and forty-two states in the course of his tenure, often with Allen by his side. Sam Brown blessed the approach. "I left John free to do what he does best: cheer up the troops. An administrator he was not. He was the voice and the

conscience. John was liberated to do what he is brilliant at doing: Tell the
stories. Raise the hopes."[11]

For all the feel-good moments, Lewis's time at ACTION was full of controversy. From the moment he arrived, the agency was under incessant
criticism from the Republicans. During the War on Poverty, the Office of
Economic Opportunity had funded a welter of community-based anti-
poverty programs, some of which had become divisive for their radical politics. Community-organizing groups were suspect because, as prescribed
by radical theorists like Saul Alinsky, they pitted organizers in direct confrontation with local officials. When Nixon came to power, he neutered
the Office of Economic Opportunity and instead created ACTION, where
the surviving programs migrated. Now, however, in 1977, with the Democrats back in power, Republicans on Capitol Hill again grew irate at the
thought of taxpayer dollars subsidizing left-wing outfits like the Association
of Community Organizations for Reform Now, or ACORN. (ACORN,
admitted Podesta, was one of the "challenging grantees.") That Brown—
the man credited with the aphorism "Never trust anyone over thirty"—was
staffing ACTION with self-proclaimed radicals inflamed them further. The
right-wing press teemed with scare stories. The Heritage Foundation issued
a report about ACTION, "The New Left in Government: From Protest to
Policy-Making."[12]

Spearheading the offensive were Robert Michel of Illinois, a rising GOP
star, and John Ashbrook of Ohio, a conservative movement darling. From
his perch as the ranking minority member of a key subcommittee, Michel
would interrogate Brown and other ACTION figures in hearings. He made
them account for activists they had hired (such as Chicago Seven member
Lee Weiner) and politicized decisions they had made (withholding training
for VISTA volunteers in states that hadn't passed the Equal Rights Amendment). The Republicans would hype the ensuing confrontations.[13]

"It was a crazy time," said Marge Tabankin, a former student radical who,
at twenty-eight, now headed VISTA. "Republicans were attacking us. The
GAO moved in and audited everything." Carter's Republican predecessors
had restricted VISTA's mission to exclude community organizing. Tabankin,
an Alinsky disciple, put it back in. Accusations flew that the volunteers were

engaging in proscribed political activity. "People wanted to get rid of me," she said. "But Sam and John stood behind me."[14]

Lewis considered the harassment of his colleagues to be more of the red-baiting he had experienced at SNCC. For all their professed radicalism, the ACTION staff were hardly implementing a revolutionary agenda. They were, Lewis believed, simply helping the poor. "If Brown and Tabankin are guilty of conspiracy," Lewis declared publicly, "I want to be identified with it. It's a conspiracy for the good."[15]

Lewis's moral standing and earnest demeanor provided some political protection for ACTION. "John was a firewall with Congress," Brown said. "He helped deflect or prevent criticism." Because Lewis was so plainly decent and gentle, his story so evidently admirable, Republicans found it hard to go after him. Congressional Democrats, for their part, trusted his honesty enough to feel comfortable defending ACTION programs that they might otherwise have viewed skeptically. "They would rally to the defense of a project because John Lewis was up there on the Hill, defending it," said Podesta.[16]

Lewis found it all draining. "The worst part was having to deal with the insensitivity of Congress," he later said. "The whole time I was there, we never received a single appropriation for our department. We made it through on the standing budget, just a continuing resolution. During those three years, the concerns of poor people were not on the congressional agenda."[17]

The ugliest donnybrook came over the Peace Corps. To direct the agency, Brown had hired Carolyn Payton, an academic psychologist, dean at Howard University, and Peace Corps veteran. Payton was no conservative, but over time she came to think that Brown was politicizing the agency to match his New Left politics. She said that Brown wanted the Peace Corps "to be engaged in a kind of political activism and advocacy" and that volunteers were steered toward using left-wing tactics, like protesting against corporations in their host countries, instead of teaching math or building bridges. Brown, in contrast, scorned the "make work" of building bridges and wanted volunteers to empower local communities to improve their own lives.[18]

Lewis mediated. "John is about as averse to confrontation as any human being I've ever met," said Brown. It pained him to see colleagues fighting. Payton appreciated his attempt. "He offered me his support," she said. "I couldn't ask him to support me too strongly in the fight because that would have put his job in jeopardy." In November 1978, after months of squabbling, Brown fired Payton. She aired her grievances in a speech to educators. "I believe it is wrong to use the Peace Corps as a means ... to export a particular political ideology," she said.[19]

The firing of the agency's first Black female head—along with two other Black Peace Corps staffers—subjected ACTION to more scrutiny. Payton insinuated that Brown had acted out of prejudice. "I don't know why he fired me," she said. "It may have to do with my age, my being female, or my being Black." This brought Lewis into the fray again. On behalf of ACTION he rebutted her claims in a letter to the *Washington Post*. His tone was firm. "There is no basis to such cynical speculation," Lewis wrote. Payton's departure "stemmed from regrettable—but nonetheless honest and irreconcilable—differences with the administration concerning policy and philosophy." He decried the "unchecked rumors" and "misinformation" coursing through the media. "Those of us, black and white, who have come through the civil rights struggle have an obligation to denounce unfounded rumors which raise the specter of racism."[20]

Lewis hoped to win a reprieve for himself and his beleaguered colleagues. The upshot of Payton's firing, however, was to furnish more ammunition to the Republicans.[21]

Still a prominent figure in the national civil rights community, Lewis found himself during the Carter years enmeshed in larger controversies. The most painful of these came in August 1979, centering on Andrew Young. On August 14, newspapers disclosed that Young, in his capacity as UN ambassador, had met with Zehdi Labib Terzi, the Palestine Liberation Organization's observer delegate. At the time, the PLO still openly championed terrorism and refused to recognize Israel's right to exist. Young's intentions had been noble: he hoped to persuade the Palestinians to drop a request to recognize the PLO as a government-in-exile—a resolution that would have spiked tensions in the region. Young held that talking to your enemies was the way to overcome differences. Carter, however, followed a long-standing American policy of denying recognition to the PLO until it acknowledged Israel's legitimacy. Worse, Young hadn't cleared the Terzi meeting with his boss, Secretary of State Cyrus Vance. Prodded by Charles William Maynes, a State Department colleague, Young acquiesced in a phony cover story about the get-together, falsely painting it as impromptu rather than planned.

Young had always been a liberal more than a radical—and an exponent of integration and racial harmony. In Atlanta, he enjoyed excellent relations with the Jewish community, and he had made clear his support for Israel many times. (It was Carter's attitudes toward Israel that Jews questioned.) But the reports of Young's colloquy with Terzi sent a chill through the Jewish community, dredging up fears that America's alliance with Israel, widely seen as an imperiled nation, was in jeopardy. Nonetheless, no major Jewish leaders called for Young's ouster. It was Cy Vance—feeling undermined, lied to, and humiliated by his subordinate—who insisted. Carter, saying Young had "lied," forced his friend to resign.[22]

The incident inflamed tensions between Blacks and Jews. Since the rise of Black anti-Semitism amid the fumes of late-1960s militancy, the once-strong marriage between these two afflicted communities had deteriorated into something like a lovers' quarrel. Sometimes rifts opened about Israel, with Black radicals tending to identify with the stateless Palestinians, Black liberals aligning with the Jews, and almost all taking umbrage at Israel's opportunistic relations with South Africa. Disputes could also arise over local politics, like the notorious monthslong ruckus over a Brooklyn teachers strike in 1968, or the ransacking of Jewish-owned businesses during urban riots. Through it all, however, Black and Jewish leaders had repaired the breaches. In the 1970s, Bayard Rustin and A. Philip Randolph would place full-page ads in the *New York Times* affirming Black support for Israel or American Jewry when Israel came under siege, securing signatures from Coretta King, James Farmer, Ralph Ellison, Pauli Murray, Jackie Robinson, Rosa Parks, Harry Belafonte, and other luminaries.[23]

Reliably, Lewis had put his name to those ads. He also spoke out independently in support of Israel, which he described as "an outpost of democracy in the Middle East," and he called for American-led "efforts toward a lasting and equitable peace in the Middle East arising from direct negotiations" between Israel and its neighbors. Those assurances had calmed Jewish anxieties about the durability of the Black-Jewish relationship.[24]

But the Young imbroglio upset the equilibrium. "Young capitulated to Jewish pressure," charged Jesse Jackson. Though inaccurate, that myth would persist. Some pro-Israel Black leaders including Coretta King, Vernon Jordan, and Bayard Rustin came to Young's defense, protesting his resignation while reiterating their desire to sustain amicable Black-Jewish relations. Others demagogued the issue—most visibly Jackson, who sneered at "our former allies, the American Jewish community" and flew to Lebanon, where he hugged and kissed PLO leader Yasir Arafat. More disturbing to Jews than Jackson's grandstanding, however, was a late-August conclave in New York that included many mainstream Black leaders, including longtime Jewish allies Vernon Jordan, Kenneth Clark, and Ben Hooks of the NAACP. Their session generated a caustic statement, which Julian Bond read to the press. It assailed Israel for its ties to South Africa and took aim at unspecified "Jewish organizations and intellectuals" for having become "apologists for the racial status quo" on affirmative action. The statement would have been harsher, it was reported, but for the moderating hands of Hooks and Jordan.[25]

As a government official, Lewis didn't attend the New York confab. But the statement—which also implied that Jewish civil rights advocates had supported the movement purely out of self-interest—distressed him. He tried to calm the waters in an interview with Jack Nelson of the *Los Angeles Times*. Without naming names, Lewis chided "some of the rhetoric coming from some quarters of the Black community, . . . doing a disservice to the Black community." He explained, "I don't want to see any leader or any organization do anything further to create tension and division. If it hadn't been for the white liberal element in this country, particularly the Jewish community, we could not have made much of the progress we have made."[26]

Like many other supporters of Israel, Lewis did not lack sympathy for the Palestinian people or their desire for statehood. It was the scapegoating of Jews for Young's ouster and the ugly insinuations seeping into the discourse that he felt it urgent to arrest. "In the whole episode, John was a moderating force," said Stuart Eizenstat, an Atlantan and top Carter adviser. "He really helped to prevent a Black-Jewish schism. He was always trying to calm things down." The Atlanta Jewish community also took notice. "During the whole affair," said Elaine Alexander, a close friend, "John was the only one who spoke up." Members of both communities concerned about preserving their historic alliance remembered Lewis's intervention.[27]

In smaller ways, too, Lewis showed a concern at ACTION for making sure that no one felt unwelcome. When morale got low around the office, he invited Dick Gregory to come deliver his trademark mix of stand-up comedy and political exhortation. "He came in, he was funny, he was encouraging," Brown said. "It was a big shot in the arm for everybody." Paget credited Lewis with "a stroke of brilliance" for knowing what the staff needed. Gregory, for his part, had long considered Lewis a special creature, "this sweet, honest-to-goodness, beautiful guy. . . . I have a son, and I can say, if my son grew up to be one-tenth as beautiful and as decent as John Lewis," Gregory said, "I would feel that I had succeeded as a father."[28]

At another point, a row broke out in the Chicago regional office after an employee underwent what was then called a sex-change operation. With such transitions almost unheard of in the late 1970s, the staff—none of whom had ever met a transgender person—was up in arms. One day their colleague had left the office regarded by the staff as male, but returned identifying and living as female and using the women's bathroom. Adding to the delicacy of the matter, the worker was white, while most of the women on staff were Black. They filed a grievance through their union, which brought the issue to Washington's attention. No one wanted to touch it.

But Lewis did. He felt strongly that the worker be treated respectfully. He also insisted that the women in the office be shown respect. He kept returning to the problem, demanding that a solution be found. Finally, the Chicago office addressed it: the transgender staffer agreed to use the women's room during designated hours, when the other women would have the choice to stay away—a solution that met, more or less, with everyone's satisfaction.[29]

The most memorable moments of Lewis's government service came on his travels. He and Archie Allen paid visits to small communities to hear people's concerns and offer assistance and inspiration. "The best part of the work in government was the time I've spent with the people," Lewis said. "For example, talking with an elderly Native American couple in Navajo, through a translator. To see them, the people, their faces, to learn what they want for their children and grandchildren, this has been the best." On one trip, to Hotevilla-Bacavi, Arizona, Lewis met with David Monongye, a Hopi leader known as Grandfather David. "It was a beautiful end of a day near sunset out in front of the hogan where Grandfather David lived," recalled Allen. "The Hopi had come in from out on the desert and were forming a semicircle around him. He was seated in the king's chair, holding court as if he were the head of a nation, and was speaking to John." Though fluent in English, Monongye spoke in the Hopi language for the benefit of those who weren't. Lewis listened attentively. "John told him that he would do everything in his power to carry this message back to the president," Allen said. "It was just a very short, compassionate response."[30]

There were also trips to Kentucky and West Virginia to spotlight poverty among Appalachian coal miners and to the Black Belt region. On one 1979 excursion to Iberia Parish, Louisiana, Lewis, Sam Brown, and other colleagues intended to visit a VISTA project involving plantation workers who were being exploited by the sugar company they worked for. The ACTION group drove along a narrow rutted road inside a sugarcane field, with stalks rising high on either side. Suddenly, they saw a pickup truck coming at them down the one-lane road, with two scowling men perched in the back with rifles. Jumping off the truck bed, the men—employees of the sugar mill—stopped Lewis's entourage and ordered them "in fairly rude language," as Brown put it, to leave. An interracial party, even in 1979, was not welcome in those parts.[31]

Fortunately, Lewis's group was traveling with a local television crew. They hopped out of the backseat of their car with their camera rolling. "At which point," Brown said, "the texture of the questioning changed dramatically from 'Get the fuck out of here' to 'Can we help you figure out where you're going?'" Brown and Lewis chose not to press the issue, fearing that the plantation workers might face retaliation. But they notified the press. "The plantation workers are in servitude—slavery," Lewis explained to reporters, "and there's no sense in mincing words." Lewis affirmed that the VISTA projects were trying to help the local people "through self-help projects such as agricultural co-ops, co-operative health clinics, sewing co-ops, and solar greenhouses for food production. . . . We will do everything in our power to assist in that effort to help them make a difference in their own lives."[32]

Lewis's journeys also brought him to Alabama, including for one trip that would affect him deeply. For years, Lewis had modeled forgiveness, professing respect and love even for his former antagonists. On the death in 1973 of Lyndon Johnson—an eternally despised figure for some anti-war leftists—Lewis eulogized him effusively for having "freed Black people from political slavery. . . . He was a people's man and he'll probably go down in history as one of our greatest presidents." Lewis had at other times mended friendships with SNCC rivals, forgiven political foes, and even embraced erstwhile segregationists.[33]

But George Wallace had never benefited from Lewis's charity of heart. In the early 1970s, when Wallace was courting Black voters in pursuit of another gubernatorial term, Lewis scoffed at his adversary's newfound egalitarianism. "I can't understand how any Black could in good conscience support George Wallace," Lewis had said. "He symbolizes all the things we fought against and tried to change for the past fifteen or twenty years."[34]

By mid-1979, however, Lewis had come to see things differently. Since leaving office in January, Wallace had been on an apology tour, recanting his segregationism before various audiences. While in Alabama for a family reunion, Lewis discussed with Archie Allen the idea of meeting with Wallace. Allen placed the call and made the arrangements.[35]

They met at Wallace's Montgomery office on July 23. The ex-governor had a sinecure with the University of Alabama, but he still displayed a nameplate that said "George C. Wallace, Governor." He was with his valet, a Black man—as if to proclaim, Lewis thought, "Some of my best friends are colored." Lewis was wearing his usual dark suit and a light-colored necktie with diagonal stripes. Wallace wore a three-piece suit, the vest buttoned snugly, with a foulard tie. He was "in a great deal of pain," Lewis observed, "because he kept moving. He had a real problem with hearing. . . . Every now and then he would grab his side and his stomach."

Allen took a few pictures as the men shook hands: Lewis was standing; Wallace—partially paralyzed by a 1972 assassination attempt—was in his wheelchair, behind his desk. Behind them was a wall-mounted, framed tapestry bearing the Alabama coat of arms.

The meeting received no news coverage. Years later, accounts of the conversation—including Lewis's own—would portray it as an apology, part of Wallace's conversion from an unabashed racist into a governor responsive to Black voters' needs. But according to a tape recording that Lewis and Allen made immediately after the visit, Wallace's comments were far short of penitent or apologetic.

After exchanging pleasantries and talking about ACTION, Wallace "went into a long and extensive discourse about his own involvement and his relationship with Black people and the different episodes that took place during the civil rights movement," Lewis recounted immediately afterward. Wallace claimed that "what he did was not so much an opposition to Black people. He never considered himself a racist. He never made a racist speech, that maybe a few things he said offended people, and he's sorry if people were offended by it. But he loved Black people because they cared for him and raised him. He played with them and went swimming with them and ate with them, but they didn't go to school together. And they were taught . . . that it was best for the Black race and it was best for the white race for people to be separated."

Then, according to Lewis's account, Wallace paused and said, "I'm not so sure why I'm saying this to you." Wallace claimed that the *New York Times* and other media had always misrepresented him. "But John," he added, "you're a leader among Black people and a leader among people."

Lewis listened. "I guess he thought that I would help set the record straight," he said to Allen after the meeting.

Wallace had offered other self-justifications. He said that in 1963 when Vivian Malone and James Hood tried to enroll at the University of Alabama, he had acted as he did in order to keep "the hoodlums and the thugs" from running wild, as they had at Ole Miss. He said, "I never supported the Klan." He said that on Bloody Sunday, he had ordered Al Lingo "to keep the marchers from crossing the bridge for their own protection."

When Allen asked Lewis for his reaction to all of these comments, Lewis replied: "I thought it was shallow, hollow, and it just didn't ring right. The weakest statement was his rationale for what happened in Selma."

In that initial conversation with Allen, Lewis didn't mention any apology from Wallace, only talk of "changes" and a "transition." But he did tell Allen that despite Wallace's self-serving account, "I was happy to have an opportunity to chat with him. We never met, our paths never crossed. He had said things about me and I have said things about him over the years. And I think it was a mutual feeling that it was good for two people who had been, who grew up near each other, at different times in different periods—he's somewhat older than I am—at least to shake hands and to say hello. It was two human beings in a sense putting some of their bitter and strange feelings behind them to say hello to another human being. . . . I felt a great deal of sympathy for the man and compassion for the man."[36]

In interviews a decade later, and again in 1998 when Wallace died, Lewis spoke and wrote about the meeting very differently, focusing on the compassion he felt and downplaying the governor's self-justifications. Lewis's later accounts were not irreconcilable with his contemporaneous one, but they were markedly different in emphasis. "I'm prepared to give him the benefit of the doubt," Lewis said in 1988. In these later accounts Lewis also said that from the moment he encountered Wallace, "I could tell that he was a changed man." He also said he heard a sincerity in the governor's voice. "It was almost like a confession," Lewis recalled, as if "I were his priest."

In these later accounts, Lewis remembered Wallace saying, "I want to ask your forgiveness for anything I've done to wrong you." Lewis now described holding hands and praying with the governor as Wallace vowed, "I want to get right with my maker."[37]

When Lewis returned to his office at ACTION after the visit, he gathered several colleagues to tell them about the meeting. "There were four or five of us. We were on the tenth floor," according to Karen Paget. "We were in a space the size of a large dining room. I remember the expression on his face. It was as if to say, 'Will wonders never cease?'" The people in the office thought this was a historic moment and deserved recognition. "But John is so modest, we worried that the moment would be lost to history."[38]

By the end of 1979, two and half years into his job at ACTION, Lewis decided to go back to Georgia. The arguments for quitting had become overwhelming. Lillian found Washingtonians to be rude. "I had a three-year-old. We'd go out. People wouldn't talk to me. I was a nonperson," she said. "In Atlanta people talk to you whether you have occupational credentials or not." John also missed Atlanta. "In Washington," Lewis said at the time, "I have found so many people unwilling to take a chance, to take a risk. So many people don't care." He was suffering from headaches and backaches. Lillian thought they were caused by his job.[39]

The Republican browbeating certainly took a toll. One trip to the Hill turned into a fourteen-hour grilling. The day began inauspiciously, Podesta recalled, with John Ashbrook urging that the ACTION witnesses "be read their Miranda rights." ("Maybe if Mr. Brown will be under oath," Ashbrook warned, "he may want an attorney at that point.") Later in the hearings, another congressman—"his voice steeped in outrage," Podesta said—professed astonishment that Lewis had been arrested forty times, as if his noble defiance of segregation rendered him unfit for office. "He didn't see how anyone who had such a 'criminal record' could serve in such an important post in government," said Podesta, who looked on in bafflement.[40]

Lewis was not so much offended as deflated, fed up with the governmental inertia and partisan jockeying. "John never really fit the image of the bureaucrat," Brown reflected. "Quite frankly, John wasn't a star in Washington.... Too often, instead of appearing at the 'right' dinner parties, he was out of town visiting the poor on Indian reservations or in Appalachia."[41]

Beyond the job's vexations, there was also the possibility of another shot at Congress. Senator Herman Talmadge was retiring; if Wyche Fowler ran for the Senate, the Fifth District congressional seat would be open, and Lewis could try again.[42]

There was a final reason, too, that Lewis was quitting. He was no longer happy working for Jimmy Carter.

When Carter had won the presidency in 1976, Lewis had supplied reporters with fulsome praise. "The things Carter has said to me make me feel his sense of understanding and commitment are deeper than Kennedy's or even Johnson's," Lewis had asserted, not quite plausibly.[43]

But Carter proved disappointing. He flailed in the face of economic setbacks, foreign policy trials, and what he called a national malaise, and he alienated important blocs of supporters, including Black Americans. Though Lewis held his tongue publicly, in 1979 he joined a group of a dozen African American administration officials who would meet quietly to share grievances about Carter. He had several gripes: the president "spread himself too thin," Lewis believed, and was inept at cultivating support from Congress and the public. "We're all reaching the point," one conspirator told the *New York Times*, letting slip the secret meetings, "where we will have to decide whether to back Carter for reelection."[44]

Lewis also complained that Carter hadn't kept his promises to the poor.

On July 15, 1979, struggling with a welter of crises, Carter had delivered a major televised address describing "a crisis of confidence . . . that strikes at the very heart and soul and spirit of our national will." The next day, Lewis met with White House aide Louis Martin to offer his own analysis. He followed up the meeting with a three-page memo, drafted by Allen, keyed to Carter's pledge the previous night "to travel this country, to hear the people of America."

Lewis's memo urged the president to visit three places: an Indian reservation, an Appalachian community, and the Black Belt. "These visits would enable President Carter to reach out personally and touch Americans in areas never before visited by a President of the United States," Lewis explained, "and to demonstrate the sincerity and depth of a personal and Presidential commitment to humanity." Having traveled himself to all these spots, Lewis volunteered to "provide all the assistance necessary in the planning of those visits" including drafting the itineraries and connecting the president to local leaders and groups.[45]

Carter never replied.

"It was frustrating to see the problems and needs of people," Lewis later said, "and also that you can only do so much as part of an administration."[46]

There were smaller vexations, too. At one point, Lewis had hoped that Carter would talk about "the beloved community," much the way Lewis himself did. Perhaps Carter would make the phrase into his slogan, like Kennedy's "New Frontier" or Johnson's "Great Society." Allen urged the idea on Carter speechwriter Hendrik Hertzberg, who took up the cause. But Carter never warmed to the phrase.[47]

Lewis wasn't the only one exasperated. In November 1979, Ted Kennedy announced that he would challenge the president for the Democratic Party nomination. The decision put Lewis in a bind. Since 1968, Lewis had grown close to Ted and the Kennedy clan. Politically, too, he was closer to Kennedy than to Carter, and the senator's aides—and even Ethel Kennedy, Robert's widow—were recruiting him for the campaign. Lewis confided to friends that in his heart of hearts, he favored Kennedy.[48]

But Lewis was loyal by temperament. For all his qualms about Carter, he knew that the president was popular in Georgia—which might matter if Lewis sought office again. Lewis decided to quit the administration, while staying neutral in what was sure to be a nasty primary duel.

Before Lewis could share this decision with Carter, rumors got around. In November, he was at a staff retreat in the Rockies when word came that the White House was looking for him. "John was ducking the call," recalled Paget. "I was ducking the call. It became excruciating." Finally, Lewis went to the phone. It was Louis Martin, who said he'd heard that Lewis was planning to sign up with Kennedy. Lewis denied it. When he returned to Washington, Carter asked him to a meeting on December 3 to hear for himself.[49]

Suffering from a bad cold, Lewis did not consider this trip one of his happier Oval Office visits. He took a seat on a striped sofa. Carter, in a cardigan, sat in a wing chair. "I am resigning, Mr. President," Lewis confirmed. "But I will not be campaigning for Senator Kennedy. I simply want to return to Atlanta."[50]

Carter had one request. "If you can't support me fully," he said, "all I ask is that you remain neutral."[51]

Lewis agreed. That had been his plan. Carter sent him a warm letter of thanks.

News of Lewis's resignation appeared three days later. Lewis described his dilemma candidly. "I have friends on both sides," he told a reporter. "I have a feeling for both of them, Senator Kennedy and President Carter. It's brutal."[52]

Wyche Fowler didn't run for Senate in 1980, and Lewis didn't mount another congressional bid. But he was happy all the same to head back to Atlanta. "I think through being in Washington, I've become more of a private person," he said. "I never got caught up in going to the parties, the receptions. I just went to work. . . . I had a few friends, and I tried to do my best."[53]

Chapter Eighteen

ATLANTA

——— ▪ ▪ ———

J ohn Lewis returned to Atlanta in 1980 with a yen to keep serving in public office. Lillian encouraged his ambitions, convinced that he had a great career ahead of him. Some friends suggested he run for mayor, but Lewis knew that his skills and temperament didn't suit him for the job—and in any case Andrew Young had made clear his own interest in the position. Instead Lewis set his sights on the city council, the elections for which would be held the next year.

In the meantime, he needed work. In the fall of 1980, he became director of community affairs for the National Consumer Cooperative Bank—a federally established depository that provided funds to housing cooperatives, farming collectives, and other nonprofits to promote economic growth in poor neighborhoods. Based in Washington, the bank had an Atlanta office.[1]

It wasn't the right job. Lewis missed the interaction with everyday Americans, and the details of lending left him cold. When the bank had to terminate its loans, the work could be unpleasant. At one point it foreclosed on an Atlanta grocery, the University West Consumers Co-op, run by a man named Jameel Kareem, who paid himself handsomely while doing little, bank officials believed, for the community. Kareem accused the bank of racism, and in Atlanta's Black wards Lewis came under fire for siding with a faceless financial institution over a well-known local figure. Lewis insisted the charge of racism was baseless and cynical—"playing the race card," he called it. "With Jameel," Lewis told a reporter, "it never became a true co-op. It became his thing, his private domain."[2]

Lewis decided to leave the job. By March 1981, speculation about the city council races was quickening, with Lewis's name in the mix. A government position would mean a loss of income—the salary was only $18,000 annually—but he and Lillian, now earning $30,000 from the university, would manage. In July, Lewis declared for an at-large council seat held by longtime incumbent Jack Summers. As in 1977, he believed he could overcome his underdog status by campaigning aggressively. Over the summer and fall he visited all of Atlanta's neighborhoods, Black and white, rich and poor, from sunrise until past dusk.

The campaign forced Lewis to adopt a more critical stance toward the city's governance. For years he had been an unabashed booster, championing Atlanta as a model of integration and interracial cooperation. Now he talked about the city's tangle of problems—problems endemic to most big cities at the time. The economic hardships of the 1970s, which persisted through the so-called Reagan Recession of the early 1980s, had ended Atlanta's boom years. De facto residential segregation persisted, with white and Black communities divided by gulfs in wealth, employment, and education. Crime was spurring whites to decamp for the suburbs, eroding the city's tax base and its political power statewide. Scholars of Black life, such as William Julius Wilson of the University of Chicago, argued that the problems African Americans faced in the 1970s and '80s now had less to do with bigotry than with transformations in the economy, including declining job opportunities, that gave rise to an "underclass."[3]

Lewis saw merit in the new scholarship. His work at ACTION had reinforced his belief in the primacy of poverty as a social issue, and he saw the many pressing urban problems as intertwined. "What you have is something like a festering sore, a white ring around a poor, black core with a few prosperous black and white neighborhoods," he said. "The city is surrounded by suburban wealth. There's a realization that we've got to do something about it. If we don't, the sore is going to burst." In Atlanta, he said, "we've been pushing an image, now we'll have to deal with it. A whole segment of the population here has been left behind."[4]

On the campaign trail, he promised to be "a voice for the voiceless," endorsing what were standard liberal policy solutions on most issues. But he also acknowledged problems within poor Black communities. He was "appalled," he said, when he saw on his campaign rounds just how many teenagers were working as "peddlers of drugs and hot stolen merchandise," and he beseeched Atlantans to foster "social pressure and a level of conscious-ness" to make these youngsters "embarrassed" to traffic in criminal activities. The desertion of the downtown areas also had to be halted. "Atlanta cannot continue to be a 9 a.m. to 6 p.m. city," he said. "People need to feel that they are safe in their neighborhoods."[5]

Lewis also made an issue of ethics in government. In Atlanta, develop-ers and commercial groups energetically wielded their money and influence. The business-friendly environment had lubricated Atlanta's robust growth, but also encouraged the neglect of poorer constituencies. Feeding the cor-ruption, city statutes allowed council members to hold jobs or collect in-come from outside business deals, creating conflicts of interest and sowing doubts about their integrity.[6]

In the end, Summers's service proved no match for Lewis's dogged cam-paigning and heroic biography. Lewis hauled in a slew of endorsements, in-cluding from the *Constitution*, and coasted to victory with 69 percent of the vote. It was his first electoral victory, the start of a long career as an elected representative of the people of Atlanta.

Young won the mayoralty in a hard-fought race, defeating a white can-didate. That race had stirred up racial tensions, which Lewis tried to defuse. Atlanta, he said after the election, must promote more than "just peaceful coexistence between Blacks and whites . . . nor can it be just people living in two different worlds—a Black world and a white world. We've got to have one world, one community, one city."[7]

On the city council, Lewis emerged as the body's most outspoken member, but also one of its most polarizing. He accumulated a roster of supporters and admirers, from a diverse mix of backgrounds, who cheered him on when-ever he struck a bold stand. But he also accrued enemies who found him self-righteous, inflexible, and—notwithstanding his oft-touted humility—more than a little self-aggrandizing. In his first elected public position, Lewis now came to appreciate the nuances and complexities of politics, the need to balance his principled positions with a measure of compromise and accommodation.

The main issue that thrust Lewis into controversy was a yearslong fight over what became known as the presidential parkway. When Jimmy Carter sought to build his presidential library on grounds near Emory University, his plans included a four-lane highway that would slice through historic neighborhoods, both Black and white, including a park designed by the great landscape architect Frederick Law Olmsted. Lewis was against it. Not only would the road destroy historic homes and greenspace, but, he feared, it would lead to congestion and pollution and a diminished quality of life for those in the affected neighborhoods. Lewis also worried that the cost of the roadway would divert funds from precincts of the city that needed government largesse. The fight over the road would become a key test of Lewis's independence, his willingness to follow his principles despite immense political pressures.[8]

Versions of the road plan had been circulating for decades, long before the Carter Library was even envisioned. As governor, Carter himself had vetoed one. During the 1981 elections, almost all of the candidates for public office had opposed a new thoroughfare, including Andrew Young. "We all ran on a no-roads platform, and that was what you needed to do to get elected," Young explained. "But once I got to be mayor . . . I had to worry about the growth of the city, and I couldn't imagine turning away President Carter's library." Lewis, however, held to his position, and his resistance pitted him against his old ally. Other African American leaders also criticized Lewis. It was a rude welcome into life as an elected official.[9]

Early in 1982, as his mayoralty got underway, Young pushed ahead. His emissaries pressured Lewis to get on board. Joseph Lowery of the SCLC, who always had an unspoken beef with Lewis, warned him sharply to "back off." Young's aides whispered to Lewis that they could relieve his campaign debt. "Absolutely everybody opposed to John's position tried to talk to him," said Stanley Wise. None made headway.[10]

Uglier methods came into play. Because the preservationists fighting the roadway were mostly white, the *Baltimore Afro-American* reported, "the difference of opinions became a race issue, with blacks turning against Lewis." One militant group drove trucks with loudspeakers through Black neighborhoods, blaring accusations of perfidy. An outfit called the Black Slate, linked to an eccentric Afrocentric church, circulated leaflets calling Lewis's position "a vote against the mayor and the Black community." "Once again," Lewis later wrote, "I was accused of not being black enough."[11]

Young John Lewis, circa 1951.

The ten Lewis siblings, probably in the early 1970s.

3

On February 27, 1960, "Big Saturday," Lewis (seated, center) and the Nashville Student Movement staged their historic lunch-counter sit-ins.

4

In April 1960, Nashville activists C. T. Vivian, Diane Nash, and Bernard LaFayette lead a march on city hall.

5

Lewis with fellow Freedom Rider Jim Zwerg after their assault by a Montgomery, Alabama, mob.

At a press conference with James Farmer, Ralph Abernathy, and Martin Luther King Jr. during the Freedom Rides. Lewis's head is bandaged.

Photographer Danny Lyon's picture of Lewis kneeling with activists in Cairo, Illinois, became a popular SNCC poster.

Lewis enjoying the SNCC folk festival in Greenwood, Mississippi, where Bob Dylan and the Freedom Singers performed performed, 1963.

Lewis loved dancing, here with SNCC friend Casey Hayden.

Lewis with fellow SNCC activists Courtland Cox (with glasses), Stokely Carmichael (behind Cox), Gloria Richardson, and Stanley Wise.

Planning the March on Washington are civil rights leaders (left to right) Bayard Rustin, Jack Greenberg, Whitney Young, James Farmer, Roy Wilkins, Martin Luther King, Lewis, and A. Philip Randolph.

Lewis (at right) editing his controversial speech at the March on Washington with (from left) Mildred Forman, Courtland Cox, and James Forman, August 28, 1963.

The many leaders of the march included (from left to right): Mathew Ahmann, Cleveland Robinson (seated with glasses), Rabbi Joachim Prinz, A. Philip Randolph (seated), Joseph L. Rauh Jr., Lewis, and Floyd McKissick.

As head of the Voter Education Project from 1970 to 1976, Lewis toured the South, often with his best friend, Julian Bond (next to Lewis), registering Blacks to vote.

23

"You're a survivor," James Baldwin told Lewis in 1976, "and a very honest man."

24

In 1977, Lewis, seen here with his wife, Lillian, and their son, John-Miles, ran for Congress and lost but resolved to run again.

On July 23, 1979, Lewis met with Alabama governor George Wallace. At the time, he called Wallace's excuses for supporting segregation "shallow," but years later described the visit as an act of reconciliation.

26

Under Jimmy Carter, Lewis was deputy director of ACTION, which oversaw federal volunteer work. His experience working for Carter wasn't a happy one.

In March 1994, before the first inclusive South African elections, Lewis led a congressional trip where he visited with Nelson Mandela, soon to be elected president.

Lewis was one of Bill Clinton's strongest boosters in 1992. In 2008, he backed Hillary Clinton for president, only to change his endorsement to Barack Obama.

29

Lewis with two of his trusted chiefs of staff, Michael Collins and Linda Earley Chastang.

30

With John-Miles.

31

After enduring racist taunts, Lewis (seen here with colleagues Steny Hoyer, Andre Carson, Speaker Nancy Pelosi, and John Larson) defied the mobs to lead Democrats to the Capitol to pass universal health care legislation in 2010.

32

The success of Lewis's graphic memoir, *March*, made him a fan favorite at Comic-Con. Illustrator Nate Powell is behind Lewis to the left and coauthor Andrew Aydin to the right.

33

President Obama and First Lady Michelle Obama, as well as former president Bush (not visible in photo) and many others, joined Lewis in Selma for the fiftieth anniversary of Bloody Sunday.

34

On *The Late Show with Stephen Colbert*, Lewis crowd-surfed, to the delight of social media users.

Lewis wept at the White House in 2016, as C. T. Vivian recounted the journey from segregation to Obama's presidency.

During the racial upheaval of 2020 in the wake of the murder of George Floyd, Lewis visited Black Lives Matter Plaza in Washington, DC. He died six weeks later.

The rhetoric stung. Ever since 1966, hard-line Black activists had from time to time deemed Lewis disloyal to his race. Sometimes the charge was subtle, nothing more than a subtext of a criticism. On occasion it was crude. (Once, a Black Los Angeles paper accused Lewis of having married "a Yankee White woman"; when called on to retract the claim, it declared, "JOHN LEWIS WILL NEVER, EVER, EVER BE BLACK, thus, we apologize for calling him Black.") Now and then, the barbs implied that Lewis's hope for an interracial "beloved community" was itself flawed, that it conceded too much sympathy to whites. Yet Lewis held to his position.

The city council was to vote on Young's road proposal in July. Two days beforehand, a councilman invited Lewis to a Saturday breakfast at a restaurant called the Canopy Castle. Lewis showed up to find not only the councilman but Young himself, along with several staff members and other councilors. In a wood-paneled room downstairs, they sat down to eggs, sausage, and grits. Young asked Lewis point-blank to abstain on the parkway vote.[12]

"No way," Lewis said. "If I'm there, I'm going to vote." No one could change his mind.

The next night, Lewis was at home when the phone rang. John-Miles, six, answered it. "Daddy!" he called as he ran into the living room. "A man's on the telephone and he says he's President Carter. But I don't believe it."

Carter was laughing on the other end. But he cut to the chase. "John, it's about that vote that's coming up. I don't believe that you love me anymore."

The attempt at humor—or manipulation—landed with a thud. "I need your help here," Carter continued. "I gave you a job, and you came up to Washington and you took it. And then you left and went and worked for Ted Kennedy."

Lewis was offended. He reminded Carter that he had stayed neutral in the primary and campaigned for Carter in the general election. "I'm sorry, Mr. President," he concluded. "But I don't think the road is needed. I made a commitment during the campaign and I have to stay with that commitment."[13]

At the council meeting the next day, Lewis rose from his seat to deliver a jeremiad against the highway. The seven-minute speech contained, the *Atlanta Daily World* reported, "the strongest and most forceful objections" of any council member. Lewis did more than lay out his concerns. He also accused Young's staff of "dirty pool . . . misrepresentation, intimidation, and harassment"—triggering a roar of applause from the galleries. Two allies of Lewis's, Myrtle Davis and Bill Campbell, both joined him—the only Black council members to do so. Five white members did so as well. But they fell short, 11–8.

There was some consolation. The council amended the plan to reduce the four-lane highway to two lanes with a grassy median. Still, Lewis had lost his first big fight.[14]

The council vote, however, turned out to be just the start. In the labyrinthine approval process that lay ahead—a slew of state and federal agencies had to weigh in—there were opportunities to reverse course. Neighborhood activists formed CAUTION (Citizens Against Unnecessary Thoroughfares in Older Neighborhoods) and staged protests, petitioned state and federal bodies, and filed lawsuits, with Lewis as their most prominent and passionate advocate. "He was instrumental in our fight," said Ruth Wall, a leading anti-road activist. "He was with us day and night." A headline over an admiring November 1982 *Atlanta Weekly* profile read "Butting Heads with the Status Quo." The *Baltimore Afro-American* called John "the honest man Diogenes was searching for." Carter kept demanding the wider road, threatening to move his library if he didn't get his way.[15]

The fight stretched on longer than anyone dreamed. In the summer of 1983, the Georgia Department of Transportation was set to render its decision about authorizing the road. On Tuesday evening, June 7, it held the last of a series of public forums, at the Atlanta Civic Center. CAUTION had rented a room nearby to use as a command post. Parkway opponents dominated the proceedings with speeches, comments, catcalls, and derisive laughter. Lewis gave a rousing call to action with all the gusto of the stemwinders of his civil rights speeches. While the stakes of a battle over a 2.4-mile roadway paled next to those of the fight against Jim Crow, these were the methods and rhetoric that Lewis knew and reached for. "We will use nonviolent protest to stop this road!" he hollered to the civic center crowd, which leapt to its feet.[16]

Lewis and CAUTION failed to persuade the Department of Transportation to kill the roadway that night, but they fired up the troops. Over the next several years, the activists tried everything they could think of. Lewis tried engaging Carter directly; when that failed, opponents protested at events where Carter spoke. They courted state legislators, throwing parties and lunches for the lawmakers' wives. They petitioned the Federal Highway Administration to block the road on historic preservation grounds. They scrutinized the "environmental impact statement" required of construction projects, spelling out the harm that construction would cause.[17]

But the road's advocates kept winning. In October 1984, workers broke ground on the library site. By January 1985, the Department of Transportation was laying groundwork for the parkway itself.[18]

As construction began, another protest group, the Road Busters, fought the project with guerrilla tactics—laying their bodies before machinery until police carried them away. "People would climb up in trees and chain themselves to the trees. They chained an old Volvo to a tree," recalled Sam Collier of the Sierra Club. (The pale orange station wagon, which had no wheels, "serves as a sort of field headquarters," the *Constitution* reported, and was "stocked with . . . apples and Celestial Seasonings tea.") Lewis taught the activists how to mount protests and get arrested nonviolently. "They had a lot of demonstrations where John was speaking," said Collier, "and saying, yes, this is exactly what you do over something unjust like this road." At rallies, Lewis always invoked the civil rights movement. "We must be prepared to use the tactics, yes, the techniques of nonviolent direct action to stop this road." The crowd chanted: "This is public land!"[19]

Political opinion eventually turned against the parkway, halting construction. Yet the Carter Center went forward, and in October 1986 the former president celebrated its opening. Amid a jolly atmosphere, guests could be spotted wearing buttons or holding balloons saying "Stop the Road." Among the VIPs invited were the Lewises. The activists in the crowd applauded the couple's arrival, bidding John to say something. "Lillian did not want him to speak at all," said Ruth Wall. "They were there to go to the opening. They were all dressed up." Bowing to the cheers, Lewis clambered onto a flatbed truck and grabbed the corded microphone of a public address machine. "We don't need unnecessary roads destroying our historic neighborhoods," Lewis declared triumphantly. There were six thousand spectators at the event, he noted—all of whom had managed to get to the Carter Center without a dedicated parkway.[20]

The road battle would drag on for five more years, long after Lewis left the city council. In 1991, with Atlanta slated to host the 1996 Olympic

Games, both sides submitted to mediation. The final agreement radically scaled back the parkway. A plaque commemorated the work of Lewis, CAUTION, and others in defeating the original plan. In 2018, the city named it the John Lewis Freedom Parkway.[21]

Lewis's opposition to the parkway earned him a following among Atlanta's engaged citizens. Many considered his principled stands to be just what the ossified city government needed. "I don't think there's ever been a person like John on the city council," said Bill Campbell, who shared an office with him. "His commitment to an ideal that is unswerving frightens some people. . . . The status quo always fears the uncontrollable."

But Lewis's moralism irritated others. Some thought him holier-than-thou, bent on elevating himself by shaming others. Most aggrieved was Marvin Arrington, the council chairman, who seethed over Lewis's relentless push for strict ethics rules. In 1981 Lewis had made ethics reform part of his campaign platform, and on the council he pressed the issue. His persistence infuriated Arrington, an attorney and avid investor in local businesses. The newspapers reported frequently on conflicts of interest on Arrington's part—doing the bidding of a church group that had retained his law firm, or pushing billboard legislation at the behest of a client. Each Arrington scandal prompted Lewis to speak out. Arrington retaliated by ensuring that Lewis never chaired a committee or received discretionary perks.[22]

One skirmish came in late 1984, amid the parkway fight. The papers reported that the city had awarded an $890,000 roadbuilding contract to a construction company that Arrington co-owned. The conflict of interest was even more flagrant than the previous scandals. With Arrington in his sights, Lewis made a display of publicly disclosing all of his outside income (less than $40,000), while theatrically challenging all of his colleagues to do the same. That spring he drafted a bill requiring all elected city officials to reveal their income sources. "So long as we have elected officials serve as consultants to developers and others seeking favors from the city," Lewis declared, "conflicts between their private interests and the public interest will continue."[23]

Arrington bottled up the bill. But in November 1984, with pressure mounting, he allowed Lewis's bill to be discussed, while also—in a shallow ploy to deflect the spotlight from his own conflicts—declaring that as council chairman he would no longer vote on any legislation. Lewis's disclosure law failed to pass. Even Bill Campbell, his good friend and ally, voted against it, calling it an insult to the members' integrity. Lewis dismissed Campbell's statement as "poppycock."[24]

Lewis's uncompromising approach left questions about his effectiveness as a legislator. "I don't know if I would've taken the same approach," said Charles Johnson, who had managed Lewis's 1981 campaign. "He was so moral and determined to do the right thing that he isolated himself. It was a stubborn, go-at-it-alone, solo style." By loudly declaring himself unbought, he implied that everyone else had been bought. "This was good for John's image," Johnson said, "but it didn't always go down well with others."[25]

If Lewis struggled to succeed as a legislative insider, he did endear himself to influential constituent groups. Broadening his profile, he became a prominent champion of a host of liberal causes. The energetic pace that had occasionally caused alarm among SNCC colleagues and even his doctors was still evident. "More than anything, I am trying to do too much," he acknowledged in a note to Archie Allen, "and trying to run too fast too early and I really don't have to." But the causes he took up mattered greatly to his constituents.[26]

The preservationists who valued his leadership in fighting the parkway came to see in Lewis a committed environmentalist. Throughout his term, he reliably voted for a green agenda. He was one of the first politicians to speak out about "environmental justice," highlighting the ways that poor and minority communities suffered most acutely from ecological hazards.[27]

Lewis also became a friend of Atlanta's increasingly visible gay and lesbian community. In the 1980s even liberal politicians kept a polite distance from the world of gay activism. Jimmy Carter, as governor ten years before, had become infamous for throwing gay activists out of his office. As mayor, Andrew Young declined to sign a city council resolution celebrating "Lesbians/Gay Males/Transpersons Pride Day." But Lewis showed no fear. A regular at the local YMCA, where he would go for massages, he had met and become friendly with a number of the city's gay leaders who frequented it. During his 1981 city council race he sought support from the First Tuesday Democratic Association, a gay political group, whose leaders took him out for a night at the Cove, a lively gay bar. Lewis stayed out with his new friends until 3:00 a.m. meeting people, dancing, and talking—having "nothing stronger to drink than a Coke," he remembered*—and even asking if they could find another bar to visit when his hosts moved to call it a night. Once on the council, Lewis advocated for a law prohibiting discrimination on the basis of sexual orientation, using the universalist language of the civil rights movement. He also took part in the city's Gay Pride marches. In 1988, the Atlanta chapter of the Human Rights Campaign Fund would award him its inaugural Dan Bradley Memorial Award. He attended the dinner with John-Miles, whom he wanted to appreciate the values of tolerance and inclusion. Lewis "had fought too long and hard against bigotry and racism," he said, to ignore this new frontier in the struggle.[28]

Jewish Atlantans, too, became some of Lewis's most loyal supporters. In 1982, Lewis and three dozen other prominent Black and Jewish Atlantans formed the Black/Jewish Coalition. Their purpose was to lead the two communities in confronting their political differences, renewing their historic alliance, and championing shared causes. Lewis cochaired the group with architect Cecil Alexander. The group hosted events, traveled to Selma, and issued various statements—denouncing, for example, Reagan's plan to visit a Nazi cemetery in 1985, or calling for a posthumous pardon of Leo Frank, a Jew lynched in 1915 by a Georgia mob. Each of these groups—the anti-roadway protesters, the gay community, the Black/Jewish Coalition—provided Lewis with both political support and deep and lasting friendships.[29]

Lewis's friends, indeed, were a truly diverse lot: Black and white, young and old, gay and straight, Christian and Jewish. He had friends from SNCC, from the political world, from the communities he represented, and from the Phi Beta Sigma fraternity, which he joined in the early 1970s (Black fraternities typically have active post-collegiate memberships). Atlantans

---

* Lewis stopped drinking alcohol in 1972.

came to know the everyday John Lewis, a man who loved his hobbies, which ranged from antiquing to Scrabble, from Braves games to used bookstores. He spent time gardening—he planted impatiens in the courtyard of his Pinehurst home—and at supporter Richard Ossoff's annual Fourth of July party, he played volleyball for hours in the blazing heat, despite not being very good, because he loved the company of his friends.[30]

For all his social activity, though, Lewis remained prone to feelings of solitude. "Maybe it is part of my makeup or chemistry to be in the thick of things, to be in the marketplace, to be involved in creative conflict," he wrote to Archie Allen. "Maybe in a real sense it is a part of my restlessness, my loneliness, my desire to reconnect with some force or source that is much larger. You know I have said on many occasions that I have a restless spirit and I need to find a way to harness my restlessness for good and for humankind."[31]

Lewis's immersion in local politics did not distract him from national issues. Chief among these was the looming expiration of the Voting Rights Act in 1982. Lewis had been involved in Voting Rights Act renewals twice before, in 1970 and 1975, but this time around the cause was urgent. Reagan's Justice Department was angling to pare back the hard-won voting protections enshrined in the law. The Supreme Court, moreover, had shown that it was no longer the staunch defender of voting rights that it had been in the 1960s.

On taking office, Ronald Reagan had chosen William Bradford Reynolds to run the Civil Rights Division of the Justice Department. Reynolds was the most conservative leader in that division's twenty-five year history. Conservatives believed that the winds of history had shifted and were blowing their way. In 1980, in *Mobile v. Bolden*, the Supreme Court had limited the scope of the Voting Rights Act by holding that if the federal government wanted to invalidate a state voting provision, it was necessary to prove not just a racially discriminatory *impact* but racially discriminatory *intent*— something that was, in practice, extremely difficult to do. In 1982, the act's supporters resolved to insert new language explicitly deeming discriminatory impact grounds for challenging state-level restrictions. For their part, Reynolds and his Justice Department staff, including a twenty-six-year-old Harvard Law School graduate, John G. Roberts, wanted to preserve the narrow application of the law. The conservatives feared that any "impact" test would lead to hard racial quotas for elected officials, since a low number of minority officeholders could be held up as proof of discrimination and thus ruled illegal.

As a councilman, Lewis had no power to shape the legislation. But he traded on his experience to influence the debate—starting with his annual march in Selma. At this point, Selma was associated with Martin Luther King as much as with Lewis, and the commemorative march had not yet become a major event. For the 1982 march, SCLC president Joseph Lowery led the way, and Selma was just one station on a longer procession across Alabama, from Carrollton to Montgomery. Lewis was present for the march over the Pettus Bridge, an emotional high point of the weeklong affair. "I came back today with a sense of hope and determination that we are on the verge of building a new movement," he said after the crossing. Joining Lowery at the front of a train of two thousand marchers, Lewis joined in songs and chants calling on Reagan to restore the Voting Rights Act to its full strength. "It pains me a great deal to know that we've got to cross that bridge again," he preached. "But I'm willing and I know you all are willing to march to Washington if necessary to preserve the Voting Rights Act."[32]

The House of Representatives, under Democratic control, had passed a bill renewing the act and reestablishing the impact test. But in the 1980 elections the Senate had fallen into Republican hands for the first time since 1955. Conservatives were poised to scrub the Democratic revisions. Ted Kennedy, however, persuaded Bob Dole, the influential Kansas Republican, to accept wording—which Kennedy slyly called the "Dole compromise"— that retained most of the House bill along with a stipulation that a lack of proportional representation wouldn't automatically constitute a violation of the act. Dole's acquiescence brought aboard other Republicans—including, remarkably, Strom Thurmond—and ensured the bill's passage.

Lewis was pleased with the compromise. Its twenty-five-year extension was the longest ever granted. "The greatest step," he said, "was to get around the question of intent, because it is very costly to prove intent in court."[33]

The bill's bipartisan support dissuaded Reagan from vetoing it. In June, the president, over the objections of his own Justice Department, renewed the Voting Rights Act for another quarter century.[34]

Voting remained a leading issue for Black Americans, who continued to lag behind their white counterparts in registration and turnout. Since Lewis had left the VEP in 1977, that once-thriving organization had fallen on hard times, struggling with funding and leadership. Into the vacuum stepped Jesse Jackson, the North Carolina–born, Chicago-based minister and activist, who had been one of Martin Luther King's junior aides at SCLC during his final years. In 1983, in anticipation of the next year's elections, Jackson barnstormed the South holding voter-registration drives. Charismatic, forceful, eloquent, and mediagenic, Jackson was a gifted orator with a magic for firing up crowds. Fueling the turnout at his events was a deep antipathy among Black Americans to Reagan: not only was his Justice Department hostile to civil rights enforcement but Black poverty and unemployment rates were climbing. Jackson seized on the discontent, and the media buzzed with chatter that the flamboyant minister might himself pursue the presidency.[35]

That would mean taking on Walter Mondale, Jimmy Carter's vice president, a stalwart civil rights liberal and the front-runner in the Democratic race. In mounting his challenge, Jackson received encouragement from several prominent Black officials, notably Marion Barry, now mayor of Washington, D.C. Also supportive was Bernard LaFayette, who had formed a relationship with Jackson in Chicago. But other civil rights veterans remained dubious about Jackson based on their history with the man.[36]

Lewis was among the skeptics. He remembered how, back in March 1965, Jackson, although uninvolved in staging the Selma campaign, had hurried down from Chicago after King's call for clergy to come, only to insinuate himself with the SCLC leadership. On the day of the Selma-to-Montgomery march, Jackson had somehow claimed a prominent place outside Brown Chapel. "Up popped Jesse," recalled one journalist present. "I thought it was strange that he would be making a speech when he was not on the SCLC staff and had not been included in any of the strategy meetings. He just seemed to come from nowhere. But he spoke so well."[37]

There were other grounds for concern. The dubious finances of "Operation Breadbasket," Jackson's Chicago-based SCLC offshoot, had raised eyebrows. His self-aggrandizing embellishment of his proximity to Martin Luther King on the evening of the assassination infuriated colleagues.

Jackson had left SCLC in 1971 after a falling-out with Ralph Abernathy, and thereafter the Atlantans—including Coretta King, Hosea Williams, Andrew Young, Julian Bond, and Lewis—distrusted Jesse as a grandstander and self-promoter. That Jackson had gone on to acquire a glitzy sheen of celebrity—and a retinue of media personalities from Bill Cosby and Quincy Jones to Hugh Hefner and Donald Trump—fueled the suspicion.

There were also personal slights. In the early 1970s, Jackson had visited Lewis in Atlanta and noticed the VEP poster saying "Hands that pick cotton now can pick our public officials." Jackson soon began using the phrase in his own speeches without giving credit. "He was enamored of that phrase, and it wasn't copyrighted," said Archie Allen, "but it was the slogan of the Voter Education Project, and he used it as a centerpiece in his speeches." In 1981, Jackson managed to wrest control of the Selma commemoration march, dominating the media coverage. These and similar gestures didn't sit well with Lewis.[38]

The distrust was mixed with rivalry. Though just a year older than Jackson, Lewis had come to prominence years before him. Then, for a spell, Julian Bond had been the younger generation's leading voice, and after him came big-city mayors like Coleman Young, Tom Bradley, and Wilson Goode. It rankled them all to watch Jackson, who had no political experience, leapfrog them to claim the media title of "leader of Black America."

Lewis's support of Mondale, however, was based on more than his dim view of Jackson. A principled liberal, Mondale was a heavy favorite to win the 1984 nomination. Backing him early could pay dividends for individual Black politicians and for the community. For those like Lewis who were transitioning from protest to politics, the calculus was clear. Even James Forman, his revolutionary days now behind him, publicly cast his lot with the former vice president.[39]

Jackson knew that he had to compete with Mondale for Black votes. Before he even announced his candidacy, he courted holdouts, including Lewis. In August 1983, at a twentieth-anniversary March on Washington event, where a gallery of civil rights heroes paraded and spoke, Jackson stole a quiet moment to lobby Lewis. Uncomfortable with being put on the spot, Lewis demurred. But Jackson kept at it. "John, don't leave me," he said. "Let's get together and pray." Lewis promised that he would consult Jackson before endorsing anyone. Privately he continued to favor Mondale.[40]

Over the next few months, Lewis was often quoted in the press deflating Jackson's pretensions. When Jackson seized headlines with his revivalist rallies, Lewis pointed out that many others were registering voters, too. "Groups do work when Jesse's not around, when the reporters and cameras aren't there," he told *Time* magazine. When Jackson claimed that low Black voter turnout resulted not from "apathy" but solely from "oppression," Lewis, who knew the issue as well as anyone, explained that the reality was more complex. When Jackson formally declared his candidacy on October 30 at Morehouse College—with Ralph Abernathy delivering a surprise endorsement—Lewis cautioned that most Blacks in the movement "didn't fight and almost give our lives for the vote to use it in 1984 in a symbolic way." When in January Jackson, at the White House's behest, secured from Syrian dictator Hafez al-Assad the release of an American hostage, Lewis generously praised Jackson's "stunning political triumph," but added: "I don't think we're going to see any quick movement of Black elected officials or black political leaders toward the candidacy of Jesse Jackson."[41]

In time, Lewis made his loyalties plain. In January 1984, he put forward his name as a Mondale delegate at that summer's Democratic National Convention. In February, he formally endorsed the vice president. And in the March 13 primary, Mondale carried Georgia handily. Jackson finished third.[42]

In the meantime, a firestorm engulfed Jackson's campaign. In February, talking to Milton Coleman, an African American *Washington Post* reporter, Jackson referred to Jews as "Hymies" and New York City as "Hymietown." The candidate had assumed he was off the record, but Coleman felt obliged to share the slurs with colleagues at the *Post*, and they appeared low down in a long, fair-minded piece about Jackson's relations with the Jewish community. Jackson compounded his mistake first by refusing to apologize, then by doing so tepidly, and finally by defending the openly anti-Semitic Nation of Islam leader Louis Farrakhan—who had, with Jackson right next to him, called for violence against the candidate's supposed persecutors and, later, called for Milton Coleman's death. By the time Jackson repudiated Farrakhan's remarks as "reprehensible and morally indefensible," he had badly damaged his prospects with not only Jews but voters of all sorts. Among the many voices condemning Farrakhan's anti-Semitism were Lewis and the Atlanta Black/Jewish Coalition.[43]

Lewis tried hard to keep Jackson in the Democratic tent. "Without question, Jesse is the undisputed symbol of Black leadership since Dr. King," Lewis gushed in April. "He has already accomplished his main goal: to energize the Black electorate." Lewis was similarly artful with the *New York Times*. "A great many people wanted to be identified with Jesse Jackson's candidacy as a protest and as a message and as a matter of pride," he said after the paper's June poll found that most Blacks now wanted Mondale to be the Democratic nominee. "Now they must play in the real world, and they know that the real fight is between the Democratic Party and Reagan."[44]

In the fall, Lewis campaigned hard for Mondale. He led rallies when Mondale came to town, spoke at Atlanta's Black colleges, and shared the stage with Jackson at events. A second Reagan term, he warned, would be disastrous for civil rights. On Election Day, Mondale won 88 percent of the Black vote. But Reagan, buoyed by a rebounding economy, trounced Mondale with almost every other group, taking forty-nine states and 59 percent of the popular vote. It was a glaring reminder of America's racial divide. "This administration and Mr. Reagan," Lewis said dejectedly, have "made some white conservatives feel they're on a roll."[45]

As Lewis looked to his own reelection the next year, he found himself weary of squabbling with the likes of Marvin Arrington. The city council was a clown show, the *Constitution* reported, its twice-monthly meetings "so lively and unpredictable that they have become a source of public entertainment." Lewis concluded, as he later wrote, that he "wasn't cut out to be dealing with water systems and sewers and roads." Even so, he declared for reelection in August, drew no serious competition, and won with 90 percent of the vote that October. He doubted he would be long for the job.[46]

Since their race against each other in 1977, Lewis and Wyche Fowler had developed a genial friendship. The same could not be said of Fowler and Julian Bond. From his perch in the state senate, Bond had joined forces with Republican Paul Coverdell after the 1980 census to redraw Georgia's congressional districts. Their plan created additional Black-majority districts and a Republican-majority district. Notably, the Fifth District—Fowler's—would become majority Black. To Fowler's irritation, Bond then announced that he would challenge the incumbent in the 1982 primary—only, however, to abruptly end his campaign after one week. Fowler was more popular with Atlanta's Black residents than Bond had reckoned. Indeed, two years later, Fowler turned back another challenge, from Hosea Williams, securing a fourth full term with 64 percent of the vote. Still, Fowler was aware that many Black leaders in the district wanted to see an African American politician succeed him.

The time came in October 1985, just after Lewis's reelection to the city council. Fowler invited Lewis to lunch. "John," he said, "I'm going to run for the Senate next year. I want you to run for my seat, and I want you to win."[47]

Lewis had been contemplating a run for a while. With his experience at ACTION and on the city council, he felt far more qualified than he had been in 1977. Lillian was pushing him to do it.[48]

Lewis felt no need this time to clear his decision with Bond. But he did see fit to discuss the move with his friend, as a courtesy. It would be a hard conversation. Though still friendly, the two had grown apart. Bond's good looks and debonair bearing had turned him into a celebrity. He hosted *Saturday Night Live*, acted in a Richard Pryor movie, and at one point declared he was leaving politics for a career in television. A fixture of the Atlanta nightlife, he had a glamorous playboy image. Lewis, in contrast, frequented sedate Atlanta house parties and threw himself into his work. His breakthrough social accomplishment in the last few years had been getting his driver's license, at forty-two, though other people continued to drive him most places.[49]

Both men valued the deep attachment they had forged through their years together in the trenches.

In late October, Bond invited Lewis to lunch. Rumors were running wild, and both men were called by reporters as they set off to meet.

They met at Portico's, a downtown hotel restaurant. Julian's son, Michael, then a teenager, joined them. After they ordered, Lewis cut to the chase.

"Senator," he said in the customary jocular tone they used, "what are you going to do?"

"I'm going to run for Congress, Mr. Chairman," Bond said. "What are you going to do?"

"I'm running, too," Lewis said.

"Well," Bond replied, "I'll see you on the campaign trail."[50]

The exchange was difficult, awkward. "I'd never really seen John that way before," Michael Bond recalled. "He was kind of pensive."

Bond seemed less rueful than annoyed. "My father, he was kind of Mr. Spockish. His emotions didn't always show. But I could feel it simmering underneath him. He was angry." Bond told his son that he and Lewis had long ago made an agreement: Lewis would run for Congress with Bond's support, but the next time around, Bond would run with Lewis's support. Lewis never made mention of such a pact.

Bond ended their conversation with a vow to his son. "You know," he said, "I'm going to kick his ass."[51]

Chapter Nineteen

JOHN VS. JULIAN

———— ■ ■ ————

J ohn Lewis and Julian Bond were best friends. They were also a study
in contrasts.

The son of an eminent Black educator, Bond hailed from the African
American elite. W. E. B. Du Bois, Albert Einstein, and Paul Robeson had visited his boyhood home. Confidence and wry wit imbued his well-wrought
sentences. Tall, lean, and jauntily handsome, with a twinkling eye and devil-
ish smile—*Cosmopolitan* named him one of its sexiest men—he dressed in a
cool preppy outfit of khakis, crisp oxfords, and penny loafers.

Lewis, the son of sharecroppers, grew up in dismal poverty and even at
forty-six struggled to be understood over his rural accent and speech impediment. Short and stocky, with big farm-boy hands, he had by 1986 developed a paunch and lost most of his hair. Though usually turned out in a
smart jacket and tie, he still often appeared a bit bedraggled.

Bond was more fun to be around. Where Lewis was a square at heart,
Bond adored the nightlife and hung out with celebrities. "I'm supporting
them both," said Fulton County commissioner Michael Lomax, "but all
other things being equal, Julian always has better-looking women around
and gives better parties." Lewis drove a Chevrolet, when he drove at all.
Bond had a Peugeot.[1]

Even their campaign headquarters looked different. Bond rented space
in a renovated auto dealership, where he laid down white plush carpeting
and displayed an enormous blowup of an *Ebony* cover sporting his face.
Lewis found a cheap, battered storefront abutting the Gospel Light Rescue

Mission and filled it with borrowed furniture and lamps. He budgeted money to rent a TV on election night and went without one until then.[2]

Their friends thought Bond had the mark of a winner. Politicians, celebrities, and donors lined up to assist him. Bill Cosby, Hugh Hefner, Jann Wenner, Mike Nichols, Quincy Jones, and Cicely Tyson all sent checks. More than half of Bond's large donations came from out of state. The Temptations headlined a fundraiser. With a few exceptions—Ralph Abernathy, Jesse Hill, Bill Campbell—Atlanta's Black political players also backed Bond. People liked Lewis, but his strident independence and righteousness on the city council had earned him enemies like Marvin Arrington and annoyed friends like Andrew Young.[3]

The defections were politically damaging and personally painful. One night on the campaign trail, Lillian asked Young, "You're with John, aren't you?" He mumbled a response, and she asked again. "He didn't answer," Lillian recalled. "All he said was, 'It's going to be all right.' That hurts." Although Young pledged to remain neutral, the *Journal-Constitution* called his tacit blessing of Bond's candidacy "the worst-kept secret in town." He shared his donor lists with Bond and let city hall aides take leaves to staff Bond's operation. One Young adviser, Eugene Duffy, managed Bond's campaign.[4]

It wasn't only the Atlanta elites. Bond nabbed the endorsement of Rosa Parks, even though she had known Lewis better and longer. Bond also got Ted Kennedy's backing; Kennedy's explanation that Bond had sided with him in 1980 when Lewis hadn't did little to ease the blow. (Nor did it stop Lewis from quoting Kennedy in his campaign mailers saying, "John Lewis represents the best of America.") Even close friends of Lewis's like Stanley Wise went with Bond. Perhaps most painfully, Coretta Scott King, who like Young publicly professed impartiality, campaigned with Bond but not Lewis.[5]

Bond's enthusiasts often let it be known that "John's was not the image they wanted to put forward, to portray to the nation," said Elaine Alexander, a friend of both men who sided with Lewis. "I was so offended by what the Black leadership said about John." An inordinate amount of media coverage focused on Lewis's speaking style—the way he dropped the *s* at the end of words or stumbled over certain combinations of consonants—and whether it befit a congressman. The class snobbery was unmistakable. Many middle-class voters, white and Black, spoke as if they were embarrassed by

Lewis's rough country manner. "All my friends were liberals, Democrats," said Clark Lemmons, a friend in the gay community. "And a bunch of them, I would hear this more than once. 'Well, John Lewis seems OK, but he just sounds so ignorant. Shouldn't we get someone more sophisticated?'" Recalled Dianne Harnell Cohen, who worked on Lewis's campaign: "They were like, 'John doesn't even speak English. Julian's our fair-haired child.'"[6]

By April, Bond had raised three times as much money as Lewis. Lewis hated asking people for money, and a few of his well-off advisers cosigned a $400,000 loan to keep the campaign afloat. Bond shot out to a thirty-point lead in the polls.[7]

But if Bond's polish and grace largely worked to his advantage, in some ways the men's differences cut in Lewis's favor—if he could capitalize on them. For many Atlantans, Lewis's simple upbringing and unassuming ways spoke to his decency, integrity, and authenticity. When Lewis walked around town, he stopped and talked to everyone—security guards, cleaning women, store clerks—treating them as he would anyone else. Once, his friend Wade Burns watched Lewis listen to a man rambling on about his screen porch when some bigwig interrupted; Lewis turned back to the first man and said, "I'm sorry. You were telling me about your screen porch?" Bond in contrast could be haughty. In his most recent state senate race, he'd gotten a scare from an upstart challenger who had publicized Bond's home answering machine recording. "I'm sorry if there is no one here to answer your phone call," Bond had said on the message, "but that is the way it is. . . . Please don't leave a message on this phone. It does not like them and will not take them." It was a remarkably tone-deaf message for a public servant to leave for constituents.[8]

Bond's arrogance sometimes mystified his friends. Once, Mills Lane, who ran the biggest bank in Atlanta, asked Young to introduce him to Bond. Young reached out. "Julian," he asked, "would you go with me to just say hello to Mills Lane?"

"I'd rather not," said Bond.

Young pushed. "He's a good guy to know."

"I don't need to know him," Bond said with finality.[9]

Love Collins, who would become Lewis's deputy campaign manager, had met Bond in the 1980s. As they shook hands, Bond was already peering over Collins's shoulder to see who else might be in the room. Collins's

introduction to Lewis—in the middle of an intersection—was very different. In order to talk at length, Lewis spun around to walk back in the direction in which Collins was headed—the mark of an uninflated ego. Anthony
Johnson, a radio reporter who later worked for Lewis, told a similar story.
He met Lewis on election night in the city hall pressroom while phoning in
for the latest returns. Lewis, giving no clue as to his stature, asked Johnson
politely to check on his race as well and then thanked him profusely. In contrast, Bond passed through the pressroom umpteen times without acknowledging Johnson's presence.[10]

Lewis held another advantage over Bond: he worked harder. He had
bottomless reserves of energy and needed little sleep. As he had since SNCC
days, he pushed himself relentlessly. Bond was an indifferent campaigner
who copped to his own laziness. Over two decades in state government, he
had an undistinguished record. Bond had even spoken publicly about quitting politics for a career in TV news. "I'm at a level beyond which I cannot
rise," he had griped to the *New York Times*. "I could possibly be a congressman, but I don't have any interest in it."[11]

Lewis stressed his industriousness in his campaign literature. "Because
the problems of Atlanta don't stop at 5 o'clock," one mailer said, "neither
does John Lewis." It went on: "Late nights at the office and John Lewis is
reading a briefing report before a crucial vote . . . Missing dinner at home
to attend a neighborhood gathering . . . A Saturday morning meeting with
factory employees facing layoffs . . . Going to a senior citizen's apartment because she can't get out of the house." It contrasted him with other politicians,
left unnamed, and obliquely made reference to Bond's answering-machine
message. "John Lewis has never hidden behind a desk. He's never left people
hanging, waiting for him to return their phone call."[12]

As important, Lewis embodied his message of hard work. As the race
got underway, Lewis did what he had done in 1977: rising early, going to
the factory gates and MARTA stations and supermarket entrances, hustling from one event to the next. After nightfall he would still be at it—
at church rallies or on busy downtown streets. Even if he went home at
midnight, he would first stop at a twenty-four-hour convenience store and
traverse the aisles, shaking hands. Reporters realized that to keep up with
him, they had to park themselves in his driveway first thing in the morning.
Bond's camp took note. "John Lewis is really beating the pavement," said

Stoney Cooks, a Young confidant working for Bond. "All the major events in the city, he's there."[13]

Lillian worked hard, too. Sherry Frank from the Black/Jewish Coalition had a son, Drew, the same age as John-Miles. On weekends the Lewises would drop John-Miles at the Franks' house and race around Atlanta while the boys played. Once, Frank brought the boys to an afternoon fundraiser for Lewis, only to let the boys wander over to a similar event nearby for Bond. "The food was ten times better at Julian's event," John-Miles reported perkily. At the end of the weekend, Frank recalled, the Lewises "would come striding into my house Sunday evening, starving and dead." She would feed them kugel or other leftovers from her fridge.[14]

The Lewis team's scrappiness gave their man an underdog appeal. Brad Lichtenstein, a high school senior who was looking to volunteer, checked out Bond's office, but it was "teeming with people," he recounted, with nothing for him to do. Lewis's office "was just barren." That's where he ended up working.[15]

A smattering of other candidates joined the race that spring, but Lewis remained solidly in second place. Still, people talked about him with condescension or pity, as if his candidacy were a sad joke. Joseph Lowery talked about friends chortling at the very idea of Lewis as Atlanta's representative. "They said, 'We're surprised he made the city council and now he's talking about Congress!'" When Lewis's campaign filings revealed that he had spent $1,000 on elocution lessons from a media consulting firm called Speakeasy, one newspaper columnist reported, "members of Julian Bond's camp sat around snickering over the disclosure." For now, the Bonds and the Lewises tried not to let the contest affect their families. "We still hugged John," Michael Bond said. But resentments were building.[16]

People urged Lewis to bow out to avoid an ugly fight and spare himself the embarrassment. Lewis bristled at what he called "a form of intimidation." Well-connected insiders whispered to reporters they would lure Lewis out of the race with a plum job offer. "I just think this race is over," one politico told journalist Frederick Allen. "We've got to find John a place." Dinky Romilly, James Forman's second ex-wife, resurfaced to praise Lewis in a letter to the *Journal-Constitution* before arguing that his talents were needed on the city council. Even Stokely Carmichael, now Kwame Ture, phoned Lewis to weigh in. He and Lewis hadn't spoken since 1966, but now

Carmichael implored Lewis not to "divide the Black community." Lewis was dumbfounded. "Stokely," he countered, "you are not a person who has the right to tell me to drop out."[17]

The apparent coronation of Bond brought out Lewis's pugnacity. Besides the class politics, there was also a personal angle. As much as he loved Bond, Lewis had never been fond of his friend's airs. Things came easily to Bond, and he took it for granted. "He approached his work," Lewis later said, "as if it were an inconvenience." Rivalry had always tinged the relationship. Though grateful to Bond for teaching him the ways of the world as a young man—how to order a highball or behave in a fancy restaurant—Bond was also a living reminder of Lewis's sense of himself as an untutored farm boy. Their very friendship summoned up Lewis's insecurities.[18]

Lewis's feeling that the congressional seat was slipping away from him, moreover, brought back painful memories of Kingston Springs. Again friends were abandoning Lewis, belittling him, telling him to step aside. As before, he felt conspired against. Yet as in 1966 he believed himself to be the right man for the job. "Never again," he told himself. He resolved to stand his ground.[19]

Lillian believed in him just as resolutely. "Lillian wanted him to be a big famous man," said Muriel Tillinghast, a SNCC friend who volunteered on Lewis's campaign, "and she got involved in every aspect of the campaign. She was selecting what clothes he should wear, how he should be presented. She was grooming him." "Lillian was the feisty one," said Lois Frank, a family friend. "She stiffened John when he found certain political confrontations distasteful."[20]

Lillian was also close to Alice Bond—as close to Alice as John had been to Julian. For months, Alice had been confiding in Lillian, sharing details about their deteriorating marriage. An incorrigible ladies' man, Bond was behaving badly. The more Alice bad-mouthed her husband to Lillian, the more convinced Lillian became that Bond had nothing on Lewis. She told her husband as much: he deserved to be congressman, she said, and shouldn't let anyone muscle him aside.[21]

Bond's destructive behavior included not only infidelity but also something much more potentially damaging to his career: cocaine use. Rumors had swirled for years about what an FBI report later called Bond's "very heavy cocaine habit." Alice at one point said her husband needed a fix every two hours, although later, under media and political pressure, she would retract that claim. Although it wasn't publicly known at the time, Bond was under federal investigation.

Lewis had been hearing the rumors for several years. He had even spoken about them to a friend who was a police officer. He also heard that Bond was suffering from physical debilities, possibly related to the drug use. Bond's weight had dropped, and during parades Lewis would tromp along energetically for miles, while Bond rode in a car. Lewis concluded that Bond's addiction must be serious. There were other stories out there, too. Bond was rumored to be having an affair with a woman who was said to be his dealer as well.[22]

In 1986, cocaine and crack were devastating all kinds of communities, especially Black ones. Liberals and conservatives, Blacks and whites—all were demanding a tough response. First Lady Nancy Reagan was pushing her "Just Say No" campaign. The Reagan administration was touting an antidrug strategy that included, to the dismay of civil libertarians, mandatory drug testing for federal employees. In June, the Boston Celtics' top draft pick, a University of Maryland star named Len Bias, died of a cocaine overdose two days after his selection. In political races everywhere, drugs topped the list of voters' concerns.

Lewis had no intention of airing Bond's private struggles. But hearing, seeing, and knowing what he did about Bond made him confident that he would be the better congressman, no matter who cut a more dashing figure in a tailored suit.

In any case, there were other issues. Lewis and Bond held similar positions on most political matters, but they were not identical. Although both men had ties to Atlanta's Jewish community, Bond had on occasion run afoul of Jewish opinion. Though he affirmed Israel's right to nationhood, he had at times described himself as "anti-Zionist"—a term that most Jews equated with enmity toward the Jewish state. At other times, he minimized the anti-Semitism in Black radical circles. Some of Bond's Jewish friends were taken aback by his ignorance of the issues, such as not knowing that Arab citizens voted in Israeli elections. Once, when a local American Jewish Committee chapter invited Bond to speak about Israel, he showed up at the synagogue

with some swaggering militant types, turning what had been meant as a conciliatory gesture into a divisive one.[23]

Lewis, by contrast, always showed heartfelt sympathy for the concerns
of Atlanta's Jews. He helped set up a program for Black and Jewish teens
where each group would listen to and learn about the other's experiences.
"We'd split into groups, Black and Jewish, and anonymously write down
questions for the other group," said Sherry Frank, who was involved. "Sometimes it would be tense—on Israel, South Africa, Jesse Jackson." Blacks
might ask Jews why they talked so much about the Holocaust; Jews might
ask Blacks if they felt they benefited unfairly from affirmative action. The
process bred mutual understanding. Lewis liked the exercise because it promoted the kind of community he remembered from Nashville. "John was
always there," Frank said. "Sometimes he'd come in a tuxedo because he'd
been speaking at a gay rights dinner. Sometimes he'd come in jeans because
he was coming from home. I'd tell him he should go home to Lillian, but
he'd stay."[24]

Lewis also maintained special ties to the gay and lesbian community. In
the mid-1980s, the cause of equal rights for gays and lesbians was still highly
controversial, and even some liberals kept their distance. For Gay Pride
Month, in June, Andrew Young would issue a generic statement on behalf of
civil rights for all. But Lewis "greeted the gay lobby more enthusiastically,"
the *Journal-Constitution* reported. "It isn't easy to be gay, particularly in the
South," Lewis said to a Gay Pride gathering.[25]

The churches, too, especially Black churches, steered clear of gay rights.
Relatively few Black men and women were out of the closet. According to
Dave Hayward, a white gay activist and journalist, most visible movement
leaders at the time were white. "A very good friend running for the Atlanta
City Council told me that he went to a party, and it was basically Black gay
men. He said, 'Dave, I was just totally astonished. All these guys they have
wives and daughters and girlfriends, and they're all on the down-low'"—a
phrase referring to the secretive lives of Black gay or bisexual men.[26]

Lewis never worried that his outspokenness on the issue would hurt him
with churchgoing voters, Black or white. "He wanted people to have the
opportunity to love who they wanted to love," said his friend Joe Larche,
who had known Lewis since arriving in Atlanta in the late 1960s, "and to
be with who they wanted to be with. I'm certain that there was conflict in

his thinking because he was raised as a strict religion person. And he had to cross that river, which was a raging river. He knew that he was going against his upbringing." Undaunted, Lewis attended an AIDS vigil in the middle of the campaign, where he won a rapturous reception. "It's a struggle, a fight, a battle, a war," he said. "But we will fight . . . and we will win."[27]

"I just remember that there was this general feeling of goodwill and beneficence, and that we had a friend we could go to," Hayward said. "And he was always somebody who would speak up for us and take our part and, at some, at some personal risk."[28]

Lewis's most controversial stand, however, was neither his sympathy for gay rights nor his support of Israel. It was his decision to back the extension of the Georgia 400 highway to ease the traffic from northern Atlanta to downtown. A few years before, on the city council, Lewis had blocked the extension. But the business community and congestion-weary commuters kept the project alive. Given Lewis's resolute opposition to the presidential parkway, residents of Atlanta's mostly white northern communities expected him to be equally adamant in fighting the extension of Georgia 400.

As the 1986 campaign got underway, Lewis and Lillian met with the friends with whom they had battled the presidential parkway. At the home of Ruth Wall, one of the group's leaders, they discussed Lewis's position on Georgia 400. The group, which was all white, wanted him to stand firm. The highway was a pet project of business interests, they said, and it would look bad for Lewis to flip-flop. On the other hand, public support for the road was growing and many Black Atlantans saw the resistance as a cause for wealthy white elites.

The Lewises listened quietly as one friend after another made the case for opposing the highway. Finally, Lillian rose out of her chair. Everyone could see she was about to let loose. "You're all a bunch of right racists!" she yelled. "This is something he needs to support!" Her husband could not constantly capitulate to white interests, she argued. The very people for whom Lewis had gone to bat in the last roadway fight should understand his predicament.

Everyone was reeling after Lillian called them all racists. Then she abruptly changed the topic, asking chirpily where they should all go to dinner. Having made her points, Lillian harbored no lasting animus toward her white friends.[29]

On May 23, Lewis announced that because of population growth and traffic in Buckhead, he now favored the Georgia 400 extension. Some activists lashed out. "It's a sad day for John Lewis," said one. "It's clear from everything I have heard that he is trying to resuscitate a failing candidacy by pandering to developers and other vested interests." But Lewis found most Atlantans forgiving. "I have to say I was disappointed with your change on 400," a voter told him in June as he was out shaking hands. But, she added, "you know I'm going to vote for you." In the next quarter, campaign contributions from developers and business interests picked up considerably.[30]

As the August 12 primary approached, the campaign got nasty. On the more benign end of the spectrum, the campaigns waged a war of yard signs, as each stole or defaced the others' placards. Men in city trucks were spotted driving around, confiscating Lewis signs, presumably on Bond's behalf. Love Collins, a West Point graduate who brought a military-style efficiency to Lewis's team, had learned that the Bond campaign was relying on volunteers for its sign operation. "We were able to recruit and pay a lot of the sign people that Julian had," Collins said. If a Bond volunteer delivered one hundred Bond yard signs to the Lewis campaign, he told them, they could join the Lewis team and get paid. "Julian was complaining his signs would be put up one day and the next day they'd be gone," Collins said. "What he didn't know was that the very people who were snatching his signs were his own yard team."[31]

More serious than the sign hijinks were the personal attacks. Still in second place, Lewis was pressed to go negative against his friend. Lillian and his top campaign aides reminded him that playing hardball was necessary in a competitive campaign. Some aides urged him to bring up Bond's drug use. It was a legitimate issue, they said, which voters cared about. But Lewis resisted.

Lewis did throw a few jabs at Bond, although in the long and sordid annals of American electioneering, they were fairly mild. He repeated Bond's description of himself as lazy and joked about having to roust his friend out of bed back in the SNCC days. He would describe himself as having been a "headlight" in the movement, and Bond a mere "taillight." Or he described himself as the "tugboat" to Bond's "showboat." Not unfairly, he contrasted his marching into danger with Bond's cerebral work from the communications desk. "Mr. Bond served as the communication director for the Student Nonviolent Coordinating Committee and did a good job. He did a superb job," Lewis said slyly on Boyd Lewis's radio program. "But he was not there on the firing line, but he played a role. And I cannot take that from him."[32]

Sometimes Lewis grazed the truth. He took to stating that Bond "worked for me" in SNCC. Technically, as chairman, Lewis held the senior position, and Bond's work with the Atlanta publicity shop had kept him away from the dangers that left Lewis bloodied. But SNCC had prided itself on its democratic decision-making, and besides, if the staff could be said to have "worked for" anyone, it was Jim Forman. Many SNCC comrades took umbrage at the way Lewis spun things. "For John to go through this thing with Julian about, you know, 'he worked for me,' was bullshit," said one. "How people rewrite history for their own ends is amazing to me." Some SNCC friends never forgave him.[33]

But Bond did his own share of negative campaigning. "If John Lewis could not get eleven of his colleagues to vote for his bills on the council," he would say, "it will be impossible for him to establish the type of relationships needed to get bills passed in Washington." At one forum, he said that Lewis wouldn't be able to answer a certain question until he spoke to Lillian.[34]

Lewis left the hardest-hitting attacks on Bond to others. In June, Charles Johnson, who was running in third place, aired a radio ad that quoted from Bond's 1972 book, *A Time to Speak, a Time to Act*, in which Bond had facetiously called on Blacks to "take over the major cities of this country and charge admission fees to suburban whites." Johnson also went on the air to say that the book had advocated "cop killing." Harsh and racially loaded, the blasts eroded Bond's popularity, especially among white voters.

As the bickering worsened, the campaign managers for Bond, Lewis, and another candidate, Jan Douglass, held a peace summit. (Johnson's campaign manager wasn't invited.) Exactly what happened was murky. Some reports said that all three camps promised to stop the sign stealing and to keep the campaign "on a high level." Other accounts said they pledged to avoid the drug issue. Yet C. T. Martin, Lewis's campaign manager, insisted that he made no such commitments. Whatever promises were made, the negativity continued.[35]

In fact, after Johnson aired his negative radio spots against Bond, C. T.

Martin realized that he could use Johnson to go after Bond while keeping
Lewis out of the fray. Martin approached Johnson with an explosive rumor:
he learned that once, while returning from Central America, Bond had been
detained at the airport for drug possession. It was clear to Johnson that Martin wanted him to do his dirty work. Johnson refused. But he did cut a radio
ad that, while omitting the airport story, nonetheless raised the temperature.

Johnson's new ad was about his exclusion from the peace summit. But
it also put the drug issue on the table. "My message said, 'I was not represented at that meeting. I don't use drugs and I will help lead the fight against
drugs,'" Johnson later explained. "The ad was not accusing anybody of drug
use, just going after the meeting."

Before the ad could air, however, columnist Frederick Allen of the *Constitution* caught wind of it and phoned Johnson. Johnson pulled the ad, but
Allen wrote about it anyway. "Venomous stories are circulating by word of
mouth between the camps of various candidates," the columnist wrote, al-
luding to the airport arrest rumor and other scuttlebutt. "Many of the candidates and their staffers are intimate, lifelong friends who grew up together,
shared the trenches together during the Civil Rights movement and know
each others' deepest secrets."[36]

"There are all sorts of vicious personal rumors being spread," said Beni
Ivey, Jan Douglass's campaign manager. "We all got to live together when
this is over."[37]

When Lewis and Bond crossed paths, they still greeted each other in
their old manner: "Hello, Mr. Chairman." "Hello, Senator." Beyond that,
they never said more than a few words.[38]

The conflict took its toll on their families. Lillian and Alice stopped
speaking for a while. "It's over," Lillian told a reporter in July. "Irretrievably
broken."

The children, too, suffered. The Bond children had regarded the Lewises
as family. Michael Bond, to whom the Lewises were godparents, cherished
memories of birthdays, vacations, and holidays together—"going to Disne-
yland together," Michael said, "riding on the airplane sitting in Lillian's lap
the whole way, looking out the window and going on all the rides." Once,
Lewis took the Bond boys to an Atlanta Braves game, arriving with a Rich's
department store bag containing his own home-cooked hot dogs, Michael
remembered, even "ketchup and mustard from home and all of that. . . . We

were just like, 'Rats, man! We don't want homemade hot dogs.'" But simply going with Lewis made it "one of the best Braves games that I have ever been to." There would be no more ball games.[39]

John-Miles, too, experienced painful moments. At the outset of the campaign, his parents hadn't yet told him that he had been adopted. He learned the news from the reporters who were always hovering around his family. Family friends said that the disclosure disturbed him and that it upset Lillian even more.[40]

On Thursday, August 7—five days before the primary—the League of Women Voters had scheduled a forum for the candidates to air on WSB-TV. Those candidates who had met a fundraising threshold qualified: Lewis, Bond, Johnson, Douglass, and a fifth candidate, Alveda Beal. A sixth candidate, former assemblywoman Mildred Glover, didn't make the cut. Angry about her exclusion, Glover enlisted Hosea Williams— always up for a publicity stunt—to set up a picket line outside the studio, from which he melodramatically decried the fundraising threshold as a modern-day "poll tax."

Bond and Johnson arrived at the studio first that night. Ignoring Hosea Williams and his bullhorn, they entered the WSB building. When Alveda Beal arrived, she took the bullhorn, and announced she would boycott the debate. Douglass also opted out. Lewis and his entourage huddled, discussing what to do. It was now 7:45 p.m. The debate was set for eight o'clock.

The debate organizers desperately wanted Lewis to participate. He was still in second place; viewers wanted to see him and Bond cross swords. His advisers were split. C. T. Martin urged him to cast his lot with the excluded candidates. But Lillian, one chronicler noted, was "raging like a bull," wanting him to go inside. "We thought, 'Oh my God, he's giving the whole thing to Julian, what the hell's the matter with him?'" recalled Sherry Frank. "But there was principled John."[41]

At a few minutes before eight, a television station executive appealed to Lewis. "John," he said, "we have gone to great lengths and great expense to bring this debate to the viewers. The entire 230,000 voters are waiting in front of their television sets to see you."

Lewis still hesitated. Finally, he said, "I would love to go inside, . . . but

I can't go unless all the candidates are invited." Johnson and Bond debated next to three empty chairs.[42]

Opinion divided over Lewis's decision. *Journal-Constitution* columnist Cynthia Tucker, normally sympathetic to Lewis, rebuked him. "He would have been better off inside the building acting like a congressman rather than an also-ran," she wrote. Others, however, admired that he stood with those on the outside.[43]

The weekend before the primary, the drug issue resurfaced. President Reagan announced that his cabinet secretaries would all be taking drug tests. Mildred Glover capitalized on her newfound attention by challenging all the Fifth District candidates to take the tests, too. TV cameras followed her Monday morning at six o'clock as she went to Peachford Hospital for a urinalysis. Three other candidates also agreed to get tested.

As a rule, Lewis didn't believe in mandatory drug testing. But he knew he was clean. He had stopped drinking. He didn't smoke pot. (He had tried it once, letting his mouth fill up with smoke, but—like another famous politician—not managing to inhale.) Lewis also didn't want anyone suspecting the worst of him if he declined. He decided to take a test. "Throughout the campaign all of us have talked of fighting drugs," he said, "and I believe we should take the leadership role."

Bond refused to be tested, accusing Glover of grandstanding.

The next day, Atlantans voted. Bond still led in every poll, with numbers close to the 50 percent that he needed to avoid a runoff. But Lewis had hidden strengths. He had won lots of endorsements, including from the *Atlanta Journal-Constitution*, the American Federation of Teachers, and environmental groups like the Sierra Club. Love Collins had also organized a tight game-day operation, with buses and cars to drive people to the polls. "We gave them orange juice and peppermint sticks, which was a huge treat. And then we talked to them about John Lewis on the route to the polls," he said. "And don't forget after you vote, you get on the bus, we take you back to the senior citizen high-rise. We had that worked out really well." At the polling stations, too, he continued, "we had food and beverages, water, sandwiches, and everything distributed. Poll workers were treated very well. So much so that poll workers for Julian Bond's campaign were throwing his signs down, coming over, and slipping on our T-shirts and eating our sandwiches."[44]

Still, the early returns looked bad. Bond was consistently clearing 50 percent. That meant he would avoid a runoff and capture the Democratic nomination outright. "John was in tears," said Kevin Ross, a top campaign adviser. "I think he thought he had lost the election."[45]

As the evening went on, however, Bond's percentage dipped ever so slightly. When tallies from the northern white neighborhoods arrived, he fell to the high forties.

In the final count that night, Bond claimed 47 percent of the vote, Lewis 35. "My staff and supporters went wild," Lewis later wrote. "You would have thought we had won." Lewis climbed on a chair as reporters scribbled in their notebooks. "Here we come!" he said. "Here we come!"[46]

Three weeks remained until the runoff.

Lewis knew that to make up a twelve-point deficit, he would have to campaign harder than ever. "I went from door to door, literally running," he said. He had worn down his favorite blue Nikes; he would go through two more pairs before the three weeks were over. "No one is going to outwork me," Lewis would tell himself. "I went into every drugstore, every theater, every place that was still open at night when the theaters are letting out, and I'm there shaking hands." He would find people mowing their lawns and push their lawn mowers for them. He shook so many hands he got "trigger thumb"—swollen tendons and ligaments that make the thumb cleave to the palm, like a spring-loaded stapler snapping shut.[47]

Television exposure mattered, too. Love Collins had saved 20 percent of the campaign's funds. "I wanted to have enough money so that at the end of the primary there would be virtually no gap between that and us being able to stay on the air," he said. If Bond had cleared 50 percent, then his frugality would have looked like a mistake. But it turned out to be a smart bet. Bond had depleted his coffers and needed time to raise more money to get back on the airwaves. He ran no ads until right before the election.[48]

Lewis gained a shot at more TV exposure when Bond challenged him to debate. Normally, the front-runner has little to gain by appearing side by side with a trailing challenger. But Bond knew that he was quicker, slicker, and more adept at discussing policy than Lewis. Lewis's halting speech was still an issue, a turnoff for some voters. Bond thought that by besting Lewis in a series of debates, he could knock his rival down for the count.

Lewis knew he had to improve. Many mornings, when he wasn't shaking hands, his advisers would gather to rehearse debate questions and train Lewis to answer them succinctly. "We had people meet at seven a.m. to pump John with the MTV answers," Sherry Frank said. "We rehearsed and rehearsed and rehearsed." Lewis took advice from Joe Roberts, the eloquent pastor of Ebenezer, and from Sandy Linver of Speakeasy. In his campaign van, Lewis could be spotted practicing his diction in the car mirror.

Lewis had also recently found another speaking coach, a woman named Shawn Reed. Reed held one- or two-hour sessions with Lewis in her living room in northwest Atlanta, practicing debate questions. The most important advice she gave him was not to try to outtalk Bond, whose suavity Lewis could never hope to match. Instead, he should relax and be himself. His plainspoken manner would look good next to Bond's arch demeanor.

The first debate was scheduled for Sunday, August 24, at the studios of WAGA-TV, Channel 5. Reed told Lewis to come to her place beforehand. He expected a last-minute cram session. Instead, she had him sit in her hot tub and meditate.[49]

Love Collins also had a pregame strategy. On Sunday, he called Dewey Crim, Lewis's driver, and told him to take the candidate to Grady Memorial Hospital for a drug test. "Tell John to take his test, fold it up, and put it in his lapel pocket," Collins ordered. "I'll explain to John when I see you guys at TV Five." Collins wanted to have the test ready to use on air.

They met up in the WAGA parking lot. Collins and Lewis entered the studio just as Bond and Eugene Duffy were walking in. As they strode down the hall, Duffy played some head games. Trailing behind Lewis and Collins, Duffy called ahead to Bond, "Congressman! Congressman!" Collins seethed. "We hadn't had the election yet!" he recalled. Lewis, seeing what Duffy was doing, told Collins to stay cool.

Collins and other advisers wanted Lewis to whip out his drug test results at an opportune moment during the debate. They believed it was perfectly legitimate for voters to want to know if their representative was a drug user. It would not be a below-the-belt hit; if it seemed that way, it was only because Lewis so rarely went negative.

Always conflict averse, Lewis couldn't do it. The first debate passed without his raising the drug issue.

Before the second debate, on Wednesday at WPBA, the local public television station, there was more psychological warfare. Lewis overheard Bond and an aide talking loudly about "the Shirley MacLaine book"—a 1970 memoir called *Don't Fall Off the Mountain*, in which the actress mentioned being "stoned" with Lewis at a SNCC party. All MacLaine had meant by that ambiguous slang term was that Lewis had had a couple of beers, but there was no telling what voters would think, and Bond seemed intent on rattling Lewis. Yet Lewis kept cool. In the event, Bond was bluffing. He didn't bring up the book.

As the second debate went on, Lewis's advisers watched nervously. They muttered to themselves as Lewis passed up one chance after another to raise the drug issue. "I remember watching John," said Kevin Ross. "I'm in the wings saying, 'John, get this drug issue in there. Get this drug issue in there.'"

At one point, Bond slammed Lewis for breaking his word by running for Congress. In seeking reelection to city council the year before, Bond reminded the audience, Lewis had promised, if reelected, to serve out his second term. That did it. "All of a sudden," Ross said, "after John had passed up two times to get this in, he got angered for a moment. And he accused Julian of being afraid to take a drug test." Lewis was picking up the gauntlet that Mildred Glover had thrown down and laying it at Bond's feet. "I challenge you to meet me at Grady Hospital tomorrow morning to take the drug test," Lewis said.[50]

As before, Bond refused. Then, seeking to downplay the whole issue, he stated that Atlanta didn't have a serious drug problem. It was an inexplicable gaffe, like Gerald Ford saying in a presidential debate in 1976 that there was no Soviet domination of Poland.

Lewis pounced. "I don't know whether Mr. Bond is living in Atlanta," he said, "but for Mr. Bond to suggest that this district is without a drug problem, I just don't understand it."[51]

Bond backpedaled, denying he had made the remark. That claim elicited laughter not only from the audience, who had just heard it, but also from the cameramen. Lewis was turning out to be a better debater than expected.

Between debates, the issue dogged Bond. One morning, reporters gathered at his house, peppering him with questions. Bond lashed out. "None of these people north of I-20 are going to tell me how to run my campaign," he said. Love Collins was elated. "I just said, 'Bingo! I needed you to say that.'" Everyone knew that "people north of I-20" meant white people.[52]

Two debates and less than one week remained. By now both men were doubting whether their friendship could be salvaged. In Bond's view, Lewis had crossed a line that friends should never cross. He felt betrayed.

Bond confided in his son Michael. "My dad said that he had things on John that would ruin him for life, not just beat him in a campaign," Michael recounted. But Bond added he wouldn't trash Lewis's reputation the way Lewis had just trashed him. "He refused to go negative," said Michael. "He could have ruined John forever given the times that we were in, in 1986, but he didn't."[53]

Here and there, Bond hinted glancingly that he held some damning information about Lewis. But he never publicly revealed what he was referring to. "I know things about John and he knows things about me," Bond said cryptically to Art Harris of the *Washington Post*, "and they're not campaign issues."[54]

It was in the third debate that the mud flew. Held Friday afternoon at city hall, it was broadcast on WGST radio. Dick Williams, a conservative columnist at the *Journal-Constitution*, and Tom Houck, a close friend of both Bond and Lewis working at WGST, were the questioners. Denis O'Hayer, another radio journalist, moderated. Although it wasn't televised in full, the local channels had cameras there to record highlights for the evening news.

The candidates sat at either end of a long table, like boxers in opposite corners of a ring.

Lewis came out swinging. He assailed a series of entanglements between Bond's campaign and city hall. Lewis charged that for Bond to have Gene Duffy running his campaign was itself a conflict of interest; Duffy's use of a city car for campaign business was an even bigger conflict. A different city official, Lewis also claimed, had strong-armed prospective city contractors into donating to Bond. Bond denied any impropriety. Andrew Young, sitting in the audience, walked out.[55]

Commercial breaks interrupted the action. "As soon as that underwriting break would take place," Kevin Ross recounted, "Gene would run over and whisper in Julian's ear. And then I would run over to John and I'd be whispering in John's ear. The two of us were like Angelo Dundee and Cus D'Amato."[56]

Bond tried to trip Lewis up on federal policy. He asked about the Gramm-Rudman bill, a proposed mechanism to avoid federal budget deficits that was being debated in Washington. When Lewis answered vaguely, Bond homed in. "Tell me what specifically you would cut out of Gramm-Rudman," he said, with Lewis on the ropes. Finally Lewis said he would "cut out the entire bill." That was what it meant to oppose a piece of legislation, wasn't it? Lewis acquitted himself passably and won sympathy in the face of Bond's bid to show him up.[57]

After failing to thrash Lewis on his weaknesses, Bond went after his strength: ethics. Bond accused Lewis of having voted to award a cable franchise to a company after taking donations from a "lobbyist" and a "lawyer." Lewis explained that the lobbyist and lawyer were Sharon Adams and Clay Long, longtime friends, and he took umbrage at Bond's insinuation that he had been bought. Bond shot back: "If it looks like a duck and quacks like a duck and waddles like a duck, then it must be a duck."[58]

His integrity impugned, Lewis was now furious. He thought to himself, as he later put it, "I'm not going to let this Negro get away with this." It was another echo of 1966, when opponents had taken away his SNCC chairmanship through devious means. He wasn't going to let that happen again.[59]

"Mr. Bond, my friend, my brother," he said, collecting himself. "We were asked to take a drug test not long ago, and five of us went and took that test. Why don't we step out and go to the men's room and take another test?"

Bond stood silent. Lewis went on. "It seems like you're the one doing the ducking."

Bond refused. Drug tests, he reiterated, were intrusions on privacy and civil liberties.

Lewis kept pushing. "Can you tell us why you will not take the test, so that people will know that you are not on drugs?"

"I will let the people know that I am not on drugs now," Bond said angrily. "I am not on drugs."

Dick Williams asked Lewis if he was accusing Bond of illegal drug use. "No," Lewis said, a bit disingenuously. "I do not suspect that he is on drugs.

I just feel like he should take the test to clear his name and remove public doubt. People need to know."[60]

Toward the end, the candidates posed their own questions. Lewis surprised Bond by asking about one of the questioners, Tom Houck. Though officially neutral, Houck was privately favoring Bond, and before the debate he had been spotted conferring with Bond.

What had they had been discussing behind closed doors? Lewis asked.

Bond was taken aback. "We talked about the friendship between you and me," he blurted out, "and how this campaign has put a strain on the relationships that our families have enjoyed. We talked about how I will disallow this campaign to destroy our friendship of twenty-five years."[61]

In his closing, Bond returned to the subject of their friendship. He made clear how much Lewis's criticisms had wounded him. "We've been friends for twenty-five years. We went to Africa together. We were in Selma together.... But never in those twenty-five years did I ever hear any of the things you are saying about me now. Why did I have to wait twenty-five years to find out what you really thought of me?"[62]

"Julian, my friend," Lewis replied, avoiding the question, "this campaign is not a referendum on friendship. This is not a referendum on the past. This is a referendum on the future of our city, the future of our country."[63]

At the final debate on Sunday at the WXIA television studios, there was no need for any more fisticuffs. Everything had been said. Both men tried to act statesmanlike on the eve of the election.

Bond had called for the debates expecting that he would intellectually overpower Lewis. But debates are not won on points alone. Perceptions of character matter, too. Lewis had come across as earnest and humble, sincerely appealing to the voters. Bond had often seemed supercilious, as if he considered himself superior to Lewis, and assumed that he would have the voters' support.

On Monday morning, his eyes red, Bond campaign manager Gene Duffy reached for his coffee as he rallied his staff and volunteers. "We are going to lose this thing unless we get out the vote," he warned them. "I am serious." Lewis was already hoofing it around Grant Park and Gresham Park.[64]

On Tuesday, September 2, the day of the runoff, it rained. In the morning, Lillian called her friend Dianne Cohen and said she had "this sinking terrible feeling in her stomach," Cohen later recalled. Lewis deemed the inclement weather a bad sign. Rain depressed turnout, and he needed every vote he could get. But in fact Bond, as the front-runner, had more to lose. Given his twelve-point margin in the first round, his voters were more likely to be complacent and more inclined to stay home. Lewis's people knew their votes were needed.

Late in the day, Lewis was still knocking on doors when a young boy answered and cried out to his parents, "Here comes John Lewis!" Lewis knew he was getting recognized.

That night, the campaign had reserved a ballroom in the Westin Hotel, in case things broke their way. In the early evening, Lewis's headquarters down the street—meant to hold perhaps 150 people—was filling up. Volunteers came in tired and damp from working the polls all day, grabbing lemonades and Cokes. Music played. There were microphones and a platform for Lewis to stand on when decision time came.

The Lewises were holed up in a little office off the main headquarters when Love Collins walked in. "John, do you have the victory speech and the concession speech?" he asked.

"I have both," Lewis said.

"I'm going to go outside and see how everything's going," Collins said, "and I'll come in periodically and let you know where we are."

Bond jumped out to an early lead. As the night went on the lead held firm. Young, interviewed on television, confessed what everyone had known. "Well, the election is over. I guess I can tell you how I voted. I voted for Julian Bond." Lewis was angry; the polls were still open. He knew that Bond's lead wasn't insurmountable.[65]

Lewis left for an interview at one of the TV studios, then came back to headquarters. Eleven o'clock came and went. Friends who were supposed to be waiting at the Westin grew impatient and came over to the headquarters, filling the space beyond its capacity. Bond still led by four points.

Richard Cohen, the campaign treasurer, told Collins, "You need to go in and tell John that he's going to have to give the concession speech. It's not looking real good."

Collins slipped through the crowd into the little office. "John, I talked to Richard Cohen and several others and they think you need to get your concession speech ready."

"Oh, gee," Lewis said. "We worked so hard, so hard. We came so close."

They sat quietly for a moment. "It was a good effort," Lewis said. "It was a good effort."

All of a sudden they heard screaming from the next room.

"Let me go out and see what's going on," Collins said. The numbers people showed him the latest tally. Lewis was at just over 51 percent. Precincts 8A, 8B, and 8C had come in—Buckhead and other northern white suburbs—putting Lewis over the top. He had also overperformed in the poorer Black neighborhoods.

Collins went back into the office. "What's going on?" Lillian asked.

He walked up to the desk, stuck his hand out, and said, "Congratulations, Congressman."

Lillian burst into tears. Lewis lost his breath. "Are you sure?" he asked.

"I'm absolutely sure," Collins said. "And you need to go outside and celebrate."

They could barely open the door to the main room. People were jumping, screaming, and hugging. Lewis mounted a podium and gave his victory speech.

A white limousine pulled up to take them to the Westin. John-Miles and a friend excitedly climbed in, but Lewis decided that arriving by limo wouldn't look right. They would walk the mile and a half up Peachtree Avenue to the hotel.

The Lewises and a train of campaign workers set off. As they marched, people flooded into the streets to join them. Horns honked. People waved and cheered. There would still be a general election race against the Republican nominee in November, but it was a formality in solidly Democratic Atlanta. John Lewis was headed to Washington.[66]

The next morning, Lewis and Bond were interviewed on the *Today* show. Bryant Gumbel, the host, was in New York, while the two of them sat inches apart in an Atlanta studio. Bond was in an immaculate cream-colored Pierre Cardin suit, Lewis in his standard blue shirt, blue tie, and blue blazer. They looked straight ahead at the camera, not once turning their heads to each other.

"You gained the nomination," Gumbel said to Lewis. "Was it worth the price, the stress on your friendship?"

"Well, this race was a very difficult race," Lewis answered. "Julian is a very good and close friend. We were friends long before this campaign and we will continue to be friends."

Gumbel turned to Bond. "Do you still see John Lewis as you did before this began?"

"Oh, no," Bond said. "I couldn't say that. There's been a real strain put on this relationship between the two of us. But, you know, time is a great healer and I'm sure in time the wounds will heal."

Bond took solace in having won 60 percent of the Black vote, although Lewis could point to large swaths of Black voters who switched from Bond to Lewis between the first and second ballots. White voters went for Lewis four to one. "That was the deciding factor," Bond told Gumbel.[67]

Later that day, to another reporter, Bond said it would take twenty-five years for the wounds to heal.

Lillian said that she and Alice would remain friends "on the level that it's always been." And Lewis reached out to others. On Friday, the leading Black ministers of Atlanta held a "Unity Breakfast" at Paschal's. A hundred religious and political leaders gathered with John and Lillian over eggs and sausages to pledge cooperation for the general election. Lewis frenemy Joe Lowery declared, "We must grow accustomed in a majority-black community to contests between friends and comrades, and not let those contests divide us." Lewis gave out hugs, including to Bond's erstwhile supporters.

Bond wasn't there. He had already left for his vacation home in Florida.[68]

Chapter Twenty

ON THE HILL

———— ▪▪ ————

oting a basket of chilled champagne, a tub of Atlanta's finest jambalaya, and a bouquet of red, white, and blue balloons, John Lewis arrived at the Peachtree train station on Sunday afternoon, January 4. Although he was a frequent flyer, Lillian was not. She hated airplanes and took the train even when going to see her family in Los Angeles. And since she and John-Miles were accompanying Lewis to Washington for his swearing-in, they all would be taking Amtrak.

Ruth Wall, the Lewises' friend from the parkway fight, turned the trip into a party on wheels. Forty-four well-wishers made the thirteen-hour journey through the South Atlantic night. The guests spread out over several cars and Lewis, now a practiced glad-hander, flitted from one to the next, laughing with friends and introducing himself to curious onlookers. In one bunk, ten-year-old John-Miles enjoyed a sleepover with his campaign-trail friend, Drew Frank. In the club car, following midnight champagne toasts, Lewis peered out into the North Carolina darkness and reflected on his life's course. "I know it's hard for some people to believe," he said, absently caressing a scar on his bald head. "But I feel truly blessed. The beatings, the arrests—it was all worth it."[1]

After day broke over Washington, Lewis, wearing a sleek camel topcoat and tan fedora, debarked at Union Station and took in the Capitol dome. He felt the same rush as he had when first seeing it in 1961. He went to his assigned office, on the third floor of the Cannon Building—a majestic 1908 Beaux-Arts palace with Doric columns modeled on the Louvre, located on

Independence Avenue just south of the Capitol. A dozen red carnations sat on his desk, along with an offering of Piper Sonoma champagne. No phones had been installed; a hulking pile of electric typewriters sat on the floor. Lewis hung an American flag over his door. A reporter noted that the Georgia state flag—which from 1956 to 2001 featured the old Confederate battle standard—was "conspicuously absent."[2]

Making his way to the House floor, Lewis found the area toward the rear of the chamber where the Georgia delegation sat by custom. Reflecting the dearth of Black Southerners, members called it "Redneck Row." (In later years, Lewis would sit with the Congressional Black Caucus, in the first rows on the left side.) That first night, the Georgia delegation threw a party in the Caucus Room of the Russell Senate Office Building.[3]

On Tuesday morning, walking from a breakfast reception to his swearing-in, Lewis got lost in the Capitol's maze of corridors; Georgia senator Sam Nunn rescued him and escorted him to the chamber. Lewis was excited to be joined in his incoming class by Joseph Kennedy II, Robert's son, and by Mike Espy, Floyd Flake, and Kweisi Mfume, whose arrival brought the size of the sixteen-year-old Congressional Black Caucus to an all-time high of twenty-three.[4]

Love Collins and Richard Ossoff led the team tasked with hiring a staff. They spent weeks opening manila envelopes and scanning resumes. Old acquaintances of Lewis's, real and self-proclaimed, were coming out of the woodwork. Knowing that other freshmen were also staffing up and that top talent would go fast, Collins and Ossoff were intent on filling the key roles, especially the chief of staff (then called the administrative assistant, or AA), the legislative director (LD), and the Atlanta district office manager. Lewis didn't share their urgency. He calmly maintained that it would all get resolved in time.[5]

Some campaign staffers were disappointed not to be offered positions. Nunn and Wyche Fowler had warned Lewis that campaign jobs and congressional jobs required different skills and that he should start afresh. The only campaign aide asked to come to Washington was Collins, whom Lillian asked to be chief of staff. But Collins had two young children, and his wife, a prominent Atlanta attorney, had her own career to pursue. Instead, Lewis hired Clarence Bishop, who had worked for an outgoing Maryland congressman, Parren Mitchell. Bishop brought on Bradley Mims as legislative director. Michael German, a Federal Emergency Management Agency administrator in Atlanta, would run the district office.[6]

Bishop soon discovered that he had two bosses. "Sometimes it was difficult to tell, honestly, who had been elected, whether Mr. Lewis had been elected or whether his wonderful wife had been elected," he said. Early on, Lillian instructed Bishop to fire Cherie Murdock, Lewis's longtime secretary. "Mrs. Lewis wanted the look and feel of Mr. Lewis's congressional office to be young and energetic. It was very early at that time, and I wanted to please everybody. So I fired the lady."

Two weeks later, when Bishop called the Atlanta office, Murdock answered the telephone. "I just said, mentally, 'Oh, isn't this nice? She's come by the office to visit her friends. And she just answers the phone.'" Then he learned that Murdock wasn't just being helpful. Lewis, a softie at heart, had hired her back.[7]

An inveterate collector and history buff, Lewis had always turned his offices into miniature museums. At ACTION and on the city council, he had covered his walls and filled his shelves with photographs of the civil rights years, campaign posters, blown-up magazine covers, framed letters from presidents, artwork from his collection, chicken artifacts, and other memorabilia.

In the spring of 1987, Lewis was still unpacking wall hangings when colleagues came knocking. A few were seeking his blessing for their presidential bids. Dick Gephardt of Missouri invited Lewis to dinner at his Virginia home and gave him an autographed picture of the two of them. At another dinner, Senator Al Gore of Tennessee cornered Lewis and outlined his own campaign plans; when Lewis arrived at work the next morning, a handwritten thank-you note awaited him.[8]

Gephardt and Gore were both founding members of the Democratic Leadership Council. Reformist politicians had established the DLC in 1985 after the Democrats had lost four of the last five presidential elections, three of them in landslides. To regain the White House—and win support broadly—they aimed to steer the party toward more electorally palatable positions. The most prominent DLC members were moderates like Nunn, whose centrism posed a sharp contrast to the liberalism of Democratic

eminences like Walter Mondale, Ted Kennedy, and Mario Cuomo. Many
DLCers hailed from the South. Political consultant Bob Squier dubbed
them the "Southern White-Boys Caucus."[9]

It wasn't quite accurate. Although Southern white moderates predom-
inated in the DLC, the organization also encompassed dyed-in-the-wool
liberals with a pragmatic streak. Many were African American: Mayors Tom
Bradley, Maynard Jackson, Kurt Schmoke, and Andrew Young; Congressmen Mike Espy, Floyd Flake, Bill Gray, and William Jefferson; Lieutenant
Governor L. Douglas Wilder; party operatives Vernon Jordan and Ron
Brown. "There was an initial perception that this was sort of a good-old-
boys' group," said Maynard Jackson, an ardent DLC booster. But after the
influx of pragmatic Black liberals, he added, that idea had "no validity."[10]

It was in this spirit that Lewis joined the DLC. He agreed that Democrats had to win back the so-called Reagan Democrats, whose defection to
the GOP had hurt them politically. That meant changing perceptions of
the party. Although Lewis never held DLC office, "he did show up at DLC
gatherings," staffer Will Marshall said. "He had this quiet moral force and
lots of pragmatic things to say about how Democrats could build biracial
coalitions in the South," as they had for Carter in 1976 and for Lewis in his
1986 congressional race.[11]

In 1987, Southern governors collaborated to create "Super Tuesday"—a
one-day regional presidential primary, to be held on March 8, 1988, in
which fourteen Southern and border states* would vote. They hoped to
produce a nominee from the political mainstream. That summer, the DLC
hosted a "Super Tuesday Education Project" to teach politicians how to
drive turnout on the pivotal primary day. Lewis participated. "You cannot
have white voters flocking to the Republican Party," he explained. "It's not
good and it's not healthy. And it's not what we've been trying to bring about
in the South in recent years. We've been trying to build a biracial society."[12]

On June 21 and 22, at the Marriott Marquis Hotel in Atlanta, three
hundred officials and activists gathered for a "Super Tuesday Summit."
Lewis welcomed them. He spoke about the importance of Atlanta, slated to

---

* The fourteen states included Maryland. Six other states and American Samoa also
voted that day.

host the next summer's Democratic convention, and argued that the party had to be a big tent. "Our party," he said, "is a very diverse party. It is Black and white. It is young and old, rich and poor. It is urban and rural. Our party is America." Super Tuesday, he said, should be a vehicle to ensure that the nominee would appeal to the full breadth of that diversity.[13]

Lewis understood that this might mean nominating a leader whose politics differed from his own. At a time when "progressive" was being rediscovered as a euphemism for "liberal," Lewis disavowed the term, calling himself an "off-the-charts liberal." But in choosing a presidential nominee, Lewis mainly wanted to find a winner. For months he touted Nunn, one of the Senate's most moderate Democrats, but he couldn't persuade his friend to run. Lewis also threw cold water on the aspirations of liberals like Patricia Schroeder of Colorado. "I think in 1988, it is going to be very difficult for a non-Southerner," Lewis said. "I don't want to come across as being chauvinistic, but it is going to be almost impossible for Pat Schroeder to overcome some of the feelings in the South and within the Democratic Party. Some white American male will be the nominee of the Democratic Party when we meet in July."[14]

Lewis was wary, too, about the return of Jesse Jackson. Since 1984, Jackson had retooled his image, downplaying race, stressing populist economics, avoiding inflammatory statements, and fashioning a more inclusive message. It seemed to work. After a sex scandal felled Colorado senator Gary Hart in the spring of 1987, Jackson rose to the top of the Democratic polls. Lewis remained dubious. "We've gone through the days of protest and now it's time to make a contribution to the party," he told Juan Williams of the *Washington Post*, in a muted dig at Jackson, who had never held office. "I spoke to a group of labor people from Georgia and other parts of the South and I got the sense from these folks that it's time to win. They really want to win the White House." Lewis also felt loyal to other contenders—not only Gore and Gephardt, but also Illinois senator Paul Simon, who had been ACTION's best friend during Lewis's government tenure. Lewis also had reason to worry about Atlanta's Jewish constituency if he backed Jackson. He decided to stay neutral among the lengthening roster of hopefuls.[15]

Just how much the civil rights landscape had changed since the 1960s was underscored in August by the death of Bayard Rustin at age seventy-five. Most movement radicals had broken with Rustin during the Black Power debates of the mid-1960s, but Lewis always regarded him as a hero, particularly with respect to nonviolence and interracial coalitions. Lewis insisted on honoring Rustin in death. Although press secretary Anthony Johnson was taking a long-delayed vacation in California, Lewis had him write a press release immediately.[16]

At a memorial service for Rustin at Manhattan's Community Church, Lewis represented the old civil rights movement. "With Bayard's death, an era of leadership has passed," Lewis said in his remarks. "He nurtured the concept of creating a truly interracial society." That language revealed something about Lewis's reluctance to endorse Jackson, whom he didn't see as a unifying figure. During the fall and winter, Lewis said little to encourage Jackson. Unlike four years earlier, though, Jackson was talking about forging a "rainbow coalition," a slogan he took from the Black Panthers. Black leaders who had snubbed Jackson in 1984 were giving him a fresh look.[17]

Lewis noticed the difference. Jackson was suddenly getting good press, appearing on the cover of *Ebony* and all over Black radio and television. "Jesse Jackson, Jesse Jackson. That's all people were talking about from the time I got there until the time I left," Lewis told a reporter after getting a haircut at the Anderson Barbershop on Martin Luther King Jr. Drive in Atlanta. At Paschal's, the conversation was the same. When Lewis got home and called his mother in Troy, he said, "The first thing she starts telling me was that she was praying for Jesse Jackson to do well." And the next morning, when he visited young students at Tilton Elementary School, "every question was about Jesse Jackson." Even John-Miles, Lewis sighed to a reporter, "runs around the house saying 'Jesse Jackson has got to win. I hope he wins.'"[18]

Lewis felt the pressure. Unlike in 1984, moreover, when he felt a kinship with Mondale, a civil rights stalwart, Lewis had no relationship with Massachusetts governor Michael Dukakis, the Democratic front-runner. And where Jackson had finished third in the 1984 Georgia primary, he was now poised to win the state. Lewis never hesitated to follow his conscience, even in the face of political headwinds. But he felt uncomfortable being out of sync with so many African Americans, including in his district.[19]

Super Tuesday—which included the Georgia primary—was scheduled for March 8. It fell one day after the twenty-third anniversary of Bloody Sunday. As the day neared, Lewis decided to endorse Jackson.

"This is the anniversary of Bloody Sunday," Lewis told a reporter on Sunday, March 6, "and it was appropriate for me to do it in this context." At a rally at Ebenezer Baptist Church, Jackson spoke about the 1965 Selma campaign, lavishing praise on Lewis, who sat in a front pew. Lewis returned the favor, stifling his concerns that Jackson might wind up as a spoiler. "He is trying to put back on the American agenda," Lewis said of Jackson, "the needs and concerns of the segment of our population that is hurting and suffering."[20]

The next night Lewis again spoke on Jackson's behalf, to three hundred supporters at the Georgia World Congress Center downtown. "We make tomorrow a super Super Tuesday, because we send a message loud and clear," Lewis hollered, burying any trace of hostility, "that we want Jesse Jackson in the White House." The message was strikingly different from what he had been saying only recently. But rallies called for full-throated, unambiguous messages.[21]

On Super Tuesday, Jackson edged out Gore in Georgia's primary. He also won Alabama, Mississippi, Louisiana, and Virginia. It was a stunning performance. "Lewis definitely made a contribution," observed state senator Gene Walker, Jackson's Georgia state chairman. Lewis's endorsement had encouraged skeptical Blacks and wavering whites to put aside their own doubts. Although Dukakis stayed in the overall lead—finishing first in Florida, Texas, and Maryland—Jackson was now able to carry his campaign through the spring. It was not the Super Tuesday outcome sought by the Southern governors who had planned it.[22]

In a second irony, however, Super Tuesday proved to be Jackson's high-water mark. In mid-March he would score an upset in Michigan, but Dukakis beat him in the other remaining big states. Dukakis humored Jackson by saying he would consider him as his vice president. But political logic dictated that he tack centerward, not leftward, for the general election, and he eventually tapped the moderate Texas senator Lloyd Bentsen.

The choice was sound, but in publicizing Bentsen's selection, Dukakis blundered. He failed to tell Jackson about the decision before it was reported, leaving his rival insulted and infuriated. Dukakis apologized, but with the Atlanta convention nearing, media speculation took hold that a wounded Jackson might withhold his backing from Dukakis, crippling the nominee in November.

Lewis tried to repair the rupture. While continuing to praise Jackson, Lewis defended Dukakis before the press and reassured Jackson voters that all was well. At times he intimated that Jackson's pouting was part of an ego trip. "Governor Dukakis and his people have been very careful to try to meet the concerns and wishes of Jesse Jackson and his supporters," Lewis said, evincing a hint of exasperation. "It's time to go on to the convention."[23]

When convention week arrived, Lewis played city booster and welcomed the out-of-town hordes. On Sunday, July 17, the day before the opening gavel, John and Lillian hosted a parade and street party in Inman Park, the old neighborhood he had fought as city councilor to protect. The Lewises envisioned a grand affair. When Anthony Johnson asked if he could help recruit guests, Lewis would say, "No, it's too, too big." Johnson stuck to alerting the media.

To match the quarter's majestic Victorian manors, Lillian chose the theme "Victorian Nights, Victorious Days." Constituents and guests suited up in fin de siècle attire—high-necked white cotton dresses, seersucker jackets, sailor outfits for the kids. Sporting a luminous white suit, a beaming Lewis rode beside Lillian in a horse-drawn carriage, followed by two marching bands and a troupe of Spelman students dressed as suffragists. Turnout, however, was far from the "too, too big" showing that Lewis had feared. "It's myself, Brad Mims, and Regina Evans," Johnson recalled—three staffers. "We're the only three people standing on the street. And all I remember is the carriage goes by and we're waving. Goes down, turns around, comes back again." Still, some big-name journalists showed up, Johnson said, and "the *Atlanta Journal-Constitution* took a great picture of him and Lillian and put it above the fold and below the fold. He was ecstatic."[24]

The next morning, at the Martin Luther King Center, Lewis and Coretta Scott King welcomed the Massachusetts delegation, celebrating the state's historic commitment to Black equality. All week long, Lewis talked up Dukakis's career-long advocacy for civil rights and talked down the notion of a rift with Jackson. On Wednesday night, on a C-SPAN call-in program, Lewis fielded queries from viewers who had just watched Jackson fold his cards and endorse Dukakis. When one caller described Lewis as "one of the most liberal congressmen in the South" and fretted that the party was veering too far leftward, Lewis replied with a smile and a dose of pragmatism. "I may be liberal, and there may be some other liberal and progressive

Democrats," he said, "but the common denominator is to win. We all want to win. And you cannot win unless you have a true coalition, liberals and conservatives working together."[25]

Lewis was slotted to speak to the convention on Thursday night, before Dukakis's acceptance speech. His job was to deliver a closing argument to any remaining Jackson holdouts. Lewis ascended the podium before a boisterous sea of delegates. In keeping with his pledge in March, he had cast his vote the night before for Jackson, but now he implored everyone to set aside grudges and reservations. "Our party is broad enough to include Jesse Jackson, Michael Dukakis, and Lloyd Bentsen," Lewis declared, repeating a line he had been uttering for two weeks. "We have come a great distance since the '60s. When we look across the convention hall, it is self-evident that we are the party of inclusion."[26]

The unity drive brought the convention to a euphoric close. Dukakis shot ahead to double-digit leads in polls over George Bush, the lackluster Republican vice president. The Democrats appeared to have recast themselves as the party of economic opportunity and growth.

But the convention bounce faded. In the fall Bush relentlessly impugned Dukakis's patriotism and fitness on defense and crime. Led by consultants Roger Ailes and Lee Atwater, Bush told the story of William Horton,* a Black felon in Massachusetts who while on furlough from prison committed rape and assault. Lewis denounced the Horton attacks as "shamelessly designed to scare white voters." But Dukakis failed to rebut the allegations effectively and Bush closed the gap. In November he defeated Dukakis resoundingly.[27]

In Atlanta's Fifth District, it was a different story. Lewis had shown his constituents that he could fill the role of U.S. congressman. Although neither of his congressional committees—Public Works and Transportation, and Interior and Insular Affairs—was a prized assignment, they allowed him to provide for his district: from the former perch, he directed funds to Atlanta's rapid transit system and its airport; from the latter, he channeled aid to the historic Sweet Auburn neighborhood, home to Martin Luther King's birthplace and grave. Lewis also mended fences with Julian Bond's camp.

---

* Horton went by "William." It was pro-Bush ads that labeled him "Willie."

"We're moving closer together," he assured the press. On Election Day Lewis was returned to office with 78 percent of the vote.[28]

After the election, Lewis concluded his brief career as a Jesse Jackson enthusiast. Electoral victories in 1989 by David Dinkins as mayor of New York and Doug Wilder as governor of Virginia signaled a new era, Lewis proclaimed. Jackson, he said, was no longer "the undisputed symbol or leader of blacks in the national political arena.... These two men have paid their dues in terms of electoral politics."[29]

By his second term, Lewis was comfortably ensconced in Washington. He was still, to be sure, a backbencher; according to a *New York Times* profile, "Mr. Lewis has no major legislation to his credit and is not regarded as an insider in Congress." Yet he continued to bring home the pork—a new congressman's first responsibility, he understood, and one he would attend to his whole career. He hosted "constituent Fridays" once a month from his district office, where Atlantans dropped in to ask about their Social Security checks or issues like U.S. aid to the Nicaraguan Contras. Though draining, the marathon sessions solidified Lewis's bond with voters. "At the end of the day," Lewis said, "I feel like a doctor who has been seeing patients."[30]

Lewis also became personally popular with Washington colleagues. The *Times* called him "one of the best-liked men in Congress" and "something of a celebrity, frequently stopped and praised by tourists and passers-by." Evincing none of the cynicism heard in casual commentary about Congress, Lewis described his colleagues as an "unbelievable group of people." He made friends in both parties. The House, Lewis went so far as to say, had become "like a family" to him—even, he said, using SNCC's slogan, "a circle of trust, a band of brothers and sisters." The fraternity of the body provided him with the community that he was forever seeking.[31]

Lewis's daily routine energized him. He had bought a hundred-year-old three-story row house at 219 Third Street SE on Capitol Hill, and each morning he rose at five thirty and was out the door within an hour. He walked to the House gym for a workout, part of his ongoing battle against an expanding waistline, although neither the hours he put in on the treadmill nor his intermittent diets tamed his love of fast food and Coca-Cola. Some friends suspected the gym trips were less frequent than he let on. "I was there every day for maybe six years in the morning, taking tae kwon do classes," said Mike Espy, a third-degree black belt. "I tried mightily to get him to exercise. If he was there, I didn't see him."[32]

Lewis went next to the House prayer breakfasts—though his attendance there, too, waned over time. Then it was back to the Cannon Building, where he logged a twelve-hour day. Lewis was so busy that he skipped meals. (Raised on Southern manners, he wouldn't eat in front of others at meetings.) The day was topped off by a slate of receptions, dinners, and speaking gigs. He was invariably behind schedule because he stopped so often to talk with the admirers who accosted him on the street or in the corridors. Some staffers called it "John Lewis Time." Occasionally it became a problem.[33]

"Mr. Lewis would go MIA," recalled Tara McDaniel, a junior staffer. "He would've walked from the congressional office across the street to the Capitol and run into some school group. I'm racing up and down the halls of the Capitol looking for this man. And he's standing out in the Rotunda, giving them a tour. The halls echo. I'd listen for kids. Sure enough, he'd be standing there pointing at stuff and telling stories. Because he thought that was as important as a meeting with the heads of the big three automakers who were waiting for him."[34]

Linda Chastang, who replaced Clarence Bishop as administrative assistant and became one of Lewis's most trusted aides, also remembered hunts for her wayward boss. "When I had to track the congressman down," she said, "which I had to do rather often, I had to send interns to do it." She would instruct them to check Statuary Hall, a resplendent yet intimate gallery next to the Rotunda, home to busts and statues of eminent Americans, that was Lewis's favorite spot on the Hill. They frequently found him there, Chastang said, "talking to groups of students, chatting with the Capitol police, catching up with colleagues, answering questions from visitors, or just wandering around looking at the statues." The children were his favorite. Years later, friends and former staffers remembered Lewis taking their kids on special tours up the steps to the top of the Capitol's dome or to have lunch in the Members' Dining Room. Staff loved watching him get down on the office carpet to play with youngsters who visited.[35]

At the workday's end, around five o'clock, Lewis would hit the receptions, thrown by whoever was lobbying on the Hill. "We'd go to five, six, maybe eight in an evening," said Anthony Johnson. "We'd walk in and look for the Georgia people and we'd spend time with them." One night they had been invited to eleven events, and Lewis became obsessed with hitting them all, as if he were trying to break some obscure Guinness world record. "We got started and we were dashing and Mr. Lewis was keeping up," as Johnson told it. "We were just going stop after stop after stop after stop. Stay there for about fifteen minutes. We'd time it out. Because he wanted to hit all eleven. And I'll never forget: we got back to Capitol Hill probably about nine thirty, ten o'clock. He was so happy. He was, like, 'Yes! We did all eleven!'"[36]

When Lewis got home on a typical night, if he hadn't dined out or filled up on hors d'oeuvres, he might microwave some frozen crab cakes, fold his laundry, or flip on the television news. The night ended with a call to Lillian. They might talk for hours, even falling asleep while on the phone. "That was the point at which the meeting of the minds came together," said Michael Collins, a subsequent chief of staff. "Everything that had gone on throughout the day, all dumped out in the late hours of the night."[37]

On weekends Lewis went back to Atlanta. "He liked those five p.m. Thursday votes so he could get home," said Bill Richardson, then a congressman, who became a good friend. "He'd spend his weekends in the district." Thanks to his patronage of Delta—whose corporate offices were in Atlanta—the ticket agents knew his voice and his flight preferences. After the weekend he would return to Washington with fresh fruits and vegetables stashed in his luggage, since they were cheaper and easier to find in Atlanta than in D.C.[38]

Lewis befriended a wide range of colleagues. On Tuesday nights he shared antipasti and carafes of wine—or sometimes it was Chinese food—with "the Italians," including Nancy Pelosi, Leon Panetta, and Marty Russo. (Plenty of non-Italians, including Chuck Schumer and Dick Durbin, were also regulars.) The group, consisting mostly of liberals, became an incubator of the party's future leadership.[39]

Other evenings he dined with Richardson at the Hawk 'n' Dove, a Capitol Hill tavern. Over dinner, Richardson observed something about Lewis that other colleagues also noticed: he had yet to develop an appetite for policy work. For all his eighteen-hour days, for all his passion about human rights and equality, Lewis wasn't inclined to burrow deep into the sinews of the issues. "He's not much of a legislator," was a line heard from many people—including his friends and staff. Lewis's life's work had made him a go-to source on civil rights and voting rights, and recently he had become a champion of AIDS funding. ("He was very concerned with issues of AIDS and equal treatment," Richardson said, "and saw it as a civil rights issue.") But he wasn't the chamber's reigning expert on housing policy or education policy or drug policy. Richardson urged Lewis to expand his portfolio, arguing that it would help his congressional career. "'Johnny,' I'd say, 'You need to get some other issues!'" Lewis would laugh and smile.[40]

Lewis did, in time, get his share of legislation passed. But as his colleague Barney Frank explained, "His role lay elsewhere." That role included putting his moral weight behind an issue, inspiring others to fight on, and articulating the ideals that had to be kept in sight. "He was a tribune," according to Frank. And at a time of public cynicism toward Congress, Frank added, the presence in the body of "one of the great moral heroes of our time" was as powerful an advertisement for a career in public service as one could hope for.[41]

In the summer of 1991 Lewis plunged into two of the biggest fights that Democrats had with President Bush: over the nomination of Clarence Thomas to the Supreme Court and over a new civil rights bill. In these battles, Lewis demonstrated to his colleagues that there was more than one way to be an effective congressman. He found that the moral authority that he had accrued from his civil rights years played extremely well in Washington and with the media, especially when the subject was race. His experience compelled people to listen when he spoke to the core principles at stake in a policy debate. Conversely, jabs at a political opponent, even the president, didn't come across as quite so partisan when launched by someone widely judged to be a hero or a saint.

The Supreme Court fight began on June 27, when Justice Thurgood Marshall, at that time the only African American ever to sit on the high court, announced his retirement after nearly a quarter century. Bush immediately chose Clarence Thomas, forty-three, as his replacement. Raised in rural Georgia by his maternal grandmother, Thomas boasted an inspiring up-from-poverty biography: he had excelled in high school (having integrated his Catholic boarding school), attended College of the Holy Cross and Yale Law School, and shot up in the Washington firmament, chairing the Equal Employment Opportunity Commission under Reagan and joining the U.S. Court of Appeals for the D.C. Circuit under Bush. His selection was plainly strategic. Bush knew that many African American groups and voters would balk at opposing a Black successor to Marshall, no matter his politics. Some prominent Black leaders gave Thomas their endorsements or stayed neutral. Polls consistently showed him with substantial African American support.[42]

Thomas's views on race, civil rights, and affirmative action, however, were fundamentally conservative. Many Black leaders believed that Bush—who had voted against the 1964 Civil Rights Act as a congressman and exploited the Horton case in his presidential race—was again playing racial politics. Lewis called out the president's tendency to use racial wedge issues. "I do see the president using the element of race in a similar manner to that used by some of the Southern white politicians during the '40s, '50s, and early '60s," Lewis said that summer. "Race for this administration is becoming a political football, and I think the president . . . is leading toward further divisions in the American people."[43]

If Thomas was unknown to the country, he was no stranger to Black leaders in Washington, who regarded him with suspicion. Four years earlier, when he was EEOC chairman, Thomas had tried to meet with the African American congressmen. Only one granted him an audience: John Lewis. In January 1987, days into Lewis's first term, he and Thomas spent forty-five minutes chatting in Lewis's half-decorated Cannon Building office. "Every other Black congressman had rebuffed him," according to Thomas's aide Charles Shanor. "He had been ostracized." Yet Lewis was welcoming. He said he found Thomas "hard-working, articulate, and likable."[44]

But Lewis's courteousness toward Thomas didn't translate into enthusiasm for his nomination. Within a day of Bush's announcement, Lewis predicted that the judge's confirmation was "not going to be easy." Thomas's legal views, not his race, would make Blacks skeptical. "I don't think the appointment of Judge Thomas will be acceptable," Lewis said, "not to the great majority of Black people or to members of the civil rights community." The next week Lewis joined eighteen other members of the Congressional Black Caucus—with Gary Franks of Connecticut, the sole Black Republican in Congress, dissenting—in condemning the nomination. Thomas, they said, was "not the person to carry on the legacy of Thurgood Marshall."[45]

Lewis spent that summer drumming up opposition to the nomination. In one interview, he spelled out the caucus's elaborate plans to fight Thomas, which included enlisting the NAACP, the Urban League, Jesse Jackson's PUSH, and Black fraternities and sororities. "We plan to lobby, to confer, to talk with members of the United States Senate," Lewis explained, "and some of us plan to testify against his confirmation. . . . We may not be able to stop his confirmation, but we need to send a message."[46]

Lewis also made the case against Thomas in a piece for the *Los Angeles Times*. After complimenting Thomas's "rise from an impoverished early life to the highest positions in our federal government," Lewis cited a series of decisions the nominee had made at the EEOC that were hostile to discrimination plaintiffs. "Judge Thomas stands poised," Lewis concluded, "to deny to others the kind of opportunities that he has enjoyed."[47]

Lewis caught flak for his harsh words. Many people told Lewis, he said, that "I had turned on a 'brother,' a fellow Georgian. . . . I had not done 'the Black thing.'" But Lewis was unswayed. On September 19, he made his arguments before the Senate Judiciary Committee. Entering the Russell Senate Office Building, amid a crush of microphones and cameras, Lewis took a seat at the far-left end of a green-felt-topped table, beside four other Black Caucus members, all set to testify. Ted Kennedy claimed the privilege of introducing Lewis, describing his friend as someone "who still bears the bruises of the physical struggles" of the 1960s, implying that Lewis knew a thing or two about civil rights that Clarence Thomas didn't. After a few more words from committee chairman Joe Biden, Lewis adjusted his gold wire-rimmed glasses and for the next seven minutes read his remarks.

"I have been advised by some that I should not testify against Clarence Thomas, because he is Black," Lewis said. "The color of Clarence Thomas's skin is not relevant. The person, his views and his qualifications are." He continued: "You cannot vote to confirm Clarence Thomas, unless you feel confident that Clarence Thomas will not bring his own agenda to the bench and that his decisions will not be burdened with his own preconceived notions about how things are or should be. You must feel confident in your gut that, as he himself put it, Thomas is fair, full of integrity, open-minded, and honest."[48]

The testimony of Lewis and the other Black congressmen swayed few if any senators. Thomas at this point was all but assured of confirmation. Yet out of public view, senators had learned about sexual harassment allegations lodged against Thomas by an employee of his at the EEOC, attorney Anita Hill. After much wavering, Hill went public with her charges in early October, prompting a new round of televised hearings. The two protagonists' dueling testimonies riveted the nation—Hill with lurid accounts of Thomas's crude sexual innuendo, Thomas with inflammatory charges of being subjected to a "high-tech lynching." Still, few senators changed their minds. On October 15, Thomas was confirmed, 52–48.

Lewis expressed his dismay. He continued to believe Thomas should not be on the court. But he also believed it was important to show respect for the new justice. The next Friday, accepting an invitation from the president, Lewis joined one thousand other guests in the White House Rose Garden for Thomas's swearing-in.[49]

To a large minority of Americans, Thomas's investiture was no cause for celebration. Many were appalled by the Senate's rough interrogation of a shy, private woman who had bravely come forward to reveal a painful case of wrongdoing, only to have her story brushed aside. One Atlanta woman watching the hearings was so incensed that she felt moved to reach out to Hill, offering solidarity. Hill responded to the overture. From then on, Anita Hill and Lillian Lewis became fast friends.[50]

The racial politics of the Thomas hearings were divisive in part because Democrats were at that same moment growing exasperated with President Bush over his refusal to sign a new civil rights bill. In 1989, in a decision called *Wards Cove*, the Supreme Court had made it harder for plaintiffs to sue companies for racial discrimination. The technical issue centered on who bore the burden of proof when a given business practice had a "disparate impact" on a minority group. Previously, businesses had borne that burden, but *Wards Cove* shifted it to the plaintiffs. Liberals considered the ruling an obstacle to bringing legitimate discrimination lawsuits and a blow against racial justice. In 1990 Democrats drafted and passed a civil rights bill to return the burden of proof to employers.

George Bush, perennially concerned about his right flank, vetoed the bill. His was the first veto of a civil rights bill since 1866.

Bush's strained explanation was that the bill would have forced businesses to adopt strict racial quotas. The claim was false. But the word *quota*, which Bush tossed about repeatedly, could be counted on to conjure up fears that deserving job candidates were being passed over in favor of undeserving minorities.

Democrats believed that such demagoguery could be rebutted. After gaining seats in the 1990 midterm elections, they attempted to pass a new civil rights bill in 1991, purposefully including an explicit ban on quotas to deny Bush his most resonant argument. This time Lewis took a prominent role in the fight.

As the battle heated up in the summer of 1991, Lewis again found his sharpest weapon to be his moral authority. He hadn't been involved in the bill's drafting, nor did he do much for its passage behind the scenes. And although he gamely tried to win over colleagues who were growing skittish over the quota charge, they would avoid his phone calls or—like his friends Marty Russo and Buddy Darden—hear him out respectfully before declining to change their votes. Lewis, it turned out, was no LBJ-style arm-twister, no back-room mover of men.

But he did become one of the bill's most effective public proponents. He spoke out with a clarity and force that made journalists take notice. "It is a shame and a disgrace that, in 1991, we are still debating whether or not we should protect our fellow American citizens from discrimination," Lewis sermonized to the *New York Times* in July. To the *Atlanta Journal-Constitution*, he explained, "There is nothing radical, there is nothing extreme, there is nothing revolutionary about this little piece of legislation. For anyone to suggest this bill has anything to do with quotas is tampering with the truth and misleading the American people."[51]

Privately, Lewis was even more indignant. "He just can't do that!" Lewis would say of the president. "That's un-American."

Bush eventually granted the Congressional Black Caucus a ninety-minute audience to present their arguments. In the White House meeting, Lewis called the president on his cynical misrepresentations. Politely but firmly, Lewis told Bush that "he should stop using the word 'quota,' saying that this bill was a quota bill. It's not helping. It's just fanning the flames of division."[52]

Bush relented. In November he signed the Civil Rights Act of 1991.

Lewis's new prominence won notice not only from the press corps but also from a key Washington player: House Speaker Tom Foley. Over the summer, Foley had been grappling with a conundrum. Bill Gray of Pennsylvania, the Democratic whip—the third-ranking position in the party leadership—had recently announced his resignation from Congress. With Dick Gephardt serving as majority leader and David Bonior of Michigan set to replace Gray as whip, the Democrats now had an all-white, all-male leadership team. It was a problematic look for a party whose identity increasingly lay in its diversity.

Foley wanted to bring a Black member onto the leadership team. The Congressional Black Caucus was pushing Alan Wheat, an eight-year House veteran from Missouri. Wheat was an up-and-comer, with a seat on the powerful Rules Committee. In contrast, Lewis "had kept a pretty low profile," according to Lorraine Miller, a Foley aide who would later work for Lewis. "Everybody was glad to have him there, but he was observing and learning those first few terms."[53]

Moreover, for all his admirers in the Black Caucus, Lewis wasn't in the group's inner circle. Some caucus members, in fact, wanted him to understand when he arrived that they had been there longer and he shouldn't expect any special treatment. A few even saw his storied independence as a cover for personal ambition—an unwillingness to abide by caucus decisions in the name of solidarity. In 1989, when CBC colleagues had nominated Edolphus Towns for a seat on a plum committee, Lewis broke with protocol and declared for the seat himself, rankling some colleagues. In 1990, he had shamed some CBC members by spurning the egregious Gus Savage, a Black Chicago representative with a track record of anti-Semitic and anti-gay statements. "I just didn't want to be associated with that type of philosophy," Lewis said, even as others backed Savage for reelection. Cynthia Tucker of the *Atlanta Journal-Constitution* wrote that some members were deriding Lewis's friends in Congress as "eclectic," which she thought meant too white—the old insinuation that Lewis wasn't "Black enough." But Lewis stuck to his universalist ideals. He even said that he hoped that someday there would be no need for the Black Caucus. "The Democratic Party has been divided and splintered into so many pieces," he said. "Somehow we have to get to the point where we can forget about race and color." To *Newsweek* he said, "I don't major in caucus."[54]

But Foley still wanted Lewis. They had developed a personal friendship.

Foley admired Lewis's outspokenness in fighting for the civil rights bill and in opposing the 1991 Gulf War. (Foley ruled out Wheat because, like Gephardt, he came from Missouri.) Gephardt and Bonior also wanted Lewis in the leadership. Bonior argued that choosing Lewis would mean he would be in attendance at leadership meetings at the White House, "where his presence would remind the president of the racial, social, and economic justice issues John had fought and almost died for." They all thought that Lewis's reputation for courage would serve the party well. "I can hear Foley now," Lorraine Miller recalled, "saying he deserved the honor because 'Would you walk across the Pettus Bridge and would you allow billy clubs to hit you across the head?'"[55]

To satisfy several different constituencies seeking a place in the leadership ranks, Foley split the position of "chief deputy whip" into three parts. He appointed Lewis, along with Barbara Kennelly of Connecticut (a woman) and Butler Derrick of South Carolina (a moderate Southerner). Shortly before announcing the arrangement, Foley pulled Lewis off the House floor to make sure he liked the plan. "Will you come in my office?" Foley asked Lewis—a joke he used to make when he would usher a member into a more secluded area of the House floor. He spelled out the arrangement. "Yes, Mr. Speaker," Lewis said eagerly. "Yes, Mr. Speaker." Lewis took pride in his selection, calling it "the most important accomplishment I have had during my tenure in the House." The CBC, at least publicly, cheered his elevation. "He is clearly on a path," said Ed Towns, "to becoming Speaker of the House."[56]

As George Bush's third year in office drew to a close, Lewis was more determined than ever to put a Democrat in the White House. Only under Democratic leadership, he believed, would it be possible to revive the liberal agenda—whether on civil rights, social programs, or other issues. Under Bush, things felt even bleaker than they had under Reagan. The economy had nose-dived, and the huge budget deficits accumulated since Reagan's first term had made it impossible even to consider using spending to stimulate growth. Bush had made clear he was a foreign policy president, justifiably proud of the American-led victory in the Gulf War and hopeful about a new liberal international order after the Soviet Union's fall, but desultory at best when it came to tending to hard times at home.

That weakness gave Democrats an opening. But the party's lineup of candidates was undistinguished. Paul Tsongas, disheveled and shambling, was a former one-term Massachusetts senator who talked like Elmer Fudd. Jerry Brown, "Governor Moonbeam," the eccentric former California governor, had run twice before. Tom Harkin, a folksy Iowan, ill-advisedly styled himself as the second coming of George McGovern. Doug Wilder of Virginia, the first African American governor since Reconstruction, was still in his first term and preoccupied with state-level crises. Senator Bob Kerrey of Nebraska was somewhat more promising, with his record of Vietnam War service and business success, but his flat style left crowds cold.

The one candidate who noticeably excited voters was Bill Clinton, a voluble, gregarious Rhodes scholar and Yale Law School graduate who had been elected governor of Arkansas in 1978 at age thirty-two. A liberal on racial issues, Clinton had come of age in the South just as African Americans were gaining political sway. Unlike Jimmy Carter—two decades his senior and a latecomer to civil rights—Clinton belonged to a progressive cohort of Southerners born after World War II; he lacked any nostalgia for the old segregationist order. Though derided by some as slick and eager to please, he offered something for everyone. Moderates were drawn to his work with the DLC, liberal intellectuals to his highly detailed policy ideas, and African Americans to his long history and visible comfort in their churches and communities.

Lewis had met Clinton early in his political ascent. "I was in and out of Arkansas a lot as the head of the Voter Education Project," Lewis recounted near the end of his life. "He was a young political leader on the rise. He was a breath of fresh air in the South, young and energetic and smart. I admired him. He was someone the South needed. I would run into him from time to time. He represented the best of the New South. I would see him at group meetings with other young political types."[57]

Clinton remembered it similarly. "I was just a young man back in the seventies," he said of their first meeting, in 1976, "held no office, wanted to get elected to something in my state, and was interested in helping a fellow from Georgia named Carter get elected president." At the time, Lewis regaled the young Arkansan with "all these stories" about the civil rights movement. "My eyes were big. I thought, one of the reasons I liked politics and one of the reasons I'm a Democrat is I can sit here, a twenty-nine-year-old kid, and talk to John Lewis about his life." The next time they talked, at a 1978 Democratic Party convention in Memphis, "we were mostly talking about health care," Clinton said, but he was still "starstruck."[58]

Over the next decade and a half, they crossed paths and developed a friendship. Lewis could see Clinton's ambition and political talent. Once, at a cocktail hour, two of Lewis's congressional staffers, Anthony Johnson and Brad Mims, were chowing down at the shrimp bowl when the Arkansas governor sidled up. "We were laughing. It was like two Black guys started eating all the shrimp, right?" Johnson recounted. "And all of a sudden, this tall white guy comes and he says, 'Excuse me, brothers, would you mind if I shared some of the shrimp with you?' We were like, 'Yeah, man, go ahead.' That was the coolest dude we ever saw."

"Clinton gives me the 'brother handshake,'" Mims remembered. "He does what the brothers do when they greet each other. And I was like, 'Holy—where'd you get this from? You been hanging with your brothers, huh?'

"And he says, 'Yeah, I'm an honorary brother.' I said, 'Oh, you all right, man!' So we sat and chatted for a while and laughed."

Lewis remembered his aides coming to him, talking about their new friend who "acts more like a brother than a lot of brothers."

"Mr. Lewis, who is that guy? He's so cool," Johnson asked.

"Oh, that's Bill Clinton," Lewis replied. "He's the governor of Arkansas. He's going to be president of the United States."[59]

In the fall of 1991, Clinton declared his candidacy for president. "Clinton solicited my help and support," Lewis recalled. "I thought he would be good for the new politics in the New South." At first, though, he didn't make an endorsement. Even though Doug Wilder's chances were seen as slim, Lewis didn't want to wound his candidacy in its infancy.[60]

Still, friends knew whose corner Lewis was in. He readily shared his high opinion of Clinton with reporters. "He may be able to put together—and I don't want to sound like a Clinton partisan—the type of organization or movement in the Black community that Jimmy Carter did," Lewis said of Clinton in November. In December, Lewis participated in a fundraiser for Clinton at the Atlanta Ritz-Carlton, where Sam Nunn and Georgia governor Zell Miller endorsed the candidate to great fanfare. After Wilder shuttered his campaign in January, Lewis dropped all restraint. Harkin and

Kerrey continued to court him, but Lewis admitted to the press, "If I endorse anyone, it will be Governor Clinton."[61]

He also reached out to colleagues on Clinton's behalf. "I called a meeting of the Congressional Black Caucus. I was one of the people who organized the meeting," Lewis said. "Along with Mike Espy and maybe one or two others. People were very impressed with him. We made a decision with four or five of us to endorse him." The pitch made a difference for some of the skeptical caucus members, like Charlie Rangel of New York. "Quite frankly, I had not gotten over my bias against white Southern males," Rangel said. In 1965 Rangel had traveled to Selma for the voting rights march. "It took John Lewis and Andy Young to force me to listen to Clinton," he said, "and I was persuaded."[62]

"Having John Lewis for me was not only a credibility booster for me," Clinton later explained, "it was also a confidence booster." It was critical to his campaign strategy as well. When Clinton had first sat down with James Carville before hiring him as campaign manager, the consultant explained, "The path to the Democratic nomination runs through Black voters, especially Southern Blacks."

"I believe I can win them," Clinton had replied. He was a Southerner who had felt comfortable around Blacks his whole life, who succeeded in Arkansas thanks to an interracial coalition, and who preached a message of racial unity. "He comes to the Black churches," Lewis said of Clinton. "He can sing the songs without even looking at the hymnal."[63]

Lewis's endorsement also sent a signal to liberal voters beyond the South who might normally distrust a Southerner who chaired the DLC. Despite the DLC affiliation, however, Clinton was politically to the left of fellow candidates Tsongas and Kerrey. "I got all sorts of grief about my involvement in the DLC," Clinton explained in January 1992. "But I never would have gotten involved if it was going to push the country to the right." Instead of forging a strictly centrist path, as some pundits mistakenly read his strategy, Clinton was seeking to fuse liberals, African Americans, and working-class whites in an alliance that Lewis compared to Robert Kennedy's famous "black and blue" coalition of 1968. Lewis's enthusiasm, for hesitant Northerners, served to validate Clinton's bona fides on race and civil rights.[64]

Clinton's strategy centered on doing well in the Southern primaries. Zell Miller had bumped up his state's primary so that it preceded Super Tuesday by one week—allowing Georgia to enjoy the spotlight all alone. The state would be Clinton's proving ground.[65]

Then disaster struck. In the depth of winter, a one-two punch of headline scandals walloped the campaign. First came reports of Clinton's extramarital affair with an Arkansas woman named Gennifer Flowers. Two weeks later came stories about his dodgy moves to avoid combat service in Vietnam. Reporters began drafting the campaign's obituaries.

Some supporters ran for cover, but Lewis stood by Clinton. On January 23, after the infidelity story broke, Hillary Clinton—who had emerged as a popular headliner on the campaign trail—flew into Atlanta for a series of events, including a fundraiser for Lewis. All day long, reporters asked her about the affair. Untroubled, Lewis didn't shy away from her. "John would stand tall politically by his friends," said Keith Mason, Clinton's Georgia organizer, who escorted Hillary to the Atlanta events on the trip. "There wasn't any weather vane when it came to John Lewis."[66]

The scandals took a toll on Clinton. Instead of winning the February 18 New Hampshire primary, as he had orignally hoped, he finished second behind Tsongas. In his remarks that night, he spun the outcome as a triumph by declaring himself the "Comeback Kid." But he still had to start winning some primaries.

That night, after the elation in New Hampshire subsided, Clinton flew to Atlanta. "We come rolling into Georgia on an all-night flight," recalled Paul Begala, a top Clinton aide. "Zell had set up a welcome event. Maynard Jackson was there. John Lewis was there. The whole panoply."[67]

Lewis threw himself into the Clinton campaign. "He was all in for Clinton," said Buddy Darden, another Clinton supporter. "There was no question about his commitment." On Friday Lewis formally endorsed Clinton before hundreds of Black students at the King International Chapel at Morehouse College. Lewis cheerfully introduced the governor as "a son of the South" who "has seen the tumult and the strife of the past. . . . On all of those issues that are dear to many of us, this man can not only talk the talk, he can walk the walk." Some students peppered Clinton with tough questions, including about his support for the death penalty, but Clinton engaged them without defensiveness. Later that week, Lewis cut ads for Clinton to run on Black radio stations around the state.[68]

As Clinton courted Black audiences, he also sought to blunt concerns that his role in the DLC made him hostile to Jesse Jackson, who had been feuding with the organization. Although Jackson had pledged to stay neutral in the 1992 race, he had begun taking shots at Clinton. Clinton downplayed any talk of a conflict, stressing the two men's shared positions on a welter of issues including the 1991 civil rights bill, universal voter registration, and gun control.

A week before the Georgia primary, however, Clinton suffered another self-inflicted wound. Clinton was in a television studio on February 26, when his staffer George Stephanopoulos told him—erroneously—that Jackson had endorsed Tom Harkin. Harkin had been running what his Georgia political director, Joe Larche (Lewis's good friend), called "Lee Atwater–type ads" that slammed Clinton for using "a Black man's death to boost his campaign."* Clinton fumed into a live mike. "It's an outrage. It's a dirty, double-crossing, back-stabbing thing to do," he said. Seized on by the media, replayed endlessly on CNN, the gaffe promised to slow Clinton's newly recovered momentum.[69]

Lewis again stepped up. "Mr. Lewis, Maynard Jackson, and others—who knew Jesse far better and did not support him—they defended Clinton," recalled Begala. "And it really mattered." Lewis downplayed Clinton's outburst as an understandable reaction to a false report, and he campaigned with Clinton at Ebenezer Baptist Church, Big Bethel AME Church, and Stone Mountain. Excited about Clinton's popularity with Black voters, Lewis confidently predicted he would win the Georgia primary with at least 40 percent of the vote.[70]

In the event, Clinton won 57 percent of the primary vote and 72 percent of the Black vote. "We gave Clinton his first primary victory," Lewis later said, "and all of us were early supporters. There is a kinship there. We are all Southern. We're like a family." A series of follow-up victories the following week confirmed Clinton as the front-runner.[71]

---

* Clinton had emphasized his support for capital punishment by returning to Arkansas to oversee the execution of a convicted murderer, Ricky Ray Rector. Rector, after murdering a policeman, had shot himself in the head in a botched suicide, necessitating a lobotomy. Critics faulted Clinton for allowing the execution of a mentally ill man, typically omitting the fact that Rector had been fully compos mentis when he murdered his victims.

Reporters began asking Clinton about his vice presidential choice. In mid-June, the campaign released a list of a dozen names. Lewis's was on it. No one, with the possible exception of Lillian, thought he would be selected; his inclusion was a thank-you from Clinton, an acknowledgment of Lewis's importance to the campaign. He responded with typical modesty. "It's news to me," he told the *Journal-Constitution*.[72]

Al Gore of Tennessee eventually got the nod. Clinton was doubling down on his bid to remake the party as youthful, given to new ideas, and hospitable to Southerners. That summer, at the Democratic convention in New York City, Lewis was asked to second Gore's nomination—"an apparent effort," according to the *Congressional Quarterly*, "to calm any qualms among black voters toward an all-Southern white ticket." Lewis rehearsed his speech repeatedly in his hotel suite that Thursday afternoon, with staff or interns sitting on the sofa as a practice audience. Lewis was concerned about getting the tone right. "Is that too 'church'?" he would ask those sitting on the couch.[73]

At 8:52 p.m., on July 16, dressed in a dark blue suit and white shirt, with a red AIDS ribbon pinned to his lapel, Lewis strode from the wings to the center-stage teleprompters. Peppy big band music filled Madison Square Garden. Lewis waved and gestured at friends in the audience, smiling, nodding, flashing the thumbs-up sign. On the floor, the Georgia delegation hoisted "Lewis for Congress" signs. Then, over the droning din, Lewis thundered in full Baptist preacher mode and "whipped the delegates into a sign-waving frenzy," *CQ* wrote. To the doubters Lewis explained, "Bill Clinton and Al Gore were part of a new generation of Southern political leaders who tore down the signs of the 'Old South' and created a community of opportunity. Today, we proudly call the region the 'New South.' . . . Just as they helped to transform the 'Old South' into the 'New South,' Bill Clinton and Al Gore will now help to transform the old America into a new America."[74]

Lewis remained a Clinton enthusiast through November. Remembering Jimmy Carter's 1976 victory, in which Black votes had enabled the Georgia governor to take the South, Lewis believed Clinton could make the Democrats competitive in the region again. With Congressmen Mike Espy and William Jefferson, Lewis planned a "Freedom Ride"—a six-day, two-thousand-mile bus tour winding through the South from which Clinton surrogates would register voters. Joined by ten other members of the Congressional Black Caucus, Lewis's convoy rolled from city to city, linking up with the candidate for rallies. As Election Day neared, Lewis returned to Atlanta, making the rounds of the city's Black churches with Maynard Jackson to get out the vote.[75]

On Election Day, Clinton handily defeated Bush, carrying thirty-two states and 370 electoral votes. His strategy of courting Blacks and moderate whites paid off with victories in unlikely states including Georgia, which went Democratic for only the second time in a presidential election since 1956. Lewis himself coasted to reelection with 72 percent of the vote. In the new Congress, he would gain a seat on the Ways and Means Committee, one of the most prestigious assignments in the chamber.

Even more important, Lewis would for the first time be returning to Congress with a Democrat occupying the White House.

Chapter Twenty-One
THE CLINTON YEARS

———— ▪▪ ————

Soon after taking office, Bill Clinton invited Lewis to a movie night at the White House—the kind of casual get-together the new president used to build friendships and trust. "It's one of the great perks of the White House, that little theater," Clinton said. Trips to the executive mansion were hardly unfamiliar to Lewis, but this invitation made him giddy. Coming after a long Republican reign, Clinton's election offered Democrats hope. His warmth and gregariousness made him easy to like; his youth signaled a break with the past and the promise of a better future. "Mr. Lewis was like a little kid," said Debbie Spielberg, his legislative assistant, of the White House invite. "He was so excited. We were all excited for him."

The next morning, the staff huddled around to hear what happened. "Well," Lewis said, "they brought out the White House china. And then they ordered Domino's Pizza." Lewis didn't consider the low-budget meal a snub. It made the event intimate: a few friends hanging out to watch a movie.[1]

The first years of Clinton's presidency, though burdened with struggles, were heady times for Lewis. White House solicitations continued. So did visits from First Lady Hillary Clinton, who came to Capitol Hill as she led the administration's drive to extend health-care coverage to all Americans. "How is my favorite congressman?" she would chirp with a smile when she came by Lewis's office. ("He *was* my favorite congressman!" she affirmed years later.) On the night of the president's 1994 State of the Union address—in which he pressed his case for health-care reform to an enthusiastic joint session of Congress—Lewis invited Mrs. Clinton to his whip's office at the Capitol. "Everyone was crowding and jockeying to see her," recalled his aide Kim Walker. "Everyone was so excited to see the First Lady. I'm short. I was climbing on people. At one point I realized I was climbing on George Stephanopoulos." When Walker pivoted to extricate herself, she ran straight into President Clinton. "There was so much buzz," said Tara McDaniel, another staffer. "There's an energy that's in the Capitol on the night of State of the Union if you're in the majority. Bill Clinton, he was young and he was energetic, and he played the saxophone. And the Black staffers loved him. We loved him."[2]

Lewis remained a loyal booster of Clinton's agenda. He was unapologetic about sharing the president's pragmatic approach to governance. "All of us should hold on to immutable principles and we shouldn't run away from our principles," he said. "But there also comes a time when you have to be realistic and be very practical. And I like winning."[3]

The president made his first order of business a radical overhaul of Reaganite fiscal policy—higher top tax brackets, antipoverty tax credits, research and education investments, reductions in the Reagan-Bush budget deficits—and Lewis eagerly lent his support. He also backed the health-care plan; a bill giving workers the right to take family or medical leave; the Brady Bill, which limited handgun access; and more. "He's a party man," said his aide George Dusenbury. "He believes in the Democratic Party." Clinton viewed it in more personal terms. "When I looked over at John Lewis, I didn't think, 'Oh, good, I have a political ally,'" he said years later. "I thought, 'There's an old friend.'"[4]

Yet Lewis didn't relinquish the righteous adherence to principle that had sometimes led him to break with erstwhile allies. ("Every now and then," he acknowledged, "I'm out of sync.") He opposed the North American Free Trade Agreement, a pact with Canada and Mexico that Clinton championed but that Lewis feared would drive away manufacturing jobs. He would later oppose a compromise welfare reform plan that Clinton agreed to after vetoing two Republican versions. Lewis also argued in White House meetings against a Democratic plan to rein in political action committees, or PACs, which he argued were vital fundraising tools for candidates who lacked wealthy donor bases. If party loyalty ran deep, so did the claims of conscience.[5]

In Lewis's lifetime, no foreign country's struggles had engaged his passions as much as South Africa's. Since 1948, when the country's white supremacist National Party had fastened on its people a sweeping regime of racial segregation known as apartheid, Black Americans had found common cause with South African freedom seekers. As a young man, Lewis took up the anti-apartheid struggle. In 1966 he was arrested and jailed alongside SNCC comrades for sitting in at the South African consulate in New York; in 1988, as a congressman, he was still at it, getting arrested again outside the embassy in Washington. In between, he traveled to Zambia and Lesotho to meet with apartheid opponents—South Africa denied him a visa—and pressured Republican and Democratic presidents alike to take tougher measures against the government.[6]

Lewis especially admired Nelson Mandela, an early disciple of Gandhian nonviolence who, since his 1964 imprisonment on Robben Island, had nobly embodied Black South Africans' aspirations. "He is a hero to many of us. It is very important for Blacks to have that kind of hero," Lewis said of Mandela in 1990, reiterating his long-held belief in the value of charismatic leadership. "With the loss of Martin Luther King, Jr., John F. Kennedy, and Bobby Kennedy, there no longer was that kind of individual."[7]

Change finally came in 1990, when a new prime minister, F. W. de Klerk, began dismantling apartheid and freed the long-suffering Mandela. By early 1994, de Klerk had agreed to hold elections without regard to race—a landmark step toward multiracial democracy. But uncertainties remained. Mangosuthu Buthelezi, whose Inkatha Freedom Party commanded the allegiance of the country's 7 million Zulus, called for an election boycott, lest his people lose their autonomy within the KwaZulu-Natal province. Their abstention risked undermining the elections, and as the April 26 vote neared, deadly violence flared around the country.

From Washington, Lewis followed the worrisome news. To encourage peaceful elections, he wanted to visit. His aide Rob Bassin organized a congressional delegation—a "codel," in Capitol Hill terminology—to push the parties forward with the balloting. On Saturday, March 26, 1994, Lewis led six other members of Congress first on a short trip to Ghana, and then on a longer visit to Johannesburg, Durban, and Cape Town, to meet with de Klerk, Buthelezi, Archbishop Desmond Tutu, and Mandela, whose African National Congress was expected to prevail in the upcoming vote.

The trip began inauspiciously. On Monday, as the delegation flew to Johannesburg, panic gripped the city. Earlier that day, lethal gun battles had broken out in the downtown streets, where Zulu nationalists were demonstrating. As the Zulus marched toward Shell House, the ANC headquarters, the party's security forces opened fire, killing eight protesters. The Zulus retaliated, and for hours, militias, police officers, and snipers blasted away amid the downtown high-rise canyons. Fifty-three people were killed.[8]

Journeying into the city from the airport that evening, Lewis surveyed the aftermath. "While we were riding into Johannesburg, I felt like I was going into Mississippi during the Freedom Rides in 1961," he reported. "We saw people running and running, going into their shops and pulling down their steel gates and doors. Downtown was very, very tense." He added, "It was somewhat eerie, a strange feeling, so quiet . . . just a strange sense that something was about to happen."

Nonetheless, Lewis pressed ahead with the next day's plans, which included a meeting with ANC leaders at Shell House. On Tuesday morning, he and his colleagues boarded a coach bus from their hotel for their appointment downtown. He could see debris, broken windows, and the wreckage of the previous day's carnage strewn about.

When they were a block away from Shell House, gunshots rang out from a rooftop.

"It was truly a frightening moment," said James Waller, who had succeeded Linda Chastang as Lewis's chief of staff. "You're in another country. People probably knew who we were." The Americans worried they might be the targets.

Lewis and other passengers pressed their faces against the windows to see what was happening. Some people were firing guns, some running with weapons, others running for their lives. But as the politicians gawked at the bedlam, one rider—Carl Swann, a staffer of Kweisi Mfume's, raised in a rough Baltimore neighborhood—hit the floor. Everyone else, realizing their initial mistake, followed suit. "It takes a while to compute that they're shooting at you," said Pat Schroeder, a House member on the trip. The staffers, Waller recalled, "almost became like Secret Service" in shielding the members. "Because nothing can happen to a member of Congress on this trip. . . . We got down and the bus sped away." The meeting was canceled.[9]

By Wednesday things had quieted down enough for the Americans to meet at their hotel with Thabo Mbeki and Cyril Ramaphosa, Mandela's deputies. Apologetically, Mbeki explained that Mandela wouldn't be joining them. He had the flu, Mbeki said. Or perhaps he was playing it safe.

Toward the end of the session, Mbeki took a phone call. Moments later, he returned to the Americans. "That was Mandela," he said. "He's feeling better, if we go right now."

They hurried to Mandela's house, a gated estate in the leafy neighborhood of Houghton. In the high-ceilinged living room, they lined up with Lewis at the front. Mandela entered the room, wearing a bright, multicolored sweater and a tie, slacks, and loafers, flashing his trademark squinty-eyed, toothy smile. "It was a magical moment," Waller said.

"He looked in great health and in great spirits," said Butler Derrick, a delegation member, later that day. "He looked relaxed and very positive about what was going to be done between now and the election."

Mandela had previously met Lewis only briefly, in June 1990, when the ANC leader had addressed a joint session of Congress and Lewis had brought John-Miles, then fourteen, to see him. But when he arrived to greet the Americans, according to Waller, "he and Congressman Lewis had a big embrace. They embraced like old friends."

Mandela's living room opened onto a veranda, where they took tea. The African leader spoke to the Americans in "calming" tones, Schroeder later wrote, with "no bombast, no oratory. We kept expecting him to build to a crescendo," but he held forth "in the cooler British tradition."

"We feel very blessed, really, that we have had an opportunity to be here at this particular time," Lewis recounted that afternoon. "It is a rare moment to see the forces of history moving."

Afterward, Lewis and the Americans held a press conference. Lewis expressed confidence that a vote would go forward. Schroeder and Mfume invoked Lewis's personal history and the American South's metamorphoses from a segregated redoubt to an interracial democracy—as if to embolden the South Africans to overcome their fears and seize their own future. Lewis, too, talked about his past. The civil rights movement remained his lodestar, his lens for viewing the world. "We conducted a nonviolent revolution in America," he told the audience. "People shed some blood. Some people were beaten. Some were shot. Some were killed. But we didn't give up. We kept coming. We kept organizing. . . . In America, we spoke a great deal about the creation of an interracial democracy back in 1960, '61 and '62. And I think today in America, we are on our way. . . . And we would like to see that happen here in South Africa and around the world."[10]

That night the delegation traveled to Durban, on the east coast—Buthelezi's home. At a white-tie dinner with the local chamber of commerce, U.S. ambassador Princeton Lyman rebuffed the chief's demands to postpone the election. When Lyman finished speaking, Lewis and his colleagues "clapped frantically," according to Schroeder, and the audience leapt to its feet. Buthelezi seethed. The Americans would meet him first thing in the morning.

Over breakfast Thursday, they gathered at the offices of Inkatha, the Zulu political party. Brooding and suspicious, Buthelezi had his people record the meeting. Dismissively, he told his guests that they had been duped by Lyman's "philosophical pollution." Buthelezi also made clear that he didn't like to be lectured. "If looks could kill," Schroeder recalled, "I would have been struck dead."[11]

Lewis wasn't intimidated. The Americans hadn't come to lecture or preach, he assured. But, he said, "South Africa is not an island. We're all in this thing together." Lewis told Buthelezi that "the whole world is watching," that "it is important, very important, that the process be allowed to work." Violence would not be tolerated. "Not just you, Chief," Lewis said, "but all the parties—Mr. Mandela, the king, and the state president—should all call on people to cease the violence and urge people to get out and participate in these elections."

The other members echoed Lewis's message. Buthelezi raised the specter of violence. Then some of the Americans noticed Lewis stiffening, his jaw becoming firm. He looked the chief in the eye, looked around the table, and stood up.

"Chief Buthelezi," Lewis said, "I don't know how much you know about my history. But I know what violence is. I have been a victim of violence. Enough is enough. Too many people have been beaten and shot and killed in this country, and we will not stand by. My country will not stand by and let anyone interfere with free and fair elections. You can help shape or mold history, or make history, or you can become a footnote to history."

Lewis assured him that the Americans were not on anyone's side. "We are on the side of what we think is right and what we think fair."

Lewis closed by quoting his hero. "Dr. Martin Luther King said it best, Chief: 'If we don't learn to live together as brothers, we will perish as fools.'" They shook hands and left.

Days later, Buthelezi agreed to participate in the elections. Robert Gosende, a State Department Africa specialist, called Lewis to thank him, saying he attributed the shift to Lewis's performance.[12]

At home, Lewis briefed Clinton at the White House. "The reason I wanted to talk to him," Clinton later said, "is I wanted to know whether he thought they could pull this election off with minimum violence. And he said, 'Yeah, there might be some trouble. But I don't think you'll see much because they haven't voted for three hundred years.'"[13]

In early May, Lewis again made the fifteen-hour journey to South Africa—this time joining a forty-four-person delegation led by Vice President Gore and First Lady Hillary Clinton to celebrate Mandela's historic inauguration.

The competing pressures of party loyalty and personal conscience presented Lewis with a difficult dilemma in the summer of 1994, when Democrats were trying to pass a bill to curb the scourge of violent crime.

Crime had been bedeviling politicians since the 1960s. In the 1970s and '80s, in response to skyrocketing rates of lawlessness, Nixon and Reagan had adopted harsh law-and-order rhetoric and punitive measures. But while they succeeded in tarring Democrats as weak-kneed, their policies failed to arrest the problem. To the contrary, in the 1980s the illegal traffic in crack cocaine and other narcotics led to an explosion of murders, carjackings, and gunplay, the worst of it devastating Black communities, where homicide tallies reached historic highs. Grisly stories led the local news everywhere.

Clinton came to office touting a new approach to policymaking. His updated liberalism retained the goals of the New Deal and Great Society, but sought innovative policy solutions to reach them. Later called the Third Way, and sometimes misconstrued as mere political positioning or "triangulation," his strategy relied on devising a mix of policies that, defying neat ideological categorization, would appeal to different constituencies for different reasons.

The Violent Crime Control and Law Enforcement Act, which Congress debated throughout 1993 and 1994, fit the Third Way mold. Some provisions were liberal, some conservative, some both, some neither. The grab-bag bill included a ban on assault weapons; a section targeting violence against women; incentives to promote community policing; funding for one hundred thousand new police officers; programs like "midnight basket-ball" leagues to provide urban youth with alternatives to criminal mischief; monies for state-level prison construction; and the expansion of the death penalty to cover a host of federal crimes. Most important, the $30 billion bill for the first time promised massive federal help to state and local governments, whose leaders had long bemoaned being unable to fight crime within their own budgets.

Lewis had always believed the government had to do more to alleviate the poverty and despair that gave rise to crime. But the death tolls of the 1980s and early '90s upset him deeply, and he shared the common perception that the urban crime problem had reached a dire state. "What is happening in the inner cities and what is happening to the young African Americans, especially young African American males, is an emergency," he said in 1993. "What is happening now is probably the greatest threat to African Americans probably since slavery." The horror stories of gang violence or innocent children caught in the cross fire sometimes involved people Lewis knew personally, and he became convinced of the need for direct anti-crime measures along with a focus on root causes. "I'm sick and tired of people saying they don't have jobs, that they grew up in poverty" to explain turning to crime, Lewis said despairingly. "I don't care how poor you are, there's no way to justify what's going on in many of these communities." He added: "People fail to value human life anymore. People just shoot people, just kill people, just to get some money or to get a fix or maybe because of some personal conflict. And I think we have to say there must be a revolution of values, a revolution of attitude, and we have to lead that."[14]

Nonetheless, as the House considered an early version of the crime bill in 1993, Lewis refused to back it. As a lifelong death penalty opponent, he couldn't countenance the creation of dozens of new capital offenses. Every human life held "a spark of the divine," Lewis often said, that no human being or institution should have the power to snuff out. Lewis also thought about the racist ways of the old South, where state officials or all-white juries used flimsy pretexts to execute innocent Blacks. He lobbied Clinton to strike these new capital crimes from the emerging bill, sending the president a long brief against the death penalty. "While the rest of the world is moving away from death as a form of punishment," he argued, "capital punishment is becoming *more* entrenched in some parts of our country." But the provisions remained.[15]

By the summer of 1994, surveys were listing crime as voters' number one concern. Clinton's first eighteen months had been rocky, with legislative victories like the 1993 budget bill and NAFTA blemished by high-profile setbacks and Republican investigations of various ginned-up scandals. The crime bill became a referendum on the administration's viability. It might even decide the party's fate in the November midterm elections.

Democratic leaders had trouble corralling the votes they needed. Rural Democrats disliked the bill's gun-control provisions, while Lewis and other liberals resisted the expanded death penalty measures. Most Republicans denounced the bill as a liberal boondoggle and ridiculed the social programs like midnight basketball.

On August 11, the House voted on whether to take up the bill. In a shock to the White House, fifty-eight Democrats joined all but eleven Republicans to block the bill's consideration. Headlines the next day trumpeted the "stunning setback" and "stinging defeat for Clinton."[16]

Two paths remained. Clinton could negotiate with either the bill's conservative opponents or its liberal foes. The former course would mean scuttling the widely popular assault-weapon provisions and much of the social spending. So instead the administration approached Lewis and six other Congressional Black Caucus members, inviting them to the White House for a Wednesday meeting.

Pressure mounted on Lewis to back the bill. Polls revealed strong African American support for it. "There were black pastors, black mayors, black mamas, black elected officials lined up in the hallway during this time saying, do something," said Lewis aide Tara McDaniel. "Everybody thought they were doing the right thing at that time. When you have that level of devastation, you want to do something drastic."[17]

Phone calls to Lewis's office ran two-to-one in favor. Lewis was known to answer his phone himself sometimes, and when callers got him on the line, they would rant about the out-of-control gun violence in his district. If he mentioned the death penalty, an aide noted, "They would say, 'Look around Atlanta, three people were killed the night before. You've got to represent Atlanta.'" Meanwhile, much of the Black Caucus endorsed the bill. Washington sages berated Lewis for his insubordination. "When . . . party whips like John Lewis inexcusably abandon their party on a tough vote on a rule," wrote congressional analyst Norman Ornstein in the *Washington Post*, it showed that the Democrats lacked discipline.[18]

Lewis felt uneasy breaking with Clinton. "I don't like voting against my president, against my party, against the leadership of the House," he said. But his conscience compelled him.[19]

On the night before his White House visit, Lewis sat alone in his Capitol Hill townhouse. "Yes, I prayed," he told a reporter. "I prayed and I prayed. We have buried too many young people. Personally, I've gone to the funerals of too many young people, too many children. My son just graduated from high school. I've gone to the funerals of three or four of his classmates."[20]

On Wednesday morning, Lewis and the other Black Caucus members filed into the Cabinet Room. Clinton took a seat at the huge oblong table, immediately to Lewis's left. Turning on the charm, he made his pitch to the members that they should at least allow the bill to come to a vote.

"I remember well," Lewis said later. "He was very convincing in getting us to let it out of committee to get it to the floor for a vote."[21]

At the meeting, Lewis spoke his mind. "I told him I had to protect against the death penalty," he recalled. "I told him that from my earliest days in the civil rights community, with a philosophy of nonviolence, I've been against the death penalty. I believe there is a spark of divinity in every person. I told him that this was a tough one for me." Then he paused. "But I'm inclined to support the rule."[22]

Clinton thanked Lewis. Two other congressmen, Charles Rangel of New York and Cleo Fields of Louisiana, also agreed to back the rule. All three said they still intended to vote against the bill itself.

"It's been one of the most difficult decisions I've had to make in the eight years since I've been here," Lewis said afterward. "It was much easier to march across the bridge in Selma or go on the Freedom Rides. Everything then was clearly black and white." But, he explained, "I was seeing proposals moving [the bill] further and further to the right. What was in the making was something worse than what you have now."[23]

The bill went forward. The Democrats still had to make concessions—mainly cutting funds for Clinton's crime-prevention programs—to secure a few last votes. It cleared the House, 235–195.

Lewis voted against it.[24]

Two months after Clinton signed the crime bill, the Republicans scored a landslide victory in the midterms. In local, state, and national races, voters turned out Democrats en masse, including stars like Governor Mario Cuomo of New York and Speaker of the House Tom Foley. Republicans seized both chambers of Congress, the House for the first time in forty years. Lewis held his safe seat, but other Georgia Democrats, including his friend Buddy Darden, were swept away.

Lewis's staff called it "the Tsunami." Debbie Spielberg, demoralized like Democrats everywhere, approached her boss, knowing he was an eternal optimist and hoping that his implacable positivity might buoy her spirits.

"Mr. Lewis," she said, "please tell me there's a silver lining."

"Debbie," he replied, "there is no silver lining."[25]

Many factors had produced the Democrats' debacle. Some were short-term, including Clinton's unpopular health-care plan (which he failed to pass), his middling approval ratings, a House banking program that let members overdraft their accounts (Lewis had done so on occasion), and a "throw the bums out" disaffection. Other causes were longer in the making. Veteran Democratic incumbents who had for years been winning reelection in right-leaning districts retired in 1994, opening up seats that Republicans captured. The historical tendency for the party in the White House to lose seats in the midterms also played a role.

Ironically, some Democratic losses could be traced to the 1982 Voting Rights Act renewal. By making it easier to create Black-majority districts, the 1982 legislation had encouraged state-level gerrymanders that concentrated Blacks in certain districts—thereby making other districts whiter and more Republican. Lewis had been ambivalent about this development. In 1992, he had celebrated the arrival of thirteen new Black members of Congress from new majority-Black districts. But he also recognized even then the vital role of left-of-center moderates in maintaining Democratic majorities. The goal, he said, should be "to create an interracial democracy in America . . . not separate racial enclaves." Those warnings had gone for naught.[26]

Georgia's case was emblematic. In 1990, Lewis was the only African American in a state delegation that included seven white Democrats and one white Republican (Newt Gingrich, from nearby Marietta). Just four years later, the delegation contained three Black Democrats, but now only one white Democrat—the four of them outnumbered by seven white Republicans. Similar shifts took place across the South.

Of all the horribles that confronted Lewis and the Democrats in the new Congress, the most distressing was Gingrich's imminent election as speaker. The eccentric bomb thrower with the Dickensian name and Hobbesian worldview had been a thorn in Democrats' side since the mid-1980s. He rose to power trashing congressional norms with rhetoric that demonized his opponents, parliamentary maneuvers that enraged party elders, and cynical scandal-mongering that in 1989 brought down House Speaker Jim Wright, Foley's predecessor. With Foley now also gone, Gingrich claimed the throne.

Gingrich promised to implement his "Contract with America," a 1994 campaign platform that called for cutting taxes, social programs, and government operations. He also pledged to overhaul the way Congress conducted its business—including a vow to defund the Congressional Black Caucus. When Lewis denounced the move as "punitive," Gingrich scoffed, "A number of these unofficial organizations were potential scandals waiting to explode."[27]

Gingrich never killed off the Black Caucus. But other perks that Democrats had enjoyed vanished. Under a Democratic majority, Lewis—owing to his position as chief deputy whip—had enjoyed a hideaway office in the Capitol Building where his floor assistant Rob Bassin worked. Painted yellow and white, it had an elegant marble fireplace, a grand gold-framed mirror, and a beautiful oval table with inlaid green leather. When the Republicans took over, Lewis found a spot for Bassin on his regular staff, but he lost the office.

"Mr. Lewis," Bassin said as he planned to move out, "there's all that really nice furniture in the office. What should we do?"

"Strip it to the walls!" Lewis replied.

In the quiet hours, Bassin found himself rolling the beautiful table through the underground tunnels to the Cannon Building.[28]

The despair that Lewis expressed to Debbie Spielberg after the election was real. But it didn't last. His optimism returned. Around the office he began singing a different tune. "He saw our needs for hope and optimism in him, and we asked for it regularly," said Kim Walker. "And he gave us that." "He would say, 'It's not going to last forever, and we just need to be ready,'" recalled Chastang. "I remember conversations about what we're going to do when we take back the House."[29]

Lewis said his first priority was "to protect some of those hard-won gains that we've made in the last few years." He acknowledged that "Americans want changes," but he added, "they don't want to do away with services for senior citizens, low-income people, the disabled. They want to be fair." Safeguarding the edifice of the New Deal and the Great Society was essential. The "era" of big government might be over, Lewis said, in that it would be impossible now to pass sweeping bills like Medicare. But the "role" of a big federal government was still important.[30]

Lewis called on the Democrats to fight back. "I'm a partisan," he said proudly. "I'm a Democrat. I'm in the minority. I don't like being in the minority." David Bonior, the Democratic whip, organized a brigade of fired-up House members to go after Gingrich. Dozens of members showed up at Bonior's initial strategy sessions, eager to strike back at their tormentor. Their numbers dwindled over time, but Lewis remained a regular. "John just stepped up," Bonior said. "He saw what I saw."[31]

That included Gingrich's own sketchy financial arrangements. In 1989, he had toppled Wright as speaker by forcing an ethics investigation into schemes under which Wright's donors bought bulk copies of his book to evade House rules on honoraria. Yet Gingrich was doing similar things. One charge before the House Ethics Committee alleged that Gingrich used his political action committee, GOPAC, to raise money for a college course he taught, which was in reality a vehicle for training Republican operatives. Then, after the election, Gingrich signed a $4.5 million book deal with HarperCollins, the publishing house owned by conservative mogul

Rupert Murdoch. It smelled bad. "These are some of the same fires he used to burn us," Lewis said. "I'm not saying it's payback time, but it's a question of fairness."[32]

Bonior, Lewis, and a small squad began by using what were called "one minutes" to keep Gingrich's dealings in the public eye. According to House rules, each day, before regular business began, members could speak about any subject for sixty seconds. Usually the topics were anodyne or ceremonial. (In 1993, Lewis opened one of his one minutes by declaring, "Mr. Speaker, I rise today, not to speak about a crisis on foreign soil, or NAFTA, or even health care. I rise today to speak about Justice—David Justice and the rest of America's team, the Atlanta Braves." A devoted baseball fan, Lewis was cheering that his team had reached the National League playoffs.) Now, however, Lewis used one minutes to shine a light on Gingrich's foul-smelling deals. One day Lewis listed the huge sums that Gingrich's wealthy donors gave to GOPAC. The next day he slammed the speaker's refusal to divulge his contributors. A week later he jabbed at Gingrich's entanglements with a right-wing cable station. "A television station, a political organization, a foundation, even a $4.5 million book deal," Lewis said. "It is amazing Speaker Gingrich has any time at all to be speaker of the House."

"John gave it a boost every time he spoke," Bonior said.[33]

Lewis was gunning so hard for Gingrich that his staff began to worry. Normally, members preserved amicable relations with their in-state colleagues, the better to collaborate in bringing home federal dollars. Lewis was leading a drive to fund the King Historic District and a new federal building in Atlanta. The city would also be hosting the Olympic Games the next year. Georgia's Republicans insinuated that Lewis's campaign against Gingrich could backfire. "On things like the Olympics, we're going to have to work together as a delegation," said Gingrich ally John Linder, adding that Lewis was "not helping that process. It makes it harder to cooperate."[34]

Even the news media, normally smitten with Lewis, were critical. "Once viewed by members on both sides of the aisle as a moderating influence in the House," wrote Kevin Merida of the *Washington Post*, "Lewis has sharpened his sword and is regularly taking swipes at the head of Speaker Newt Gingrich." The *Atlanta Journal* editorialized that Lewis was "potentially jeopardizing a united congressional front that could benefit their constituents and all Georgians."[35]

Aides advised Lewis to let others take the flak. "It made people uncomfortable," said Waller. "'You're doing the right thing, but do *you* have to do it?'"

"It's the principle," Lewis would reply. "If the speaker wants to hurt the world looking at Atlanta, because of principles, then that says something about the speaker." On the House floor, an undaunted Lewis blasted "the nerve, the gall" of Gingrich's allies "to hold the people of Atlanta, the citizens of Georgia, and the athletes of the world hostage" to suppress criticism of the speaker.[36]

"It was particularly awkward," Waller said, "when they went on the same plane back home."[37]

In the spring and summer of 1995, Lewis and Bonior ratcheted up the pressure. They held press conferences laying out Gingrich's ethical lapses. Lewis began hammering the speaker on other issues, too.[38]

In March, when the Republicans introduced a harsh welfare reform bill, Lewis took to the House floor to recite the German theologian Martin Niemöller's famous warning about the Nazis ("First they came for the socialists . . ."). He sounded his own alarm. "This Republican proposal certainly isn't the Holocaust," he said. But "they are coming for the children. They are coming for the poor. They are coming for the sick, the elderly, and the disabled. This is the Contract with America." It was strong rhetoric.

Staffer George Dusenbury asked James Waller, "Was that as bad as it seemed from the gallery?"

"Yeah, it was," Waller said. But when Lewis came back to his office, he was beaming.[39]

What followed was one of the partisan flaps that periodically convulses Washington for a few days. Republicans indignantly accused Lewis of likening welfare reform to the Holocaust. Lewis held his ground, rejoining in the *Washington Post* that "my critics have misinterpreted my speech . . . at best and . . . distorted it for political gain at worst." Lewis, his aides felt, had discovered the full power of his voice as a moral authority.[40]

Gingrich came into Lewis's sights again that summer when the speaker outlined a plan to slash projected Medicare spending by $270 billion over seven years. On August 7, Gingrich was set to unveil the policy with a speech at the Stouffer Waverly Hotel in northern Atlanta. Lewis and a local labor group had packed the room with a hundred protesters. "I arrived around 9:15," Lewis said, "and whole busloads of community activists, primarily labor union representatives and senior citizens, arrived around 9:30." Event organizers tried to shunt them into the satellite room, but they occupied the chairs in the main hall instead. "We must tell the speaker and the Republicans to take their greedy hands off of Medicare," Lewis said to his allies in impromptu remarks. "Medicare is not a bank to be used to pay for a tax break for the wealthy." His event hijacked, Gingrich slinked away via a back elevator. The crowd chanted, "Where's Newt? Where's Newt?"[41]

Later that day, he lit into Lewis. "At some point he needs to realize that he's now a congressman, not a protester," Gingrich fumed. "It seems to me as a member of the delegation he ought to be involved in solving the problem, not just shouting about it." But to Lewis, protest techniques were important tools. He saw no reason to stow them away just because he was an elected official. "When you're in the minority in Congress, you have to reach beyond parliamentary procedure and legislative action," he told a reporter. "You have to use certain techniques and certain tactics to dramatize an issue.... What I've fallen back on is some of the things I know best, things that I learned from the early days of the civil rights movement."[42]

That fall, the Republicans' Medicare reforms became the central point of contention in their feud with Clinton over the budget. Earlier in the summer, Lewis and his staff had fumed over a chummy television appearance Clinton had made with Gingrich, in which they agreed on the need to hold down Medicare spending. But over the summer, the president sharpened his divisions with the speaker, promising to protect Medicare, Medicaid, and Social Security from Gingrich's axe. The standoff led to a government shutdown, in which only essential employees reported to work. Some eight hundred thousand others were furloughed.[43]

On November 18, amid the shutdown, Congress held a rare Saturday session. The Republicans agreed to allow Social Security, Medicare, and Veterans Affairs employees to resume work. The Democrats then tried to pass additional measures, hoping to convey a solemnity about conducting the people's business while painting the GOP as out of touch. But the Republicans surprised them by moving to adjourn. Stunned, the Democrats chanted, "Work! Work! Work!"

Unable to win enough votes for adjournment, the GOP called a recess, suspending legislative business indefinitely. They filed out of the chamber. The Democrats stayed behind and took to the well to make speeches.

Bill Thomas, a senior Republican, was incensed. "Turn that mike off!" he growled at a House technician. "Off now, and keep it off!" Republicans also shut off the cameras and closed the House restaurant. But Democrats stayed on the floor. Tourists looked on dumbfounded.[44]

"There were a lot of Democratic members sitting on the floor of the House in protest," recalled Barney Frank. "And it's at that point, as I remember, that John made a speech."

Like a coach giving a halftime pep talk, Lewis stepped to the podium to fire up the caucus. "I stood up to Bull Connor in Birmingham," he roared. "I stood up to Sheriff Clark in Selma. I stood up to George Wallace in Alabama. And I'm not about to run from Newt Gingrich." He urged his fellow Democrats not to relent in their battles with the Republicans. "He talked about how he was used to this," Frank said, "and you stay with your cause if it's right. It was an inspirational speech." Dick Gephardt, the minority leader, also found it stirring. "I remember that speech. And I remember the phrase that he always used when we got into a situation like that. 'We cannot give up and we cannot give in.'"[45]

Lewis also continued to spotlight Gingrich's business dealings. In 1995 the Ethics Committee agreed to investigate the GOPAC arrangements and the book deal and later appointed a special counsel. In December 1996, the counsel's office released its report, finding that Gingrich had violated House rules and lied to the committee.* By now, Clinton had been reelected, though the Republicans held the House. The Gingrich revolution wasn't over, but it had stalled. "The Republicans will have a smaller margin to work with in the House," Lewis said. "Newt and his cadres now must realize that they went too far, that they are looked upon by the American people as too extreme."

---

* In 1997, Gingrich said he would pay his ethics penalty with a $300,000 loan from Senate Majority Leader Bob Dole. Outraged, Bonior, Lewis, and others called for another ethics investigation. In the ensuing debate, Lewis charged Gingrich with "lying"—a charge that House rules forbade from being leveled at a fellow member. Refusing to withdraw is his remarks, Lewis was suspended for a day.

Needing to move on, Gingrich admitted his guilt. In January the House voted 395–28 to reprimand him and make him pay $300,000 in sanctions.[46]

While Lewis bucked home-state pressure in taking on Gingrich, he faced a different kind of pressure from within the Black community by speaking out against the Nation of Islam leader Louis Farrakhan. Since coming to fame during the 1984 Jesse Jackson campaign, Farrakhan had intermittently returned to the national headlines, usually after he or one of his acolytes was heard trafficking in anti-Semitic rhetoric. Lewis would call out Farrakhan's prejudice and remind everyone that the minister didn't speak for most African Americans.[47]

Lewis was sticking up for his long-held vision of a racially integrated beloved community. But he was also motivated by a lifelong identification specifically with the Jewish people. Over the years this philo-Semitism translated into steadfast support for causes of importance to American Jews: the plight of Soviet Jews, the survival and security of the state of Israel, the separation of church and state at home, the fight against persistent anti-Semitism in certain corners of American and African American culture.

Lewis's solicitude for the Jewish people dated to childhood. "When I was growing up," he told an interviewer, "I would visit the little town of Troy from time to time, and there was a little department store called Rosenberg, owned by a Jewish merchant. And from time to time, I would hear white people speak evil about this Jewish merchant. And to me, the way I heard it—and I was very young, only nine or ten years old—I knew there was something wrong. When they said 'Jew,' it sounded to me like saying 'nigger.' So I grew up as a child trying not ever to say Jew, which was really strange. I tried to say Jewish this, Jewish that, never saying or using the term Jew. Because it was, to me, like nigger—because of the way I'd heard people pronounce it."[48]

Lewis's identification with Jews had positive sources as well. "I grew up hearing songs as a young child saying, 'Go down, Moses, way down in Egypt land. Tell old Pharaoh to let my people go,'" he said in another interview. "We cannot erase that from our conscience. We have an obligation—almost a mission—to look out for the children of Israel." Learning about the Holocaust also made a searing impression. "I get into discussions with some of my friends, even when I was younger, in the '50s and '60s: How did this happen? How did people allow this to happen? . . . I said to people over and over again, we must not allow a modern-day holocaust to take place."[49]

In the civil rights movement, John couldn't help noticing the ubiquitous presence of Jews: local women in Nashville, Freedom Ride volunteers, sympathetic reporters like David Halberstam and Calvin Trillin, SNCC friends like his roommate Danny Lyon, rabbis at the March on Washington, Jewish leaders like Arnold Aronson and Joseph Rauh who helped pass the Civil Rights Act and the Voting Rights Act, the students of the Mississippi Freedom Summer like Mickey Schwerner and Andrew Goodman, whose murders still haunted Lewis. "He felt that people put their lives on the line for something that they didn't have to," said Debbie Spielberg. "And I think that's really what he felt like about the Jewish community. He felt a real kinship."[50]

As he had in Atlanta, in Congress Lewis fostered dialogue between Blacks and Jews. One informal caucus he organized in the 1980s and '90s included Barney Frank, Howard Berman, Martin Frost, and Alcee Hastings. "Sometimes I will convene a breakfast meeting. Sometimes we get together and have a minister and a rabbi come in." In the late 1980s, when Black members were disturbed by Israel's arms sales to South Africa, the Jews in Lewis's group agreed to pressure the Israeli government to end the sales, while the Black members agreed not to make too public a fuss. They raised the issue with a group of Israeli officials over breakfast in the members' dining room. Eventually, Israel phased out the arms sales and joined in worldwide sanctions against the regime. Over many decades, even as talk of a Black-Jewish rift made for perennial news stories, the cooperation in Congress remained strong. "Of any two distinct groups, there's probably no two groups of members as close together in the Congress than Black and Jewish members," Lewis said.[51]

Lewis's philo-Semitism also included a passionate defense of Israel. This commitment endured even after a faction of left-wing Democrats began expressing antagonism to the Jewish state. A regular at events hosted by the American Israel Public Affairs Committee and other pro-Israel groups, Lewis also made frequent trips to the Holy Land. In 1991, he lobbied African nations to repeal the United Nations' notorious 1975 resolution equating Zionism with racism (the repeal passed), and in 1995 he spearheaded a congressional drive to relocate the American embassy to Jerusalem, the seat of Israel's government.* Some people attributed his stands to the influence of the Jewish community in his district or, in an ancient anti-Semitic trope, to their campaign contributions. Lewis denied it. He had Jewish constituents and contributors, but insisted, "If I didn't have any, my feeling would be the same. It's a very principled one."[52]

Jews—and other Americans troubled by anti-Semitism—turned to Lewis in the early 1990s as Farrakhan was boosting his profile. In 1991, the Nation of Islam published a widely read tract of pseudo-history falsely claiming that Jews drove the African slave trade. Then, in late 1993, a deputy to Farrakhan, Khalid Muhammad, delivered an anti-Semitic, anti-gay, anti-white diatribe at a New Jersey college that was written up in the *New York Times*, leading to weeks of public recrimination. From the House floor, Lewis urged a resolution condemning the remarks.[53]

As the furor continued, Lewis went on the Charlie Rose show on PBS to argue against Farrakhan's message. Despite dramatic strides in the social and political position of Blacks since the 1960s—the integration of neighborhoods, workplaces, halls of power, and even families—the intractable problems of poverty, crime, drugs, education, and family breakdown in the inner cities were spurring many people to seek out new spokesmen. These included Farrakhan, whose emphasis on self-reliance and strict renunciation of drugs, alcohol, and other corrupting influences resonated with some Black Americans fed up with conditions in the ghettos. Some were drawn to Farrakhan's scapegoating of Jews; others merely thought his anti-Semitism, sexism, and his intolerance of homosexuality were outweighed by what they considered his positive model of behavior.

But Lewis held, as always, that the means must match the ends. "Any time we see expressions of racism, bigotry, anti-Semitism, we have a moral

---

* The U.S. had kept the embassy in Tel Aviv, even though it wasn't Israel's capital, because for years Jordan and then the Palestinians staked a claim to East Jerusalem. In 1995 Clinton signed a bill to move the embassy. The new embassy in Jerusalem opened in 2018.

obligation to speak out," Lewis said on the Charlie Rose show, as he argued with the New York City activist Al Sharpton. "I saw young Blacks and young Jews dying together, shedding blood together, for the right to vote, to end segregation and discrimination at lunch counters and restaurants in the South. I'm not about to stand by and see anyone, whether that person is Black or white, Jewish or non-Jewish, create a schism within our communities."[54]

Later that year Farrakhan made a play for still greater prominence by unveiling plans to hold a "Million Man March" on the Washington Mall the following fall. One million Black men—he urged women to stay home—would gather and take responsibility for the violence, drug use, and broken homes afflicting their communities. Ignored at first, the plan steadily gained followers, aided by the endorsement of Ben Chavis, a recently deposed NAACP president. Lewis's long-estranged friend James Bevel, who had struggled with mental health issues for decades and joined forces with the crackpot politician Lyndon LaRouche, was also now advising Farrakhan.[55]

The march was scheduled for October 16, 1995. At first, Lewis didn't know what to make of it. "What is the goal?" he wondered. "Is it to display a sense of solidarity? Or is it to be one of these things like in the stadium where you have sort of a Jesus thing?" (The Promise Keepers, an Evangelical Christian organization, had been holding mass rallies in which men would recommit themselves to their families.) As the date drew near, African American leaders debated whether to promote the march's goals of Black male uplift and self-responsibility, or to shun it because of its noxious captain. Fascinated by the story—the eccentric Farrakhan was nothing if not good copy—reporters pressed every prominent Black leader to take a stand. To Lewis's surprise, the Black Caucus decided to back the march. So did civil rights legends such as Rosa Parks and Dorothy Height. Some distanced themselves from Farrakhan's vile doctrines, stipulating that they were endorsing only the message of self-reliance. But their participation lent the publicity-seeking minister a margin of legitimacy.[56]

On Thursday, October 12, Gary Franks of Connecticut became the first Black Caucus member to publicly assail the march—a fact the *New York Times* reported. But the same *Times* article also noted, as if by way of reproach, "the noticeable silence of Representative John Lewis, . . . one of the most respected civil rights leaders in Congress."[57]

Lewis was quiet because he was deliberating. He personally liked some ideas that the march was purporting to uphold: its appeal to Black pride, its emphasis on self-sufficiency, its goal of inspiring more Black men to help repair broken families and solve the urban crisis. On the other hand, Farrakhan remained anathema to him, and he knew that his Jewish friends and constituents—as well as members of the gay and lesbian communities— would consider his participation a betrayal.[58]

At a staff meeting in his Cannon office, Lewis asked about sentiment in his district. An aide replied that the march was popular, and Black constituents especially wanted him to endorse it. If he didn't, he risked drawing a primary challenger the next year.

Without betraying emotion, Lewis asked each person at the table what he should do. Almost to a person, the staff urged him to stay away. They couldn't reconcile Farrakhan's views—separatist, hateful, angry—with Lewis's belief in the beloved community.

Playing devil's advocate, Lewis rehearsed the counterarguments. Supporters said the event was about morale and responsibility in the Black community, not the Nation of Islam's politics. He also mentioned how Martin Luther King had once organized under the slogan "I <u>AM</u> A MAN"—a sentiment similar to that of the march. But the staff believed he had had his mind made up all along. He would not attend.[59]

Lewis gave an interview to the Associated Press. "I don't want to be associated with or identified with anything that tends to demonstrate signs of racism, bigotry, or antisemitism," he said unequivocally. He also explained his position in an essay for *Newsweek*. "I am not going to attend," he said, "because it goes against what I have worked for—tolerance, inclusion, integration."[60]

Lewis wasn't alone in boycotting the march. Coretta Scott King spoke out against it, as did a diverse set of eminent Black leaders including, many reports noted, Julian Bond, now a board member of the NAACP. But Lewis still caught flak. Letters, faxes, and phone calls flooded his office in protest.[61]

One person who felt differently about the march was James Waller, Lewis's chief of staff. He wanted to participate but was nervous about telling his boss. All week long, Waller avoided the subject. Then Waller's father, who lived in Philadelphia, told his son that he was coming to Washington for the event. Waller decided he had to broach it with Lewis.

Not knowing what to expect, Waller said, "I explained to him why I wanted to go. And he said, 'You should. If that's what you want to do, you should participate.' He said, 'I've been through many experiences in my life and I've learned a lot, but I support you in making this decision that you've made.'"[62]

Also struggling with his response was Bill Clinton. The president knew he should castigate Farrakhan's bigotries, but he had relied on African American support and didn't want to alienate the march's Black enthusiasts. On the day of the Million Man March, Clinton was scheduled to speak at the University of Texas at Austin. He decided to talk about race relations.

Two days before, on Saturday morning, Clinton called Lewis at home. "I remember that he thought it was imperative that, as president, I had an aggressive position on race and that we not basically cede the field to Farrakhan," Clinton recalled. "I asked him to walk me through how he thought I should say things. I said, 'I'm not going to say anything I don't believe. But you know what I believe, and so let's talk about it.' I'll never forget it."[63]

They agreed that for all the progress made toward racial equality since the 1960s, the races seemed to be pulling apart culturally. The popular phrase "It's a black thang; you wouldn't understand" captured a sense that the statistical markers of Black advancement masked deeper, unbridgeable divides. In the murder trial that month of football player O. J. Simpson, many Blacks had cheered his acquittal, while whites tended to judge it a miscarriage of justice. (Lewis himself did not celebrate the verdict.) "We're very troubled by this division in America," Lewis said of his conversation with Clinton. "As a nation we cannot continue to go down that road."[64]

When Monday morning arrived, Lewis looked out the window of his Third Street townhouse to see waves of participants hoofing it over to the National Mall. "It was a sea of humanity," he said. "It was very impressive." He himself went to the office, where he watched the speeches on TV. Local and cable television broadcast remarks from Stevie Wonder, Maya Angelou, Jesse Jackson, and others, along with Farrakhan's own two-hour "lecture," as he called it, which ended only as the sunshine gave way to twilight.[65]

Afterward, Waller took some friends back to the congressman's office. "He was there," Waller said, "and we had conversations about the march." Lewis was not judgmental; he wanted to hear people's impressions. "It was always comfortable in the D.C. office to have those conversations," recalled

George Dusenbury. "There was a really good diversity of perspectives. Congressman Lewis enjoyed that. I think that's what the civil rights movement was like for him. People talking and getting through their feelings and their strategy and their perspective."

The House photographer had taken a dramatic panoramic picture of the march, which members could purchase. Waller asked for two copies. "I gave one to my parents and framed it. I have one." Even though the congressman had opposed the event, he said, "we got them under the name of John Lewis."[66]

Lewis's busy schedule left him with less time for his family than he wished. He went home to Atlanta on weekends, but as his relationships in Congress multiplied, he spent more weekends headlining fundraisers for Democratic colleagues, who counted on his star power to fill a room. Demands rose for him to give talks, accept awards, attend museum openings, and lend his name to causes. He never liked to say no. "Well, the saint is not home much to take out the garbage," Lillian told a reporter. "But when he's home, he's saintly."[67]

His absence had an impact on John-Miles. As a boy, John-Miles had struggled with a learning disability and emotional issues. He was rambunctious and often difficult. Lewis was on occasion heard to threaten his recalcitrant son with a "nonviolent spanking." Lillian dealt with his needs constantly. "He was more Lillian's son than John's," said a friend. Lewis clearly loved his son and was playful and gentle with him. "He was instrumental in showing me what it was like to be a father the way he was interacting with John-Miles," said Love Collins. "He helped me see the softer side and the human side of things." But he was not at home very much.[68]

Living in the shadow of his revered father also created expectations for John-Miles. Strangers would tell him about his father's greatness. Friends of the Lewises who knew John-Miles well cherished his sweetness and warmth and became attached to him. But colleagues who met the youth only in passing were struck by the difficulty he had engaging with them—putting on headphones and retreating into his music, for example, during a dinner with his parents and their friends. Lewis often seemed disappointed, frustrated, and unsure of what to do.

As a teenager John-Miles wanted to be a rapper. Lewis recoiled at the thought. He disliked rap—the lack of melody, the misogyny and vulgarity of the lyrics. When John-Miles was a little older, he began drinking and smoking, which Lewis disliked even more. If he walked into the room and smelled cigarettes or saw beer cans all over, Lewis would reprimand his son that he wasn't allowed to smoke in the house. One time Lewis lectured his son that, at his age, he had been involved in a nonviolent revolution; later he realized the comment had been a mistake, that it could only make his son feel inadequate. At the time, John-Miles had merely replied, "Oh, Dad, it's another day." Years later, however, he told an interviewer that the stories he heard about his father influenced his own hip-hop lyrics. "You know it's hard as hell growing up in the house and, you know, you got pictures of your pops getting hit with billy clubs and getting dogs sicced on him, that shit goes into your head," he said. So he "merged" his understanding of the civil rights movement into his own music.[69]

When John-Miles was nineteen, he was hanging out with some friends John and Lillian considered unsavory. Lillian was having health problems, including serious kidney issues, and was hard-pressed to regulate her son's behavior. In December, John-Miles was driving on Cobb Parkway in northern Atlanta near the Cumberland Mall with a friend. After running a red light, they were stopped by the police, who found loaded handguns and an open can of beer pouring out on the floor. John-Miles was charged with possession of a concealed weapon and underage possession of alcohol. Buddy Darden, who was serving as Lewis's attorney, got the charges dropped. Lillian called Ruth Wall to ask her if Ruth's husband, a restaurateur, could hire John-Miles to do some work, just to give him some responsibilities. Eventually he enrolled at Clark Atlanta University, though he would not graduate.[70]

Since the mid-1960s, Lewis had thought about writing a memoir. In 1991, he was approached by a prominent New York literary agent, David Black, and decided it was time. "I wanted to give a source of inspiration to young people and those not so young who maybe don't remember the struggles of the civil rights movement," Lewis told journalist Robert Scheer. "And hopefully, it would inspire people to act again, to move.... I want people to know that during another period, we did have people working together across racial lines, blacks and whites."[71]

As his coauthor, Lewis selected Larry Copeland, a former *Atlanta Journal-Constitution* reporter. They drafted a five-page proposal, tentatively titled "The John Lewis Story," which was shown to publishers. He signed a contract for $165,000 with Alice Mayhew of Simon & Schuster.

Copeland traveled with Lewis to Nashville and Selma and sat with him scribbling notes as the congressman recounted his memories. But after nearly a year, the book wasn't coming together and Copeland left the project. In early 1995, Black asked another client of his, Michael D'Orso, who had written an acclaimed history of the 1923 racial violence in Rosewood, Florida, to take over. D'Orso, too, took weekend road trips with Lewis to Troy, Nashville, Selma—"every one of the hot spots," D'Orso said, "just to walk the ground"—and interviewed the congressman in his office and his home.[72]

By late 1997, they were nearing completion. "I've been getting up at 2 or 3 in the morning," Lewis told a *Journal-Constitution* reporter, "and part of it has been difficult to re-read. You get into 1964 and the Mississippi Summer and the killing of the three civil rights workers or 1968 and I have to relive the assassinations of Dr. Martin Luther King and Bobby Kennedy and it gets painful." But it was also a labor of love. Lewis had made it his mission to convey to the public, and especially younger generations, the story of the movement—its ideals, its struggles, its triumphs. The desire to keep alive that flame lay behind Lewis's attendance at all the anniversaries, his authorship of so many op-ed pieces, even legislative work like getting the Selma-to-Montgomery route designated a National Park Service historic trail. The memoir would be a way to share the story with new generations. It could imbue in young people those same childhood passions—for school, for reading, for civil rights—that Lewis had harbored as a boy.[73]

Published on June 1, 1998, as *Walking with the Wind: A Memoir of the Movement*, the book was a critical and commercial success, selling thirty thousand copies in hardback in its first year and winning several major awards. It catapulted Lewis to even greater celebrity, as he was afforded long interviews by TV and radio hosts and profiled in *Jet* and *People*. Vice President Gore threw him a book party in Washington; Governor Zell Miller hosted one in Atlanta. Lewis's busy speaking schedule grew busier.[74]

Lewis loved talking to audiences about the book. Rob Bassin took a leave of absence from the congressional office to set up events. Bassin called the chiefs of staff of other Black Caucus members and asked if they would appear with Lewis at independent bookstores in their districts. "I think we did maybe thirty cities, just going around," Bassin said. "And he would sit for hours and sign books. If there were two hundred people, he would do every one." Linda Chastang and Lillian also lined up events, sometimes calling up former staff members to ask for help in setting up a talk in one city or another.[75]

The book contained a few errors. Normally, Lewis had an eerily accurate recall of dates; he could cite exactly when a given sit-in or march or speech took place. But in a strange confusion, Lewis had misremembered being present for the original "Freedom Day" in Selma in October 1963, when in fact he had been in jail. He also misremembered being with Martin Luther King on the night of LBJ's "We Shall Overcome" speech on March 15, 1965. There were a handful of other incorrect dates or details as well.

Not everyone liked the book. Though never nasty or harsh, Lewis's tone toward some former adversaries was critical in places, and a few reacted angrily. Ekwueme Mike Thelwell, who was assisting Carmichael with his own memoir (he would complete it after Stokely died), wrote scathingly that *Walking with the Wind* exposed Lewis as a man of "unbridled ambition, an instinct toward the establishment, and a certain lightness of principle"— qualities Thelwell alleged Lewis had also shown in his rough-and-tumble campaign against Bond. Bond himself said that while he hadn't read the book, "I've had people read parts of it to me" and that from their account, he inferred that Lewis "says things about the campaign that I think are just not true.* . . . I think he's just having trouble with the fact that the election is over [and] he's proven to be the best man."[76]

Others charged, with bitterness or disappointment, that as Lewis's star rose, he forgot about old comrades. They questioned his political pragmatism and his comfort with the Democratic establishment. Muriel Tillinghast, a SNCC friend who had worked on both of Lewis's congressional

---

* Bond wrongly alleged that Lewis claimed in *Walking with the Wind* to have won the Black vote in their 1986 race. Lewis never made such a claim.

campaigns, said she considered him "a decent person," but that "his goal became to stay in office, which is the agenda that most politicians have. Once he was in office, he turned his back on SNCC. He was unwilling to acknowledge SNCC. I really never forgave John for that. His life bears out the detriment of getting involved in politics from the inside."[77]

An especially pained reaction to the book came from Archie Allen, Lewis's friend and colleague from Nashville, the VEP, ACTION, and Atlanta. In researching a never-completed biography of Lewis, Allen had conducted 242 pages of interviews with his subject, as well as others with family members, associates, and friends. He had shared these materials with Lewis and was certain that Lewis had used them in writing *Walking*—there were many similarities—although Copeland and D'Orso both stated that they hadn't done so. More troubling, when Allen looked in the book's index, he didn't see his name. It appeared only once in the book, in a photo credit. When Allen called to ask why, Lewis could only protest feebly that it was "an oversight." Lewis did send an inscribed copy, "to my dear friend Archie," with thanks for "your friendship and all of your help and support." But the omission of one of Lewis's closest associates over almost twenty years was hard to explain.[78]

D'Orso later said that "Lillian had no hand, no word, no say in the book." Allen, however, suspected that she was responsible for his omission. Jealous of his closeness to her husband, she had never hidden her dislike of Allen. Also absent from the book was Lewis's longtime administrative assistant Cherie Murdock, whom Lillian also disliked. Joan Browning, another SNCC colleague, had been with Lewis when Robert Kennedy announced his candidacy in 1968 and worked as treasurer of Kennedy's Georgia operation, but she, too, was left out of the memoir. "If you got on Lillian's bad side, you were written out of the story," Browning said years later, although she ultimately held Lewis responsible, calling him a "conniver."[79]

But these criticisms were confined largely to a handful of old associates. The popular reception was quite different. The encomiums propelled Lewis, already a historic figure, into something more like legend status. "I thought that the book was the beginning of the transformation of Congressman Lewis to an icon," said George Dusenbury. "He was not an icon before then. He was a respected member of Congress." *Time* magazine had two decades earlier dubbed him a saint, but even then he was not really a household name. The novelist Alice Walker had dedicated *Meridian*, a 1976 novel, to "John Lewis, the unsung." In 1996, when he spoke at the Democratic convention, there was little coverage or comment. Historian Sean Wilentz, in a 1996 *New Republic* profile, quoted Bond as saying, admittedly with some lingering acrimony, "John ought to be in the top ranks of black leadership, but he's probably not, if you ask a hundred people on the corner." As late as 1998 it was possible to describe Lewis—as Clinton aide Paul Begala did when asked by *Esquire* to name a personal idol—as "one of the least-known heroes of the civil-rights movement."[80]

With the memoir's publication, the adjective "least-known" would not be applied to Lewis any longer.

As Lewis hopscotched the country to promote *Walking with the Wind*, Washington was transfixed by the campaign to impeach Bill Clinton over his trysts with Monica Lewinsky. The salacious story of the randy president and the former intern had dominated the airwaves since it broke in January 1998. Clinton's foes rejoiced that they finally had a scandal that might deliver his presidency's death blow, while friends writhed in consternation that he had handed the Republicans a weapon to bring him down. After weeks of round-the-clock news coverage, however, Clinton's popularity rebounded. Americans drew a distinction between private and public morality, and however harshly they judged Clinton's infidelity (which he continued implausibly to deny), they rejected the drive to impeach him as politically motivated and incommensurate with his sins.

Through it all, Lewis stood by Clinton. Part of his motivation was personal loyalty; part was a recognition of Clinton's robust popularity within Black communities. "This president understands African Americans better than any other president in modern times," Lewis said in February as the yearlong donnybrook was getting underway. Black solidarity with the beleaguered president helped him survive months of frenzied media grilling and legal jockeying. But after independent counsel Ken Starr produced DNA evidence of the affair, in the form of a semen-stained dress, the president agreed to testify before a grand jury. That same night, August 17, on national television Clinton admitted to the affair, calling it "wrong" and a "personal failure" and professing "regret" for having misled everyone.[81]

Most Americans accepted the apology and agreed with Clinton's call "to move on." But Washington pundits deemed the speech insufficiently penitent. With the political fallout hard to gauge, most Democratic officials kept their heads down. But not Lewis. "The president is a friend of mine, and I'm not going to run from him," he said. "You don't run from your friends when they're down, when they need your help."[82]

August 28 would be the thirty-fifth anniversary of the March on Washington. Chastang had organized a book event for Lewis in Oak Bluffs, Martha's Vineyard, home to a large Black community. Clinton, who had been vacationing there in recent summers, planned to participate. But as the date approached he called Lewis to ask if he should still attend.

"You have to be here," Lewis replied.[83]

"Well, John," Clinton said, "if I come what should I say?"

"We all need forgiveness," Lewis said. "People will identify with you if you're vulnerable." Lewis said the public sided with Clinton over Ken Starr, "but they want you to ask them for forgiveness."[84]

Lewis passed the morning of the event at Bickerton & Ripley Books in Edgartown on the island, signing copies of his memoir. White House speechwriter Jeff Shesol had prepared remarks for Clinton that touted Lewis's heroism and called on Americans to finish the work that Lewis and the movement had begun. But the president, waking up late, flipped over the speech draft and wrote out a new talk by hand. He fiddled with it as he rode to the church where he would speak.[85]

At two o'clock, Lewis and Clinton met at Union Chapel, a five-minute walk from the ferry dock. Dating to 1871, the wood-framed, octagonal church, with its steeply pitched roofs and tall triangular gables in the Eastlake style, was an iconic gathering point in the Oak Bluffs community. Several others took seats alongside Lewis and Clinton in front of the altar, including Harvard law professor Charles Ogletree, who moderated the event.

After preliminaries, Lewis rose to speak. "Mr. President, my friend and my brother, thank you so much for being here. You didn't have to come, but you came. And thank you so much," he began as Clinton's eyes turned moist and the audience applauded. "Mr. President, you have been my friend and you will always be my friend. I was with you in the beginning and I will stand with you from now till the end." The audience applauded wildly again. Lewis and Clinton shook hands and patted each other on the back. Lewis

then gave a ten-minute book talk about the march and his memoir, concluding with a call to the audience to "walk with the wind, and let the spirit of
history be your guide."[86]

Next, Clinton stood up, to another raucous ovation, which lasted a full
minute. "John Lewis has been my friend for a long time—a long time," he
said. "And he stood with me in 1991 when only my mother and my wife
thought I had any chance of being elected. . . . I treasure the years of friendship we have shared. I have boundless admiration for him." Originally allotted ten minutes to speak, Clinton held forth for thirty.

He listed three lessons he had learned from Lewis and the movement.
He ticked off each one, digressing into examples and stories, then circling
back to the next item: the mutual dependence of all people; the wisdom
of nonviolence; and, finally, the need for forgiveness. "All of you know, I'm
having to become quite an expert in this business of asking for forgiveness,"
Clinton said. "It gets a little easier the more you do it. And if you have a
family, an administration, a Congress, and a whole country to ask, you're
going to get a lot of practice." The next day's *New York Times* headline read:
"Embraced by the Forgiving, Clinton Talks of Forgiveness."[87]

Afterward, Lewis signed a copy of *Walking with the Wind* to Chastang,
who had labored for weeks to organize an event that ended up focusing on
Clinton more than Lewis. "In a way," he wrote, "you helped save the President."[88]

Lewis's belief in forgiveness was sincere and profound. That fall, Stokely
Carmichael died and Lewis offered a tribute to his old adversary. "I last saw
him this past spring, at a tribute to Stokely," Lewis wrote in *Newsweek*. "We
hugged, and after so many years I discovered the personal hurt had faded.
He held my hand for a while, and seemed happy, and in that moment I was
no longer sitting next to the revolutionary Kwame Ture, but my old friend
and brother Stokely Carmichael."[89]

The fall also witnessed the passing of George Wallace. Lewis eulogized
him, too. "With all his failings," Lewis wrote in the *New York Times*, "Mr.
Wallace deserves recognition for seeking redemption for his mistakes, for
his willingness to change and to set things right with those he harmed and
with his God. . . . When I met George Wallace, I had to forgive him, because
to do otherwise—to hate him—would only perpetuate the evil system we
sought to destroy."[90]

Chapter Twenty-Two

AMBITIONS

———— ▪ ■ ————

O ne decade into his congressional tenure, Lewis was a mainstay of the Democratic leadership, a favorite of the president, a sought-after headliner, and an unrivaled moral voice. "The conscience of the Congress"—a phrase originally applied to the Black Caucus as a whole—now referred to Lewis alone. The moniker fit so well that no one noticed the shift.

But Lewis, at fifty-eight, was still full of energy and drive. Lillian, always his greatest booster, believed he could rise still higher—become speaker of the House, senator, vice president, even president. In 1997, she had urged him to challenge Senator Paul Coverdell, a Republican who had unseated Wyche Fowler in 1992. But his political soundings suggested he couldn't win.[1]

Instead, at Lillian's instigation, he set his eyes on the House leadership. The Democrats' rebounding popularity in the mid-1990s fed the party's hopes of reclaiming majority status. If Dick Gephardt, the party leader, became speaker—or ran to succeed Clinton in 2000—then David Bonior would move up to become leader, opening the whip position. In 1998, Lewis started talking to colleagues about the whip job, even though no one knew when or even if it would become available.

As Lewis felt out colleagues, Nancy Pelosi charged into the race. Hailing from a Baltimore political family, transplanted to Northern California decades before, she had entered Congress a few months after Lewis and established herself as a staunch liberal and cagey strategist. On August 13, 1998, Pelosi circulated a letter to colleagues saying she expected the Democrats to capture the House in November. "If we expect to win, we must act like winners," she argued. "I, therefore, want you to know that I intend to run for a leadership position in the new Congress."[2]

Lewis was caught off guard. So was Steny Hoyer of Maryland, another canny insider, who had lost the whip race to Bonior in 1991 and was hoping his time had come.

In November 1998, in a backlash against the Republicans' impeachment drive, the Democrats defied historical trends to gain seats in the House. But they fell short of a majority, meaning the whip race would have to wait another cycle. But where Lewis relaxed his campaigning, Pelosi pressed on. "When I got in, I had every intention of winning," she said. By the summer of 1999 she was hosting discreet dinner meetings with an army of loyalists—roughly twenty-five members—at her favorite Hill eateries, Barolo's and Hunan Dynasty.[3]

In August, word of Pelosi's strategy sessions leaked. "The whip's race is starting way, way too early," Hoyer charged. "This shouldn't be going on right now." He added, "Quite honestly, since it has started, I don't intend to sit on the sidelines." Lewis sent a letter urging that all three candidates "cease and desist" until after the next election. But he, too, kept campaigning.[4]

Lewis had many strengths to recommend him. Everyone admired his heroism and moral voice, and he was well-liked, even beloved. He had ties to different party factions, including the Black Caucus, Southerners, liberals, and New Democrats. But he was neither a legislative strategist nor a pitiless vote counter nor a wily horse trader. In fact, he wasn't the sort of person usually elected whip at all. Nor was he sure that he wanted to campaign for the job relentlessly for the next fifteen months—or possibly longer, depending on what happened in 2000.

"I won't do any unilateral disarmament in terms of the campaign itself," Lewis said in September 1999. "But it's not going to be every waking moment."[5]

"Those who snooze, lose," Pelosi countered.[6]

Pelosi kept announcing endorsements. So did Hoyer. "You've got to do things for people," Bonior noted. "This one wants an office. This one wants to go on a trip. Steny had done that his whole career. Nancy's very good at that, too." Lewis lagged.[7]

His staff knew that any path to victory went through the Black Caucus. Sanford Bishop, Lewis's fellow Georgian, promised his vote. But Cynthia McKinney, the state's third Democrat, backed Pelosi. So did Eleanor Holmes Norton, the District of Columbia representative, who had known Lewis since the March on Washington. Old lions Charles Rangel, John Conyers, and Julian Dixon sided with Lewis, but James Clyburn of South Carolina and Marylanders Elijah Cummings and Albert Wynn went with Hoyer. "I love John Lewis," said Carolyn Kilpatrick of Detroit. "John Lewis is my hero. But he hasn't given me a reason to vote for him for whip."[8]

At one point Hoyer announced that he had seventy commitments, and ninety if the vote went to a second ballot. Lewis muttered weakly that he wouldn't "play the numbers game" and that no one could "say right now that they have a hard, fast count." When Pelosi talked up the prospect of becoming the first female whip (and possibly speaker), Lewis reluctantly cited his race as a credential, something he had usually been loath to do. "I don't want to see a caucus with only white Americans in the leadership," he said.[9]

Lewis's staff saw that his heart wasn't in the fight. Pelosi and Hoyer were treating the race as a bare-knuckles contest. Lewis had to be badgered into making calls. His aides—and Lillian—were more fired up than he was. In the past, others had had to push him into accepting assignments that most members would jump at. When his Georgia colleague Ed Jenkins retired in 1993, opening a slot on the Ways and Means Committee, Tom Foley and Dan Rostenkowski of Illinois, the committee chairman, had to twist Lewis's arm to join it. When his time came to chair the Congressional Black Caucus, Lillian wanted him to take it, but he declined, seeing it as a thankless post where he would get bogged down in petty squabbles and make enemies.[10]

At bottom, Lewis feared that becoming whip—or becoming speaker one day—would rewrite his place in history. He now stood as a living embodiment of the civil rights movement, known for his surpassing courage. The lead paragraph of his obituary had in effect been written. His performance as whip or speaker, especially a middling performance, might one day eclipse those experiences or render them in a less admirable light. Being a legend provided him a better platform than would being whip.[11]

Staff changes introduced more challenges to his campaign. His chief of staff Rob Bassin left for a job at AIPAC. Bassin's successor, James Williams, stayed for only a few months, with Linda Chastang returning temporarily in January 2000. Michael Collins, a Boston-born Morehouse College alumnus, came on board as floor assistant.[12]

Collins noticed Lewis's half-heartedness about the whip race. But in his first week on the job, he learned that Lewis wasn't the only one who mattered. Lillian, on a rare trip to Washington, came to Collins's desk and asked sternly, "Mr. Collins, can I see you in the congressman's office?" When he walked in, her tone became icy. "I don't know why you forced your way onto the staff," she said. "But if my husband loses this race, it's going to be because of you."[13]

Collins did his best under the circumstances. With Pelosi having staked out the liberal ground and Hoyer styling himself a moderate, Lewis crafted a new message. He now billed himself as "a builder of bridges," someone beholden to neither wing of the party.

"I bring people together," he would say. Lewis assembled a steering committee of twenty members, campaigned for colleagues in their districts, and hosted soul food or Chinese dinners at his townhouse. He made the rounds to colleagues' offices and wrote them personal notes.[14]

But the endorsements never came. "People's political futures had deeper ties than their love for John," Charles Rangel said. Seeing Lewis's path to winning blocked, Pelosi and Hoyer both wooed him, encouraging him to play kingmaker. Lewis considered both of them friends, but he turned to Hoyer first, asking his honest assessment of who would win.

Hoyer said he had eighty-five commitments. Pelosi had only sixty-five. He was confident he would prevail.[15]

In July, Lewis withdrew and backed Hoyer. "I have concluded that the votes are simply not there for me," he said. "My candidacy for the leadership was never based on personal ambition, only on a desire to serve."[16]

In the fall of 2000, the Democrats again fell short of winning back the House. After more than two years of jockeying, Pelosi and Hoyer would have to wait another cycle for their final showdown, with Pelosi ultimately carrying the day. Lewis remained chief deputy whip.[17]

Lewis's staff and close friends weren't surprised at the outcome of the whip race. They knew that the driving force behind it had not been John but Lillian.

Lively, dynamic, and sharp-witted, Lillian had in the last decade moved on from her job as a librarian to take on different administrative posts at Clark Atlanta University. Though she avoided Washington, and Lewis's House colleagues rarely saw her, she had many friends in Atlanta, who knew her as cultivated, elegant, and ambitious. One acquaintance said she aspired to "the *Ebony* magazine view of the world"—an interest in middle-class Black society, culture, and politics, coupled with a concern for social attainment. She loved art and books and was a fixture on the Atlanta scene. "She would see a play, go to a movie, go to a book signing, just do something almost every day," said Lyn Vaughn, a CNN anchor and a friend. "She enriched her life." Lillian also liked to gossip, in a playful way, and kept abreast of the city's social doings. "If somebody famous was in town," said Vaughn, "she would want to know about it."[18]

Shopping was her favorite pastime. She delighted in outings to Saks Fifth Avenue and other ritzy stores. "She loved to shop," said Mignon Morman Willis, another Atlanta friend. "She had an affinity for unique purses, handbags, and shoes. I would just watch her in amazement." Early in her marriage, she met Carl Nelson, who worked in the couture department at Saks. Nelson noticed that Lillian, despite her frequent patronage, hadn't been given the store's select membership card that alerted customers to advance sales and special events—because, he suspected, she was Black. Nelson got her the special card and doted on her whenever she came into the store. They became close friends.[19]

But if Lillian had one defining trait, it was that she was utterly devoted to her husband.

The relationship was in some ways unusual. They were physically apart from each other more than most couples. "My niece said that I've made a life that's comfortable for me, as he has for himself," Lillian told a reporter in a rare act of self-disclosure. "John was that person before I met him. I'm not a clingy person. His life makes him happy." Yet deep down, Lillian's friend Carol Dove said, "they were just totally connected." They talked on the phone every morning and night, and often in between. If he had a decision to make, she would weigh in; if he were unsure about an opportunity, she would invariably have him seize it.[20]

Vigilantly minding her husband's interests, Lillian was, everyone said, his "protector." She protected him from rivals, from aides proffering bad advice, even from his own agreeable nature. She called the office regularly and kept track of who was competent, reliable, and loyal. "You were either in or out," said Brad Lichtenstein, an intern who stayed close to the Lewises and was one of the ins. To those on her good side, she was warm and generous. "Mr. Lewis was a gem," said Rachelle O'Neil, who worked in the Atlanta office for nearly twenty years. "Mrs. Lewis was actually the first one to befriend me of the two, honestly. She was just a very sweet person." Lichtenstein remembered her trips to New York, where he lived, when she would take him and John-Miles to see *Jelly's Last Jam* on Broadway or to a gala headlined by her friend Anita Hill. On his answering machine she would leave cheery messages saying, "Now, Brad, I'm sure you're up there in New York tripping the light fantastic. Well, call your old pal Lillian when you get back." When Lichtenstein announced he was getting married, Lillian insisted on meeting the bride to give her approval.[21]

Tuere Butler, another veteran of the Atlanta office, was learning to work the phones as a new hire and feared she would bungle the transfer if Lillian called. "I think I dropped the line a couple times," Butler said. "But she had mercy." One year, Butler, who had been reared in Washington in a political family, hoped to attend the Congressional Black Caucus's Legislative Weekend, a star-studded annual event. "I answered the phone, and Lillian was like, 'Do you have tickets for everything?' And I was like, 'No, I have a few tickets.' She sent me tickets to everything."[22]

Even Lillian's favorites, however, detected the no-nonsense undercurrent in her voice and knew to respond to her queries with alacrity. "She had this soothing voice," Butler said, "but it was a little bit intimidating." Those who didn't respond quickly wound up in her doghouse, which could become crowded. "She set very high expectations, which were wonderful to try to accomplish, you know?" said Michael Collins, who became chief of staff after Chastang's second tour of duty. "But she just had a level of expectation for everybody, no matter who you were, and nothing was ever to that degree. And so she challenged everybody. She made everybody's life miserable."[23]

One could run afoul of Lillian by letting the congressman down—or, conversely, by growing too close to him, forming a bond that might threaten her. Friends who had backed Julian Bond in 1986 noticed that even after John welcomed them back into the fold, Lillian was unforgiving. "She would always say to me, 'Well, well, if it isn't the guy that put the knife in John's back!'" said Ron Zirpoli, who had worked for Lewis in 1977 but switched to Bond in 1986. Some of Lewis's friends from the 1960s believed that their relationship with him changed after she entered the picture, that she was leery of their preexisting friendships. Some felt he became less accessible, more remote, even a different person.[24]

For the office staff, a call from Lillian was rarely good news. "Lillian cracked down on the staff," said Buddy Darden, Lewis's close friend in the Georgia delegation who later became his attorney and campaign treasurer. Her voice on the line usually meant that someone had made a mistake. She obsessed about the details of local fundraising events. "She would call me all the time," said Kristin Oblander, Lewis's Atlanta fundraiser. "And she'd say, 'My *husband* . . .'"—elongating the word husband—"and act like it was coming from him. I knew it wasn't. He didn't have the bandwidth to worry about table linens or all the specifics. She was definitely in charge of that side of the operation."[25]

Lillian also had firm opinions about her husband's Washington office. "There was one year we had an opportunity to move to the Rayburn building," James Waller recalled. The Rayburn offices were bigger than those in Cannon; the Ways and Means Committee met there as well. "I kept trying to convince him, this is a better building. You're closer to the committee. This is more prestigious when the constituents come." Lewis eventually agreed. The next day Lillian weighed in. "My husband," she said flatly, "does not want to move." They didn't.

The issue resurfaced a few years later during a lottery for offices, when veteran lawmakers could upgrade their digs. Rob Bassin, who was chief of staff at the time, reached into a velvet cap and pulled out the ball marked "1." He had twenty minutes to choose a new office. The most appealing option was a spacious suite in Rayburn that included a separate room for the chief of staff. (In Cannon, Bassin doubled up with the scheduler.) A second option was in Cannon, in quarters slightly nicer than Lewis's existing chambers. Bassin wanted to ask Lewis his preference, but the congressman was nowhere to be found—probably caught up talking to a school group. With the clock ticking, Bassin was nagged by a hunch that Lillian would disapprove of a move to Rayburn, so he went with the smaller Cannon quarters. The next day she phoned telling him he had done the right thing, before adding a tart comment about "other" chiefs of staff who needed their own offices.[26]

To cope with Lillian's directives, especially those of dubious advisability, aides developed subtle strategies. Lillian might call and ask for help in getting appointed to corporate boards, or in securing lodgings within the national parks where the Lewises could stay. With feigned innocence, the aides would mention the odd request to the congressman. Aware of his wife's proclivities, Lewis would reply, "Oh, no, don't worry about that."

The chiefs of staff bore the brunt of it all. "Things had to be done a certain way," Michael Collins said. "Mr. Collins, I want this done. Mr. Collins, I want this done." She was unhappy if Lewis heeded an aide's advice rather than her own. "People always said this, just in general, that the spouses of members get very little time with their husbands and wives," said Collins. "And that the chiefs of staff get more. There's always this dynamic, a power play of sorts. We literally fought for years. There wasn't a moment she gave me any grace," Collins added. "And I always had the congressman's back. And he always had mine when it came to her. But she and I just had a terrible relationship."[27]

Some in the Washington office noticed that when Lewis returned after a weekend in Atlanta, "he would be in a little bit of a mood" that would fade in the course of the day as he became his cheerful self. Yet he never bad-mouthed his wife. Aides knew that Lillian's tough-cop posture was a reflection of her dedication to him. "She always had his back," said Dusenbury. Lewis reciprocated.[28]

"Lillian is the one who made John believe he could be elected," said Buddy Darden. "She made John believe in himself and gave him confidence."[29]

Lewis himself credited Lillian with turning him into the luminary that he had become. "She picked up a country boy," he said toward the end of his life, "and helped me build an incredible life."[30]

———

The life Lewis built was now centered on politics. But his workhorse tendencies did not deprive him of ordinary pleasures. He harbored a charmingly boyish side, taking delight in everyday diversions and hobbies. "He liked to do normal things," said Anthony Johnson. "He was a superstar who liked normal things."[31]

His list of pastimes, like Lillian's, began with shopping. After they married, Lewis said goodbye to the secondhand suits he wore in his Nashville days. He began visiting the tailor and haberdasher William Thourlby, formerly the Marlboro Man of cigarette billboards, who ran a shop on Peachtree and boasted of giving wardrobe advice to Richard Nixon and Jimmy Carter. Lewis developed a style that was conservative and classy, befitting a politician, with a preference for various shades of blue, his favorite color. Over the years, he shared his love of fine clothing with staff members like Archie Allen, whom he sent to see Thourlby, and, later, his social media assistant Andrew Aydin. "He took me shopping at Dillard's," said Aydin, who was raised by a single mother, "and taught me how to buy a suit." And if Lewis left behind thrift stores for high-end department stores, he was still a sucker for a sale. "He *loved* that Nordstrom sale," said Keith Washington, a close friend in Lewis's later decades. Constituents would be tickled to run into him on the day after Thanksgiving at Atlanta's Lenox Square shopping mall, eating at the food court Panda Express after hunting for Black Friday bargains.[32]

Lewis liked browsing as much as buying—in bookstores, furniture stores, even strip malls. In Dallas once for a book event, he was being driven to a fancy dinner by his former staffer Tara McDaniel when he got a yen for Jason's Deli, a national franchise, and had her pull off the highway for a quick bite, the impending dinner notwithstanding. After eating, he wandered into a half-price bookstore, where he thumbed through volumes and told yarns, guaranteeing that they would be late for their event. "This is Mr. Lewis," McDaniel said to her perplexed husband. "This is how he rolls." Other staffers described Lewis chatting up the clerks in the boutiques of Vineyard Haven or passing forty-five minutes in a Natchez, Mississippi, antique emporium while in town for a documentary shoot.[33]

Antiques were a special passion. Lewis frequented furniture stores long after his Pinehurst home had run out of room for even a footstool. "I once spent seven hours with John Lewis in an ABC Carpet and Home in New York," said Bassin. "Just looking at carpets and furniture."

Gardening was another prized pursuit. Anthony Johnson was once driving Lewis back from a talk at Delaware State University when the congressman spied a roadside flower shop and asked to stop; he bought so many plants that there was barely room left for him to sit. But he took them home and nurtured them. The Pinehurst home had a courtyard where John lovingly oversaw the garden, buying and planting flowers. In Washington he tended window boxes and a modest backyard patch. When asked by *The Hill*, a newspaper that covered Congress, if he gambled, Lewis said, "I plant flowers. I gamble by planting flowers. Last night I stayed up in my yard planting flowers until 11:16. I water the flowers. I fertilize the flowers and hope and pray that they will be beautiful."[34]

In fact, he also enjoyed real gambling. Every week Lewis bought a lottery ticket, despite never winning big, and when packing for trips to Las Vegas or Tunica, Mississippi, where the Black Caucus held conferences, he would hide rolls of quarters in his balled-up socks so he could play the slot machines—sometimes donning a baseball cap and sunglasses as he set out for the casino in the hope of avoiding detection. Once, on a congressional trip to Egypt, he was cheerfully gambling away his coins when he hit the jackpot, only to realize there might be ethics implications if he collected the money that came spewing forth. "Oh my God, Debbie, you take it," he said in a mild panic to his aide Debbie Spielberg, who was with him. "I don't know what to do with it."[35]

There were other hobbies, too. Lewis collected stamps, dragging John-Miles—or, if he was in Washington, congressional aides—to buy the first-day issues of stamps featuring African American figures like James Baldwin or Harriet Tubman. John-Miles connected his father's philately to his earliest involvement in the civil rights movement. "Imagine being eighteen and writing a letter to Martin Luther King . . . and to get a response, in the mail," John-Miles said years later. "A stamp being put on two envelopes—changed the course of history."[36]

Lewis's joy in ordinary pursuits was of a piece with his humility. "Deep down," said Michael Collins, "he's still the little boy from the farm." As high as Lewis rose, he always thought of himself as a simple country kid. Late into his career he continued to express disbelief that he was a high official who consorted with presidents and celebrities. "I can't believe I go to Congress every day," he would say to Ruth Berg, his Atlanta receptionist. In 1991, he greeted Queen Elizabeth on her visit to Washington. "Can you believe it that this sharecropper's son just got to meet the queen of England?" Lewis gushed on returning to the office.[37]

Stories abounded about Lewis's refusal to avail himself of the privileges of status. He never acquired airs. He declined to let aides carry his bags or fetch him a glass of water. At Mary Mac's Tea Room, an Atlanta restaurant where his photograph adorned the walls, he disliked being seated before customers who had been waiting longer and chatted with everyone in the anteroom before taking his table. For years after most congressional colleagues adopted the autopen to affix their signatures to bulk mail, he signed letters by hand, carting stacks of documents onto an airplane and spending the flight scribbling his name. Even after email arrived, he continued for years to give his correspondents a hand-signed response. Aides had to convince him that a form letter generated by a political website didn't merit a personal reply.[38]

Other tasks that his peers might shun or delegate, Lewis took on without complaint. If the receptionist had gone home, Lewis would answer the phone. If a maintenance man came to the office to change a lightbulb or fix a chair, Lewis would help. Once, several years after he had moved out of (but not sold) his Pinehurst home, he returned from Washington to find it ransacked, the refrigerator stolen and the basement copper pipes ripped out. "Looks like we have some work to do," he said matter-of-factly to his friend Wade Burns, who was with him, before they drove to Home Depot to buy rubber gloves, trash bags, and cleaning supplies.[39]

Lewis's uninflated sense of self allowed him to interact easily with people from all walks of life. He felt comfortable with everyone. Once, on a drive back to Atlanta along a rural back road, he and Michael German were invited to dinner by strangers. German thought the invitation peculiar, but Lewis said to him, "Come on, we are going to go eat. My mama said, 'Eat where you're at.'" The family was "a typical, rural Black family," German said, and served "a traditional Sunday meal, chicken and greens and cornbread—country cooking." Lewis treated them with the utmost respect. German noted that Lewis felt so much at ease that "he asked for another piece of the chicken"—the kind of thing one might feel constrained from doing with strangers. "He didn't stop. He ate with them." Lorraine Miller, who accompanied Lewis on a codel to Africa, marveled at how "he just melted in with the Africans, like he was at home. 'I've been gone a couple of years, but I'm back.'"[40]

In his working life, Lewis adhered to the same egalitarian values. His office desk was pushed into a corner, and when he met with guests in his office,

they all sat around his leather-topped coffee table. He knew the Capitol elevator operators, security guards, and janitors by name and would ask about
their children or spouses. "He knew the people who were wiping down the
sinks in the ladies' room," said Tara McDaniel. "The people who were cooking the food in the cafeteria." Bassin recalled rushing with Lewis to a meeting in the speaker's office when a Capitol policeman saw them. "Mr. Lewis?"
the cop asked. "What is it, brother?" Lewis replied. As the men talked, Bassin tugged at his sleeve. "Rob, it's OK," he said. "The speaker can wait."[41]

Lewis's unfeigned humility could give the impression of dharmic egoless-
ness. But he was too self-aware and modest to put credence in his reputation
as a saint. George Dusenbury was watching a Capitol Hill press conference
when a legislator known for hogging the limelight grabbed the microphone.
"Man, he has the biggest ego," Dusenbury said. "Now, George," came Lewis's
reply, "we all have egos." For all his self-abnegation, Lewis took pleasure in
his fame and in the attention of others. Nor was he without his vanities. He
was conscious of his hair loss and quietly relied on trusted female staffers to
daub his head with a little makeup when the situation warranted. ("He was
always concerned about his head being shiny in photos," said Kim Walker.
"He carried a compact.") Rachelle O'Neil teasingly called Lewis her "little
narcissist" when she caught him wallowing in the accolades showered on
him. "I'm like, 'John Robert Lewis, are you up here being a narcissist?'"[42]

The teasing was standard for the office, a reflection of Lewis's own sense
of humor and mischief. There were always occasions for singing and dancing. Sometimes, Lewis said, Michael Collins or another staffer would begin
reciting "Invictus" and everyone would join in. "He broke down those work
barriers," said Jamila Thompson, his legislative director for many years, "and
he welcomed our parents, our spouses, our children, our grandchildren, our
nieces and nephews, our godchildren, and our friends into the circle." He
performed staffers' weddings and went to their parents' funerals. He also enjoyed "stirring things up in the office," Thompson said. "You might call him
a little bit of an instigator. He would get us in trouble with Michael, try and
corner us with questions, and stir things up. And with time, you knew not
to take the bait, and you would learn to say, 'Oh, no, Congressman, you're
not going to get me today.' And he would laugh. . . . Not the one that you see
on television, but the one where he would be sitting back and shooting the

wind, and he would throw back his head and he would just laugh from his heart, from his belly, from his soul."[43]

As Bill Clinton prepared to leave office after eight years, Lewis was concerned that the next president be just as strongly committed to racial equality. Choosing a candidate in 2000 turned out to be an easy call.

Lewis had known Vice President Al Gore since his days in the Senate. In 1992, the two of them—Congress's leading civil rights advocate and its leading environmentalist—had cosponsored the first legislation to address "environmental racism," the ways that pollution and environmental harm hit Black neighborhoods harder than white ones. The legislation stalled, but when Clinton became president, Lewis took the issue to the White House to push for an executive order. Lewis, Clinton said, was "the first person who ever talked to me about environmental justice for Black people. Because all these toxic waste dumps in America were in Black neighborhoods. . . . And in four years, we closed three or four times as many dumps as they had in the previous twelve years. And that was all John Lewis."[44]

Gore's only competition in the Democratic primary that winter was Senator Bill Bradley of New Jersey, a former professional basketball player with unremarkable centrist politics and a bland demeanor that made Gore look like William Jennings Bryan. Bradley's African American support consisted mostly of former NBA stars like Julius Erving and Willis Reed. "There's a loyalty to Gore that Senator Bradley cannot shake," Lewis told the *New York Times* in January 2000. "It's just impossible." Lewis himself had nothing but praise for Gore, whom he called "one of the most effective vice presidents we've had." Gore won every primary and caucus and cruised to the nomination. He would face off against presidential scion George W. Bush in the fall.[45]

For his vice president, Gore chose Senator Joe Lieberman of Connecticut, the first Jew on a national ticket. Gore hoped that Lieberman's pious denunciation of Clinton's liaison with Monica Lewinsky two years before would inoculate the ticket from any taint by association. But Lieberman turned out to be vulnerable on a different front. His vocal criticisms of affirmative action troubled Black political leaders. Maxine Waters of California announced she was "withholding" her endorsement of the ticket, while others protested behind the scenes.[46]

But the objections to Lieberman were in the end few and mild—and muted by Lieberman's agreement to back Gore's pro-affirmative action policies. Still, the media hyped the perennial story of a Black-Jewish rift. ("I just think that so much of the media is just hellbent and determined to look for some controversy," James Clyburn complained.) Lewis was again deputized to quell the fracas. Around the Staples Center in Los Angeles, the site of the Democratic convention, he could be seen jawboning Jesse Jackson. He also took on the assignment of formally introducing Lieberman to the assembled delegates. From the podium on a warm Wednesday night in July, Lewis returned once more to the well of civil rights history: As a Yale undergraduate in 1963, he reminded the delegates, Lieberman had gone to Mississippi to help run the Freedom Democrats' historic mock elections. "He came to the heart of the delta of Mississippi to help tear down the walls of segregation and racial discrimination," Lewis boomed. "As a young student, he left the comfort of Connecticut and New Haven to be a foot soldier in the drive to register black voters."[47]

There was nothing to worry about. Whatever their opinion of Lieberman, African Americans turned out in 2000 in greater numbers than they had in 1996. Gore won an even bigger percentage of the Black vote than Clinton had. It was enough to propel Gore to victory—at least in the national popular vote.*

In the Electoral College tally, however, neither Gore nor Bush secured enough votes on election night to declare victory. Florida's outcome remained undetermined, to be settled by a dizzying series of recounts that stopped and started according to the ever-shifting whims of local election boards and state and federal courts. Throughout the monthlong recount drama, Gore pointed out that if every legitimately cast vote were counted, he might well prevail. Bush pressed to halt the recounts before too many votes were reassigned to Gore.

The saga revived memories of Lewis's fight for the ballot decades earlier. "As I watched election night 2000 turn into this controversy over counts

---

* Gore got 90 percent, compared to 84 percent for Clinton in 1996.

and recounts," he wrote, "my mind went back to that day on the bridge." It pained him to see pundits arguing glibly when people's votes were going uncounted; it angered him that politicians, election officials, and judges were calling for ballots to be rejected for technical errors, or on the impulses of local election boards.[48]

As the process dragged on past Thanksgiving, Lewis tried to make himself heard above the din. "Every morning it was an internal and a vocal cry for justice at the television, at what was happening in the office. He wanted to make sure that he personally could do everything possible to make a difference," said Collins. "Every television was turned on, all the time. In his office, we had a box of TVs that had four television screens so he could see all the different channels and what was happening. We were finagling the remotes—'Turn this one on!' He was intent on having his voice heard wherever necessary."[49]

Lewis placed an anguished cri de coeur in the *New York Times* on December 2. Neither partisan nor legalistic, the essay drew on his history to argue for the "one man, one vote" axiom that he had endorsed at the 1963 March on Washington. "Friends of mine died for this principle," Lewis wrote. "I was beaten and jailed because I stood up for it." There was only one solution: "The makers of the ballot machines have told us that the most accurate way to count the ballots is by hand. So, count them by hand we must, even if it means recounting all six million ballots cast in Florida."[50]

That would be up to the Supreme Court. Nine days later, on December 11, Lewis arrived at the court's neoclassical edifice on First Street NE to listen to oral arguments in the case of *Bush v. Gore*. The Bush campaign was appealing a Florida court ruling mandating a statewide manual recount. Lewis took a seat in the crowded courtroom, "almost unrecognized," according to Elaine Sciolino of the *New York Times*. He was there, he told Sciolino, because "it's important to bear witness. This day is as important for me as March 7, 1965. . . . We won that battle and we come back 35 years later and see that people's votes aren't counted. This is why the right to vote means so much to me."[51]

Lewis had another worry. "I was at home in Atlanta last weekend," he wrote, "and I'd go into a grocery store, or to city hall, or just walk down the street, and folks would say, 'Congressman, they're trying to steal the election.' Rank-and-file, middle-class people, white, black, Hispanic—not partisans." The loss of faith in the system to determine the rightful president could have corrosive effects. "My greatest fear today is that the perception our votes were not counted may usher in a period of great cynicism," he concluded.[52]

The Supreme Court voted 5–4 to halt the recount, awarding Bush the presidency. Gore gamely went on national TV to accept the decision. Lewis spoke for the millions who considered it a travesty. "It's going to be very difficult, almost impossible," he said a few days later, "for many of us to forget what happened."[53]

He was even more forthright in a later interview. "I truly believe in my heart," he said, "that if all of the votes had been counted in Florida, and if all of the African Americans had had an opportunity to cast a vote, then George Bush would have never been president of the United States."[54]

He skipped Bush's inauguration.

Chapter Twenty-Three

IN OPPOSITION

———— ■ ▨ ————

J ohn Lewis first met George W. Bush at a House Democratic retreat in Farmington, Pennsylvania, in February 2001. Hoping to heal the rancor of recent years, the Democrats had invited the new Republican president to join them at what was normally a partisan rally. Seeking to pad his slender congressional majorities, Bush accepted.

At a receiving line, Lewis introduced himself to the new president as if he were one of 435 unfamiliar faces. "Hi, Mr. President, I'm John Lewis," he said. "It's a pleasure to meet you."

Bush smiled. "I know who you are!" he blurted out. The president then extended his forefinger and gently poked the congressman in the belly, emitting a loud "Boop!" as if Lewis were the Pillsbury Doughboy. Lewis made a face. This was, he surmised, the callow new president's way of making friends.[1]

On the second Tuesday in September 2001, Lewis was lingering at his Capitol Hill townhouse. His morning workouts had given way to watching the *Today* show. He was putting on his suit when the anchors reported that airplanes had crashed into the World Trade Center and the Pentagon. No one knew exactly what had happened.

He called Michael Collins at home. Collins also heard from Jacob Gillison, the scheduler and office manager, who had put the office on lockdown. Collins told Gillison to close the office and send everyone home.

To Lewis, he said, "Congressman, don't come in."

"I'm not coming in," Lewis assured him.

"You shouldn't even come out," Collins said. "You should stay in the house."

But then, Lewis recalled, "I heard all these people running, running, running." He wanted to see things for himself, to talk to people. He kept calling Collins, telling him, "I need to go out."

Collins, who lived near Meridian Hill in Northwest Washington, decided to go to Lewis's townhouse. But when he went outside he couldn't find his car; it had been towed. "So the only thing I could do is get on the phone and keep him at bay," Collins remembered. "And then I honestly don't know how I got to him. But I told him I'm coming over and I'll go outside with you."

They went outside. "He just wanted to walk up and down Pennsylvania Avenue, you know?" Collins said. "The neighborhood."

"I came out and walked to the corner of the street," Lewis remembered. "There was a little restaurant on the corner of the street, and all these staffers started saying, 'Congressman, do you need a telephone? Do you need a telephone?'"

Lewis told them he was okay. He could see smoke rising from the Pentagon. "I was terrified," he said. He stayed outside, talking with people, telling them he was sorry. In 1996, Lewis had been in Atlanta when a bomb went off at the Olympic Games. He had gone to the Olympic Park just to hug and comfort people. Now he did the same thing. "He just wanted to extend his condolences," said Collins. "He wanted to do what he normally does, which is be a symbol. And so we did all of that."[2]

Outside the Library of Congress, he ran into Senator Pat Leahy of Vermont, who had just closed his office. There was speculation that the terrorists had meant to crash one of the hijacked airplanes into the Capitol. "I had three or four people with me," Leahy said. "And everybody's kind of moving. We wanted to get away from anything that could be a target." Lewis and Leahy were happy to see each other but at a loss about what to do.

"It's madness," Lewis said. Leahy nodded.

"Brother Patrick," Lewis continued, "can we stand and pray?" They held hands tightly and prayed, each taking strength from the other. "We stood there holding hands and praying," said Leahy, an observant Catholic.

"Different religions. Different skin colors. Totally irrelevant. That was the one thing we could do."[3]

Later in the day, the House Democrats held a conference call. They planned a vigil that night on the Capitol steps and a prayer session the following night in the Rotunda. Everyone agreed that Lewis should speak. His voice was respected; he could be trusted to be nonpolitical. "When the country is in peril, they always asked Brother John to say something," Collins said. "I can hear [California congresswoman] Anna Eshoo saying, 'It's John who has to speak.' So that's why he would be the one. It was just clear, to take the politics out of it."[4]

Wednesday night, after a chaplain convened the members, Lewis stood behind the lectern in a black suit, white shirt, dark tie, and reading glasses, and looked out at the Rotunda, crowded with members. Despite having been ordained decades before, he seldom delivered sermons. "I do not hide or try to get away from the fact that I am a licensed, ordained Baptist minister; I am a minister," Lewis had said in 1976. "But on the other hand, I don't see myself going to a pulpit every Sunday morning and preaching; I just don't see that as my role." He wasn't even a regular churchgoer anymore. In Congress, he spent Sunday mornings watching the political roundup programs like *Meet the Press* and *Face the Nation*, not in the pews. He prayed alone at home, but, as he acknowledged in his memoir, "I don't as a rule engage in formal prayer."[5]

Yet that night, the spirituality that had animated Lewis as a youth was on display. Speaking slowly, with a faint tremor in his voice, he gave a stirring appeal for divine guidance. "We turn to you tonight for there's no one else for us to turn to in our hour of need. We ask that you continue to watch over America and shed thy grace on thee." His eyes were trained on the papers before him. "We stand in need of your presence, O God. We are your people. We are your children. We are hurting. . . . Help us, O God. See us through this storm and hold us in the palm of your powerful hands tonight."[6]

The assault on the United States, committed by the Islamist terrorist group al-Qaeda, temporarily brought partisan politics in Washington to a halt. Democrats and Republicans passed long-stalled anti-terrorism legislation, calling it the Patriot Act, and authorized an invasion of Afghanistan, whose Taliban regime was sheltering al-Qaeda leader Osama bin Laden. Lewis was one of sixty-six House members, almost all liberal Democrats, to vote against the Patriot Act, which he believed intruded too much on civil liberties. The vote to allow the president to use military force against the Taliban was a harder call. Some friends expected Lewis to oppose it. He had voted against most other military interventions, opposed military appropriations bills, and regularly sponsored a bill to let citizens keep their tax dollars from funding wars. But Lewis never entirely abjured force as a tool of foreign policy. He had favored using the military to deliver humanitarian aid to famine-struck Somalia in 1992 and again to stop the Serbian slaughter in Kosovo in 1999. In 2006 and 2009 he would get arrested demanding a stronger response to the genocide in Darfur. As much as Lewis hated violence, he understood that sometimes only American military might could prevent horrendous suffering.

On the vote to use force against the Taliban, he voted aye.[7]

Lewis had never styled himself a policy wonk. He cared about health care, and his legislative directors often were health policy experts, but he rarely burrowed into the finer points of legislation dealing with taxes, drugs, housing, crime, welfare, or other such issues.

But he used his standing and moral authority to get bills passed and from time to time made a piece of legislation truly his own. In particular, he championed laws dealing with the history and legacy of the Black freedom struggle. "Mr. Lewis was a history buff," said Lorraine Miller. Lewis believed in the importance of teaching the public, most of all young people, about the American past and especially the civil rights movement. To know history, he believed, was an essential part of citizenship and a precondition for completing the unfinished work of the struggle for equality.[8]

Lewis called attention to the history of the civil rights movement whenever he could. In 1995, when Gerald Solomon, a Republican committee chairman, sought to hang the portrait of Howard W. Smith of Virginia—an unrepentant segregationist—in the committee room, Lewis educated Solomon about Smith's sordid past and persuaded him to change course. Later, Lewis sponsored the Emmett Till Unsolved Civil Rights Crime Act, allowing the FBI to reopen "cold cases" from the civil rights years—murders and other violent crimes that corrupt local judicial systems had let go unpunished. He spoke at anniversaries of the great events of the 1960s, attended openings of civil rights museums, and wrote prefaces to history books. If a colleague from the movement died, Lewis would be on television or radio, talking about the deceased's contributions.[9]

Of all these endeavors, none occupied him more than the drive to create a museum of Black history on the National Mall. The idea had long preceded Lewis's arrival in Congress; Robert Wilkins, an attorney who worked on the project, discovered versions of the idea dating back to 1915. In the 1980s Mickey Leland of Texas had led the charge, but in 1989 he died in a plane crash in Africa, leaving Lewis, then in his second term, as the chief advocate. Lewis would introduce a bill to create the museum in every Congress thereafter.

Twice in the early 1990s Lewis and his allies nearly got a bill passed. In 1992, the Senate approved a bill, but in the House Gus Savage, demanding that any Black history museum have its own new building, refused to allow the Smithsonian's Arts and Industries Building—a three-story Renaissance revival–style pavilion of deep red brick—to serve as its temporary home. In the next Congress, the House passed the bill, but this time Jesse Helms of North Carolina blocked it in the Senate. Then in 1994 the Republicans took control of Congress, leaving the bill to languish. Lewis kept reintroducing it, but now did so as a ritual reminder, with no prospect of near-term success. "We always had to put the museum bill in, every year, every Congress," said Miller. "If nothing else was put in with John Lewis's name on it, the museum bill was."[10]

Help arrived in 2000 from an unlikely ally: Sam Brownback, a religious Christian and staunchly conservative Republican senator from Kansas. Brownback, forty-four, liked to jog on the Mall, where he would draw inspiration from the many museums there, including the recently opened Holocaust Museum and National Museum of the American Indian (which was still being built). One day, Brownback recalled, "just as I was praying about this in the little Catholic church there across the street from the Senate, the thought came to me about putting together an African American museum on the Mall to tell the story of what had happened to African Americans. And it startled me." Brownback had entered the House in 1995 and moved to the Senate in 1996; he had missed all the activity around the museum in the 1980s and '90s. He asked an African American aide, LaRochelle Murray, to research whether anything had ever been attempted. She uncovered the project's long history, including Lewis's role.

Brownback hesitated to approach Lewis. "My experience with John Lewis to date was him giving fiery speeches on the House floor where he is mostly yelling, I thought," Brownback said. "I just had no relationship there." But he found himself moved by a voice—what he took to be the Holy Spirit—urging him to go to Lewis.

Brownback and Murray called on Lewis in his Cannon office. As they walked in, they were overcome by the scores of historic photographs, documents, and memorabilia adorning the walls and shelves. "Every space was covered with his photos, the sacrifice of his life," Murray recalled. "It was absolutely overwhelming, larger than life." The two men discussed their visions for the museum. Brownback had imagined an exhibition focused on slavery, but Lewis won him over to a more expansive conception that would chronicle the whole African American experience. They agreed that the spirit of the museum should be one of racial reconciliation, that a visit there should spur reflection about America's racial wrongs and a commitment to do better.

The weight of history in the room was palpable. "He's got all of these books and things," said Robert Wilkins, who visited the office often, "and when you're in there, if he sees you looking at something he'd say, 'Oh yeah, that was this. Let me tell you what happened.' And he might pull a book off the shelf." As they were about to leave, Brownback and Murray set their eyes on an oversized book resting on the coffee table. Lewis lifted it up and began to gently thumb its thick, glossy pages. Recently published, with a foreword by Lewis, it was called *Without Sanctuary*. It told the history of lynching through the gruesome photographs and postcards made of these killings. They slowly turned the pages, lingering on one photograph in particular. "One of the pictures that I just so vividly remember," Brownback said, "there's these two young white children, probably ten years of age, straw hats on, standing with their dad in front of a lynched Black man like they were at the county fair. Just smiling and grinning." Murray, too, could not forget it. "There was a boy that couldn't be more than thirteen years old, smiling with his gun as if this was a prize deer that he had killed," she said. "Mr. Lewis showed us this book because he wanted us to understand that this is the history, the telling of this history that we were going to do."[11]

They agreed to relaunch the museum bill with a team that was biracial, bipartisan, and bicameral. In the House, Lewis turned to J. C. Watts, a Black forty-three-year-old former Oklahoma University football star in the Republican leadership. On being elected in 1994, Watts—who grew up in segregated Oklahoma and whose uncle had led the state NAACP chapter— had placed having a meal with John Lewis on his bucket list, wanting to "pick his brains about being on the front lines of the civil rights movement." He got his wish. They lunched in the members' dining room, talking for hours. That encounter formed the basis of a working relationship, and they joined forces in 1999 on a bill to address racial disparities in health care. Watts signed on to the museum bill. To round out the quartet, John enlisted his fellow Georgian, Senator Max Cleland.[12]

Each lawmaker assigned a staff member to the project. All were Black women. "It became my full-time job," said Tammy Boyd, Lewis's legislative director. "Meetings trying to unlock different committees, different blocs. We met all the time. Nights, weekends, just trying to piece different things together."[13]

The first task was to get the White House on board—a tall order. Conservatives typically objected to projects—including museums—devoted to specific ethnic groups, arguing that they fostered racial division; the existing American History Museum, they said, already encompassed all strands of the nation's history, including Black history. Watts, who as part of the GOP leadership visited the White House regularly, was tasked with enlisting President Bush. Bush deputized Vice President Dick Cheney to meet with the quartet in his Capitol office. To the quartet's delight, Cheney pledged the administration's support in writing.[14]

If the White House proved surprisingly accommodating, other stakeholders were unexpectedly resistant. Local African American history museums—including Washington's Anacostia Community Museum— feared that a big Smithsonian gallery would lure away their patrons and donors. Members of Congress decried the exorbitant cost. The Black community wasn't wealthy enough to provide the necessary private funding, others warned; only a few major donors, such as Oprah Winfrey and Bill Cosby, were on board.

The biggest obstacle was the Smithsonian itself. A few months into their work, when the quartet and their staff sat with Smithsonian secretary Larry Small in his hideaway, he shocked them by opposing their plans. His institution, he said, was too overburdened to take on such a project. The National Museum of the American Indian, authorized in 1989, remained unfinished and behind schedule; Smithsonian staff called it "the $400 million hole in the ground." Lewis would be better off creating an independent museum, Small said, like the privately financed Holocaust Museum.

Lewis, who thought it essential that the museum bear the imprimatur of the U.S. government, argued back. Small refused to budge. Brownback stormed out.

In the following weeks, Small's message was reinforced by sotto voce communications from staff at the Smithsonian, who warned Tammy Boyd and the others that to revive the museum would be hubris. The bill would never pass and would end up as a failure, a black eye.[15]

Boyd was demoralized, but Lewis demanded that they forge ahead. Persistence would carry the day. Brownback scored a coup by securing the cooperation of Senate Appropriations Committee chairman Ted Stevens of Alaska, who controlled the purse strings. On the House side, Watts won over another crucial gatekeeper, Ralph Regula of Ohio, who chaired a key appropriations subcommittee. With those two Republicans in their corner—and Cheney's letter in their back pocket—Lewis saw no reason to back down. They enlisted grassroots supporters, drafted the legislation, and circulated "Dear Colleague" letters to bring on new cosponsors, including the new junior senator from New York, Hillary Rodham Clinton. In May 2001, the expanded group introduced the bill with an outdoor press conference in the springtime air. Amid lush trees and budding flowers, Lewis proclaimed, "Until we understand the full and complete African American story we cannot understand ourselves as a nation. . . . This is our chance to create an America that values the dignity of every individual, an all-inclusive community that is at peace with itself, a beloved community, a beloved nation."[16]

Still, obstacles remained. Southern legislators, concerned about the South's portrayal, stayed aloof. Participants fought over the museum's purpose and scope; at one point, Charles Rangel revived the idea that it should be a slavery museum. "They were having to put out different fires all the time," Boyd said. "I don't think people get how hard it was to bring everyone together."

Lewis scheduled countless individual meetings with fellow members and outside parties. "All these different Democrats had their own conversations with Lewis," said Boyd. "The Republicans had their own conversations. And the members had to be personally really involved. They spent numerous hours in meetings with members, going on the floor. . . . The members had to physically give of themselves. And Congressman Lewis was the bridge. If it wasn't for Congressman Lewis, I don't know if anybody could have done it. He put a lot of 'sweat equity' into it." Wilkins called Lewis "a true tactician in getting this through. Because this was a triple bank shot to the side pocket." Said Boyd: "Mr. Lewis comes across as a very simple Southern guy. But strategically, he was very complicated and very smart."[17]

Pressure built on the holdouts. Larry Small and the Smithsonian came around. In October 2001, Lewis and Watts met with Regula to say they wanted to get a bill passed before the legislative session ended in December. Regula—whose subcommittee funded the Smithsonian and who sat on its board of regents—insisted that too many issues remained unresolved, including the museum's location. He offered a deal: if Lewis and Watts would scale back this year's bill to simply create a commission to study the issues, he would promise to fund the museum in the next Congress. Lewis and Watts took the deal.[18]

When Brownback heard that a deal had been struck, he was incensed. Also unhappy were the staff members who had worked relentlessly for more than a year. Boyd shared her dismay with Lewis. "Oh my God," she said, "you just agreed to this in the room." Lewis replied that they would get there eventually if they didn't let up. Whether the authorization passed in 2001 or 2003 mattered less than the fact that it was now destined for passage. "His thing was pace yourself," Boyd said. "For whatever reason he knew that we had to do this to be able to get here."[19]

To Wilkins, "he just said, 'Robert, we're just going to keep introducing the bill, until the time is right. And we'll get it through at some point.' You know his mantra, keep the faith and never give up. And that was his attitude with this museum." Wilkins was also reassured that the newly created commission would be required to issue an action plan—concrete steps toward getting the museum built.[20]

The Senate Appropriations Committee still had to sign off on the deal. But at a meeting with the quartet, Ted Stevens and the ranking Democrat, Robert Byrd, proved amenable. After they rose from their chairs, Byrd and Lewis embraced in a prolonged hug—the onetime Klansman and the civil rights hero finding common cause in a museum devoted to racial reconciliation.[21]

In a nod to his years of work, Lewis was named as the lead sponsor. Watts and Regula were cosponsors. The bill passed the House on December 11 and passed the Senate six days later by unanimous consent.[22]

There was little doubt that the presidential commission would return a favorable verdict. Lewis appointed allies like Wilkins, and he and the rest of the quartet served as ex officio members. But the ultimate location remained a question. In 1992 Gus Savage had killed the museum because it was going to be housed in the Arts and Industries Building; Savage insisted that it have its own building. Lewis had come around to that position. Visits to the various proposed sites had convinced him that the Arts and Industries Building was small, run-down, technologically antiquated, and inadequate for the task. Yet other proposed sites were too far away from the Mall, and Lewis thought it would be an affront to African Americans to shunt the museum to a distant location.

In April 2003, when the presidential commission filed its report, it listed four possible sites. Ranked first was a plot on Constitution Avenue between First and Third Streets, northwest of the Capitol and east of the National Gallery of Art. Though technically on the Capitol Grounds and not the Mall, the Capitol site was a good location. But Lewis and Brownback wanted to keep other options open, including a highly appealing spot between Fourteenth and Fifteenth Streets near the Washington Monument. In the bill they introduced that spring, they delegated the Smithsonian regents to choose among the four sites. When the time came, Lewis could lean on the regents to select one of the sites he liked best.[23]

The Senate passed the bill as Lewis and Brownback had drafted it. But resistance in the House endured. In July the Committee on House Administration held hearings to settle the outstanding issues.

Shortly after the proceedings began, committee member John Mica, a

Florida Republican, declared himself "adamantly opposed to any site on the Mall" that would "set a precedent that would be unfair to all the other racial and ethnic groups that make up the family of the American community." He explained: "My mother's side is Italian American. They have made incredible contributions to this country. My father's side was Slovak American, and they have done the same. But at some point we have to be fair to all racial and ethnic groups. If we put on the Mall a specific building dedicated to one group, I believe that is unfair."

Lewis countered with a powerful argument. "In the South, many, many years ago," he began, "I remember it very well when people of color could not enter through the front door of many homes and businesses. A national African American Museum should be in the front yard of the United States Capitol. The National Mall and the space around it is the front door to America; it is a symbol of our democracy. I firmly believe that a national African American Museum should not be off the National Mall at some back door." He reminded the committee that the current bill included four possible sites, allowing the regents to choose.[24]

Lewis was up against more than the Republicans. Preservationists, who tended to be politically liberal, had formed a powerful coalition to forbid any new development along the whole strip from the Lincoln Memorial to the Capitol. The coalition had recently lost a bitter fight to block a World War II memorial near the Reflecting Pool and didn't want to lose again. During that previous fight, Eleanor Holmes Norton, congresswoman from the District of Columbia, had adopted the coalition's stance against all new construction on the Mall. To carve out an exception for a Black history museum, she worried, risked seeming unprincipled. The *Washington Post*'s influential architecture critic, Benjamin Forgey, also warned against "A Giant Step That Could Trample Mall."[25]

At the July hearings, Norton threaded the needle by arguing for the Capitol site. She reiterated her strong excitement about the museum and voiced sympathy for the idea that "we have allowed every other kind of museum to get there and so it would come very hard on African Americans to say you're too late because we made you too late, so you can't go to the Mall."

But she added, "I am not one of the devotees of putting everything on the Mall. I think our generation will go down in infamy for having tried to use up the Mall, meant for perpetuity, for our own egos. . . . The Mall is overcrowded and overdeveloped." Choosing the Capitol site, she said—"not technically the Mall," but still a prime location—was the best solution.

On the next panel, however, Charles Cassell of the National Coalition to Save Our Mall called for scotching the Capitol site from consideration altogether. The July hearing ended without consensus. Suddenly the bill's future seemed—again—in doubt.[26]

Lewis was nearing the end of his rope. "Meetings on top of meetings with members of the House and Senate to get it moving," he said later. "Sometimes we thought we had dotted all the i's and crossed all the little t's and it was supposed to be out of committee and on the floor and it didn't happen for some reason. Then you have to go back."[27]

"There were times he was doubtful about its passage because of his past experience," said office manager Jacob Gillison. "I watched him. It was a learning moment for me. I saw one day you could be up and down the next day." But Lewis rolled up his sleeves. "He had to go talk to Eleanor Holmes Norton," Tammy Boyd said. Norton concluded that her constituents would approve of the Mall site. "One by one, he had to knock those things down. He was very invested in it."[28]

On November 17, the amended bill passed the House, 409–9. Three days later, it passed the Senate on a voice vote. On December 16, Lewis went to the White House to watch George W. Bush sign the bill into law. In the Oval Office, he stole a moment to speak with the president. He thanked him, while pressing him to fully fund the museum in the next year's budget.[29]

To celebrate, Lewis invited everyone to dinner at his townhouse. After a decade and a half, his residence was now magnificently arranged, with the original hardwood floors restored, Persian, Sarouk, and Mashad rugs in different rooms, and custom draperies tailored to match the color schemes. For the dinner, Lewis staged an elegant affair with "white tablecloths and everything," Wilkins recalled, "beautifully decorated and extremely classy." Guests marveled at Lewis's artwork and historic photographs covering the walls. But the sophistication did not create a stuffy mood. "It felt like he just had invited us over for Thanksgiving," Wilkins said. "He's serving us and he's making sure we got something to drink. I'm like, 'Congressman Lewis, you don't need to worry if I've got my food.' It was like I was having dinner at my uncle's house."[30]

Even after the celebration, Lewis knew his work wasn't done. He planned to shepherd the museum through to its opening. Indeed, on a wintry morning in 2005, he climbed into Collins's Volkswagen and they drove around downtown Washington to check out the possible sites once more. They got out at the Monument site—between Fourteenth and Fifteenth Streets—where a group of boys were playing soccer, and Lewis took in the expanse of green. "Of all the places yet, this would be the best," he said.[31]

On February 22, 2010, ground for the National Museum of African American History and Culture was broken on that very spot.

In 2003, before Bush signed the museum bill into law, Willie Mae Carter Lewis, John's mother, died at her home outside Troy. For all the distance John had traveled in his life, he still felt the pull of his roots and a powerful attachment to his mother. "He enjoys when he comes here and hates to leave," his sister Rosa Mae said. "He is always talking about, 'I'm going to retire and build me a house down here.'"[32]

Willie Mae was almost never interviewed by the press. But in 2000, at a sixtieth birthday party dinner honoring her son where President Clinton spoke, she talked to Rebecca Carr of the *Atlanta Journal-Constitution.* "John had his own ideas that the Lord instilled in him—they were that one day he would do better for himself and his people," she said.

Her death was a terrible loss. One reporter, who brought him a gift bag with a sympathy card and an inspirational book, watched as he walked over and put his head against the wall and started weeping.[33]

Lewis also had to contend with Lillian's health problems. Her kidney ailments had many debilitating side effects, including making it hard to walk. She now used a walker or a wheelchair or stayed in her room.

Making matters worse, by the early 2000s the Lewises' house on Pinehurst had grown overcrowded. The Lewises were, if not quite hoarders, very avid collectors, and they filled their rooms and cluttered the floors with books, magazines, art, and antique furniture. Their closets and bureaus were overstuffed. Lillian had stopped inviting friends over out of embarrassment; a friend who had to pick something up would be told to retrieve it from the car. The Lewises decided it was time to move.[34]

They found a beautiful one-story home with ten rooms and four bath-rooms, in a well-heeled Black neighborhood at 2015 Wallace Road SW. It was owned by Larry Thompson, the general counsel for Pepsi. Built in 1967, it sat on an acre of wooded land, set back from the street, fenced by a black iron gate. Lush hedges bordered the path to the house, and French doors opened onto a backyard terrace. The gardens included rosebushes, crape myrtles, azaleas, and hydrangeas.[35]

The parties and fundraisers at the house were less frequent now, but friends and guests still visited. Everyone remarked on the Lewises' collec-tion of art, mainly by African American artists. "He had original Romare Beardens, Jacob Lawrence paintings," said Kristin Oblander. "It was just in-credible." Lewis called buying art his "greatest extravagance."[36]

At the Pinehurst abode, many of the Lewises' canvases had lain unhung, but as they prepared to move, Lillian enlisted their friend and interior de-signer Howard Brown to "help us decide what we're going to take and what we're not going to take," as he recalled her words, "because this new house will not look like this." Brown made a point of ensuring that the Wallace Road home showcased the Lewises' artwork properly. Paintings graced the walls of every room and hallway. "I lost count," Brown said, "but at one point, I had hung over four hundred pieces of his art in the combined living and work spaces. His collection consisted of original paintings, rare photo-graphs, limited editions, rare antique furniture, a set of dining chairs that were hand-carved by a slave, various American and African sculptures from all over the world."[37]

"The house was totally renovated and he loved it," said Stephen Mc-Daniel, a close friend of Lewis's since the 1970s. "I said, 'John, this is how you're supposed to live.' I would go into the house and we would sit in his most beautiful living room and just look at the art on the wall. He just loved being there." Once, McDaniel said, Lewis told him, "If I had another life, I would be an artist."[38]

Lewis considered his art connoisseurship to be of a piece with his ac-tivism. "The stories of African Americans are some of the most inspiring stories of human history," he told Danielle Isaacs, an African American art specialist at Weschler's, a Washington auction house, who advised him on his purchases. "They speak of pain and suffering, the ongoing struggle for human dignity, the hopes, aspirations and dreams of a people. These are universal concepts and ideas expressed beautifully and innovatively by African American artists. Perhaps some museums and collectors have finally realized that we all have stories to share, and it is not possible to tell the whole story of this nation without including African American art."

Lewis had discovered his love for art in a class at Fisk with Aaron Douglas, a major figure in the Harlem Renaissance who founded the university's art department in 1944. "During the height of the civil rights movement, African American art served as an inspiration to us all," Lewis later said. "Seeing our work, in the struggle, depicted on canvas or in other forms of fine art was very uplifting. My appreciation for African American art grew out of these experiences." He never considered collecting, however, until he married Lillian. "She loved books and art," Lewis said, "and they became my passions also."[39]

Although his tastes ranged widely, Lewis's favorite pieces were those with a connection to the civil rights movement or Black history. He didn't use the vocabulary of a scholar or professional curator, but, according to Steve Slotin, an Atlanta dealer, "he knew what he was looking for." Favorites included some of the twentieth century's most esteemed African American painters, including Bearden, Lawrence, and Charles White. Lewis's fondness for Bearden was so great that when the National Gallery partnered with other museums to mount a traveling retrospective of the Harlem artist's work in 2003, Lewis went from city to city to see precisely how each museum staged it.[40]

"He liked narrative art of the civil rights struggle and of the Black diaspora," said Isaacs. "And figurative. African Americans' depictions of their lives, like Romare Bearden and his Odyssey series comparing their struggle to the Homeric epic, or Elizabeth Catlett, who explored individuals living in society from sharecroppers to men and women in the 1970s riding the bus and the subway in New York." Some artists Lewis collected painted scenes of Selma or other historic events in which he himself had taken part. (When Lillian discovered that her friend Carol Dove owned a print of Lawrence's *Confrontation at the Bridge*, she demanded that her friend give it to her; Dove refused, but Lillian scoured the art world to find another copy for her husband.) Benny Andrews, an acclaimed Atlanta artist who was also a friend of the Lewises, composed a series of collages and ink drawings about Lewis, including one of him preaching to the chickens, which Lewis kept for his collection.[41]

Lewis also collected folk art by self-taught painters such as Mose Tolliver, known as Mose T, and Jimmy Lee Sudduth. "The style was super colorful, blocky, bold, kind of abstract," Slotin said. The folk artists tended to have elements in common with Bearden and Lawrence, even though they lacked professional training." Lewis sought out folk art everywhere. On weekends staff drove him to go "treasure hunting," as Michael German called it. "We went up to North Georgia. We'd go to a flea market, or we'd go to an art league. We'd drive up in the mountains and buy art." At Weschler's auction house in Washington, not far from Capitol Hill, Lewis was a regular at weekly Tuesday sales. "He would always pick up the phone for Weschler's," Isaacs said. "If you called his office, they would put you on with him directly. All the emails were always answered." When a new auction catalog arrived in the mail, Lewis would get downright giddy, the way he had as a boy when he got his hands on the latest Sears, Roebuck catalog.[42]

Several artists became personal friends. Lewis had an affinity for those like himself who grew up in the segregated rural South. Aides would drive the congressman over dusty back roads to visit with these men or women, usually coming home with something for the walls. Once, coming back from a trip to Montgomery, German recalled, Lewis decided to go see Mose T, a factory worker who had turned to painting after his legs were crushed in a shop floor accident. "We drove up Sunday evening, maybe nine o'clock at night," German said. "We had his address, no GPS. We came off the expressway, and we went over, knocked on the door." Tolliver and Lewis struck up a warm conversation. "They started bringing stuff out from under the bed," German recounted. "And so there we are, going through all this stuff. And pretty much it's on wood, plywood." Lewis bought a piece and convinced German to do so as well.[43]

Other aides had similar experiences. "He took us to see a folk artist in the backwoods of Alabama—Mose," recalled Kim Walker. "And he just sat down and had lemonade with him. I was wondering, 'Where are we going? What are we doing?' It was so John Lewis." Another time, remembered Debbie Spielberg, "he knew of a woman somewhere. I don't know her name anymore, but she was undiscovered." Spielberg drove Lewis to the woman's house. "We sat in the basement where her studio was, this very modest little house. It was the three of us, just talking. He loved her art and then he bought something. And I bought something because I thought I should."[44]

One important friendship for Lewis was with Thornton Dial, a sculptor born to a sharecropping family in 1928. They would share stories of growing up in rural Black Alabama. "He takes ordinary, what some people would consider throwaway, materials," Lewis said, explaining his fondness for Dial's work, "and makes it some of the most colorful and some of the most moving pieces. He makes it real, he brings it home to you." In 1996, at the invitation of the Freedom Park Conservancy, Lewis chose Dial to create an outdoor installation for the Freedom Parkway—the road constructed to the Carter library after activists blocked the planned eight-lane highway. Titled *The Bridge*, Dial's playful, busy, forty-two-foot-long assemblage combined steel with found objects like tires and barrels, painted black, to create an abstracted depiction of a person advancing over an enormous hump. Lewis said that Dial told him that the sculpture evoked "traveling from one place to another place, and along the way, you come in contact with different parts of human life." It captured a precise moment in history, while also signaling "we're still crossing a bridge."[45]

The sculpture was dedicated in a September 2005 public ceremony. "It's a beautiful tribute to him in my opinion," said Shirley Franklin, Atlanta's mayor and an art connoisseur herself, "maybe even more important than a portrait or a lifelike sculpture, because it reflects his aspirations and hopes."[46]

In the summer of 2005, with the retirement of Sandra Day O'Connor and the death of William Rehnquist, President Bush had the opportunity to appoint two justices to the Supreme Court. His first choice was John G. Roberts, a judge on the U.S. Court of Appeals for the District of Columbia, who after Rehnquist's death was nominated for the position of chief justice. The nomination divided Democrats. Some feared that with the departure of O'Connor—a relative moderate in her jurisprudence next to her colleagues Antonin Scalia and Clarence Thomas—the addition of any clear-cut conservative, such as Roberts, would move the court to the right and thus had to be blocked. Others held to the view that a president deserved a degree of deference in his choice, and that a well-credentialed nominee who was neither plagued by scandal nor ideologically extreme—again, like Roberts—deserved confirmation.

Lewis couldn't vote on the nomination, but he knew which side he was on. In the Reagan Justice Department, Roberts had led the unsuccessful fight to water down the Voting Rights Act. The Bush White House felt obliged to release thousands of pages of records relating to his tenure. Vetting the material, Democrats saw their worst fears confirmed about Roberts's hostility to that historic law, which at the time he said was becoming "a quota system for electoral politics."

Lewis believed the Senate's charge was clear. "I think the senators on both sides should really grill him on not just his commitment to the Voting Rights Act," he told the *New York Times*, "but his understanding of what the fight was all about—the spirit of the act, not just the letter."[47]

On the Senate Judiciary Committee, Pat Leahy, the ranking Democrat, wanted Lewis to be a witness. "He was honored to be asked," according to Michael Collins. "And he was up for it. It was a lot of scrutiny, a lot of drama, but as always, he loved a good fight to get in the way." As he had against Clarence Thomas fourteen years earlier, on September 15, Lewis walked over to the Senate hearing room—room 216 of the Hart Building—to try to persuade his colleagues to keep an avowed critic of the Voting Rights Act off the Supreme Court.

Many of Lewis's remarks that day—recounting the "white men" and "colored men" signs of his youth, or the literacy tests that asked "the number of bubbles in a bar of soap"—were familiar, lines he could recite in his sleep. But they were still relevant and powerful in underscoring Roberts's Reagan-era positions. "Judge Roberts' memos reveal him to be hostile toward civil rights, affirmative action, and the Voting Rights Act," Lewis said. "He has even said that Voting Rights Act violations, and I quote, 'should not be made too easy to prove.'" Roberts, Lewis said, "was on the wrong side of history."[48]

But if Clarence Thomas's hearings had riveted the country, with the nominee's fate hanging in the balance, the Roberts hearings were Kabuki theater. The partisan lines were drawn; few were open to persuasion. With Roberts's impeccable credentials and choirboy persona having convinced many Democrats to vote for him, the judge's confirmation was assured. When Lewis spoke, the C-SPAN camera zoomed in on his face, but discerning viewers noted in the background a troubling number of empty chairs and the occasional pair of legs walking by, as if there were somewhere more important to be. According to the *Washington Post*, only four committee members were in the room and only sixteen reporters populated a press gallery that seated 120. "Lewis's testimony," Dana Milbank wrote, "was passionate, poignant—and pretty much irrelevant to the outcome."[49]

On September 29, the Senate approved Roberts's appointment as chief justice by a vote of 78–22.

The fight over Roberts's nomination coincided with the fortieth anniversary of the enactment of the Voting Rights Act, and the question of its future loomed over the judge's confirmation. In 2007, the 1982 Voting Rights Act renewal would be expiring. Republicans now controlled both houses of Congress as well as the White House, and it seemed possible that where Nixon and Reagan had failed, Bush might succeed. When Bush met in early 2005 with the Black Caucus and was asked about renewing the act, he said he didn't know enough about it to comment. Members of the caucus were shocked—and worried.[50]

Protests on behalf of the act got underway that summer in Atlanta. On Saturday, August 6, the anniversary of the signing of the Voting Rights Act, Lewis joined ten thousand people on a two-mile hike from the Russell Federal Building downtown to Herndon Stadium in Vine City. A rally and concert followed. Old movement friends like Harry Belafonte and Dick Gregory flew in for the occasion; Nancy Pelosi, Maxine Waters, Dick Durbin, and other congressional allies came, too. "Forty years later we're still marching for the right to vote," Lewis bellowed at the football stadium. "We're being too quiet with this administration. We've got to talk back to the Bush Administration. Keep your eyes on the prize!"[51]

Lewis published an op-ed essay that day in the *New York Times* arguing for the act's renewal. The conservative claim that it was no longer needed, he said, was belied by new gambits in many states to restrict the ballot. There were "hundreds of contemporary challenges to the right to vote that need our attention," Lewis wrote, from new voter-identification laws in Georgia to a South Dakota county's machinations to limit Native American representation. "Unless we re-authorize and strengthen every vital provision of the act," Lewis concluded, "we risk the advances we have achieved."[52]

Lewis had reason for optimism. The Bush administration was struggling politically. Voters were unhappy over the president's failed attempt to partially privatize Social Security and the protracted military occupation of Iraq. Eyeing gains in the upcoming midterms, Democrats were painting Republicans as hostile to African American interests—a reputation Bush could ill afford.

In a stroke of good timing, Republican Jim Sensenbrenner of Wisconsin was now chairing the House Judiciary Committee. Sensenbrenner was no liberal; he had even voted against the African American history museum, citing its cost. But he believed in the Voting Rights Act and in 1982 had urged Reagan to sign that year's reauthorization over the objections of John Roberts. Sensenbrenner wanted to renew the act before the 2006 election, after which he would have to cede his committee chairmanship.[53]

Sensenbrenner spoke with John Conyers, the committee's ranking Democrat. They agreed that with Republicans controlling the government, "strengthening" the act—as Lewis had demanded in his August *New York Times* op-ed—was not in the cards. Instead, the 2006 reauthorization should stick closely to the terms of the 1982 bill. They would reject proposals to alter it from either the left or the right.[54]

Conyers called Lewis to tell him of his talks with Sensenbrenner. Lewis signed on. "John was involved from the beginning," Sensenbrenner said. "Because everybody on both sides of the aisle knew that there would be no voting rights extension bill passed without the enthusiastic input and support of John Lewis."[55]

Lewis favored the bipartisan strategy. He knew that historically all the Voting Rights Act renewals—indeed, all major civil rights bills of the modern era—had had powerful GOP backers. "If it hadn't been for both Democrats and Republicans working together, the Civil Rights Bill of 1964 would not have passed the Congress," he said years later. "It was a bipartisan effort." The 2006 Voting Rights Act renewal should be no different.[56]

Steve Chabot of Ohio, who chaired the subcommittee on the Constitution, held ten sets of hearings. Forty witnesses testified about continuing attempts to revise state voting laws to limit Black participation. The committee accumulated a massive trove of evidence to argue that the act—including its all-important preclearance provisions—was still needed. Armed with these findings, Sensenbrenner won the endorsement of House Speaker Dennis Hastert and Senate Majority Leader Bill Frist. The Republicans were falling in line.

To lend moral heft to the cause, Lewis accompanied Sensenbrenner and Conyers when they testified before the Senate Judiciary Committee in April 2006. "We said we had a good bill that ought to pass unamended and be sent to the president," Sensenbrenner recalled. "John referred to me as 'bro,' which was a high, high honor." The Bush administration, which had come under fire for neglecting Black poverty amid its botched response to Hurricane Katrina in 2005, was now on board as well.[57]

But opposition was brewing—from Lewis's home state. For more than a year, Georgia Republicans had been trying to redraw the state's congressional districts in their favor. Lewis and the Democrats were fighting them. Spearheading the Republicans' attack was Representative Lynn Westmoreland, a stone-faced ultraconservative from Atlanta best known for calling on the House and Senate to display the Ten Commandments. Westmoreland and his faction believed that Georgia and the other states required by the Voting Rights Act to submit redistricting plans or voting changes for federal preclearance had long since overcome their history of discrimination and should no longer suffer scrutiny. Westmoreland said he would consider renewing the Voting Rights Act, but only with changes. "Renewing the law as it is would keep Georgia in the penalty box for 25 more years," Westmoreland complained in the *Atlanta Journal-Constitution*. "It doesn't make sense to subjugate Georgia to the whims of federal bureaucrats until 2031 based on the turnout of an election featuring Barry Goldwater and Lyndon Johnson."[58]

Lewis and Sensenbrenner had been counting on a smooth passage. But Westmoreland and his allies took their fight to the House floor. On July 13, 2006, the final day of debate, they demanded amendments to the bill. Westmoreland—who had just supported a redistricting plan in Georgia to reduce the number of majority-Black districts—again claimed that his state was now treating voters fairly, without respect to race.

To drive home his point, he dug up a statement from Lewis. If the Democrats could cloak themselves in Lewis's aura, so could the Republicans. "Don't just take my word for it on Georgia's progress," Westmoreland said tauntingly on the House floor. "Listen to this ringing endorsement from my colleague from Georgia, Congressman John Lewis, an icon of the civil rights movement. Under oath in federal court five years ago, Congressman Lewis testified: 'There has been a transformation. It's a different state, it's

a different political climate, it's a different political environment. It's altogether a different world we live in. We've come a great distance. It's not just
in Georgia, but in the American South, I think people are preparing to lay
down the burden of race.'"

Westmoreland not only appropriated Lewis's moral authority. He also
implied that Lewis was being dishonest. "If he said that under oath, sworn
to tell the whole truth and nothing but the truth, why is he telling the House
something different today?" Westmoreland asked. "The reason he was under
oath was because he was testifying in front of the Department of Justice that
it was OK for the majority-minority districts in Georgia to be diluted, in
direct violation of the Voting Rights Act."

Lewis's testimony had come in a 2002 case, when he and the Georgia
Democrats—who at the time controlled the state assembly—had, in a bitter irony, been accused of violating the Voting Rights Act because their redistricting plan sought to spread the Black vote around to more districts,
in the hope of creating more seats where Democrats could win. Lewis and
the Democrats had won the case, called *Georgia v. Ashcroft*, at the Supreme
Court in a 5–4 decision, with the conservative justices upholding the plan
and the liberal justices dissenting. But despite the unusual alignment of
forces, Lewis hadn't been trying to weaken Blacks' voting power. On the
contrary, the plan he favored had sought to maximize that power statewide.[59]

When Lewis heard Westmoreland throwing his own words back at him
from the well, he became furious. He called on Westmoreland to "yield"—a
parliamentary term for giving someone else a chance to speak. "My dear colleague, you called my name," Lewis protested, straining to be polite. Westmoreland talked over him.

Only when Westmoreland's time expired did Conyers yield fifteen seconds of his own time to Lewis. "Mr. Chairman, let me say to my friend and
to my colleague from the State of Georgia," Lewis began, "it is true that years
ago I said that we are in the process of laying down the burden of race. But it
is not down yet and we are not asleep yet." He waggled a finger at Westmoreland. "The Voting Rights Act was good and necessary in 1965 and it is still
good and necessary today." His voice grew loud and trembled as he spoke
over the gavel. "So don't misquote me. Don't take my words out of context."

Lewis was still fuming. Michaeleen Crowell, his legislative director,
described "a mad scramble" in the office to mount a reply, "one of those

all-hands-on-deck moments where he was mad. He was personally affronted."

About an hour later, for his closing arguments, Lewis came back to the floor with two enormous blown-up black-and-white photographs of himself at Selma. The first showed him and Hosea Williams leading the marchers to the bridge. The second showed Lewis fallen to the ground, shielding his head, his trench coat gripped by a helmeted state trooper. "He always had those posters at the ready," Crowell said. "Those were in his office and he used them often to educate and to show people the experience that he had."

School his opponents is what Lewis did. "Yes, we have made some progress. We have come a distance," he said. "We are no longer met with bull-whips, fire hoses, and violence when we attempt to register and vote. But the sad fact is, the sad truth is discrimination still exists, and that is why we still need the Voting Rights Act."

He returned to the importance of history. "We cannot separate the debate today from our history and the past we have traveled. When we marched from Selma to Montgomery in 1965, it was dangerous. It was a matter of life and death." Now his voice was rising, reverberating throughout the chamber. "I was beaten, I had a concussion at the bridge. I almost died. I gave blood, but some of my colleagues gave their very lives. We must pass this act without any amendment. . . . When historians pick up their pens and write about this period"—here, he pounded the lectern—"let it be said that those of us in the Congress in 2006, we did the right thing. . . . Let us pass a clean bill without any amendment." Applause cascaded from the gallery.[60]

The House rejected the conservatives' amendments. In the final vote, all but one of Georgia's seven Republican congressmen voted against the bill. Lewis and the other Democrats voted for it. It passed easily, 390–33.[61]

The next week came the Senate's turn. Ted Kennedy invited Lewis to watch from the Senate floor. The bill passed unanimously. He and Kennedy exchanged congratulations in the President's Room, where both men had watched Johnson sign the Voting Rights Act in 1965. Bush signed the new bill one week later on the White House South Lawn.[62]

Chapter Twenty-Four

"BECAUSE OF YOU"

———— ■ ■ ————

F or his sixty-fifth birthday in February 2005, John Lewis invited a special guest: Barack Obama.

Like millions of Americans, Lewis was wowed by Obama's talent from the moment he burst on the scene at the 2004 Democratic convention in Boston. The Illinois state senator and candidate for U.S. Senate had delivered a rousing, inspirational keynote address that immediately pegged him as a presidential prospect. After winning his Senate race that November, Obama was inundated with speaking requests. He declined most of them, not wanting to earn a reputation for publicity-seeking when he should be learning the Washington ropes. Still, Obama knew that he needed to raise his profile in the South. Besides, John Lewis—one of his heroes—was asking.[1]

Obama credited Lewis, in part, with giving him the confidence to pursue a political career. When Obama had been president of the *Harvard Law Review*, Lewis gave the keynote speech at the journal's annual dinner. "I was nervous," Obama recounted years later, since it was "probably the first time that I really gave a public speech that was recorded." Having Lewis in the audience raised the stakes. "I'm thinking, 'Well, this is a guy who was at the March on Washington,'" Obama said. "So it's a little bit of pressure. And I don't recall what my remarks were, but I do recall afterwards John coming up and saying, 'You've got a great gift and I am looking forward to you doing great things in the future.'"[2]

The star-studded birthday party for Lewis, held at the Georgia Tech Hotel and Conference Center, attracted Coretta Scott King, Harry Belafonte, Andrew Young, and, by video, Bill Clinton. For all the excitement around Obama, not everyone considered him the most exciting draw. Herman Russell, a construction magnate who was probably the wealthiest Black man in Atlanta, was talking to Buddy Darden when someone beckoned him to meet Obama. "Not right now," Russell demurred. Russell replied. "Buddy's going to introduce me to Ethel Kennedy."[3]

Still, Obamamania was in full flower. Lewis spent time getting to know his new colleague. "We walked the streets of Atlanta together and Blacks and whites were asking him to run for president," Lewis said. "When we got to the restaurant, the waiters and waitresses were asking him to run. And when I introduced him that night, I said, 'One day this man will be president of the United States.'"[4]

Obama returned the love. He recounted meeting Lewis as a younger man and credited Lewis with having made his own rise possible. "There is a direct line between his courage and my current station," Obama said.[5]

Over the next two years, the Obama love-in mushroomed. By March 2007, the Illinois senator had announced he was running for president. So had Hillary Clinton, now in her second Senate term from New York. Both coveted Lewis's endorsement. Lewis had become a power player nonpareil.

Artur Davis, the congressman who represented Selma, asked Obama to speak on Bloody Sunday at Brown Chapel. When Clinton learned of the invitation, she arranged to speak at the First Baptist Church down the street at the same time. For good measure, Bill Clinton announced that he was coming, too, to be inducted into Selma's Voting Rights Hall of Fame. "It was a real high-stakes moment," Hillary Clinton remembered, given "the significance of the first maybe viable Black candidate, the first maybe viable woman candidate. Dueling speeches in two different churches at the same time, and then the walk across the bridge. It was pretty exciting."[6]

Lewis was in a bind. He decided to attend Obama's speech because he traditionally went to Brown Chapel, but he made clear that Hillary's supporters were free to go hear her. They would all cross the bridge together— the two candidates' first side-by-side appearance of the campaign. Lewis was frank about his quandary. "One day I lean one way, the next day I lean

another way," he said. "Isn't it healthy that we have the luxury to choose between two wonderful, gifted politicians?"

On most days, he leaned toward Clinton because he knew her better
and longer and considered her a friend. He said as much to Obama. "John
had already communicated to me that it would be difficult for him to go
against Hillary," Obama later disclosed. "His view was that he had been in
the foxhole with the Clintons throughout Bill Clinton's presidency and had
become very close to them. They had been important allies on a whole host
of fights." Still, Lewis's gut told him that the young phenom might well prevail and he made no endorsement.[7]

The weekend went smoothly, with egos in check. Bill Clinton, called on
to speak, demurred, saying, "All the good speaking has been done by Hillary
and Senator Obama." Obama played the part of the dutiful youngster. At
one point, Bill Clinton knelt down to get onto eye level with an eighty-five-
year-old Fred Shuttlesworth, who was sitting in a wheelchair, having been
diagnosed with a brain tumor. Clinton rested his clasped hands on Shuttlesworth's knee; the minister placed his hands on Clinton's, and they locked
eyes. Standing behind them, sleeves rolled up, pushing Shuttlesworth's chair,
was Barack Obama.[8]

When it was all over, Lewis later recounted, "I said we cannot do this
again. . . . It was too much drama. I think it probably took something away
from the essence of our trip." He stopped inviting presidential candidates on
the pilgrimage.[9]

The weekend also brought him no closer to an endorsement. On March
30, he spoke to Juan Williams of National Public Radio, who told Lewis that
the political world was waiting on his endorsement. "It's a tough decision,"
Lewis confessed. "And so we like to put the decision off as long as possible."[10]

By the fall, Clinton had established a clear lead over her rival. Black and
white Americans alike were breaking her way, judging her as more experienced, better versed in the issues, and readier to be president. Obama had a
magnetic charisma and an appealing message of generational change, but it
seemed that his turn would come another day. Even Obama accepted that
Lewis would probably endorse Clinton. "I really didn't squeeze him hard
on it because I couldn't argue with his basic position," Obama later said. "I

would not have wanted a white colleague and friend of mine who I was very close to, who thought I would be the better candidate, not to endorse me because there was a white candidate in the race. And it wouldn't have made sense for me to expect the reverse."[11]

In October, Lewis formally cast his lot with Hillary. A backlash against the Iraq War had damaged Bush and his swaggering foreign policy; Democrats were debating if they wanted to scale back America's foreign involvements (Obama) or to maintain a prominent leadership role abroad (Clinton). Experience and knowledge of international affairs loomed large.

On October 12 at Paschal's in Atlanta (relocated from its historic site), Lewis joined Clinton for a rally. "I have looked at all the candidates, and I believe that Hillary Clinton is the best prepared to lead this country at a time when we are in desperate need of strong leadership," he said. "She will restore a greater sense of community in America and reclaim our standing in the world." When asked about picking a white candidate over a Black one, Lewis said, "I've always preached biracial politics. That's what the civil rights movement was all about." He joined Clinton again that night for an event in South Carolina.[12]

Despite having expected it, Obama reportedly told aides it felt like a stab in the back. Publicly, he implied that Lewis was motivated more by his debts to Bill Clinton than by Hillary's strengths. "I can't expect to be getting every single endorsement, given the eight years of a Clinton presidency" and "the favors that he's done," he told National Public Radio.[13]

With his campaign struggling, Obama went negative. His team devised a plan to paint Clinton as untrustworthy, dishonest, and captive to outdated establishment thinking while ensuring that Obama preserved his image as the opposite: a breath of fresh air, an antidote to the phoniness and compromises of Washington. On October 30, at a debate in Philadelphia, Obama and the other five trailing candidates—united in their need to derail Clinton—went after her. She parried their thrusts poorly, and at the evening's end her front-runner status was suddenly shaky. Over the next two months Obama gained ground, culminating in a historic triumph in the Iowa caucuses on January 3, 2008.[14]

Iowa scrambled the race. Black voters, most of whom had favored Clinton, now saw Obama as viable, even likely to become the first Black president, and flocked to his banner. Clinton was further damaged when the Obama campaign seized on a series of comments by her surrogates—such as warnings that Obama's admission of youthful cocaine use might cost him votes in the fall election—to impute racism. One Obama staffer drafted a memo coaching people on how to frame various Clintonites' remarks as offensive. Each episode, though trivial in and of itself, dominated the media coverage for days, turning the campaign into a donnybrook about race and racism—something both candidates had wanted to avoid.[15]

The racial recriminations spiked after a comment Hillary made the day before the January 8 New Hampshire primary. Contrasting her experience with Obama's newness, she argued that oratory and organizing alone wouldn't bring change, that skilled executive leadership was also needed. "Dr. King's dream began to be realized when President Johnson passed the Civil Rights Act of 1964, when he was able to get [it] through Congress," she said by way of analogy. "It took a president to get it done." Although Clinton eked out a surprise win in New Hampshire the next day, her remark got almost as much attention as her historic win. Obama's people spun the comment as a snub of Martin Luther King. Obama himself deftly stoked the controversy while plying his trademark cool, calling it "an unfortunate remark, an ill-advised remark."[16]

Lewis was upset by the negativity. He had always disliked ill-founded accusations of racism, especially against people he knew to be decent. He couldn't fathom how anyone could truly believe that Hillary was playing the race card.

So far he had avoided the ginned-up controversies. He had framed his endorsement of Hillary in terms of loyalty. "If I make it a commitment, I keep my commitments," he said. "If he gets the nomination, I'll go out and campaign for him." Now, though, he spoke out.[17]

Suddenly, he was all over the media. He went on the *PBS NewsHour* to debate with Joe Lowery, an Obama ally. Lowery had been trash-talking Lewis, and on the show he condescended to the congressman as if he were still an impudent Nashville student. In return, Lewis was atypically blunt. "I think there's been a deliberate, systematic attempt on the part of some people in the Obama camp to really fan the flame of race and really try to distort what Senator Clinton said," Lewis argued. He pointed to the news reports of behind-the-scenes messaging. "The Obama camp," he reminded viewers, was "sending out memos to members of the media, trying to suggest that the Clintons are playing the race card."

In another interview, with the *Washington Post*, Lewis upped the ante. He called Obama "a friend," but then stated harshly, "He is no Martin Luther King Jr. I knew Martin Luther King. I knew Bobby Kennedy. I knew President Kennedy. You need more than speech-making. You need someone who is prepared to provide bold leadership." The words—echoing Lloyd Bentsen's famous put-down of Dan Quayle in the 1988 vice presidential debate—were harsh, perhaps harsher than he intended.[18]

Far from helping Hillary, Lewis's foursquare defense of her only elicited more criticism of him. Over the next weeks, he and other Black Clinton supporters were admonished to fall in line behind Obama. An Atlanta political operative named John Garst placed fifty thousand automated phone calls to local voters, exhorting them to pressure Lewis to switch to Obama. "Don't be afraid to call, and remember, King Day is on Jan. 21 this year. And we shouldn't have a congressman in King's own home city refusing to endorse a member of the Black Caucus." The Obama campaign denounced Garst, who was acting on his own, but it was clear that the pressure campaign had spun out of control.[19]

Lewis's friends and aides could see him struggling. "It was a difficult time for him," said Michael Collins. "The congressman wanted people to understand that he was true to his friends. And the Clintons were his friends. They go a long way back. And that was really where he lay."[20]

Super Tuesday fell early in 2008, on February 5. Twenty-two states and territories were voting that day. They ended up dividing almost evenly, Obama winning twelve and Clinton ten. She took the big states including New York and California, but he won most of the South, boosted by Black voters. In Georgia, Obama won 67 percent of the vote, including Lewis's Fifth District.

Lewis hoped that the conclusion of the Georgia primary would end the drama. But the opposite happened. The Clinton-Obama race was now shaping up as the closest Democratic nomination fight since the advent of the primary-dominated system in 1972. For the first time, it seemed, the outcome might hinge on the ballots not of regular voters but of the superdelegates—the hundreds of party officials who by dint of their position could cast votes at the summer convention on top of those of the popularly chosen delegates. And while Obama was winning the Black vote, Clinton was winning with Black superdelegates.

Party leaders had devised the superdelegate system in 1982 to counter the bandwagon effect of the elections of the 1970s, when primary voters' sudden and lightly held enthusiasms had produced what insiders judged to be weak nominees. For Obama supporters in 2008, however, the notion that superdelegates' judgments might prove decisive reeked of unfairness. Complicating matters, many pro-Obama superdelegates—like Ted Kennedy in Massachusetts and Bill Richardson in New Mexico—had constituents who favored Clinton. There was no simple solution.

Some Obama allies resorted to hardball tactics. Jesse Jackson Jr., a Chicago congressman, warned Emanuel Cleaver of Missouri, a Clinton partisan, "If it comes down to the last day, and you're the only superdelegate, do you want to go down in history as the one to prevent a Black from winning the White House?" When Cleaver aired the threat, Jackson doubled down. "Many of these guys have offered their support to Mrs. Clinton, but Obama has won their districts. So you wake up without the carpet under your feet. You might find some young primary challenger placing you in a difficult position." Sure enough, Black Clinton supporters began drawing challengers who argued that the incumbents were too old and too cautious.[21]

Lewis suffered another blow when an anonymous source, described in the *Journal-Constitution* as "a former admirer of Lewis" who had grown "disillusioned" over his Clinton endorsement, leaked the news that, many months before, Lovelean Williams, Lewis's Atlanta office manager, had quietly settled a lawsuit against Lewis and Michael Collins. Williams claimed she had been passed over for promotion; after complaining to the congressman, she said, she was fired, eight months short of retirement. Although the settlement included no admission of wrongdoing—Lewis settled, his office said, to avoid a costly lawsuit—the bad publicity couldn't have come at a worse time. Joseph Beasley, a Rainbow/PUSH employee representing Williams, lambasted Lewis as "the personification of everything that's bad in the workplace." It was a painful episode for Lewis, who prided himself on his upright behavior. He didn't know what other negative attacks might follow.[22]

Grassroots discontent was also brewing among young Black activists in Atlanta. Jelani Cobb, a Spelman College history professor, wrote a newspaper essay lacerating Lewis and the "civil rights gerontocracy" for defending "the interests of Democratic Party insiders more than those of the Black community." In these and other criticisms, Lewis heard echoes of his rejection at Kingston Springs in 1966. Again he faced jibes that his day had passed, accusations that he was out of step with the times, questions about his racial bona fides.[23]

Critical calls flooded the office. "The pressure was on every day," Collins said. "They said he was out of touch, and he was an old guy. And there was always this reference to the Bible, Joshua and Moses. And this is now the Joshua Generation. And Congressman Lewis was not part of it."[24]

Malaika Moses, a daughter of SNCC's Bob Moses, joined Cobb and others in a drive to force the congressman to pledge his superdelegate vote to Obama. They circulated a petition and lobbied the *Journal-Constitution* to publicize their effort. Some of their allies were even more hostile to Lewis than they were. At one meeting, Cobb recalled, "one person said, 'John Lewis stood up to white people on the Edmund Pettus Bridge and has never stood up to any white people since.' I was like, 'Ouch!' But that was the tone."[25]

Even as Lewis agonized, however, he showed no rancor. He still lived by the old Gandhian precepts. When his Atlanta aide Rachelle O'Neil heard some broadcasters "just trashing Mr. Lewis at the very radio station that always wanted him to go on air," she phoned in to complain. "He fought and nearly died for all of us to have the right to vote," she chided the hosts. "And now you guys are telling him that his vote is not his choice? How dare you."

The congressman took a different tack. "Call the radio station," he instructed O'Neil. "We're going up there." They drove over. "So next thing, he marched right up to the radio station," O'Neil recalled, "and everybody was all nice and kind. And so I said, 'Mr. Lewis, how do you do it, sir? How do you subdue people who are so nasty and negative towards you?'"

"Rachelle," he replied, "You've got to learn how to love the hell out of people."[26]

On February 14, Lewis told reporters that a change of his endorsement "could happen," the Associated Press reported. He wasn't abandoning Clinton, he reiterated, but he didn't want the people's will contravened by superdelegates. He was inching toward supporting Obama, but was not yet there.

Lewis had confided in Jim Clyburn that he was worried he was "on the wrong side of history." Clyburn, who was for Obama, invited Lewis to talk things over in his office. In the meeting, Lewis said that he was probably willing to switch, but needed to find a way to do so diplomatically, with dignity for everyone involved. He had to consult his staff and figure out how and when to announce a decision.

What happened next is disputed. As Lewis recounted it to aides, he was walking back to his office through the Cannon Tunnel when his cell phone rang. It was a reporter from the *New York Times*. Lewis was surprised. His office never gave his private cell number to reporters, who always paid him the respect of going through his press office. Could someone in the Clyburn meeting have leaked his cell number? Caught off guard, Lewis took the call. He felt a little queasy, having had no time to plan his remarks.

Jeff Zeleny, the *Times* reporter who spoke to Lewis, recalled it differently. Zeleny, who was covering the Obama campaign, was in Milwaukee, getting off the Obama bus and checking into a Courtyard Marriott, when a call came from a regular source of his, someone "who is active in African American politics and was close to Lewis." The source asked if Zeleny would be free in a few minutes to take a call from the congressman. "Of course," Zeleny said. He went to his room and waited for his phone to ring. ("I definitely did not call him," Zeleny added. "I'd never had Mr. Lewis's cell phone number.") Someone—not from Lewis's staff—then phoned Zeleny and put the congressman on the line.

Either way, in the conversation that followed, Lewis indicated his readiness or perhaps intention to switch his superdelegate vote—conveying more certainty than he had to other reporters that week and probably more than he wished to. Zeleny and Patrick Healy, who was covering Clinton for the *Times*, jointly wrote a story stating unequivocally in the lede that Lewis "planned to cast his vote as a superdelegate" for Obama. Later in the piece, they noted that Lewis hadn't yet withdrawn his endorsement of Clinton, but might do so soon. Their editors posted the story online that night and showcased it on Friday's front page.

Word traveled fast. Before Lewis returned to his office on Thursday, journalists were phoning with new questions. By Friday they were camping out in front of his office.

When Lewis arrived Friday morning, he darted into his office with a copy of the *Times* and shooed everyone else out. Publicly, Brenda Jones, his press secretary, shot down the *Times* report, but it still made its way into other outlets. Lewis then said nothing for many days.[27]

The heat was cranked up the next week when Markel Hutchins, a twenty-nine-year-old Atlanta minister and activist, announced he would challenge Lewis in the Fifth District primary, scheduled for July 15. Questioning Lewis's "decision to separate himself from his own electorate" by standing by Clinton, Hutchins belittled Lewis as old and irrelevant. It was Lewis's first primary challenge since 1992. Some people suspected that Obama's people had put Hutchins up to it. He certainly looked like one of the "young primary challengers" being talked about. Few expected Hutchins to win, but for the first time in ages Lewis looked politically mortal.[28]

"It was a very direct, personal threat," according to Hillary Clinton. Lewis was told, "We'll basically run somebody who's with us, namely, the Obama campaign, and will be young and vigorous and make the case as Obama made, that it's time for a new generation. And I think that really was so disappointing to John and so almost inexplicable that after everything he'd done, that would be the end of his political career, or at least it would be a very difficult reelection."[29]

Lewis continued his deliberations. Lillian, who also felt great affection for the Clintons, told her husband that she saw a lot of the young John Lewis in Obama and that Obama represented the future.[30]

Finally, Lewis later recounted, "I had an executive session with myself." He concluded that he didn't want to stand apart from the enthusiasm that was sweeping America. "It was very difficult for me," he later told Oprah Winfrey. "But I saw the Barack Obama campaign as a movement. It was very similar to the civil rights movement, and I said I wanted to be on the right side of history, and that's why I made that change."[31]

"It was a great time in Black history," explained Jacob Gillison. "Obama's winning the primaries. The congressman's constituents are supporting Obama. Be on the right side of history. He had to make some phone calls behind closed doors and say, 'Hey, I'm going to have to do this.' But he did it."[32]

Lewis called Bill Clinton first. He told Clinton that he loved both him and Hillary and that he valued their long friendship, but he was going to change his endorsement.

"I talked to Hillary about it," Bill Clinton recalled. "I said, 'We need to let John go. It's not going to change what happens now in this primary. He's a wonderful person. He has been great to me, and he's been great to you, and he'll never say a bad word about you. And that's what really matters.'

"And she said, 'I agree with you.' She said, 'We can't afford to lose him in Congress. What he means symbolically to America. It's just not right. He's too big a figure. It's wrong.'"

Bill Clinton and Lewis spoke again. "John," Clinton said, "we love you, and we're going to love you whatever you do, you do what you need to do."

Lewis and Hillary also spoke. "He talked to Bill and then I don't remember when I connected with John, but it wasn't very long after that," she later said. "I told him, 'Look, John, I understand. I really regret that you're being put through this. I am not worth it for you to go down over this. Or even to have to be fighting for your seat when you are such an important member of Congress.'

"So I told him that I understood. It was painful. I don't want to sugar-coat it. We'd been friends a long time. And yet I got it. Politics is a contact sport." It wasn't easy for Bill Clinton, either. "I hated it," he later said. "But they were playing to win, and they realized that they could do better with the superdelegates than we would otherwise have thought. And so it happened. But it never caused any problems with us. Between him and me or with Hillary."[33]

Given the unrelenting media glare, Lewis and Brenda Jones planned a strategy for releasing the news. Lewis would speak with one local reporter, Monica Pearson of WSB-TV, and one national reporter, Andrea Mitchell of NBC, both of whom he trusted. He met with them separately on Wednesday, February 27. Pearson hurried onto the air first, speaking to CNN, with which WSB was affiliated. Mitchell's interview aired later on *NBC Nightly News*. To both women, Lewis described how hard the decision was—harder than confronting Wallace's troopers on Bloody Sunday.

LEWIS: Forty-three years ago, I marched across a bridge in Selma. That was much easier than the decision that I have to make. But I had to make it.

MITCHELL: You're saying this decision was harder than the Selma march?

LEWIS: It was much tougher.

MITCHELL: Congressman, you got your head beaten in. Your face
was covered with blood.

LEWIS: But this is tougher. I'm dealing with friends, people that I
love, people that I admire, part of my extended family.[34]

Obama could hardly contain his delight. "John Lewis is an American hero
and a giant of the civil rights movement, and I am deeply honored to have
his support."

Clinton tried to show grace. "I understand he's been under tremendous
pressure," she said. "He's been my friend. He will always be my friend."[35]

Lewis felt at peace. Constituents praised him for getting on board. But some
resentment lingered. A second congressional challenger, state representative "Able" Mabel Thomas, who had run against him in 1992, now jumped
in the primary. Thomas took aim at Lewis's tardy switch to Obama.[36]

As the front-runner, Lewis followed a conservative strategy and declined
to debate his rivals. His campaign manager unconvincingly cited scheduling
conflicts. At one point, Hutchins showed up at Lewis headquarters, with reporters in tow, histrionically challenging Lewis to a debate. "I'm here to talk
to John Lewis! Where is he?" Hutchins demanded. "He's at work," quipped
Andrew Aydin, the campaign press secretary. Hutchins held up an envelope.
"Well, give him a letter for me," he said. Aydin pointed to a heap of constituent mail. "You can put it right over there," he said. The news crews loved
the theater.[37]

When debate time came, Hutchins and Thomas sparred on television
next to an empty podium. Lewis was blasted for abjuring a democratic ritual. But he was seasoned enough to know that he was likely only to hurt
himself if he stumbled onstage.

Instead, he hit the streets. "No one but no one will out-work or out-
campaign me," he vowed. Aides who thought of themselves as hale and spry
would struggle to keep up. Young volunteers would show up in the morning,
recalled Juliana Illari, an Atlanta activist and Lewis supporter, "and I would
say, 'You need more water. You need better shoes. You're not prepared.' At
the end of the day, they would be completely exhausted." Lewis again got out
there and pushed homeowners' lawn mowers for them. The gay community,

which had been solid behind Hillary, turned out in force, providing a counterweight to disaffected Obama supporters. Lewis stole the show at the Gay Pride parade in June. "He would walk the whole way," Illari said. "His staff would get grumpy because he would shake hands with everybody and it would slow down the whole parade."

On July 15, Lewis won 69 percent of the primary vote.[38]

The Democratic National Convention was held in the last week of August in Denver. Obama planned to accept the nomination in Mile High Stadium, the Denver Broncos' football field, on Thursday, August 28—the forty-fifth anniversary of the March on Washington. The sole speaker from the march who was still alive, Lewis was slated to introduce a film tribute to Martin Luther King.

In the late morning, two members of the convention speechwriting team, Kenneth Baer and Paul Orzulak, were walking through a stadium tunnel when they saw Lewis. "How are you doing?" asked Orzulak, who knew Lewis from his years on the Hill.

"I've been crying all day," Lewis said.

The two men chatted with Lewis, who was happy to linger.

Lewis associated freely, as if on a psychoanalyst's couch. He reminisced about his visits to the White House that summer as the twenty-three-year-old chairman of SNCC. He spoke about all the people who had died since the march, saying how much he wished they could be alive to witness Obama's nomination. His tone was excited—almost disbelieving—about Obama's breakthrough, yet also wistful. He was making sense of the American journey since 1963.

"What do you remember about that day?" Orzulak asked.

"White boys in trees," Lewis said—the kids who had shinnied up the trees lining the Reflecting Pool to glimpse the action.

Later that day, Baer and Orzulak had to edit Lewis's remarks. They were told to cut his speech for length and make sure he stuck to the convention's themes. "All of us were, 'Nope, we're not touching this,'" Baer said. "No one was going to tell him he's going to be too long." That night, Lewis roared out his remarks to the eighty-thousand-person crowd. His fiery style was all wrong for the cavernous outdoor venue. No one complained.[39]

Lewis campaigned for Obama in the fall, but he was never admitted into the candidate's inner circle. Some staff members thought that as effusive as Obama was about Lewis in public, his camp retained a residual pique, believing that Lewis had backed their man only when he had to. The decision had been agonizing, the primary challenge disconcerting, the leaked news of the legal settlement upsetting. Aydin, who became the congressman's digital director and policy adviser, remembered Lewis at a nadir. "I'm worth more dead than alive," he told Aydin.[40]

But if 2008 was a low point for Lewis, Election Day brought a new high. Ever since the financial system's near-collapse in mid-September, leading to the worst economic conditions since the Great Depression, Obama had opened up a comfortable lead over Republican John McCain. Voters were embracing the Democrats' message of change. Oddsmakers forecast an Obama victory. Yet many doubted that the nation would really choose a Black president.

On November 4, Lewis rose at 4:00 a.m. and voted early. At Westlake High School in Atlanta, a five-minute drive from his house, he shook hands with people waiting to vote—all two hundred of them. He kept calling it a "historic day."[41]

He spent the evening at Ebenezer Baptist Church. By seven o'clock, the sanctuary was packed beyond capacity. Crowds were massing on the lawn and sidewalks. Some people jostled and strained to peer through the windows at the giant television screens inside broadcasting the returns. Even before Obama reached the magic number of 270 electoral votes, swing states were breaking his way. Everyone smelled victory.

An emotional Lewis stepped to the pulpit. He told the crowd that he could barely believe that just four decades ago he was beaten senseless marching for voting rights and now he had just voted for the first African American president. "This is a great night," he declared. "It is an unbelievable night. It is a night of thanksgiving." Soon after, the networks reported that Pennsylvania would go for Obama, putting him over the top. At that, Lewis told Oprah Winfrey the next day, "I had what I call an out-of-body experience. I jumped so high I started shouting. I was at Ebenezer Church. I just embarrassed myself. I was just overcome."[42]

The news media were calling: Michele Norris of NPR, Brian Williams of NBC. "I felt that Dr. Martin Luther King, Jr. was looking down on all of us saying hallelujah," Lewis said.[43]

The excitement lasted for months. Each congressman was allotted 193 tickets to the inauguration. Lewis's office received fourteen thousand requests. Close friends who wanted two got one.[44]

The Sunday before Inauguration Day, Lewis preached at the Shiloh Baptist Church in Washington. Over several days he sat in his office greeting constituents and handing out tickets, along with coffee, hot chocolate, and donuts. At one point he went for a stroll down the Mall, commingling with the sea of humanity. Tourists asked for signatures and pictures. "Barack has lifted people," Lewis told the journalist David Remnick, who accompanied him on his walk. "Old people, young people, children, black and white. Look out on the Mall here. You can see it in their walk, can't you?"

For the swearing-in, Lewis had a seat of honor on the stage erected on the Capitol steps. "Congratulations, Mr. President," Lewis said as Obama walked by, about to be inaugurated.

"Thank you, John," Obama said. "You're the first person to call me that." He added, "I'll need your prayers."

"I love you," Lewis said.

"I love you, too," Obama said.

After the ceremonies came a celebratory lunch. Lewis, so often asked to sign photographs, now handed Obama one to sign. "Because of you, John," Obama wrote.[45]

Chapter Twenty-Five

ROCK STAR

——— ▪ ▪ ———

The day after Obama's inauguration, Andrew Dys of the Rock Hill, South Carolina, *Herald* wrote a piece about the local men and women who had fought segregation in the 1960s—and how proud they felt now on the election of America's first Black president. Elwin Wilson, a seventy-two-year-old former Klansman who had harassed and beaten up some of those protesters, read Dys's article. He decided it was time to apologize.

"I hated Blacks," Wilson told Dys in an interview. "Hated 'em." When the Freedom Riders had come to town in 1961, he confessed, he had punched out two men at the bus station—Albert Bigelow and John Lewis. Now, Wilson said, watching Obama's inauguration, "I saw people come together, all these people, and I knew that I had done wrong. . . . I need to tell people I'm sorry." Dys wrote a follow-up story for the *Herald* about Wilson's apology.

Dys called Lewis for a comment. "I accept that apology," Lewis said, "and would love to have the opportunity someday to talk to that man if he wants to. I have no ill feelings. No malice. This shows the distance we have come. It shows grace on his part. It shows courage."

Amid the optimism of Obama's inauguration, Wilson's story captured readers' imaginations. His journey seemed to confirm the hope that the country had turned a corner in its quest for a tolerant society, a beloved community. It was also a storybook example of how nonviolence was supposed to work: by modeling love, people like Lewis could lead a violent bigot—even after forty-eight years—to change his ways.

ABC's *Good Morning America* brought Wilson to Washington to meet

Lewis. On Tuesday, February 3, in Lewis's office—surrounded by civil rights memorabilia and with cameras rolling—Wilson apologized to the man he had punched at the Rock Hill bus station.

"I forgive you," Lewis said. They hugged and talked. Wilson's son looked on in tears.

"I never had any idea this would occur," Lewis said. "This shows the power of love. Of grace. Of people being able to say I am sorry."[1]

Wilson's was one of dozens of conciliatory gestures tendered to Lewis by dyed-in-the-wool racists over many years. George Wallace had unburdened himself to Lewis in 1979. On *The Oprah Winfrey Show* in the 1990s, Joe Smitherman, Selma's mayor since 1965, begged forgiveness from Lewis for his actions back in the day. A few years later, a middle-aged white man in Birmingham walked up to Lewis and apologized "on behalf of all the white people of Alabama." Years after that, Montgomery police chief Kevin Murphy would repent on behalf of his police force and hand Lewis his badge. When Senate Majority Leader Trent Lott caught flak in 2002 for praising Strom Thurmond's 1948 segregationist presidential bid, he too visited Lewis's office to seek forgiveness.[2]

It became a familiar ritual, with Lewis as the nation's father confessor, a wise and loving elder to whom racists turned for absolution. The publicity redounded to Lewis's benefit. But he wasn't dispensing pardons to get good press. He believed these reformed racists had been brave. His friend Bonnie Myers, Archie Allen's ex-wife, at one point told Lewis how much she admired him for sharing a stage with Elwin Wilson when the two men received an award together. Lewis shrugged. "It just took so much courage for him to do that," he said.[3]

As a venerated congressman in the twenty-first century, Lewis encountered little overt racism anymore. He had no illusions that Obama's election heralded the consummation of the beloved community, or that Americans had set down the burden of race. But things had improved. Now most of the racism he dealt with was unintentional—unconscious biases, unthinking slights.

One incident occurred when he was driving with Michael Collins and a *Journal-Constitution* reporter, Melanie Eversley, from Atlanta to an event in Chattanooga. Along the way, they saw one of Lewis's favorite menswear stores, an Alabama-based chain called Parisian. They pulled off the highway and went in. While Lewis was waiting for a clerk, a woman picked up a shoe and asked if he had it in her size. Eversley was horrified. "This is a congressman!" she blurted out. The customer said only, "I didn't know." Lewis remained unruffled. "You have to let these things roll off your back," he told Eversley.[4]

Another time, Lewis was at the black-tie wedding of Paige Alexander, the daughter of his friends Miles and Elaine, at Atlanta's Swissôtel. The bride was in the receiving line, shaking hands, badly in need of a drink. Lewis brought her a glass of white wine. Seeing him deliver the drink, a guest asked Lewis, "May I please have a white wine, too?" Lewis fetched the woman a glass of wine. As he handed it to her, Alexander said to the woman, "Oh, I didn't know you knew Congressman Lewis." A mortified look swept across the guest's face. Alexander, realizing what had happened, got upset as well. Lewis whispered in her ear not to worry. "It's happened my whole life," he said. Sometimes, he said, people see a Black man in a tuxedo and they order a white wine. Having faced brutal macroaggressions, Lewis wasn't one to be troubled by microaggressions.[5]

That explicit racism was diminishing in everyday life indicated some measure of progress in America. But it also made it all the more shocking when unvarnished racism reared its head. Obama's election, even as it showed many Americans ready to accept a Black president, also sparked an ugly, hateful backlash.

Lewis saw that ugliness early in Obama's second year, when Congress was trying to pass the president's long-promised health-care legislation, the Affordable Care Act. The death of Lewis's friend Ted Kennedy the previous summer, and his replacement in the Senate by a Republican, had confounded the Democrats' strategy. Nancy Pelosi, now the House speaker, decided to pass a version of the bill already approved by the Senate, even though many Democrats considered it imperfect. Passage looked iffy.

Opposition came even from Lewis's district. "People were angry, calling up the office and saying horrible, racist things," recalled Michaeleen Crowell. "The phones were off the hook. The vitriol being spewed out of those phones was vile. The poor kids that were answering the phones at the time. They couldn't keep up with the calls. They were bouncing back into the 'lege' room"—the legislative room—"and we were picking up calls all day. It was awful."[6]

One nasty caller left a message, Rachelle O'Neil recounted, in which "he called Mr. Lewis all kinds of n-words and mf-words. And Mr. Lewis called the man back!" Lewis's personal reply stunned the constituent, who immediately apologized and began talking respectfully. "We were like, 'Where was the man that was going ballistic? That was the person you're talking to?'" O'Neil said. "Completely subdued."[7]

On Saturday, March 20, Pelosi was corralling the final votes to pass the bill. For months, Republicans had been denouncing the legislation as an unaffordable government intrusion into the marketplace that would cost nearly $1 trillion over ten years. Thousands of right-wing demonstrators, many of them affiliated with the Tea Party, a right-wing movement that arose after the 2008 crash, flooded Washington. The crowd was seething—much angrier than the typical swarms of activists who from time to time descended on Capitol Hill.

Lewis was walking to the Capitol from the Cannon Building with Michael Collins and his colleagues Andre Carson and Emanuel Cleaver, both also African Americans. The crowd was in a lather, yelling, "Kill the bill!" Lewis politely engaged with them. "I'm voting for the bill," he said.

"Kill the bill, nigger!" someone yelled. Several yards behind Lewis, Cleaver was spat upon. Others jeered "faggot" and "homo" at Democrat Barney Frank as he walked by. "I heard people saying things today I've not heard since March 15th, 1960," said James Clyburn, who had joined sit-ins as a college student. "It was like going into a time machine with John Lewis," Carson said.

"They were shouting, sort of harassing," Lewis told a reporter. "But it's OK. I've faced this before. It reminded me of the Sixties. It was a lot of downright hate and anger and people being downright mean." He counseled his staff to stay calm. "We've done this before," Jacob Gillison remembered Lewis saying. "People yelled at us, they threw things at us, and we were able to proceed in a nonviolent way."[8]

When the Democrats caucused the next day, the protesters were back, chanting and picketing on the Capitol grounds. Inside Cannon, where the

Democrats were meeting, John Larson of Connecticut, the chair of the Democratic caucus, said to Lewis, "John, we're going to need to fire everybody up, so I'm going to call on you after people speak."

Lewis told Larson not to bring up the previous day's racist incident.

"But, John," Larson said, "everybody will be so infuriated. How could they do this?"

"My young man," Lewis said (Larson was only eight years younger than Lewis), "keep your eyes on the prize. We do not want to distract from the moment. If you do, they win. We're out to get health care for the American people."

At the caucus meeting, all the heavyweights spoke: Pelosi, Hoyer, Clyburn. John Dingell, a fifty-five-year House veteran and longtime health-care advocate, presented Pelosi with an oversized gavel used during the passage of Medicare. Then came Lewis's turn. The caucus gave him a standing ovation.

Lewis reminded the Democrats that it was forty-five years ago in March—"on a Sunday like this"—that he had marched for voting rights in Selma. It took a lot to walk across that bridge, he said, "but we knew what we were walking for. In this caucus today, we know what we are fighting for." He laid out what the bill would mean for millions of Americans who lacked health care and linked Selma to the fight to take care of every American.

When Lewis finished, Larson and Pelosi looked at each other. They knew intuitively that it was time to move. Larson banged the gavel.

"Let's lock arms, walk down these steps across that street, and pass healthcare for the American people," Lewis said.[9]

The Capitol police in the room objected. "The security for the leadership, especially for Nancy Pelosi," Lewis remembered, "they were saying, 'You can't do that. You cannot walk. It's an angry crowd.'" Alexandra Pelosi, the speaker's daughter and a filmmaker, told her mother she was crazy. The police ordered them to use the underground tunnel.

Lewis was having none of it. "Mr. Lewis was like, no, I'm not hiding, and I'm not doing that," Michaeleen Crowell said. Pelosi saw that he was right. She and Hoyer and Lewis locked arms and, with other Democrats in their train, walked out of the building, past the hostile mobs, and into the Capitol. The mood was buoyant. Pelosi carried the big Medicare gavel. A trumpeter played "We Shall Overcome."[10]

At 7:50 p.m., Lewis took the podium. Calling the vote "the most important vote that we cast as members of this body," Lewis boomed, "We have a moral obligation to make health care a right and not a privilege." By this point, Pelosi, a consummate vote counter, knew the bill would pass. The margin was slim, 219–212, but it was enough to give President Obama the biggest legislative victory of his presidency.[11]

Along with the emergence of an angrier, populist right, the early Obama years also saw political ferment on the left. Though most of these young radicals professed admiration for Lewis, they didn't always pay lavish respect to his heroism of yore. In the fall of 2011, activists frustrated with deepening economic inequality in America—a condition exacerbated by the 2008 crash—took over Zuccotti Park near Wall Street in Manhattan. Calling themselves "Occupy Wall Street," they encamped for months. Copycat movements sprang up around the country, including in Atlanta.

On Saturday, October 8, in a show of solidarity, Lewis visited the Atlanta site, sprawled out across Woodruff Park. He came, he explained, "to say, 'I stand with you, I support you, what you're doing.'" Leading the proceedings when he arrived was a bearded, bespectacled man in a red T-shirt wielding a megaphone, who announced Lewis's appearance to the crowd. People cheered and clapped excitedly.

The bearded man—after chiding the group that applause was out of order (wiggling fingers was preferred)—asked if the group wished to hear Lewis. In keeping with Occupy practices, the bearded man spoke only three or four words at a time, pausing to let the crowd repeat each snatch of his sentences.

A second bearded man with glasses and a red T-shirt raised his hand. He praised Lewis, but added—again uttering fragments of three or four words that the crowd would echo—that no one was more valuable than anyone else, and a large agenda lay ahead of the group. Lewis, he said, should wait his turn. The first bearded man then claimed there was a "consensus" that Lewis should wait. The crowd howled and cried, "Let him speak." A woman in a billowy skirt and fuchsia jacket argued for hearing Lewis. By now five minutes had elapsed.

Lewis stood by good-naturedly. The spectacle was not unfamiliar to him; SNCC had also been enamored of radically democratic decision-making and went to excruciating lengths to make decisions. He continued to wait through more comments, more call-and-response, more shows of hands. Lewis had a seven o'clock meeting to get to. The sun was setting.

Finally, the man with the megaphone said again that there was no consensus to hear Lewis. With that, John and his aide Jared McKinley said thank you and walked away. Reporters trailed them. "What do you feel it says about this organizational process?" one asked. "It will work out," Lewis said with a smile. "They're growing, maturing. It will come of age."[12]

In late 2012, Lewis's staffers noticed that he was spending more time than usual in Atlanta, not returning to Washington immediately after the weekend, as he usually did. He didn't talk about it much, but the reason was Lillian's health.

Lillian had been suffering from kidney disease for more than a decade. She had stopped working in 2003. Since moving to Wallace Road in 2006, she had been housebound. Over the years she had gone through dialysis treatments, a kidney transplant, and more dialysis. On a couple of occasions, she was at death's door, and Lewis, John-Miles, and other loved ones came to Emory University Hospital to say goodbye. Once, Buddy Darden said, they had to don "space suits" because Lillian was immunocompromised. "She was in this room, and you had to put on this yellow thing all over yourself to go in," said Lyn Vaughn. "We just boo-hooed." John sobbed, convinced the end was near. "He wept. I mean, he just really wept." Lillian recovered, but the hospital stays continued, including a long sojourn in a nursing home.[13]

Lillian kept her medical condition private. Respecting her wishes, John also said little about her condition. Occasionally, to those few aides closest to him, he might say, "Mrs. Lewis is really sick. Got to pray for her." But her illness was never mentioned in the news. (Without any ballyhoo, Lewis sponsored legislation to fund research on kidney disease.) He did his best to take care of her. If Tom Houck was coming to visit, Lillian would ask him to smuggle in pizza from her favorite place. "You need to stop bringing her this," Lewis would chide Houck. "She's not supposed to be eating this."[14]

Yet Lewis still had duties in Washington or on the road. The Lewises hired a full-time caregiver, and others stepped in to help. John-Miles, now in his early thirties and a skilled cook, tended to his mother. So did several close female friends such as Carol Dove, Mignon Morman Willis, and Lyn Vaughn. Michael Collins was also conscripted. Their relationship had softened over time, and Lillian explained to him that her husband simply couldn't handle the logistics of her medical care. "I ended up talking to doctors," Collins later said. "And then I went down to Atlanta to find a nursing home with Mignon. By the end, I was literally feeding her."

At the end of December 2012, Congress had a full calendar, keeping everyone in session until New Year's Eve day. A late vote was scheduled. Afterward, Lewis planned to catch a 10:00 p.m. flight home.

At eight o'clock that morning, Dr. Antonio Guasch, Lillian's doctor at Emory Hospital, tried to call Lewis. After several unsuccessful attempts, he called Collins instead. He told him that Lillian had died.

Collins hurried over to Lewis's house. The congressman was still getting dressed.

"Congressman, come here," Collins said. "Sit down."

"No, I've got to get ready. I'm late," Lewis replied.

The two went back and forth. Finally Lewis sat down.

"I have some news for you," Collins said.

"What?"

"Mrs. Lewis passed."

Lewis was disbelieving. "How do you know?"

Collins explained that Guasch had called him after failing to reach Lewis. He took out his cell phone and called the doctor back, tapping the speakerphone icon. Guasch confirmed the news and shared the details.

Lillian's funeral was to be held at Ebenezer, where the Lewises had been married forty-four years earlier. Collins planned the funeral. One night in Atlanta, he and Lewis were sitting around. "That's why it's so important to be good to people," Lewis said. "Because you never know who's going to feed you your last supper."[15]

Lewis brought Lillian's casket to his home the night before the funeral. "I'm going to stand at attention," he said. "John-Miles and I. And I'm going to talk to her all night." In driving to the funeral, he said, he planned to follow a route that would include all of her favorite places.

On Monday, January 7, Raphael Warnock, the pastor at Ebenezer, presided over the funeral. Jennifer Holliday, star of the musical *Dreamgirls*, sang. Andrew Young, Jesse Jackson, Xernona Clayton, and Anita Hill all spoke. To the surprise of many, one old friend who showed up and even served as a flower bearer was Alice Clopton Bond.[16]

Lillian and Alice Bond had reconciled without public fanfare. Lewis also rebuilt a warm relationship with Michael Bond, Julian's son, who became a successful Atlanta politician. But John and Julian never fully reconstituted their friendship.

After losing his race in 1986, Bond had seen his life unravel. In early 1987, Alice had gone to the Atlanta police and reported his cocaine problems, setting off a tawdry scandal that turned their lives upside down. She retracted the worst of her accusations, but they soon divorced. Bond remarried, to Pamela Horowitz, and moved to Washington. He quit drugs and straightened out his life, teaching at the University of Virginia and American University. In 1998 the NAACP named him chairman.

Occasionally he and Lewis crossed paths. At first the encounters were awkward. Boyd Lewis, the journalist and photographer who had traveled the South with them in the 1970s, exhibited his photos in 1991 in an Atlanta gallery. Lewis and Bond both came to the opening. They smiled and joked. Bond said it was inevitable that they would come together sooner or later, Boyd Lewis recalled, "because they were both on the same team." Later, a visitor to the gallery noticed on the wall a photo depicting Bond and Lewis standing together—parallel vertical lines rising in the frame. Several paces back from the photograph stood the two men in the flesh, unconsciously mimicking the photo. Both stared straight ahead, gazing at the picture, silently.[17]

Three years later, Bond and Lewis both came to a dinner celebrating the seventy-fifth anniversary of the Southern Regional Council. Joan Browning saw Lewis arrive and motioned for him to join her table. On her other side was Bond. The two barely spoke. "It was frosty," Browning said. "They gave each other cold nods."[18]

In 1999, Michael Lomax, then president of Dillard University in New Orleans, decided to broker a reconciliation. He granted honorary degrees to both men, along with the historian Taylor Branch, a mutual friend. The three honorees, along with Pamela Bond, spent the weekend together in

New Orleans. Knowing how prim Lewis could be, Bond mischievously suggested that they dine at Lucky Cheng's, a gay bar and drag cabaret. Whether he hoped to make Lewis squirm or simply to foster an air of levity wasn't clear, but at first things went badly. "Our waiter was clearly a man in a dress and high heels and stockings and flamboyant makeup," Branch said. With an "instinct for who was the most squeamish person," the waiter "plopped down in John Lewis's lap at our table." Lewis was visibly uncomfortable, but he gamely bantered with the waiter.

When the waiter left, Lewis scolded Bond. "Whose idea was this?" he demanded. But in the course of the evening his irritation faded and the conversation flowed. He and Bond were able to relax with each other for the rest of the weekend. If it wasn't quite old times, Branch said, "it broke the ice."[19]

After that, they saw one another once in a while. In 2005, Bond interviewed Lewis for a series he was conducting for the University of Virginia, with no apparent signs of ill feeling. In later years Bond would take his students through the South on civil rights tours, and Lewis would talk to the group at Paschal's. In Washington, Lewis would sometimes invite Julian to meet constituent groups visiting the Capitol. They would also see each other at events like SNCC's fiftieth reunion. "He would say, 'Oh, we talked about it, we're all right,'" Michael Bond remembered about his father. "But he wouldn't say specifically, 'John apologized to me.'"[20]

Lewis liked to think they had patched up their rift. Though he never directly apologized to Bond, he came close to stating that he had been wrong to raise his friend's drug use in the 1986 campaign. "That probably was a low blow," he told filmmaker Kathleen Dowdey for her 2017 documentary *Get in the Way*. "Probably if I had to do that over again, I probably wouldn't do it."[21]

Bond, however, never fully forgave Lewis. "It was a break in the relationship that never healed," he told his colleague Phyllis Leffler in 2002. "We see each other from time to time, and I would like to think we're cordial. But it has never healed." Nonetheless, the same year, the NAACP, with Bond as chairman, gave Lewis its highest honor, the Spingarn Medal.[22]

In April 2014, the Lyndon Johnson Presidential Library held a multiday event on the fiftieth anniversary of the passage of the Civil Rights Act. Presidents Carter, Clinton, Bush Jr., and Obama all spoke. Lewis agreed to be on a panel with Bond, as well as Andrew Young. Beforehand, in the greenroom,

Bond began talking to Andrew Aydin and they ended up exchanging contact information. The next February, on Lewis's birthday, Bond called Aydin and told him not to pick up his phone the next time it rang; Bond wanted to leave a birthday voicemail for Lewis. He then called back. "Mr. Chairman," he said on the recording, "I was just calling to wish you a happy birthday." Aydin played it for Lewis, who seemed surprised but pleased by the gesture.[23]

Bond died in August 2015. Lewis posted a message on Twitter. "We went through a difficult period during our campaign for Congress in 1986," he wrote, "but many years ago we emerged even closer." The last part wasn't true. Lewis was not invited to Bond's funeral.[24]

On June 25, 2013, John Lewis was in the House cloakroom with Sean Patrick Maloney of New York, an up-and-coming Democratic star. Adjacent to the House floor, the cloakroom provided members a place to relax and talk, sometimes to plan strategy. There was a lunch counter with a TV perched above it. A report came on the TV about a Supreme Court ruling, in an Alabama case called *Shelby County v. Holder*, deeming key parts of the Voting Rights Act to be unconstitutional. Lewis's warnings about John Roberts had been prescient. Lewis turned to Maloney, calling him "little brother." He recounted standing behind LBJ's desk when the Voting Rights Act was signed in 1965. "And if you told me all these years later that we would still be fighting for voting rights," he added, "I just wouldn't believe you." He began to walk away but then turned back to Maloney. "And that's why it's going to be up to people like you," he said, "to make sure that we keep up the fight."[25]

The court's 5–4 decision, written by Roberts, was a clever piece of legal reasoning—a bank shot. It did not strike down Section 5 of the law, which required federal preclearance of any proposed changes to voting rules in the parts of the country under scrutiny. Rather, it terminated Section 4, which set forth how those localities subject to preclearance were chosen. But with Section 4 invalidated, Section 5 was hollowed out, rendered inert. The effect was to end the preclearance process, a bulwark against discrimination in voting.

In the years since Roberts's appointment, Lewis had closely watched the many new state-level attempts to limit ballot access. After the 2010

midterms, when Democrats lost control of many statehouses and gover-
norships as well as the House of Representatives, those efforts multiplied.
Thirty-four states were proposing restrictions. Lewis warned from the
House floor that "voting rights are under attack in America." He tried to get
the Obama administration to take action. But, he noted ruefully, "no one
seemed to be listening." The votes weren't there.[26]

Earlier in 2013, as he watched *Shelby County* wend its way to the Supreme Court, Lewis had filed an amicus brief supporting the government in
which he laid out myriad ways that the preclearance provision was still pre-
venting racial discrimination. The next month he attended oral arguments
in the case, almost breaking down in tears when he heard Justice Antonin
Scalia compare the Voting Rights Act to a "racial entitlement." He could see
which way the court was leaning.[27]

Still, the decision came as a blow. In the *Washington Post*, Lewis called
it "a dagger in the heart of the Voting Rights Act." He tried to organize the
House to pass legislation that would make the preclearance provisions of
the Voting Rights Act functional again. A few Republicans, like Jim Sensenbrenner, lent support. Nancy Pelosi wanted to name it the John Lewis Voting
Rights Act. But with Republicans in the majority, the idea went nowhere.[28]

Like Mike Campbell going bankrupt in Hemingway's *The Sun Also Rises*,
John Lewis's stature had risen two ways: gradually and then suddenly. Early
in the new century, he had noticed a spike in speaking invitations, awards,
honorary degrees, and other recognitions. "The demands on his time are
just stunning," George Dusenbury, Lewis's district director, told a reporter.
"If he wanted to, he could be speaking 24 hours a day." Lewis was mystified.
"I don't know why it's happening," he said. The bestowal of laurels only ac-
celerated as the years went on, culminating—though not ending—with his
receipt of the Presidential Medal of Freedom in February 2011.[29]

This lionization had many sources, including his sheer longevity. As eminent colleagues from the movement died, Lewis was now the most visible
link to an era passing into history. But instrumental, too, were Lewis's own
activities, which he undertook to keep alive knowledge of the movement
and his role within it.

Lewis did so purposefully and even strategically. It was not because he adored the limelight—although he wasn't immune to the blandishments of fame—but rather because he wanted to equip Americans with the knowledge, the will, and the tools to continue the fight. Lewis, said Michael Collins, "drilled into the conscience of America that the civil rights movement had meaning and had a place when everybody forgot about it, when people didn't recognize it, and the people were not valued. And it became a whole new movement for people to recognize and to use. And I really believe that he single-handedly gave a rebirth to the civil rights movement in the modern day."[30]

One unlikely role for Lewis in this regard was that of comic book author. In 2008, after the agony of the Obama-Hillary ordeal and ensuing primary challenge, Lewis's aide Andrew Aydin, a self-professed "comic book nerd," had mentioned that he planned to relax by going to a comic book convention. His office mates mocked him.

"You shouldn't laugh," Lewis interjected. Back in 1957, Lewis said, the Fellowship of Reconciliation had published a ten-cent comic book, *Martin Luther King and the Montgomery Story*, about the bus boycott, which had helped inspire Lewis and other young people to get involved.

A while later, Aydin proposed that Lewis write a comic book himself—a graphic memoir—about his movement years. It would be another way to teach the history to younger generations. Lewis demurred, but Aydin persisted. "Yes, I'll do it," Lewis finally said, "but only if you write it with me."[31]

They began working in 2009. Two years later they had signed a contract with Top Shelf Productions in Atlanta, a publisher of graphic novels. The publisher recruited illustrator Nate Powell. Lewis got permission from the House Ethics Committee for a contract that would give the three coauthors royalties.[32]

Lewis threw himself into the project with such vigor that Aydin and Powell strained to keep pace. "He works so hard it's a constant struggle to keep up with him," Aydin said. "It taught me to stay up late and to get up early, but it was hard to keep my game face on when I was holding eighteen-hour days." As Michael D'Orso had done for *Walking with the Wind*, Aydin traveled with Lewis to Nashville, Selma, and other stations of his personal cross. Powell often joined them. Given everyone's demands, it was hard to find time when all three could focus on the book. But Lewis made it a priority. The work gave him an outlet for his energies, especially after Lillian's death.

The first manuscript draft came to around three hundred pages. Top Shelf decided to publish a trilogy instead of a single book. The first installment would be released in August 2013, on the fiftieth anniversary of the March on Washington. The later volumes would be pegged to commemorations of the Civil Rights Act and Voting Rights Act.[33]

A month before its publication, Lewis previewed *March: Book One* at the San Diego Comic-Con. The annual comic book convention had recently exploded into a colossal jamboree for not just industry professionals but also fans of comics, superheroes, video games, and science fiction. Top Shelf had scheduled an hour-long question-and-answer discussion with Lewis, as well as multiple book-signing sessions. But the level of interest dwarfed everyone's expectations. Fans camped out for hours to meet Lewis. NBC News showed up to interview him. Lou Ferrigno, who played the Incredible Hulk on TV, waited in line to shake his hand.[34]

"There were thousands of people there, not just from the U.S., but from Europe, from Japan, from Central and South America," Lewis said. "A lot of people were in costume, looking like Batman or Superman or whatever. I was almost moved to tears by some of them. They would come up and start crying and saying, 'I never thought I would meet you.' . . . It was very, very moving."[35]

March: Book One became an instant bestseller. Schoolteachers used it in their classrooms, librarians in their community programming. Lewis and his collaborators realized they had to finish the next two volumes quickly. And because *March* was now being taught in history classes, the authors felt an extra obligation to ensure its accuracy. They took pains to set the record straight.[36]

Adding to their burden, they had to write and draw the remaining volumes while promoting the first volume at bookstores and festivals. "From 2014 to 2016, we traveled pretty much every week," Nate Powell said. Lewis hit speaker series and universities, news programs and late-night shows. He found a following in the younger generations. On *The Late Show with Stephen Colbert*, he crowd-surfed, allowing the enthralled studio audience to hold his body aloft and propel it from row to row. The video went viral. In

2015, he returned to Comic-Con garbed in his own costume, based on his Bloody Sunday outfit—black suit, skinny tie, white trench coat, backpack— and led a throng of starstruck children through the convention center. Kids came to his book events dressed in their own John Lewis uniforms. He had become a superhero.[37]

Powell and Aydin exhausted themselves in the race to finish. Powell, who had two young kids, developed shingles; his wife quit her job because he needed to work six full days a week. Aydin also got sick, with an auto-immune disorder. "It took two years for each of us separately to move to a healthy mental and physical state," Powell said. But *March* had reached a whole new generation of Americans, educating them about Lewis and the movement.[38]

The *March* phenomenon peaked in November 2016 when Lewis, Aydin, and Powell won the National Book Award for Young People's Literature, for the third volume. Dressed in a tuxedo, Lewis fought back tears in accepting the award at the New York City ceremony. He spoke about his childhood love of reading and his own wish as a young boy to obtain a library card in Troy, only to be turned away because he was Black. The video of that event, too, went viral.[39]

As important as March *in* launching Lewis into superstardom were his an-nual trips to Selma. John rarely missed an anniversary commemoration— whether of the March on Washington or other high points of the civil rights era. He went to reunions of the Freedom Riders and SNCC. "The congress-man wasn't a historian, but he was history," said Collins, who spent a good part of his two decades with Lewis planning and attending anniversaries. "And he wanted to mark occasions. He was very, very clear about that."[40]

Of all the milestones that Lewis observed, Bloody Sunday stood apart. "I think every student should know that Selma changed America forever," he explained in 2014. "Selma, this little town on the banks of the Alabama River, made it possible for all our citizens to become participants in a dem-ocratic process." He called his trips *pilgrimages*. "The word, it's very im-portant," he explained. "We're not tourists. In a sense, we're seekers, seeking inspiration, seeking to learn, to know, . . . in a sense to be renewed."[41]

Ever since his first trip back with journalist Pat Watters in 1969, Lewis

had returned to Selma annually to cross the Edmund Pettus Bridge, sometimes in small groups, sometimes in large demonstrations. At first, the Voter
Education Project had organized the events. Later, SCLC took the lead.
Then in the early 1990s, Hank and Rose Sanders, Harvard Law School
classmates who had married and settled in Selma in 1971, took charge of an
annual "jubilee" that drew big crowds, including Lewis.[42]

Interest in the Selma trips surged after 1997, when Lewis became co-
chair, with Republican Amo Houghton, of the board of the Faith and Politics Institute, a Washington-based organization that worked to surmount
racial, religious, and ideological differences among politicians. Run by Doug
Tanner, a Methodist minister, Faith and Politics hosted retreats and workshops for members of Congress. At one weekend retreat in Hershey, Pennsylvania, in March 1997, Lewis bade an early goodbye to Tanner, explaining
that he was due in Selma for the bridge-crossing.

"I wish I could come, too," Tanner said.

"I'd bet a lot of your colleagues would, too," Kathy Gille, Tanner's wife,
said to Lewis. The idea of a congressional outing was born.

Lewis liked the idea of bringing colleagues with him. Here was another
way to spread knowledge about the movement's history, one that might
also salve the partisan wounds that festered under Gingrich. The next year,
Lewis invited a passel of his colleagues to join him under the Faith and Politics banner on a trip to Montgomery, Birmingham, and Selma. It would
conclude with a march across the Pettus Bridge.

The group was small enough to fly together on Southwest Airlines. Over
three days they visited historic sites across Alabama, including the Sixteenth
Street Baptist Church in Birmingham and the statehouse in Montgomery,
traveling in a single coach bus, whose monitors played clips from the documentary *Eyes on the Prize*. "John had real enthusiasm. He was providing a
running commentary all the way," Tanner said afterward. "It's like going to
Normandy with Dwight Eisenhower," Amo Houghton said.[43]

On Friday, in Montgomery, the group visited an ailing George Wallace,
who was lying in a hospital bed in his house, smoking a cigar, watching a
documentary about himself, and using a computer to communicate. A few
Northern liberals on the trip balked at entering the room, not wanting to
be photographed or seen with the notorious segregationist. Earl Hilliard, a
Black congressman who represented Selma, laughed. "You white boys have

to get over this," he said, waltzing in. In Selma, they all attended services at Brown Chapel and lunched with Mayor Smitherman.[44]

When the members returned to Washington, Lewis set aside an hour of floor time for them to talk about their journey. Houghton compared it to "my trip to the Holy Land. It was a religious experience." Sheila Jackson Lee of Texas called it "another singular moment in our history." Sherrod Brown, Eliot Engel, and Fred Upton expressed awe over Lewis's lack of rancor toward old adversaries like Wallace and Smitherman. "We love him," Upton said. "We love all that he did for America and for this House . . . then and now." Republican John Shimkus of Illinois, who was wielding the gavel during all these speeches, was so bowled over by the testimony that he signed up to go himself. In 1999, when Faith and Politics repeated the ritual, twenty members came along.[45]

For Selma's thirty-fifth anniversary, in 2000, Lewis brought along Bill Clinton—the first sitting president to come. Press attention mushroomed. Scores of civil rights veterans signed on, including Coretta Scott King, Hosea Williams, Andrew Young, Jesse Jackson, and Julian Bond. C-SPAN broadcast Clinton's speech and others from the foot of the bridge. Joining hands with Lewis and Mrs. King, the president led the walk up the bridge's slope. On the other side, state troopers were lined up, as in 1965. This time they saluted.[46]

Thereafter the pilgrimage became a hot ticket. Members brought their families. Selma would run out of hotel rooms. The programming expanded. Guests heard from Selma heroes like Amelia Boynton, F. D. Reese, and J. L. Chestnut. One year Jack Valenti and other Johnson administration officials came. Another year it was David Halberstam and the civil rights reporters. Or it was Bishop Tutu. A film about the pilgrimages, *Come Walk in My Shoes*, was screened in the Lyndon B. Johnson Room of the Capitol and aired on PBS.[47]

Lewis took pains to make sure his colleagues—especially the Republicans—got the most out of their trips. Eric Cantor, the House Republican leader, once brought his son, who was learning in school about Ruby Bridges, the six-year-old who in 1960 had integrated a New Orleans grade school; the Cantors were overwhelmed when they met Bridges herself. Another time, Kevin McCarthy, Cantor's successor, was moved when Lewis slowed down the entire march so that McCarthy and his family, walking by Lewis's side, wouldn't be separated from him. For Sam Brownback, who one year had to leave the pilgrimage early, Lewis rose at 5:30 a.m. to provide a personal predawn escort across the bridge. He did the same years later for John Larson and his children, who had to go home early because school exams beckoned.[48]

Lewis was always at the center of it—planning, organizing, preaching, teaching, hugging, crying, marching. "I spend a great deal of time" getting colleagues to come, he told an interviewer in 2014. "Even on the floor today, several members asked me about it, said they were going. They're going to bring their children, going to bring their wives or husbands or someone from their church." The Selma campaign was now firmly linked in the public mind with Lewis.[49]

The pilgrimages provided Lewis with their share of headaches as well. Not everyone checked their egos, and some guests would elbow their way to the front row of the marching column. "Jesse Jackson would always try to get to the head of the parade, get his Rainbow Coalition situated ahead, as if he'd been there," said Steny Hoyer, who made the pilgrimage sixteen times. "John was annoyed. He didn't say anything. He didn't do anything. But you could tell." One friend of Lewis's, confused by Jackson's recurring presence, asked, "What did Jesse do at Selma?" Lewis replied, "He watched."[50]

Friction also developed between Faith and Politics and Rose and Hank Sanders. Rose, who in later years went by Faya Ora Rose Touré, chafed when the elected officials were shepherded to the head of the line, insisting that "foot soldiers"—other participants from the 1965 marches—have a space at the front. She also resented that Faith and Politics and the congressional visitors didn't give more money to her cash-strapped local organization. The conflicts tried Lewis's tolerance. Sometimes in later years he would ask his staff, "Do we really have to go this year?" Knowing the ritual's importance, Lewis continued to go.

For the fiftieth anniversary, in 2015, Lewis wanted something extra special. The *Shelby County* decision had made safeguarding voting rights urgent. The feature film *Selma*, released in December 2014, had piqued public interest in the town's history and significance. Recent high-profile killings by police officers of Michael Brown and Eric Garner, unarmed Black men, had made national issues again of police brutality and racial justice. Lewis also knew that anniversaries could train media and public attention on an event and "create a new resurgence to go forward," as Collins said. "The conversations were about making sure as many people as possible could have access to this opportunity to be renewed. He believed young people should have an opportunity to learn and witness firsthand. He believed in drama, and he wanted to dramatize this. He wanted to show it front and center, everything it could be."[51]

Lewis wanted President Obama and all the living former presidents to come to Selma. "The congressman was clear," recalled Collins, who oversaw the arrangements. "He wanted all the presidents to be there. And I invited all of them." But problems arose. By the time invitations went out, Clinton was committed to a major event for his foundation. Carter and the elder George Bush were too frail to attend.

One invitee who accepted was George W. Bush. Bush asked only that he not be asked to speak. "If my presence is going to make any difference," he said, "I need to be on that bridge with John. And I don't need to say a thing."

Obama's participation was more complicated. Lewis had scheduled the festivities for March 7, the actual anniversary of Bloody Sunday, which fell on a Saturday, and invited Obama. But Rose Sanders, determined to hold the jubilee on Sunday, sent the White House her own invitation, for March 8. "The White House was in a pickle," said Collins said, who had to "massage this relationship and all the drama with it." After excruciating negotiations, they agreed that Obama would "speak but not march" on Saturday, as the *Atlanta Journal-Constitution* reported, while the official march would occur on Sunday.[52]

To build interest, Lewis made an early trip to Selma with journalists. "We had to get him in front of everybody who might be vying for the spotlight," Brenda Jones explained. Lewis spent ten hours with reporters and photographers cooperating with advance stories that would build interest in the anniversary. Back in Washington, he recruited a record number of colleagues—one hundred—to join the pilgrimage, "including a bumper crop of Republicans," the *Journal-Constitution* noted. Lyndon Johnson's daughters, Lynda Bird and Luci, came, as did the 103-year-old Amelia Boynton. President Obama brought not only Michelle but also his daughters, Malia and Sasha. On Saturday, March 7, forty thousand people converged on the small city's downtown to hear the president and Lewis speak.[53]

Obama opened his remarks with a tribute to Lewis and the other Selma

marchers of 1965. Playing the role of historian, he painted the scene from
fifty years before in which "John Lewis led them out of the church on a mission to change America." He then wove together trials and triumphs from
throughout American history to render a story of persistent if fitful progress
toward freedom. The second half of his speech connected the story to the
present and the ongoing quest for true racial equality. "If Selma has taught
us anything," Obama said, in a line that Lewis could have spoken, "it's that
our work is never done." He gestured at the killings that had relaunched conversations about race and racism—the police killings of Brown in Missouri
and Garner in New York and, two years before that, a vigilante's slaying of
teenager Trayvon Martin in Florida. Obama concluded with a pitch to restore the Voting Rights Act to its pre-*Shelby* potency.[54]

When the speeches were done, a token crew of fifty VIPs queued up
behind Lewis and the Obamas. Before setting off, Lewis once again narrated
his memories of the fateful encounter. The group walked, as the *Washington Post* noted, "partway" across the bridge—a gesture designed to honor
the compromise with Rose Sanders. At the front, Lewis stood between the
Obamas, holding their hands. George and Laura Bush disappeared into the
middle of the pack. They all sang "Keep Your Eyes on the Prize," one of Lewis's favorite freedom songs.[55]

It all made for great television, but those in attendance experienced the
power of the event at a personal level. In 2015, as in other years, colleagues
told Lewis afterward of the journey's transformative power. "They feel like
it's a conversion, that they are changed," Lewis explained, "and they'll say
to their fellow members who didn't go, 'You need to go. . . . If you don't do
anything else over your congressional career, go to Selma, Alabama, with
John Lewis.'"[56]

Obama continued to work with Lewis in keeping alive the memory
of the Black freedom struggle. During Black History Month of 2016, the
White House invited Lewis and C. T. Vivian, along with Black activists of
younger generations, to a meeting in the Roosevelt Room. "We called it an
intergenerational civil rights meeting," said Valerie Jarrett, a close adviser to
Obama. One purpose was to help the young radicals appreciate how hard it
had been to secure the gains of the 1960s and afterward. "It was one of the
best meetings we've ever had," Jarrett recalled, with fruitful conversations
across boundaries of age and ideology.

What Obama remembered most vividly was a moment when Lewis and Vivian "started bringing up what it meant for them to be there in the White House with me," he said. Lewis and Vivian both started choking up. "To see the physical, emotional response for them, of the distance they traveled, the inevitable doubts that they must've carried, the decades of backlash. . . . For them to feel, not that we've made it, but just that we could all be sitting there together—and this is a person who could be their child who was actually running the federal government—it was just a reminder of how hard they had worked and how much they had sacrificed. And to hear that in their voices, that meant a lot."[57]

Besides March and the pilgrimages, Lewis's office undertook other stratagems to raise the congressman's already-lofty profile and, with it, public interest in the movement. For years, the staff had tried to interest filmmakers in documenting his life and career. But the deals foundered on questions of editorial control and royalties. Would-be film directors expected broad access to Lewis and discretion to make the films they wished. But Lewis and his aides envisioned a coauthored project like *Walking with the Wind* or *March* in which as co-creators they would shape the film and reap some royalties. Despite these conflicts, two independent documentaries were ultimately made, Kathleen Dowdey's *Get in the Way* (2017) and Dawn Porter's *Good Trouble* (2020).

Lewis also became a popular television guest, and not just on news programs. On *Finding Your Roots*, Harvard professor Henry Louis Gates Jr. and his staff traced Lewis's genealogy back to their enslavement; on the kids' cartoon *Arthur*, an animated Lewis and the show's eponymous aardvark staged a sit-in to help a beleaguered lunch lady. The city of Atlanta also honored Lewis with a series of tributes, including a permanent display at Hartsfield-Jackson Airport and, in a delicious irony, by renaming the roadway to the Carter Center "John Lewis Freedom Parkway."

Leading the communications operation, Brenda Jones kept Lewis in the news. "What I was hired to do was to build his status and influence within the press," she acknowledged, "so that his iconic status is something people were aware of—not just on Capitol Hill or in Atlanta, but nationally and internationally." With Lewis, she wrote *Across That Bridge*, a compact book of his life's wisdom, which further spread the Lewis gospel. Andrew Aydin built a social media presence that included the newly coined hashtag #goodtrouble. The phrase, which Lewis had been using for only a few years, suddenly became his tagline, a staple of every speech and talk-show chat.[58]

Lewis's online fan base grew to the point where it could produce unintended viral moments. In March 2014, after a belated birthday celebration for Lewis in the Atlanta office that featured a Caribbean buffet and dessert from a local bakery, Lewis and his staff were feeling punchy. Someone played Pharrell Williams's song "Happy," a Lewis favorite, and after a brief protest—"I'm so full I can't even move"—he began snapping and swinging his hips in the hallway, to everyone's delight. "Break it down, Congressman," cheered on Rachelle O'Neil, who recorded his impromptu shimmy on her phone. "I usually don't make things public," O'Neil later said. "But my office staff members begged me to make it public so they could share it with their friends." She posted it on Facebook with the hashtag #TooMuchCake. "Once I made it public, it took on a life of its own." The next morning, when she awoke to go to the gym, "people were still calling me at like five or six in the morning." Internet sites picked it up; so did news shows like CNN's *Inside Politics*. The joyfully dancing John Lewis that friends had loved for years was now revealed to the American public. "You wouldn't put him on a Broadway stage," said his friend Shirley Franklin, the two-term mayor of Atlanta, "but he had a ball doing it."[59]

The cumulative effect of all of these activities—March, the Selma trips, the awards, the viral videos—propelled Lewis to a celebrity of a different order. It became hard for him to walk in public without being accosted. In 2016, as Lewis was ambling through Greenwich Village after speaking at New York University's commencement, a burly truck driver stopped his rig in the middle of West Fourth Street and hopped out to shake the congressman's hand, snarling traffic. Once, in Atlanta, O'Neil watched as a man in the window of a sandwich shop glimpsed Lewis strolling by. "We're literally walking and you can look in the window of Quiznos and see it in real time. This person was like putting the sandwich up to their mouth to eat, threw the entire sandwich down, and ran outside just to shake his hand." A little later, "this car just comes to a screeching halt and that person jumps out of their car"—also to pay respects. On public occasions, the attention was even more intense. On the fiftieth anniversary of the March on Washington, said Danny Lyon, who spent the day with Lewis on the Mall, "he did TV interviews all day. Everyone wanted him. The security guard wants to shake his hand. He was like Madonna." Visitors wept after ordinary encounters. "I nicknamed him Baby Jesus," O'Neil said. "I said, 'They want to come and touch the hem of your garment.'"[60]

Lewis didn't make his aides' lives easier by shaking every hand, posing for every picture, signing every autograph. His friend Don Harris once invited Lewis to keynote a Kennedy-King dinner that Harris organized, imagining they would have time to catch up afterward. "He spoke to six hundred or seven hundred people," Harris recalled. "Every single one wanted to shake his hand or get his autograph. You just have to let that go on for an hour. I was standing around while he said hi to all seven hundred before we could go out together." Even when Lewis would go out for a quiet dinner with a friend, a steady stream of patrons would come by the table; Stephen McDaniel, who witnessed many such moments, would think to himself, "The man's in the middle of eating. Can't this wait?" Airports were an obstacle course of exuberant admirers and chatty families, a sea of outstretched hands and cell phones. Asked to describe walking with his father to his plane, John-Miles gave a one-word response: "Tedious."[61]

But if Lewis enjoyed the recognition, he was never motivated by the trappings of celebrity. "There's several athletes I've met over the years who were superstars, but they just refused to be superstars," said J. C. Watts. They never let fame go to their heads. Lewis, he said, was exactly that way. "If John's not in front of a microphone," Watts said, "I don't know if you would know that that was John Lewis, if you didn't know it was John Lewis."[62]

Chapter Twenty-Six

CONSCIENCE OF
THE CONGRESS

■ ■

The occupation of Iraq was over. The economy was fairly strong. But as Barack Obama's presidency entered its final year, tremors triggered by the war and the 2008 crash were still rattling the body politic.

Obama's policies had averted economic catastrophe. They had revived growth and brought down unemployment. The Affordable Care Act had fortified the social safety net. But other major proposals—to arrest global warming, curb gun violence, and solve the immigration crisis—had failed. More surprising, given the early hopes, racial strife in America was worsening. On the right, the anger that had fueled the Tea Party in 2010 was still boiling, especially in areas untouched by the recovery. On the left, outrage over inequality had birthed the improbable presidential candidacy of the dyspeptic Vermont senator Bernie Sanders, a seventy-five-year-old unabashed socialist.

Never one to chase bandwagons, Lewis in the presidential race remained bound to Hillary Clinton, who was running again. Lewis felt bad about having forsaken her eight years ago—though he still believed that supporting Obama had been the right thing to do—and he refused to let another upstart steal her thunder. Lewis endorsed Clinton early, in October 2015, with a heartfelt statement describing her as "tireless in her advocacy for those who have been left out and left behind."

Since her 2008 slugfest with Obama, Clinton had mostly repaired the reputational damage she had incurred among African Americans. But

Lewis's full-throated testimonial still furnished some additional validation. Later that October, he stood beside her onstage at Clark Atlanta University as she reeled off ideas for criminal justice reform, including revised sentencing guidelines and an end to racial profiling—a direct response to the newly urgent demand to purge racism from the penal system.

The event didn't go well. After the introductions, young Black Lives Matter demonstrators, indignant about the 1994 crime bill that she (and Sanders) had supported, heckled and taunted Clinton. "By this time," Clinton recalled, "I was alone on the stage. John had gone to sit in the first row along with all the other dignitaries.

"Usually with hecklers," Clinton continued, "you wait for them to kind of quiet down or be escorted out, you don't engage them. But all of a sudden, John and a few others came back up on the stage, kind of walked up to the microphone and just began trying to take them to school." Lewis and Kasim Reed, the mayor of Atlanta, implored the activists to hear her out, to no avail. "It was so touching to me," Clinton said, "because he knew my record, he knew the trenches we'd been in together, he understood what I was trying to do, and he wasn't going to sit idly by." As the disruptions continued, the Clinton fans in the room—an overwhelming majority—loudly chanted, "Let her speak!" until guards ushered the protesters away amid celebratory applause. Afterward, Lewis was charitable toward the students. "They were trying to make a point," he said empathically, "to dramatize what they're concerned about."[1]

Over the next months, Sanders channeled the anger of the radical left and alienated youth. Ratcheting up his attacks on Clinton, he sent her unfavorable ratings soaring. Although he posed nothing like the threat to her nomination that Obama had, Hillaryland veterans flashed back to the winter of 2007 when her front-runner status had dissipated. She eked out a one-point win in the 2016 Iowa caucuses on February 1, but the narrowness of that victory, followed by Sanders's triumph in New Hampshire on February 9, sparked a full-blown panic.

Black voters' allegiances kept Clinton ahead. With primaries approaching in Georgia and South Carolina, Sanders knew he had to make inroads with African Americans. He talked up his role fifty-four years earlier in sit-ins at the University of Chicago, when he was an undergraduate, protesting the university's ownership of segregated apartments. Some journalists doubted Sanders's account. An old black-and-white photo of him sitting in was circulating online, but some of his friends said the picture was actually of a classmate.[2]

Lewis believed that Sanders held honorable, liberal views on race. But having known friends who had devoted years to the movement, he was bothered that Sanders was exaggerating his role—pointing to one campus action as if to imply that he had been deeply immersed in the yearslong struggle.

On February 11, to shore up Clinton after her New Hampshire loss, Lewis and other Black Caucus members held a press conference. In response to a question, Lewis gently scoffed at the notion of Sanders as a pioneer in the fight for racial justice. "I never saw him. I never met him," Lewis said. "I chaired the Student Nonviolent Coordinating Committee for three years from 1963 to 1966. I was involved in the sit-ins, the Freedom Rides, the March on Washington, the march from Selma to Montgomery and directed the Voter Education Project for six years. I met Hillary Clinton. I met President Clinton."[3]

The remarks infuriated Sanders's devotees. On Twitter—which political reporters now followed obsessively—so-called Bernie Bros labeled Lewis a sellout. When Lewis's staff posted to his public Facebook page a picture of the congressman cuddling a puppy, a barrage of mean-spirited jibes littered the comments.

Danny Lyon, who as a University of Chicago student had photographed the 1962 housing protests, realized he had taken the photo of Sanders that was making the rounds. He dug up his contact sheets to make sure. On his blog, Lyon vouched that it was Sanders. The blog, which normally drew maybe twenty viewers a day, got eighty-five thousand hits. *Time* magazine ran a story. Lewis was counseled to walk back his comments.

Three days later, he did so. "The fact that I did not meet him in the movement does not mean I doubted that Senator Sanders participated in the civil rights movement," Lewis said. "Neither was I attempting to disparage his activism. Thousands sacrificed in the 1960s whose names we will never know, and I have always given honor to their contribution." The comments quelled the furor.[4]

Lewis's own annoyance with Sanders took longer to subside. Shortly before the Nevada primary in February, Lewis served as a media surrogate for Clinton after a joint appearance with Sanders in Las Vegas. "John would just get so frustrated," Clinton recalled, "because he had known Sanders in the in the House, and he would just go, 'No, no, he shouldn't be president!'" As Lewis spoke to the press that night, Clinton and her staff were a little startled by the harshness of his criticisms of Sanders. "He almost went too far in a way," she said. Afterward, she and her staff took Lewis for "pizza and hamburgers and French fries at this Las Vegas hotel" and teased him about his over-the-top rhetoric. "We were saying, 'Now, John, you're a Christian. You shouldn't be saying those things!' I was laughing. We had such a good time. I mean, he's remembered for literally putting his body on the line for civil rights. But he was also fun. He was fun to be around. He was fun to talk to."[5]

Clinton defeated Sanders in Nevada and then trounced him in South Carolina, Georgia, and other states. Her nomination was secure. But the Sanders challenge—and the rage behind it—was not abating.[6]

Far more disturbing was the ressentiment fueling the candidacy of real estate mogul turned reality show host Donald Trump. Though Trump had flirted with politics for decades, he had only lately become serious about it, amassing a huge following thanks to his scathing contempt for both parties' establishments and his willingness to tear into anyone who stood in his way. Racial as well as cultural and economic grievances powered the Trump phenomenon; if past Republican leaders had used dog whistles to speak to white disgruntlement, Trump preferred a megaphone, heedless of reproof from any liberal arbiters.

To Lewis, Trump's style reeked of George Wallace. Both men thrived on sticking it to the authorities, drawing strength from their delight in transgressing rules of fair play. Both celebrated the violence at their rallies, the better to inspire a frisson of fear. "It's a reasonable comparison," Lewis told the *New York Times*. "See, I don't think Wallace believed in all that stuff he was preaching. I think Wallace said a lot of stuff just to get ahead. I don't think Trump really believes in all this stuff. But he thinks this would be his ticket to the White House—at least to get the Republican nomination."

Lewis lamented that Trump's surge was driving a right-wing Republican Party further right. Partisanship had been thwarting constructive policymaking since Gingrich's ascent, but now—except maybe for the Selma pilgrimages—almost no one socialized or interacted across the aisle. With

Obama's election, the Beloved Community had seemed, if not at hand, then discernible on the horizon. Now it was receding from view.[7]

Nowhere did the stranglehold of partisanship prove more tragic than in the failure to achieve gun-control measures like those that had passed under Clinton. A spate of high-profile mass shootings in the 2000s—at Virginia Tech University in 2007, a Connecticut grade school in 2012, a Black church in Charleston in 2015, a San Bernardino government center also in 2015—aroused an intense desire for federal action. But with power split between the parties and Republicans all but uniformly opposed to new firearm restrictions, nothing happened.

In the early hours of June 12, 2016, a twenty-nine-year-old Afghan American named Omar Mateen, who had pledged fealty to the jihadist group ISIS, walked into Pulse, a gay nightclub in Orlando, Florida, where 320 revelers were drinking, talking, and dancing. Mateen carried a semiautomatic rifle and a semiautomatic pistol. He opened fire, killing forty-nine people and wounding fifty-three in a massacre that immediately took its place as the deadliest shooting in United States history.* Mateen was killed by the police.

As had become typical after these slaughters, Democrats repeated their call for gun-control measures. Republicans denied that new restrictions would deter homicidal maniacs; they said the problems were mental illness and Islamist extremism. Desperate to make headway, Democrats rallied behind a bill they called "no fly, no buy," which would prevent people on the government's list of terrorist suspects from purchasing guns, and a second bill mandating background checks for all gun buyers. But they knew that their chances of passing the bills were slim.

About a week after the Pulse killings, a small group of Democrats—David Cicilline of Rhode Island, Katherine Clark of Massachusetts, John Larson of Connecticut, Robin Kelly of Illinois—met to brainstorm. They were searching for an offbeat or dramatic idea to break the logjam. One idea was to attempt a discharge petition, an arcane congressional maneuver

---

* It would be surpassed sixteen months later by a massacre in Las Vegas.

used to force a bill out of committee. But that would require getting roughly thirty Republican votes. It had no chance.

On Tuesday, June 21, they held another meeting, with a larger contingent of Democrats present, including Lewis. Cicilline rolled out a new idea: One after another, members of their crew would descend to the well of the House and make one-minute speeches about Congress's failure to act. Then each one of them would simply stay in the well. "We would just say, 'We're not going to leave until action is taken,'" Cicilline recalled.

Lewis offered an amendment. "Maybe we should sit down," he said.

Everything clicked. "I just remember thinking, 'Oh, my God, of course!'" Cicilline said. "That was the way to annex this struggle to this incredibly powerful history of sit-ins in the civil rights movement that John Lewis was just such an important leader of. That was actually the genius of that moment." Lewis would be the gambit's public face.[8]

For Lewis, the air of hushed anticipation around the preparations evoked the sit-in planning in Kelly Miller Smith's church basement in 1960. No more than two dozen colleagues were in on the plan. "Most of the members didn't even know what was ahead for us," Lewis said. "We never said anything or shared anything." Because the plan would violate House rules, they kept it secret from Pelosi and Hoyer. Lewis also kept it secret from his staff, though they suspected something was up. On Wednesday morning, June 22, when most House Democrats were toasting Hillary Clinton, who was visiting the Hill, Larson was furtively asking the House parliamentarian what would happen if they occupied the House. It was "hard to know," the parliamentarian said: it had never been done.[9]

When the House convened at 10:00 a.m., things began normally. Republicans and Democrats alternated five-minute speeches. Clark, Cicilline, Kelly, and others spoke about the Orlando murders. They called for action on the Democrats' "commonsense" bills.

At 11:18 a.m., Lewis claimed the podium. He wore a dark blue suit, a light blue square-patterned tie, and a rainbow Gay Pride ribbon in honor of the Pulse victims. "Mr. Speaker," he began, "I will ask that all of my colleagues join me on the floor." With that, twenty-six members walked forward and stood with him in a long cordon, two or three people deep.

"We have lost hundreds of thousands of innocent people to gun violence," he cried. "What has this body done? Mr. Speaker, nothing. Not one thing." Lewis continued for five minutes, modulating his voice, sometimes thunderous, sometimes quietly quavering. "Give us a vote! Let us vote!" he said, pounding the lectern.

Lewis gave his colleagues their marching orders. "Now is the time to find a way for us to dramatize it, to make it real," he said. "We have to occupy the floor of the House until there is action."[10]

Lewis stepped forward and bent on one knee. He settled his seventy-six-year-old body onto the blue carpeting. About fifteen others joined him, gently lowering themselves as well. Several others stood in the well in support.

The presiding officer, Republican Ted Poe, was flummoxed. He gaveled the session into recess. In a throwback to their 1995 conflict, the Republicans shut off the C-SPAN cameras. Democrats chanted, "No bill, no break."

At noon, Poe tried reopening the session. But after a prayer and the Pledge of Allegiance, the Democrats resumed their chants, and Poe had to recess again. The Democrats held the floor unencumbered.

At first, Pelosi and Hoyer were unhappy with the guerrilla theater. "We got some sense," Cicilline said, "that they were furious." But the leaders quickly shifted course. "We'll be here as long as it takes," Pelosi told the press.[11]

From the back of the room, Hoyer watched with satisfaction. Kevin McCarthy, his Republican counterpart, walked up to him. "We need to stop this," McCarthy said.

"Well," Hoyer said with a smile, "you can have him carried off the floor." He need only call the Capitol Police.

McCarthy shot Hoyer a baffled look. "I'm going to have John Lewis carried off the floor?" he asked. "Are you crazy?"[12]

The alternative, Hoyer said, was to take up the Democrats' legislation.

The GOP scored one tactical victory. Shutting off the cameras had denied the Democrats an audience. But an aide to Scott Peters of California had an idea. He messaged the congressman to download onto his phone an app that could live stream the drama. Filming on the floor violated House protocols, but Peters went ahead anyway. "If John Lewis is going to sit on the House floor, that's against the rules, so I thought it's better for people to know about it," he said. C-SPAN picked up his feed. Other members also started live streaming. Soon the story was all over cable and the internet.[13]

The chamber took on a merry atmosphere. Senators popped in to watch the action or bring donuts. Larson told his colleagues to postpone their flights home; they might be needed for a few days. Lewis rested his back against the clerk's desk, his legs outstretched. Some colleagues parked themselves next to him; others took chairs. Occasionally Lewis strolled outside to talk to the press.[14]

It went on for hours. Debbie Wasserman Schultz of Florida fought back tears as she read a message from Gabby Giffords, a former colleague who had been brain damaged in a shooting five years earlier. Speaker Paul Ryan complained on CNN about the "publicity stunt." Democrats were just trying to raise money off the issue, he said. To the tune of "We Shall Overcome," Democrats sang, "We shall pass a bill someday."

At 7:55 p.m. Lewis spoke again, drawing a standing ovation from representatives and onlookers in the galleries. The applause roared on as if Lewis had hit a World Series–winning home run. He waved appreciatively. "Thank you for getting in trouble, good trouble, necessary trouble," he said, using his familiar new line. "Sometimes by sitting down, by sitting in, you're standing up," he added, using a much older one.[15]

At 2:30 a.m., the Republicans, seizing on a reduced Democratic presence, reconvened to push through a few appropriations bills. "And then," Cicilline said, "they did something we never contemplated. They adjourned." Having finished their business, they announced that Congress would be on hiatus until July 5, twelve days later. "We're done," they yelled, exiting the chamber.[16]

Lewis and Pelosi huddled. They decided to continue the sit-in into Thursday, but saw no point in remaining much longer with Congress adjourned. They could declare victory and go home.

Through the night, two dozen Democrats soldiered on. Republicans had shut off the heat, and members slept under blankets and rugs. At noon on Thursday, after more than twenty-four hours, Lewis and a die-hard corps of lieutenants, still wearing Wednesday's clothes, celebrated. Lewis closed out the sit-in, promising that the struggle would continue after the recess. There were hugs and photographs.

Congress passed neither background checks nor "no fly, no buy." But Lewis believed the sit-in had done some good. He reminded everyone that

the first Selma-to-Montgomery march had failed. It took three attempts to
get over the bridge.[17]

The fall of 2016 brought personal satisfactions for Lewis: the opening of
the National Museum of African American History and Culture in September, the National Book Award for *March* in November, a continuing stream
of awards, profiles, and tributes. But the presidential race was always top
of mind. Lewis campaigned as hard for Hillary as he had for any nominee.
"When she got the nomination," he later said, "I did everything I could for
her." He also headlined rallies and fundraisers for House and Senate colleagues and lent his name to all manner of text and email solicitations from
the party. It was necessary to keep Trump out of the White House.[18]

It wasn't just Trump. There was a dark, nasty mood among the people.
Renewed racial hostility was flourishing amid other tribal conflicts: red
against blue, liberals against conservatives, young against old, secular against
religious, rural against urban, populists against the establishment. "This current division caused by an undercurrent of fear in America is the worst I've
seen," Lewis said in Chicago, stumping for Senate candidate Tammy Duck-
worth. "We can't let them win." In the campaign's final days, the Clinton
team dispatched him to Florida and North Carolina, crucial swing states.
"Vote like you've never voted before," Lewis would say. It was another old
line, delivered with utter sincerity.[19]

On election night, Lewis watched the returns with friends in a suite at
the Hyatt Regency in Atlanta. "It was a train wreck in slow motion," recalled
Will Anderson, a former staffer who stayed in touch with Lewis. As soon
as returns began coming in, it was clear that Clinton was underperforming.
"We were still always just hoping that it wouldn't get as terrible as it did,"
Anderson said. "And that was the most depressed I'd seen Mr. Lewis since
Mrs. Lewis died. And I remember that evening having to tell *John Lewis*
to keep the faith." It was a role reversal. Like many staffers and colleagues,
Anderson knew that it was usually Lewis's job to reassure everyone "that the
key was to keep the faith and keep marching forward. And here *I* was trying
to give Mr. Lewis a pep talk about how we have to focus on bending that arc
towards justice."[20]

Trump's upset victory on November 8 sent Democrats reeling. The thought of entrusting the presidency to such a cruel, willful, vindictive, and corrupt man inspired fear and not a little hysteria. People burst out into the streets; some protests gave rise to violence. Amid the despair, Lewis summoned up his ingrained sense of hope. His counsel might have seemed bromidic had it not been necessary. "I would say to the young people, the young protesters, and those not so young: Accept a way of peace, believe in the way of love, believe in the philosophy and the discipline of nonviolence," he pleaded. Extremism would only play into Trump's hands. "The struggle is not a struggle that lasts one day or a few weeks or a few years," he said. "It is a struggle of a lifetime."[21]

Many Americans desperately sought a moral leader to guide them. They wanted someone who could provide comfort, nurture their better angels, remind them of hard times overcome, and hold out a vision of hope. It was a role made for Lewis. He became the anti-Trump, a symbol of charity over spite, gentleness over anger, compassion over discord, hope over fear. Demands for his presence grew even greater: he spoke at Yale's and Harvard's commencements, tossed the coin at the start of the Super Bowl, introduced the Best Picture–winning film *Green Book* at the Oscars. Seeing Lewis helped people retain hope.

Individual Americans turned to him for solace. Samira Mehta, a thirty-eight-year-old religious studies professor at Albright College, described to the *Washington Post* touring the African American history museum and seeing an exhibit about Lewis that inspired her to soldier on. "That's where my despair turned into something like resolve," she said. Ingrid Anderson, a thirty-nine-year-old physical therapist, was in the Atlanta airport when she saw Lewis getting a shoeshine. "I said thank you for everything you do, and I just started crying," she recounted. Lewis stepped off the pedestal and hugged her. She told the Associated Press that she left with a replenished fund of hope.[22]

On Friday, January 13, 2017, Lewis sat for an interview with Chuck Todd of NBC News. Todd wanted to ask him about how a country that had so recently elected Obama could now choose Trump. The conversation was supposed to air on *Meet the Press* two days later.

Todd asked Lewis if he would "forge a relationship" with Trump.

"You know," Lewis said, "I believe in forgiveness. I believe in trying to work with people. This is going to be very hard. It's going to be very difficult. I don't see this president-elect as a legitimate president."

Todd asked why.

Lewis explained that the Russians "participated in helping this man get elected" and "destroyed the candidacy of Hillary Clinton." Trump had cozied up to Russia's Vladimir Putin during the campaign, and U.S. intelligence agencies concluded that Russia had interfered in the election. As a result, Lewis said, "I don't plan to attend the inauguration. It'll be the first one that I miss since I've been in the Congress." (In fact, he had skipped George W. Bush's first inauguration, too, but forgot that in the moment.) "You cannot be at home with something that you feel that is wrong."[23]

When he sat down with Todd, Lewis hadn't planned to call Trump illegitimate. The remark was spontaneous. But when asked the question, he felt obliged to answer truthfully.[24]

NBC hyped the interview. Producers rushed the key segment onto the airwaves Friday, two days ahead of schedule. Breathlessly, Todd said at the start of Friday's program that Lewis's statement amounted to "a bombshell declaration" and "a serious inflection point in the American democracy."[25]

The fanfare got Trump's attention. Never able to let criticisms pass, he went after Lewis on Twitter, his weapon of choice. "Congressman John Lewis should spend more time on fixing and helping his district, which is in horrible shape and falling apart (not to mention crime infested) rather than falsely complaining about the election results. All talk, talk, talk—no action or results. Sad!"[26]

Lewis was unfazed. Trump's bullying had become unremarkable. Substantively, too, Trump's criticism was wide of the mark: as a congressman, Lewis had always done well by the Fifth District, which included neighborhoods that were rich as well as poor, white as well as Black. The furor only made Trump look petty and Lewis noble. Dozens of Democrats now pledged to join him in skipping the inauguration. *March* shot up to number one on Amazon's nonfiction bestseller list. *Walking with the Wind*, a twenty-five-year-old book that had been ranked at 15,918, surged to number two.[27]

On January 20, Lewis stayed in Atlanta. The next day he joined the city's Women's March, one of hundreds of demonstrations convened worldwide to protest Trump's election and defend women's rights. Striding at the head of the parade, Lewis enjoyed "a hero's welcome," the *Atlanta Journal-Constitution* reported, "drawing chants of support as he offered his own encouragement: 'Speak up, speak out, and find a way to get in the way.'"[28]

Cheering crowds and surging book sales scarcely compensated for the injury Lewis saw being done to democracy. Every day of the Trump administration brought new outrages: gratuitous insults of foreign leaders, high-handed power grabs, naked conflicts of interest, coldhearted policies. The bevy of scandals made it hard to organize against Trump. Where to direct one's energies?

One place was the continuing fight for racial equality. Lewis was a living reminder of just how recently segregation had been the law of the land. As white supremacism emerged from the shadows, he admonished Americans not to lose their way. But he found his faith in progress tested. In August 2017, neo-Confederates, neo-Nazis, and other right-wing extremists paraded through Charlottesville, Virginia, to protest the removal of a statue of Robert E. Lee. The nightmarish weekend ended with a white supremacist plowing his car through a crowd, killing one counterprotester and injuring dozens. Lewis wept over the young woman's death. "I cannot believe in my heart what I am witnessing today in America," he said. "I wanted to think not only as an elected official, but as a human being that we had made more progress. It troubles me a great deal." The very future of interracial democracy seemed in doubt. "I don't want to go back. I want to go forward. I want to continue to be part of an effort to make America one."[29]

Lewis believed Trump had fostered the culture in which open racial hatred was flourishing. "His message arrested that movement toward goodness and openness," Lewis said in an interview. "People stopped respecting the worth and dignity of all of us." In the days of Reagan and the Bushes, Lewis had never branded his political adversaries as racist; even at the start of Trump's campaign, he had described him as a demagogue, not an outright racist. But he changed his mind. Asked by Jamil Smith of *Rolling Stone* what he might say to Martin Luther King today, Lewis imagined telling his old mentor, "There have been so many setbacks since you left. We have someone, the head of our government, who, in the finality, is a racist. He doesn't understand the meaning of your life and the significance of the civil rights movement. But I truly believe, somehow and some way, we will not give up, we will not give in. We will continue to do what we must to create what you called the beloved community."[30]

Lewis also became a spokesman for other groups who found themselves under siege—Jews, immigrants, gays and lesbians. The latter group had until recently been making major strides toward social acceptance. Lewis remained active in the fight.

In the summer of 2015, David Cicilline had sponsored the Equality Act, which would have amended the 1964 Civil Rights Act to make sexual orientation a protected class alongside race and sex. Lewis immediately asked to become a cosponsor. "It wasn't even like I had to persuade him," Cicilline said. "He volunteered and approached me about making sure he was on the bill."

Some Black leaders wavered over the Equality Act, not because they opposed gay rights but because they worried, Cicilline said, "that opening up the Civil Rights Act would then invite Republicans to engage in all kinds of mischiefs." Cicilline brought Lewis to meet with the civil rights organizations, who were reluctant to tinker with the sacrosanct 1964 legislation.

The meeting began tensely. "I was trying to make the point that separate but equal is not a good strategy," Cicilline recounted. "But also there was a whole bunch of jurisprudence around the Civil Rights Act that we would have the benefit of, if we just included the civil rights architecture. To say that this is a category of protected classes like race and religion and ethnic origin." But his arguments weren't working.

Just as Cicilline prepared to give up, Lewis stood up and banged the table, not angrily but forcefully, commanding everyone's attention. He said that the discussion reminded him of what people used to say in 1963 and 1964—go slow, be incremental. The advice was shortsighted then, he maintained, and shortsighted now. "We need to be bold," he said, "and we need to do this now."

Lewis's speech had an immediate effect. "I wanted to turn and be like, 'I agree with Mr. Lewis!'" Cicilline later said. "The sentiment in the meeting changed. And shortly after that, everyone came out with statements and expressions of support."[31]

The Equality Act faltered under Trump. But Lewis kept speaking out for gay rights, drawing on his knowledge of the Black church. "I think it's important for members of religious communities to understand and know that members of the gay community are part of the human family. I grew up in a Baptist Church. I attended churches of all kind in Atlanta, in Nashville. . . . Many of the members in our churches, in our religious institutions, are gay. The church is supposed to preach the gospel of love, the gospel of peace, the gospel of sisterhood and brotherhood, that we are one family. . . . The church needs to learn and understand that there is not any room in our society—or any society—to discriminate against someone because of sexual orientation."[32]

Lewis's sensitivity to the concerns of American Jews also made him alert to the spread of anti-Semitism. The emergence of white supremacism from the shadows had brought with it a revival of overt and even lethal Jew-hatred, including mass shootings at synagogues in Pittsburgh and Poway, California. The left's new radicalism also sometimes encompassed a more subtle form of anti-Semitism, problematically enmeshed with extreme anti-Israel politics, as ugly insinuations about excessive Jewish money and power found voice from prominent Americans, including members of Congress.

Lewis recognized the difference between criticism of Israel and anti-Semitism. He not only favored a Palestinian state but yearned for a peaceful resolution to the decades-old conflict. Once he even got caught up in playing PeaceMaker, a video game in which users played the parts of the Israeli prime minister and Palestinian president to forge an accord. Nor was he afraid to criticize Israel. In 2015, along with several Democratic colleagues, he had boycotted a speech to Congress by the Israeli prime minister Benjamin Netanyahu, which House Republicans had arranged without consulting Obama. Yet Lewis also knew that the most vicious attacks on Israel frequently had an anti-Semitic component. He supported a bill labeling the so-called BDS movement, which sought Israel's isolation and economic strangulation, "morally bankrupt."[33]

What brought the issue to the halls of Congress was a string of comments in early 2019 by Representative Ilhan Omar of Minnesota, a recently elected Democrat. On Twitter, Omar insinuated that pro-Israel politicians supported Israel because they had been bought off by Jewish lobbyists. On another occasion, she charged American Jews with "an allegiance to a foreign

country." Her Jewish colleagues—almost all of them liberal Democrats—
were livid. To reassure voters on their party's stance, they passed a resolution
condemning anti-Semitism and "all attempts to delegitimize and deny Israel's right to exist." But sniping within the Democratic caucus continued.[34]

Lewis wanted to do something. He joined Brenda Lawrence of Michigan and several Jewish colleagues in founding a new bipartisan Black-Jewish
Caucus, to renew the interpersonal contacts that in the past had kept the
two groups' alliance strong. He cosponsored a bill condemning BDS, which
passed the House, 398–17—an important assurance to American Jews that
legitimate criticisms of Israel would not cross over into demonization and
anti-Semitism. And to reassure Israel's critics on the left, he also put his name
to a second bill, pushed by Omar, defending the *right* to engage in boycotts,
a form of protest he had always supported. This last gesture brought criticism from the right; one conservative Jewish outlet accused him of sending
"mixed messages." But Lewis noted that Omar's measure "makes no mention
of Israel," only "the right to protest," and added, correctly, that there was no
contradiction in voting for both bills.[35]

Of all the cruelties that Lewis observed in the Trump years, what disturbed him most was the inhumane treatment of immigrants. For two decades, millions of immigrants had been entering the United States illegally
and yet in that time Congress had never passed any comprehensive reform.
The inaction had led Lewis in 2013 to join House colleagues in blocking
traffic outside the Capitol in a show of protest against the inaction, notch-
ing him one more arrest on his record. Although as a candidate Trump had
promised to solve the crisis, it worsened during his tenure. Most scandalous
were the revelations of immigrant children being taken away from their parents and kept in pens with wire walls that resembled huge cages. Lewis declared the scenes to be as upsetting as anything he witnessed in all of Trump's
presidency. "Taking young kids from their parents and putting them in cages
made me cry," he said with pain in his voice. In 2018, Lewis joined two thousand protesters in Lafayette Square under a banner reading "Families Belong
Together," part of a coast-to-coast series of demonstrations against Trump's
family separation policies.[36]

The public pressure led Trump to stop breaking up immigrant families,
but there remained the problem of how to house children who entered the
country alone. In July 2019, Lewis and House colleagues visited an army

installation where the government was holding kids in custody. "I visited a place in Florida that had been an old camp, a military ground. It made me sick. All these little girls were there. It was so sad and painful." Tens of thousands of underage immigrants couldn't be left on their own, but the shabbiness of the facilities bespoke a callousness unbefitting the United States. "Some of these kids would never see their mothers or fathers again. I kept saying, 'How can we do something like this? How can we be so mean?' History won't be kind to us because of what we are doing to the children. This is one of the dark marks on America in modern history. As a nation, when you commit a great sin, a great evil, you pay a price."[37]

On Saturday, July 28, 2018, Lewis was flying on Delta flight 513 from Detroit to Atlanta after spending the day campaigning for a colleague. Midway through the two-hour flight, he felt dizzy and sweaty. Flight attendants came to see what was wrong. Lewis told the crew that he had the bad habit of skipping meals, only to have his hunger later catch up with him. They brought him some food and drink and watched over him. When they landed, he wanted to walk off the plane, but they insisted he use a wheelchair.

Rachelle O'Neil had come to meet Lewis. She had been planning to take him to a white-linen party and fundraiser hosted by Hank Stewart, an Atlanta community activist. She was dressed for the event, wearing all white and chic sunglasses, drawing puzzled looks from the crew. "I guess I didn't look like a person who should have been with him," she recalled, "because I had on all white, I had these shades on, I'm looking like some fly person." She was shocked to see Lewis in the wheelchair. "Is that my boss?" she wondered.

Lewis had always had staff help him with things: driving him around, getting him lunch, handling various tasks. Since Lillian's sickness and death, they had also taken on more personal roles, with Michael Collins, the staffer to whom he was closest, taking him to doctor's appointments. Lewis had diabetes, as well as what O'Neil called "normal old people illnesses, high blood pressure, stuff like that." There had been an incident on an airplane once before, in 2013 en route to Nelson Mandela's funeral. And, unbeknownst to almost everyone, because Lewis had never missed so much as a day of work for treatment, he had overcome prostate cancer as well. But overall his staff and his doctors considered him healthy. He was famous for never calling in sick. "In the sixteen years I was there," said Brenda Jones, "I probably could count on one hand the number of times" when he left the office early with a cold. Nor did he take vacations. When his friend Stephen McDaniel took him on a cruise, Lewis said it was his first vacation in twenty years. Still, aides were mindful of his advancing age and his health.[38]

At the Atlanta airport, when O'Neil saw Lewis being wheeled off the plane, "I immediately went into protection mode," she said. "I made them take him to a private area. I made them triage him. They wanted to get a gurney and wheel him through the airport. I said, 'Absolutely not. Nope. That's not happening.' I made them wheel him to the freight elevator." She got them to conceal his identity.[39]

Lewis stayed overnight at the hospital for observation. Jones issued a brief statement. Despite the paucity of hard information, local TV stations sent reporters to stand in front of Lewis's darkened Atlanta offices to issue their reports. Online news outlets posted squibs about the episode. At the hospital, doctors ran tests and found nothing seriously wrong. He was released on Sunday evening with what Jones described as a "clean bill of health." A few days later, Lewis gave the flight crew congressional certificates of appreciation.[40]

Over the next several months, Lewis began losing weight. Since he had always struggled with his waistline, often joking about having been "a few pounds lighter" back in his civil rights days, people were at first happy for him, complimenting him on his slimmer profile. One aide quipped that he could have a second career sharing his weight-loss tips. But over time his staff began to worry. In October 2018 Danny Lyon visited John to interview him for a movie he was making. "He was drinking something in a plastic cup to make him gain weight," Lyon recalled. "He looked horrible." Lewis said that he had mentioned the weight loss to his doctor, who didn't detect any problem; people in their late seventies often experience weight loss without having a serious illness. Lewis was sensitive about the issue and didn't discuss it much.[41]

There were other strange signs. Once, Lewis made a speech on the House floor and his hand was shaking. Friends called the office to ask if everything was all right. On other occasions, Lewis would come to the office without having slept; he would be up all night, watching MSNBC. He said it was because Trump was president, but that couldn't explain the extent of the insomnia. One friend told him, "John, something is wrong. You've got to get to the bottom of it." He continued to work unflaggingly.[42]

Lewis concluded that stopping Trump required retaking control of Congress. As much as possible in 2018, he traveled the country, bringing his star power to aid endangered incumbents and boost promising challengers. He traveled to Massachusetts to help Michael Capuano, to Texas for Colin Allred and Lizzie Fletcher, to Illinois for Betsy Londrigan and Brendan Kelly, to Arkansas for Clarke Tucker. In Georgia, he stumped for Stacey Abrams, a dynamic activist carrying on Lewis's work of voter registration, who was running for governor. At rallies and fundraisers, Lewis found, the mood was different from most midterm elections. People were energized. They were desperate to exercise a check on Trump or send a message of repudiation.

When Lewis went to vote on Election Day, a CNN documentary crew accompanied him. Applause rose up as he approached the school, then more as he entered the building. His mood was light. "I'm happy to see so many people participating," he told the press. "And I truly believe we're going to take back the House of Representatives."

Lewis again watched the returns from a large suite in the Hyatt Regency hotel downtown, where hundreds gathered in the downstairs ballroom in hopes of an Abrams victory. He sat upstairs with Atlanta friends and various staff members. They drank white wine and San Pellegrino. The early signs were inauspicious. In the first races called, Republicans claimed victories. Memories of two years earlier, when disappointment had followed upon disappointment, sent Democratic feet pacing. "I think it's going to be a long night," Lewis said to Reverend Raphael Warnock, the Ebenezer pastor, who was also there for the hoped-for celebration.

With the TV commentary given over to idle gabbing, Lewis would ask Collins for updates. "So we picked up fifteen already?" As the night went on, the numbers improved. When Lizzie Fletcher ousted an incumbent Republican, Lewis jumped out of his seat and clapped, then called her on his cell phone to offer congratulations. For his friends sitting on the sofa with him, he kept up a running commentary. At one point MSNBC reported on the race of Steve King of Iowa, a far-right conservative known for racist remarks. Lewis couldn't contain himself. "Oh, I hope we can rid of this guy here, King," he told his friends. "King is a racist. He is so bad."

Shortly after 9:30 p.m., MSNBC projected that Democrats were going to win the House. The room burst out in celebration. Lewis jumped up from his seat again. Collins fairly sprinted the length of the suite, hugging other guests.

"In the majority again!" Collins cheered.

"That's the best feeling," Lewis said.

The mood was dampened a bit when it became clear that Stacey Abrams was likely to lose. Shortly before 10:00 p.m., as she trailed by 250,000 votes, Lewis went down to the ballroom to speak to her supporters, telling them not to "get lost in a sea of despair."[43]

Having put his muscle into recapturing the House, Lewis now turned his energies to Nancy Pelosi's bid to regain the speakership. Insiders acknowledged Pelosi to be one of the most effective congressional leaders in decades, if not of all time. But two years earlier, she had faced a serious challenge to her leadership, and people were again gunning for her. As the party's public face, Pelosi had become anathema to Republicans, who ran against her the way Democrats had run against Gingrich in the 1990s. In the 2018 campaign, many Democrats in tight districts had pledged not to back her as speaker. Some on the far left also wanted her out, considering her too moderate.

Pelosi worked to put down the challenge. She convinced Alexandria Ocasio-Cortez, a newly elected twenty-nine-year-old progressive, that any other speaker would be to Pelosi's right. To the moderate members, she dispensed favors and promises.

When the caucus met on November 28, Pelosi took no chances. She lined up a murderers' row of members, representing a cross section of the party, to argue for her election. She saved Lewis for last.

"Nancy, Nancy, Nancy," John said, when his turn came. "Believe in me. I would not lie to you. I've seen the struggle," he said to any members who might be wavering. He did not hesitate to invoke Selma. "I've been beaten, left bloodied, left unconscious. I almost died on that bridge in Selma." It might have seemed hackneyed or exploitative to those who had heard this pitch many times before, and there was something incongruous about the high moral dudgeon Lewis brought to the most insiderly of debates. Yet hearing such testimony from Lewis in the flesh was powerful, especially for new members. "Nancy's been with us, and she will be with us now, tomorrow, and in the years to come. I ask for you"—now his voice rose suddenly to a loud cry—"I beg of you, I plead with you to go and do what we must do, and cast your vote for Nancy Pelosi as the next speaker of the House of Representatives."[44]

Pelosi won easily, 203–32, with three abstentions. Her election as speaker wouldn't be official until the new Congress met and voted in January, but the rebellion was over. To fight Trump, the Democrats now had their commander back in place.

Lewis and Pelosi had a special relationship. The two of them and Steny Hoyer—also reelected that fall, as majority leader—were nearly alone in the caucus in having served since 1987. "I loved him from the start. I was in awe of him from the start," Pelosi said. The Tuesday night Italian and Chinese dinners of the 1980s had led to decades of collaboration and a genuine friendship. "Over time, in the trenches, your bond grows stronger," Pelosi said.[45]

Pelosi appreciated how valuable Lewis was to the Democrats. Whenever he spoke out, everyone in Congress paid attention. So did the news media. Pelosi never presumed to tell him what to say, but she was aware that a powerful, well-timed statement from him could be useful to whatever cause the Democrats were rallying behind.

One such moment came in September 2019. Over the summer, a whistleblower from the National Security Council (later revealed as European Affairs director Alexander Vindman) had told the congressional intelligence committees that Trump had pressured the Ukrainian president, Volodymyr Zelensky, to investigate former vice president Joe Biden. Biden's son Hunter had enjoyed an egregious sweetheart deal with a Ukrainian energy company, and Trump wanted to tarnish the elder Biden—who seemed likely to be the Democrats' nominee in 2020—with the scandal. In a July 25 phone call, Trump had warned Zelensky that he might withhold $300 million in military aid if Ukraine didn't play ball. News of the phone call brought forth calls for Trump's impeachment.

Lewis was focused on the implications for American democracy.

Trump was attempting almost exactly what he'd been accused of in 2016: courting a foreign power to meddle in the presidential election. This was an assault on the integrity of the vote, the cause Lewis had fought for his whole life.

Still, Lewis hesitated to join the pro-impeachment chorus. That was mainly because one other important holdout remained: Nancy Pelosi. The speaker knew that with Republicans controlling the Senate, Trump would never be removed from office; she also believed that for the House to impeach him might appear petty and partisan and alienate independent and moderate voters. Lewis wouldn't cross Pelosi lightly. Yet the caucus now regarded him as a leader in his own right, someone whose position would influence others. As the days passed, Washington waited on his words.

On September 12, *Politico* ran a long article spotlighting Lewis's key role in the House. It described him as a uniquely influential voice within the party, someone whose silence on impeachment had only enhanced his power. Colleagues stated that his decision, when he made it, would be critical.

"There's no one more respected than John Lewis in the caucus," said Ro Khanna of California. "He has greater moral weight than anyone in this body, and I think he would make a big, big difference speaking out."

"No question about it," said Emanuel Cleaver. "Who wants to be on the other side of John Lewis?"

Yet no one lobbied him. To do so would be disrespectful. Given his well-known independent streak, it was also unlikely to yield the desired results.

Lewis's comments to *Politico* were cryptic. "My time is growing near," he said. "I've never been supportive of this so-called president. Before he was inaugurated I said he was not legitimate. So I have some very strong feelings." Strong feelings weren't the same thing as a judgment on the wisdom of impeachment. But he declined to say more.[46]

Over the next ten days, reporters unearthed incriminating details of Trump's July 25 phone call. The White House released a summary of the call in the hope of exonerating Trump, but the details largely confirmed Vindman's account. By Monday, September 23, Pelosi shifted her stance. She confided to certain members that they could back impeachment. That evening, after informing the speaker, seven freshman House Democrats from swing districts collectively endorsed impeachment in a *Washington Post* essay. Several Pelosi allies added their voices to the chorus.[47]

The next day, any lingering doubt about the Democrats' plans vanished when Lewis broke his silence. "People approach me everywhere I go," he said on the House floor. "They truly believe that our nation is descending into darkness. They never dreamed that the United States, once seen as a beacon of hope and as an inspiration to people striving for equality and justice, would be falling into such disgrace." Lewis told his colleagues that he had trouble sleeping at night. "I am afraid to go to sleep for fear that I will wake up and our democracy will be gone."

The Ukraine scandal rekindled fears that Trump meant to sabotage the democratic process. "The people have a right to know whether they can put their faith and trust in the outcome of our elections," Lewis said. "They have a right to know whether the cornerstone of our democracy was undermined by people sitting in the White House today. They have a right to know whether a foreign power was asked to intervene in the 2020 election." He reached back to an idea he had learned about in college, one that had often occupied his thoughts. "There comes a time when you have to be moved by the spirit of history," he said, "to take action to protect and preserve the integrity of our nation. I believe, I truly believe the time to begin impeachment proceedings against this president has come."[48]

It was a bravura performance. Television replayed clips of it. Newspapers reprinted the text.

Later that day, Pelosi announced that the House would open a formal inquiry into impeaching Trump. If Lewis was not known as one of the chamber's preeminent experts on Ukraine or national security, he was its chief defender of democracy and the sanctity of the vote. But Lewis wouldn't end up playing much of a role in the fall's impeachment hearings. He discovered that he had an even more urgent battle to fight.

Chapter Twenty-Seven
LION IN WINTER

———— ■ ■ ————

In two decades of working for Lewis, Michael Collins had become closer to the congressman than any family member. "Wherever you saw Congressman Lewis, Collins was never far behind, beside, or leading him," a Washington profile noted. He not only ran the congressional office but administered to many aspects of Lewis's personal life. "I literally took care of him," Collins recalled. "I was taking him to the doctor." Collins felt bad that he could never get Lewis to forgo his love of McDonald's and Wendy's and Chick-fil-A, but on the whole the congressman remained vigorous, working harder than people decades younger. His physical exams set off no alarm bells.[1]

Yet by the fall of 2019 Lewis's weight loss had become increasingly worrisome. "You don't always notice it when you see someone day-to-day," Collins said. "But I was playing doctor, and I noticed one day when I came to pick him up."[2]

Jacob Gillison, Lewis's former scheduler, went to Lewis's house in October to plan a visit to Benedict College in Columbia, South Carolina, Gillison's alma mater. Gillison had arranged for Lewis to give the keynote talk at the school's homecoming.

"Jake, I don't know," Lewis said to him. "I don't feel right. Something doesn't feel right."

"What do you mean?"

"Oh, I just feel a lot of pressure here," Lewis said, touching a spot on his midsection. "Congressman," Gillison said, "you should go get yourself checked."

"I will, sonny," Lewis said.

"No, really, Congressman," Gillison reiterated. "Really, you need to get yourself checked."

"I will," Lewis promised.

On the trip to Benedict, Gillison said, "I was watching him close, and I could see a difference in Mr. Lewis." Gillison asked, "Congressman, did you go get yourself checked?" Lewis said that he had. But he mentioned the pressure and discomfort again.

Collins made an appointment with Brian Monahan, the attending physician for the Congress and Supreme Court. Monahan recommended some tests. Collins thought the issue might be Lewis's diet. "Well, let's get him eating right," Collins said. "Let's get him on an eating plan, get his sugar up, regulate the diabetes, and then we'll do these tests."

"Look, I have a different suggestion," Monahan countered. "I think we should do the tests, do the ultrasound, and then we can worry about eating right."

On December 4, Collins picked Lewis up at home and drove him to a radiology clinic on K Street. He helped Lewis into his hospital garment and waited. When Lewis came walking out, the director of the clinic was with him.

"What are they saying?" Lewis asked. He seemed confused, almost bewildered. Collins himself didn't know what was going on.

"Make sure you've got fight in you," the director said to Lewis. "Make sure you're ready to fight."

Collins was concerned. "I'll figure it out," he said. "We'll talk to Dr. Monahan."

They were in Collins's car driving back to Capitol Hill when his phone rang. Collins had a rule never to answer the phone in the car by putting the speakerphone on. You never know what's meant to be private. But in this case, he recalled, "I did it. I answered the phone on speakerphone."

It was Monahan. "I need you to bring the Congressman to me immediately. We have some life-changing decisions to make."

They went to see Monahan. He took them through the images and charts and explained what was going on. It was Stage 4 pancreatic cancer, the most advanced stage—metastatic. Although treatments for the disease were improving, they remained far from effective. Three-fourths of people diagnosed with Stage 4 pancreatic cancer died within a year. Only one in ten went on to live for five years or longer.[3]

Back on the Hill, Lewis was due in the House chamber for some votes. Collins was "just trying to keep it together," he said. "I talked to Steny Hoyer, who is his closest friend." He shared the news.

"Michael and I both teared up," Hoyer remembered. "We didn't break down. But we both teared."

"I'm here for you," Hoyer said.[4]

Lewis called Pelosi. He wanted to tell her the news face-to-face. "He said he wanted to see me, just the two of us. I didn't have the faintest idea what it was about. Was it something personal? Political? Some issue he wanted to get ahead of?" They scheduled a meeting for one week later, December 11.

Sitting across from her, Lewis broke the news. "I had no thought other than his recovery," Pelosi said. "I practice medicine on the side, without a diploma. I told him which doctors I thought he should see." She was determined that he receive "beautiful attention. They know they have someone very precious to protect."[5]

Collins and Lewis notified family and a few friends. In the meantime, Lewis showed no signs of flagging. When the House took up Trump's impeachment, Lewis was as commanding as ever. In a tub-thumping speech from the floor, he tied Trump's lawlessness to the recent assault on civil rights and the rebirth of white supremacist–style racism. "Our children and their children will ask us, what did you do? What did you say?" he bellowed. "For some, this vote may be hard. But we have a mission and a mandate to be on the right side of history."[6]

For Christmas break, Lewis went back to Atlanta. He told Stephen McDaniel about the diagnosis. McDaniel, who shared Lewis's love of art, bought his friend a set of paints, brushes, and canvases as a Christmas present. On December 23, he and Sam Burston, a Clark Atlanta University official who was also an accomplished artist, brought over the gift. "And I said, 'John, look, now you got your art piece, so just do your art.'" Lewis dabbed out a small watercolor, abstract and colorful, which his friends photographed for posterity.[7]

On December 29, Collins and Brenda Jones—who in October had left as communication director but had now come back to help—arranged a conference call with the staff to break the news. Everyone was devastated. "I remember that call when Michael got us all on the phone," said Tuere Butler of the Atlanta staff. "And it was heavy, and it was dark. And I thought, if I'm feeling this way, how much more heavy is Michael feeling?" Butler was walking home from a lunch when the call came. "I had to stop and sit down. And then my husband had to come and get me because I was like, what is happening?"[8]

Rachelle O'Neil had already left for vacation in Ghana, bringing items for the president that Lewis had autographed. She missed the conference call. "I just remember getting back to the hotel that day, and I had all these messages in my phone. And I was like, what's going on?" she recounted. She called Lewis. "He was like, 'Are you OK?' I was like, 'Yeah, I'm fine. Why wouldn't I be fine?' And he dropped the news. So he's announcing to the world that he's sick and he's checking on his staff, even as far away as in Africa."[9]

Later that day, Lewis disclosed his cancer diagnosis in a press release:

I have been in some kind of fight—for freedom, equality, basic human rights—for nearly my entire life. I have never faced a fight quite like the one I have now.

This month in a routine medical visit, and subsequent tests, doctors discovered Stage IV pancreatic cancer. This diagnosis has been reconfirmed.

While I am clear-eyed about the prognosis, doctors have told me that recent medical advances have made this type of cancer treatable in many cases, that treatment options are no longer as debilitating as they once were, and that I have a fighting chance.

So I have decided to do what I know to do and do what I have always done: I am going to fight it and keep fighting for the Beloved Community. We still have many bridges to cross.

To my constituents: being your representative in Congress is the honor of a lifetime. I will return to Washington in coming days to continue our work and begin my treatment plan, which will occur

over the next several weeks. I may miss a few votes during this period, but with God's grace I will be back on the front lines soon.

Please keep me in your prayers as I begin this journey.[10]

Calls, texts, and emails started coming in. On his personal cell phone, Lewis
got 154 calls within a few hours. Everyone wanted an interview. Jones recommended that Lewis give a single, exclusive interview to a trusted reporter.
They chose Ernie Suggs of the *Atlanta Journal-Constitution*, who published
his story on January 1. To Suggs, Lewis displayed his usual optimism, explaining again that the treatments were "no longer as debilitating as they
once were" and that he would be "talking and learning" from friends who
had battled cancer. He said he had no plans to retire.[11]

Chemotherapy treatments started in the new year. Lewis went on Mondays;
every fourth week he had a break. Even at the hospital, his reputation preceded him. "Going to the chemotherapy appointment, people saw him coming in, and all the workers knew him," said his friend Howard Brown, who
accompanied him once. "And he would speak to them and took his time."
Lewis handled it better than some people his age, but the chemicals still
took a toll on his body, his energy, and his alertness. For the first time in his
career, he was regularly absent from the office.[12]

Collins drove Lewis to his appointments and practically lived with him
at his townhouse. Knowing that Collins needed help, Lewis asked Jacob
Gillison and Keith Washington to assist with his care. Washington, a friend
of twenty years, was a fellow political junkie who for years would call Lewis
each morning to share polling data from political races around the country. The three friends took turns staying with Lewis, cooking or bringing
in meals. They moved his bed into the downstairs parlor and set it by a
window, with a good view of the TV. Next to the bed was a photograph of
Lewis's mother.[13]

So many friends bombarded Lewis with calls that he often had to say no.
Even so, the steady stream kept him busy. Barack Obama, Bill and Hillary
Clinton, Joe Biden, even French president Emmanuel Macron called. His
brothers and sisters visited. So did friends from different chapters of his life.

"John should put a 'do not disturb' sign on his door," said Tom Houck, who made the trip up from Atlanta.[14]

In January, Danny Lyon flew in from New Mexico and stayed for three days. The visit reminded him of when they roomed together in the SNCC days. The old friends took short walks around the neighborhood. "It reminded me of taking care of my grandfather," Lyon said. "We'd go .001 miles an hour." Lewis donned a knit hat and they sat on a park bench, watching the squirrels and the people playing with their dogs. "We're just two old guys in the park. He looked like an old homeless guy."

At first no one recognized him. Then Lewis and Lyon walked some more, Lyon said, and "a bunch of people recognized him and jumped up to shake his hand. He's shaking everyone's hand." Lyon half suspected that Lewis was pacing back and forth *until* people noticed him. The next day, when some Phi Beta Sigma brothers visited, Lewis took pleasure in recounting the excitement of the people in the park.

Lyon made a few videos and pictures of Lewis. Along with his art and antiques, John also collected African American quilts. Lyon took one photo of Lewis in a V-neck T-shirt, lying in bed, under a pair of gorgeous multi-colored quilts. His left hand propping up his head, his wrist adorned by a gold-colored watch, as his right arm stretched out before him on the quilt. His lined face looked neither pained nor sad, but sober and dignified, a lion in winter.[15]

In mid-January, Lewis went to the Hill for an hour to cast some votes— his first appearance since disclosing his illness. When he entered the chamber, everyone clustered around him. "When I got on the floor, we were just at that point of affection and love," Lewis told Lyon a few days later. People seemed to forget about his weakened immunity. Lewis would put his hands in his pockets or fold his arms to remind himself to keep his distance, but the human pull was powerful. "There was a young lady from Cleveland, Ohio who acted like a den mother of the Congress," Lewis said, referring to Representative Marcia Fudge, who was twelve years his junior. "And apparently someone had told her that I would be coming through the doors, and she sort of guarded the doors and said, 'Welcome, John. Welcome.' And she kept saying to the members, 'No touching, no hugging. You're going to find him a comfortable seat.' And so I took my seat."

Nancy Pelosi came by to say hello. So did Kevin McCarthy, who leaned in for an embrace—only to hear Fudge remind him, "No hugging!"

"I want to hug John," McCarthy protested.

"You're not supposed to hug him," Fudge countered.

Lewis appreciated the gesture. "No one told her to be there," he said, "but she was just trying to shield me."[16]

Lewis's monotonous days at home were spelled by moments of levity. During a visit from Don Harris in February, Lewis and some friends were chatting when the doorbell rang. No one knew who it was. Collins answered the door. It was a pastor whom someone had invited to talk to Lewis. Lewis summoned Harris upstairs. He explained sotto voce that he didn't want to talk to this woman. "She was there to save his soul," Harris later said. But Harris didn't want to deal with her, either, and, in the good-natured way that friends can rib each other, said, "Sorry, I'm leaving." Then Collins and the other guest left, too, leaving Lewis—always the gentleman, unfailingly polite—to indulge the pastor for an hour.

Howard Brown, who also visited, joked about how often Lewis would do his laundry. "If he had five T-shirts, he would put that load in. I would be like, 'Congressman, you just washed yesterday.'" Lewis countered that his doctors told him to exercise, and going up and down the steps to the washer and dryer kept the juices flowing. "He was diligent about getting his exercise and putting those clothes in the wash," Brown said. "He loved clean clothes."[17]

Mostly, Lewis watched the news. In January, it was coverage of Trump's Senate impeachment trial; in February, it was the presidential primaries. He never tired of it. When Brown stayed with Lewis, he said, he "watched more TV in those two weeks than I had in the last twenty-five years. It was MSNBC all day, every day, morning, noon, and night."[18]

Gillison was also amused by his old boss's appetite for MSNBC. "They're just repeating the same information over and over," he said to Lewis.

"Well," Lewis replied, "sometimes they tell it a little differently."

The 2020 primaries were in full swing, and Lewis followed developments avidly. He had planned to endorse Biden—whom he had known the longest and the best. The previous summer, when Biden had been roasted on the internet for boasting of his ability to work with segregationists like James Eastland or Strom Thurmond, Lewis had come to his defense. "I don't think the remarks are offensive," Lewis told reporters, explaining that he, too, had found ways to work with white supremacists. "During the height of the civil rights movement, we worked with people and got to know people that were members of the Klan—people who opposed us, even people who beat us and arrested us and jailed us." Still, despite his esteem for Biden, Lewis didn't make any endorsement, out of respect for his many colleagues in the race. Lewis's hope was simply to nominate someone who could defeat Trump. After Biden finished poorly in Iowa and New Hampshire and his candidacy appeared doomed, Lewis flirted with endorsing former New York mayor Michael Bloomberg. Despite his controversial "stop and frisk" policing methods, which targeted high-crime Black and Hispanic neighborhoods, Bloomberg had been fairly popular with New York's African American voters for much of his mayoralty, and in 2020 he had endorsements from Black mayors like Muriel Bowser of Washington, D.C., and London Breed of San Francisco, who admired his nonideological approach to urban problems. In the end, however, Lewis chose to wait to see if Biden bounced back.[19]

The late winter was a time of milestones for Lewis: his eightieth birthday on February 21 and the fifty-fifth anniversary of Bloody Sunday on March 7. Xernona Clayton, still energetic at eighty-nine, planned a party in Atlanta, but he asked her to cancel it. He wasn't even sure he wanted to go to Selma. The jubilee was scheduled for Sunday, March 1, the Faith and Politics outing for the weekend after.

In late February, Lewis told Collins he wanted to visit Atlanta. He wanted to see John-Miles. He had also adopted a gaggle of fifteen or so stray cats. John-Miles and various others were feeding the cats, but Lewis, an animal lover ever since his chicken-preaching youth, wanted to check on his feline friends. Atlanta was also where he had to file to run for reelection.

His doctors advised him to avoid public spaces. But they gave Collins permission to drive Lewis down. So, along with David Bowman and Marcus Sawyers, two other aides from the Washington office, they made the ten-hour trip. Lewis stayed awake the whole time. They played gospel music and talked and laughed.[20]

Lewis had a recliner in his D.C. townhouse that he loved, and Collins bought him another one for his Atlanta home. "It was there for him when he got there," Collins said. "And so when he got in the house, he just plopped in the chair and looked at me and said, 'Thank you for bringing me home.'" He still wasn't sure about Selma.[21]

On March 1, it appeared that the jubilee would proceed without him. Unlike in previous years, which had featured a single march over the bridge, this year's proceedings were disorganized. Stacey Abrams led one march; Jesse Jackson led another. Biden had just romped the day before in the South Carolina primary, reclaiming the front-runner's mantle, but the presidential race was still crowded. Other than Bernie Sanders, all the remaining candidates were coming to Selma: Biden, Bloomberg, Elizabeth Warren, Pete Buttigieg, Amy Klobuchar, even the little-known financier Tom Steyer. Biden and Bloomberg spoke at Brown Chapel, with Biden waxing tender about his long friendship with Lewis. The congressman was nowhere to be seen.

Tia Mitchell, who covered Lewis for the *Atlanta Journal-Constitution*, was sitting in Brown when Michael Collins texted her. He was notifying reporters that he and Lewis were en route. They would meet the press at the apex of the bridge.

The bridge, mostly empty, filled up again. Collins and Lewis, joined by Stephen McDaniel, pulled up in a black car. When people realized who it was, they crowded the vehicle, peering through the tinted windows, taking photos. "Oh my God, that's John Lewis!" they shouted.

Lewis stepped out of the car at about 3:20 p.m. He was wearing a handsome burgundy sweater over a shirt and tie, looking gaunt but not weak. Collins helped him mount a small stand. The presidential candidates and other VIPs—Jesse Jackson, Stacey Abrams, Al Sharpton—surrounded him. Lewis balanced himself with one arm around Collins's shoulders, the other grasping Sharpton's arm.

"Fifty-five years ago, a few of God's children attempted to walk from Brown Chapel Church across this bridge," Lewis began. "We were beaten. We were tear-gassed. I thought I was going to die on this bridge." These were words he had said many times before. But then his remarks took a personal turn. "But somehow, in some way, God Almighty helped me." Lewis implored the crowd not to give up, not to give in, to "vote like we never, ever voted before." He offered a spontaneous shout-out to the fraternity and sorority students in the crowd—"You look good! You look colorful!"—and then shifted and spoke about himself. At one level, he was still talking about his lifelong fight to protect the vote; on another, he was speaking to his own fight for survival. "I'm not going to give up. I'm not going to give in. We're going to continue to fight. We need your prayers now more than ever before."[22]

Within a few minutes he was back in the car.

For some it was all too fast. "We did not get to see you because there were so many others who wanted 'a piece of you'!" Peggy Wallace Kennedy wrote him in a personal note. "But I was not far away. . . . Your voice was strong and your spirit was soaring. I was proud to see it and feel it."[23]

On the drive back, on I-85 from Montgomery to Atlanta, Lewis was hungry. They stopped at a Cracker Barrel. While they were eating, two buses pulled up and a large group of Delta Sigma Theta members who had been at Selma entered the restaurant. Many of the women recognized Lewis, and a few waved or said hello, but no one disturbed his meal. Then, when Lewis, Collins, and McDaniel got up to leave, McDaniel recalled, "everyone at the restaurant stood up and applauded. And they just applauded as he walked through the restaurant on the way out. It was tear-jerking. He was visibly touched by the affection of the moment."

Collins and McDaniel drove Lewis back to Wallace Road. He plopped down again in his recliner and said, "Thank you."[24]

On Monday, March 2, Lewis went to the state capitol to file his reelection papers. "I never considered not running," he told reporters. The next day was Super Tuesday, with fourteen states voting. Biden won big again, cementing his front-runner status. Lewis was back in Washington, where his Democratic colleagues threw him a surprise belated-birthday party. "I feel honored and blessed to be in your presence," Lewis said on entering the Capitol meeting room where Pelosi, Hoyer, and dozens of others—including some Republicans—gathered. "And to be still here."[25]

There remained the question of whether to go back to Selma for the Faith and Politics weekend. Collins kept asking Lewis if he wanted to go. They both knew it could be his last time crossing the bridge. Lewis kept saying no. "In my heart, all I kept thinking was 'I've got to get him there. I don't know how,'" Collins said.

Finally, Collins broached the taboo topic. "Congressman," he said, "I don't know if we're going to get another chance to go back. I want to take you to the bridge. And I will drive. We will go straight to the bridge and we will get out. And we'll do exactly what we did last time. And you can say a few words and get back in the car and we'll come right back home."

It was probably the fifth time he had asked Lewis. This time Lewis shook his head yes. Back to Selma they went.[26]

No presidential candidates came this time, but there was a large congressional delegation, including Pelosi and Hoyer. On Sunday, March 8, they gathered on the Pettus Bridge. Lewis wore a light blue sweater and a charcoal topcoat. Several pilgrims donned leis, in tribute to those worn on the 1965 Montgomery march. When Lewis spoke, people wept. "It was like nothing I'd ever seen," said Jonathan Capehart, a *Washington Post* journalist who had been on four Selma pilgrimages. "You could feel it. This might be the last time he's on the bridge and the last time we get to be a part of it."

In crossing the bridge, Lewis locked arms on his right side with Nancy Pelosi, who wore a stylish tartan windbreaker. Holding Lewis's left arm was an old friend who at age ninety-one had come to Selma all the way from Los Angeles, the Reverend James Lawson.[27]

Saturday, March 7, 2020, was also the day that the first case of Covid-19, a highly contagious and dangerous coronavirus, was diagnosed in Washington, D.C. Four days later, the World Health Organization declared the disease a global pandemic. Washington mayor Muriel Bowser announced a public health emergency. People began avoiding large gatherings and then small gatherings and then working from home. Schools moved their classes online. In mid-May, the House would vote to allow proxy voting and remote hearings for the first time.[28]

People with weakened immune systems and the elderly were especially vulnerable to the virus. As a chemotherapy patient, Lewis had to be extra careful. He still took visitors at Third Street, but guests wore masks and kept a safe distance. Sherry Frank and other friends from Atlanta sent shipments of food. There were lots of phone calls. He spoke to John-Miles every day. On Sunday nights, the night before chemo treatments, Lewis would often have trouble sleeping and passed the time on the phone with friends like Tom Houck, who could gab for hours.[29]

Lewis stayed engaged with politics. On April 7, he formally endorsed Biden for president, bringing on some now-predictable Twitter abuse from the Bernie Bros but otherwise surprising no one. Lewis also seconded James Clyburn's suggestion that Biden pick an African American woman as his running mate.

In May, Lewis appeared in a pair of ads, one for television and one for online platforms, to promote the thirty-three-year-old Jon Ossoff, who was running in Georgia's Democratic Senate primary. Lewis had known Ossoff's parents since his city council years; as a high school student Ossoff had interned in Lewis's office. He had since become a protégé. One of his ads used footage of an affecting face-to-face conversation the two men had had in 2017, when Ossoff had unsuccessfully sought a seat in Congress. The other ad used film of a September 2019 rally at a community center in Atlanta's Sweet Auburn district, where Lewis enthusiastically endorsed Ossoff for Senate. The spots would help propel Ossoff to victory in the June primary.[30]

On Memorial Day, May 25, Minnesota police stopped a man named George Floyd for allegedly using a counterfeit bill at a grocery store. In apprehending Floyd, Officer Derek Chauvin pressed his knee into the man's neck for almost nine minutes. Floyd gasped, "I can't breathe," and onlookers warned Chauvin that he was about to kill Floyd—which he ultimately did. Seventeen-year-old Darnella Frazier recorded the gruesome scene on her cell phone. Her video rocketed around the world. Lewis watched it. "The way this young man died, watching the video, it made me so sad," he said on TV days later. "It was so painful. It made me cry. I kept saying to myself, how many more? How many more young Black men will be murdered? The madness must stop."[31]

Fifty-five years earlier, films and photographs of Lewis's own beating by police had triggered a wave of national outrage. Now the Floyd video did the same. Millions of Americans, cooped up in their homes since the pandemic began, vented their pent-up energy by pouring into city streets to demand an end to police abuse and entrenched forms of racism.

Most protesters behaved peacefully, but looting, arson, and violence led twenty-one states to activate their National Guard units. The night of Friday, May 29, violence was especially bad in some cities, including Atlanta, where rioters smashed windows and stormed the CNN building, the Omni Hotel, and the College Football Hall of Fame. Cars, including a police squad car, were set ablaze.

Lewis had returned to Atlanta for another visit. When Collins greeted him the next morning, the congressman was in tears. "What's the matter?" Collins asked.

"It's too much. It's too much," Lewis said. The TV was on, showing footage of the rioting. From one standpoint, it seemed that a new generation was picking up the mantle of the civil rights movement and fighting to fulfill its goals. But from another perspective, it seemed that the ideals of nonviolence and the beloved community were slipping away.[32]

Lewis wanted to honor the frustration of the protesters while steering them away from destructive acts. "I'm deeply moved and touched and really inspired by the determination of the young people. The children, young men, young women, all the people prepared to get out there and say enough is enough," he said to the local CBS station. But, he added—referring to violence from the police as well as from protesters—"the violence must stop. How many more people will be murdered? How many more young men, women, must we lose?" A reporter asked him what advice he had. "I would say follow the way of peace. Follow the way of love. Follow the philosophy of discipline and nonviolence, and never become bitter or hostile," he said.[33]

Later, Lewis posted a statement on his website and on Twitter:

To the rioters here in Atlanta and across the country: I see you, and I hear you. I know your pain, your rage, your sense of despair and hopelessness. Justice has, indeed, been denied for far too long. Rioting, looting, and burning is not the way. Organize. Demonstrate. Sit in. Stand up. Vote. Be constructive, not destructive. History has proven time and again that nonviolent, peaceful protest is the way to achieve the justice and equality that we all deserve.

His comments were broadly welcomed. A few voices criticized him for continuing to advocate nonviolence, which they claimed didn't work. But the historical record showed that it had.[34]

Besides the street violence, Lewis was also uncomfortable with the extreme positions that some protesters and even politicians were taking. "Defund the Police" was the new motto, and in the wake of the George Floyd protests, some cities voted to slash their law enforcement budgets. Lewis worried that the slogan would send the wrong message and imply that Democrats were indifferent to public safety. Earlier that year, on a trip to the Hill, he had shared his dismay with Clyburn as they discussed the 1960s refrain "Burn, baby, burn," chanted during the 1965 Watts riots. "John Lewis and I were very concerned when these slogans came out about 'defund the police,'" Clyburn later said. "We sat together on the House floor and talked about how that slogan ... could undermine the Black Lives Matter movement, just as 'burn, baby, burn' destroyed our movement back in the '60s."[35]

Lewis never compromised his commitment to nonviolence. To Brenda Jones, he said, "Brenda, the longer I live, the more I come to believe that nonviolence is an immutable principle, which should never be violated." "Those were his exact words," she recalled.[36]

He wanted nonviolence to be the foundation of the new surge in activism for Black equality. When he returned to D.C. in early June, Lewis sat for interviews with Al Roker, Gayle King, Ellen DeGeneres, and Jonathan Capehart. He praised the protest movements and tried to buck up his listeners. King, having heard that Lewis had seen his cats for the first time in months, asked their names. Lewis paused before deciding not to explain that this particular clowder consisted of adopted strays. "Well," he said, "we don't—we call them 'kitty,' 'kitty cat,' and they know each other. But when I went back home this past weekend, I was somewhat disappointed. I don't think they recognized me." King wrapped up the interview.[37]

On Friday, June 5, Washington mayor Muriel Bowser declared a stretch of Sixteenth Street north of Lafayette Square to be "Black Lives Matter Plaza." City employees painted the words "Black Lives Matter" in huge yellow capital letters on the asphalt. Lewis watched it on TV.

"I want to go there," he told Collins.

Collins had other things to focus on. "Well," he said, "I'll take you there on your way to chemo. We'll have a look." Then he thought about Lewis's love of art and how he seemed taken with the visuals of the Black Lives Matter Plaza. "I then had second thoughts," he said, "and I thought this is a bigger story than just doing a drive-by."

On Saturday, Collins texted Capehart. Collins said that Lewis wanted to visit the plaza and felt it should be documented. But he didn't want to issue an all-points bulletin. He asked Capehart to find a photographer. Capehart agreed, on the condition that he could come along. They agreed to meet Sunday at 6:30 a.m. at Sixteenth and K Streets. They would visit before the crowds arrived, to protect the immunocompromised Lewis.

"I'm going to take you to Black Lives Matter Plaza," Collins told Lewis on Saturday night. "The thing is we have to go very early."

"How early?"

"Well, I'm going to get you up at 4:30 in the morning so we can get there by about six." Lewis wasn't thrilled about it, but he agreed.

Sunday morning, Lewis put on his favorite T-shirt, which said "Too busy to hate." He chose a hat that said "1619." Collins had bought some clothes that were easy to take on and off, including pants with a drawstring. They drove off.

In the car, Collins wondered if Lewis should be dressed more formally. Though Lewis was never above wearing a campaign T-shirt, he always looked dignified in public. Collins realized that this trip could turn out to be a big event. He turned the car around, darted back in the house, and retrieved a navy-blue quarter-zip sweater. He helped Lewis into it right on the street, arranging the fabric to somewhat conceal the congressman's frail physique. They drove to the plaza.

A small group met them there, including Capehart and two photographers—Gary Williams, whom Capehart had recruited, and someone the mayor's office had hired. Everyone was masked. Lewis was walking with a cane. One TV crew, from the local Fox 5 station, was on hand.

Bowser had arranged access to a building with a rooftop terrace. They rode the elevator up to take some pictures with the enormous yellow "Black Lives Matter" lettering visible on the street behind them. Collins helped Lewis onto a small platform for a better view of the plaza.

Lewis didn't say much. He just took it all in, "digesting it all," Williams later said. "I was wondering, 'What is Mr. Lewis thinking?' It was a very tender time, a time of reckoning for America. I felt grateful just to see and witness." Williams spoke to Lewis briefly, thanking him for all he had done, "for paving the way, for showing how to create change."

Downstairs, they said hello to the mayor. A city sanitation truck pulled up to block the road so the photographers could climb on it to take photos. Lewis and Bowser were standing by the yellow "B" in "Black Lives Matter."

Williams asked the truck driver to back up a bit and then climbed up. He was stepping in dirt and garbage in order to get a good shot.

By now people were coming to the square. "People start realizing, 'Holy shit, it's John Lewis,'" Capehart said. They started applauding. Some thrust their cell phones toward the photographers, asking them to take pictures. One of the photographers agreed to take a photo for someone, opening the floodgates to endless requests.

Lewis also accommodated everyone's requests for pictures. He stood with city workers, with Williams's family, with admirers who had the good luck to be walking by. He talked to Stephanie Ramirez of Fox 5. "It's very moving. Very moving. Impressive," he said. "I think the people in DC and around the nation are sending a mightily powerful and strong message to the rest of the world that we will get there."

Shortly after 7:30 a.m., Lewis and Collins headed back to the car. A crowd followed them. "It was as if the crowd was literally walking him to his car," Williams said. Finally, they got in and drove home.

From there, the internet took over.[38]

The next morning, Lewis had a chemo treatment. The doctors told Lewis and Collins that things weren't looking as they should.

On the way home, Lewis asked for a milkshake. Collins stopped at a restaurant called Ted's Bulletin for a strawberry shake. The chemo had been draining, and Lewis got into bed to rest.

When Collins came back to check on Lewis, the congressman was upside down in his bed and shaking. Collins called Dr. Monahan, who said to go to an emergency room. Getting Lewis out of bed was difficult. Things didn't seem right. Collins called an ambulance and rode with Lewis to the hospital.

The doctor who saw Lewis was a young African American woman. After some tests, she told Collins that Lewis had a blood infection. Lewis stayed in the hospital that night. His condition stabilized, but later his blood pressure suddenly dropped. "All these buzzers are going off," Collins recalled. The hospital moved Lewis to an intensive care unit for four days.

At one point during those days, Collins went out to get coffee. When he came back, Lewis said, "We need to talk."

Collins wasn't ready. But Lewis began describing what he wanted for his funeral service. "I want Jim Lawson to do my eulogy," he said. He wanted Jennifer Holliday to sing. He mentioned a couple of people he didn't want there.

After going on for a while, he looked up at Collins and said, "You're not writing this down." Collins laughed and made sure to pay attention.

The next day, Lewis left the ICU, but was still in the hospital. At times he would wake up from a sleep, babbling and incoherent. "The chemo just isn't working," Dr. Monahan explained. "He needs to gain weight. We need to figure out a different treatment plan because this is no longer working."

Collins went home to shower and change. When he came back, a twenty-four-hour nurse was stationed by Lewis. "What happened?" he asked.

"Well, he thought he was in the airport," he was told. Lewis had hallucinated that he was late for a plane and had gotten up to run for his gate, when he tripped and fell. The hospital wanted someone with him at all times.

A couple of days later, Lewis was released. Collins got him a hospital bed for the downstairs parlor. Lewis asked when his next treatment would be.

"Well, there is no more treatment," Collins said.

Lewis was confused.

"Don't you remember when Dr. Monahan came in and explained this to us?"

Lewis didn't remember.

"Well, he believes you first have to get your strength back before we do more chemo and we figure out a new plan."[39]

Meanwhile, on June 9, Lewis fended off a primary challenge to be re-nominated for his Fifth District seat. He won 82 percent of the vote. Atlanta was not ready to let him go.

Collins organized a conference call with Lewis's doctors, his family, and a few close friends. He wanted to know how much time Lewis had left and what could be done. Lewis told Collins that he wanted to know whether resuming treatment would extend his life and, if so, for how long.

Collins patched together the various parties. Then he turned to Lewis. "You had a question?"

"How much time do I have with treatment, and without treatment?" Lewis asked.

The doctors told him it would probably be a difference of three to six months.

A couple of days later, Lewis said to Collins, "I want to go home"—meaning Atlanta.

"Well, when?" Collins asked.

"I want to go home now," he said. He was ready to stop treatment and prepare for his death.

"Well, I can't take you right now, but we can get you there." Collins began making arrangements.[40]

In Atlanta, Stephen McDaniel had a friend who knew Ed Bastian, the CEO of Delta Air Lines. The friend offered to help. Around six in the evening, McDaniel's phone rang. Bastian himself was on the phone, offering a private plane. McDaniel passed the offer on to Collins and Lewis.

"No," Lewis said. "I want to fly commercial." He turned down the private jet.

On June 24, Lewis and Collins flew to Atlanta. Delta gave them the royal treatment. The airline arranged for transportation to the airport, made sure Lewis was the last person to board and the first person to deplane, and drove him home.[41]

Nurses were at the house to handle his hospice care. John-Miles was also there; he and his father would have fun cooking their favorite dishes. But when he first arrived, Lewis had the odd sensation of not knowing what to do with himself. Collins told him to make some phone calls.

His first call was to Barack Obama. They talked about the "grandkids," meaning the young people out protesting. They shared a note of hope about what these protests might accomplish.

Next, Lewis called Pelosi. She insisted on coming to Atlanta. Over the July Fourth weekend, she sat with Lewis for two hours. At one point she asked him to sign a picture, but when he tried he was too weak. She then gave him a brooch, a replica of one she herself wore, engraved with the words "One country, one destiny"—a phrase that had been sewn into the lining of Lincoln's coat. That night, Pelosi called Collins again, crying. "I didn't realize this could be the last time I see him," she said.[42]

Bill Clinton also spoke to Lewis. "I was so afraid [it would be] the last time I'd ever get to talk to him," Clinton later said. But "it was wonderful. It was just like no time had ever passed. Everything was the way it always had been." They talked about "mostly our friendship and the life we had. How fortunate we'd both been and the lives we'd had and the families we had. And they have one child, and we did. But it was just like we were two old friends and compelled to run the last lap of our race, which we all have to do."[43]

Jacob Gillison also felt a need to say one last goodbye. He flew to Atlanta. Lewis was drifting in and out of sleep. "But he knew it was me. And I said, 'Congressman, I really want to thank you. I want to thank you for giving me this opportunity to work in your office, to work for you, to understand our history so much better. I learned all that from you. And I thank you for the trips to Selma, Alabama, to help me see, visualize, what our people went through.'" Lewis expressed appreciation. "And I said, 'Congressman, I know you're tired. And I know you have a lot on your mind and you're fighting so much. But it's OK.'"

Lewis said thank you. "And I said, 'I love you.' And I just left the room. It was my way of saying goodbye without saying goodbye. And I just watched him drift off to sleep."[44]

Even on his deathbed, Lewis remained solicitous of his visitors. Micheal Cristal, the president of Phi Beta Sigma, came to pay respects. "Is there anything I can do for the fraternity?" Lewis asked. Cristal was taken aback. "Congressman, no," he said. "You've done enough for all mankind."

One day Michael Bond visited, but when he arrived at Wallace Road, Lewis was asleep. He told his mother that Lewis was back in Atlanta. "She ran over," Michael said, "to sit with him for a day or so, helped to support him. And he was very pleased to see her. She hadn't seen him in a long time, maybe ten or fifteen years. They had some good moments together, kind of healing."[45]

In Washington, Lewis's staff continued to work hard. The congressman would from time to time put his name to a statement or a resolution. He signed on with Republican leader McCarthy to a letter seeking funding for a new initiative to revive education about civics and government. It was issued on July 17.[46]

There were also funeral plans to make. Lewis had always paid attention to his media coverage. His staff, too, was mindful of his legacy. The funeral should be done right.

For help, Collins brought in several others, including Anthony Coley, who had been Ted Kennedy's communications director when the senator died. At Kennedy's funeral in 2009, Cardinal Theodore McCarrick had read aloud a letter that the senator had written to the pope, allowing those assembled at the grave site to hear his final words after his passing. The experience had been emotionally overwhelming, moving mourners to tears. Coley proposed something similar. He drafted a letter to the American people from Lewis, to be published after his death. Brenda Jones rewrote it, using several of Lewis's trademark ideas and phrases while making sure it addressed the political moment and said something new. Collins gave the letter to Lewis, who approved it.

Coley got in touch with Kathleen Kingsbury, recently appointed as opinion editor of the *New York Times*. As he read Kingsbury the draft, she teared up. She immediately agreed to run it. Coley emailed the piece to her on Monday, July 12. She didn't think it needed much editing, but she insisted that Lewis personally approve the final wording of any piece bearing his name. "We had known, both from Brenda Jones and Anthony Coley, but also just from our own newsroom," Kingsbury said, "that we were talking about hours, possibly hours versus weeks of his life left. We sent over the edits not knowing if we were going to get them back, and we went back and forth a few times." One version of the piece had Lewis saying, "I'll be watching you," but it was nixed as too mawkish. Kingsbury and her deputy, Mary Suh, "were literally editing it ourselves, fact-checking it ourselves," Kingsbury said. "Because we just wanted it to be totally confidential. We didn't even tell the newsroom." On Friday, July 17, Kingsbury put the piece to bed.[47]

Lewis spent the day talking to friends, including old movement comrades such as Bernard LaFayette, James Lawson, and Bettie Mae Fikes. During the day, there was nothing out of the ordinary with his condition. He was in his bed, under his nurses' care. Collins and John-Miles were on hand. Then, that evening, "things just turned for the worse," Collins said. In the peace of his own bed, John Lewis drew his last breath.[48]

Chapter Twenty-Eight

INVICTUS

——————— ■ ■ ———————

To plan Lewis's memorial services, Michael Collins assembled what Stephen McDaniel called "the most amazing team" of staffers, friends, and communications professionals. In March, Anthony Coley had drawn up a multiday itinerary with events in multiple cities. In the week after Lewis died, the team met nightly over Zoom at seven o'clock, planning the events and figuring out whom to contact. All sorts of logistical matters needed attention: working with television teams and newspaper reporters, managing public crowds and private ceremonies, choosing friends and relatives for designated roles. In the midst of the planning, Nancy Pelosi told Collins that she had arranged for an honor guard to be with Lewis throughout the process—meaning the military would take charge of handling and transporting the casket, among other details. "It's unbelievable, in my opinion, that we put together what we did in a matter of seven to eight days," McDaniel said.[1]

The celebration of Lewis's life surpassed anything ever seen for a U.S. congressman. Not even the towering figures from the civil rights era who had died in recent years had received a comparable send-off. The farewell spanned six days and five cities, with speakers ranging from Lewis's siblings to former presidents. Television networks covered it as they had the Royal Wedding or the moon landing.

The rites began on Saturday, July 25, with a ceremony at Troy University, the formerly segregated college where a young Lewis had once hoped to enroll. It was an occasion for Americans to meet and hear from his surviving siblings—Henry Grant, Sam, Freddie, Rosa Mae, and Ethel

Mae—some of whom still lived on or near the old family farm. That evening, Lewis's body was chauffeured to Selma, ninety miles away, for another tribute, at Brown Chapel.

Sunday morning was called the Final Crossing. A pair of steeds pulled Lewis's flag-draped casket across the Pettus Bridge, trundling over a trail of red rose petals—meant to symbolize the bloodshed on the site. Family members walked behind it; well-wishers bowed their heads from the edge of the route. From there it was on to Montgomery, where Lewis lay in state in the Alabama capitol. As the motorcade traveled from city to city, mourners lined the route, much as they had for Robert Kennedy's funeral train in 1968. "Police cars with policemen standing outside, fire trucks with firemen standing outside," recalled McDaniel. "Just lined with people."[2]

After its Alabama sojourn, Lewis's casket was flown by military jet to Washington, where it lay in state in the Capitol, resting on the same catafalque that had once held Lincoln's coffin. Following a ceremony, it was moved to the East Front steps, which the public could file past on the Capitol's East Plaza. Friends and colleagues from every stage of Lewis's life offered goodbyes. One person who did not show was the president of the United States, who couldn't even bring himself to issue a statement. "He chose not to come to my inauguration," Trump later explained.[3]

On Wednesday, amid sweltering heat, Lewis's hearse joined a convoy on a final circuit around Atlanta, including along John Lewis Freedom Parkway. In the gay neighborhood of Midtown it halted at an intersection adorned with rainbow crosswalks, an acknowledgment of Lewis's ceaseless support for gay and lesbian rights. A synagogue was also on the route, in tribute to Lewis's affinity for the Jewish community. The procession drove past a sixty-five-foot-tall mural of Lewis, captioned with the word "Hero"—by now something of an Atlanta landmark. Atlanta's own statehouse provided one more resting place where neighbors and constituents could pay last respects.

On the morning of Thursday, July 30, *New York Times* readers and internet news consumers everywhere saw the message John Lewis had left for them. "Together, You Can Redeem the Soul of Our Nation," read the headline on his essay. One final time, he underscored the importance of history and the continuities between the struggles of his youth and those of the present day. "Democracy is not a state," he wrote. "It is an act, and each generation must do its part to help build what we called the Beloved Community, a nation and world society at peace with itself." For his own part, he said, "In my life I have done all I can to demonstrate that the way of peace, the way of love and nonviolence is the more excellent way."[4]

The funeral was held at Ebenezer, where Lewis had been a long-standing if irregular parishioner and whose pastor, Raphael Warnock, was running to be Georgia's first Black senator. Covid protocols limited the number of guests, but in the sanctuary were fifty House colleagues, including Pelosi, Hoyer, and Clyburn, as well as the African American senators Cory Booker and Kamala Harris.

Two of Lewis's nieces spoke. So did Bernice King, Martin's daughter. Bill Campbell and Xernona Clayton represented his vast constellation of friends. Pelosi extolled his service to the Congress and the Democratic caucus. From the civil rights movement, James Lawson recounted Lewis's precocious emergence as a leader in what Lawson described as not the civil rights movement but "the Nonviolent Movement of America." Jamila Thompson, Lewis's longtime legislative director, spoke for the staff, which she called "a little family, a little enclave," that Lewis had nurtured. "I don't think that there are many offices where you have the opportunity to hold your boss's hand and to adjust his tie," she said, "and to tell every person that you loved them."

In an extraordinary occurrence, three former presidents—Bill Clinton, Barack Obama, and George W. Bush—delivered eulogies. Introduced as the "president the last time we authorized the Voting Rights Act," Bush reminded the audience of Lewis's ability to cooperate with his political rivals, noting their work together on creating the National Museum of African American History and Culture and passing the Emmett Till Unsolved Civil Rights Crimes Act. Obama reviewed Lewis's acts of heroism in the movement, celebrating his preternatural persistence, courage, and determination. Obama also brought into the sanctuary the urgent events of the outside world: the pandemic, the racial activism, the presidential election. Decrying Republican steps to restrict voting, he advocated a comprehensive campaign to make voting easier through automatic registration, new polling places, and an Election Day holiday. "You want to honor John? Let's honor him by revitalizing the law that he was willing to die for."

If Obama's speech was the most political, Clinton's was the most personal. He reminisced about their friendship dating back to the 1970s, shared memories of Lewis scolding a younger John-Miles about his unruly Afro ("I said, 'John, Let's don't get old too soon. If I had hair like that, I'd have it down to my shoulders'"), and meditated on Lewis's fondness for Thomas Merton, whose *Seven Storey Mountain* sat in his backpack when he faced the troopers' batons on Bloody Sunday. Clinton also dared to raise the issue of Lewis's separation from SNCC, gently acknowledging that "there were two or three years there where the movement went a little bit too far towards Stokely." Some people on Twitter rebuked Clinton for rehashing a story of division at a ceremony devoted to warm remembrance. But Clinton understood that Kingston Springs had been a formative experience for Lewis. "He showed us as a young man, there are some things that you cannot do to hang on to a position, because if you do them, you won't be who you are anymore," Clinton said. "We are here today because he had the kind of character he showed when he lost an election."

Given Lewis's love of children—the hours he spent with them at schools, at Comic-Con, or in the halls of the Capitol—it was fitting that one speaker was Tybre Faw, a twelve-year-old from Tennessee who had befriended Lewis after persuading his grandmother to drive seven hours to attend a Selma pilgrimage. Faw read "Invictus," the poem that Lewis had recited as a child, which in later years his staff would occasionally join him in chanting around the office.

Out of the night that covers me,
    Black as the pit from pole to pole,
I thank whatever gods may be
    For my unconquerable soul.

In the fell clutch of circumstance
    I have not winced nor cried aloud.
Under the bludgeonings of chance
    My head is bloody, but unbowed.

Beyond this place of wrath and tears
    Looms but the Horror of the shade,
And yet the menace of the years
    Finds and shall find me unafraid.

It matters not how strait the gate,
>How charged with punishments the scroll,
I am the master of my fate,
>I am the captain of my soul.[5]

Lewis was buried next to Lillian at Atlanta's South-View Cemetery. In death, he continued to exert an outsized influence. In a summer when the names of statesmen were being stripped off buildings in penance for their racism and other imputed sins, Lewis was someone everyone wished to honor. For months to come, his name would be affixed to schools and centers, bridges and parks, streets and post offices, fellowships and awards. An ice cream parlor in Decatur, Georgia, debuted a flavor called "Good Trouble" (chocolate with brown sugar cake, coconut pecan crunch, and a salted caramel swirl). Lewis appeared in a Superman comic and in the online video game Minecraft. "Georgia Farmers Create 40-Acre Portrait of John Lewis," read a headline in a Milwaukee newspaper. "Why I Have a John Lewis Tattoo on My Leg," read another one, in the *Tennessean*.[6]

The most significant retitling was that of the voting rights bill languishing in Congress. Since the 2013 *Shelby County* decision, Democrats had tried unsuccessfully to establish new voting protections, only to face Republican opposition. After Lewis died, James Clyburn revived a suggestion from some years before. "It should be the John R. Lewis Voting Rights Act of 2020," he said. "That's the way to do it." The GOP did not yield, but the bill would for years thereafter bear Lewis's name.[7]

Lewis's spirit also hovered over the fall election. The presidential race had become, in Joe Biden's formulation, a battle for America's soul. Trump's reelection, the nominee warned, would bring more meanness and contempt for the norms of liberal democracy—a descent into darkness. Repudiating Trump would signify the triumph of the nation's better angels.

But to save their democracy, Americans would have to use it. Democrats needed high turnout, especially from African Americans, in order to prevail in swing states like Pennsylvania, Wisconsin, Michigan, and—competitive again in 2020—Georgia. They blitzed the electorate with pleas to register and to vote, sprinkling Lewis's name throughout their emails, texts, and other appeals. In August, the Democratic National Convention—whose proceedings, owing to the pandemic, were moved online—included a five-minute video tribute to Lewis's fight for the ballot. Over four nights, twenty different speakers invoked his legacy.

With the pandemic lingering and no vaccines yet available, many states had expanded the use of absentee ballots, to ease crowds at polling places. But the resort to the mails meant that on Election Day—Tuesday, November 3—several states didn't finish counting their votes. Expectant citizens were deprived of their usual late-night verdict.

By Wednesday, however, a decision was coming into view. According to the Associated Press tally, Biden had now won 264 electoral votes, just seven shy of victory. By Friday, he had surged ahead of Trump in Pennsylvania and Georgia. Here, too, Lewis's spirit seemed somehow to be at work: what catapulted Biden to his imminent Georgia victory was a trove of ballots from Clayton County in Lewis's Fifth District. "I love the idea that Clayton County could put Biden over in GA," said former Missouri senator Claire McCaskill. "That's John Lewis' district. He would do one of his trademark happy dances in heaven."[8]

In an unprecedented act of defiance, Trump not only refused to concede but schemed to repeal the outcome. When his legal challenges failed, he tried illegal ones: pressuring Michigan legislators to override Biden's victory in the state; leaning on the Pennsylvania assembly speaker to appoint pro-Trump electors; badgering the Georgia secretary of state to "find" the extra votes that he needed to win the state. Those efforts, too, failed. As a last resort, on January 6, 2021, Trump egged on a mob shortly before the special session of Congress was to notarize the electoral count. Two thousand riled-up vigilantes, some of them armed, overpowered police, broke the windows and doors of the Capitol, and rampaged through the halls as lawmakers fled for cover. Only after six hours of mayhem and the arrival of the National Guard and police reinforcements could Congress resume its duty and declare Biden the forty-sixth president.

The Capitol riot showed that the shades of reaction would not be swept back easily into their crypts by the fresh winds of a new presidency. The agonies and discord of the Trump years stood as a cruel reminder that the Beloved Community, like all utopias, would, for all its nobility, remain a Platonic ideal—sometimes appearing near and palpable on the horizon, sometimes dissolving into wisps like a desert mirage.

John Lewis had always chosen hope. Even as Trump's paramilitaries stormed the citadel of democracy on January 6, news arrived from Georgia of a pair of resounding victories. In two Senate runoffs, Raphael Warnock and Jon Ossoff, two men who had yoked their fortunes to Lewis's legacy, his pastor and his protégé, a Black man and a Jew working in tandem, had both won their races. Their victories gave the Democrats a bare majority in the next Senate—and President Biden a fighting chance to govern. Embattled but resilient, the guardians of liberalism would, for many years to come, draw sustenance and inspiration from John Lewis's unconquerable soul.

ACKNOWLEDGMENTS

My first thanks go to the late John Lewis. He invited me to meet with him in his Atlanta office in February 2019 and promised his cooperation with this book. Later, during the pandemic, when conditions made in-person interviews impossible, he spoke to me in telephone conversations with great feeling about his life. His longtime chief of staff, Michael Collins, not only sat for many interviews but trusted in an author whom he didn't know. Michael opened doors, encouraging friends and colleagues to cooperate with me. He patiently reviewed facts, chronologies, and other details. John Lewis's trusted press secretary Brenda Jones similarly assisted me in making sure I understood the congressman in all his complexity.

In the bibliography readers will find a list of roughly 250 people I interviewed, who generously gave of their time to share with me their knowledge and memories of John Lewis. They include Lewis's staff, family members, friends, and colleagues from throughout his career, including President Obama, President Clinton, Secretary of State Hillary Clinton, and House Speaker Pelosi. For the sake of brevity, I won't repeat all of their names here, but they have my profoundest thanks. Their knowledge of and insights into John Lewis form the core of the book's second half, for which few archival materials were available. My appreciation goes as well to their assistants who helped with arrangements. An extra thanks to many people who gave me multiple interviews—in some cases dozens—including Michael Collins, Linda Earley Chastang, Brenda Jones, Archie Allen, Tom Houck, and Danny Lyon. They helped me get to know John Lewis beyond his public image and provided deep context about his life and career.

The bibliography also contains lists of "Private Materials Shared with Author" and "Private Interviews, Shared with Author." These items came either from friends of John Lewis or historians or journalists who interviewed him. Again, I am listing their names in the bibliography, but with no less appreciation than if I had cited them here. I owe a special mention to a few. Archie Allen, who knew John Lewis since their time together in the Nashville Student Movement in the early 1960s, began a biography of Lewis in 1968 that he never wrote. He also worked closely with Lewis at the Voter Education Project and ACTION. He gave me exclusive access to seventeen binders of materials and a box of cassette tapes from his archives. Archie also gave me several of his wonderful photographs to use. Henry Louis Gates and his team at *Finding Your Roots* shared the research materials for their episode about Lewis, including archival research into his family history. Danny Lyon shared a dozen private recordings of Lewis. Sean Wilentz shared seventeen cassettes containing interviews with Lewis and others that he conducted for a 1996 *New Republic* profile. Neal Bennett generously digitized the Allen and Wilentz tapes for me.

The bibliography contains, too, a list of archives I consulted. I wish to thank all the archivists and librarians at those repositories who allowed me and my research assistants to use their resources, who answered questions, and who in many cases identified and scanned materials to spare me an onsite visit. A special shout out to Matthew Wasniewski, Amelia Frappolli, and their colleagues in the House of Representatives History Office, who helped me on a dozen occasions. I thank the many librarians at Rutgers University and at the New York Public Library for their assistance in finding materials. Rutgers history librarian Tom Glynn arranged for my use of the ProQuest database "The Black Freedom Struggle in the 20th Century," which includes the SNCC papers among other collections. Caroline Mann conducted an extensive literature review for me dealing with Lewis's congressional career.

Many scholars and journalists have shared with me their knowledge and insights into John Lewis and the civil rights movement or gave advice on other matters. I am in their debt, both for their scholarship on which I relied and for taking time to talk with me. These include Ari Berman, Taylor Branch, Dan T. Carter, Robert Cohen, Matt Cooper, Joe Crespino, Matt Dallek, John D'Emilio, Don Doyle, Jonathan Eig, Juliet Eilperin, Eric Etheridge, Evan Faulkenbury, Michael Flamm, Eric Foner, Sam Freedman, Brett Gadsden, David Garrow, Todd Gitlin, Sage Goodwin, David Grann, Ben Hedin, Heather Hendershot, Wesley Hogan, Ben Houston, Carl Hulse, Gregg Ivers, Will Jones, David Karol, Frances Lee, Phyllis Leffler, Fredrik

Logevall, Michael Long, Nancy Weiss Malkiel, Andrew Maraniss, David Margolick, Jon Meacham, Aldon Morris, Maureen Orth, Tracy Parker, Garth Pauley, Betsy Phillips, Gary Pomerantz, Andrew Pope, Todd Purdum, Bill Rankin, Nico Slate, Timothy Stewart-Winter, Gil Troy, Milton Viorst, Mark Whitaker, Leon Wieseltier, Sean Wilentz, Bob Woodward, Carla Yanni, and Julian Zelizer. The names of other journalists and historians, who gave me interviews about their own relationships with John Lewis, appear among the interviewees.

At Rutgers University, my chairs and deans there have been exceptionally supportive, as have senior university officials. Thanks to Jonathan Holloway, Francine Conway, Amy Jordan, Susan Keith, Jonathan Potter, Dafna Lemish, Mark Aakhus, Karen Novick, Alastair Bellany, Melissa Feinberg, Rebecca Walkowitz, and Henry Turner. My gratitude extends to my colleagues in those departments as well. Saladin Ambar, Ross Baker, and Steven Lawson have been especially helpful. For indispensable administrative help, I thank Narda Acevedo, Marisol Porter, Vinny Andoldi, Mary Demeo, Candace Walcott-Shepherd, Marilyn Reyes, Amanda Gravenhise, Ronette Henry, Jennifer Schenk, and Tejal Talati.

The Rutgers Research Council awarded me its "Social and Racial Justice Award." I also have been fortunate to receive external grants and fellowships that enabled me to write this book: I thank Kai Bird, Thad Ziolkowski, and the Leon Levy Center for Biography at the Graduate Center of the City University of New York and Anthony Marx, William Kelly, Martha Hodes, Paul Delaverdac, and the Cullman Center for Scholars and Writers at the New York Public Library—as well as the fellows with whom I served, whose ideas and comments helped me immeasurably. I am grateful also to the Guggenheim Foundation for awarding me a fellowship to finish this book and the National Endowment for the Humanities for a summer stipend and a Public Scholar Fellowship. Eric Foner, Annette Gordon-Reed, Peniel Joseph, Laura Kalman, and Sean Wilentz have my thanks for writing supporting letters.

A remarkable group of assistants has helped me throughout the research process. Foremost is Katherine Thai, who began assisting me while an undergraduate at Rutgers and became an indispensable part of this project. A standout in my course on literary journalism, she went on to pursue a Ph.D. in computer science, which is almost in hand. That she should excel in a third discipline, history, is a testament to her extraordinary range and intelligence. Other Rutgers students who provided great help through the Aresty Research Assistant program include Adam Ahmadi, Swasti Jain, Grace Lewis, Olivia Mezzarina, David Ogilvie, Adam Panish, Andrew Roberts, Sarah Samdani, and Emily Trujillo. Visiting remote archives or providing other forms of research help were Jay Driskell, Kelsey Ensign, Kate Kelley, Maxime Minne, Joseph Riley, Glenn Speer, Ben Welton, and Alexandria Yen. Jill Cowan assisted me with photo research and video research and discovered the extraordinary footage of John Lewis in his hospital bed on Bloody Sunday. My thanks to all.

For several years, I've had the pleasure of being part of a writing group of journalists and historians (with a slightly changing cast) who meet each month to share and comment on one another's work. They have commented on many chapters of this book, talked through bigger problems about themes, structure, tone, and writing, and provided delightful companionship. Thanks to Matthew Connelly, James Goodman, Nicole Hemmer, James Ledbetter, Dahlia Lithwick, Kati Marton, Michael Massing, Nara Milanich, Natalia Mehlman Petrzela, Claire Bond Potter, Clay Risen, James Traub, Ted Widmer, and Brenda Wineapple—treasured friends all.

Several colleagues have read the manuscript in whole or in part and offered ideas to improve the it. My deep thanks to Saladin Ambar, Ann Fabian, David Garrow, and Brian Rosenwald, who read complete drafts of the manuscript, and to Jeff Shesol and Mark Whitaker, who read portions of it. All offered insightful and incisive feedback. Thank you to Rob Sternitzky and Lisa Healy for a meticulous copyedit.

My agent, Peter Matson, took me on as a client when I was a graduate student writing my first book. For twenty-five years he has been a great champion and friend. Thanks to him, Christopher Combemale, and the team at Sterling Lord Literistic.

Bob Bender of Simon & Schuster signed this book in 2019. We have developed a felicitous working relationship, talking through together what the book can and should be. He has improved it in countless ways. When he retired earlier this year, Dawn Davis ably carried the book to publication. CEO Jonathan Karp, whom I met years ago when we were starting out in our respective businesses, has been a great supporter. Thanks as well to so many others at Simon & Schuster including associate editor Johanna Li, Maria Mendez, Julia Prosser and Anne Tate Pierce in publicity, Tyanni Niles in marketing, art director Jackie Seow, and designer Lewelin Polanco.

As the page proofs for this book arrived, my father, Robert Greenberg, died at the age of eighty-nine. A philosopher and the most rigorous of thinkers, he instilled in me not only a love of scholarship but also a devotion to freedom, equality, and human rights for all. In some ultimate sense, he and my mother, Maida Greenberg, thus inspired me to write this book. He was proud to know that this life of John Lewis would be published soon. For unfailing love and support, I thank him and my mom and the rest of my family: Judith, Ira, Claire, and Sasha; Jonathan, Megan, Hank, and Maggie; and the whole Nossel family. My wife, Suzanne Nossel, and my children, Leo and Liza, have been deeply involved in this project from the beginning, joining me on a tour of Atlanta, Montgomery, Birmingham, and Selma early on as we all deepened our knowledge about civil rights and African American history. Suzanne was usually the first person to read each chapter (when I needed a simple answer to the question "Is this any good?"), and Leo and Liza provided encouragement and at least feigned a modicum of interest when I held forth about my research. They have my enduring gratitude and love.

NOTES

ONE: THE BOY FROM TROY

1. Eddie Lewis, interview with Archie Allen, Mar. 15, 1969, NPL-AAC, box 3, folder 31; Willie Mae Lewis, interview with Archie Allen, NPL-AAC, box 3, folder 33; *Harper's*, Oct. 1961, 136.

2. Ethel Mae Tyner, interview with Archie Allen, NPL-AAC, box 3, folder 33; *Los Angeles Times*, July 26, 1998, 3.

3. Sarah Antoinette Sellers Abernathy, "Memories," FYRRM, 76–77; "Land Purchases and Sales by Tobias and Elizabeth Carter, 1869–1891," FYRRM; Lewis with D'Orso, *Walking*, 24–25.

4. *Finding Your Roots*, season 1, episode 2, PBS, Mar. 25, 2012.

5. Litwack, *Been in the Storm So Long*, 238–40; Kolchin, *First Freedom*, 56–59; *Finding Your Roots*, season 1, episode 2, Mar. 25, 2012.

6. Fitzgerald, *Reconstruction in Alabama*; Litwack, *Storm*, 546–57; "Final Script: Episode 102—Booker/Lewis," FYRRM.

7. "Verification of Birth Record," Alabama State Department of Health, Feb. 19, 1957, AAPP; John Lewis, interview with David Halberstam, #1, BU-DHP, box 59, folder 4.

8. Lewis with D'Orso, *Walking*, 25–36.

9. Eddie Lewis, interview with Archie Allen, NPL-AAC, box 4, folder 21.

10. John Lewis statement, NPL-AAC, box 3, folder 2.4; Lewis with D'Orso, *Walking*, 28; Willie Mae Lewis, interview with Archie Allen, NPL-AAC, box 3, folder 23; John Lewis, interview with David Halberstam, #1, BU-DHP, box 59, folder 4.

11. John Lewis, interview with Archie Allen, Feb. 14, 1969, NPL-AAC, 2. (Allen's interviews with Lewis are not in the archives but shelved at Special Coll B. L6746A v. 2 NCR.)

12. Eddie Lewis, interview with Archie Allen, NPL-AAC, box 3, folder 21; Raines, *Rested*, 72; John Lewis interview with Sean Wilentz, June 12, 1995, tape 1, SWT.

13. Lewis with D'Orso, *Walking*, 31–32; John Lewis, interview with David Halberstam, #1, BU-DHP, box 59, folder 4.

14. John Lewis, interview with Archie Allen, Feb. 14, 1969, NPL-AAC, 1.

15. *New South*, Spring 1971, 17; John Lewis, interview with David Halberstam, #1, BU-DHP, box 59, folder 4.

16. John Lewis, author interview, May 8, 2020; John Lewis, interview with Archie Allen, Feb. 14, 1969, NPL-AAC, 18–22; John Lewis, interview with David Halberstam, #1, BU-DHP, box 59, folder 4.

17. John Lewis, interview with David Halberstam, #1, BU-DHP, box 59, folder 4; *New Republic*, July 1, 1996, 23; Lewis with D'Orso, *Walking*, 59; Beardslee, *Way Out*, 2.

18. John Lewis, interview with David Halberstam, #1, BU-DHP, box 59, folder

4; John Lewis, interview with Sean Wilentz, June 12, 1995, tape 1, SWT; John Lewis, author interview, May 8, 2020.

19. John Lewis interview with David Halberstam, #1, BU-DHP, box 59, folder 4; John Lewis, interview with Sean Wilentz, June 12, 1995, tape 1, SWT; *Atlanta Constitution*, Nov. 4, 1977, 18.

20. *Southern Exposure*, Fall 1976, 15–16.

21. John Lewis, interview with Archie Allen, Feb. 14, 1969, NPL-AAC, 11–12; Lewis statement, NPL-AAC, box 3, folder 2.4; Lewis with D'Orso, *Walking*, 34–35.

22. Willie Mae Lewis, interview with Archie Allen, NPL-AAC, box 3, folder 23; *New York Times Magazine*, June 25, 1967, 44; John Lewis, interview with Archie Allen, Feb. 14, 1969, NPL-AAC, 14; *Washington Post*, Feb. 4, 1996, L8.

23. John Lewis, OH with Katherine Shannon, Aug. 22, 1967, RJBOHC, 7–8.

24. John Lewis, interview with Archie Allen, Feb. 14, 1969, NPL-AAC, 16.

25. Egerton, *Mind to Stay Here*, 53; John Lewis, interview with David Halberstam, #1, BU-DHP, box 59, folder 4; *Washington Post*, June 9, 1998, D2.

26. John Lewis, interview with Archie Allen, Feb. 14, 1969, NPL-AAC, 19–22; *Southern Exposure*, Fall 1976, 16. In *Walking with the Wind* and *March*, Lewis says that he put the drowned bird in the sun and it revived. This is not a story he had told before, however, and for obvious reasons it is suspect.

27. John Lewis, interview with David Halberstam, #1, BU-DHP, box 59, folder 4.

28. John Lewis, interview with Archie Allen, Feb. 14, 1969, NPL-AAC, 19–20; Lewis with D'Orso, *Walking*, 61; *New Republic*, July 1, 1996, 23.

29. Lewis statement, NPL-AAC, box 3, folder 2.4.

30. John Lewis, interview with Archie Allen, Feb. 14, 1969, NPL-AAC, 14.

31. Deutsch, *Schoolhouse*; Lewis with D'Orso, *Walking*, 44–46; John Lewis, interview with David Halberstam, #1, BU-DHP, box 59, folder 4; John Lewis, interview with Archie Allen, Feb. 14, 1969, NPL-AAC, 7–9.

32. Lewis with D'Orso, *Walking*, 49–50.

33. John Lewis, interview with Archie Allen, Feb. 16, 1969, NPL-AAC, 31; Viorst, *Fire*, 96.

34. John Lewis, interview with Archie Allen, Feb. 14, 1969, NPL-AAC, 31; John Lewis, interview with David Halberstam, #1, BU-DHP, box 59, folder 4; Lewis with D'Orso, *Walking*, 50–51.

35. *Southern Exposure*, Fall 1976, 16.

36. "Morning Edition," NPR, Jan. 17, 2020; John Lewis, interview with David Halberstam, #1, BU-DHP, box 59, folder 4; John Lewis, interview with Julian Bond, Sept. 26, 2005, UVA-EBL, 15.

37. John Lewis, interview with David Halberstam, #1, BU-DHP, box 59, folder 4.

38. John Lewis, interview with Archie Allen, Feb. 14, 1969, NPL-AAC, 23; Lewis with D'Orso, *Walking*, 59–60.

39. John Lewis, interview with David Halberstam, #1, BU-DHP, box 59, folder 4; Eddie Lewis, interview with Archie Allen, NPL-AAC, box 3, folder 31; John Lewis, interview with Archie Allen, Feb. 14, 1969, NPL-AAC, 21; *Atlanta Constitution*, Nov. 4, 1977, 18; Raines, *Rested*, 72; Lewis with D'Orso, *Walking*, 70–72.

40. John Lewis, interview with David Halberstam, #1, BU-DHP, box 59, folder 4; Lewis with D'Orso, *Walking*, 57.

41. Martin Luther King Jr., "Paul's Letter to American Christians, Sermon Delivered to the Commission on Ecumenical Missions and Relations, United Presbyterian Church, U.S.A.," Martin Luther King, Jr. Research and Education Institute, June 3, 1958.

42. John Lewis, interview with Randall

Kennedy, Apr. 14, 2003, jfklibrary.org; John Lewis, OH with Katherine Shannon, Aug. 22, 1967, RJBOHC; Viorst, *Fire*, 98; Raines, *Rested*, 73; Lewis with D'Orso, *Walking*, 56.

43. John Lewis, OH with Katherine Shannon, Aug. 22, 1967, RJBOHC, 5–7; John Lewis statement, NPL-AAC, box 3, folder 2.4, 2; Egerton, *Mind to Stay Here*, 53.

44. John Lewis, interview with Julian Bond, Sept. 26, 2005, UVA-EBL, 15; John Lewis, interview with Archie Allen, Feb. 16, 1969, NPL-AAC, 27; John Lewis, interview with David Halberstam, #1, BU-DHP, box 59, folder 4; *Southern Exposure*, Fall 1976, 15–17; Lewis with D'Orso, *Walking*, 63; John Lewis to American Baptist Theological Seminary, Dec. 10, 1956, Mar. 12, 1957, and Apr. 4, 1957, Charles Fitzgerald to John Lewis, Dec. 17, 1956, John Lewis Application for Admission, Apr. 4, 1957, W. H. Abernathy to "Whom It May Concern," Mar. 20, 1957, John Lewis high school transcript, May 27, 1957, all AAPP.

45. Lewis with D'Orso, *Walking*, 64.

TWO: NASHVILLE

1. John Lewis to American Baptist Theological Seminary, Aug. 29, 1957, AAPP; John Lewis, interview with Archie Allen, Feb. 16, 1969, NPL-AAC, 32; Halberstam, *Children*, 69; Lewis with D'Orso, *Walking*, 69.

2. *Tennessean*, Sept. 15, 1924, 9; *Southern Exposure*, Fall 1976, 17.

3. John Lewis, interview with Archie Allen, Feb. 16, 1969, NPL-AAC, 33–34; Lewis with D'Orso, *Walking*, 69–71.

4. Barry E. Lee, "The Nashville Civil Rights Movement," doctoral dissertation, Georgia State University, Atlanta, GA, 2010, 91–93; Lewis with D'Orso, *Walking*, 69; Halberstam, *Children*, 68.

5. Meacham, *Truth*, 48; John Lewis,

OH with Katherine Shannon, Aug. 22, 1967, RJBOHC, 35; John Lewis, interview, Sept. 26, 2005, UVA-EBL, 15; Lewis with D'Orso, *Walking*, 72–82.

6. Kelly Miller Smith, interview with Archie Allen, Aug. 5, 1969, NPL-AAC, 5; John Lewis, interview with David Halberstam, #1, BU-DHP, box 59, folder 4.

7. John Lewis, interview with David Halberstam, #1, BU-DHP, box 59, folder 4; Lovett, *Tennessee*, 120.

8. *New York Times*, Sept. 12, 1957, 24; *Chicago Defender*, Sept. 21, 1957, 12; *Southern Exposure*, Fall 1976, 18; John Lewis, interview with David Halberstam, #1, BU-DHP, box 59, folder 4, 18; Doyle, *Nashville*, 237–42.

9. John Lewis, interview with Archie Allen, Feb. 16, 1969, NPL-AAC, 33; Egerton, *Mind to Stay*, 54.

10. *Southern Exposure*, Fall 1976, 17; John Lewis, interview with Archie Allen, Feb. 16, 1969, NPL-AAC, 30; John Lewis, interview with David Halberstam, #1, BU-DHP, box 59, folder 4, 19–20; Lewis with D'Orso, *Walking*, 81; Viorst, *Fire*, 103.

11. Lewis with D'Orso, *Walking*, 70–71, 74; John Lewis, interview with Archie Allen, Feb. 16, 1969, NPL-AAC, 41.

12. Angeline Butler, author interview, Apr. 29, 2020; Colia Clark, author interview, June 4, 2020; Bernard LaFayette, author interview, June 17, 2020.

13. Lewis with D'Orso, *Walking*, 72.

14. Marian Fuson, author interview, June 2, 2020; Doyle, *Nashville*, 225; *Jet*, Dec. 5, 1963, 14–22; C. T. Vivian, interview with Blackside, Jan. 23, 1986, WU-HHC.

15. Houston, *Nashville Way*, 1–2, 13–14.

16. Doyle, *Nashville*, 159; Halberstam, *Children*, 23.

17. Dunne, "Next Steps," 1–34.

18. Houston, *Nashville Way*, 35; Doyle, *Nashville*, 225–28.

19. "Pursuit of a Dream," VU-KMSP, box 28, folder 7; *Ebony*, July 1954, 26–30; *Time*, May 26, 1961, 19.

20. "Background of the Nashville Christian Leadership Conference," VU-KMSP, box 75, folder 8; "Toward the Beloved Community," VU-KMSP, box 75, folder 13; Walker, *Challenge and Change*, 26.

21. "Toward the Beloved Community," VU-KMSP, box 75, folder 13; Lovett, *Tennessee*, 119–20; Hogan, *Many Minds*, 16.

22. Harvey Cox, author interview, Dec. 16, 2020; James Lawson, OH with William Barnes, Oct. 21, 2002, NPL-CROHC; Branch, *Parting*, 204–5; Halberstam, *Children*, 13–17, 25–50.

23. James Lawson, author interview, Mar. 30, 2020; *Tennessean*, Mar. 24, 1958, 4; History of NCLC, VU-KMSP, box 76, folder 6; "Sit-In," liner notes, Folkways Records Album no. FH5590, VU-KMSP, box 76, folder 24.

24. *Southern Exposure*, Fall 1976, 19; John Lewis, author interview, May 8, 2020; Halberstam, *Children*, 71; C. T. Vivian, interview with Archie Allen, Aug. 15, 1968, 1, NPL-AAC, box 3, folder 35.

25. John Lewis, interview with David Halberstam, #1, BU-DHP, box 59, folder 4, 23; Morris, *Origins*, 175.

26. In *Walking with the Wind*, Lewis erroneously places his application to Troy State in his freshman year. Lewis with D'Orso, *Walking*, 76.

27. John Lewis, interview with Archie Allen, Feb. 16, 1969, NPL-AAC, 27; Viorst, *Fire*, 101.

28. John Lewis, interview with David Halberstam, #1, BU-DHP, box 59, folder 4, 19; Ralph Abernathy, interview with Archie Allen, Aug. 17, 1968, NPL-AAC, box 3, folder 1.

29. Fred Gray to John Lewis, June 9, 1959, 28–29, AAPP; John Lewis, interview with Archie Allen, Feb. 16, 1969, NPL-AAC, 28; Lewis with D'Orso, *Walking*, 76–77.

30. John Lewis, interview with Callie Crossley, John F. Kennedy Library, August 18, 2013.

31. Lewis with D'Orso, *Walking*, 77.

32. Fred Gray to John Lewis, Aug. 14, 1959, AAPP; John Lewis, interview with Archie Allen, Feb. 16, 1969, NPL-AAC, 28–29.

33. Ralph Abernathy, interview with Archie Allen, NPL-AAC, box 3, folder 1.

34. Branch, *Parting*, 261.

35. John Lewis, interview with Archie Allen, Feb. 16, 1969, NPL-AAC, 29.

36. Lewis with D'Orso, *Walking*, 78–79.

37. Kelly Miller Smith, interview with Archie Allen, NPL-AAC, box 3, folder 29; James Lawson, OH with William Barnes, May 23, 2003, NPL-CROHC; Hogan, *Many Minds*, 17–19; Morris, *Origins*, 177; "Background of the Nashville Christian Leadership Conference," VU-KMSP, box 75, folder 8.

38. Kelly Miller Smith, interview with Robert Penn Warren, Feb. 13, 1964, VU-WSNC; John Lewis, interview with Archie Allen, Feb. 16, 1969, NPL-AAC, 35; Morris, *Origins*, 176.

39. Lewis placed his first encounter with Lawson in the fall of 1958. But Lawson insists that he met Lewis in September 1959, when he began hosting nonviolence workshops for students. Historians have written different things. When I asked Lewis about the discrepancy in 2020, he told me to trust Lawson's memory over his own. "If that's what Jim Lawson says, he's right." One possibility is that Lewis heard Lawson speak at one or more NCLC meetings in 1958 and 1959—meetings that featured, as Lewis recalled, "ministers and laypeople and people in the NAACP," but that were separate from the famous workshops. John Lewis, author interview,

May 8, 2020; James Lawson, author interview, Mar. 30, 2020; John Lewis, interview with Clayborne Carson, Apr. 17, 1972, 3, CRMVET; Carson, *In Struggle*, 22; Halberstam, *Children*, 60; Hogan, *Many Minds*, 19; Lewis with D'Orso, *Walking*, 83–84; Viorst, *Fire*, 103–4; Branch, *Parting*, 262.

40. Lewis with D'Orso, *Walking*, 83–84.

41. James Lawson, author interview, Mar. 30, 2020; Kelly Miller Smith, interview with Robert Penn Warren, Feb. 13, 1964, VU-WSNC; Kelly Miller Smith, OH with Lewis Britton, Dec. 22, 1967, RJBOHC; John Lewis, interview with Archie Allen, Feb. 16, 1969, NPL-AAC, 34; John Lewis, interview with Clayborne Carson, Apr. 17, 1972, 3; Lewis with D'Orso, *Walking*, 83–91; Lovett, *Tennessee*, 122.

42. "Bibliography," VU-JLP, box 38, folder 1; C. T. Vivian, interview with Archie Allen, Aug. 15, 1968, NPL-AAC, box 3, folder 35, 1; James Lawson, OH with William Barnes, Oct. 21, 2002, NPL-CROHC; Isaac et al., "Movement Schools and Dialogical Diffusion of Nonviolent Praxis," 171; Viorst, *Fire*, 104; Carter, "C. T. Vivian," 46. Some felt that Lawson claimed too much credit. Angeline Butler said that she and C. T. Vivian agreed that Lawson has elevated his own role over that of other equally important minsters in the group, including Vivian, Smith, and Metz Rollins. Angeline Butler, author interview, May 21, 2020. Archie Allen expressed a similar opinion. Archie Allen, author interview, Nov. 18, 2021.

43. Kapur, *Prophet*, 155; Carson et al., eds., *Papers of Martin Luther King, Jr.*, vol. 5, 423.

44. Jensen, "The Growing Edges of Beloved Community," 239–58; Carson et al., eds., *Papers of Martin Luther King, Jr.*, vol. 5, 322–27. Introducing Lawson in 1961, King said, "Some time ago I read that Jim

Lawson was a disciple of Martin Luther King on the philosophy of nonviolence. This is very interesting to me because I'm sure Jim Lawson knew about nonviolence before Martin Luther King and he knows more about it than Martin Luther King.... If anything, I am a disciple of Jim Lawson." Lee, "The Nashville Civil Rights Movement," 205.

45. Powledge, *Free at Last*, 234.

46. Halberstam, *Children*, 60; John Lewis, interview with Archie Allen, NPL-AAC, 35; Viorst, *Fire*, 105; John Lewis, interview with David Halberstam, #1, BU-DHP, box 59, folder 4, 23–24.

47. James Lawson, author interview, Mar. 30, 2020.

48. Will Campbell, interview with Archie Allen, Sept. 11, 1968, NPL-AAC, box 4, folder 7, 6.

49. John Lewis, interview with Archie Allen, Feb. 16, 1969, NPL-AAC, 39; *Into America*, podcast, July 21, 2020.

50. John Lewis, interview with Archie Allen, Feb. 16, 1969, NPL-AAC, 39; Colia Clark, author interview, June 4, 2020; Bill Harbour, OH with K. G. Bennett, Aug. 19, 2004, 4, NPL-CROHC; James Bevel, Bernard LaFayette, and Rip Patton, OH with K. G. Bennett, Jan. 17, 2003, 9, NPL-CROHC; James Bevel, interview with David Halberstam, BU-DHP, box 58, folder 13, 12.

51. James Lawson, OH with William Barnes, Oct. 21, 2002, NPL-CROHC; Holsaert et al., eds., *Freedom Plow*, 40.

52. Morris, *Origins*, 218; Matthew H. Ahmann, ed., *The New Negro*, 45; Powledge, *Free at Last*, 204; Branch, *Parting*, 559; Halberstam, *Children*, 59, 62–63, 143–45; Lewis with D'Orso, *Walking*, 92.

53. Viorst, *Fire*, 103–5; Kelly Miller Smith, interview with Archie Allen, NPL-AAC, box 3, folder 29; Paul LaPrad, interview with K. G. Bennett, Mar. 7, 2003, 9,

NPL-CROHC; John Lewis, interview with David Halberstam, #1, BU-DHP, box 59, folder 4, 24; Halberstam, *Children*, 77–81.

54. Hogan, *Many Minds*, 25; Lewis with D'Orso, *Walking*, 93.

55. Angeline Butler, author interview, Apr. 29, 2020; Halberstam, *Children*, 66–67; Kelly Miller Smith, interview with Archie Allen, Aug. 5, 1969, NPL-AAC, box 3, folder 29, 3.

56. James Bevel, Bernard LaFayette, and Rip Patton, OH with K. G. Bennett, Jan. 17, 2003, 18, NPL-CROHC; Hogan, *Many Minds*, 25; Marian Fuson, author interview, June 2, 2020.

57. Lewis with D'Orso, *Walking*, 94–95; James Lawson, "Report on Nashville" (handwritten notes), VU-JLP, box 45, folder 2; Kelly Miller Smith, "Dear Friend," Nov. 25, 1959, VU-JLP, box 62, folder 19.

58. John Lewis, interview with Archie Allen, Feb. 16, 1969, NPL-AAC, 56; *Chicago Defender*, Jan. 5, 1960, 5; Lovett, *Tennessee*, 123; Lewis with D'Orso, *Walking*, 95.

59. Lewis, author interview, May 8, 2020.

60. Lewis with D'Orso, *Walking*, 96–97; Bernard LaFayette, author interview, June 17, 2020.

THREE: THE SIT-INS

1. *Chicago Defender*, Jan. 5, 1960, 5, Jan. 10, 1960, 2.

2. Angeline Butler, author interview, Apr. 29, 2020; James Lawson, unpublished manuscript, VU-JLP, box 45, folder 26, ch. 6; *New York Herald Tribune*, Mar. 13, 1960, 18.

3. Chuck McDew, OH with Katherine Shannon, Aug. 24, 1967, RJBOHC, 14; *Chicago Defender*, Mar. 9, 1960, 9; Morris, *Origins*, 188–94; Zinn, *SNCC*, 17–18.

4. *New York Times*, Feb. 3, 1960, 22; Lovett, *Tennessee*, 123; Ella Baker, interview with Clayborne Carson, May 5, 1972,

CRMVET; *New York Times*, Feb. 11, 1960, 22.

5. James Lawson, unpublished manuscript, VU-JLP, box 45, folder 26, ch. 6; "Chronology," VU-JLP, box 45, folder 2; Wynn, "The Dawning of a New Day," 45; *New York Herald Tribune*, Mar. 13, 1960, 18; *Nashville Banner*, Mar. 21, 1960, 10; *Tennessean*, Mar. 21, 1960, 2; John Lewis, interview with Clayborne Carson, Apr. 17, 1972, CRMVET.

6. "Chronology," VU-JLP, box 45, folder 2; Doyle, *Nashville*, 245; Raines, *Rested*, 98; Wynn, "The Dawning of a New Day," 46.

7. *Tennessean*, Feb. 14, 1960, 10; Lewis with D'Orso, *Walking*, 100.

8. *Southern Exposure*, Fall 1976, 19; Viorst, *Fire*, 107; Lovett, *Tennessee*, 125.

9. John Lewis, interview with David Halberstam, #1, BU-DHP, box 59, folder 4.

10. Bernard LaFayette, interview with David Halberstam, BU-DHP, box 58, folder 17; *New York Times*, Feb. 14, 1960, 30; *Tennessean*, Feb. 14, 1960, 10; Houston, *Nashville Way*, 92–93; Lovett, *Tennessee*, 125.

11. John Lewis, interview with David Halberstam, #1, BU-DHP, box 59, folder 4.

12. Lewis with D'Orso, *Walking*, 103.

13. James Lawson, unpublished manuscript, VU-JLP, box 45, folder 26, ch. 6, 4; John Lewis, interview with Archie Allen, May 28, 1969, NPL-AAC, 44; Lewis with D'Orso, *Walking*, 103–4.

14. Houston, *Nashville Way*, 125; Hampton and Fayer, *Voices of Freedom*, 57.

15. Branch, *Parting*, 275; Hogan, *Many Minds*, 31; Morris, *Origins*, 202, 210. The first chair, Luther Harris, was not spending enough time with the movement and Nash was chosen to replace him. Diane Nash, interview with August Meier, Jan. 31, 1961, NYPL-SC-AMP, box 4, folder 70, 4.

16. *Newsday*, Mar. 19, 1960, 1; *New*

York Times, Mar. 20, 1960, 1, 45; Time, Apr. 11, 1960, 64; New York Times, Feb. 21, 1960, E21; Morris, "Black Southern Student Sit-in Movement," 758.

17. Tennessean, Feb. 16, 1960, 3; Lewis with D'Orso, Walking, 106–7.

18. Tennessean, Feb. 21, 1960, 2; Viorst, Fire, 108.

19. Houston, Nashville Way, 93–94.

20. Journal of Southern Religion 10 (2007); Houston, Nashville Way, 95.

21. James Lawson, unpublished manuscript, VU-JLP, box 45, folder 26, ch. 6; press release, VU-JLP, box 62, folder 14; "Lunch Counter Sit-In Suggestions," VU-KMSP, box 75, folder 14; John Lewis, interview with Archie Allen, Feb. 16, 1969, NPL-AAC, 44–45; John Lewis, interview with David Halberstam, #1, BU-DHP, box 59, folder 4; John Lewis, OH with Katherine Shannon, Aug. 22, 1967, RJBOHC, 34; New York Times, Mar. 2, 1960, 28; Nashville Banner, Feb. 2, 1993, 7; King, Stride Toward Freedom, 156–57.

22. Kelly Miller Smith, manuscript, VU-KMSP, box 28, folder 8; Kelly Miller Smith, interview with Archie Allen, Aug. 5, 1969, NPL-AAC, box 3, folder 29; Beardslee, Way Out, 7; Halberstam, Children, 128; Morris, Origins, 206.

23. Angeline Butler, author interview, Apr. 29, 2020; Holsaert et al., eds., Freedom Plow, 42; Kelly Miller Smith, manuscript, VU-KMSP, box 28, folder 8; Kelly Miller Smith, interview with Archie Allen, Aug. 5, 1969, NPL-AAC, box 3, folder 29; Morris, Origins, 206.

24. John Lewis, interview with David Halberstam, #1, BU-DHP, box 59, folder 4, 27.

25. Kelly Miller Smith, manuscript, VU-KMSP, box 28, folder 8; Houston, Nashville Way, 92.

26. Which store Lewis visited first is not certain. Butler confidently placed both

John and Paul LaPrad in her group, which went to McLellan's, and in 1967 Lewis vividly described being with LaPrad. But in other accounts Lewis consistently said that he went to Woolworth's first and McLellan's later. Adding to the confusion, LaPrad wrote a short while later that he had gone to Woolworth's. But news reports placed him at McLellan's, as does Candie Carawan's diary entry. On Lewis going to McLellan's: Angeline Butler notes, NPL-ABD, box 2, folder 2; Angeline Butler, author interview, Apr. 29, 2020; Holsaert et al., eds., Freedom Plow, 42. On Lewis at Woolworth's: John Lewis, interview with Archie Allen, May 28, 1969, NPL-AAC, 45; Lewis with D'Orso, Walking, 106–7; Hampton and Fayer, Voices, 58; Nashville Banner, Feb. 2, 1993, 7. On LaPrad at McLellan's: Candie Carawan, email to author, June 29, 2021; "Sit-Ins: The Students Report," CRMVET; New York Times, Feb. 28, 1960, 51; Nashville Banner, Mar. 1, 1960, 1, 8.

27. Reporter, Mar. 31, 1960, 19.

28. James Lawson, unpublished manuscript, VU-JLP, box 45, folder 26, ch. 6; John Lewis, interview with Archie Allen, May 28, 1969, NPL-AAC, 45; Reporter, Mar. 31, 1960, 19.

29. John Lewis, interview with David Halberstam, #1, BU-DHP, box 59, folder 4; Reporter, Mar. 31, 1960, 19; Viorst, Fire, 109.

30. James Lawson, unpublished manuscript, VU-JLP, box 45, folder 26, ch. 6; John Lewis, interview with Archie Allen, Feb. 16, 1969, NPL-AAC, 46; John Lewis, OH with Katherine Shannon, Aug. 22, 1967, RJBOHC, 41–42; Kelly Miller Smith, interview with John Britton, Dec. 22, 1967, 31; Knoxville News-Sentinel, Feb. 28, 1960, 1; Tennessean, Feb. 29, 1960; Beardslee, Way Out, 8; Halberstam, Children, 131–33; Houston, Nashville Way, 99; Lewis with D'Orso, Walking, 108–9.

31. John Lewis, interview with Archie Allen, Feb. 16, 1969, NPL-AAC, 47; John Lewis, OH with Katherine Shannon, Aug. 22, 1967, RJBOHC, 40; Egerton, *Mind to Stay Here*, 57; Houston, *Nashville Way*, 99; Morris, *Origins*, 209; *Nashville Globe*, Mar. 11, 1960, 1, 4.

32. John Lewis, interview with David Halberstam, #1, BU-DHP, box 59, folder 4, 29; Raines, *Rested*, 99; Viorst, *Fire*, 110.

33. Hampton and Fayer, *Voices*, 59; Beardslee, *Way Out*, 8; *Chicago Defender*, Mar. 22, 1960, 9.

34. Raines, *Rested*, 100; Halberstam, *Children*, 237–38.

35. Young, dir., *NBC White Paper: Sit-In*; *Nashville Banner*, Mar. 1, 1960, 8; *Southern Exposure*, Fall 1976, 20; Lewis with D'Orso, *Walking*, 109–10; *Nashville Globe*, Mar. 11, 1960, 1; Kelly Miller Smith, "Introduction," *The Nashville Sit-In Story*, Folkways Records, Album no. FH5590. See liner notes in KMSP, box 76, folder 24. On October 19, 1960, the charges were finally dismissed. *Philadelphia Tribune*, Oct. 22, 1960, 1.

36. John Lewis, OH with Katherine Shannon, Aug. 22, 1967, RJBOHC, 45.

37. *Tennessean*, Mar. 6, 1960, 6; James Lawson, unpublished manuscript, VU-JLP, box 45, folder 26, ch. 6; *Nashville Banner*, Feb. 29, 1960, 1.

38. Lawson statement, VU-JLP, box 62, folder 9; *Nashville Banner*, Mar. 1, 1960, 1, 2, 6; *Chicago Defender*, Mar. 2, 1960, 3; *Washington Post*, Mar. 3, 1960, D5.

39. *Nashville Banner*, Mar. 3, 1960, 1; *Tennessean*, Mar. 3, 1960, 1; Letter, Mar. 2, 1960, VU-JLP, box 62, folder 10; "Brushfire," *Time*, Mar. 14, 1960, 21.

40. J. Robert Nelson to James Lawson, Mar. 8, 1960, VU-JLP, box 62, folder 10; Letters, VU-JLP, box 62, folder 6; Doyle, *Nashville*, 248; *New York Times*, Mar. 2, 1960, 28; *Chicago Defender*, Mar. 3, 1960; *Washington Post*, Mar. 6, 1960, A16.

41. Houston, *Nashville Way*, 107; Lewis with D'Orso, *Walking*, 110–11; *Tennessean*, Mar. 8, 1960, 1; *Newsweek*, Mar. 21, 1960, 50.

42. *Tennessean*, Mar. 6, 1960, 1; *Tennessean*, Mar. 17, 1960, 1; *Tennessean*, Mar. 27, 1960, 12; Houston, *Nashville Way*, 111; John Lewis, interview with Archie Allen, Feb. 14, 1969, NPL-AAC, 48; *Tennessean*, Mar. 29, 1960, 2.

43. Frankie Blakely, interview with Archie Allen, Sept. 9, 1968, NPL-AAC, box 4, folder 5, 1.

44. NCLC and student representatives, Statement, VU-JLP, box 62, folder 6; *Tennessean*, Apr. 7, 1; Doyle, *Nashville*, 248; Lewis with D'Orso, *Walking*, 113; Houston, *Nashville Way*, 112; *Tennessean*, Mar. 27, 1960, 12.

45. Walker, *Challenge and Change*, 29; Wynn, "The Dawning of a New Day," 50; Houston, *Nashville Way*, 111; *Tennessean*, Apr. 3, 1960, 1.

46. Will Campbell, interview with Archie Allen, Sept. 11, 1968, NPL-AAC, box 3, folder 7; Lewis, Allen interview, #1, 51.

47. *New York Herald Tribune*, Mar. 13, 1960, 1; *Chicago Defender*, Mar. 21, 1960; *Reporter*, Mar. 31, 1960, 18; *Nashville Banner*, Apr. 7, 1960, 37; *Tennessean*, Apr. 7, 1960, 14; Viorst, *Fire*, 119.

48. Lewis with D'Orso, *Walking*, 114.

49. Lewis with D'Orso, *Walking*, 115–16; Houston, *Nashville Way*, 114; Walker, *Challenge and Change*, 30; Betsy Phillips, author interview, May 19, 2021; Phillips, *Dynamite Nashville*.

50. John Lewis, interview with Archie Allen, NPL-AAC, Feb. 14, 1969, 53; John Lewis, OH with Katherine Shannon, Aug. 22, 1967, RJBOHC, 58; Hampton and Fayer, *Voices*, 65; Young, dir., *NBC White Paper: Sit-In*; Lewis with D'Orso, *Walking*, 115–16.

51. John Lewis, interview with Archie

Allen, Feb. 16, 1969, NPL-AAC, 54; James Lawson, interview with Blackside, Dec. 2, 1985, WU-HHC; Lewis with D'Orso, *Walking*, 116; Viorst, *Fire*, 115; *New Yorker*, Mar. 27, 1965, 38–39.

52. *Tennessean*, Apr. 20, 1960, 1, 2; Doyle, *Nashville*, 249; Houston, *Nashville Way*, 116; Halberstam, *Children*, 237.

53. *Tennessean*, Apr. 19, 1960, 2; *Tennessean*, Apr. 21, 1960, 1; *Nashville Banner*, Apr. 21, 1960, 4; Lewis with D'Orso, *Walking*, 116–17.

54. *Tennessean*, Apr. 21, 1960, 1; *Nashville Banner*, Apr. 21, 1960, 4.

55. *Tennessean*, May 11, 1960, 7; *New York Times*, May 11, 1960, 1; Laue, *Direct Action*, 77.

56. "Where Do We Go from Here?" VU-KMSP, box 89, folder 16; Wallace Westfeldt, "Settling a Sit-In," July 1960, NYPL-SC-AMP, box 70, folder 5.

57. Lomax, *Negro Revolt*, 121; Lovett, *Tennessee*, 155. The Greensboro students didn't become full-time activists, but many Nashville students went on to play key roles in the movement. Isaac et al., "Movement Schools and Dialogical Diffusion of Nonviolent Praxis."

58. Rip Patton, OH with K. G. Bennett, July 11, 2003, NPL-CROHC; James Lawson, remarks at the funeral of John Lewis, C-SPAN, July 30, 2020, https://www.c-span.org/video/?474223-1/repre sentative-john-lewis-funeral-service-atlan ta-georgia.

59. John Lewis, interview with Archie Allen, May 29, 1969, NPL-AAC, 61.

60. Young, dir., *NBC White Paper: Sit-In*.

FOUR: SNCC

1. Laue, *Direct Action*, 77; *Tennessean*, Apr. 3, 1960, 6; Septima Clark, "The New Generation Fights for Equality," NPL-HFSC, box 5, folder 17. On Highlander, see Adams with Horton, *Unearthing Seeds of Fire*; and Glen, *Highlander*.

2. Martin Luther King Jr., "Leadership Training Program and Citizenship Schools," VU-JLP, box 39, folder 36; "The Trouble at Highlander," *Concern: A Biweekly Journal*, Oct. 23, 1959, NPL-HFSC, box 5, folder 7.

3. Lewis with D'Orso, *Walking*, 89–90; Septima Clark, interview with Archie Allen, Sept. 21, 1968, NPL-AAC, box 4, folder 9, 1; Angeline Butler, interview with Rachel Lawson, Mar. 21 and 30, 2005, 12, NPL-CROHC; John Lewis, interview with Sean Wilentz, June 12, 1995, tape 1, SWT.

4. Meeting notes, UW-HRECR, mss. 265, box 78, folder 9; Adams, *Unearthing*, 144; Clark, "New Generation," NPL-HFSC, box 5, folder 17; *Tennessean*, Apr. 3, 1960, Apr. 4, 1960, AAPP.

5. Myles Horton, "Class on Nashville Sit-Ins," VU-JLP, box 62, folder 16; "Excerpt from College Workshop," UW-HRECR, mss. 265, box 78, folder 9; Clark, "New Generation," NPL-HFSC, box 5, folder 17; *Tennessean*, Apr. 3, 1960, 6; Angeline Butler, author interview, Apr. 29, 2020; Holsaert et al., eds., *Freedom Plow*, 43.

6. UW-HRECR, mss. 265., box 78, folder 9; John Lewis, interview with Archie Allen, Feb. 14, 1969, NPL-AAC, 49–50; Clark, "New Generation," NPL-HFSC, box 5, folder 17.

7. Phil Schechter, author interview, July 6, 2021; John Lewis, interview with Julian Bond, Sept. 26, 2005, UVA-EBL, 15; Clark, "New Generation," NPL-HFSC, box 5, folder 17; John Lewis, remarks, UW-HRECR, mss. 265, box 78, folder 9.

8. Alice Cobb, interview with Archie Allen, Sept. 14, 1968, NPL-AAC, box 3, folder 10, 1–2.

9. Ella Baker, interview with Archie

Allen, Nov. 7, 1968, 3, NPL-AAC, box 3, folder 4; Lovett, *Tennessee*, 137; Zinn, *SNCC*, 31; Branch, *Parting*, 291. On SNCC, see Carson, *In Struggle*; Hogan, *Many Minds*; Laue, *Direct Action*; Stoper, *Student Nonviolent Coordinating Committee*; and Zinn, *SNCC*.

10. Angeline Butler, author interview, May 21, 2020; "Report of the Raleigh Conference," VU-JLP, box 38, folder 2; *New York Times*, Apr. 18, 1960, 21; John Lewis, interview with Archie Allen, Feb. 14, 1969, NPL-AAC, 52; *Tennessean*, Apr. 16, 1960, AAPP; Lewis with D'Orso, *Walking*, 113–15; Hampton and Fayer, *Voices*, 64. The 126 figure comes from the cited contemporaneous SNCC document. A contemporaneous *New York Times* account said 142. As early as 1972, Lewis told an interviewer, Clayborne Carson, that he did attend the Raleigh conference. He told the same to Milton Viorst and other interviewers. But most accounts, including his memoir, put him in Nashville. An April 15, 1960, *Tennessean* article by David Halberstam lists all the Nashville attendees, but does not list Lewis. John Lewis, interview with Clayborne Carson, Apr. 17, 1972, CRMVET; Viorst, *Fire*, 120.

11. Martin Luther King Jr., "Statement to the Press," Apr. 15, 1960, VU-JLP, box 40, folder 1; "Report of the Raleigh Conference," VU-JLP, box 38, folder 2; *New York Times*, Apr. 16, 1960, 15; *New Republic*, May 2, 1960, 16; Carson, *In Struggle*, 19–25; Garrow, *Cross*, 132; Hogan, *Many Minds*, 35; Morris, *Origins*, 215–21.

12. Marion Barry, interview with Blackside, May 15, 1979, 7–8, WU-HHC; Julian Bond, interview with David Halberstam, BU-DHP, box 58, folder 14.

13. Ella Baker, interview with Archie Allen, Nov. 7, 1968, NPL-AAC, box 4, folder 4, 7; Greenberg, ed., *A Circle of Trust*, 34; Carmichael with Thelwell,

Ready for Revolution, 186–87; Halberstam, *Children*, 216.

14. "Report of the Raleigh Conference," VU-JLP, box 38, folder 2; *New Leader*, September 12, 1960, 11; Hampton and Fayer, *Voices*, 62.

15. Raines, *Rested*, 102; Grant, *Baker*, 127–30; Ransby, *Ella Baker*, 242–43; Viorst, *Fire*, 120.

16. SNCC Memo, VU-JLP, box 44, folder 1; "Draft of Statement of Purpose," VU-JLP, box 44, folder 1; "Recommendations," LC-SNCCP, series 1, reel 1; *New York Times*, Apr. 17, 1960, 32, Apr. 18, 1960, 21; Garrow, *Cross*, 132–34; Morris, *Origins*, 216–17.

17. "Some NCLC Landmarks," VU-KMSP, box 75, folder 13; John Lewis, interview with Archie Allen, Feb. 14, 1969, NPL-AAC, 58; Fisk University Application for Admission, Feb. 25, 1961, NPL-AA, box 3, folder 2.2; Lewis with D'Orso, *Walking*, 121–22.

18. Marion Barry and Jane Stembridge to Bayard Rustin, June 17, 1960, LC-SNCCP, series 1, reel 1; Rorabaugh, *Real Making*, 108.

19. James Farmer, interview with Sheldon Stern, Apr. 25, 1979, 6–7, JFKL-OHP; SNCC to Sen. John F. Kennedy, June 27, 1960, LC-SNCCP, series 1, reel 1; *New York Times*, June 25, 1960, 13; documents on party conventions, LC-SNCCP, series 1, reel 1.

20. Brauer, *Kennedy*, 39; *New York Herald Tribune*, Oct. 7, 1960, 2; Carson, ed., *Student Voice*, 6.

21. John Lewis, interview with Archie Allen, Feb. 14, 1969, NPL-AAC, 58; Washington Butler, interview with Archie Allen, Sept. 23, 1968, NPL-AAC, 1; *New York Times*, Sept. 4, 1960, 71; Lewis with D'Orso, *Walking*, 122–23.

22. John Lewis, OH with Katherine Shannon, Aug. 22, 1967, RJBOHC, 54;

SNCC staff meeting minutes, HV 252253-003-0903; Workshop assignments, LC-SNCCP, series 1, reel 1; Lewis with D'Orso, *Walking*, 125–26.

23. SNCC press release, VU-JLP, box 44, folder 1; *New York Times*, Oct. 27, 1960, 22; Hampton and Fayer, *Voices*, 69; Garrow, *Cross*, 148–49; Branch, *Parting*, 351–78; Wofford, *Of Kennedys and Kings*, 11–28; Kuhn, "There's a Footnote to History," *Journal of American History*, 583–95. This version of Kennedy's words comes from Coretta Scott King's direct recollection.

24. Notes, VU-JLP, box 38, folder 1.

25. *Tennessean*, Oct. 18, 1960, 2.

26. *Tennessean*, Nov. 11, 1960, 1, 26; *Chattanooga Times*, Nov. 11, 1960, 9; Houston, *Nashville Way*, 124–25; Lewis with D'Orso, *Walking*, 126–27.

27. John Lewis, interview with Archie Allen, Feb. 16, 1969, NPL-AAC, 59; Lewis with D'Orso, *Walking*, 127–29; *Daily Home News*, Nov. 11, 1960, 19.

28. John Lewis, interview with Archie Allen, Feb. 16, 1969, NPL-AAC, 59; *Tennessean*, Nov. 11, 1960, 1, 26; Lewis with D'Orso, *Walking*, 127–29.

29. *Tennessean*, Nov. 13, 1960, 12, Nov. 22, 1960, 5, Nov. 24, 1960, 15, Dec. 8, 1960, 24; Raines, *Rested*, 99–100; Houston, *Nashville Way*, 125.

30. Angeline Butler, author interview, Apr. 29, 2020; John Lewis, interview with David Halberstam, #1, BU-DHP, box 59, folder 4, 22.

31. Candie Carawan, email to author, July 11, 2021; Petrus and Cohen, *Folk City*, 204–14; Carson, ed., *Student Voice*, 17; "The Nashville Sit-In Story," Folkways Records, Album no. FH5590, VU-KMSP, box 76, folder 24; (Rosa) Mae Lewis, interview with Archie Allen, Mar. 16, 1969, NPL-AAC, box 3, folder 22.

32. Young, dir., *NBC White Paper: Sit-In*; Cunningham, ed., *The Art of*

Documentary, 293–99; Al Wasserman, interview with Fordham University, May 12, 1998, FU-MCTVOH; Young, "Nothing but a Man," 93–94; Barnouw, *Tube of Plenty*, 287.

33. "Student Workshop," VU-KMSP, box 89, folder 15; Andrew Young, interview with author, May 20, 2020; Young, *An Easy Burden*, 125–34; Torres, *Black, White, and in Color*, 42–44; Lewis with D'Orso, *Walking*, 195–96.

34. Andrew Young, author interview, May 20, 2020; Holsaert et al., eds., *Freedom Plow*, 483.

35. John Lewis, OH with Katherine Shannon, Aug. 22, 1967, RJBOHC, 56; James Bevel, "To the Community," Feb. 1, 1961, VU-KMSP, box 75, folder 4.

36. John Lewis, interview with Archie Allen, May 28, 1969, NPL-AAC, 62; John Lewis, OH with Katherine Shannon, Aug. 22, 1967, RJBOHC, 56; "February 1, Freedom Day Action," VU-JLP, box 44, folder 2; Student Non-Violent Movement statement, Feb. 1, 1961, VU-KMSP, box 89, folder 15; *Tennessean*, Feb. 5, 1961, 13A; Lewis with D'Orso, *Walking*, 129–30.

37. *Tennessean*, Feb. 26, 1961, 21.

38. Student movement statement, VU-KMSP, box 89, folder 15; Frankie Blakely, interview with Archie Allen, Sept. 9, 1968, NPL-AAC, box 3, folder 5; *Santa Fe New Mexican*, May 6, 2021, 8; Halberstam, *Children*, 280–81.

39. Will Campbell, interview with Archie Allen, Sept. 11, 1968, NPL-AAC, box 3, folder 7; *Tennessean*, Feb. 22, 1961, 1, 8.

40. *Tennessean*, Feb. 23, 1961, 7; "Chapel Service," Mar. 7, 1961, NPL-AAC, box 3, folder 2.3; John Lewis, interview with Archie Allen, May 28, 1969, NPL-AAC, 63; *Harper's*, Oct. 1961, 137.

41. *Tennessean*, May 8, 1961, 30; *New York Times*, Apr. 30, 1961, 72; Branch, *Parting*, 394–95; Houston, *Nashville Way*, 126.

FIVE: THE FREEDOM RIDES

1. Fisk University Application for Admission, Feb. 25, 1961, NPL-AAC, box 3, folder 2.2; Untitled statement, NPL-AAC, box 3, folder 2.4.

2. Fred Shuttlesworth to John Lewis, Mar. 23, 1961, NPL-AAC, box 3, folder 2.7.

3. *New York Times*, May 5, 1961, 17; Arsenault, *Freedom Riders*, and Catsam, *Freedom's Main Line*, are sources throughout the chapter. The plaintiff in the case, Bruce Boynton, was the son of Amelia Boynton, an activist in Selma, Alabama.

4. John Lewis, interview with Archie Allen, May 28, 1969, NPL-AAC, 65; John Lewis, interview with *Freedom Rides*, June 4, 2009, WGBH-OV-FRI, 3; "Freedom Ride," Carson, ed., *Student Voice*, 41; Bernard LaFayette, author interview, June 17, 2020; Meier and Rudwick, *CORE*, 136.

5. Bernard LaFayette, author interview, June 17, 2020; John Lewis, interview with Archie Allen, May 29, 1969, NPL-AAC, 66; John Lewis, OH with Katherine Shannon, Aug. 22, 1967, RJBOHC, 62; Lewis with D'Orso, *Walking*, 132–36.

6. "Freedom Ride Itinerary," NPL-AAC, box 3, folder 1.1.

7. Halberstam, *Children*, 248–50; Farmer, *Lay Bare*, 198; John Lewis, interview with Danny Lyon, July 15, 2016; Beardslee, *Way Out*, 10; Person, *Buses*, 140, 145.

8. John Lewis, interview with *Freedom Rides*, June 4, 2009, WGBH-OV-FRI, 5; *Bridgeport Telegram*, May 5, 1961, 2; *Chattanooga Daily Times*, May 5, 1961, 30; Lewis with D'Orso, *Walking*, 139–40; Roberts and Klibanoff, *Race Beat*, 243.

9. Genevieve Hughes, interview with *Freedom Rides*, May 27, 2009, WGBH-OV-FRI, 5–6; *Harper's*, Oct. 1961, 136.

10. Halberstam, *Children*, 261.

11. John Lewis, interview with Archie Allen, May 29, 1969, NPL-AAC, 68; *New York Times*, May 9, 1961, 29.

12. Farmer, *Lay Bare*, 199; Halberstam, *Children*, 256.

13. Albert Bigelow, OH with Elise Randolph, 1978, CU-OHC, 26; John Lewis, interview with *Freedom Rides*, June 4, 2009, WGBH-OV-FRI; John Lewis, interview with Archie Allen, May 29, 1969, NPL-AAC, 69; Hank Thomas, interview with *Freedom Rides*, Feb. 8, 2009, WGBH-OV-FRI, 10; *New York Times*, May 11, 1961, 25; *Rock Hill Herald*, Feb. 4, 2009.

14. John Lewis, interview with Archie Allen, May 29, 1969, NPL-AAC, 69–71; Albert Bigelow, OH by Elise Randolph, 1978, CU-OHC, 27.

15. Lewis with D'Orso, *Walking*, 142–381.

16. John Lewis, interview with Archie Allen, May 29, 1969, NPL-AAC, 71; John Lewis, interview with *Freedom Rides*, June 4, 2009, WGBH-OV-FRI, 7.

17. Farmer, *Lay Bare*, 200–201.

18. Arsenault, *Riders*, 125–35.

19. Hank Thomas, interview with *Freedom Rides*, Feb. 8, 2009, WGBH-OV-FRI, 19; *New York Times*, May 15, 1961, 1, 22.

20. Catsam, *Main Line*, 151–53.

21. Carson, ed., *Student Voice*, 45; *Washington Post*, May 16, 1961, A1, A4; Hank Thomas, interview with *Freedom Rides*, Feb. 8, 2009, WGBH-OV-FRI, 20–21; Halberstam, *Children*, 263.

22. *New York Times*, May 15, 1961, 1, 22; Peck, *Freedom Ride*, 126–27.

23. *Washington Post*, May 15, 1961, A1, May 17, 1961, A1; Arsenault, *Riders*, 144–57.

24. Peck, *Freedom Ride*, 129; Roberts and Klibanoff, *Race Beat*, 245–50.

25. John Lewis, interview with *Freedom Rides*, June 4, 2009, WGBH-OV-FRI, 10; Jim Zwerg, author interview, Sept.

20, 2021; Lewis with D'Orso, *Walking*, 144–46.

26. Arsenault, *Riders*, 166–76.

27. Jim Zwerg, author interview, Sept. 20, 2021; William Harbour, interview with *Freedom Rides*, Feb. 8, 2009, WGBH-OV-FRI, 3; *Tennessean*, May 18, 1961, 2; *Christian Science Monitor*, Feb. 28, 1985, 1; Lewis with D'Orso, *Walking*, 150–52.

28. James Lawson, interview with *Freedom Rides*, Mar. 20, 2009, WGBH-OV-FRI, 15–18; Diane Nash, interview with *Freedom Rides*, May 27, 2009, WGBH-OV-FRI, 2.

29. Farmer, *Lay Bare*, 203; Diane Nash, interview with *Freedom Rides*, May 27, 2009, WGBH-OV-FRI, 4–7.

30. NCLC executive board minutes, May 18, 1961, VU-KMSP, box 74, folder 12; John Lewis, interview with Archie Allen, May 29, 1969, NPL-AAC, 72; John Lewis, interview with *Freedom Rides*, June 4, 2009, WGBH-OV-FRI, 8; John Lewis, OH with Katherine Shannon, Aug. 22, 1967, RJBOHC, 67–68; Halberstam, *Children*, 275, 286.

31. Arsenault, *Riders*, 183–86.

32. John Lewis, interview with *Freedom Rides*, June 4, 2009, WGBH-OV-FRI, 9; Halberstam, *Children*, 290–93.

33. John Lewis, interview with Archie Allen, May 29, 1969, NPL-AAC, 73–76; John Lewis, interview with *Freedom Rides*, June 4, 2009, WGBH-OV-FRI, 9; John Lewis, OH with Katherine Shannon, Aug. 22, 1967, RJBOHC, 70; William Harbour, interview with *Freedom Rides*, Feb. 8, 2009, WGBH-OV-FRI, 7.

34. John Lewis, interview with Archie Allen, May 29, 1969, NPL-AAC, 76.

35. John Lewis, interview with Archie Allen, May 29, 1969, NPL-AAC, 77; John Lewis, interview with *Freedom Rides*, June 4, 2009, WGBH-OV-FRI, 13; John Lewis, OH with Katherine Shannon, Aug. 22, 1967, RJBOHC, 71–73; Catherine Burks-Brooks, interview with *Freedom Rides*, Feb. 11, 2009, WGBH-OV-FRI, 8–10.

36. William Harbour, interview with K. G. Bennett, Aug. 19, 2004, NPL-CROHC, 9.

37. John Lewis, interview with Archie Allen, May 29, 1969, NPL-AAC, 77–78; Catherine Burks-Brooks, interview with *Freedom Rides*, Feb. 11, 2009, WGBH-OV-FRI, 10–11; William Harbour, interview with *Freedom Rides*, Feb. 8, 2009, WGBH-OV-FRI, 9; Halberstam, *Children*, 295–96. In different interviews, Lewis assigns the couple different ages—fifties, sixties, seventies.

38. John Lewis, interview with Archie Allen, May 29, 1969, NPL-AAC, 77–78; John Lewis, interview with *Freedom Rides*, June 4, 2009, WGBH-OV-FRI, 13; John Lewis, OH with Katherine Shannon, Aug. 22, 1967, RJBOHC, 73–75; Catherine Burks-Brooks, interview with *Freedom Rides*, Feb. 11, 2009, WGBH-OV-FRI, 10–11.

39. John Lewis, interview with Archie Allen, May 29, 1969, NPL-AAC, 78–79; John Lewis, OH with Katherine Shannon, Aug. 22, 1967, RJBOHC, 75–76.

40. John Lewis, interview with David Halberstam, #2, BU-DHP, box 59, folder 5, 3.

41. John Lewis, interview with Archie Allen, May 29, 1969, NPL-AAC, 79; John Lewis, OH with Katherine Shannon, Aug. 22, 1967, RJBOHC, 76–77; John Lewis, interview with Sean Wilentz, tape 2, June 12, 1995, SWT; Halberstam, *Children*, 297–98, 305; Forman, *Revolutionaries*, 153.

42. John Lewis, interview with *Freedom Rides*, June 4, 2009, WGBH-OV-FRI, 15; John Seigenthaler, interview with *Freedom Rides*, Mar. 19, 2009, WGBH-OV-FRI, 14; Hampton and Fayer, *Voices*, 84–85.

NOTES TO PAGES 82-87

584

43. John Lewis, interview with Blackside, #1, May 14, 1979, WU-HHC, 11; *U.S. News & World Report*, Oct. 23, 1961, 77–78; Schlesinger, *Robert Kennedy*, 296.

44. John Lewis, OH with Katherine Shannon, Aug. 22, 1967, RJBOHC, 79.

45. *New York Herald-Tribune*, May 21, 1961, 1; William Harbour, interview with *Freedom Rides*, Feb. 8, 2009, WGBH-OV-FRI, 11–16; Lewis with D'Orso, *Walking*, 158–59; Beardslee, *No Way*, 12; Forman, *Revolutionaries*, 155.

46. John Lewis, interview with Blackside, #1, May 14, 1979, WU-HHC, 12; Hampton and Fayer, *Voices*, 90.

47. *Time*, May 26, 1961, 16–17; Branch, *Parting*, 446.

48. Silver, *Freedom Rider Diary*, 21.

49. John Lewis, interview with Archie Allen, May 29, 1969, NPL-AAC, 80; Lewis with D'Orso, *Walking*, 159–60; Halberstam, *Children*, 311–12.

50. John Lewis, OH with Katherine Shannon, Aug. 22, 1967, RJBOHC, 81; John Lewis, interview with *Freedom Rides*, June 4, 2009, WGBH-OV-FRI, 16–17.

51. John Lewis, interview with David Halberstam, #2, BU-DHP, box 59, folder 5; Jim Zwerg, author interview, Sept. 20, 2021; *New York Herald Tribune*, May 21, 1961, 1; *New York Times*, May 22, 1961, 26; *Santa Fe New Mexican*, May 6, 2021, 8; Beardslee, *Way Out*, 13.

52. John Lewis, interview with Archie Allen, May 29, 1969, NPL-AAC, 61; John Lewis, interview with *Freedom Rides*, June 4, 2009, WGBH-OV-FRI, 17; *Huntsville Mirror*, Sept. 16, 1961, 1; Lewis with D'Orso, *Walking*, 163–64; Halberstam, *Children*, 318.

53. *New York Herald Tribune*, May 21, 1961, 1, 26–27.

54. *New York Times*, May 21, 1961, 78; Viorst, *Fire*, 153.

55. *Into America* podcast, July 21, 2020.

56. John Lewis, interview with Archie Allen, May 29, 1969, NPL-AAC, 81; John Lewis, interview with *Freedom Rides*, June 4, 2009, WGBH-OV-FRI, 18; Lewis with D'Orso, *Walking*, 163–65.

57. Hampton and Fayer, *Voices*, 92.

58. Branch, *Parting*, 454–62.

59. John Lewis, interview with Archie Allen, May 29, 1969, NPL-AAC, 23–25; John Lewis, interviews with David Halberstam, #2, 10, #4, 1, BU-DHP, box 59, folder 5; *Tennessean*, May 24, 1961, 1; Forman, *Revolutionaries*, 156; Branch, *Parting*, 463–65.

60. John Lewis, OH with Katherine Shannon, Aug. 22, 1967, RJBOHC, 89; John Lewis, interview with Archie Allen, May 30, 1969, NPL-AAC, 83; Chuck McDew, OH with Katherine Shannon, Aug. 24, 1967, RJBOHC, 69; *New York Times*, May 23, 1961, 27; *Chicago Defender*, May 24, 1961, 1; *Tennessean*, June 9, 1961, AAPP; Jim Zwerg, author interview, Sept. 20, 2021; Rick Momeyer, author interview, Sept. 22, 2021; Forman, *Revolutionaries*, 146. On Farmer's view that SCLC took too much credit, see Powledge, *Free at Last*, 314–17. Lewis himself said, "No question about it. The Nashville movement then had emerged as the center for the movement. In a sense, the Nashville Student Movement, in terms of being a movement, was more of a viable organization than its parent group, in a sense, SNCC." John Lewis, interview with Archie Allen, May 28, 1969, NPL-AAC, 58.

Many historians have conflated the Nashville Student Movement with SNCC. But at this point in SNCC's short life it was still a coordinating committee, and the Nashville students acted after consulting one another and the NCLC but not with anyone at SNCC. "This was not a SNCC project; it was a project of the Nashville students," wrote Judy Kay Anderson, an early researcher of the Nashville movement. Judy Kay Anderson, "Nashville's Contribution: The Original Leadership of SNCC," unpublished paper, 1965, VU-SMP, box 2, folder 10, 28–29.

61. Branch, *Parting*, 466–68; Lewis with D'Orso, *Walking*, 165–67; Farmer, *Lay Bare*, 206–7.

62. *New York Times*, May 22, 1961, 26; John Lewis, interview with David Halberstam, #2, BU-DHP, box 59, folder 5.

63. Arsenault, *Riders*, 248; Lewis with D'Orso, *Walking*, 164–66.

64. *New York Herald Tribune*, May 24, 1961, 1; Branch, *Parting*, 468.

65. *New York Times*, May 25, 1961, 1, 24.

66. John Lewis, OH with Katherine Shannon, Aug. 22, 1967, RJBOHC, 89–90; Branch, *Parting*, 470–74.

67. John Lewis, interview with Archie Allen, May 29, 1969, NPL-AAC, 83–84; Arsenault, *Riders*, 273. Freedom Riders who were jailed in Mississippi and wrote up their experiences include John Lewis, Bernard LaFayette, and James Bevel, "Appeal for Freedom Riders," *Voice of the Movement*, June 30, 1961, VU-KMSP, box 75, folder 11; Judith Frieze, as told to Lois Daniels, *Boston Globe*, July 30–Aug. 6, 1961; Frank Holloway, *New South*, July/Aug. 1961, 3–8; William Mahoney, *Liberation*, Sept. 1961, 7–11; Carol Ruth Silver, *Freedom Rider Diary*; and Joan Trumpauer Mulholland, in Holsaert et al., eds., *Freedom Plow*, 67–76.

68. "Freedom Ride Coordinating Committee," VU-KMSP, box 75, folder 11; Arsenault, *Riders*, 282–84.

69. JFKL-JFKPP-WHSF-HW, Alphabetical File, 1956–1962, Interstate Commerce Commission, 1961: 29 May–22 June.

70. *New York Times*, May 27, 1961, 1, 8.

71. John Lewis, interview with Archie Allen, May 29, 1969, NPL-AAC, 88; "Appeal for Freedom Riders," VU-KMSP, box 75, folder 11; *Nashville Banner*, June 1, 1961, 1; *Liberation*, Sept. 1961, 8; *New South*, July/Aug. 1961, 3–8; Diane Liederman, "Jean Thompson of Amherst Recalls Her Time as a Freedom Rider," MassLive, May 3, 2011.

72. "Appeal for Freedom Riders," VU-KMSP, box 75, folder 11; Peck, *Freedom Ride*, 143; Farmer, *Lay Bare*, 21; Catsam, *Main Line*, 277.

73. Forman, *Revolutionaries*, 157; Catsam, *Main Line*, 271; Lewis with D'Orso, *Walking*, 170–73.

74. Arsenault, *Riders*, 300–301, 308–9, 362; Holsaert et al., eds., *Freedom Plow*, 73–75; Lewis with D'Orso, *Walking*, 172–73; Carmichael with Thelwell, *Ready for Revolution*, 182, 196.

75. "Appeal for Freedom Riders," VU-KMSP, box 75, folder 11; Peck, *Freedom Ride*, 145.

76. Halberstam, *Children*, 345; Carmichael with Thelwell, *Ready for Revolution*, 202.

77. John Lewis, OH with Katherine Shannon, Aug. 22, 1967, RJBOHC, 92–93; Raines, *Rested*, 127; Arsenault, *Riders*, 325–28.

78. John Lewis, OH with Katherine Shannon, Aug. 22, 1967, RJBOHC, 93–94; John Lewis, interview with Archie Allen, May 29, 1969, NPL-AAC, 89; "Appeal for Freedom Riders," *Voice of the Movement*, June 30, 1961, VU-KMSP, box 75, folder 11; John Lewis to Mrs. Jones, June 2, 1961, AAPP; *Boston Globe*, Aug. 3, 1961, 28; Silver, *Diary*, 62; Peck, *Freedom Ride*, 150; Lewis with D'Orso, *Walking*, 172–73.

79. John Lewis, interview with *Freedom Rides*, June 4, 2009, WGBH-OV-FRI, 23–24; Fred Leonard, interview with *Freedom*

Rides, Mar. 19, 2009, WGBH-OV-FRI, 12–15; *Liberation*, Sept. 1961, 10.

80. *Boston Globe*, Aug. 4, 1961, 19; Silver, *Diary*, 65–66; Farmer, *Lay Bare*, 9; Arsenault, *Riders*, 358–60; Catsam, *Main Line*, 283.

81. *Time*, June 9, 1961, 15; *New York Times*, Sept. 23, 1961, 1; Catsam, *Main Line*, 278, 290; Etheridge, *Breach of Peace*, 29; "Freedom Ride Questionnaire," VU-KMSP, box 75, folder 11; *Boston Globe*, July 30, 1961, 24.

82. Lewis with D'Orso, *Walking*, 174.

SIX: OPEN CITY

1. *Pittsburgh Courier*, July 15, 1961, 5; John Lewis, interview with Archie Allen, Aug. 8, 1969, NPL-AAC, 97.

2. *Christian Science Monitor*, July 5, 1961, 6; Baltimore *Afro-American*, July 1, 1961; *Pittsburgh Courier*, July 8, 1961, 24.

3. SNCC minutes, June 9–11, 1961, VU-JP, box 44, folder 2; Carmichael with Thelwell, *Ready for Revolution*, 216–18.

4. SNCC minutes, July 14–16, 1961, VU-JLP, box 44, folder 2; *New York Times*, June 20, 1961, 30; Powledge, *Free at Last*, 295–300; Carson, *In Struggle*, 41; Laue, *Desegregation*, 114–17.

5. SNCC minutes, June 9–11, 1961, VU-JLP, box 44, folder 2; SNCC Executive Committee meeting minutes, UW-HRECR, mss. 265, box 71, folder 16; Lewis with D'Orso, *Walking*, 181–84; Lovett, *Tennessee*, 173.

6. John Lewis, OH with Katherine Shannon, Aug. 22, 1967, RJBOHC, 97–99.

7. Metz Rollins, interview with David Halberstam, BU-DHP, box 59, folder 12, 10; *Baltimore Sun*, Aug. 7, 1961, 7, Aug. 8, 1961, 4; Kelly Miller Smith, statement, and "Emergency Bulletin," VU-KMSP, box 77, folder 2; Carmichael with Thelwell,

Ready for Revolution, 236–40; Lewis with D'Orso, *Walking*, 178–81.

8. Forman, *Revolutionaries*, 145–60.

9. Lewis with D'Orso, *Walking*, 180–81.

10. James Lawson to Charles McDew, Sept. 15, 1961, VU-JLP, box 44, folder 2.

11. John Lewis, interview with Archie Allen, Aug. 8, 1969, NPL-AAC, 93–97; John Lewis, interview with David Halberstam, #2, BU-DHP, box 59, folder 5, 14; "Belafonte," VU-KMSP, box 74, folder 10; NCLC meeting minutes, Sept. 12, 1961, VU-KMSP, box 74, folder 12; Martin Luther King Jr. and Wyatt Tee Walker to Fisk University registrar, Sept. 27, 1961, AAPP; *Nashville Banner*, Sept. 26, 1961, 3, Sept. 28, 1961, 18; Lewis with D'Orso, *Walking*, 184–86; Egerton, *A Mind to Stay*, 61.

12. Edward B. King to SNCC members, Sept. 12, 1961, VU-JLP, box 44, folder 2.

13. Archie Allen, interview with Kathy Bennett, Mar. 31, 2003, NPL-CROHC, 13–14; John Lewis, OH with Katherine Shannon, Aug. 22, 1967, 105; John Lewis, interview with Archie Allen, Aug. 8, 1969, NPL-AAC, 97; NCLC letter, Nov. 21, 1961, VU-KMSP, box 76, folder 22; "Meeting of 'Operation Open City' Planning Group," Nov. 10, 1961, AAPP; NCLC meeting minutes, Nov. 15, 1961, VU-KMSP, box 74, folder 12; *Nashville Banner*, Nov. 20, 1961, 31.

14. Andrew Young, author interview, May 20, 2020; John Lewis, interview with Archie Allen, Aug. 8, 1969, NPL-AAC, 101–2.

15. John Lewis, interview with David Halberstam, #2, BU-DHP, box 59, folder 5, 16; Lewis with D'Orso, *Walking*, 185–86.

16. Charles McDew, OH with Katherine Shannon, Aug. 22, 1967, 71; Halberstam, *Children*, 357–58, 396–98; Carson, *Struggle*, 78; Angeline Butler, author interview, Apr. 29, 2020.

17. John Lewis, interview with Archie

Allen, Aug. 8, 1969, NPL-AAC, 99; John Lewis, OH with Katherine Shannon, Aug. 22, 1967, 105; John Lewis, interview with David Halberstam, #2, BU-DHP, box 59, folder 5, 15; Anderson, "Nashville's Contribution," VU-SMP, box 2, folder 10, 36; Harriet Tanzman, interview with Archie Allen, Sept. 21, 1968, 1.

18. Richard Momeyer, author interview, Oct. 11, 2021.

19. NCLC minutes, Jan. 17, 1962, VU-KMSP, box 74, folder 12; *Voice of the Movement*, Apr. 21, 1962, May 25, 1962, VU-KMSP, box 76, folder 9; *New York Times*, Feb. 3, 1962, 8; Lovett, *Tennessee*, 176–77.

20. *Tennessean*, Feb. 15, 1962; *Michigan Chronicle*, Mar. 3, 1962, 7; Richard Momeyer, author interviews, July 21, 2021, Oct. 11, 2021.

21. Richard Momeyer, author interviews, July 21, 2021, Oct. 11, 2021; *Tennessean*, Feb. 11, 1962, NPL-AAC, box 3, folder 15.

22. *Tennessean*, Mar. 6, 1962, 26, Mar. 9, 1962, Apr. 13, 1962, May 22, 1962, 4.

23. *Student Voice*, June 1962, 2; *Chicago Defender*, May 26, 1962, 4; form letter to Harry Nichols [*sic*], May 11, 1962, RMPP; SNCC press release, May 16, 1962, HV 252253-013-0713; Richard Momeyer, author interview, Oct. 11, 2021; *Tennessean*, May 20, 1962, May 21, 1962, in NPL-AAC, box 3, folder 5.

24. SNCC press release, May 21, 1962, HV 252253-014-0001; *Nashville Banner*, May 22, 1962, 26; *Tennessean*, May 22, 1962, 4; Richard Momeyer, email to author, Oct. 17, 2021.

25. Charles McDew to John Lewis, Mar. 15, 1962, HV 252253-007-0545.

26. John Lewis, interview with Danny Lyon, Oct. 27, 1989, DLT; Julian Bond, "James Forman," UVA-HJB, box 11, folder 35; King, *Freedom Song*, 35.

27. SNCC conference documents, CRMVET; *Student Voice*, June 1962, 3; Carson, *In Struggle*, 51, 67, 69.

28. Lewis with D'Orso, *Walking*, 189–90; *Student Voice*, June 1962, 3; *Chicago Defender*, Dec. 30, 1961, 18.

29. SCLC Board-Staff Consultation, January 4–5, 1962, HV 001565-004-0201; Colia Clark, author interview, June 4, 2020; John Lewis, interview with Danny Lyon, Oct. 27, 1989, DLT; *New York Times*, Dec. 18, 1961, 1, 31; Carson, *In Struggle*, 63; Garrow, *Cross*, 189, 199; Lewis with D'Orso, *Walking*, 190–91; Fairclough, *To Redeem*, 85–91.

30. John Lewis, interview with Archie Allen, Aug. 8, 1969, NPL-AAC, 98–99; John Lewis to Richard Momeyer, Sept. 19, 1962, and Oct. 12, 1962, RMPP.

31. Katherine Jones, interview with Archie Allen, Oct. 4, 1968, 5–6. On Lewis's constant search for financial help, see, for example, Martin Luther King to John Lewis, Mar. 5, 1963, NPL-AAC, box 4, folder 17; and John Lewis to C. T. Vivian, June 30, 1962, EU-CTOVP, box 12, folder 1.

32. Paul Good, "John Lewis—Vanishing American," unpublished manuscript, AAPP; John Lewis, interview with Archie Allen, Sept. 23, 1969, NPL-AAC, 136; John Lewis, interview with David Halberstam, #1, BU-DHP, box 59, folder 4 29–31; (Rosa) Mae Lewis, interview with Archie Allen, Mar. 16, 1969.

33. John Lewis to James Forman and Charles McDew, June 7, 1962; Norma Collins to John Lewis, June 9, 1962, HV 252253-007-0545; John Lewis to Richard Momeyer, June 6, 1962, RMPP.

34. James Forman and Charles McDew, June 27, 1962, HV 252253-007-0545; SNCC press release, July 13, 1962, HV 252253-013-0713; Salynn McCollum, OH with K. G. Bennett, Mar. 27, 2004, and July 2, 2004, NPL-CROHC, 22–24; *Chicago Defender*, June 27, 1962, 4;

Charles E. Koen, "My Story of the Cairo Struggle," doctoral dissertation, Union Institute and University, Cincinnati, Ohio, 1980, 31–35; Pimblott, *Faith in Black Power*, 79–92.

35. John Lewis to Richard Momeyer, July 8, 1962, RMPP; John Lewis, interview with Archie Allen, Aug. 8, 1969, NPL-AAC, 99–100; Salynn McCollum, OH with K. G. Bennett, Mar. 27, 2004, and July 2, 2004, NPL-CROHC, 30; *Chicago Defender*, July 2, 1962, 2.

36. SNCC press release, Aug. 16, 1962, HV 252253-013-0713; John Lewis, interview with Archie Allen, Aug. 8, 1969, NPL-AAC, 99–100; *Chicago Defender*, July 3, 1962, 2, July 5, 1962, 2, July 19, 1962, 3, July 28, 1962, 2, Aug. 2, 1962, 2, Aug. 16, 1962, 2; *Chicago Tribune*, July 15, 1962, 21; *Carbondale Southern Illinoisan*, Oct. 8, 2017.

37. SNCC press release, July 13, 1962, HV 252253-013-0713; Lewis with D'Orso, *Walking*, 192–93; Lyon, *Memories*, 22–27.

38. Mary (Salynn) McCollum, "SNCC Report of Rollerbowl Incident," HV 252253-003-0287; Salynn McCollum, interviews with K. G. Bennett, March 27, 2004, and July 2, 2004, 28–29, NPL-CROHC; *Chicago Tribune*, Aug. 18, 1962, B9; *New York Times*, Aug. 18, 1962, 11; *Carbondale Southern Illinoisan*, Oct. 8, 2017; Pimblott, *Faith in Black Power*, 90–91.

39. *New York Times*, Aug. 21, 1962, 28, Sept. 7, 1962, 10; *Chicago Defender*, Aug. 21, 1962, 1–3.

40. Richard Momeyer, author interview, Sept. 22, 2021; *Carbondale Southern Illinoisan*, Oct. 8, 2017.

41. John Lewis to James Forman, Aug. 13, 1962, HV 252253-007-0545.

42. FBI report, Sept. 12, 1962, HV 104868-001-0001; *Sikeston Daily Standard*, Aug. 14, 1962, 1, Aug. 15, 1962, 1, Aug. 17, 1; Aug. 29, 1962, 1, 8; *Atlanta Constitution*, Aug. 16, 1962, 31; *Chicago Defender*, Aug. 16, 1962, 2, Aug. 23, 1962, 10; John Lewis to Richard Momeyer, June 6, 1962, July 8, 1962, July 27, 1962, Aug. 22, 1962, Aug. 24, 1962, RMPP.

43. John Lewis to Richard Momeyer, Sept. 19, 1962; John Lewis to James Forman, Sept. 21, 1962, HV 252253-007-0545; FBI report, Sept. 12, 1962, HV 104868-001-0001; SNCC press release, Aug. 23, 1962, HV 252253-014-0001.

44. Branch, *Parting*, 637–72.

45. John Lewis to Richard Momeyer, Sept. 28, 1962, RMPP.

46. John Lewis to Richard Momeyer, Sept. 28, 1962, RMPP; Houston, *Nashville Way*, 136.

47. John Lewis, interview with Archie Allen, Aug. 8, 1969, NPL-AAC, 100–101; John Lewis to Jim Forman and Ruby Smith, Oct. 30, 1962; Ruby Doris Smith to John Lewis, Nov. 2, 1962, both HV 252253-007-0545; SNCC press release, NPL-AAC, box 3, folder 4; *Tennessean*, Oct. 23, 1962, 2, Nov. 18, 1962, 19A.

48. SNCC press release, Nov. 16, 1962, HV 252253-013-0713; *Tennessean*, Nov. 24, 1962, 2, Nov. 25, 1962, 1; *Atlanta Daily World*, Dec. 2, 1962, A1; John Lewis, interview with Danny Lyon, Oct. 27, 1989, DLT; Lyon, *Memories*, 50.

49. Vencen Horsley, author interview, Jan. 4, 2022; David Kotelchuck, author interview, Dec. 20, 2021; SNCC press release, Nov. 27, 1962, HV 252253-013-0713; *Tennessean*, Nov. 25, 1962, 1; Danny Lyon, email to author, Oct. 26, 2021; Lyon, *Memories*, 49; Carson, *Student Voice*, 61.

50. Stanley Wise, interview with Archie Allen, May 31, 1969, NPL-AAC, box 4, folder 37; *Main Street Nashville*, July 29, 2021.

51. C. T. Vivian, interview with Archie Allen, Aug. 15, 1986, NPL-AAC, box 4, folder 35; Vivian with Fiffer, *It's in the Action*, 64.

52. Richard Momeyer, author interview, Sept. 22, 2021; Colia Clark, author interview, June 4, 2020; John Lewis to Richard Momeyer, Dec. 12, 1962, RMPP; *Tennessean*, Dec. 9, 1962, 10.

53. *Tennessean*, Jan. 28, 1963, 2, Feb. 12, 1963, 5, Feb. 27, 1963, 6 (YMCA); *Nashville Banner*, Oct. 22, 1962, 10, Mar. 15, 1963, 8; *Tennessean*, Mar. 6, 1963, 7, Mar. 7, 1963, 11, Mar. 9, 1963, 3, Mar. 14, 1963, 74, Mar. 19, 1963, 5; SNCC press release, Feb. 19, 1963, HV 252253-013-0713; SNCC Newsletter, Mar. 22, 1963, HV 252253-013-0713; John Lewis, interview with Archie Allen, Aug. 8, 1969, NPL-AAC, 102; Lovett, *Tennessee*, 179.

54. "Proposals of NCLC to the Nashville Community," KMSP, box 76, folder 22; NCLC flyer, VU-KMSP, box 75, folder 10; *Voice of the Movement*, Mar. 15, 1963, VU-KMSP, box 75, folder 10.

55. SNCC press release, Mar. 22, 1963, HV 252253-013-0713; Archie Allen, OH with K. G. Bennett, Mar. 31, 2003, NPL-CROHC, 10; John Lewis, OH with Katherine Shannon, Aug. 22, 1967, RJBOHC, 106; *Nashville Banner*, Mar. 5, 1963, 1, Mar. 22, 1963, 1; *Tennessean*, Mar. 22, 1963, 1.

56. John Lewis to Richard Momeyer, Mar. 15, 1963, RMPP; newsletter, Mar. 22, 1963, VU-KMSP, box 77, folder 6; "Dear Friend," NCLC letter, Mar. 29, 1963, NPL-AAC, box 4, folder 3; J. E. Lowery letter, Apr. 27, 1963, VU-KMSP, box 75, folder 10; Archie Allen, OH with K. G. Bennett, Mar. 31, 2003, NPL-CROHC, 11; John Lewis, interview with Archie Allen, Aug. 8, 1969, NPL-AAC, 104; *Tennessean*, Mar. 24, 1963, 1, 15, Mar. 27, 1963, 10; *Nashville Banner*, Apr. 29, 1963, 8; Houston, *Nashville Way*, 139–40.

57. John Lewis, interview with Archie Allen, Aug. 8, 1969, NPL-AAC, 104; David Kotelchuck, author interview, Dec. 20, 2021; Vencen Horsley, author interview, Jan. 5, 2022; Branch, *Parting*, 750.

58. On Birmingham, see Branch, *Parting*, 756–91; McWhorter, *Carry Me Home*.

59. John Lewis, interview with Archie Allen, Aug. 8, 1969, NPL-AAC, 104; Lewis with D'Orso, *Walking*, 196–98.

60. Kelly Miller Smith Jr., "Achieving a Goal," VU-KMSP, box 76, folder 9; *Nashville Banner*, May 7, 1963, 6, May 8, 1963, 8; *Tennessean*, May 8, 1963, 6; *New York Times*, May 9, 1963, 17; *Daily Northwest Alabamian*, May 9, 1963, 1.

61. John Lewis, interview with Archie Allen, Aug. 8, 1969, NPL-AAC, 104; Metz Rollins, Halberstam interview, BU-DHP, box 59, folder 12, 3; *New York Times*, May 9, 1963, 17, May 10, 1963, 14, May 11, 1963, 1, 10; *Tennessean*, May 11, 1963, 1–2; *Nashville Banner*, May 9, 1963, 16, May 10, 1963, 1, 8; *Chattanooga Daily Times*, May 11, 1963, 1; *Daily Northwest Alabamian*, May 9, 1963, 1, May 10, 1963, 1.

62. Chronology of Events re: Nashville Racial Crisis, USM-WCP, box 56, folder 18; *Nashville Banner*, May 11, 1963, 1–2; *Tennessean*, May 11, 1963, 1–2; *New York Times*, May 11, 1963, 1, 10; Powledge, *Free at Last*, 450–51.

63. *Tennessean*, May 13, 1963, 1, May 14, 1963, 1, 4; *Nashville Banner*, May 13, 1963, 2; *Knoxville News-Sentinel*, May 14, 1963, 1, 12.

64. *New York Times*, May 14, 1963, 27; *Nashville Banner*, May 14, 1963, 1, 10.

65. John Lewis, interview with Archie Allen, Aug. 8, 1969, NPL-AAC, 104.

66. *Tennessean*, May 14, 1963, 1, 4, May 15, 1963, 1, 2; *Nashville Banner*, May 14, 1963, 1, 10; *New York Times*, May 16, 1963, 25; Houston, *Nashville Way*, 145.

67. James E. Jackson, "Three Brave Men," July 1963, AAPP.

68. Jackson, "Three Brave Men."

69. Office of the Mayor, News Release,

May 16, 1963, USM-WCP, box 56, folder 18; "Human Relations Committee," USM-WCP, box 56, folder 18; *Voice of the Movement,* June 4, 1963, VU-KMSP, box 76, folder 10; *Kingsport Times,* May 16, 1963, NPL-AAC, box 3, folder 19; *New York Times,* May 17, 1963, 15; Doyle, *Nashville,* 252–53.

70. John F. Kennedy, "Remarks in Nashville at the 90th Anniversary Convocation of Vanderbilt University," May 18, 1963, UCSB-APP; Bryant, *Bystander,* 397–98.

71. *Peterson v. City of Greenville,* 373 U.S. 244 (1963); *New York Times,* May 21, 1963, 1; *Nashville Banner,* May 20, 1963, 1. In April 1965, the Supreme Court would reverse the convictions of Lewis and seven others for their October 1962 B&W sit-in.

72. Archie Allen, aide-mémoire, NPL-AAC, box 3, folder 4; *Tennessean,* May 31, 1963, 43.

73. NCLC minutes, press release, June 12, 1963, NPL-AAC, box 3, folder 4; *Voice of the Movement,* June 4, 1963, VU-KMSP, box 76, folder 10; *Tennessean,* June 11, 1963 , 1, 2, Sept. 15, 1963, 37–38; Joseph Lowery, OH with Robert Wright, Oct. 19, 1970, RJBOHC, 14–15; *Jet,* Dec. 5, 1963, 14–22.

74. David Kotelchuck, author interview, Dec. 20, 2021.

75. "Lawson Resigns NCLC Post," VU-KMSP, box 76, folder 10; *Tennessean,* July 8, 1963, 2, July 27, 1963, 7; Houston, *Nashville Way,* 151. Unhappy in his Cleveland position, Smith would return to Nashville in 1964.

76. David Kotelchuck, author interview, Dec. 20, 2021; Lovett, *Tennessee,* 179. Surprisingly, few civil rights historians have taken note of the strides made in Nashville in May 1963. Don Doyle, Bobby Lovett, and Ben Houston make brief mention of them, with Houston stressing how much work remained unfinished. Raymond Arsenault summarizes the activity in Nashville after the Freedom Rides thus: "The Bevels, Lester McKinnie, and others had long since moved on to continue the struggle in other parts of the South." This was not true in McKinnie's case, who returned to Nashville in 1962 after some time spent in Mississippi, and who in June 1963 would soon take over as chairman of the Nashville Student Movement from Lewis. Arsenault continues: "Even Lewis spent the summer of 1962 as an organizer in Cairo, Illinois, and after his election as SNCC national chairman in June 1963, he too moved on." While correct, this account completely omits Lewis's activities in 1962–63, from organizing the November 1962 SNCC conference to his spring 1963 activism (Arsenault, *Freedom Riders,* 503). David Halberstam mentions in passing Lewis's "constant assaults on two recalcitrant restaurants in Nashville, Crosskeys [*sic*] and Morrison's," calling the Nashville Movement "virtually the only major urban SNCC chapter still engaged in daily local protests." But Beverly Briley's name does not appear in his index (Halberstam, *Children,* 445). Taylor Branch does not mention Nashville's 1963 desegregation at all in *Parting the Waters.* Amazingly, not even John Lewis and Michael D'Orso in *Walking with the Wind* discuss the Nashville gains of May 1963, focusing largely on Lewis's reaction from afar to the Birmingham crisis.

SEVEN: THE MARCH ON WASHINGTON

1. *Kingsport Times,* June 8, 1963, June 19, 1963, NPL-AAC, box 3, folder 20; *Tennessean,* June 8, 1963, 5, June 18, 1963, 5, June 19, 1963.

2. Powledge, *Free at Last,* 523–31.

3. *New York Times,* June 17, 1963, 1; Carson, *In Struggle,* 90.

4. John F. Kennedy, "Radio and Television Report to the American People on Civil Rights," June 11, 1963, UCSB-APP.

5. Garrow, *Cross*, 268–69; LaFayette and Johnson, *In Peace and Freedom*, 74–77; *New York Times*, June 13, 1963, 14.

6. NCLC board minutes, June 12, 1963, VU-KMSP, box 74, folder 14; SNCC press release, June 15, 1963, NPL-AAC, box 3, folder 4.

7. John Lewis, interview with Emily Stoper, 1966, CRMVET, 5; Chuck McDew, OH with Katherine Shannon, Aug. 24, 1967, RJBOHC, 125; Ella Baker, interview with Archie Allen, Nov. 7, 1968, NPL-AAC, box 3, folder 4; James Bolton to James Donbrowski, June 27, 1963, HV 252253-009-0535; Beardslee, *Way Out*, 16; Forman, *Revolutionaries*, 331; King, *Freedom Song*, 182, 186. Two versions of Lewis's 1966 interview with Emily Stoper exist. Oddly, the one she published in *The Student Nonviolent Coordinating Committee: The Growth of Radicalism in a Civil Rights Organization* (Brooklyn, NY: Carlson, 1989) is incomplete. The longer version appears on the CRMVET website.

8. John Lewis, interview with Archie Allen, Aug. 8, 1969, NPL-AAC, 105; Sue Thrasher, author interview, Dec. 9, 2021; David Kotelchuck, author interview, Dec. 20, 2021; Lukas, *Don't Shoot*, 148.

9. SNCC executive committee meeting minutes, June 14–15, 1963, HV 252253-003-0903; John Lewis, OH with Katherine Shannon, Aug. 22, 1967, RJBOHC, 116.

10. SNCC minutes, June 14 and 15, 1963, HV 252253-0030903; SNCC press release, June 15, 1963, NPL-AAC, box 3, folder 4; *New York Times*, June 17, 1963, 1, 12; Murphree, *Selling*, 44–45.

11. Watters, *Down to Now*, 24.

12. John Lewis to NCLC, June 20, 1963, VU-KMSP, box 74, folder 14.

13. *Tennessean*, June 19, 1963; Lewis with D'Orso, *Walking*, 200; MacLaine, *Don't Fall*, 138.

14. John Lewis, OH with Katherine Shannon, Aug. 22, 1967, RJBOHC, 107–8; Carson, *In Struggle*, 69–71.

15. John Lewis, "Six Month Report," Dec. 27, 1963, HV 252253-003-001; SNCC press release, July 8, 1963, HV 252253-013-0713; John Lewis, interview with Archie Allen, Aug. 8, 1969, NPL-AAC, 108; John Lewis, OH with Katherine Shannon, Aug. 22, 1967, RJBOHC, 122; John Lewis, interview with Ben Hedin, May 19, 2010, BHI; Mary King, author interview, Feb. 9, 2020; Archie Allen, author interview, Feb. 8, 2022; Lewis with D'Orso, *Walking*, 206–11.

16. John Lewis to Rick Momeyer, June 6, 1962, RMPP.

17. Carson, *In Struggle*, 29; Rachelle Horowitz, OH with Megan Rosenfeld, Nov. 24, 2003, LC-VCRPC; Taylor, *Randolph*, 185.

18. Rachelle Horowitz, OH with Megan Rosenfeld, Nov. 24, 2003, LC-VCRPC.

19. Forman, *Revolutionaries*, 332–33.

20. James Farmer to A. Philip Randolph, Apr. 1, 1963, Julian Bond to A. Philip Randolph, Apr. 1, 1963, HV 001581-007-0089; Lewis with D'Orso, *Walking*, 202–3; D'Emilio, *Lost Prophet*, 327–29.

21. Clarence B. Jones to A. Philip Randolph, May 6, 1963, HV 001581-007-0089; "Committee for the Emancipation March on Washington for Jobs," May 7, 1963, HV 001581-008-9563; Branch, *Parting*, 816–17.

22. *New York Times*, June 12, 1963, 25; *Washington Post*, June 12, 1963; *Christian Science Monitor*, June 14, 1963, 1.

23. *Washington Post*, June 14, 1963, A9, July 3, 1963; Fairclough, *To Redeem*, 152; Hampton and Fayer, *Voices*, 161.

24. John Lewis, interview with Archie Allen, Sept. 23, 1969, NPL-AAC, 122; Garrow, *Cross*, 270; Farmer, *Lay Bare*, 239; Height, *Open Wide the Freedom Gates*, 140. On the Council for Unity, see Eagles and Lewis, eds., *American Civil Rights*, 39–55; Faulkenbury, "An Uncommon Meeting of Minds," 392–414.

25. *Washington Post*, June 22, 1963, B2.

26. John Lewis, interview with Archie Allen, Aug. 8, 1969, NPL-AAC, 110.

27. Courtland Cox, author interview, Jan. 11, 2022; John Lewis, interview with Archie Allen, Aug. 8, 1969, NPL-AAC, 111; Lewis with D'Orso, *Walking*, 201–2; King, *Freedom Song*, 183–85.

28. President's Agenda, June 22, 1963, JFK-POF-097-003-p0088; *Washington Post*, June 23, 1962, A1; Garrow, *Cross*, 273–75; Fairclough, *To Redeem*, 151.

29. Purdum, *Idea*, 87; Bruce, *From the Door*, 95. The account of the Cabinet Room meeting is based on: Arthur Schlesinger Jr. journal entry, June 22, 1963, 1069–76, and mail chart, June 20, 1963, NYPL-AMSP, box 312, folder, June 1963; Lee White, "Memorandum for the President," June 22, 1963, JFK-POF-097-003-p0069; President's Agenda, June 22, 1963, JFK-POF-097-003-p0089; John Lewis, interview with Archie Allen, Aug. 8, 1969, NPL-AAC, 109–10; John Lewis, interview with Clayborne Carson, Apr. 17, 1972, 11; John Lewis, interview with Vicki Daitch, Mar. 19, 2004, JFKL-OHP, 2–3; John Lewis, interview with Davis Halberstam, #2, BU-DHP, box 59, folder 5, 17–18; Rachelle Horowitz, interview with Archie Allen, NPL-AAC, box 3, folder 15, 8–9; James Farmer, OH with Sheldon Stern, Apr. 25, 1979, JFKL-OHP, 27; *New York Times*, June 23, 1963, 1; *Boston Globe*, June 23, 1963, 10; *Los Angeles Times*, June 23, 1963; Schlesinger, *A Thousand Days*, 968–72; Lewis with D'Orso, *Walking*,

203–4; Wilkins with Mathews, *Standing Fast*, 290.

30. "John F. Kennedy Public Approval," UCSB-APP. Some accounts say Kennedy was citing a private poll, but Schlesinger's journals, the most proximate source, quote him as citing Gallup, and no private poll has been found.

31. President's Agenda, June 22, 1963, JFK-POF-097-003-p0089; Halberstam, *Children*, 446.

32. Forman, *Revolutionaries*, 366.

33. John Lewis, interview with Archie Allen, Sept. 24, 1969, NPL-AAC, 142; *Atlanta Daily World*, Nov. 26, 1970, 2.

34. John Lewis, interview with Blackside, May 14, 1979, WU-HHC, 14; *New York Times*, July 3, 1963, 10; Forman, *Revolutionaries*, 332; Garrow, *Cross*, 277.

35. John Lewis, interview with Blackside, May 14, 1979, WU-HHC, 14; *Washington Post*, July 4, 1963, B2.

36. *Washington Post*, July 3, 1963, A1.

37. John Lewis, interview with Nancy J. Weiss, Aug. 3, 1983; Eagles and Lewis, *American Civil Rights*, 44; *New York Times*, July 3, 1963, 10; *Washington Post*, July 3, 1963, A1; *Tennessean*, July 3, 1963, 4; Forman, *Revolutionaries*, 364–70; Height, *Open Wide the Freedom Gates*, 142; Garrow, *Cross*, 278.

38. John Lewis, interview with Julian Bond, Sept. 26, 2005, UVA-EBL, 15; Rachelle Horowitz, author interview, June 16, 2020; *Chicago Defender*, Aug. 9, 1963, A9; *New York Times*, July 24, 1963, 15; *Time*, Aug. 30, 1963; *Nation*, Sept. 7, 1963, 104; D'Emilio, *Lost Prophet*, 340–41.

39. John Lewis, OH with Katherine Shannon, Aug. 22, 1967, RJBOHC, 122; FBI report, July 15, 1963; "Racial Situation, State of Alabama, Selma, Alabama," July 16, 1963, HV 001339-006-01718; John F. Kennedy, "The President's News Conference," July 17, 1963, UCSB-APP.

40. *Tennessean*, July 19, 1963, 6.

41. John Lewis, author interview, Feb. 22, 2019; John Lewis, interview with Archie Allen, Sept. 23, 1969, NPL-AAC, 127; John Lewis, interview with David Halberstam, #2, DHP-BU, box 59, folder 5, 21; Carson, ed., *Student Voice*, 69; Robnett, *How Long*, 162; Lewis with D'Orso, *Walking*, 213. In some accounts, Lewis says the fight was on TV, but to Allen he insists they listened on radio. Moreover, the fight was shown on closed-circuit, not broadcast, television. Also, the fight did not start until 10:30 p.m. Eastern time, an unlikely hour for the attorney general to be holding meetings. *New York Times*, July 21, 1963, 120.

42. Hampton and Fayer, *Voices*, 161.

43. Paul Anthony, interview with Archie Allen, May 28, 1969, NPL-AAC, box 3, folder 2; Pauli Murray to A. Philip Randolph, Aug. 21, 1963, HV 001581-007-0708; D'Emilio, *Lost Prophet*, 343; Hedgeman, *Trumpet Sounds*, 178–80.

44. John Lewis, OH with Katherine Shannon, Aug. 22, 1967, RJBOHC, 133; King, *Freedom Song*, 163.

45. Nancy Stearns, interview with Archie Allen, Nov. 8, 1968, NPL-AAC, box 3, folder 30, 3; Nancy Stearns, author interview, Jan. 12, 2022.

46. Joy Reagon Leonard to John Lewis, Aug. 13, 1963; Gerald L. Davis to Lewis, Sept. 2, 1963, HV 252253-001-0523; NAACP-NCLC-SNCC memo, VU-KMSP, box 75, folder 10.

47. *Nation*, Sept. 7, 1963, 107.

48. Roy Wilkins and A. Philip Randolph, telegram to John Lewis, Aug. 7, 1963, HV 252253-010-0314; *Democratiya*, Winter 2007, 204; Dorie Ladner and Joyce Ladner, OH with Joseph Mosnier, Sept., 20, 2011, CRHPC-AFC, 5.

49. *Pittsburgh Courier*, Aug., 24, 1963, 1. Robert Kennedy's aides opposed the indictments, but the attorney general concluded that overruling the U.S. attorney who brought them would smack of political interference.

50. David Kotelchuck, author interview, Dec. 20, 2021. Dorie and Joyce Ladner, OH with Joseph Mosnier, Sept. 20, 2011, CRHPC-AFC, 3–5, 11–12; Rachelle Horowitz, interview with Archie Allen, Nov. 8, 1968, NPL-AAC, box 3, folder 15; Rachelle Horowitz, author interviews, June 16, 2020, Jan. 11, 2022; Egerton, *A Mind to Stay Here*, 62.

51. Lewis with D'Orso, *Walking*, 215–16; John Lewis, interview with David Halberstam, #3, Dec. 10, 1995, BU-DHP, box 59, folder 5, 1; John Lewis, OH with Katherine Shannon, Aug. 22, 1967, RJBOHC, 129.

52. Rachelle Horowitz, interview with Archie Allen, Nov. 8, 1968, NPL-AAC, box 3, folder 15.

53. Rachelle Horowitz, author interview, June 16, 2020. Meier went on to become a major education reformer.

54. *New York Times*, Aug. 26, 1963, 18; John Lewis, interview with Archie Allen, Sept. 24, 1969, NPL-AAC, 171; Notes, NAACP Papers, HV 001473-019-0528; Jones, *March*, 172–73.

55. The account of the controversy over Lewis's speech is based on: Courtland Cox, author interview, Jan. 11, 2022; Norman Hill, author interview, May 25, 2020; Rachelle Horowitz, author interviews, June 16, 2020, Jan. 11, 2022; John Lewis, interview with Archie Allen, Sept. 23, 1969, 113–21; John Lewis, interviews with Blackside, May 14, 1979, 13–18, and Nov. 5, 1985, WU-HHC, 14–16; John Lewis, interview with Clayborne Carson, Apr. 17, 1972, 8–9; John Lewis, interview with David Halberstam, #3, Dec. 10, 1995, BU-DHP, box 59, folder 5, A1–3, B1–2; John Lewis, OH with Katherine Shannon, Aug. 22, 1967, RJBOHC, 125–29; Jack T. Conway, interview with Larry

Hackman, Dec. 29, 1972, JFKL-OHP, 80–81; Courtland Cox, interview with Blackside, May 14, 1979, WU-HHC, 2–6; James Forman, interview with Blackside, Dec. 11, 1985, WU-HHC, 1–4; Roberta Jones, interview with Archie Allen, NPL-AAC, box 3, folder 19, 2; Francis O'Boyle, OH with Katherine Shannon, Oct. 30, 1967, RJBOHC, 27–32; Bayard Rustin, interview with Blackside, Oct. 26, 1979, WU-HHC, 4–9. Secondary sources include: Carmichael with Thelwell, *Ready for Revolution*, 331–33; Lewis with D'Orso, *Walking*, 218–25; Forman, *Revolutionaries*, 333–38; Sellers, *River*, 64–66; Wilkins, *Standing Fast*, 292–93; Branch, *Parting*, 878–80; Carson, *Struggle*, 91–97; D'Emilio, *Prophet*, 353–55; Euchner, *Nobody Turn*, 45–49, 150–54; Garrow, *Cross*, 281–83; Gentile, *March*, 164–83; Halberstam, *Children*, 451–53; Hampton and Fayer, *Voices*, 159–70; Hansen, *Dream*, 140–46; Nussbaum, *Undelivered*, 17–37; Powledge, *Free at Last*, 533–42; Viorst, *Fire*, 229; Zinn, *SNCC*, 190–215. Notable articles include Fairclough, "Civil Rights and the Lincoln Memorial," 408–16; *Dissent*, Spring 2013, 75–79; *Dissent*, Summer 1998, 285–91; Pauley, "John Lewis's 'Serious Revolution,'" 320–40; and Pauley, "John Lewis, Speech at the March on Washington," 18–36.

56. "Contact Sheet," NAACP Papers, HV 001473-019-0528; Lyon, *Memories*, 84; Danny Lyon, author interview, July 29, 2019.

57. Young, *Uneasy Burden*, 272; Hampton and Fayer, *Voices*, 161–64; Jones, *March*, 178; Viorst, *Fire*, 227.

58. Roberts and Klibanoff, *Race Beat*, 346.

59. Gentile, *March*, 201.

60. Gentile places this change on Tuesday night. Drafts of the speech show a version whose only change is the addition of that word, but it is unclear when it was

added. LC-JFP, box 35, folder 1; Gentile, *March*, 175–76.

61. Lewis would skip over the word "unfinished" when delivering it.

62. John Lewis, "Six Month Report," Dec. 27, 1963, HV 252253-003-001.

63. Rachelle Horowitz, author interview, June 16, 2020. Most accounts say that Forman typed the draft. Photographs show no typewriter, and Cox believes he erroneously mentioned the typewriter in previous interviews, leading to its appearance in many narratives. But other witnesses, including Lewis, remember a typewriter. Cox, author interview, Jan. 11, 2022. *Jet* magazine reported that Lewis said he "wrote and rewrote the speech five times to satisfy the leadership committee." Forman's papers contain at least five different drafts (all typed). *Jet*, Sept. 12, 1963, 28–29; speech drafts, LC-JFP, box 35, folder 1. Versions also exist in HV 252253-002-001. Garth Pauley analyses the differences between the first and final drafts in "John Lewis's 'Serious Revolution,'" 327–29. A side-by-side comparison of versions is in Nussbaum, *Undelivered*, 30–31.

64. Sellers, *River*, 64–65; Bond, *Time to Teach*, 251.

65. After the March, organizers published a pamphlet and fundraising appeal that contained a complete, accurate version of Lewis's delivered remarks. "Speeches by the Leaders," NAACP Papers, HV 001473019-0528. The speech can be found on YouTube, including at https://www.youtube.com/watch?v=TCqR9LbT1_w.

66. A. Philip Randolph to John F. Kennedy, Aug. 13, 1963, Kenneth O'Donnell to A. Philip Randolph, Aug. 22, 1963, JFK-WHCF-0365-007; "Leadership Itinerary," NAACP Papers, HV 001473019-0528; Gentile, *March*, 250–51; Wilkins, *Standing Fast*, 292; Bruce, *From the Door*, 97.

NOTES TO PAGES 149–154

595

67. John Lewis, interview with Archie Allen, Sept. 23, 1969, NPL-AAC, 125; John Lewis, interview with David Halberstam, #3, Dec. 10, 1995, BU-DHP, box 59, folder 5; John Lewis, OH with Vicki Daitch, Mar. 19, 2004, JFKL-OHC.

68. *Washington Post*, Aug. 29, 1963, D14; *Atlanta Daily World*, Sept. 1, 1963, 1; Jones, *March*, 199; Wilkins, *Standing Fast*, 293.

69. "John F. Kennedy, Meeting with Civil Rights Leaders, Aug. 28, 1963," JFK Meeting Tape 108.1 and 108.2, PRDE. Popular lore holds that Rockefeller's standing fell because of his divorce, but historical evidence suggests Birmingham mattered more. *Politico*, May 26, 2015.

70. Jack Lynn to John Lewis, Aug. 22, 1963, HV 252253-0100314; Transcript of "March on Washington . . . Report by the Leaders," Aug. 28, 1963, JFK-WHCF-0365-008.

71. John Lewis, interview with David Halberstam, #3, Dec. 10, 1995, BU-DHP, box 59, folder 5.

72. Viorst, *Fire*, 230.

73. *Nashville Banner*, Aug. 29, 1963; *Christian Science Monitor*, Aug. 30, 1963, 12; *New York Times*, Aug. 29, 1963, 16, 20; *Washington Post*, Aug. 29, 1963, Aug. 30, 1963, A18; *Time,* Sept. 6, 1963, 10–15; *Wall Street Journal*, Aug. 29, 1963, 2; John Lewis, interview with Archie Allen, Sept. 23, 1969, NPL-AAC, 128; John Lewis, "Six Month Report," Dec. 27, 1963, HV 252253-003-001.

74. Francis O'Boyle, OH with Kathleen Shannon, Oct. 30, 1967, RJBOHC, 31.

EIGHT: ONE MAN, ONE VOTE

1. *New York Times*, Sept. 16, 1963, 1; *Los Angeles Times*, Sept. 16, 1963, 17; *Time*, Sept. 27, 1963, 17; Branch, *Parting*, 889; McWhorter, *Carry Me*, 5, 501–12, 516.

2. John Lewis, interview with David Halberstam, #3, Dec. 10, 1995, BU-DHP, box 59, folder 5, 5–6.

3. John Lewis, interview with Archie Allen, Sept. 23, 1969, NPL-AAC, 129; Lewis with D'Orso, *Walking*, 226–27.

4. John Lewis, OH with Katherine Shannon, Aug. 22, 1967, RJBOHC, 117; *Washington Post*, Sept. 23, 1963, A7.

5. Broderick and Meier, *Negro Protest Thought*, 317.

6. "Proposed Plan of Action," JFKL-BMPP 008-004; *Washington Post*, Sept. 23, 1963, A7, Sept. 25, 1963, A6.

7. *New York Times*, Sept. 25, 1963, 33; *Washington Post*, Sept. 23, 1963, A7; McWhorter, *Carry Me*, 520; Munis, *Shuttlesworth*, 406.

8. Garrow, *Cross*, 294; McWhorter, *Carry Me*, 537; Branch, *Pillar*, 143–44; *Parting*, 896–98.

9. Gerald Davis to John Lewis, Oct. 2, 1963, HV 252253-0010-523.

10. *Southern Patriot*, Oct. 1963, NPL-AAC, box 3, folder 21; York (Pa.) *Gazette and Daily*, Oct. 9, 1963, 23.

11. Anne Braden to Julian Bond, Sept. 25, 1963, Anne Braden to Mike [no last name given], Oct. 2, 1963, Julian Bond to Anne Braden, Oct. 2, 1963, HV 252253-009-0535.

12. Bruce Gordon, "Field Report," Nov. 9, 1963, HV 252253-045-0862; LaFayette and Johnson, *In Peace*, 95.

13. "Special Report: Selma, Alabama," Oct. 11, 1963, HV 252253-014-0001; Zinn, *SNCC*, 153.

14. SNCC press release, Sept. 25, 1963, HV 252253-013-0713; "Special Report: Selma, Alabama," Oct. 11, 1963, HV 252253-014-0001; John Lewis, interview with David Halberstam, #3, Dec. 10, 1995, 10, int. #4, July 8, 1996, 3, BU-DHP, box 59, folder 5; John Lewis, interview with Blackside, #2, Nov. 5, 1985, WU-HHC, 11.

15. "Special Report: Selma, Alabama," Oct. 11, 1962, HV 252253-014-0001; *Atlanta Constitution*, Sept. 17, 1963, 6; *Atlanta Daily World*, Sept. 18, 1963, 6; *Baltimore Sun*, Sept. 18, 1963, 8; Pace, *Prathia Hall*, 83; May, *Bending*, 29.

16. FBI documents, Sept. 25, 1963, HV 00139-006-0718.

17. FBI documents, Sept. 24, 1963, Sept. 25, 1963, HV 00139-006-0718; "Special Report: Selma, Alabama," Oct. 11, 1962, HV 252253-014-0001.

18. FBI documents, Sept. 25, 1963, HV 00139-006-0718; SNCC press release, Sept. 25, 1963, HV 252253-013-0713; John Lewis, interview with Archie Allen, Sept. 23, 1969, NPL-AAC, 130–31; *Atlanta Daily World*, Sept. 18, 1963, 6; *New York Times*, Sept. 25, 1963, 32, Sept. 27, 1963, 30; *Selma Times-Journal*, Sept. 26, 1963, 1, 8; Carson, *Student Voice*, 77; Lewis with D'Orso, *Walking*, 232–36.

19. SNCC press release, Oct. 2, 1963, HV 252253-013-0713; *Baltimore Sun*, Oct. 3, 1963, 16; John Lewis, interview with Archie Allen, Sept. 23, 1969, NPL-AAC, 131.

20. John Lewis, OH with Katherine Shannon, Aug. 22, 1967, RJBOHC, 119; *Selma Times-Journal*, Oct. 6, 1963, 1, 2; *New Republic*, Oct. 26, 1963, 11–12; Zinn, *SNCC*, 151.

21. *Selma Times-Journal*, Oct. 7, 8, 1963; *New York Times*, Oct. 8, 1963, 37; *Washington Post*, Oct. 8, 1963, 7; *New York Amsterdam News*, Oct. 19, 1963, 15; *New Republic*, Oct. 26, 1963, 11–12; *New Yorker*, Sept. 22, 2020; Zinn, *SNCC*, 147–66; May, *Bending*, 30–36. Neither in *Walking with the Wind* or in any interview does Lewis say explicitly that he was in jail on Freedom Day. But neither does he ever discuss his own activities that day. To Katherine Shannon he said, in 1967, "Some of us got arrested earlier during the day for trying to get people in line."

(John Lewis, OH with Katherine Shannon, Aug. 22, 1967, 119.) To James A. DeVinney he said, "I can never forget that day. . . . Sheriff Jim Clark and others stood there and later some of us were arrested." (Lewis, interview with Blackside, #2, Nov. 5, 1985, WU-HHC, 2.) But the *Selma Times-Journal* reported daily on his status during this period, noting each day that he remained in jail and reporting his release only on Oct. 10. His memo to SNCC on Dec. 27, 1963, talks of a two-week stay in jail, which would span from Sept. 25 to Oct. 9. It is likely that Lewis was mixing up the Freedom Day activities with his own efforts to get Selma voters registered on Oct. 15. See King, *Freedom Song*, 223–28; *Selma Times-Journal*, Oct. 6, 7, 8, 9, 10, 11, 15, and 16, 1963; John Lewis, memo, Oct. 15, 1963, HV 252253-007-0545; John Lewis, "Six-Month Report," Dec. 27, 1963, HV 252253-002-0001.

22. John Lewis, memo, Oct. 15, 1963, HV 252253-007-0545; John Lewis, "Six-Month Report," Dec. 27, 1963, HV 252253-002-0001; *Selma Times-Journal*, Oct. 16, 1963, 1, 2; John Lewis, OH with Steven Lawson, USF-SFLP, box 6, folder 1, "Oral History Interview—John Lewis," 16–19; John Lewis, interview with Blackside, #2, Nov. 5, 1985, WU-HHC, 2; King, *Freedom Song*, 223–25.

23. June Fair, author interview, Oct. 14, 2021; Rick Momeyer, author interview, July 21, 2021; Lewis, "Six-Month Report," Dec. 27, 1963, HV 252253-002-0001; Itinerary, Nov. 18, 1963, HV 252253-002-0001; Rick Momeyer, "Remembering John Lewis and His Place in Allegheny College History," Allegheny College, July 20, 2020; Rick Momeyer, email to author, Jan. 26, 2022.

24. John Lewis, interview with Archie Allen, Sept. 23, 1969, NPL-AAC, 133; Beardslee, *Way Out*, 20.

25. John Lewis, interview with David

Halberstam, #3, Dec. 10, 1995, BU-DHP, box 59, folder 5, 8–9; John Lewis, interview with Emily Stoper, 1966, 6, CRM-VET.

26. *New York Times*, Nov. 25, 1963, 12; Bryant, *Bystander*, 458–59; Schlesinger, *Thousand Days*, 1027. Polling data showed that Black Americans were especially upset about Kennedy's killing. Brauer, *Second Reconstruction*, 312–13.

27. Conference program, HV 252253-014-0001; "Press information," "Statement on the Death of John F. Kennedy," HV 252253-056-0433; Lyon, *Memories*, 119–23.

28. John Lewis, OH with Jack Bass and Walter DeVries, Nov. 20, 1973, UNC-SOHP, 65–66; John Lewis, interview with David Halberstam, #3, Dec. 10, 1995, BU-DHP, box 59, folder 5, 9; *New York Times*, Nov. 29, 1963, 25; Lewis with D'Orso, *Walking*, 241–42.

29. *York (Pa.) Gazette and Daily*, Nov. 30, 1963, 1.

30. Danny Lyon, author interview, July 29, 2019.

31. *Young Socialist*, Dec. 1963/Jan. 1964, 1–2; *Detroit News & Letters*, Dec. 1963, 6; Carson, ed., *Student Voice*, 88, 90.

32. John Lewis, interview with Archie Allen, Aug. 8, 1969, NPL-AAC, 106–8.

33. John Lewis, interview with Archie Allen, Sept. 23, 1969, NPL-AAC, 136.

34. John Lewis, interview with David Halberstam, # 4, July 8, 1996, BU-DHP, box 59, folder 5, 9; Danny Lyon, author interview, July 29, 2019.

35. Muriel Tillinghast, author interview, Dec. 13, 2022.

36. John Lewis, interview with David Halberstam, #4, July 8, 1996, BU-DHP, box 59, folder 5, 1; Halberstam, *Children*, 447.

37. Nancy Stearns, author interview, Jan. 12, 2022; Rick Momeyer, author interview, Sept. 22, 2021.

38. John Lewis, interview with David Halberstam, #4, July 8, 1996, BU-DHP, box 59, folder 5; Julian Bond, interview with David Halberstam, BU-DHP, box 58, folder 14, 5–6; John Lewis, interview with Danny Lyon, #5, Oct. 27, 1989, DLT; Courtland Cox, author interview, Jan. 11, 2022; Matthew Jones, interview with Archie Allen, Nov. 9, 1969, NPL-AAC, box 3, folder 18, 10; Danny Lyon, author interview, July 29, 2019; Archie Allen, author interview, Feb. 8, 2022; MacLaine, *Don't Fall*, 137.

39. Hogan, *Many Minds*, 105; Curry et al., eds., *Deep in Our Hearts*, 153.

40. Carson, ed., *Student Voice*, 91; Brown-Nagin, *Courage to Dissent*, 228–31; Grady-Willis, *Challenging U.S. Apartheid*, 41–53.

41. Judy Richardson, author interview, Aug. 14, 2019; SNCC executive committee minutes, Dec. 27–31, 1963, HV 252253-003-0287; *Atlanta Constitution*, Dec. 23, 1963, 3; *Nashville Banner*, Dec. 23, 1963; Carson, ed., *Student Voice*, 95–96, 99; Forman, *Revolutionaries*, 360–61; King, *Freedom Song*, 164–69, 172–73, 186.

42. John Lewis, interview with Archie Allen, Sept. 23, 1969, NPL-AAC, 136–37.

43. SNCC press releases, Jan. 10, 1964, Jan. 16, 1964, "Atlanta Fact Sheet," HV 252253-019-0500; *New York Times*, Jan. 8, 1964, 28; Carson, ed., *Student Voice*, 101–3, 107; Lyon, *Memories*, 124; King, *Freedom Song*, 181–82, 186.

44. "Agreement Settles Atlanta Sit-Ins," SNCC press release, Jan. 6, 1964, HV 252253-019-0500; *Atlanta Constitution*, Jan. 3, 1964, 7; *New York Times*, Jan. 22, 1964, 28, Jan. 29, 1964, 18; *Christian Science Monitor*, Jan. 27, 1964, 10; *New York Times*, Feb. 11, 1964, 1; *Nation*, Feb. 3, 1964, 117–20; Carson, ed., *Student Voice*, 107, 116; Brown-Nagin, *Courage to Dissent*, 234.

45. SNCC executive committee minutes, Dec. 27–31, 1963, HV 252253-003-0287; SNCC executive committee minutes, Apr. 19, 1964, HV 252253-003-0903; John Lewis, interview with Emily Stoper, 1966, CRMVET, 2.

46. Robert Moses, author interview, June 26, 2020; *San Francisco Chronicle,* Dec. 7, 1963, 4; *Chicago Defender,* Dec. 18, 1963, 9; Carson, *In Struggle,* 96–99.

47. Julia Prettyman, interview with Archie Allen, Nov. 11, 1968, NPL-AAC, box 3, folder 26, 3; John Lewis, interview with Emily Stoper, 1966, 214; *Nation,* Feb. 3, 1964, 119; Dittmer, *Local People,* 209; Carson, *In Struggle,* 99; Carson, ed., *Student Voice,* 131.

48. *Nation,* Feb. 3, 1964, 118; Hogan, *Many Minds,* 157–58. According to the Tuskegee Institute, lynchings in the South numbered in the double digits almost every year until 1935. No year saw zero lynchings until 1952.

49. Broderick and Meier, *Negro Protest Thought,* 313–21.

50. John Lewis, press release, Apr. 17, 1964, HV 252252-001-1210; Martin Luther King Jr. to Dorothy Height et al., Apr. 21, 1964, HV 252253-001-0523; John Lewis, interview with Archie Allen, Sept. 24, 1969, NPL-AAC, 146–47; *Nashville Banner,* Apr. 17, 1964; *New York Times,* Apr. 24, 1964, 1, 20; Forman, *Revolutionaries,* 368; Meier and Rudwick, *CORE,* 252–53; Jacoby, *Someone Else's House,* 15–32.

51. Theodore H. White, "Power Structure, Integration, Militancy, Freedom Now!" *Life,* Nov. 29, 1963, 86–87; King, *Freedom Song,* 283. Forman wrote an irate letter to *Life* carefully if testily rebutting White's insinuations. The editors declined to run it, owing to, they said, the volume of letters about Kennedy's assassination. James Forman to *Life* magazine, Dec. 9,

1963; Jacqueline Lapidus to James Forman, Dec. 20, 1963, HV 252253-007-0545.

52. SNCC executive committee minutes, Dec. 27–31, 1963, HV 252253-003-0287; Frank Wilkinson, OH by Dale Trelevan, Sept. 18, 1985, UCLA-COHR, 773–74; Sherrill, *First Amendment Felon,* 77; *New York Times,* Jan. 4, 2006.

53. SNCC executive committee minutes, Mar. 29, 1964, HV 252253-003-0287; Klehr, *Far Left,* 160–67; Dittmer, *Local People,* 229–34; Carson, *In Struggle,* 104–7.

54. SNCC press release, Apr. 30, 1964, HV 252253-014-0003; *Atlanta Daily World,* Feb. 15, 1964, 1, 7; *Washington Post,* Apr. 15, 1964, A23; *New York Times,* Apr. 22, 1964, 30; John Lewis, interview with Archie Allen, Sept. 24, 1969, NPL-AAC, 159–60; John Lewis, OH with William Chafe, Apr. 25, 1989, CU-OHC, 3.

55. Bill Hansen, author interview, Nov. 23, 2022.

56. Lewis itinerary, Mar. 1964, HV 252253-025-0336; Spring conference summary, Mar. 27–29, 1964, HV 252253-001-0523; Penny to Jim, Nancy, Jimmy, Mary, Julian, Dec. 11, 1963, HV 252253-001-1063; James Bolton, memo, Apr. 18, 1964, HV 252253-003-0287. In *Walking with the Wind,* Lewis dates the letter to 1965, but the letter is addressed to people, including Nancy Stearns, who had left SNCC by 1965.

57. *Tennessean,* Apr. 28, 1964, 1, 2, Apr. 29, 1964, 1, 4, Apr. 30, 1964, 1, 2, May 1, 1964, 10, May 2, 1964, 1, 3, May 3, 1964, 1; *Nashville Banner,* May 1, 1964; John Lewis, interview with Archie Allen, Sept. 24, 1969, NPL-AAC, 140, 149; Archie Allen, author interview, Feb. 8, 2022; Houston, *Nashville Way,* 153–60; Carson, ed., *Student Voice,* 143–50.

58. *Tennessean,* May 3, 1964, 1–3, May 4, 1964, 1, 4, May 5, 1964, 1, 2, May 6,

1964, 1, 11, May 9, 1964, 2; *Newsweek*, May 11, 1964, 21–22.

59. John Lewis, interview with Archie Allen, Sept. 24, 1969, NPL-AAC, 143; *New York Times*, Mar. 16, 1964, 26.

60. *Christian Science Monitor*, May 19, 1964, 13.

61. A. Philip Randolph to John Lewis, Apr. 7, 1964, HV 252253-001-0523; *New York Times*, Mar. 14, 1964, 10, Apr. 26, 1964, E6.

62. Staff Meeting Minutes, June 9–11, 1964, HV 252253-003-0903; *Atlanta Constitution*, June 13, 1964, 5; *Freedom Song*, 318–25; Ransby, *Baker*, 324; Hogan, *Many Minds*, 349, fn9.

63. Staughton Lynd, author interview, Feb. 12, 2020; Hogan, *Many Minds*, 159.

64. SNCC press release, June 12, 1964, HV 252253-002-0001; *Pittsburgh Post-Gazette*, Mar. 7, 1964, 1.

NINE: FREEDOM SUMMER

1. Sugarman, *Stranger at the Gates*, 12.

2. Belfrage, *Freedom Summer*, 1–20.

3. *Saturday Evening Post*, July 25, 1964, 15–19; *Esquire*, Sept. 1, 1964, 105–6, 190.

4. Branch, *Parting*, 351–53; Dittmer, *Local People*, 242–44; Visser-Maessen, *Moses*, 201.

5. John Lewis, interview with Archie Allen, Sept. 24, 1969, NPL-AAC, 150.

6. *New York Times*, June 21, 1964, 64.

7. Key histories of Freedom Summer include Belfrage, *Freedom Summer*; Cagin, *We Are Not Afraid*; McAdam, *Freedom Summer*; Mills, *Holy Crusade*; Sugarman, *Stranger at the Gates*; Sutherland, *Letters from Mississippi*; and Watson, *Freedom Summer*.

8. Farmer, *Lay Bare*, 271–78.

9. John Lewis, interview with Archie Allen, Sept. 24, 1969, NPL-AAC, 150; *Chicago Defender*, June 25, 1964; Lewis with D'Orso, *Walking*, 257.

10. John Lewis, interview with David Halberstam, #3, Dec. 10, 1995, BU-DHP, box 59, folder 5, 11.

11. John Lewis, interview with Archie Allen, Sept. 24, 1969, NPL-AAC, 155; *Washington Post*, June 26, 1964, A18; Carson, ed., *Student Voice*, 164; Mills, *Holy Crusade*, 102; Cagin, *Not Afraid*, 347; Lewis with D'Orso, *Walking*, 259. The search for the three men discovered corpses of other Black men killed by white supremacists. Each was a one-day story. Dittmer, *Local People*, 251–52.

12. John Lewis, interview with Archie Allen, Sept. 24, 1969, NPL-AAC, 150; Robert Moses, author interview, June 26, 2020; *New York Times*, June 28, 1964, 1.

13. *Washington Post*, June 29, 1964, A17.

14. John Lewis, interview with Clayborne Carson, Apr. 17, 1972, CRMVET, 10.

15. John Lewis, interview with David Halberstam, #3, Dec. 10, 1995, BU-DHP, box 59, folder 5, 11; Visser-Maessen, *Moses*, 203.

16. "Statement of John Lewis from Greenwood," July 2, 1964, HV 252253-015-0401; press release, July 3, 1964, HV 252253-039-0390; King, *Freedom Song*, 409–10.

17. John Lewis, interview with Archie Allen, Sept. 24, 1969, NPL-AAC, 152; John Lewis, interview with David Halberstam, #3, Dec. 10, 1995, BU-DHP, box 59, folder 5, 13; John Lewis, interview with Adam Clymer, May 8, 2008, DCC-TPP, 1, 3.

18. *Los Angeles Times*, July 24, 1964, 21; *New York Times*, July 25, 1964, 9; Carson, ed., *Student Voice*, 175, 178; Paul Good, "John Lewis—Vanishing American," unpublished manuscript, AAPP; John Lewis, interview with David Halberstam, #3, Dec. 10, 1995, BU-DHP, box 59, folder 5, 12; *Dissent*, Winter 1985, 14–15;

Beardslee, *Way Out*, 20–21; Dittmer, *Local People*, 251.

19. SNCC press release, July 9, 1964, HV 252253-014-0001; SNCC WATS reports, July 5, 1964, July 6, 1964, and "Report from Marshall Jones," July 7, 1964, HV 252253-015-0401; *New York Times*, July 7, 1964, 20; Carson, ed., *Student Voice*, 167, 169.

20. James Farmer to Roy Wilkins, July 6, 1964, HV 001487-015-0328; *Chicago Defender*, July 13, 1964, 1, 3; *New York Times*, July 13, 1964, 18.

21. "John Lewis Speech," undated, LC-JFP, box 35, folder 1.

22. John Lewis, interview with Archie Allen, Sept. 23, 1969, NPL-AAC, 151; Branch, *Pillar*, 403–4.

23. Flamm, *In the Heat of the Summer*, 1, 10–16.

24. *Crisis*, Aug.–Sept. 1964, 467; D'Emilio, *Lost Prophet*, 382–83.

25. *New York Times*, July 30, 1964, 1, 12; Wilkins with Mathews, *Standing Fast*, 304.

26. James Farmer, interview with Taylor Branch, Nov. 18, 1983, UNC-TBP, folder 66, 7; Farmer, *Lay Bare*, 298; D'Emilio, *Lost Prophet*, 383–85.

27. John Lewis, interview with Archie Allen, Sept. 24, 1969, NPL-AAC, 154; *New York Times*, July 31, 1964, 1, 11.

28. *Crisis*, Aug.–Sept. 1964, 469.

29. John Lewis, interview with Archie Allen, Sept. 24, 1969, NPL-AAC, 154.

30. *New York Times*, July 31, 1964, 11; *New Republic*, Sept. 5, 1964, 22; Carson, ed., *Student Voice*, 179, 182.

31. Bob Moses et al., "Emergency Memorandum," July 19, 1964, CRMVET.

32. Dittmer, *Local People*, 272–81; Viorst, *Fire*, 260–62.

33. Mills, *Holy Crusade*, 141; Cagin, *Not Alone*, 395–98.

34. Carson, ed., *Student Voice*, 183.

35. Lewis with D'Orso, *Walking*, 276–77.

36. Carson, ed., *Student Voice*, 183; Joseph Rauh, interview with Anne Romaine, WHS-ARI, 4–6. A roll-call vote was necessary because a presiding officer in a large hall, such as at a national convention, can typically deem a voice vote to go whichever way he pleases.

37. Moses and Cobb, *Radical Equations*, 79; Visser-Maessen, *Moses*, 228–30.

38. Lewis with D'Orso, *Walking*, 269–70.

39. John Lewis, interview with Archie Allen, Sept. 24, 1969, NPL-AAC, 158; Carson, ed., *Student Voice*, 190; Mills, *Holy Crusade*, 144.

40. Visser-Maessen, *Moses*, 234; Donaldson, *Last Hurrah*, 213.

41. Lyndon Johnson and Hubert Humphrey, Aug. 20, 1964, Conversation WH6408-29-5045, UVA-PRDE.

42. Schedule entry, Aug. 19, 1964, LBJL-PDD; Lyndon Johnson and Douglass Cater, Aug. 19, 1964, Conversation WH6408-28-5038, UVA-PRDE; *New York Times*, Aug. 20, 1964, 1, 18; *Washington Post*, Aug. 20, 1964, A4; Garrow, *Cross*, 346.

43. Daily Diary, Aug. 19, 1964, LBJL-PDD; John Lewis to Lyndon B. Johnson, Aug. 19, 1964, HV 252253-039-0390; Lee White to John Lewis, Aug. 20, 1964, CRMVET; Garrow, *Cross*, 346.

44. "Lyndon Johnson and George Reedy," Aug. 19, 1964, Conversation WH6408-28-5030, PRDE; Wilkins testimony, HV 001487-015-0328; *New York Times*, Aug. 20, 1964, 1, 18.

45. Lewis with D'Orso, *Walking*, 275.

46. Larson, *Walk with Me*, 166–76.

47. Lyndon B. Johnson, "Remarks to Democratic Governors," Aug. 22, 1964, UCSB-APP.

48. Skipper, *Showdown*, 108.

49. Joseph Rauh, interview with Anne Romaine, June 16, 1966, WHS-ARI, 6, 16; Lewis with D'Orso, *Walking*, 279–80.

50. NAACP rally materials, HV 001487-015-0328; *New York Times*, Aug. 25, 1964, 24; John Lewis, OH with Katherine Shannon, Aug. 22, 1967, RJBOHC, 130–31; Robert Moses, author interview, June 26, 2020; Hampton and Fayer, *Voices*, 199–200; Forman, *Revolutionaries*, 388; Lewis with D'Orso, *Walking*, 280–81.

51. Young, *Easy Burden*, 308.

52. *New York Times*, Aug. 26, 1964, 1, 28; Lewis with D'Orso, *Walking*, 281–82; Donaldson, *Last Hurrah*, 223.

53. Dittmer, *Local People*, 300–302; Forman, *Revolutionaries*, 390–95; Holsaert et al., *Freedom Plow*, 234–35; Larson, *Walk with Me*, 184; Bruce Hartford, "The Mississippi Movement & the MFDP," CRMVET.

54. Johnson and Humphrey lost five Southern states but won every other state except Arizona. They took 61 percent of the popular vote, the largest percentage since 1820.

55. *Chicago Defender*, Aug. 31, 1964, 4; Forman, *Revolutionaries*, 357–59, 388–96.

56. Skipper, *Showdown*, 166; D'Emilio, *Lost Prophet*, 391; Aaron E. Henry, "Position Paper," Aug. 29, 1964, CRMVET; Holsaert et al., *Freedom Plow*, 235; Theresa del Pozzo to John Lewis, Sept. 19, 1964, HV 252253-001-0523.

57. John Lewis, interview with Clayborne Carson, Apr. 17, 1972, CRMVET, 10–11.

58. John Lewis, OH with Katherine Shannon, Aug. 22, 1967, RJBOHC, 130–31; John Lewis, interview with David Halberstam, #3, Dec. 10, 1995, BU-DHP, box 59, folder 5, 12; Lewis with D'Orso, *Walking*, 281–82; Garrow, *Cross*, 351.

59. Lewis with D'Orso, *Walking*, 283–85.

TEN: AFRICA

1. Willie Mae Lewis to John Lewis, Sept. 9, 1964, HV 252253-001-0523.

2. John Lewis, interview with Archie Allen, Sept. 24, 1969, NPL-AAC, 164.

3. John Lewis to Bayard Rustin, June 2, 1964, HV 252253-001-0523.

4. Peter Weiss to John Lewis and Donald Harris, Sept. 8, 1964, AAPP; John Lewis to Peter Weiss, Sept. 29, 1964, AAPP; John Lewis to Peter Weiss, Jan. 1, 1965, HV 252253-001-0782; Peter Weiss to John Lewis and Donald Harris, Sept. 8, 1964, AAPP; John Lewis, interview with Archie Allen, Sept. 24, 1969, NPL-AAC, 160; Peter and Cora Weiss, author interview, Mar. 5, 2022; Harry Belafonte, author interview, July 15, 2020; Belafonte, *My Song*, 291. The $250 sum was equivalent to about $2,500 in 2024. The foundation was run by Peter and Cora Weiss.

5. SNCC executive committee minutes, Sept. 4, 1964, HV 25253-003-00287; John Lewis, interview with Archie Allen, Sept. 24, 1969, NPL-AAC, 161–62; Nancy Stearns, interview with Archie Allen, Nov. 8, 1968, NPL-AAC, box 3, folder 30; Fleming, *Soon We Will Not Cry*, 146.

6. John Lewis, interview with Archie Allen, Sept. 24, 1969, NPL-AAC, 162; Bill Hansen, author interview, Nov. 23, 2022.

7. John Lewis, interview with Archie Allen, Sept. 24, 1969, NPL-AAC, 165–66; John Lewis, OH with Katherine Shannon, Aug. 22, 1967, RJBOHC, 134; Forman, *Revolutionaries*, 408.

8. James Forman, "Brief Report on Guinea," Sept. 23–24, 1964, WHS-SAVF-SNCC, mss. 577, box 47, folder 4; John

Lewis, interview with Archie Allen, Sept. 24, 1969, NPL-AAC, 166; Gritter and Bond, "Interview with Julian Bond," 85; Don Harris, author interview, Mar. 25, 2022.

9. John Lewis, interview with Archie Allen, Sept. 24, 1969, NPL-AAC, 164; James Forman, "Brief Report on Guinea," Sept. 23–24, 1964, WHS-SAVF-SNCC, mss. 577, box 47, folder 4; Belafonte, *My Song*, 292–93; Don Harris, author interview, Mar. 25, 2022.

10. James Forman, "Brief Report on Guinea," Sept. 23–24, 1964, WHS-SAVF, SNCC Papers, mss. 577, box 47, folder 4; Donald Harris, OH with Shaun Illingworth et al., Feb. 28, 2013, RUOH, 39; John Lewis, OH with Katherine Shannon, Aug. 22, 1967, RJBOHC, 135.

11. Hamer, *To Praise Our Bridges*, 24.

12. Matthew Jones, interview with Archie Allen, Nov. 9, 1969, NPL-AAC, box 3, folder 18, 4–5.

13. James Forman, "Brief Report on Guinea," Sept. 23–24, 1964, WHS-SAVF-SNCC, mss. 577, box 47, folder 4.

14. Forman, *Revolutionaries*, 411.

15. John Lewis, OH with Katherine Shannon, Aug. 22, 1967, RJBOHC, 136.

16. John Lewis and Donald Harris, "The Trip," HV 252253-001-1210, 1–5; SNCC press release, Oct. 18, 1964, HV 252253-014-0198; John Lewis, interview with Archie Allen, Sept. 24, 1969, NPL-AAC, 168; Donald Harris, OH with Shaun Illingworth et al., Feb. 28, 2013, RUOH, 39; Donald Harris, author interview, Apr. 16, 2020.

17. John Lewis, interview with Archie Allen, Sept. 24, 1969, NPL-AAC, 170–71.

18. John Lewis, interview with Archie Allen, Sept. 24, 1969, NPL-AAC, 171; Donald Harris, OH with Shaun Illingworth et al., Feb. 28, 2013, RUOH, 41; Hampton and Fayer, *Voices*, 206; Lewis

with D'Orso, *Walking*, 287–88. In 1951, the Congress for Civil Rights, an American Communist organization, had tried to get the UN to indict the U.S. for lynching and other forms of violence toward African Americans with a document called "We Charge Genocide."

19. SNCC press release, Oct. 27, 1964, HV 252253-014-0198; John Lewis, interview with Archie Allen, Sept. 24, 1969, NPL-AAC, 171–174; Lewis and Harris, "The Trip," HV 252253-001-1210, 6–7.

20. David Du Bois to Lewis, Feb. 28, 1965, HV 252253-001-0782; John Lewis interview with Archie Allen, Sept. 24, 1969, NPL-AAC, 174–76; Lewis and Harris, "The Trip," HV 252253-001-1210, 8–12; Donald Harris, OH with Shaun Illingworth et al., Feb. 28, 2013, RUOH, 39–40.

21. John Lewis, interview with Sean Wilentz, tape 2, June 12, 1995, SWT; "Community Salute to Dr. Martin Luther King, Jr.," WNYC Archive Collections.

22. John Lewis to Don Harris, Dec. 19, 1964, AAPP.

23. Donald Harris, OH with Shaun Illingworth et al., Feb. 28, 2013, RUOH, 41; Donald Harris, interview with Emily Stoper, 1967; Forman, *Revolutionaries*, 427.

24. John Lewis, interview with Archie Allen, Sept. 24, 1969, NPL-AAC, 177–78; John Lewis, OH with Katherine Shannon, Aug. 22, 1967, RJBOHC, 139; John Lewis, interview with Emily Stoper, 1966, CRMVET, 23; Lewis with D'Orso, *Walking*, 292–93, 296–97.

25. Broderick and Meier, *Negro Protest Thought*, 318.

26. Smith [Robinson] to Forman, Mar. 5, 1964, LC-JFP, box 16, folder 16; Marion Barry, interview with Clayborne Carson, Apr. 7, 1972, CRMVET, 6. One instance of sexual harassment was from Sheila Kessler

Michaels, lodged against Marion Barry. See Sheila Kessler Michaels, "Complaint to Executive Committee," HV 252253-001-0523, and John Lewis, interview with David Halberstam, #3, Dec. 10, 1995, and #4, July 8, 1996, BU-DHP, box 59, folder 5.

27. King, *Freedom Song*, 452; Fleming, *Soon We Will Not Cry*, 153. On SNCC and emerging feminism, see Evans, *Personal Politics*, 60–101. On Waveland, see, among other sources, Carson, *In Struggle*, 133–52; Hogan, *Many Minds*, 197–218; King, *Freedom Song*, 437–74; Lewis with D'Orso, *Walking*, 291–302.

28. Donald Harris, OH with Shaun Illingworth et al., Feb. 28, 2013, RUOH, 41–42; Joan Browning, author interview, July 28, 2022.

29. "Proposal for the Structure of SNCC," WHS-SEP, mss. 531, box 1, folder 4; Mary King to John Lewis, Jan. 10, 1965, HV 252253-001-0782.

30. John Lewis, interview with Archie Allen, Sept. 24, 1969, NPL-AAC, 176; John Lewis, OH with Katherine Shannon, Aug. 22, 1967, RJBOHC, 138; *Washington Post*, Dec. 2, 1964, A21, Dec. 7, 1964, A16; Lewis with D'Orso, *Walking*, 298–301; Beardslee, *Way Out*, 24. On liberal concerns about SNCC's direction, see Curtis Gans to Leon Shull, Nov. 20, 1964, LC-JFP, box 19, folder 16.

31. SNCC press releases, Dec. 1, 1964, Dec. 3, 1964, HV 252253-033-0001.

32. Mary King to John Lewis, Jan. 10, 1965, HV 252253-001-0782; Forman, *Revolutionaries*, 439; Lewis with D'Orso, *Walking*, 365; Hampton and Fayer, *Voices*, 281.

33. John Lewis, interview with Laura Visser-Maessen, Nov. 16, 2009, LVMI, 4, 6; Curry et al., eds., *Deep in Our Hearts*, 368; Branch, *Pillar*, 588.

34. "Statement by John Lewis, Chairman," Feb. 1965, WHS-MEKP, mss.

82-445, box 1, folder 20; SNCC meeting minutes, Feb. 1965, WHS-MEKP, mss. 82-445, box 3, folder 2; John Lewis, interview with Archie Allen, Jan. 20, 1979, NPL-AAC, 184; John Lewis, interview with Emily Stoper, 1966, CRMVET, 31; Ed Hamlett, interview with Archie Allen, Nov. 6, 1968, NPL-AAC, box 3, folder 13, 2; Forman, *Revolutionaries*, 439; Lewis with D'Orso, *Walking*, 365–66; Curry et al., eds., *Deep in Our Hearts*, 368.

ELEVEN: SELMA

1. On Selma, key books include Fager, *Selma, 1965*; Garrow, *Protest at Selma*; Pratt, *Selma's Bloody Sunday*; and Branch, *Pillar*, 552–699, and *Canaan's Edge*, 5–202.

2. Mark Suckle, interview with Archie Allen, Nov. 10, 1968, NPL-AAC, 17.

3. Frank Smith, author interview, Nov. 22, 2022.

4. Fager, *Selma, 1965*, 9–10.

5. *Washington Post*, Jan. 5, 1965, A1.

6. Harriet Tanzman, interview with Archie Allen, Sept. 21, 1968, NPL-AAC, box 3, folder 32, 6; Fay Bellamy, OH with Ron Grele, Nov. 10, 1984, CU-OHC, 28–29; Greenberg, ed., *Circle of Trust*, 95–96; Fairclough, *To Redeem*, 230.

7. "SNCC Alabama Drive Enters 3rd Year," Jan. 9, 1965, HV 252253-045-0862; "Selma Freedom Day Set," Jan. 15, 1965, HV 252253-014-0198.

8. *Reporter*, Apr. 8, 1965, 24.

9. "SNCC, King, Nazis Clash in Selma Vote Push," Jan. 22, 1965, HV 252253-045-0862.

10. SNCC press releases, Jan. 15, 1965, Jan. 22, 1965, HV 252253-045-0862; John Lewis, interview with Archie Allen, Jan. 20, 1979, 182; *New York Times*, Jan. 19, 1965, 1, 20; *Washington Post*, Jan. 19, 1965, A1, 3; Lewis with D'Orso, *Walking*, 310.

11. *New York Times*, Jan. 20, 1965, 1, 18; *Chicago Defender*, Jan. 20, 1965, 1, 3, 10.

12. SNCC "Special Report," HV 252253-031-0001; John Lewis, interview with Archie Allen, Jan. 20, 1979, NPL-AAC, 179; *New York Times*, Jan. 21, 1965, 1, 22.

13. John Lewis, OH with Katherine Shannon, Aug. 22, 1967, RJBOHC, 140.

14. Branch, *Pillar*, 578-79; Hampton and Fayer, *Voices*, 221-22; Holsaert et al., eds., *Freedom Plow*, 473-74; "Malcolm X's Selma Speech," Budget Films Stock Footage, Feb. 5, 1965, https://www.bud getfilms.com/clip/14023/; C. T. Vivian, interview with Blackside, Jan. 23, 1986, WU-HHC, 35.

15. *New York Times*, Feb. 5, 1965, 15.

16. *Atlanta Constitution*, Feb. 6, 1965, 1; *New York Times*, Feb. 5, 1965, 1, 17, Feb. 7, 1965, 1, Feb. 10, 1965, 1, 18.

17. "Selma, Alabama—Statement by John Lewis, Chairman of SNCC," Feb. 10, 1965, HV 252253-053-0001; *New York Times*, Feb. 11, 1965, 1, 19.

18. Audio recording, Feb. 10, 1965, UNC TBP, series 6, cassette 5047-351, tape 7.

19. John Lewis, statement, Feb. 21, 1965, HV 252253-001-0782; Lewis with D'Orso, *Walking*, 317.

20. John Lewis, interview with Archie Allen, Jan. 20, 1979, NPL-AAC, 186; Garrow, *Cross*, 390.

21. James Bevel, OH with Blackside, WU-HHC, 12-16; *New York Times*, Feb. 27, 1965, 1; LaFayette, *In Peace*, 122; Branch, *Pillar*, 599.

22. Executive committee meeting notes, Mar. 5-6, 1965, HV 252253-003-0287; Harriet Tanzman, interview with Archie Allen, Sept. 21, 1968, NPL-AAC, box 3, folder 32, 7; Fay Bellamy, OH with Ron Grele, Nov. 10, 1984, CU-OHC, 32; John Lewis, interview with Archie Allen, Jan. 20, 1979, NPL-AAC, 185.

23. Executive committee meeting notes, Mar. 5-6, 1965, HV 252253-003-0287; John Lewis, interview with Archie Allen, Jan. 20, 1979, NPL-AAC, 186; John Lewis, OH with Katherine Shannon, Aug. 22, 1967, RJBOHC, 143.

24. Executive committee meeting notes, Mar. 5-6, 1965, HV 252253-003-0287; JRL and Silas Norman to Martin Luther King, Jr., Mar. 7, 1965, HV 252253-001-0782; John Lewis, interview with David Halberstam, #3, Dec. 10, 1995, BU-DHP, box 59, folder 5, 16.

25. Courtland Cox, author interview, Mar. 14, 2022.

26. Lewis with D'Orso, *Walking*, 320.

27. John Lewis, interview with Archie Allen, Jan. 20, 1979, NPL-AAC, 186; John Lewis, OH with Katherine Shannon, Aug. 22, 1967, RJBOHC, 144.

28. The account of "Bloody Sunday" comes from the aforementioned Selma books; Lewis's interviews and oral histories, especially with Archie Allen, Katherine Shannon, and David Halberstam; and James Forman's SNCC report, HV 252253-031-0001.

29. See Martin Luther King Jr., "Behind the Selma March," n.d., HV 252253-033-0001.

30. Maria Varela, author interview, Apr. 22, 2020; Fager, *Selma, 1965*, 99.

31. News reports estimated six hundred marchers, SNCC between two and three thousand.

32. John Lewis, interview with Archie Allen, Jan. 20, 1979, NPL-AAC, 187-88.

33. Baker's police force, on the chief's orders, did not take part.

34. John Lewis, interview with David Halberstam, #4, July 8, 1996, BU-DHP, box 59, folder 5, 17; John Lewis, interview with Clayborne Carson, Apr. 17, 1972,

CRMVET, 29. Footage of the march is included in Gorsuch, dir., *Selma: The City and the Symbol*. See also "Selma: The Real Selma Footage," YouTube, accessed June 17, 2022, https://www.youtube.com/watch?v=smx-Sk3PzzI.

35. Lewis testimony, Mar. 11, 1965, NARA-FBI record group 65, series 44, file unit 28492, section 1, serials 1–42 (NAID 7634471); John Lewis, interview with David Halberstam, #3, Dec. 10, 1995, BU-DHP, box 59, folder 5, 1.

36. SNCC report, HV 252253-031-0001; Fay Bellamy, OH with Ron Grele, Nov. 10, 1984, CU-OHC, 34.

37. John Lewis, OH with Katherine Shannon, Aug. 22, 1967, RJBOHC, 146.

38. John Lewis, interview with Archie Allen, Jan. 20, 1979, NPL-AAC, 191; John Lewis, OH with Katherine Shannon, Aug. 22, 1967, RJBOHC, 146–47; *Newsday*, Mar. 8, 1965, 66.

39. SNCC report, HV 252253-031-0001.

40. SNCC report, HV 252253-031-0001; John Lewis, interview with Archie Allen, Jan. 20, 1979, 192.

41. *Newsday*, Mar. 8, 1965, 66.

42. SNCC report, HV 252253-031-0001.

43. "USA: Selma Racial—Sidebar Stories for Vislib (1965)," British Pathé, https://www.britishpathe.com/asset/125312/.

44. Roberts and Klibanoff, *Race Beat*, 386.

45. Pratt, *Selma's Bloody Sunday*, 70; *New York Times*, Mar. 8, 1965, 1; *Boston Globe*, Mar. 8, 1965, 1; *Los Angeles Times*, Mar. 8, 1965, 1.

46. Lewis testimony, Mar. 11, 1965, NARA-FBI record group 65, series 44, file unit 28492, section 1, serials 1–42 (NAID 7634471). See also FBI report, Mar. 16, 1965, HV 001339-008-0308.

47. SNCC press release, Mar. 8, 1965, HV 252253-031-0001; John Lewis, interview with Archie Allen, Jan. 20, 1979, NPL-AAC, 193; Carson, ed., *Student Voice*, 211.

48. Beardslee, *Way Out*, 26.

49. The term "Bloody Sunday" had been used often in the past to refer to other events.

50. SNCC documents, HV 252252-018-1079.

51. Report, HV 252253-031-0001; *Afro-American*, Mar. 20, 1965, 17; *Cleveland Call and Post*, Mar. 20, 1965, 3C; *Pittsburgh Courier*, Apr. 10, 1965, 9; *Christian Century*, May 12, 1965, 614–16; *New York Times*, Mar. 10, 1965, 22; John Lewis, interview with Sean Wilentz, tape 3, June 12, 1995, SWT.

52. *Chicago Defender*, Mar. 10, 1965, 3.

53. Forman, *Revolutionaries*, 441; Garrow, *Cross*, 404–5.

54. *New York Times*, Mar. 10, 1965, 28; *Philadelphia Inquirer*, Mar. 22, 1965, 3; *Washington Post*, Mar. 28, 1965, A7; *Reporter*, Apr. 8, 1965, 23–26; *Christian Century*, May 12, 1965, 614–16; John Lewis, interview with Blackside, #2, Nov. 5, 1985, WU-HHC, 10; King, *Freedom Song*, 477–78; Raines, *Rested*, 213.

55. *Chicago Defender*, July 8, 1965, 4; "CORE-SNCC New York Marches with Selma," HV 2525252-018-1079; *New York Times*, Mar. 15, 1965, 1.

56. C. T. Vivian, interview with Blackside, Jan. 23, 1986, WU-HHP, 36–37; Jackson, *House by the Side*, 118.

57. *Atlanta Voice*, Feb. 2, 1973, 2; John Lewis, interview with Archie Allen, Jan. 20, 1979, NPL-AAC, 193; Beardslee, *Way Out*, 26; John Lewis, interview with David Halberstam, #3, Dec. 10, 1995, BU-DHP, box 59, folder 5; Lewis with D'Orso, *Walking*, 337.

58. John Lewis, interview with David

Halberstam, #3, Dec. 10, 1995, BU-DHP, box 59, folder 5, 3; Lyndon B. Johnson, "Special Message to the Congress," March 15, 1965, UCSB-APP; Forman, *Sammy Younge*, 99.

59. Lawson, *Black Ballots*, 312.

60. John Lewis, interview with Archie Allen, Jan. 20, 1979, 199; John Lewis, interview with Vicki Daitch, JFKL-OHC, 16; Lewis, "Reflections on Judge Frank M. Johnson, Jr.," 1253–56; Garrow, *Selma*, 112.

61. Bill Moyers to Lyndon Johnson, Mar. 19, 1965, UNC-TBP, series 04, folder 383; Metz Rollins, interview with Archie Allen, Nov. 5, 1968, NPL-AAC, box 3, folder 27, 18; Sellers, *River*, 128.

62. John Lewis, interview with Archie Allen, Jan. 20, 1979, NPL-AAC, 202–6; *New York Times*, Mar. 22, 1965, 1.

63. John Lewis, interview with Archie Allen, Jan. 20, 1979, NPL-AAC, 199.

64. *Militant*, Apr. 5, 1965, 2.

65. *New Yorker*, Apr. 10, 1965, 151–52; *New Amsterdam News*, Apr. 3, 1965, 2.

66. John Lewis, interview with Archie Allen, Jan. 20, 1979, NPL-AAC, 207.

67. Mark Suckle, interview with Archie Allen, NPL-AAC, box 3, folder 31, 18; John Lewis, interview with Archie Allen, Jan. 20, 1979, NPL-AAC, 207; John Lewis, interview with Blackside, #2, Nov. 5, 1985, WU-HHC, 18.

68. Lewis with D'Orso, *Walking*, 346.

69. While under cover, Rowe had also been involved in the Anniston, Alabama, attack on the Freedom Riders in 1961. Following his outing, which was necessary to testify against Liuzzo's killers, controversy ensued about the ethics of allowing an FBI informant to participate in such violent crimes. On Rowe, see May, *The Informant*. On Liuzzo, see Stanton, *From Selma to Sorrow*.

70. John Lewis, interview with Archie Allen, Jan. 20, 1979, NPL-AAC, 209–10; Joan Mooney, author interview, Sept. 11, 2020; "Funeral of Viola Liuzzo," YouTube video, https://youtu.be/1iZCyoMi3hg, accessed July 22, 2020.

TWELVE: REVOLT AT KINGSTON SPRINGS

1. *New York Herald Tribune*, May 24, 1965, 4; *Commentary*, Jan. 1965, 29. "Our job is to help educate, help prepare people for political action," Lewis told Lerone Bennett Jr. of *Ebony* magazine around the same time. "Our job is to organize the unorganized into a vital force for radical, social, economic, and political change. Our job is to create what I like to call pockets of power and influence, where the people can say, 'This is what I want and need.'" *Ebony*, July 1965, 149.

2. *Atlanta Constitution*, May 6, 1965, June 17, 1965, 1; Neary, *Bond*, 74–78; Carson, *In Struggle*, 166–68; Lewis with D'Orso, *Walking*, 360.

3. John Lewis, interview with Archie Allen, Jan. 20, 1979, NPL-AAC, 212. Forman and King made a show of patching things up at the end of April, but the truce was not destined to last. *Chicago Defender*, May 5, 1965, 4.

4. Lawrence F. O'Brien Jr. to John Lewis, Aug. 5, 1965, LBJL-WHCF, box 181; President's Daily Diary, Aug. 6, 1965, LBJL-PDD; White House Photo Office, LBJL, A1031-17a, A1031-21a, A1031-4a; John Lewis, interview with Archie Allen, Jan. 20, 1979, NPL-AAC, 213; *Washington Post*, Aug. 12, 1965, A17. The Twenty-Fourth Amendment, ratified the year before, had outlawed poll taxes in national elections. In 1966, the Supreme Court would hold state poll taxes to be unconstitutional as well, under the Fourteenth Amendment.

5. John Lewis, interview with Archie Allen, Jan. 20, 1979, NPL-AAC, 213.

6. John Lewis, interview with Archie Allen, Jan. 20, 1979, NPL-AAC, 213.

7. Lawrence F. O'Brien Jr. to John Lewis, Aug. 6, 1965, LBJL-WHCF, box 181, name file: John Lewis; Beardslee, *Way Out*, 28; Wilkins with Mathews, *Standing Fast*, 312; John Lewis to Lyndon B. Johnson, Aug. 6, 1965, LBJL-WHCF, HU, box 55, folder 1; Carter, *Music*, 53; Lawson, *Black Ballots*, 321, 329.

8. John Lewis, interview with Archie Allen, Jan. 20, 1979, NPL-AAC, 216.

9. *Atlanta Constitution*, Aug. 9, 1965, 1; *Chicago Defender*, Aug. 9, 1965, 9.

10. SNCC press release, Sept. 11, 1966, HV 252253-056-0433.

11. "Statement by John Lewis on Los Angeles and Chicago," HV 252253-016-0405; *Atlanta Constitution*, Aug. 17, 1965, 3; Lewis with D'Orso, *Walking*, 348.

12. John Lewis, OH with Katherine Shannon, Aug. 22, 1967, RJBOHC, 165–66; Meier and Rudwick, *CORE*, 329; *Commentary*, Jan. 1965, 25–31; John Lewis to SNCC staff, Oct. 7, 1965, LC-JFP, box 19, folder 20.

13. Lyndon B. Johnson, "Commencement Address at Howard University: To Fulfill These Rights," June 4, 1965, UCSB-APP; Carter, *Music*, 75–101; Yuill, "The 1966 White House Conference on Civil Rights," 259–82.

14. *Cleveland Call and Post*, Nov. 27, 1965, B8; *Norfolk New Journal and Guide*, Nov. 27, 1965, 11. Transcript of discussion, Microfilm Series LBJL-CRDJA, Part IV, WHCCR, reel 7, pages 157–58; Lawson, *In Pursuit*, 26–28. Lewis also spoke for a federal law to stop racial bias in jury selection, noting that Viola Liuzzo's killers were tried by all-white juries. *New York Times*, Nov. 17, 1965, 1; *Chicago Defender*, Nov. 18, 1965, 14.

15. Title VI of the Civil Rights Act prohibits racial discrimination in programs receiving federal funds.

16. John Lewis, Marion Barry, and Betty Garman to A. Philip Randolph, Morris Abram, and William Coleman, Dec. 14, 1965, HV 252253-002-001.

17. *New York Times*, Aug. 29, 1965, E4; John Lewis to Cleve Sellers et al., July 29, 1965, LC-JFP, box 19, folder 18.

18. John Lewis to Cleve Sellers et al., July 29, 1965, LC-JFP, box 19, folder 18; John Lewis, interview with Archie Allen, Jan. 20, 1979, NPL-AAC, 216–17; Forman, *Revolutionaries*, 445; Carson, *In Struggle*, 187–88.

19. "SNCC Statement Against the Vietnam War," UVA-HJBP, box 56, folder 8; John Lewis, interview with Archie Allen, Jan. 28, 1979, 218. Lewis wrote an angry letter to President Johnson, noting the White House's solicitude toward the family of James Reeb, but the president's failure to call Younge's parents or even to make a public statement. "Are you color conscious? Do you care [only] about white deaths in the struggle?" John Lewis to Lyndon Johnson, Jan. 11, 1966, HV 252253-056-0433.

20. *Atlanta Constitution*, Jan. 7, 1966, 1, 12; *New York Times*, Jan. 7, 1966, 2; *Newsday*, Jan. 7, 1966, 7; Neary, *Bond*, 89–91; Lewis with D'Orso, *Walking*, 343–44.

21. John Lewis, OH with Katherine Shannon, Aug. 22, 1967, RJBOHC, 169–70; *Atlanta Constitution*, Jan. 11, 1965, 6; Beardslee, *Way Out*, 29; Neary, *Bond*, 92–97, 102–3.

22. SNCC press release, Jan. 11, 1966, HV 252253-014-0467; *Atlanta Constitution*, Jan. 12, 1965, 1, 7; Neary, *Bond*, 124; Martin Luther King Jr., Address, Jan. 14, 1966, UVA-HJBP, box 53, folder 5.

23. John Lewis, OH with Katherine Shannon, Aug. 22, 1967, 169–70; Beardslee, *Way Out*, 29.

24. Jeffries, *Bloody Lowndes*, 146–47, 152–53; Carson, *Student Voice*, 232; May, *Bending*, 179–80. The state Democratic Party dropped the "White Supremacy" banner weeks later. *Newsweek*, Feb. 7, 1966, 20–21.

25. May, *Bending*, 181–82; Jeffries, *Bloody Lowndes*, 167–68.

26. *Ivory Tower*, May 2, 1966, 46; Carmichael with Thelwell, *Ready for Revolution*, 479; Viorst, *Fire*, 367–68.

27. "Speech by John Lewis, Memorial Dinner of Council for American-Soviet Friendship," Jan. 26, 1966, HV 252253-002-0001; "Speaker Ban at North Carolina College Revoked," Feb. 7, 1966, HV 252253-014-0467; *Norfolk New Journal and Guide*, Feb. 19, 1966, 11.

28. Carter, *Music*, 88; *New York Times Magazine*, June 25, 1967, 45. White House aide Harry McPherson knew that with Lewis in charge, SNCC was "an organization that you could invite to the White House without getting a hand grenade thrown through the window before they came."

29. War Resisters' International newsletter, Oct. 19, 1965, WHS-WRIP, 5; War Resisters' International newsletter no. 45, Apr. 29, 1966; Schedule, spring 1966, AAPP; John Lewis, interview with Archie Allen, Jan. 28, 1979, NPL-AAC, 223–24; Prasad, *War Is a Crime*, 367–70; Paul Good, "John Lewis—Vanishing American," unpublished manuscript, AAPP.

30. John Lewis, interview with Archie Allen, Jan. 28, 1979, NPL-AAC, 223–24.

31. Thomas Powers to author, email, Mar. 7, 2022; Bob Kaiser and Hannah Jopling, author interview, May 22, 2022.

32. Paul Good, "John Lewis—Vanishing American," unpublished manuscript, AAPP.

33. John Lewis, interview with Emily Stoper, 1966, CRMVET, 222–23.

34. Nils Petter Gliditsch to John Lewis, Mar. 25, 1966, Apr. 4, 1966, AAPP; "Visit of John Lewis," Apr. 5, 1966, AAPP; John Lewis, interview with Archie Allen, Jan. 28, 1979, NPL-AAC, 222–25.

35. John Lewis, interview with Archie Allen, Jan. 28, 1979, NPL-AAC, 225–226; Whitaker, *Saying It Loud*, 38.

36. Newfield, *Prophetic Minority*, 104; Forman, *Revolutionaries*, 452–53; John Lewis, interview with Archie Allen, Jan. 28, 1979, NPL-AAC, 226.

37. John Lewis, interview with Archie Allen, Jan. 28, 1979, NPL-AAC, 228; Whitaker, *Saying It Loud*, 115.

38. "SNCC Staff Conference" and "Suggestions for Directions of SNCC," May 11, 1966, HV 252253-003-0903.

39. Hampton and Fayer, *Voices*, 280.

40. John Lewis, OH with Katherine Shannon, Aug. 22, 1967, RJBOHC, 155; John Lewis, interview with Archie Allen, Jan. 28, 1979, NPL-AAC, 226.

41. The election account draws from Branch, *Canaan's Edge*, 465–67; Carmichael with Thelwell, *Ready for Revolution*, 481–83; Fleming, *Soon We Will Not Cry*, 160–63; Forman, *Revolutionaries*, 452–56; Lewis with D'Orso, *Walking*, 365–68; Newfield, *Prophetic Minority*, 104–5; Sellers, *River*, 158–59; Viorst, *Fire*, 369–70; as well as primary sources.

42. John Lewis, interview with Archie Allen, Jan. 28, 1979, NPL-AAC, 228.

43. Courtland Cox, OH with Joseph Mosnier, July 8, 2011, CRHPC-AFC, 27–28.

44. Jennifer Lawson, interview notes, UNC-TBP, series 4, folder 913; John Lewis, interview with Emily Stoper, 1966, CRMVET, 222; John Lewis, interview with Archie Allen, Jan. 28, 1979, NPL-AAC, 228; Stokely Carmichael, interview with Blackside, May 5, 1986, WU-HHC, 18; Ed Hamlett, interview with Archie Allen, Nov. 6, 1968, NPL-AAC, box 3,

folder 13, 4. Hamlett remembered the quote a bit differently: "Whoever is chairman [should] . . . tell Johnson to go to hell on the White House conference [and] go for King's balls."

45. Lewis with D'Orso, *Walking*, 366.

46. Slightly different vote totals were reported. No account exists in the minutes. The 60–22 figures are the most commonly cited numbers. See, for example, Newfield, *Prophetic Minority*, 105.

47. Carmichael with Thelwell, *Ready for Revolution*, 480; Lewis with D'Orso, *Walking*, 365–66.

48. John Lewis, OH with Katherine Shannon, Aug. 22, 1967, RJBOHC, 157–58; John Lewis, interview with Clayborne Carson, Apr. 17, 1972, CRMVET, 16; Sellers, *River*, 158.

49. Lynn Wells, interview with Archie Allen, Sept. 15, 1968, NPL-AAC, box 3, folder 36, 7.

50. Jennifer Lawson, interview notes, UNC-TBP, series 4, folder 913; Julius Lester, interview with Archie Allen, Nov. 7, 1968, NPL-AAC, box 3, folder 20, 6; John Lewis, OH with Jack Bass and Walter DeVries, Nov. 20, 1973, UNC-SOHP, 58.

51. Sellers, *River*, 158–59; Carmichael with Thelwell, *Ready for Revolution*, 481; Grant, *Ella Baker*, 194; Julius Lester, interview with Archie Allen, Nov. 7, 1968, NPL-AAC, box 3 folder 20, 6; Ed Hamlett, interview with Archie Allen, Nov. 6, 1968, NPL-AAC, box 3 folder 13, 5.

52. Carmichael with Thelwell, *Ready for Revolution*, 481.

53. John Lewis, interview with Archie Allen, Jan. 28, 1979, NPL-AAC, 229; John Lewis, interview with Clayborne Carson, 16; John Lewis, interview with Emily Stoper, 1966, 221; Marion Barry, interview with Clayborne Carson, Apr. 7, 1972, CRMVET, 9; Jennifer Lawson, interview notes, UNC-TBP, series 4, folder 913;

Holsaert et al., eds., *Freedom Plow*, 309; Grant, *Ella Baker*, 194; Charles Cobb, author interview, Mar. 16, 2020; Staughton Lynd, author interview, Feb. 12, 2020.

54. Matthew Jones, OH with K. G. Bennett, July 25, 2006, NPL-CROHC, 17.

55. Maria Varela, author interview, Apr. 22, 2020; Watters, *Down to Now*, 351.

56. Maria Varela, author interview, Apr. 22, 2020; John Lewis, interview with Archie Allen, Jan. 28, 1979, NPL-AAC, 229; John Lewis, interview with Emily Stoper, 1966, 221; Forman, *Revolutionaries*, 453; *People*, Aug. 24, 1998, 125.

57. Egerton, *A Mind to Stay*, 66.

58. Arlie Schardt, author interview, Apr. 1, 2020; Halberstam, *Children*, 524.

59. Lewis with D'Orso, *Walking*, 367–68.

60. "Motions, Recommendations, Mandates," May 14–17, 1966; "Central Discussion of Trips," SNCC Papers, HV, Folder 252253-003-0903.

61. Carson, *In Struggle*, 204.

62. *New York Times*, May 17, 1966, 22; *Atlanta Constitution*, May 17, 1966, 1, 6; *Norfolk New Journal and Guide*, May 21, 1966, C1.

63. "Statement by John Lewis," May 23, 1966, HV 252253-014-0467; *New York Times*, May 24, 1966, 28; *Washington Post*, May 26, 1966, A1; John Lewis, interview with Archie Allen, Jan. 28, 1979, NPL-AAC, 235; WSB-TV news clips, https://dlg.usg.edu/record/ugabma_wsbn _wsbn38936.

64. John Lewis, interview with Archie Allen, Jan. 28, 1979, NPL-AAC, 232; *New York Times*, May 24, 1966, 28; *Washington Post*, May 25, 1966, A1; *Atlanta Constitution*, May 20, 1966, 16.

65. Good, "The Meredith March," 3; Bernstein and Matusow, *Interpretations*, 513.

66. John Lewis, interview with Archie Allen, Jan. 28, 1979, NPL-AAC, 231;

John Lewis, interview with Clayborne
Carson, Apr. 17, 1972, CRMVET, 18;
John Lewis, OH with Katherine Shannon, Aug. 22, 1967, RJBOHC, 151;
Lewis with D'Orso, *Walking*, 370. In one
account, Sellers and Carmichael were having this discussion with Johnny Wilson of
SNCC, who was on the phone from Mississippi.

67. Halberstam, *Children*, 529.

68. *New York Times Magazine*, June 25,
1967, 44; Egerton, *A Mind to Stay*, 67.

69. Carson, *In Struggle*, 205; Lewis with
D'Orso, *Walking*, 376.

70. Weisbrot, *Freedom Bound*, 205;
Commentary, Sept. 1966, 35; *Los Angeles
Times*, July 3, 1966, B5.

71. Lewis with D'Orso, *Walking*, 371–
72; *Washington Star*, June 30, 1966, B4;
Nashville Banner, June 30, 1966; John
Lewis, "Notice of Resignation," June 11,
1966, AAPP; Central Committee meeting
minutes, June 10–11, 1966, HV 252253-
003-0903.

72. John Fischer to John Lewis, July 6,
1966, AAPP; John Lewis, personal notes,
HV 252253-001-1063; John Lewis, interview with Archie Allen, Jan. 28, 1979,
NPL-AAC, 234.

THIRTEEN: LOST
IN NEW YORK

1. Letters can be found at HV 252253-
002-0474.

2. *New York Times Magazine*, Sept. 25,
1966, 128.

3. John Lewis, interview with Archie
Allen, Jan. 28, 1979, NPL-AAC, 230;
Matthew Jones, OH with K. G. Bennett,
July 25, 2006, NPL-CROHC, 17; Frank
Smith, author interview, Nov. 22, 2022.

4. *New York Times*, Sept. 7, 1966, 1, 38,
Sept. 9, 1966, 1, 30; Joseph, *Stokely*, 139–
46; Carson, *In Struggle*, 229–32.

5. *Los Angeles Times*, July 29, 1966, 5;
New York Times, Aug. 5, 1966, 1, 10.

6. Julius Lester, interview with Archie
Allen, Nov. 7, 1968, NPL-AAC, box 3,
folder 20, 8; Elizabeth Sutherland to James
Forman, n.d., LC-JFP, box 17, folder 23;
Forman statement, Apr. 1993, LC-JFP,
box 35, folder 1; "Memo from Elizabeth
Sutherland," Sept. 15, 1966, HV 252253-
032-0118.

7. John Lewis, interview with David
Halberstam, #4, July 8, 1996, BU-DHP,
box 59, folder 5, 7.

8. Leslie Dunbar to John Lewis, July 12,
1966, Carl Holman to John Lewis, July 13,
1966, Leslie Dunbar to John Lewis, July
26, 1966, AAPP; John Lewis, interview
with Archie Allen, Jan. 28, 1979, NPL-
AAC, 235–36; Beardslee, *Way Out*, 30;
Gene Roberts, email to author, June 10,
2022; Vernon Jordan, author interview,
Nov. 11, 2019.

9. John Lewis and Sukap Realty, lease,
Aug. 31, 1966, AAPP; *People*, Aug. 24,
1998, 125.

10. John Lewis, interview with Archie
Allen, Jan. 28, 1979, NPL-AAC, 237–40;
Berman, *Ballot*, 66; Joel Fleishman to John
Lewis, Oct. 13, 1966, Elting Morrison to
John Lewis, Oct. 18, 1966, AAPP; *Yale
Daily News*, Oct. 7, 1966, 1, 3; John Lewis,
interview with Archie Allen, Jan. 28, 1979,
NPL-AAC, 24.

11. Staughton Lynd, author interview,
Feb. 12, 2020; Kennedy, *Ripples of Hope*,
175; Lewis with D'Orso, *Walking*, 378.

12. John Lewis to Oswald Schrag, Apr.
13, 1964, "Application for Readmission to
Fisk University," July 5, 1966, John Lewis
to Wilson Welch, Oct. 4, 1966, Oswald
Schrag to John Lewis, Dec. 7, 1966, Oswald Schrag to John Lewis, Feb. 13, 1967,
AAPP; Oswald Schrag, interview with
Archie Allen, Oct. 1968, NPL-AAC, box
3, folder 28; *New York Amsterdam News*,

Nov. 5, 1966, 39; *Tennessean*, June 6, 1967; *Jet*, July 20, 1967, 27; Archie Allen, author interview, June 28, 2022.

13. John Lewis, OH with Jack Bass and Walter DeVries, Nov. 20, 1973, UNC-SOHP, 13; Wilson Welch to John Lewis, May 10, 1967, Oswald Schrag to John Lewis, May 12, 1967, AAPP; *Tennessean*, June 6, 1967; *Time*, Apr. 19, 1968, 70.

14. Julian Bond to John Lewis, n.d., AAPP; John Lewis, interview with Archie Allen, Jan. 28, 1979, NPL-AAC, 237–41; John Lewis, interview with Clayborne Carson, Apr. 17, 1972, CRMVET, 19; John Lewis, interview with David Halberstam, #4, July 8, 1996, BU-DHP, box 59, folder 5, 9; Mark Suckle, interview with Archie Allen, Nov. 8, 1968, NPL-AAC, box 3, folder 31, 21–22; *People*, Aug. 24, 1998, 125.

15. *Dissent*, July 1967, 461–66; Irving Howe notes, WNPP.

16. Lewis with D'Orso, *Walking*, 378–79.

17. Martin Luther King Jr. to John Lewis, Aug. 5, 1967, AAPP; John Lewis, interview with Ben Hedin, #3, Mar. 23, 2017, BHI, 1–2; Lewis with D'Orso, *Walking*, 377; *New Yorker* online, Apr. 3, 2017; *Mic*, Jan. 18, 2018.

18. Charles S. Johnson III, interview with Archie Allen, Aug. 16, 1968, NPL-AAC, box 3, folder 16, 1–3.

19. *SNCC Newsletter*, June–July 1967, CRMVET, 4–5; *New York Times*, Aug. 15, 1967, 1, 16, Aug. 16, 1967, 28, Aug. 17, 1967, 27, Aug. 22, 1967, 24; *Newsday*, Aug. 16, 1967, 3; *Newsweek*, Aug. 28, 1967, 22; *Los Angeles Times*, Sept. 2, 1967, B4; Forman, *Revolutionaries*, 492–97; Sellers, *River*, 201–3; Adams and Bracey, eds., *Strangers and Neighbors*, 36–48; Fischbach, *Black Power and Palestine*, 18–26; Norwood, *Antisemitism*, 1–4.

20. Charles S. Johnson III, interview with Archie Allen, Aug. 16, 1968, NPL-AAC, box 3, folder 16, 1–3.

21. Peter Bent to John Lewis, June 19, 1967, AAPP; Mark Suckle, interview with Archie Allen, Nov. 8, 1968, NPL-AAC, box 3, folder 31, 21.

22. Paul Anthony, interview with Archie Allen, Nov. 8, 1968, NPL-AAC, box 3, folder 2, 6.

23. Paul Anthony to SRC Personnel Committee, Aug. 4, 1967; Paul Anthony to Ruth Alexander, Oct. 2, 1967, AUC-RWWL VEPP, series 1, box 48, folder 16; John Lewis, interview with Clayborne Carson, Apr. 17, 1972, CRMVET, 20; Lewis with D'Orso, *Walking*, 380–81.

24. John Lewis, interview with Evan Faulkenbury, EFI, 6.

25. John Lewis, interview with Marc Lipman, MLI, 3; Cohen and Lipman, dirs., *Arc of Justice*.

26. John Lewis, interview with David Halberstam, #4, July 8, 1996, BU-DHP, box 59, folder 5; Lewis with D'Orso, *Walking*, 382; *Atlanta Journal-Constitution*, July 11, 2002, B1.

FOURTEEN: RFK

1. Joan Browning, author interview, July 28, 2022; Curry et al., eds., *Deep in Our Hearts*, 80.

2. John Lewis, OH with Vicki Daitch, Mar. 19, 2004, JFKL-OHC, 5; John Lewis, interview with David Margolick, 2004, DMI.

3. Beardslee, *Way Out*, 31; Peter Edelman, OH with Larry Hackman, Aug. 5, 1969, JFKL-OHC, 24; Lewis with D'Orso, *Walking*, 384.

4. *Chicago Defender*, Apr. 20, 1968, 7.

5. *New York Times*, Apr. 5, 1968, 33, 34; Margolick, *Promise and the Dream*, 535–51.

6. Lewis with D'Orso, *Walking*, 386.

7. Porter, dir., *Bobby for President*, Radical Media, 2018.

8. Egerton, *A Mind to Stay Here*, 68.

9. Earl Graves, OH with Roberta W. Greene, #1, July 17, 1969, JFKL-RFKOH, 23, 30; Vanden Heuvel and Gwirtzman, *On His Own*, 338.

10. Schlesinger, *Robert Kennedy*, 876; Earl Graves, OH with Roberta W. Greene, #1, July 17, 1969, JFKL-RFKOH, 26.

11. Earl Graves, OH with Roberta W. Greene, #1, July 17, 1969, 27, #2, July 18, 1969, 89–91, and #3, Aug. 28, 1969, 103–4, JFKL-RFKOH.

12. Earl Graves, OH with Roberta W. Greene, #3, August 28, 1969, JFKL-RFKOH, 123–24.

13. Lewis with D'Orso, *Walking*, 391.

14. Two years later his body would be moved to a special memorial site near Ebenezer.

15. Lewis with D'Orso, *Walking*, 392. Julian Bond described Paschal's as "an Atlanta institution, where some Black politicians and businessmen gather for breakfast and coffee but mostly to talk and gossip about what's what and who's doing what to whom." Election diary, UVA-HJBP, box 5, folder 28.

16. Kelly, dir., *'68: The Year Nebraska Mattered*; Earl Graves, OH with Roberta W. Greene, #4, Aug. 30, 1969, JFKL-RFKOH, 171–82; Clarke, *Last Campaign*, 223. Historians debate the depth of Kennedy's working-class white support. Most hold that he was assembling a "Black and blue" coalition, but others argue that the idea is a myth. What is unarguable is that believers in an interracial liberal coalition like Lewis thought that, with Humphrey tarnished by his association with LBJ and the war, Kennedy was the best hope for such a politics. "If there was one politician, one person, I thought could hold the community in a sense together and continue to give black people and poor people in this country a sense of hope, that was Robert Kennedy," Lewis said. John Lewis, OH with Jack Bass and Walter DeVries, Nov. 20, 1973, UNC-SOHP, 67.

17. Steven Isenberg, author interview, July 9, 2022; Earl Graves, OH with Roberta W. Greene, #3, Aug. 28, 1969, JFKL-RFKOH, 117.

18. Steven Isenberg, author interview, July 9, 2022; *American Scholar*, Summer 2018, 35.

19. John Lewis, interview with Vicki Daitch, Mar. 19, 2004, JFKL-OHP, 7.

20. *Los Angeles Sentinel*, June 9, 1968, A3; Kennedy, *Ripples*, 178.

21. *Atlanta Constitution*, June 6, 1968, 21; John Lewis, interview with Jean Stein, Sept. 9, 1968, JFKL-JSPP, box AU02; John Lewis, OH with Vicki Daitch, Mar. 19, 2004, JFKL-OHC, 7; Kennedy, *Ripples*, 178.

22. Morison and Morison, *From Camelot to Kent State*, 34–35.

23. Egerton, *Mind to Stay Here*, 68.

24. Beardslee, *Way Out*, 32; Lewis with D'Orso, *Walking*, 395–97; Porter, dir., *Bobby for President*, Radical Media, 2018; "Kennedy family" telegram to John Lewis, June 7, 1968, AAPP; History.com, June 7, 2021; Margolick, *Promise*, 575.

25. John Lewis, interview with Jean Stein, Sept. 8, 1968, JFKL-JSPP; Witcover, *85 Days*, 313.

26. Archie Allen, author interview, Aug. 14, 2019; *Los Angeles Times*, June 20, 1968, 10; Beardslee, *Way Out*, 33; Halberstam, *Children*, 568; Lewis with D'Orso, *Walking*, 406. In *Walking with the Wind*, Lewis mistakenly places his hospital visit after the Democratic National Convention rather than before it.

27. Taylor Branch, author interview, Apr. 14, 2020; Taylor Branch, OH with Gregg Ivers, Sept. 7, 2018, AU-JBOHP.

28. *Atlanta Journal-Constitution*, Aug. 11, 1968, A6; *Atlanta Constitution*, Aug. 13, 1968, 12, Aug. 14, 1968, 17; Hudson, unpublished memoir, 187–88, 192–96, PHPP; Summerlin, "We Represented the Best of Georgia in Chicago," 64–66; Hendershot, *When the News Broke*, 83–88.

29. Taylor Branch, author interview, Apr. 14, 2020; Taylor Branch, OH with Gregg Ivers, Sept. 7, 2018, AU-JBOHP; Neary, *Bond*, 189–90, 193.

30. Nancy Schwartz, email to author, July 28, 2022; Parker Hudson, unpublished memoir, 204–44, PHPP; Summerlin, "We Represented the Best of Georgia in Chicago," 64–66; Taylor Branch, author interview, Apr. 14, 2020; Mixner, *Stranger Among Friends*, 50.

31. Summerlin, "We Represented the Best of Georgia in Chicago," 77–78; Parker Hudson, author interview, May 1, 2020; Hudson, unpublished memoir, PHPP, 399.

32. Summerlin, "We Represented the Best of Georgia in Chicago," 81; *Presidential Nominating Conventions, 1968*, 139, 141; Neary, *Julian Bond*, 211.

33. *New York Times Magazine*, Oct. 20, 1968, 71, 72; Bruner, *Black Politicians*, 22.

34. Gritter and Bond, "Interview with Julian Bond," 88; Summerlin, "We Represented the Best of Georgia in Chicago," 83–84; Mixner, *Stranger Among Friends*, 53; Walters, *Black Presidential Politics*, 54–56.

35. Egerton, *A Mind to Stay Here*, 69; Lewis with D'Orso, *Walking*, 398.

36. Hudson, unpublished memoir, PHPP, 451–55.

37. Hudson, unpublished memoir, PHPP, 458; Summerlin, "We Represented the Best of Georgia in Chicago," 89; Parker Hudson, author interview, May 1, 2020. On Thursday night, Bond was nominated for vice president, although, as he pointed out, he was seven years shy of the constitutional age limit.

FIFTEEN: THE VOTER EDUCATION PROJECT

1. *Jet*, Nov. 21, 1968, 28; Lewis with D'Orso, *Walking*, 264–65; Rosa Mae Lewis, interview with Archie Allen, Mar. 16, 1969, NPL-AAC, box 3, folder 22, 6; Ethel Lewis Tyner, interview with Archie Allen, Mar. 15, 1969, NPL-AAC, box 3, folder 33, 7.

2. Wedding invitation, AAPP; Archie Allen, author interview, Aug. 25, 2022; Tom Houck, author interview, Oct. 31, 2022; Lewis with D'Orso, *Walking*, 405.

3. Tom Houck, author interview, Oct. 31, 2022.

4. *Atlanta Constitution*, Feb. 17, 1969, 6; *Ebony*, Nov. 1976, 142.

5. Archie Allen, author interviews, Aug. 15, 2019, Aug. 25, 2022; Carol Dove, author interview, July 17, 2023.

6. Archie Allen, author interview, Aug. 15, 2019; Bonnie Myers, author interview, Oct. 16, 2019.

7. *Atlanta Constitution*, Sept. 20, 1979, 2B.

8. Watters, *Down to Now*, 325.

9. Watters, *Down to Now*, 375–76.

10. *Atlanta Constitution*, May 18, 1969, 27.

11. *Washington Post*, Mar. 15, 1970, A14; Fleming, *Soon We Will Not Cry*, 183–89; *Orangeburg Times and Democrat*, Mar. 29, 1968; Sellers, *River*, 226.

12. *Tennessean*, Feb. 28, 1970, 28; Lewis with D'Orso, *Walking*, 408; Young, *Easy Burden*, 503–4.

13. John Lewis, OH with Jack Bass and Walter DeVries, Nov. 20, 1973, UNC-SOHP, 31; *Christian Science Monitor*, July 15, 1969, 5; Lewis, *Shadows*, 265. On Cliff Alexander's TV show, Lewis added, "A great many of the community people who worked

with SNCC and became a part of SNCC see the political arena as an extension of their involvement in the civil rights movement." "Black and White" transcript, Sept. 30, 1972, UVA-HJBP, box 60, folder 2.

14. Jacoby, *Someone Else's House*, 365.

15. John Lewis to Julian Bond, Nov. 12, 1969, UVA-HJBP, box 29, folder 4; *GQ*, Sept. 1970, 160; Lewis with D'Orso, *Walking*, 408; Young, *Easy Burden*, 504–8.

16. "Minutes of the Board of Directors," series 1, box 34, folder 10, AUC-RWWL-VEPP; *Atlanta Constitution*, Feb. 8, 1970, 42; Paul Anthony to Southern Regional Council personnel committee, Aug. 4, 1967, Marilyn Adamson to John Lewis, Feb. 10, 1971, Bill Jessup to John Lewis, Aug, 10, 1973, Jan. 11, 1974, all AUC-RWWL-VEPP, series 1, box 148, folder 16.

17. *Atlanta Constitution*, June 6, 1970, 4.

18. John Lewis, OH with Jack Bass and Walter DeVries, Nov. 20, 1973, UNC-SOHP, 38; John Lewis and Archie E. Allen, "Black Voter Registration Efforts in the South," *Notre Dame Law Review*, 48:1 (Oct. 1972): 114.

19. U.S. Congress, House of Representatives, *The Enforcement of the Voting Rights Act: Hearings Before the Committee on Environment and Public Works*, 92nd Cong., 1st Sess., 1971, 242–43 (statement of John Lewis); *Atlanta Constitution*, June 11, 1971, 12; Tuck, *Beyond Atlanta*, 215–16; Lewis and Allen, "Black Voter Registration Efforts in the South," 121.

20. Faulkenbury, *Poll Power*, 126.

21. U.S. Congress, House of Representatives, *The Enforcement of the Voting Rights Act: Hearings Before the Committee on Environment and Public Works*, 92nd Cong., 1st Sess., 1971, 243 (statement of John Lewis); Lawson, *In Pursuit*, 177.

22. John Lewis, interview with Evan Faulkenbury, July 18, 2013, EFI, 10; *Atlanta Constitution*, May 16, 1970, 39,

June 5, 1970, 12; Faulkenbury, *Poll Power*, 118–26.

23. John Lewis, summary of annual report, 1970, Jan. 29, 1971, AUC-RWWL-VEPP, series 1, box 34, folder 11; *Atlanta Constitution*, June 5, 1970, 12; *New York Times*, June 7, 1970, 46.

24. John Lewis, summary of annual report, Jan. 29, 1971, AUC-RWWL-VEPP, series 1, box 34, folder 11; "Attachment to January 29, 1971 Minutes," UVA-HJBP, box 59, folder 9; Faulkenbury, *Poll Power*, 126–27.

25. *Washington Post*, June 18, 1970, A1, A6; *New York Times*, June 20, 1970, 10, June 23, 1970, 1. The 1970 law also banned literacy tests in all states; the 1965 law had banned them only in the South.

26. Lewis with D'Orso, *Walking*, 413.

27. *Tennessean*, Sept. 2, 1968, 13; Archie Allen to Julian Bond, Aug. 27, 1969, box 29, folder 2, UVA-HJBP; John Lewis to VEP Board of Directors, Oct. 28, 1971, AUC-RWWL-VEPP, series 1, box 34, folder 13; *Atlanta Constitution*, May 3, 1971, 5.

28. Michael Bond, author interview, Feb. 27, 2023. In 1971, Julian wrote to his brother James about an "out-of-sight party" jointly celebrating his own and Lewis's birthdays. Julian Bond to James Bond, Feb. 1, 1971, UVA-HJBP, box 115, folder 5.

29. Michael Bond, author interview, Feb. 27, 2023; *Times of Zambia*, Dec. 15, 1973, 1, Dec. 16, 1973, n.p., AUC-RWWL-VEPP, oversize series 1, folder 3; Lewis with D'Orso, *Walking*, 448.

30. John Lewis, interview with Evan Faulkenbury, July 18, 2013, 1, EFI.

31. VEP press release, June 11, 1971, AUC-RWWL-VEPP, series 1, box 68, folder 3; see also documents, UVA-HJBP, box 59, folder 9; *New York Times*, Mar. 24, 1971, 37, May 27, 1971, 22; *Atlanta Voice*, July 10, 1971, 4.

32. John Lewis to John Mitchell, AUC-RWWL-VEPP, series 1, box 95, folder 1; U.S. Congress, House of Representatives, *The Enforcement of the Voting Rights Act: Hearings Before the Committee on Environment and Public Works,* 92nd Cong., 1st Sess., 1971, 243–45 (statement of John Lewis).

33. VEP Annual Report, 1971, AUC-RWWL-VEPP, series 1, box 162, folder 1; *Ebony,* Oct. 1971, 106; *Newsweek,* Aug. 2, 1971, 22; Lawson, *In Pursuit,* 162–73, 180–81; *Atlanta Constitution,* June 13, 1971, 59; Berman, *Ballot,* 91–92. In September, the Nixon Justice Department would instruct Mississippi to accept prior registrations at the polls in 1971 and would issue guidelines requiring states to show that new voting rules were not discriminatory.

34. Archie Allen, author interview, Oct. 27, 2022.

35. Itinerary, AUC-RWWL-VEPP, series 1, box 68, folder 3; *Atlanta Constitution,* June 13, 1971, 59, July 2, 1971, 28; *Atlanta Daily World,* June 27, 1971, 8, July 8, 1971, 2; *Atlanta Voice,* July 10, 1971, 4, Apr. 22, 1972, 8; *Ebony,* Oct. 1971, 104–10; Lewis with D'Orso, *Walking,* 414; Berman, *Ballot,* 92–93.

36. *Harrisonburg Daily News-Record,* Feb. 9. 1971, AUC-RWWL-VEPP, box 4, folder 19; *Christian Science Monitor,* Feb. 29, 1972, 11; John Lewis, interview with Evan Faulkenbury, July 18, 2013, 2, EFI; Lewis and Allen, "Black Voter Registration Efforts in the South," 117; Halberstam, *Children,* 571.

37. *Atlanta Constitution,* July 2, 1971, 72; Berman, *Ballot,* 93–94.

38. *Shreveport Times,* July 25, 1971, 18; *New York Times,* Aug. 8, 1971, 44; *Chicago Defender,* Sept. 4, 1971, 10; John Lewis, interview with Evan Faulkenbury, July 18, 2013, EFI, 4; "Report of Field Activities,"

Nov. 17, 1972, AUC-RWWL-VEPP, series 1, box 31, folder 11; Tom Houck, author interview, Aug. 7, 2019; Archie Allen, author interview, Aug. 15, 2019.

39. *Atlanta Voice,* Apr. 8, 1972, 1.

40. Boyd Lewis, author interview, Oct. 5, 2022; *Atlanta Voice,* Apr. 15, 1972, 1, 8.

41. *Chicago Defender,* Apr. 11, 1972, 10; *Atlanta Voice,* Apr. 29, 1972, 1, May 6, 1972, 1, 2; Halberstam, *Children,* 571.

42. *New York Times,* Sept. 21, 1971, 28; Norman Siegel, author interview, Dec. 9, 2022; David Morrison, author interview, June 26, 2020; Archie Allen, author interview, Oct. 27, 2022; *Ebony,* Nov. 1976, 134. Third floor is in VEP documents, e.g., memorandum, Jan. 31, 1974, AUC-RWWL-VEPP, series 1, box 32, folder 7. The morning *Constitution* and the afternoon *Journal* shared an owner and a building since 1950. For years they published a combined Sunday paper. They fully merged in 2001. In these notes, the *Constitution* or the *Journal* alone is cited when a printed source was used. Online newspaper databases, however, combine the papers' archives from the pre-merger years, often making it impossible to know whether a story ran in one paper or both. In such cases, the *Atlanta Journal-Constitution* is listed as the source.

43. David Morrison, author interview, June 26, 2020; Norman Siegel, author interview, Dec. 9, 2022; Archie Allen, author interview, June 5, 2022; *Atlanta Constitution,* Oct. 5, 1972, 9; *Atlanta Daily World,* Oct. 6, 1974, 2; Lewis with D'Orso, *Walking,* 414.

44. VEP board of directors meeting minutes, Apr. 6, 1973, AUC-RWWL-VEPP, series 1, box 35, folder 1; Bill Jessup to John Lewis, Aug. 10, 1973, and Jan. 11, 1974, AUC-RWWL-VEPP, series 1, box 148, folder 16; *Atlanta Constitution,* Mar. 9, 1977, 11.

45. Recommendations for new board members, AUC-RWWL-VEPP, series 1, box 32, folder 5; Julian Bond to John Lewis, Dec. 18, 1972, UVA-HJBP, box 60, folder 2; AUC-RWWL-VEPP, series 6, box 45, folder 2; VEP 1976 annual report, AAPP; Faulkenbury, *Poll Power*, 128–29; Berman, *Ballot*, 118.

46. *Atlanta Daily World*, Jan. 27, 1972, 2; John Lewis, interview with Evan Faulkenbury, July 18, 2013, EFI, 13; VEP board of directors meeting minutes, Sept. 16, 1972, AUC-RWWL-VEPP, series 1, box 34, folder 16.

47. John Lewis, interview with Evan Faulkenbury, July 18, 2013, EFI, 7.

48. Janet Wells, "Voting Rights in 1975," *Civil Rights Digest*, Summer 1977, 15–18.

49. U.S. Congress, Senate, *Extension of the Voting Rights Act of 1965: Hearings Before the Subcommittee on Constitutional Rights of the Committee on the Judiciary*, 94th Cong., 1st Sess., 108; John Lewis, "Voter Registration in the South, 1972," Sept. 24, 1971, AUC-RWWL-VEPP, series 6, box 45, folder 19; "The Voter Education Project: A Past Perspective," AUC-RWWL-VEPP, series 6, box 45, folder 10; John Lewis, interview with Clayborne Carson, Apr. 17, 1972, 23.

50. John Lewis, interview with Evan Faulkenbury, July 18, 2013, EFI, 2; *New York Times*, Aug. 8, 1971, 44; Lewis with D'Orso, *Walking*, 415; Berman, *Ballot*, 102–3.

51. *Christian Science Monitor*, Dec. 2, 1970, 11; *New York Times*, Aug. 30, 1970, 66; *New York Times*, Nov. 18, 1973, 40; *Atlanta Voice*, Dec. 1, 1973, 3.

52. *New York Times*, Aug. 29, 1973, 1, 16; *Atlanta Constitution*, Sept. 17, 1972, 6.

53. Archie Allen, author interviews, Aug. 15, 2019, June 5, 2022; Julian Bond to John Lewis, Nov. 14, 1973, Julian Bond to Charlayne Hunter, Nov. 2, 1973, UVA-HJBP, box 60, folder 4.

54. "Black on White" transcript, Sept. 30, 1972, UVA-HJBP, box 60, folder 2; *Atlanta Constitution*, Mar. 3, 1974, 28–32; "Firing Line" video and transcript at https://digitalcollections.hoover.org/objects/6302/politics-and-black-progress.

55. *Atlanta Voice*, May 19, 1973, 11; John Lewis, interview with Evan Faulkenbury, EFI, 9. In an August 15, 1973, damage-control speech, Nixon bizarrely traced the contempt for the law that his subordinates showed during Watergate to the civil disobedience of the civil rights movement. "It became fashionable in the 1960s," Nixon claimed, "as individuals and groups increasingly asserted the right to take the law into their own hands, insisting that their purposes represented a higher morality. Then their attitude was praised in the press and even from some of our pulpits as evidence of a new idealism." Lewis was infuriated by the comparison. "I think it's unfortunate and tragic for the president of the United States to suggest that Watergate is an outgrowth of the human rights movement of the 1960s. . . . It's very insulting to those of us who participated in that movement." *Atlanta Constitution*, Aug. 16, 1973, 9.

56. John Lewis, interview with Maureen Orth, MOVI. When in his 1973 mayoral race Maynard Jackson claimed to have the VEP's endorsement, Lewis took to the press to deny it. *Atlanta Constitution*, Sept. 3, 1973, 7; *New York Times*, Apr. 24, 1974, 22.

57. John Lewis speech, May 17, 1971, audio cassette, AUC-RWWL-VEPP, series 7, box 11, cassette 3; John Lewis to Bayard Rustin, June 21, 1973, AUC-RWWL-VEPP, series 1, box 70, folder 15; "Join John Lewis and Julian Bond for Another Selma March," 1972, AAPP; *Atlanta Journal*, Apr. 12, 1972; *Atlanta Constitution*, Apr. 12, 1972,

50, Apr. 15, 1972, 9, Apr. 16, 1972, 1, 16; *Selma Times-Journal*, Apr. 16, 1972, 1–2.

58. VEP executive committee meeting notes, Nov. 15, 1974, AUC-RWWL-VEPP, series 1, box 32, folder 8; VEP executive committee meeting notes, Apr. 18, 1975, AUC-RWWL-VEPP, series 1, box 32, folder 10; *Atlanta Daily World*, Jan. 16, 1975, 1; John Lewis press conference, Feb. 26, 1975, UGA-WJBMA-WSB; *Atlanta Constitution*, Feb. 27, 1975; *Washington Post*, Mar. 9, 1975, 3; *New York Times*, Mar. 9, 1975, 50.

59. Julian Bond to John Lewis, June 28, 1976, UVA-HJBP, box 82, folder 1.

60. *Time*, Dec. 29, 1975, 47–56; Lewis with D'Orso, *Walking*, 416.

61. VEP executive committee meeting notes, Dec. 14, 1974, Apr. 18, 1975, AUC-RWWL-VEPP, series 1, box 32, folders 9 and 10; *Atlanta Constitution*, Dec. 9, 1974, 1; *Chicago Defender*, Mar. 19, 1975, 6; *Atlanta Voice*, Mar. 29, 1975, 4; U.S. Congress, Senate, *Extension of the Voting Rights Act of 1965: Hearings Before the Subcommittee on Constitutional Rights of the Committee on the Judiciary*, 94th Cong., 1st Sess., 110 (statement of John Lewis); Berman, *Ballot*, 110–11; Lawson, *In Pursuit*, 224–51; *Atlanta Constitution*, Aug. 7, 1975, 12.

62. *Extension of the Voting Rights Act of 1965*, 111; Wells, "Voting Rights in 1975," 19; Lawson, *In Pursuit*, 190; Lewis with D'Orso, *Walking*, 413.

63. *Time*, Apr. 5, 1976, 17; Berman, *Ballot*, 116.

64. *New York Times*, Apr. 7, 1975, 23; *Nation*, Apr. 17, 1976, 454–55; Bond election diary, UVA-HJBP, box 5, folder 28; *Today* transcript, Apr. 12, 1976, UVA-HJBP, box 84, folder 2; Long, ed., *Race Man*, 105–23; Julian Bond, election diary, UVA-HJBP, box 5, folder 28; Lewis with D'Orso, *Walking*, 413, 417.

65. *New York Times*, Apr. 15, 1976, 18;

John Lewis to Andrew Young, May 25, 1976, AUC-RWWL-VEPP, series 1, box 72, folder 18; *Ebony*, Nov. 1976, 136, 140; *Atlanta Constitution*, Aug. 31, 1976, 10-C; Lewis with D'Orso, *Walking*, 416–17.

66. *Los Angeles Times*, Oct. 10, 1976, E2; *Christian Science Monitor*, Nov. 9, 1976, 2; *Time*, Nov. 22, 1976; Berman, *Ballot*, 119–20.

67. VEP annual report, 1976, AAPP; *Black Scholar* (Jan./Feb. 1977): 6–15; Lewis with D'Orso, *Walking*, 417; Berman, *Ballot*, 119.

68. James Baldwin to John Lewis, June 23, 1976, AUC-RWWL-VEPP, series 1, box 72, folder 15.

SIXTEEN: THE FIRST RACE

1. *Atlanta Constitution*, Dec. 16, 1976, 1, 19, Dec. 21, 1976, 1, 12; Lewis with D'Orso, *Walking*, 418. The Southern Blacks in Congress then were William Clay of Missouri, Harold Ford of Tennessee, and Barbara Jordan of Texas.

2. *Ebony*, Nov. 1976, 133–42.

3. Archie Allen, author interview, Aug. 15, 2019; Sharon Adams, author interview, Oct. 31, 2022.

4. Tom Houck, author interview, Nov. 18, 2022; Nick Taylor, author interview, Oct. 18, 2022; Lewis with D'Orso, *Walking*, 419.

5. Julian Bond to Andrew Young, Aug. 25, 1971, UVA-HJBP, box 29, folder 26; *Atlanta Constitution*, Dec. 24, 1976, 7; Halberstam, *Children*, 571; Lewis with D'Orso, *Walking*, 419. After Lewis left, the VEP went on a downward trajectory, hampered by a lack of funds, and ceased to play a major role in voter registration in the 1980s. It closed its doors in 1992.

6. David Morrison, author interview, June 26, 2020; *Atlanta Constitution*, Dec. 19, 1976, 2, Dec. 21, 1976, 1, 12, Dec. 23,

1976, 14. Houston was later renamed John Wesley Dobbs Avenue.

7. "Statement by John Lewis," Dec. 21, 1976, AAPP, binder 7; Flyer, AUC-RWWL-LMLP, box 1, folder 10; Mailer, AUC-RWWL-LMLP, box 1, folder 10; *Atlanta Constitution*, Dec. 22, 1976, 1, 22, Dec. 23, 1976, 14, Feb. 8, 1977, A9; *Atlanta Voice*, Mar. 12, 1977, 15.

8. Clipping, AUC-RWWL-LMLP, box 1, folder 7.

9. Wyche Fowler, author interview, Nov. 20, 2022; Wyche Fowler, OH with Bob Short, Dec. 18, 2008, UGA-RBRL.

10. *New Republic*, Mar. 5, 1977, 19.

11. *Boston Globe*, Mar. 10, 1977, 31.

12. Nick Taylor, author interview, May 20, 2020, Oct. 18, 2022; Sharon Adams, author interview, Oct. 31, 2022.

13. Nick Taylor, author interview, Oct. 18, 2022; *Atlanta Constitution*, Mar. 13, 1977, 1, 6; *New Republic*, Mar. 5, 1977, 19–21; *In These Times*, Apr. 13, 1977, 4.

14. Nick Taylor, author interview, May 20, 2020; *Atlanta Constitution*, Feb. 17, 1977, 3A.

15. Nick Taylor, author interview, Oct. 18, 2022; Ted Kennedy speech, Jan. 15, 1977, AAPP, binder 7; *Atlanta Constitution*, Jan. 16, 1977, Mar. 5, 1977, 7; *Atlanta Voice*, Jan. 18, 1977, 1, 6, Jan. 22, 1977, 1.

16. Nick Taylor, author interview, Oct. 18, 2022; Sharon Adams, author interview, Oct. 31, 2022; Hyatt, *Zell*, 381.

17. *New Republic*, Mar. 5, 1977, 20.

18. *Atlanta Constitution*, Jan. 6, 1977, Jan. 8, 1977, 5A.

19. *Atlanta Constitution*, Mar. 9, 1977, A11.

20. *Atlanta Constitution*, Mar. 9, 1977, 11, Mar. 13, 1977, 1, 6, Mar. 17, 1977, 6.

21. *Atlanta Constitution*, Jan. 30, 1977; *Atlanta Voice*, Jan. 8, 1977, 1, 11.

22. Ron Zirpoli, author interview, Jan. 6, 2023.

23. *Atlanta Constitution*, Mar. 13, 1977, 1, 6; Nick Taylor, author interview, Oct. 18, 2022.

24. *Atlanta Voice*, Apr. 2, 1977, 1.

25. Campaign speech, n.d., AUC-RWWL-LMLP, box 1, folder 18.

26. "John Lewis Schedule," Feb. 13, 1977, AUC-RWWL-LMLP box 1, folder 17.

27. Sharon Adams, author interview, Oct. 31, 2022; *Southern Israelite*, Mar. 4, 1977, 5.

28. *Atlanta Constitution*, Mar. 5, 1977, 12; *Atlanta Voice*, Mar. 12, 1977, 15.

29. *Atlanta Constitution*, Mar. 1, 1977, 4.

30. *Atlanta Constitution*, Mar. 10, 1977, 4, Mar. 14, 1977, 4; Nick Taylor, author interview, Oct. 18, 2022.

31. *Atlanta Constitution*, Mar. 16, 1977, 6; Sharon Adams, author interview, Oct. 31, 2022.

32. *Atlanta Constitution*, Mar. 16, 1977, 2.

33. *People's Crusader*, Mar. 25, 1977, AAPP; *Atlanta Constitution*, Mar. 20, 1977, 16, Mar. 27, 1977, 6.

34. Nick Taylor, author interview, May 29, 2020; David Morrison, author interview, June 26, 2020; Don Harris, author interview, Apr. 16, 2020; Scott Harris, author interview, May 19, 2020; Michael Bond, author interview, Feb. 27, 2023; Frank Smith, author interview, Nov. 22, 2022; Sharlene Kranz, author interview, Nov. 14, 2022; *New York Times*, Nov. 8, 1976, 19; Lewis with D'Orso, *Walking*, 417–21.

35. *Atlanta Constitution*, Mar. 23, 1977, 16, Mar. 24, 1977, 4.

36. *Atlanta Constitution*, Mar. 22, 1977, 1, 7.

37. *Atlanta Constitution*, Mar. 20, 1977, 23.

38. *Boston Globe*, Mar. 20, 1977, A7.

39. *Atlanta Daily World*, Feb. 11, 1977, 1, Feb. 13, 1977, 1, 4, Apr. 3, 1977, 4; Pomerantz, *Peachtree*, 465–66; Harmon, *Beneath the Image*, 299.

40. Nick Taylor, author interview, Oct. 18, 2022.

41. Wyche Fowler, author interview, Nov. 20, 2022; *Atlanta Constitution*, Apr. 4, 1977, 10, Apr. 11, 1977, 6.

42. *Atlanta Constitution*, Apr. 11, 1977, 6.

43. *Atlanta Constitution*, Apr. 8, 1977, 4; Nick Taylor, author interview, Oct. 18, 2022; Sharon Adams, author interview, Oct. 31, 2022.

SEVENTEEN: ACTION

1. Arnie Miller, author interview, July 1, 2020; Sam Brown, author interview, Feb. 12, 2020.

2. *Atlanta Constitution*, May 1, 1977, 3B.

3. U.S. Congress, Senate, *Hearing Before the Committee on Human Resources*, 95th Cong., 1st Sess., July 21, 1977, 10 (statement of John Lewis).

4. *Atlanta Constitution*, June 14, 1977, C10; Lewis with D'Orso, *Walking*, 425.

5. *Pittsburgh Courier*, Sept. 10, 1977, 1.

6. *Atlanta Constitution*, Aug. 7, 1977, 4; *Washington Post*, Feb. 5, 1978, SM10.

7. *Pittsburgh Courier*, Sept. 10, 1977, 1; Halberstam, *Children*, 572.

8. Sharlene Kranz, author interview, Nov. 14, 2022; Sam Brown, author interview, Feb. 12, 2020; *Washington Post*, Feb. 3, 1980, H5.

9. John Podesta, author interview, Jan. 30, 2023; Karen Paget, author interview, Mar. 4, 2020.

10. Archie Allen, author interview, Aug. 15, 2019; Karen Paget, author interviews, Mar. 4, 2020, Jan. 23, 2023; Karen Paget, email to author, Feb. 17, 2020; *Atlanta Constitution*, Nov. 4, 1977, 18.

11. Sam Brown, author interview, Feb. 12, 2020.

12. John Podesta, author interview, Jan. 30, 2023; *New York Times*, May 13, 1978,
22, July 17, 1978, A12, Aug. 8, 1978, C2; *New Republic*, Feb. 10, 1979, 18.

13. *Washington Post*, Feb. 17, 1978, A7.

14. Karen Paget, author interview, Mar. 4, 2020; Marge Tabankin, author interview, June 9, 2020; *New York Times*, Apr. 5, 1979, A17.

15. Lewis with D'Orso, *Walking*, 428; *Washington Post*, Feb. 3, 1980, H5.

16. Sam Brown, author interview, Feb. 12, 2020; John Podesta, author interview, Jan. 30, 2023.

17. Beardslee, *Way Out*, 166.

18. *Washington Post*, Dec. 8, 1978, A8.

19. Sam Brown, author interview, Feb. 12, 2020; *Washington Post*, Dec. 8, 1978, A8; Feb. 3, 1980, H5.

20. *New Republic*, Feb. 10, 1979, 19; John Lewis to editor, Jan. 29, 1979, AAPP; *Washington Post*, Feb. 18, 1979, C6; Lewis with D'Orso, *Walking*, 427.

21. *Human Events*, Jan. 6, 1979, 19; 96 *Congressional Record*, House, Feb. 27, 1979, 3444–46.

22. Eizenstat, *President Carter*, 845–53; Fischbach, *Black Power and Palestine*, 182–91; Bird, *Outlier*, 463–72; Jones, *Flawed Triumphs*, 129–52.

23. "An Appeal by Black Americans for United States Support to Israel," June 28, 1970, HV 001581-001-0050; *New York Times*, Sept. 12, 1975, 66.

24. *Atlanta Constitution*, July 2, 1970, 10; *Southern Israelite*, Mar. 4, 1977, 5; Fischbach, *Black Power and Palestine*, 170–82.

25. *Atlanta Constitution*, July 15, 1984, C1; *Commentary*, Nov. 1979, 25–33; *New York Times*, Aug. 23, 1979, 12; *Washington Post*, Aug. 23, 1979, 1, 31; *Los Angeles Times*, Aug. 24, 1979, 1, 24; *New Directions*, Oct. 1979, 10; Jones, *Flawed Triumphs*, 148. Bernard LaFayette, who had come to work closely with Jackson in Chicago, warned his colleague not to appear

too chummy with Arafat, but Jackson didn't listen. Frady, *Jesse*, 297.

26. *Los Angeles Times*, Aug. 24, 1979, 1, 24.

27. Stuart Eizenstat, author interview, June 11, 2020; Elaine Alexander, author interview, June 10, 2020.

28. Dick Gregory, interview with Archie Allen, Aug. 17, 1968, NPL-AAC, box 3, folder 12.

29. John Podesta, author interview, Jan. 30, 2023; Karen Paget, author interview, Feb. 22, 2023.

30. Beardslee, *Way Out*, 166; Archie Allen, author interview, Feb. 18, 2023.

31. Sam Brown, author interview, Jan. 26, 2023; *Shreveport Journal*, Sept. 1, 1979, 24.

32. ACTION press release, undated, AAPP; Sam Brown, author interview, Jan. 26, 2023; *Atlanta Daily World*, Sept. 25, 1979, 2.

33. *Atlanta Voice*, Feb. 3, 1973, 2.

34. *Washington Post*, Nov. 16, 1975, 81.

35. *New York Times*, Jan. 7, 1979, 26. Allen is certain that the idea of a meeting originated with him and Lewis. But in the late 1990s, Lewis repeatedly said that it was Wallace who reached out. Karen Paget also recalls Lewis recounting the meeting that way in 1979. Archie Allen, author interview, Feb. 18, 2023; Paget, author interview, Mar. 4, 2020.

36. Recording of conversation between John Lewis and Archie Allen, July 23, 1979, AAPT; *Atlanta Constitution*, Aug. 19, 1979, SM10; Carter, *Politics of Rage*, 461. In 2023, Allen, recalling the meeting, asserted, "I don't think there was any substance to the idea that Wallace was seeking forgiveness." Archie Allen, email to author, Jan. 12, 2023.

37. John Lewis, interview with Dan T. Carter, n.d., EU-DTCP, box 9, folder 64; Terry, dir., *George Wallace: A Politician's Legacy*; *Atlanta Daily World*, Sept. 17,

1998, 1; *New York Times*, Sept. 16, 1998, A29; Carter, *Politics of Rage*, 462.

38. Karen Paget, author interview, Mar. 4, 2020. Wallace would run again for governor in 1982 and win a fourth term.

39. *Washington Post*, Jan. 7, 1987, D1, Feb. 3, 1980, H1.

40. Lewis with D'Orso, *Walking*, 428; John Podesta, author interview, Jan. 30, 2023; Podesta, *Power of Progress*, 79; U.S. Congress, House of Representatives, *Oversight and Reauthorization of ACTION Agency, 1979: Hearings Before Committee on Education and Labor. House, Subcommittee on Education. Committee on Education and Labor*, 96th Cong., 1st Sess., 1979, 297, 370.

41. *Atlanta Constitution*, Jan. 18, 1980.

42. *Atlanta Constitution*, Nov. 22, 1979, 1, 19.

43. *Time*, Nov. 22, 1976, 16; *New York Times*, Apr. 15, 1976, 18.

44. *New York Times*, May 16, 1979, A14; *Atlanta Constitution*, Dec. 3, 1981, 4. Carter did not use the word "malaise" in his July 15 "crisis of confidence" speech, but he did use it on other occasions. See, for example, Jimmy Carter, "National Federation of Democratic Women Remarks at a White House Reception," Apr. 28, 1979, UCSB-APP.

45. John Lewis to Louis Martin, July 16, 1979, binder, "John Lewis Speeches, Action," AAPP.

46. *Atlanta Constitution*, Dec. 3, 1981, 4.

47. Archie Allen, author interview, June 5, 2022; Hendrik Hertzberg, author interview, Apr. 18, 2023; Hendrik Hertzberg to James Fallows, Jan. 5, 1977, AAPP; James Fallows, email to author, Mar. 5, 2023.

48. *Baltimore Sun*, Dec. 6, 1979, 6; *Richmond Times-Dispatch*, Dec. 16, 1979, 9; Frank Moore, author interview, Mar. 8, 2023; Tom Houck, author interviews, Aug. 7, 2019, Feb. 13, 2023.

49. Karen Paget, author interview, Mar. 4, 2020.

50. Lewis with D'Orso, *Walking*, 428–29.

51. *Richmond Times-Dispatch*, Dec. 16, 1979, 9.

52. *Los Angeles Times*, Dec. 11, 1979, 6.

53. Beardslee, *Way Out*, 167.

EIGHTEEN: ATLANTA

1. *Atlanta Daily World*, Oct. 3, 1980, 1, 6.

2. *Atlanta Constitution*, Dec. 3, 1981; Lewis with D'Orso, *Walking*, 430–32.

3. Wilson, *Declining Significance*; Wilson, *When Work Disappears*; Auletta, *Underclass*.

4. *Atlanta Journal-Constitution*, Jan. 20, 1980; *New York Times*, Oct. 26, 1981, A16.

5. *Atlanta Daily World*, Oct. 4, 1981, 11; *Atlanta Constitution*, Dec. 3, 1981, 4.

6. Lewis with D'Orso, *Walking*, 433.

7. *Atlanta Constitution*, Oct. 1, 1981, 4, Dec. 3, 1981, 1; *Atlanta Weekly*, Nov. 7, 1982, 14.

8. Andrew Riley, *C.A.U.T.I.O.N. Inc.: The Fight for Atlanta's Olmsted Parks and Historic Neighborhood, Druid Hills*, manuscript, self-published online, Apr. 14, 2017, 14, academia.edu.

9. *Atlanta Constitution*, July 20, 2020, A0.

10. *Atlanta Weekly*, Nov. 7, 1982, 16.

11. *Baltimore Afro-American*, Nov. 20, 1982, 5; *Black Slate Bulletin*, July 1982, AAPP, binder 8; *Atlanta Weekly*, Nov. 7, 1982, 16; Lewis with D'Orso, *Walking*, 435.

12. *Atlanta Weekly*, Nov. 7, 1982, 14–15.

13. Lewis with D'Orso, *Walking*, 435–36.

14. Statement by Councilman John Lewis, July 6, 1982, AAPP, binder 8; *Atlanta Daily World*, July 8, 1982, 1, 4, July 15, 1982, 1.

15. Ruth Wall and Cathy Bradshaw, author interview, Feb. 14, 2023; *Atlanta Weekly*, Nov. 7, 1982, 14–20; *Baltimore Afro-American*, Nov. 20, 1982, 5.

16. *Atlanta Constitution*, June 8, 1983, 1A; Riley, *C.A.U.T.I.O.N. Inc.*, 17.

17. John Lewis to Jimmy Carter, Nov. 10, 1983, AAPP, binder 9.

18. *Chicago Tribune*, Feb. 28, 1984, 2.

19. Ruth Wall and Cathy Bradshaw, author interview, Feb. 14, 2023; Sam Collier, author interview, Feb. 7, 2023; Riley, *C.A.U.T.I.O.N. Inc.*, 36–44; *New York Times*, Feb. 23, 1985, 6; *Atlanta Constitution*, Feb. 27, 1985, B1; "Stop the Road," YouTube video, https://www.youtube.com/watch?v=Z7sYa7aCfJE; "This Is Your Land" video, RWPP.

20. Ruth Wall, author interview, Feb. 14, 2023; Riley, *C.A.U.T.I.O.N. Inc.*, 55; *Atlanta Constitution*, Oct. 2, 1986, A9; *New York Times*, Oct. 3, 1986, A10.

21. *Orlando Sentinel*, Sept. 29, 1991.

22. *Atlanta Journal-Constitution*, Mar. 17, 1985, M12; *Atlanta Journal-Constitution*, Apr. 27, 1985, B3.

23. *Atlanta Journal-Constitution*, Jan. 14, 1985, E1, Jan. 16, 1985, A1, Jan. 26, 1985, A23, Apr. 27, 1985, B3; Lewis with D'Orso, *Walking*, 433–34.

24. *Atlanta Journal-Constitution*, Dec. 18, 1985, C8.

25. Charles Johnson, author interview, July 14, 2022; *Atlanta Weekly*, Nov. 7, 1982, 14.

26. John Lewis to Archie Allen, Oct. 24, 1984, AAPP, binder 9.

27. *Georgia Sierran*, Fall 2013, 6, 11; Sam Collier, email to author, July 19, 2021.

28. Dave Hayward, author interview, Feb. 28, 2023; Terry Bird, author interview, Mar. 13, 2023; *Atlanta Constitution*, June 16, 1982, 12A, Feb. 25, 1986, D2, June 28, 1987, B5; Aug. 13, 1987, A1, May 23, 1988, B1; Pope, *Living in the Struggle*, doctoral dissertation, 160. On Lewis stopping drinking in 1972, see John Lewis,

interview with Sean Wilentz, tape 3, June 12, 1995, SWT.

29. *Atlanta Constitution*, Apr. 5, 1982, 15A; *Atlanta Daily World*, Apr. 22, 1982, 6; *Atlanta Constitution*, Mar. 5, 1984, 14A; *Atlanta Daily World*, Mar. 10, 1985, 1, 4; *Atlanta Constitution*, May 1, 1985, A10; Richard Cohen, author interview, Oct. 18, 2023.

30. Heather Fenton, author interview, Mar. 15, 2023.

31. John Lewis to Archie Allen, Oct. 24, 1984, AAPP.

32. *New York Times*, Feb. 15, 1982, A10; *Washington Post*, Feb. 15, 1982, A1, A16.

33. *Atlanta Constitution*, May 6, 1982, A33.

34. Berman, *Ballot*, 141–57.

35. Frady, *Jesse*, 303–7.

36. Frady, *Jesse*, 308.

37. *New York Times*, June 27, 1983, A10; Colton, *The Jackson Phenomenon*, 138.

38. Archie Allen, author interview, Feb. 18, 2023; *Tri-State Defender*, June 17, 1972, 4; *Atlanta Constitution*, Apr. 6, 1981, 1A, 6A; *Washington Post*, Apr. 6, 1981, A4.

39. *New York Times*, Apr. 29, 1984, E4.

40. *Atlanta Constitution*, Oct. 2, 1983, C1.

41. *Time*, Aug. 22, 1983, 22; *New York Times*, Sept. 22, 1983, B14; *Atlanta Constitution*, Oct. 31, 1983, 1A, 4A; *New York Times Magazine*, Nov. 27, 1983, 52; *Atlanta Daily World*, Jan. 6, 1984, 3; *Boston Globe*, Jan. 8, 1984, 16.

42. *Atlanta Constitution*, Jan. 19, 1984, A21; John Lewis, Statement, Feb. 6, 1984, AAPP, binder 9; *Atlanta Daily World*, Feb. 9, 1984, 1.

43. *Washington Post*, Feb. 13, 1984, A1, A4; Frady, *Jesse*, 343–56; *Atlanta Constitution*, July 10, 1984, A1, A16.

44. *Los Angeles Times*, Apr. 12, 1984, 1, 17; *New York Times*, July 10, 1984, A1, A16.

45. *Atlanta Constitution*, Sept. 2, 1984,

1A; *Boston Globe*, Sept. 8, 1984, 4; *Atlanta Daily World*, Oct. 9, 1984, 1; *Washington Post*, Nov. 12, 1984, A16.

46. *Atlanta Constitution*, Mar. 17, 1985, M12, Aug. 7, 1985, C32, Oct. 9, 1985, A9.

47. Wyche Fowler, author interview, Nov. 20, 2022.

48. Lewis with D'Orso, *Walking*, 436–37.

49. *New York Times*, Mar. 20, 1978, A18; *Atlanta Weekly*, Nov. 7, 1982, 14.

50. Lewis with D'Orso, *Walking*, 438.

51. Michael Bond, author interview, Feb. 27, 2023; *Atlanta Journal-Constitution*, Oct. 31, 1985, A1.

NINETEEN: JOHN VS. JULIAN

1. *Washington Post*, July 21, 1986, D2.

2. Kevin Ross, author interview, Aug. 18, 2023; Berman, *Ballot*, 184–85; Lewis with D'Orso, *Walking*, 441.

3. *Atlanta Journal-Constitution*, July 17, 1986, C1.

4. *Washington Post*, July 21, 1986, D2; *Atlanta Journal-Constitution*, June 30, 1986, E1.

5. John Lewis campaign flyer, AARL-AJYP, subseries 3B, box 46, folder 16; *Atlanta Journal-Constitution*, July 10, 1986, D14; *Atlanta Magazine*, Mar. 1990.

6. Elaine Alexander, author interview, June 10, 2020; Clark Lemmons, author interview, Mar. 13, 2023; Dianne Harnell Cohen, author interview, Oct. 18, 2023.

7. Russ Marane, author interview, Aug. 21, 2023; Richard Cohen, author interview, Oct. 18, 2023; *Atlanta Journal-Constitution*, Apr. 16, 1986, C1, Apr. 18, 1986, A20.

8. *Atlanta Journal-Constitution*, Aug. 18, 2015, B1.

9. Andrew Young, author interview, Mar. 14, 2023.

10. Love Collins, author interview, Mar. 28, 2023; Anthony Johnson, author interview, June 2, 2023.

11. *Atlanta Journal-Constitution*, Nov. 3, 1985, M14, Feb. 9, 1986; *New York Times*, Mar. 20, 1978, A18.

12. Campaign mailer, AARL-AYP, subseries 51, box 208, folder 9.

13. Morse Diggs, author interview, Aug. 8, 2023; *Atlanta Journal-Constitution*, Mar. 3, 1986, 8; Berman, *Ballot*, 184–85; Ball, *Bond vs. Lewis*, 2–3.

14. Sherry Frank, author interview, Mar. 16, 2023.

15. Brad Lichtenstein, author interview, Oct. 28, 2019.

16. *Atlanta Magazine*, Mar. 1990; *Atlanta Journal-Constitution*, Apr. 27, 1986, E1; Michael Bond, author interview, Feb. 27, 2023.

17. *Atlanta Journal-Constitution*, Apr. 27, 1986, E1, May 18, 1986, D4; Halberstam, *Children*, 648.

18. Lewis with D'Orso, *Walking*, 437.

19. John Lewis, interview with Sean Wilentz, May 8, 1996, tape 12, SWT.

20. Muriel Tillinghast, author interview, Dec. 13, 2022; Lois Frank, author interview, June 5, 2020.

21. Lewis, *Shadows*, 276; Halberstam, *Children*, 649.

22. "Horace Julian Bond," FBI-V, HJB.

23. *New York Times*, July 11, 1975, 29; Miles Alexander, author interview, June 10, 2020; American Jewish Committee mailer, undated, MAPP.

24. Sherry Frank, author interview, Feb. 22, 2019; *Atlanta Daily World*, Aug. 9, 1988, 1.

25. *Atlanta Journal-Constitution*, Aug. 13, 1987, A1.

26. Dave Hayward, author interview, Feb. 28, 2023.

27. Joe Larche, author interview, Mar. 14, 2023; invitation, EU-CTOVP, box 5, folder 1; *Atlanta Journal-Constitution*, May 27, 1986, E1.

28. Dave Hayward, author interview, Feb. 28, 2023.

29. Ruth Wall et al., author interview, Mar. 15, 2023.

30. *Atlanta Journal-Constitution*, June 22, 1986, B2, July 17, 1986, C1; *Southwinds* radio program, no. 161, WABE, June 12, 1986, AHC-KRCDR.

31. Love Collins, author interview, Mar. 28, 2023.

32. *Washington Post*, July 21, 1986, D2; *Southwinds* radio program, no. 161, WABE, June 12, 1986.

33. Judy Richardson, OH with Adele Oltman, Nov. 10, 1986, CU-OH, 25–26.

34. Ball, *Bond vs. Lewis*, 6; Buddy Darden, author interview, Mar. 15, 2023.

35. Charles Johnson, author interviews, July 14, 2022, July 11, 2023; *Atlanta Journal-Constitution*, July 8, 1986, C1, July 9, 1986, A9.

36. Charles Johnson, author interview, July 11, 2023; *Atlanta Journal-Constitution*, July 15, 1986, A2.

37. *New York Times*, Aug. 9, 1986, 5.

38. *Wall Street Journal*, Aug. 8, 1986, 36.

39. Michael Bond, author interview, Feb. 27, 2023.

40. Ruth Wall, author interview, Feb. 14, 2023.

41. Sherry Frank, author interview, Mar. 16, 2023; Ball, *Bond vs. Lewis*, 41–54.

42. Ball, *Bond vs. Lewis*, 47.

43. *Atlanta Journal-Constitution*, Aug. 9, 1986, A14.

44. *Atlanta Journal-Constitution*, July 22, 1986, A10; *Georgia Sierran*, Oct./Nov./Dec. 2013, 5, 11; Rachelle Horowitz, author interview, June 16, 2020; Love Collins, author interview, Mar. 28, 2023.

45. Kevin Ross, author interview, Aug. 18, 2023.

46. Lewis with D'Orso, *Walking*, 446.

47. John Lewis, interview with David Halberstam, #4, July 8, 1996, BU-DHP, box 59, folder 5; *Atlanta Journal-Constitution*,

Sept. 3, 1986. A8; Lewis with D'Orso, *Walking*, 448.

48. Love Collins, author interview, Mar. 28, 2023.

49. Charles Johnson, author interview, July 11, 2023; Sherry Frank, author interview, Feb. 22, 2019; Elaine Alexander, author interview, June 10, 2020; *Washington Post*, Aug. 31, 1986, A4; Lewis with D'Orso, *Walking*, 449–53.

50. Kevin Ross, author interview, Aug. 18, 2023; Ball, *Bond vs. Lewis*, 65; Lewis with D'Orso, *Walking*, 451.

51. *Atlanta Journal-Constitution*, Aug. 28, 1996, 38.

52. Love Collins, author interview, Mar. 28, 2023.

53. Michael Bond, author interview, Feb. 27, 2023; Blake, *Children of the Movement*, 64.

54. *Washington Post*, July 21, 1986, D2.

55. Ball, *Bond vs. Lewis*, 56.

56. Kevin Ross, author interview, Aug. 18, 2023.

57. Ball, *Bond vs. Lewis*, 57–58.

58. Lewis with D'Orso, *Walking*, 451.

59. Halberstam, *Children*, 649.

60. Ball, *Bond vs. Lewis*, 65.

61. Ball, *Bond vs. Lewis*, 57.

62. *Walking* states incorrectly that this exchange occurred in the first debate.

63. *Atlanta Journal-Constitution*, Aug. 30, 1986, B1, B7.

64. *Atlanta Journal-Constitution*, Sept. 2, 1986, A1.

65. Dianne Harnell Cohen, author interview, Oct. 18, 2023; John Lewis, interview with David Halberstam, #4, July 8, 1996, BU-DHP, box 59, folder 5; Love Collins, author interview, Mar. 28, 2023.

66. Love Collins, author interview, Mar. 28, 2023; Love Collins, email to author, July 14, 2023; Russ Marane, author interview, Aug. 21, 2023; Lewis with D'Orso, *Walking*, 452–54.

67. Porter, dir., *Good Trouble*; *Atlanta Journal-Constitution*, Sept. 4, 1986, D2.

68. *Atlanta Journal-Constitution*, Sept. 4, 1986, C10, Sept. 6, 1986, D2.

TWENTY: ON THE HILL

1. Sherry Frank, author interview, Mar. 16, 2023; email with Ruth Wall, Mar. 9, 2023; *Atlanta Journal-Constitution*, Jan. 4, 1987, G1, Jan. 6 1987, A11.

2. *Washington Post*, Jan. 7, 1987, D1; *Atlanta Journal-Constitution*, May 20, 1992, A1, A10.

3. Buddy Darden, author interview, Mar. 15, 2023; Brian Higgins, author interview, Sept. 7, 2020; *Washington Post*, Jan. 5, 1987.

4. *Asbury Park Press*, Jan. 7, 1987, 1; *Ebony*, Feb. 1987, 87–94.

5. Richard Ossoff, author interview, Mar. 20, 2023.

6. *Atlanta Journal-Constitution*, Jan. 7, 1987, A10; Love Collins, author interview, Mar. 28, 2023.

7. Clarence Bishop, author interview, July 24, 2023.

8. *Atlanta Journal-Constitution*, Apr. 10, 1987, A1, May 3, 1987, A1.

9. Al From, author interview, Feb. 28, 2023.

10. Carter, *Brother Bill*, 40–41; Baer, *Reinventing Democrats*, 82–85.

11. Will Marshall, email to author, Feb. 24, 2023.

12. *New York Times*, June 24, 1987, A25; Norrander, *Super Tuesday*, 24–31.

13. "Super Tuesday Summit," June 22, 1987, 10–12, NU-AFP, box 16, folder 3; From, *New Democrats*, 90.

14. James Waller, author interview, Apr. 29, 2023; *Washington Post*, June 9, 1998, D3; *New York Times*, Jan. 4, 1987, 31; *Time*, Aug. 31, 1987, 17; *Atlanta Journal-Constitution*, June 25, 1987, C1.

15. *New Republic*, Aug. 3, 1987, 15–20; *Washington Post*, May 31, 1987, C1, C4; *Atlanta Journal-Constitution*, Sept. 11, 1987, A24; *New York Times*, Jan. 25, 1988, B6; Kimball, *Keep Hope Alive!*, 143.

16. Anthony Johnson, author interview, June 13, 2023.

17. *Baltimore Afro-American*, Sept. 12, 1987, 4; D'Emilio, *Lost Prophet*, 492–93.

18. *New York Times*, Feb. 28, 1988, 29; *Los Angeles Times*, Apr. 24, 1988, A1.

19. On a C-SPAN call-in show in July he said that while he was happy to be a super-delegate to the Democratic National Convention, "I prefer it not to be placed in a position where I would have to [be] against some of the voters in my district." "Call-In with Rep. John Lewis," C-SPAN, July 20, 1988, https://www.c-span.org/video/?3521-1/call-rep-john-lewis&start=36.

20. *Atlanta Journal-Constitution*, Mar. 7, 1988, A1; *New York Times*, Mar. 7, 1988, A16.

21. *Atlanta Journal-Constitution*, Mar. 8, 1988, A7.

22. Kimball, *Keep Hope Alive!*, 143.

23. *Atlanta Journal-Constitution*, July 12, 1988, A6.

24. Anthony Johnson, author interview, June 13, 2023; *Atlanta Journal-Constitution*, July 18, 1988, C22, July 24, 1988, K2; *Charlotte Observer*, July 31, 1988, C1.

25. *Springfield Republican*, July 19, 1988, 7; "Call-In with Rep. John Lewis," C-SPAN, July 20, 1988.

26. *Atlanta Journal-Constitution*, July 22, 1988, A1, C5.

27. *Washington Post*, Aug. 5, 1990, D5.

28. Bradley Mims, author interview, June 14, 2023; *Atlanta Journal*, Feb. 2, 1987, E1, E4; *Washington Post*, Mar. 6, 1990, A3; "Election Statistics," History, Art & Archives, https://history.house.gov/Institution/Election-Statistics/Election-Statistics/.

29. *Los Angeles Times*, Nov. 11, 1989, 1; *New York Times*, Nov. 5, 1989, 4:1; *Wall Street Journal*, Nov. 9, 1989, A1.

30. Bradley Mims, author interview, June 14, 2023; *Atlanta Journal*, Feb. 2, 1987, E1, E4; *New York Times*, July 6, 1991, 8; *Washington Post*, Mar. 6, 1990, A3; *Atlanta Journal-Constitution*, Aug. 24, 1987, A1.

31. *New York Times*, July 6, 1991, 8; "Call-In with Rep. John Lewis," C-SPAN, July 20, 1988.

32. Mike Espy, author interview, May 2, 2023.

33. Jamila Thompson, remarks, John Lewis funeral, C-SPAN, July 30, 2020, https://www.c-span.org/video/?474223-1/representative-john-lewis-funeral-service-atlanta-georgia; Michael Collins, author interview, Aug. 31, 2023; *Atlanta Journal-Constitution*, Aug. 24, 1987, A1; *Atlanta Constitution*, May 20, 1992, A1, A10.

34. Tara McDaniel, author interview, June 23, 2023.

35. Linda Chastang, remarks at Representative John Lewis Stamp Unveiling Ceremony, C-SPAN, June 21, 2023, https://www.c-span.org/video/?528893-1/representative-john-lewis-stamp-unveiling-ceremony.

36. Anthony Johnson, author interview, June 2, 2023, June 13, 2023; Bradley Mims, author interview, June 14, 2023.

37. *New York Times*, Dec. 12, 1986, B6; *Atlanta Journal-Constitution*, Aug. 24, 1987, A1; *Atlanta Constitution*, May 20, 1992, A1, A10; Michael Collins, author interview, June 20, 2023.

38. Bill Richardson, author interview, Apr. 13, 2020; *Atlanta Journal-Constitution*, May 20, 1992, A1, A10, July 6, 1994, C1; Lewis with D'Orso, *Walking*, 455.

39. Ruth Berg, author interview, Mar. 6, 2023; *Atlanta Journal-Constitution*, May 20, 1992, A1, A10.

40. Bill Richardson, author interview, Apr. 13, 2020.

41. Barney Frank, author interview, Jan. 29, 2020.

42. Polls showed shifting approval levels for Thomas among African Americans, usually with more Blacks supporting than opposing him.

43. *Boston Globe*, July 14, 1991, 69–70.

44. *Washington Post*, Sept. 9, 1991, A1; *Los Angeles Times*, Aug. 12, 1991.

45. *Atlanta Journal-Constitution*, July 2, 1991, A5; *New York Times*, July 11, 1991, A1.

46. *Philadelphia Tribune*, July 23, 1991, 3A.

47. *Los Angeles Times*, Aug. 12, 1991.

48. Lewis with D'Orso, *Walking*, 468–69; Thomas Confirmation Hearing, Day 7, Part 3, C-SPAN, Sept. 19, 1991, https://www.c-span.org/video/?21780-1/thomas-confirmation-hearing-day-7-part-3; U.S. Congress, Senate, *Nomination of Clarence Thomas to Be Associate Justice of the Supreme Court of the United States: Hearings Before the Committee on the Judiciary*, 102nd Cong., 1st Sess., 1991, 697–717.

49. *Atlanta Daily World*, Nov. 3, 1991, 8.

50. Mignon Morman Willis, author interview, Mar. 7, 2023.

51. *New York Times*, July 6, 1991, 8; *Atlanta Journal-Constitution*, June 5, 1991, A10.

52. *Washington Post*, June 26, 1991, A7; Congressional Black Caucus at White House, C-SPAN, June 25, 1991, https://www.c-span.org/video/?18575-1/congressional-black-caucus-white-house.

53. Lorraine Miller, author interview, June 17, 2023.

54. *New Republic*, Jan. 29, 1990, 21–22; *Washington Post*, Sept. 17, 1989, A22–A23, Mar. 6, 1990, A3, Mar. 29, 1990, A2; *New York Daily News*, Apr. 10, 1990, 32;

Atlanta Journal-Constitution, Sept. 21, 1991, A21; *Newsweek*, July 5, 1993, 26.

55. George Kundanis, author interview, May 15, 2023; David Bonior, email to author, June 9, 2020; Richard Gephardt, author interview, May 19, 2023; Lorraine Miller, author interview, June 17, 2023; Lewis with D'Orso, *Walking*, 469.

56. John Lewis, interview with Sean Wilentz, June 13, 1995, tape 4, SWT; *Atlanta Journal-Constitution*, Aug. 3, 1991, A1; *Black Enterprise*, Nov. 1991, 15; *Jet*, Aug. 26, 1991; "Majority Party Deputy Whip Appointments," C-SPAN, Aug. 2, 1991, https://www.c-span.org/video/?20061-1/majority-party-deputy-whip-appointments.

57. John Lewis, author interview, May 15, 2020.

58. Bill Clinton, "Remarks at a Dinner for Representative John Lewis in Atlanta," Apr. 14, 2000, UCSB-APP; Bill Clinton, author interview, Oct. 18, 2023.

59. "Rep. John Lewis Weighs Endorsement Options," NPR, Mar. 30, 2007; Anthony Johnson, author interview, June 13, 2023; Bradley Mims, author interview, June 14, 2023; Bill Clinton, author interview, Oct. 17, 2023.

60. John Lewis, author interview, May 15, 2020.

61. *Washington Post*, Nov. 20, 1991, A4, Jan. 10, 1992, A4, Jan. 19, 1992, A14; *Atlanta Journal-Constitution*, Dec. 20, 1991, A4, Feb. 3, 1992, A7.

62. John Lewis, author interview, May 15, 2020; Charles Rangel, author interview, May 31, 2023.

63. Paul Begala, author interview, Mar. 20, 2023; Bill Clinton, author interview, Oct. 18, 2023; *New York Times*, Feb. 16, 1998, A11.

64. *New Republic*, Feb. 3, 1992, 27; *Atlanta Constitution*, Mar. 11, 1992, A10; *Philadelphia Inquirer*, May 4, 1992, A3.

65. Gordon Giffin, author interview, Apr. 5, 2023.

66. Keith Mason, author interview, Mar. 7, 2023; *Atlanta Journal-Constitution*, Jan. 25, 1992, A1.

67. Paul Begala, author interview, Mar. 20, 2023.

68. Buddy Darden, author interview, Mar. 4, 2023; *Atlanta Journal-Constitution*, Feb. 21, 1992, A1, Feb. 26, 1992, A4; *Los Angeles Times*, Feb. 22, 1992, A18; *Washington Post*, Feb. 22, 1992, A8.

69. *Atlanta Journal-Constitution*, Feb. 26, 1992, A4; *Washington Post*, Feb. 27, 1992, A10, Feb. 29, 1992, A12.

70. Paul Begala, author interview, Mar. 20, 2023; *New York Times*, Mar. 3, 1992, A19.

71. *Atlanta Journal-Constitution*, Nov. 4, 1992, B3.

72. *Washington Post*, June 22, 1992; *Atlanta Constitution*, June 23, 1992.

73. *CQ Almanac 1992*, 48th ed., 51-A–53-A; Brad Lichtenstein, author interviews, Oct. 28, 2019, May 23, 2023.

74. *CQ Almanac 1992*, 48th ed., 51-A–53-A; John Lewis, "Vice Presidential Nomination Speech," C-SPAN, July 16, 1992, https://www.c-span.org/video/?c4896512/john-lewis-nominates-al-gore.

75. *Baltimore Sun*, Oct. 13, 1992, 5A; *Philadelphia Tribune*, Oct. 20, 1992, 3C; *Atlanta Journal-Constitution*, Nov. 2, 1992, A1, A10.

TWENTY-ONE:
THE CLINTON YEARS

1. Debbie Spielberg, author interview, Apr. 29, 2023; Bill Clinton, author interview, Oct. 18, 2023.

2. George Dusenbury, author interview, Nov. 19, 2021; Kim Walker, author interview, June 1, 2020; Tara McDaniel, author interview, June 23, 2023.

3. John Lewis, interview with Sean Wilentz, May 8, 1996, tape 12, SWT.

4. George Dusenbury, author interview, Nov. 19, 2021; Bill Clinton, author interview, Oct. 18, 2023.

5. John Lewis, interview with Sean Wilentz, June 13, 1995, tape 4, SWT; *Washington Post*, July 1, 1994, A25.

6. SNCC press release, Mar. 24, 1966, HV 252253-014-0467; *New York Times*, Mar. 22, 1966, 37; *New York Daily News*, Mar. 22, 1966, 36; *Washington Post*, Mar. 3, 1988, B3; *Atlanta Daily World*, Dec. 16, 1976, 1, 4; *New York Times*, Oct. 25, 1985, A16.

7. *Boston Globe*, June 20, 1990, 1–2.

8. "Events in South Africa," press conference, C-SPAN, Mar. 30, 1994, https://www.c-span.org/video/?55728-1/events-south-africa; *New York Times*, Mar. 29, 1994, A1; *Philadelphia Tribune*, Apr. 12, 1994, 3E.

9. James Waller, author interview, Apr. 28, 2023; Rob Bassin, author interview, Apr. 27, 2023; *Atlanta Constitution*, Mar. 30, 1994, 13; "Events in South Africa," press conference, Mar. 30, 1994; Schroeder, *24 Years*, 89; Mfume, *No Free Ride*, 314.

10. C-SPAN interview with John Lewis, Mar. 29, 1994, https://www.c-span.org/video/?55619-1/events-south-africa; "Events in South Africa," press conference, Mar. 30, 1994; *Atlanta Journal-Constitution*, June 27, 1990, A8; James Waller, author interview, Apr. 28, 2023; Rob Bassin, author interview, Apr. 27, 2023; Schroeder, *24 Years*, 90; Mfume, *No Free Ride*, 314–15.

11. Lyman, *Partner to History*, 200–202; Schroeder, *24 Years*, 91; *Atlanta Journal-Constitution*, Apr. 1, 1994, A12. Lyman recalls a standing ovation, while Schroeder says they "remained frozen and silent."

12. *Atlanta Journal-Constitution*, Apr. 1, 1994, A12; Rob Bassin, author interview, Apr. 27, 2023.

13. Bill Clinton, author interview, Oct. 18, 2023.

14. *Newsweek*, Dec. 6, 1993, 20; *Emerge*, Aug. 1993, 15.

15. *Washington Post*, May 8, 1993, A21; Kim Walker, author interview, May 25, 2023; Paul Begala, author interview, Mar. 20, 2023.

16. *Washington Post*, Aug. 12, 1994, A1; *New York Times*, Aug. 12, 1994, A1.

17. Tara McDaniel, author interview, June 23, 2023.

18. *Chicago Tribune*, Aug. 18, 1994, 1, 18; Marshall Project website, Oct. 7, 2015; *Washington Post*, Sept. 2, 1994, A23.

19. *Wall Street Journal*, Aug. 18, 1994, A2.

20. *Chicago Tribune*, Aug. 18, 1994, 1, 18.

21. John Lewis, author interview, May 15, 2020.

22. *Chicago Tribune*, Aug. 18, 1994, 1, 18.

23. *New York Times*, Aug. 18, 1994, A1, B10.

24. After the bill passed, violent crime fell precipitously. Clinton and many others credited the bill, in part, though policy analysts debate how much the new measures contributed to the drop in crime. On the other hand, the bill's critics blamed it for rising incarceration rates, but those rates had shot up in the 1970s and '80s and grew comparatively less thereafter. See Pfaff, *Locked In*.

25. Debbie Spielberg, author interview, Apr. 29, 2023.

26. *New York Times*, Aug. 3, 1992, A14; Bloodworth, *Losing the Center*, 89; Lublin, *Paradox*, 3; Berman, *Ballot*, 188, 194; Sleeper, *Liberal Racism*, 66.

27. *Atlanta Journal-Constitution*, Dec. 7, 1994, A6.

28. Rob Bassin, author interview, Apr. 27, 2023.

29. Linda Chastang, author interview, May 2, 2023.

30. *Atlanta Journal-Constitution*, Nov. 20, 1994, H4; *USA Today*, Nov. 11, 1994, 3A; John Lewis, interview with Sean Wilentz, Nov. 8, 1996, tape 17, SWT.

31. *Atlanta Journal-Constitution*, Feb. 8, 1995, A6; David Bonior, author interview, June 3, 2020; Bonior, *Whip*, 390.

32. *Atlanta Journal-Constitution*, Feb. 8, 1995, A6.

33. "Go, Atlanta Braves," Oct. 5, 1993, 139 *Cong. Rec.*, House, 7384; "What a List," Jan. 31, 1995, 141 *Cong. Rec.*, House, 898; "The Truth Is Loose," Feb. 1, 1995, 141 *Cong. Rec.*, House, 979; "What a Dinner," Feb. 7, 1995, 141 *Cong. Rec.*, House, 1296; *Washington Post*, Feb. 16, 1995, A21; David Bonior, author interview, June 3, 2020.

34. *Atlanta Journal-Constitution*, Feb. 8, 1995, A6.

35. *Washington Post*, Feb. 16, 1995.

36. "I Will Not Be Silenced," Feb. 9, 1995, 141 *Cong. Rec.*, House, 1471.

37. James Waller, author interview, Apr. 28, 2023; Kim Walker, author interview, May 25, 2023.

38. "Speaker Gingrich Ethics Investigation," C-SPAN, Feb. 3, 1995, https://www.c-span.org/video/?63507-1/house-speaker-ethics-investigation; June 21, 1995, https://www.c-span.org/video/?65841-1/speaker-gingrich-ethics-investigation; Sept. 12, 1996, https://www.c-span.org/video/?75007-1/house-speaker-ethics-investigation; and Sept. 28, 1996, https://www.c-span.org/video/?75528-1/house-speaker-ethics-investigation.

39. "Personal Responsibility Act of 1995," Mar. 21, 1995, 141 *Cong. Rec.*, House, 8498; George Dusenbury, author interview, Nov. 19, 2021.

40. *Washington Post*, May 5, 1995, A25; George Dusenbury, author interview, Nov. 19, 2021.

41. *Wall Street Journal*, July 25, 1995, A13; John Lewis, interview with Sean Wilentz, [Summer 1995], tape 7, SWT.

42. John Lewis, interview with Sean Wilentz, [Summer 1995], tape 7, SWT; *Atlanta Journal-Constitution*, Aug. 7, 1995, A1, Nov. 27, 1997, D4; *New York Times*, Aug. 8, 1995, B6.

43. John Lewis and staff discussion, recorded by Sean Wilentz, June 13, 1995, tape 4, SWT; *New York Times*, June 13, 1995, 1.

44. *Washington Post*, Nov. 19, 1995, A1; *New York Times*, Nov. 19, 1995, 1.

45. John Lewis, interview with Sean Wilentz, Dec. 8, 1995, tape 9, SWT; *New York Times*, Nov. 19, 1995, 1; Barney Frank, author interviews, Jan. 29, 2020, May 16, 2023; Richard Gephardt, author interview, May 19, 2023.

46. *New York Times*, Sept. 19, 1996, A20; *Dissent*, Winter 1997, 10.

47. *Washington Post*, May 7, 1990, D1; "Nation of Islam," *Charlie Rose*, Feb. 7, 1994, https://charlierose.com/videos/7359.

48. *Fellowship*, Dec. 2000, 10.

49. John Lewis, interview with Aaron David Miller, July 19, 2006, ADMI.

50. Debbie Spielberg, author interview, Apr. 29, 2023.

51. John Lewis, interview with Sean Wilentz, [Summer 1995], tape 7, SWT; *Forward*, June 26, 1998; Barney Frank, author interview, Jan. 29, 2020. Lewis seemed to think it was Peres, the finance minister, whom the group had met with, although it may have been Prime Minister Yitzhak Shamir.

52. Troy, *Moynihan's Moment*, 248; John Lewis, interview with Aaron David Miller, July 19, 2006, ADMI; John Lewis, interview with Sean Wilentz, June 13, 1995, tape 4, SWT.

53. *New York Times*, Dec. 29, 1993, B1; Lewis with D'Orso, *Walking*, 470.

54. "Nation of Islam," *Charlie Rose*, Feb. 7, 1994.

55. *Philadelphia Inquirer*, Sept. 25, 1994, B4; *New York Times*, June 12, 1995, B7; Halberstam, *Children*, 682.

56. John Lewis, interview with Sean Wilentz, [Summer 1995], tape 7, SWT.

57. *New York Times*, Oct. 13, 1995, A1, A30.

58. Rob Bassin, author interview, Apr. 27, 2023.

59. *Democracy*, July 22, 2020.

60. *Washington Post*, Oct. 14, 1995, A11; *Newsweek*, Oct. 23, 1995, 3.

61. *New Republic*, July 1, 1996, 22; Bond, *Race Man*, 196–99.

62. James Waller, author interview, Apr. 28, 2023.

63. Bill Clinton, author interview, Oct. 18, 2023.

64. *Atlanta Journal-Constitution*, Oct. 17, 1995.

65. John Lewis, interview with Sean Wilentz, Dec. 8, 1995, tape 9, SWT; *Washington Post*, Oct. 17, 1995, C4; *New York Times*, Oct. 17, 1995, A19.

66. George Dusenbury, author interview, June 9, 2023; James Waller, author interview, Apr. 28, 2023.

67. *Philadelphia Inquirer Magazine*, Jan. 3, 1999, 15.

68. Howell Raines, author interview, May 5, 2020; Love Collins, author interview, Mar. 28, 2023; Judi Gerhardt, author interview, Sept. 5, 2023.

69. Halberstam, *Children*, 652; Alridge, "From Civil Rights to Hip Hop," 232.

70. Buddy Darden, author interview, Mar. 15, 2023; Ruth Wall, author interview, Feb. 14, 2023; *Atlanta Daily World*, May 4, 1995, 3, Dec. 12, 1995, 1.

71. *Los Angeles Times*, July 26, 1998, 3.

72. "The John Lewis Story," May 9,

1991, UNC-TBP, series 4, folder 722; Michael D'Orso, email to author, July 9, 2019; Michael D'Orso, author interview, May 25, 2023.

73. Michael D'Orso, author interview, May 25, 2023; David Black, author interview, June 2, 2023; *Atlanta Journal-Constitution*, Dec. 25, 1997, A3.

74. Robert Bender, email to author, June 23, 2021; "Talking Points for Vice President Al Gore, John Lewis Event," June 10, 1998, WJCPL-JSP, box 19943; *Atlanta Daily World*, June 14, 1998, 4.

75. Rob Bassin, author interview, Apr. 27, 2023; Tara McDaniel, author interview, June 23, 2023; Kim Walker, author interview, May 25, 2023.

76. Carmichael with Thelwell, *Ready for Revolution*, 482–83. See also criticism from SNCC alumnus Mike Miller in *Social Policy*, Summer 1998, 46–51; *Progressive*, Aug. 1998, 32–35.

77. Muriel Tillinghast, author interview, Dec. 13, 2022.

78. Archie Allen, author interviews, Aug. 15, 2019, May 18, 2023.

79. Michael D'Orso, author interview, May 25, 2023; Larry Copeland, author interview, Apr. 25, 2023; Archie Allen, author interview, Aug. 15, 2019; Cherie Murdock, author interview, Nov. 17, 2022; Joan Browning, author interview, July 28, 2022.

80. George Dusenbury, author interview, June 9, 2023; *Washington Post*, June 9, 1998, D2; Halberstam, *Children*, 651–52; *New Republic*, July 1, 1996, 22; *Esquire*, Nov. 1998, 108; Michael D'Orso, author interview, May 25, 2023.

81. *New York Times*, Feb. 16, 1998, A11.

82. *CQ Weekly*, Aug. 22, 1998, 2279–80.

83. *Washington Post*, Aug. 29, 1988, A1.

84. Bill Clinton, author interview, Oct. 18, 2023; *New Republic*, Oct. 5, 1998, 12.

85. Linda Earley Chastang, press release, Aug. 20, 1998, WJCPL-JSP, box 19943; Jeff Shesol, draft remarks, Aug. 27, 1988, WJCPL-JSP, box 19943; *Philadelphia Inquirer*, Aug. 29, 1998, A2; *Washington Post*, Aug. 29, 1988, A1.

86. "Walking with the Wind," C-SPAN, Aug. 28, 1998, https://www.c-span.org/video/?110527-1/walking-wind.

87. "March on Washington 35th Anniversary," C-SPAN, Aug. 28, 1998, https://www.c-span.org/video/?116045-1/march-washington-35th-anniversary; *New York Times*, Aug. 29, 1998, A10.

88. Linda Chastang, author interview, Apr. 7, 2022; *New Republic*, Oct. 5, 1998, 12.

89. *Newsweek*, Nov. 30, 1998, 35.

90. *New York Times*, Sept. 16, 1998, A29.

TWENTY-TWO: AMBITIONS

1. *Atlanta Journal-Constitution*, July 10, 1997, A3, Aug. 6, 1997, B4.

2. *Roll Call*, Sept. 3, 1998, 1.

3. Nancy Pelosi, author interview, Apr. 30, 2020; *Washington Post*, Jan. 6, 2002, W27.

4. *Roll Call*, Aug. 2, 1999, 1, Aug. 9, 1999, 1.

5. *Roll Call*, Sept. 6, 1999, 1.

6. *New Republic*, Oct. 18, 1999, 8.

7. David Bonior, author interview, June 3, 2020.

8. James Williams, author interview, July 21, 2021; Page, *Madam Speaker*, 178.

9. *Roll Call*, Nov. 22, 1999, 1; *New Republic*, Oct. 18, 1999, 8.

10. Lorraine Miller, author interview, June 17, 2023.

11. Rob Bassin, author interview, May 26, 2020; James Williams, author interview, July 21, 2021; Linda Chastang, author interview, Apr. 7, 2022.

12. *Roll Call*, Sept. 29, 1999, 1, Jan. 13, 2000, 1.

13. Michael Collins, author interview, June 20, 2023.

14. *Atlanta Journal-Constitution*, Feb. 13, 2000, B3.

15. *Washington Post*, Jan. 6, 2002, W27.

16. *Roll Call*, July 20, 2000, 1.

17. In early 2001, Bonior announced he would leave Congress to run for governor of Michigan. The Democratic caucus elected Pelosi over Hoyer on October 11, 2001. She assumed the position on January 15, 2002, when Bonior quit Congress to campaign for governor full-time. He lost his primary race to state attorney general Jennifer Granholm.

18. Archie Allen, author interview, May 18, 2023; Mignon Morman Willis, author interview, Mar. 7, 2023; Lyn Vaughn, author interview, Mar. 14, 2023.

19. Lyn Vaughn, author interview, Mar. 14, 2023; Carl Nelson, author interview, July 15, 2023.

20. Carol Dove, author interview, July 18, 2023; *Atlanta Magazine*, Aug. 2003.

21. Rachelle O'Neil, author interview, June 15, 2023; Brad Lichtenstein, author interviews, Oct. 28, 2019, May 23, 2023.

22. Tuere Butler, author interview, June 5, 2023.

23. Michael Collins, author interview, June 20, 2023; Tuere Butler, author interview, June 5, 2023.

24. Ron Zirpoli, author interview, Jan. 6, 2023.

25. Buddy Darden, author interview, Mar. 15, 2023; Ruth Berg, author interview, Mar. 6, 2023; George Dusenbury, author interview, Nov. 19, 2021; Kristin Oblander, author interview, June 2, 2023.

26. Rob Bassin, author interview, Apr. 27, 2023.

27. Michael Collins, author interview, June 20, 2023.

28. Anthony Johnson, author interview, June 13, 2023; George Dusenbury, author interview, Nov. 19, 2021.

29. Buddy Darden, author interview, Mar. 15, 2023.

30. *Vanity Fair*, Dec. 6, 2019.

31. Anthony Johnson, author interview, June 13, 2023.

32. Archie Allen, author interview, May 25, 2023; Rachelle O'Neil, author interview, June 15, 2023; Stephen McDaniel, author interview, Mar. 17, 2023; Keith Washington, author interview, July 24, 2023; Paige Alexander, author interview, Mar. 17, 2023; Andrew Aydin, author interview, June 22, 2021.

33. Tara McDaniel, author interview, June 23, 2023; Kim Walker, author interview, May 25, 2023; Brad Lichtenstein, author interview, May 23, 2023.

34. Rob Bassin, author interview, Apr. 27, 2023; Anthony Johnson, author interview, June 13, 2023; Carol Dove, author interview, July 17, 2023; *The Hill*, May 18, 2006, 26.

35. Archie Allen, author interview, May 25, 2023; Debbie Spielberg, author interview, Apr. 29, 2023.

36. John Lewis Commemorative Forever Stamp Dedication Ceremony, July 21, 2023, USPS channel, YouTube.

37. Michael Collins, author interview, May 14, 2020; Ruth Berg, author interview, Mar. 6, 2023; Anne Tumlinson, author interview, July 5, 2023.

38. Stephen McDaniel, author interview, Mar. 17, 2023; Debbie Spielberg, author interview, Apr. 29, 2023.

39. Wade Burns, author interview, Aug. 18, 2020.

40. Michael German, author interview, Feb. 9, 2023; Lorraine Miller, author interview, June 17, 2023.

41. Anne Tumlinson, author interview, July 5, 2023; Rob Bassin, author interview, May 26, 2020.

42. George Dusenbury, author interview, Nov. 19, 2021; Kim Walker, author interview, June 1, 2020; Rachelle O'Neil, author interview, June 15, 2023.

43. John Lewis, author interview, May 8, 2020; Jamila Thompson, eulogy, John Lewis funeral, C-SPAN, July 30, 2020, https://www.c-span.org/video/?c4896653/user-clip-john-lewis-remembered-legislative-director-jamila-thompson.

44. John Lewis, interview with Sean Wilentz, Dec. 8, 1995, tape 9, SWT; S. 2806, 102d Cong., 2d Sess. (1992); H.R. 5326, 102d Cong., 2d Sess. (1992); *Atlanta Journal-Constitution*, June 3, 1992, A5; Al Gore, "Rolling Stone Interview," July 23, 2020; Bill Clinton, author interview, Oct. 18, 2023.

45. *New York Times*, Jan. 16, 2000, 1; John Lewis, interview with Sean Wilentz, Nov. 8, 1996, tape 17, SWT.

46. *Los Angeles Times*, Aug. 15, 2000, 3; *Washington Post*, Aug. 12, 2000, 21.

47. *Atlanta Journal-Constitution*, Aug. 17, 2000, A12, Aug. 18, 2000, B4; Melanie Eversley, author interview, Jan. 25, 2020.

48. *Newsweek*, Dec. 11, 2000, 38.

49. Michael Collins, author interview, June 20, 2023.

50. *New York Times*, Dec. 2, 2000, A19.

51. *New York Times*, Dec. 12, 2000, A1.

52. *Newsweek*, Dec. 11, 2000, 38.

53. *New York Times*, Dec. 15, 2000, A1; Berman, *Ballot*, 213. When the electoral votes were counted in January in the Congress, Lewis and the rest of the Black Caucus protested. But because no senator cosigned their objections, Al Gore—who as vice president had to preside over the process—ruled each one out of order, certifying his own defeat.

54. Inaba, dir., *American Blackout*.

TWENTY-THREE:
IN OPPOSITION

1. Michael Collins, author interview, Apr. 27, 2023.

2. John Lewis, interview with Danny Lyon, Jan. 14, 2020, DLPT; James Waller, author interview, Apr. 28, 2023; Michael Collins, author interview, June 20, 2023.

3. Patrick Leahy, author interview, July 11, 2023; Leahy, *Road Taken*, 273.

4. Michael Collins, author interview, June 20, 2023.

5. *Southern Exposure*, Fall 1976, 14–24; James Waller, author interview, Apr. 28, 2023; Lewis with D'Orso, *Walking*, 474.

6. "John Lewis Remarks at Sept. 12 Vigil," C-SPAN, Sept. 12, 2001, https://www.c-span.org/video/?c5074017/user-clip-john-lewis-remarks-sep-12-vigil.

7. *CQ Weekly*, Dec. 5, 1992, 3760; Associated Press Newswires, May 8, 1999; *New York Times*, Apr. 27, 2009.

8. Lorraine Miller, author interview, June 17, 2023.

9. Tuere Butler, author interview, June 5, 2023; William Clay, email to author, May 20, 2020; *Washington Post*, Jan. 25, 1995, A23; *New York Times*, Jan. 25, 1995, A19; *National Parks*, Sept.–Oct. 1991, 22.

10. *Washington Post*, Oct. 8, 1994, C1; *Crisis*, 1998, 8–13; Wilkins, *Long Road*, 57–66; Lorraine Miller, author interview, June 17, 2023.

11. Sam Brownback, author interview, June 6, 2023; LaRochelle Murray Young, author interview, June 8, 2023; Robert Wilkins, author interview, June 29, 2023; Wilkins, *Long Road*, 80.

12. J. C. Watts, author interview, June 6, 2023; *Jet*, July 17, 2000, 4–5.

13. Tammy Boyd, author interview, June 25, 2023.

14. Robert Wilkins, author interview, June 29, 2023; Tammy Boyd, author interview, June 25, 2023; Wilkins, *Long Road*, 82.

15. Wilkins, *Long Road*, 82; Tammy Boyd, author interview, June 25, 2023.

16. "African-American History Museum," C-SPAN, May 3, 2001, https://www.c-span.org/video/?164059-1/african-american-history-museum.

17. Tammy Boyd, author interview, June 25, 2023; Robert Wilkins, author interview, June 29, 2023.

18. Wilkins, *Long Road*, 88.

19. Tammy Boyd, author interview, June 25, 2023.

20. Robert Wilkins, author interview, June 29, 2023.

21. Wilkins, *Long Road*, 88.

22. Wilkins, *Long Road*, 89.

23. In 2002, Watts retired from Congress and Cleland was defeated for reelection. Jack Kingston of Georgia and Chris Dodd of Connecticut filled their places in the quartet.

24. U.S. Congress, House, *Hearing Before the Committee on House Administration*, 108th Cong., 1st Sess., July 9, 2003, 3, 4; "African-American History Museum," C-SPAN, July 9, 2003, https://www.c-span .org/video/?179161-2/house-session.

25. Eleanor Holmes Norton, author interview, July 10, 2023; *Washington Post*, July 12, 2003, C1. The preservationists had gotten a bill introduced in Congress that, while making no mention of the proposed African American history museum, forbade future construction on the Mall. Lewis and Brownback got wise to it and had it amended to make an exception for their museum.

26. U.S. Congress, House, *Hearing Before the Committee on House Administration*, 108th Cong., 1st Sess., July 9, 2003, 19, 40–41; "African-American History Museum," C-SPAN, July 9, 2003; Wilkins, *Long Road*, 117.

27. *St. Petersburg Times*, Apr. 4, 2004.

28. Jacob Gillison, author interview, Apr. 29, 2020; Tammy Boyd, author interview, June 25, 2023.

29. *New York Times*, Dec. 17, 2003, A34.

30. Howard Brown to author, email, Dec. 18, 2023; Robert Wilkins, author interview, June 29, 2023.

31. *Roll Call*, Mar. 15, 2005, 1; *Washington Post*, Jan. 31, 2006, A1.

32. *Atlanta Journal-Constitution*, July 18, 2020.

33. *Atlanta Journal-Constitution*, Apr. 14, 2000, B1; Melanie Eversley, author interview, Jan. 25, 2020.

34. Carol Dove, author interview, July 17, 2023.

35. Howard Brown to author, email, Dec. 18, 2023.

36. Kristin Oblander, author interview, Mar. 27, 2023; Howard Brown to author, email, Dec. 18, 2023; *Vanity Fair*, Dec. 2019.

37. Howard Brown, author interview, Aug. 9, 2023; Howard Brown, email to author, Dec. 18, 2023.

38. Stephen McDaniel, author interview, Mar. 17, 2023.

39. *Sugarcane Magazine*, Apr. 12, 2016; *Vanity Fair*, Dec. 2019.

40. *New York Review of Books*, Feb. 13, 2020.

41. Danielle Isaacs, author interview, July 4, 2023; Carol Dove, author interview, July 17, 2023.

42. Steve Slotin, author interview, Mar. 2, 2023; Michael German, author interview, Feb. 9, 2023; Danielle Isaacs, author interview, July 4, 2023; Keith Washington, author interview, July 24, 2023; *Craftsmanship*, Feb. 18, 2022.

43. Michael German, author interview, Feb. 9, 2023.

44. Kim Walker, author interview, June 1, 2020; Debbie Spielberg, author interview, Apr. 30, 2023.

45. *Atlanta Journal-Constitution*, Aug. 28, 2005, L7, Sept. 10, 2005, A1, Dec. 22, 2012, D1.

46. Shirley Franklin, author interview, Mar. 21, 2023.

47. *New York Times*, Aug. 4, 2005, A14.

48. U.S. Congress, Senate, *Confirmation Hearing Before the Committee on the*

Judiciary: Confirmation Hearing on the Nomination of John G. Roberts, Jr., to Be Chief Justice of the United States, 109th Cong., 1st sess., Sept. 15, 2005, 458–60, 469 (statement of John Lewis); Roberts Confirmation Hearing, Day 4, Part 3, C-SPAN, Sept. 15, 2005, https://www.c-span.org/video/?188799-3/roberts-confirmation-hearing-day-4-part-3; *Washington Post*, Sept. 16, 2005, A6.

49. *Washington Post*, Sept. 16, 2005, A6.

50. Berman, *Ballot*, 233.

51. *Atlanta Journal-Constitution*, Aug. 5, 2005, A1; *Atlanta Inquirer*, Aug. 13, 2005, A13; Berman, *Ballot*, 222.

52. *New York Times*, Aug. 6, 2005, A13.

53. *New York Times*, Nov. 23, 2003, N29.

54. Berman, *Ballot*, 234–35.

55. James Sensenbrenner, author interview, June 10, 2023.

56. John Lewis, interview with Matthew Wasniewski, Dec. 11, 2014.

57. James Sensenbrenner, author interview, June 10, 2023; U.S. Congress, Senate, *Hearing Before the Committee on the Judiciary*, 109th Cong., 2nd sess., Apr. 27, 2006, 5–6 (statement of James Sensenbrenner); Tucker, "Politics of Persuasion," 234.

58. *Roll Call*, Feb. 7, 2005, 1, Mar. 10, 2005, 1, May 4, 2005, 1; *Atlanta Journal-Constitution*, May 29, 2006, A17. For Lewis's rebuttal, see *National Journal*, July 8, 2006.

59. *Georgia v. Ashcroft*, 539 U.S. 461 (2003); *New Yorker*, Sept. 20, 2004, 56–61.

60. 152 *Cong Rec.*, House, 5150; 152 *Cong Rec.*, House 5164; House Session, C-SPAN, July 13, 2006, https://www.c-span.org/video/?193337-1/house-session; Michaeleen Crowell, author interview, June 22, 2023.

61. *New York Times*, July 14, 2006, A13; *Atlanta Journal-Constitution*, July 14, 2006, A1.

62. *New York Times*, July 28, 2006, A16. Lewis did not attend the signing. He went instead to Michael Collins's father's funeral.

TWENTY-FOUR:
"BECAUSE OF YOU"

1. Kristin Oblander, author interviews, Mar. 27, 2023, June 2, 2023.

2. Barack Obama, author interview, Jan. 23, 2024.

3. Buddy Darden, author interview, Mar. 15, 2023.

4. *Atlanta Journal-Constitution*, Feb. 22, 2005, B1; *Jet*, Mar. 14, 2005, 36.

5. Remnick, *Bridge*, 485–86.

6. Hillary Clinton, author interview, Jan. 18, 2024.

7. Doug Tanner, author interview, June 21, 2023; Barack Obama, author interview, Jan. 23, 2024; *New York Times*, Mar. 4, 2007, 1, 23.

8. Photograph, Mar. 4, 2007, DJTPP; Obama, *Promised Land*, 142–48.

9. John Lewis, OH with Matthew Wasniewski and Jackie Burns, Dec. 11, 2014, HROH.

10. "Morning Edition," National Public Radio, Mar. 30, 2007.

11. Barack Obama, author interview, Jan. 23, 2024.

12. *New York Times*, Oct. 12, 2007; *Atlanta Journal-Constitution*, Oct. 13, 2007, A1.

13. Remnick, *Bridge*, 492; *Atlanta Journal-Constitution*, Oct. 13, 2007, A1; National Public Radio, Oct. 13, 2007.

14. *New Yorker*, Nov. 17, 2008, 47–48.

15. Obama, *Dreams*, 93; *Huffington Post*, Mar. 28, 2008.

16. Brenda Jones, author interview, Aug. 25, 2023; *New York Times*, Jan. 11, 2008; *Atlanta Journal-Constitution*, Jan. 15, 2008.

17. *Atlanta Journal-Constitution*, Jan. 14, 2008, B2.

18. *The News Hour with Jim Lehrer*, Jan. 14, 2008; *Atlanta Journal-Constitution*, Jan. 15, 2008, A5; *Washington Post*, Jan. 15, 2008, A4. See also Lewis's op-ed for Hillary, *Atlanta Journal-Constitution*, Jan. 27, 2008, E1, E4. "It is unfortunate that people have tried to distort what Mrs. Clinton had to say about Dr. King," Lewis also said. "There has been a deliberate, systematic attempt to distort what she said." *Atlanta Journal-Constitution*, Jan. 15, 2008, A5.

19. *Atlanta Journal-Constitution*, Jan. 24, 2008, A1.

20. Michael Collins, author interview, June 20, 2023.

21. Associated Press News Service, Feb. 15, 2008, 1.

22. *Atlanta Journal-Constitution*, Mar. 7, 2008, D3.

23. *Atlanta Journal-Constitution*, Jan. 16, 2008, A15.

24. Jacob Gillison, author interview, July 5, 2023; Michael Collins, author interview, June 20, 2023.

25. Jelani Cobb, author interview, July 6, 2023; Malaika Moses, author interview, July 9, 2023.

26. Rachelle O'Neil, author interview, June 15, 2023.

27. Brenda Jones, author interview, Aug. 25, 2023; Jeff Zeleny, author interview, Aug. 30, 2023; Associated Press News Service, Feb. 15, 2008, 1; *New York Times*, Feb. 15, 2008, 1; *Atlanta Journal-Constitution*, Feb. 16, 2008, A1.

28. *Atlanta Journal-Constitution*, Feb. 20, 2008.

29. Hillary Clinton, author interview, Jan. 18, 2024.

30. Carl Nelson, author interview, July 11, 2023.

31. Michael Collins, author interview, June 20, 2023; *Atlanta Journal-Constitution*, Feb. 26, 2008, A7; "A New Day," Oprah.com, n.d., https://www.oprah.com/world/oprah-talks-about-president-elect-barack-obama/; Remnick, *Bridge*, 507.

32. Jacob Gillison, author interview, July 5, 2023.

33. Hillary Clinton, author interview, Jan. 18, 2024; Bill Clinton, author interview, Oct. 18, 2023.

34. *NBC Nightly News* transcript, Feb. 27, 2008; Newsroom transcript, Feb. 27, 2008.

35. *Atlanta Journal-Constitution*, Feb. 28, 2008, A1.

36. *Atlanta Journal-Constitution*, June 8, 2008.

37. Andrew Aydin, author interview, June 22, 2021.

38. Maria Saporta, author interview, Mar. 15, 2023; James Waller, author interview, Apr. 28, 2023; Juliana Illari, author interview, Mar. 27, 2023; *New York Times*, July 1, 2008, B1; *Atlanta Journal-Constitution*, May 13, 2008, B1, June 30, 2008, July 3, 2008, D4, July 6, 2008, July 16, 2008, D5.

39. Kenneth Baer and Paul Orzulak, author interview, July 14, 2023; "Martin Luther King, Jr. Tribute," C-SPAN, Aug. 28, 2008, https://www.c-span.org/video/?280566-5/martin-luther-king-jr-tribute.

40. Andrew Aydin, author interview, July 25, 2019.

41. Berman, *Ballot*, 246.

42. *Essence*, Jan. 2009, 86, 98; "A New Day," Oprah.com; *New York Times*, Nov. 6, 2008, P6.

43. NPR, Election Night Special Coverage, Nov. 4, 2008; *New York Times*, Nov. 5, 2008, P6; "Rep. John Lewis: The Struggle Was Worth It," Nov. 4, 2008, YouTube, https://www.youtube.com/watch?v=o6rLIJpXK_o.

44. *New York Times*, Jan. 18, 2009, 27.

45. Wade Burns, author interview, Aug. 18, 2020; *New Yorker*, Feb. 2, 2009, 21–23; Remnick, *Bridge*, 575–79.

TWENTY-FIVE: ROCK STAR

1. *Rock Hill Herald*, Jan. 21, 2009, B1, Jan. 24, 2009, A1, Jan. 27, 2009, A1, Feb. 4, 2009, B1, Feb. 6, 2009, B1.

2. *Washington Post*, June 9, 1998, D1–3; *Fellowship*, Dec. 2000, 10; *Montgomery Advertiser*, Mar. 3, 2013, 1; *Atlanta Journal-Constitution*, Dec. 17, 2002, A12.

3. Bonnie Myers, author interview, Oct. 9, 2019.

4. Melanie Eversley, author interview, Jan. 25, 2020.

5. Paige Alexander, author interview, Mar. 17, 2023; Miles and Elaine Alexander, author interview, June 10, 2020.

6. Michaeleen Crowell, author interviews, Mar. 28, 2022, June 22, 2023.

7. Rachelle O'Neil, author interview, June 15, 2023.

8. McClatchy New Service, Mar. 20, 2010; Associated Press, Mar. 21, 2010; Jacob Gillison, author interview, July 5, 2023.

9. John Larson, author interview, July 18, 2023.

10. Michaeleen Crowell, author interview, June 22, 2023; John Larson, author interview, July 18, 2023; *New York Times*, Mar. 22, 2010, A17; Dowdey, dir., *Get in the Way*.

11. House Session, C-SPAN, Mar. 21, 2010, https://www.c-span.org/video/?29 2637-1/house-session.

12. "Occupy Atlanta Silences Civil Rights Hero John Lewis!," YouTube, Oct. 8, 2011, https://www.youtube.com/watch ?v=3QZlp3eGMNI; "Congressman John Lewis Visits Occupy Atlanta," YouTube, Oct. 8. 2011, https://www.youtube.com /watch?v=_XCLBNkBvL0.

13. Buddy Darden, author interview, Mar. 15, 2023; Lyn Vaughn, author interview, Mar. 14, 2023.

14. Jacob Gillison, author interview, July 5, 2023; Tom Houck, author interview, Oct. 31, 2022.

15. Michael Collins, author interview, June 20, 2023.

16. Carol Dove, author interview, July 17, 2023; Michael Bond, email to author, July 19, 2023; *Atlanta Journal-Constitution*, Jan. 8, 2013, B1.

17. Boyd Lewis, author interview, Oct. 5, 2022; Maria Saporta, author interview, Mar. 15, 2023.

18. Joan Browning, author interview, July 28, 2022.

19. Taylor Branch, author interview, Apr. 14, 2020; Taylor Branch, interview with Gregg Ivers, Sept. 7, 2018, AU-JBOHP.

20. 11alive.com, July 29, 2020; Michael Bond, author interview, Feb. 27, 2023.

21. Dowdey, dir., *Get in the Way*.

22. Bond, *Race Man*, 167.

23. Andrew Aydin, author interview, Oct. 23, 2023.

24. *New York Times*, Aug. 16, 2015, A1, B6.

25. Sean Patrick Maloney, author interview, July 28, 2023.

26. Berman, *Ballot*, 265.

27. *Shelby County v. Holder*, brief amicus curiae of John Lewis, Jan. 2013; Berman, *Ballot*, 278.

28. *Washington Post*, June 25, 2013; *Nation*, July 22–29, 2013, 6; Berman, *Ballot*, 300.

29. *Atlanta Journal-Constitution*, July 11, 2002, B1.

30. Michael Collins, author interview, Apr. 27, 2023.

31. *Publishers Weekly*, July 19, 2013; *Atlanta Journal-Constitution*, Aug. 13, 2013, D1.

32. *Atlanta Journal-Constitution*, Feb. 10, 2011, D1.

33. Nate Powell, author interview, Sept. 25, 2019; *Publishers Weekly*, July 19, 2013; *Atlanta Journal-Constitution*, Aug. 13, 2013, D1.

34. *Roll Call*, July 21, 2013; *New York Times*, Aug. 14, 2013, A11, A13.

35. *Chicago Tribune*, Aug. 23, 2013.

36. Nate Powell, author interview, Sept. 25, 2019; *Arkansas Times*, Jan. 5, 2017.

37. *Roll Call*, July 9, 2015; *American History*, Dec. 2015, 26–35.

38. Andrew Aydin, author interview, June 22, 2021; Nate Powell, author interview, Sept. 25, 2019.

39. "2016 National Book Awards," C-SPAN, Nov. 16, 2016, https://www.c-span.org/video/?417974-1/2016-national-book-awards.

40. Michael Collins, author interview, Apr. 27, 2023.

41. John Lewis, OH with Matthew Wasniewski and Jackie Burns, Dec. 11, 2014, HROH.

42. Faya Ora Rose (Sanders) Touré, author interview, Sept. 1, 2023.

43. Doug Tanner, author interviews, Apr. 23, 2020, June 21, 2023; Doug Tanner, OH with Jacqueline Burns, May 15, 2013, HROH.

44. John Lewis, OH with Matthew Wasniewski and Jackie Burns, Dec. 11, 2014, HROH; Doug Tanner, author interview, Apr. 23, 2020.

45. Doug Tanner, author interview, June 21, 2023; 144 *Cong. Rec.*, House, Mar. 17, 1998, H1211-1218.

46. *Philadelphia Inquirer*, Mar. 6, 2000, A2.

47. *Roll Call*, June 23, 2008; Smith, dir., *Come Walk in My Shoes*.

48. Eric Cantor, author interview, June 29, 2020; Kevin McCarthy, "Representative John Lewis Stamp Unveiling Ceremony," C-SPAN, June 21, 2023, https://www.c-span.org/video/?528893-1/repre sentative-john-lewis-stamp-unveiling-ceremony; Sam Brownback, author interview, June 6, 2023; Melanie Eversley, author interview, Jan. 25, 2020; John Larson, author interview, July 18, 2023; Richard Gephardt, author interview, May 19, 2023. Mike Pence, too, called crossing the bridge with his family alongside Lewis "one of the greatest memories I have of serving in the United States Congress," NBC News, YouTube, https://www.youtube.com/watch?v=AJETwSsGXc4.

49. John Lewis, OH with Matthew Wasniewski and Jackie Burns, Dec. 11, 2014, HROH.

50. Steny Hoyer, author interview, June 20, 2023.

51. Michael Collins, author interview, Apr. 27, 2023; *Atlantic*, Dec. 15, 2014.

52. Michael Collins, author interview, Apr. 27, 2023; Rachelle O'Neil, author interview, June 15, 2023; Faya Ora Rose (Sanders) Touré, author interview, Sept. 1, 2023; *Atlanta Journal-Constitution*, Mar. 1, 2015, B1.

53. *National Journal Online*, May 20, 2015.

54. Barack Obama, "Remarks at the Selma Voting Rights March Commemoration in Selma, Alabama," Mar. 7, 2015, APP-UCSB.

55. *Washington Post*, Mar. 7, 2015.

56. John Lewis, OH with Matthew Wasniewski and Jackie Burns, Dec. 11, 2014, HROH.

57. Barack Obama, author interview, Jan. 23, 2024; Valerie Jarrett, author interview, Jan. 31, 2024.

58. *National Journal Online*, May 20, 2015; Lewis with Jones, *Across That Bridge*; Andrew Aydin, author interview, July 25, 2019; Rachelle O'Neil, author interview, June 15, 2023.

59. Rachelle O'Neil, author interview, June 15, 2023; Shirley Franklin, author interview, Mar. 21, 2023.

60. Robert Cohen, email to author, Oct. 25, 2020; James Devitt, email to author, Sept. 21, 2022; Rachelle O'Neil, author interview, June 15, 2023; Danny Lyon, author interview, July 29, 2019.

61. Don Harris, author interview, Apr. 16, 2020; Stephen McDaniel, author interview, Mar. 17, 2023; Porter, dir., *Good Trouble*.

62. J. C. Watts, author interview, June 16, 2023.

TWENTY-SIX: CONSCIENCE OF THE CONGRESS

1. *Atlanta Journal-Constitution*, Oct. 7, 2015, B2, Oct. 31, 2015, A1, Nov. 8, 2015, B2; Hillary Clinton, author interview, Jan. 18, 2024.

2. Danny Lyon, author interview, July 29, 2019; *Time*, Nov. 12, 2015, Feb. 13, 2016; *Washington Post*, Feb. 13, 2016.

3. *Atlanta Journal-Constitution*, Feb. 12, 2016, A10.

4. Danny Lyon, author interview, July 29, 2019; *Jacobin*, Feb. 15, 2016; *Salon*, Feb. 22, 2016; John Lewis, "It was good to spend a few moments today playing with puppies brought to the Hill by the ASPCA," Facebook, Feb. 12, 2016; *Bleak Beauty* blog, Jan. 30, 2016, Feb. 13, 2016; *Time*, Feb. 13, 2016.

5. Hillary Clinton, author interview, Jan. 18, 2024.

6. *Atlanta Journal-Constitution*, Feb. 15, 2016. Months later, Briahna Joy Gray, a left-wing attorney and activist, tweeted about a picture of Lewis and his cats, "We know how Lewis will throw cats under the bus if it helps the DNC." Briahna Joy Gray, Twitter post, Jan. 4, 2016, https://www.tumblr.com/vettingsanders/189955184888/image-description-a-screenshot-of-a-twitter.

7. *New York Times*, Jan. 19, 2016, A18.

8. David Cicilline, author interview, June 28, 2023; John Larson, author interview, July 18, 2023; Nancy Pelosi, author interview, Apr. 30, 2020; *Politico*, June 22, 2016.

9. Nancy Pelosi, author interview, Apr. 30, 2020; Brenda Jones, author interview, Aug. 25, 2023; *Politico*, June 22, 2016.

10. "U.S. House of Representatives, Morning Hour," C-SPAN, June 22, 2016, https://www.c-span.org/video/?411500-1/morning-hour; 162 *Cong. Rec.*, House, 4065, June 22, 2016.

11. *Roll Call*, June 22, 2016.

12. Steny Hoyer, author interview, June 20, 2023.

13. David Cicilline, author interview, June 28, 2023; *Politico*, June 22, 2016.

14. *Atlanta Journal-Constitution*, June 23, 2016; "Representative John Lewis on House Sit-In," C-SPAN, June 22, 2016, https://www.c-span.org/video/?411626-101/representative-john-lewis-house-sit.

15. *Roll Call*, June 23, 2016.

16. David Cicilline, author interview, June 28, 2023.

17. Nancy Pelosi, press conference, *Political Transcript Wire*, June 23, 2016; "House Democrats Rally at U.S. Capitol," C-SPAN, June 23, 2016, ttps://www.c-span.org/video/?411709-1/house-democrats-rally-us-capitol.

18. John Lewis, author interview, May 8, 2020.

19. *Chicago Defender*, Nov. 2, 2016, 22–23.

20. Will Anderson, author interview, Feb. 25, 2024.

21. Associated Press, Nov. 19, 2016.

22. *Washington Post*, Nov. 20, 2016; Associated Press, Dec. 23, 2016.

23. He explained his thinking in more detail to *Time*. "I still believe there was a deliberate, systematic effort to subvert the political process, and I think it was a foreign power—the Russians—involved with the Trump campaign," he said. "I strongly feel that we need an independent

commission to find out what happened and how it happened, so it will never happen again. I will not be satisfied until we get the truth." *Time*, Apr. 10, 2017, 56.

24. Brenda Jones, author interview, Aug. 25, 2023.

25. Transcript, "Meet the Press Daily," MSNBC, Jan. 13, 2016.

26. Donald Trump, Twitter post, Jan. 14, 2017, https://twitter.com/realDonald Trump/status/820251730407473153?lang=en.

27. *American Prospect*, Jan. 17, 2017. Lewis was not the first member to announce he would skip the inauguration. Previously, Katherine Clark, Luis Gutierrez, Jared Huffman, and Barbara Lee had done so.

28. *Atlanta Journal-Constitution*, Jan. 22, 2017, A1.

29. Fox5Atlanta.com, Aug. 15, 2017; *The View*, ABC, Jan. 15, 2018, https://abcnews.go.com/Politics/rep-john-lewis-meeting-trump-martin-luther-king/story?id=52343117.

30. FoxNews.com, May 28, 2019; *Rolling Stone*, May 2019, 70–73.

31. David Cicilline, author interview, June 28, 2023.

32. *Windy City Times*, Oct. 18, 2017, 10. In June 2020, the Supreme Court held that sexual orientation and gender identity were already protected classes under the 1964 act. Lewis's office issued a statement quoting him saying, "Today's Supreme Court decision restores my hope in Dr. Martin Luther King, Jr.'s conviction that the arc of the moral universe is long, but it bends towards justice." *Bostock v. Clayton County*, 140 S. Ct. 1731 (2020); *Advocate*, July 30, 2020.

33. *Hill*, Apr. 11, 2007; *Roll Call*, Sept. 20, 2004, 1; *Forward*, Feb. 27, 2015, 1, 6.

34. *New York Times*, Feb. 12, 2019, A1, Feb. 14, 2019, A18.

35. Jewish News Service, July 23, 2019.

36. *New York Times*, Oct. 9, 2013, A16;

John Lewis, author interview, May 8, 2020; *Seattle Post-Intelligencer*, June 13, 2018, 1. On top of his forty arrests in the 1960s, Lewis added five during his time in Congress, protesting U.S. South African policy, immigration policy, and inaction in the face of the mass slaughters in the Darfur region of Sudan.

37. John Lewis, author interview, May 8, 2020.

38. Rachelle O'Neil, author interview, June 15, 2023; Michael Collins, author interview, Apr. 8, 2022; Stephen McDaniel, author interview, Mar. 17, 2023; Brenda Jones, author interview, Aug. 25, 2023; Ghana Web, Aug. 4, 2023.

39. Rachelle O'Neil, author interview, June 15, 2023.

40. *Atlanta Journal-Constitution*, July 30, 2018, Aug. 2, 2018; *Washington Post*, July 30, 2018.

41. Danny Lyon, author interviews, Oct. 13, 2020, Aug. 21, 2023; Lyon, dir., *SNCC*.

42. Danny Lyon, author interview, Jan. 18, 2020; Brenda Jones, author interview, Aug. 25, 2023.

43. Porter, dir., *Good Trouble*.

44. Ball, *Pelosi*, 283; Pelosi, dir., *Pelosi in the House*.

45. Nancy Pelosi, author interview, Apr. 30, 2020.

46. *Politico*, Sept. 12, 2019.

47. *New Yorker*, Sept. 25, 2019; Ball, *Pelosi*, 312.

48. *Morning Hour*, C-SPAN, Sept. 24, 2019, https://www.c-span.org/video/?464571-1/morning-hour.

TWENTY-SEVEN: LION IN WINTER

1. *Washington Informer*, July 29, 2020; Michael Collins, author interview, Apr. 8, 2022.

2. Michael Collins, author interview, Apr. 8, 2022.

3. Michael Collins, author interview, Apr. 8, 2022.

4. Michael Collins, author interview, Apr. 8, 2022, June 20, 2023; Steny Hoyer, author interview, June 20, 2023.

5. Nancy Pelosi, author interview, Apr. 30, 2020.

6. U.S. House of Representatives, "House Debate on Articles of Impeachment Against President Trump," C-SPAN, Dec. 18, 2023, https://www.c-span.org/video/?467441-1/house-debate-articles-impeachment-president-trump.

7. Stephen McDaniel, author interview, Mar. 17, 2023.

8. Tuere Butler, author interview, June 5, 2023.

9. Rachelle O'Neil, author interview, June 15, 2023.

10. *Axios*, Dec. 29, 2019.

11. Brenda Jones, author interview, Aug. 25, 2023; *Atlanta Journal-Constitution*, Jan. 1, 2020.

12. Don Harris, author interview, Apr. 16, 2020; Howard Brown, author interview, Aug. 9, 2023.

13. Michael Collins, author interviews, Apr. 8, 2022, Sept. 2, 2023; Jacob Gillison, author interviews, Apr. 29, 2020, July 5, 2023; Keith Washington, author interview, July 24, 2023.

14. Tom Houck, author interview, Feb. 19, 2020.

15. Danny Lyon, author interview, Jan. 18, 2020.

16. John Lewis, interview with Danny Lyon, Jan. 14, 2020; James Clyburn, author interview, Jan. 27, 2020, DLT; Nancy Pelosi, author interview, Apr. 30, 2020.

17. Howard Brown, author interview, Aug. 9, 2023.

18. Howard Brown, author interview, Aug. 9, 2023.

19. *Washington Post*, June 19, 2021; Tom Houck, author interview, Feb. 19, 2020.

20. Michael Collins, author interview, Apr. 27, 2023.

21. Michael Collins, author interview, Apr. 27, 2023.

22. Tia Mitchell, author interview, Mar. 4, 2020; "John Lewis Returns to Selma on 55th Anniversary of March," CNN video, YouTube.

23. Peggy Wallace Kennedy to John Lewis, Apr. 17, 2020, PWKPP.

24. Michael Collins, author interview, Apr. 27, 2023; Stephen McDaniel, author interview, Mar. 17, 2023.

25. Nancy Pelosi, author interview, Apr. 30, 2020; Mike Levin, Twitter post, Mar. 3, 2020, 4:56 p.m.

26. Michael Collins, author interview, Apr. 27, 2023.

27. Jonathan Capehart, author interview, June 16, 2020; James Lawson, author interview, Mar. 30, 2020; "On the Road to Montgomery and Selma with Rev. James Lawson Jr.," UCLA Labor Center, Mar. 12, 2020 (online).

28. *New York Times*, May 16, 2020, A23.

29. Tom Houck, author interview, May 21, 2020.

30. Jon Ossoff, author interview, July 28, 2023.

31. "Rep. John Lewis Says Video of George Floyd's Death Moved Him to Tears," CBS News, June 4, 2020.

32. Michael Collins, author interview, Apr. 8, 2022.

33. CBS46.com, May 30, 2020.

34. *Atlanta Journal-Constitution*, May 31, 2020.

35. "James Clyburn Says He and John Lewis Feared 'Defund the Police' Would Undermine Black Lives Matter Movement," CBS News, Nov. 9, 2020.

36. Brenda Jones, author interview, Aug. 25, 2023.

37. "Rep. John Lewis Says Video of George Floyd's Death Moved Him to Tears," CBS News, June 4, 2020.

38. Michael Collins, author interview, Apr. 8, 2022; Jonathan Capehart, author interview, June 16, 2020; Gary Williams, author interview, June 18, 2020; Stephanie Ramirez (@RamirezReports), Twitter post, June 7, 2020, 7:46 a.m., https://twitter.com/ramirezreports/status/1269596517012307970.

39. Michael Collins, author interview, Apr. 8, 2022.

40. Michael Collins, author interview, Apr. 8, 2022.

41. Danny Lyon, author interview, July 9, 2020; Michael Collins, author interview, Apr. 8, 2022; Stephen McDaniel, author interview, Mar. 17, 2023.

42. Michael Collins, author interview, Apr. 8, 2022; Nancy Pelosi, remarks, John Lewis funeral, C-SPAN, July 30, 2020, https://www.c-span.org/video/?474223-1/representative-john-lewis-funeral-service-atlanta-georgia.

43. Bill Clinton, author interview, Oct. 18, 2023.

44. Jacob Gillison, author interview, July 5, 2023.

45. Michael Bond, author interview, Feb. 27, 2023.

46. Kevin McCarthy, "Representative John Lewis Stamp Unveiling Ceremony," C-SPAN, June 21, 2023, https://www.c-span.org/video/?528893-1/representative-john-lewis-stamp-unveiling-ceremony.

47. Anthony Coley, author interview, Sept. 11, 2023; Kathleen Kingsbury, author interview, Sept. 15, 2023; *New York Times*, July 30, 2020; Kathleen Kingsbury, Twitter posts, July 30, 2020, https://twitter.com/katiekings/status/1288813849643278337.

48. Michael Collins, author interview, Sept. 6, 2023.

TWENTY-EIGHT: INVICTUS

1. Stephen McDaniel, author interview, Mar. 17, 2023; Anthony Coley, author interview, Sept. 11, 2023.

2. Stephen McDaniel, author interview, Mar. 17, 2023.

3. *Washington Post*, Aug. 4, 2020.

4. *New York Times*, July 30, 2020, A23.

5. John Lewis funeral, C-SPAN, July 30, 2020, https://www.c-span.org/video/?474223-1/representative-john-lewis-funeral-service-atlanta-georgia.

6. CreativeLoafing.com, Aug. 20, 2020; HipHopWired.com, Oct. 29, 2020; BleedingCool.com, July 26, 2022; *Milwaukee Community Journal*, Jan. 5, 2021; *Nashville Tennessean*, Nov. 9, 2020.

7. CNN.com, July 19, 2020; *New York Times*, July 21, 2020.

8. *Washington Post*, Nov. 6, 2020.

BIBLIOGRAPHY

Government documents and primary periodical sources are listed in the notes.

ARCHIVAL COLLECTIONS

Atlanta University Center Robert W. Woodruff Library (AUC-RWWL)
   Lillian Miles Lewis Papers (LMLP)
   Voter Education Project Papers (VEPP)
Auburn Avenue Research Library (AARL)
   Andrew J. Young Papers (AJYP)
Boston University, Howard Gotlieb Archival Research Center (BU)
   David Halberstam Papers (DHP)
William J. Clinton Presidential Library (WJCPL)
   Clinton Presidential Records: Speechwriting, Jeff Shesol Papers (JSP)
Dirksen Congressional Center (DCC)
   Todd Purdum Papers (TPP)
Duke University (DU)
   Donald Harris Papers (DHP)
   Judy Richardson Papers (JRP)
Emory University, Stuart A. Rose Manuscript, Archives, and Rare Book Library (EU)
   Dan T. Carter Papers (DTCP)
   Leslie Dunbar Papers (LDP)
   Paul Good Papers (PGP)
   Jack Nelson Papers (JNP)
   Southern Christian Leadership Conference Papers (SCLCP)
   C. T. and Octavia Vivian Papers (CTOVP)
Gerald R. Ford Presidential Library (GRFPL)
   James M. Cannon Files (JMCF)
Lyndon B. Johnson Library (LBJL)
   Civil Rights During the Johnson Administration, Records of the White House
      Conference on Civil Rights, 1965–1966 (CRDJA-WHCCR)
   John Lewis Name File (JRLNF)
   President's Daily Diary (PDD)
   White House Central Files (WHCF)

John F. Kennedy Library (JFKL)
    Burke Marshall Personal Papers (BMPP)
    Jean Stein Personal Papers (JSPP)
    President's Office Files (POF)
    White House Central Files (WHCF)
    White House Staff Files, Lee White (WHSF-LW)
    White House Staff Files, Harris Wofford (WHSF-HW)
Library of Congress (LC)
    James Forman Papers (JFP)
    Student Nonviolent Coordinating Committee Papers (SNCCP)
Nashville Public Library (NPL)
    Angeline Butler Diaries (ABD)
    Archie Allen Collection (AAC)
    Civil Rights Ephemera Collection (CREC)
    Civil Rights Periodical Collection (CRPC)
    Highlander Folk School Collection (HFSC)
    Metro Government Archives, Human Relations Commission (MGA-HRC)
    Nashville Banner Files (NBF)
National Archives and Records Administration (NARA)
    ACTION Record Group 362
    FBI Record Group 65, Series 44, File Unit 28492, Section 1, Serials 1-42
    FBI Record Group 65, Series 44, File Unit 32138, Section 1, Serials X-7.
New York Public Library, Stephen A. Schwartzman Building (NYPL)
    Arthur M. Schlesinger Jr. Papers (AMSP)
New York Public Library, Schomburg Center for Research in Black Culture
    (NYPL-SC)
    Ella Baker Papers (EBP)
    Bureau of Social Science Research Files (BSSR)
    Catherine Clark Collection (CCC)
    August Meier Papers (AMP)
    Moving Image and Recorded Sound Division (MIRSD)
    Roberta Yancy Papers (RYP)
Northwestern University (NU)
    Al From Papers (AFP)
Tennessee State Library and Archives (TSLA)
    Highlander Folk School Audio Collection (HFSAC)
University of North Carolina, Wilson Library (UNC)
    Taylor Branch Papers (TBP)
University of South Florida (USF)
    Steven F. Lawson Papers (SFLP)
University of Southern Mississippi, McCain Library and Archives (USM)
    Will Campbell Papers (WCP)
    Sam Shirah Papers (SSP)
University of Virginia (UVA)
    Horace Julian Bond Papers (HJBP)

Vanderbilt University (VU)
    James M. Lawson Papers (JMLP)
    Salynn McCollum Papers (SMP)
    John Seigenthaler Papers (JSP)
    Kelly Miller Smith Papers (KMSP)
University of Wisconsin (UW)
    Highlander Research and Education Center Records (HRECR)

INTERNET-BASED ARCHIVAL COLLECTIONS, INCLUDING VIDEO ARCHIVES AND SUBSCRIPTION DATABASES

American Archive of Public Broadcasting (AAPB)
    Firing Line Broadcasts (FLB)
    Freedom Riders Interviews (FRI)
    PBS News Hour (PBSNH)
Atlanta History Center (AHC)
    Kenan Research Center Digital Resources (KRCDR)
Charlie Rose Show Archives
Civil Rights Movement Archive (CRMVET)
C-SPAN Archives
FBI Records: The Vault (FBI-V)
    H. Julian Bond (HJB)
    James Farmer (JF)
    Stokely Carmichael (SC)
Gale Archives Unbound: African American Studies (GAU-AAS)
    FBI Bureau Files (FBI-BF)
    FBI Case Files (FBI-CF)
Mississippi Department of Archives and History (MDAH)
    Mississippi State Sovereignty Commission (MSSC)
ProQuest History Vault: The Black Freedom Struggle in the 20th Century (HV)
    A. Philip Randolph Papers
    Bayard Rustin Papers
    Centers of the Southern Struggle: FBI Files on Montgomery, Albany, St. Augustine, Selma, and Memphis
    Congress of Racial Equality Papers
    Papers of the National Association for the Advancement of Colored People
    Records of the Southern Christian Leadership Conference
    Records of the Interstate Commerce Commission on Discrimination in Transportation
    Student Nonviolent Coordinating Committee Papers
SNCC Digital Gateway (SNCC-DG)
Stanford University (SU)
    Martin Luther King, Jr. Research & Education Institute
University of California, Santa Barbara (UCSB)
    American Presidency Project (APP)

University of Georgia, Walter J. Brown Media Archives (UGA-WJBMA)
    WSB-TV Newsfilm Collection
University of Virginia (UVA)
    Explorations in Black Leadership (EBL)
    Presidential Recordings Digital Edition (PRDE)
Wisconsin Historical Society (WHS)
    Stewart Ewen Papers (SEP)
    Mary E. King Papers (MEKP)
    Mississippi Freedom Democratic Party Records (MFDPR)
    Social Vertical Action File COFO Papers (SVAF-COFO)
    Social Vertical Action File SNCC Papers (SVAF-SNCC)
    Howard Zinn Papers (HZP)
    War Resisters International Papers (WRIP)

COLLECTIONS OF INTERVIEWS AND ORAL HISTORIES

American University (AU)
    Julian Bond Oral History Project (JBOHP)
William Breman Jewish Heritage Museum (WBJHM)
    Esther and Herbert Taylor Jewish Oral History Project of Atlanta (JOHPA)
Columbia University, Rare Book and Manuscript Library (CU)
    Oral History Collection (OHC)
Fordham University (FU)
    McGannon Center TV Oral History Project (MCTVOHP)
House of Representatives, Office of the Historian (HROH)
Howard University, Moorland-Spingarn Research Center (HU-MSRC)
    Ralph J. Bunche Oral History Collection (RJBOHC)
John F. Kennedy Library (JFKL)
    Oral History Collection (OHC)
    Robert F. Kennedy Oral History Collection (RFK-OHC)
Library of Congress (LC)
    Civil Rights History Project Collection, Archive of Folk Culture (CRHPC-AFC)
    Voices of Civil Rights Project Collection (VCRPC)
Nashville Public Library (NPL)
    Civil Rights Oral History Collection (CROHC)
    Archie Allen Collection (AAC)
New York Public Library (NYPL)
    American Jewish Committee, Oral History Library (AJC-OHL)
Rutgers University (RU)
    Oral History Archives (OHA)
University of California, Los Angeles (UCLA)
    Center for Oral History Research (COHR)
University of Georgia, Richard B. Russell Library for Political Research & Studies
    (UGA-RBRL)
    Oral History Program (OHP)

University of North Carolina at Chapel Hill (UNC)
    Southern Oral History Program (SOHP)
Washington University, Henry Hampton Collection (WU-HHC)
    Eyes on the Prize Interviews (EPI)
WGBH Open Vault (WGBH-OV)
    Freedom Riders Interviews (FRI)
Wisconsin State Historical Society (WHS)
    Anne Romaine Interviews, 1966–1967 (ARI)
Vanderbilt University, Robert Penn Warren Center for the Humanities (VU-RPWCH)
    Who Speaks for the Negro Collection (WSNC)

PRIVATE MATERIALS SHARED WITH AUTHOR

Miles Alexander Private Papers (MAPP)
Archie Allen Private Papers (AAPP)
Finding Your Roots Research Materials (FYRRM)
Sherry Frank Private Papers (SFPP)
Parker Hudson Private Papers (PHPP)
Peggy Wallace Kennedy Private Papers (PWKPP)
David Kotelchuck Private Papers (DKPP)
Richard Momeyer Private Papers (RMPP)
Walter Naegle Private Papers (WNPP)
Debbie Spielberg Private Papers (DSPP)
Doug Tanner Private Papers (DTPP)
Ruth Wall Private Papers (RWPM)

PRIVATE INTERVIEWS SHARED WITH AUTHOR

Archie Allen Tapes (AAT)
Evan Faulkenbury Interview (EFI)
Ben Hedin Interviews (BHI)
Mark Lipman Interview (MLI)
Danny Lyon Tapes (DLT)
David Margolick Interview (DMI)
Gregg Michel Interview (GMI)
Aaron David Miller Interview (ADMI)
Maureen Orth Video Interview (MOVI)
Laura Visser-Maessen Interview (LVMI)
Sean Wilentz Tapes (SWT)

AUTHOR INTERVIEWS

Sharon Adams; Terry Adamson; Elaine Alexander; Kent Alexander; Miles Alexander; Paige Alexander; Archie Allen; Will Anderson; Andrew Aydin; Kenneth Baer; Joan Baez; Rob Bassin; Paul Begala; Harry Belafonte; Ruth Berg; Terry Bird; Clarence

Bishop; David Black; Sidney Blumenthal; Michael Julian Bond; David Bonior; Judy Bonior; Peter Bourne; Tammy Boyd; Cathy Bradshaw; Taylor Branch; Howard Brown; Sam Brown; Sam Brownback; Joan Browning; Joe Bryan; Wade Burns; Angeline Butler; Tuere Parham Butler; Eric Cantor; Jonathan Capehart; Candie Carawan; Robert Caro; Linda Earley Chastang; David Cicilline; Colia Clark; William Clay (email); Bill Clinton; Hillary Clinton; James Clyburn; Charlie Cobb; Jelani Cobb; Dianne Cohen; Richard Cohen; Robert Cohen (email); Anthony Coley; Sam Collier; Love Collins; Michael Collins; Larry Copeland; Courtland Cox; Harvey Cox; Michaeleen Crowell; George "Buddy" Darden; Paul Delaney; Menna Demessie; James Devitt (email); Morse Diggs; Sally Dorn; Michael D'Orso; Carol Dove; Kathleen Dowdey; George Dusenbury; Stuart Eizenstat; Mike Espy; Melanie Eversley; June Fair; James Fallows; Heather Fenton; Tina Flournoy; Harold Ford; Wyche Fowler; Barney Frank; Lois Frank; Sherry Frank; Shirley Franklin; Jim Free; Al From; Marian Fuson; Richard Gephardt; Judi Gerhardt; Michael German; Gordon Giffin; Jacob Gillison; Sally Haderline; Kwanza Hall; Bill Hansen; Jane Harman; Don Harris; Scott Harris; Casey Hayden; Dave Hayward; Hendrik Hertzberg; Susannah Heschel; Brian Higgins; Phyllis Hildreth; Norman Hill; Elizabeth Holtzman; Rachelle Horowitz; Vencen Horsley; Tom Houck; Steny Hoyer; Parker Hudson; Richard Hyde; Juliana Illari; Danielle Isaacs; Steven Isenberg; Richard E. Jackson; Valerie Jarrett; Anthony Johnson; Charles S. Johnson; Brenda Jones; Rock Jones; Hannah Jopling; Kelly Jordan; Vernon Jordan; Robert Kaiser; Peggy Wallace Kennedy; Mary King; Spencer King; Kathleen Kingsbury; David Kotelchuck; Sharlene Kranz; Robert Krasner; George Kundanis; Joyce Ladner; Bernard LaFayette; Josh Lamel; Joe Larche; John Larson; John Lawrence; James Lawson; Patrick Leahy; Clark Lemmons; Boyd Lewis; Henry Grant Lewis; John Lewis; Sam Lewis; Brad Lichtenstein; Al Lingo; Miryam Lipper; Mike Long; Staughton Lynd; Danny Lyon; Sean Patrick Maloney; Ty Manning; Russ Marane; Will Marshall (email); Keith Mason; Stephen McDaniel; Tara McDaniel; Arnie Miller; Lorraine Miller; Mary Ann Miller; Mike Miller; Bradley Mims; Tia Mitchell; David Mixner (email); Richard Momeyer; Sue Momeyer; Joan Mooney; Frank Moore; David Morrison; Malaika Moses; Robert Parris Moses; Carol Muldawer; Cherie Murdock; Bonnie Myers; William Myers; Walter Naegle (email); Richard Neal; Carl Nelson; Eleanor Holmes Norton; Lynn Nottage; Barack Obama; Kristin Oblander; Denis O'Hayer; Rachelle O'Neil; Paul Orzulak; Jon Ossoff; Richard Ossoff; Karen Paget; Nancy Pelosi; Martin Peretz; John Podesta; Dawn Porter; Nate Powell; Thomas Powers (email); Howard Raines; Charles Rangel; Bill Richardson; Judy Richardson; Gene Roberts; Howard Romaine; Kevin Ross; Maria Saporta; Steve Schapiro; Arlie Schardt; Phil Schlechter; Nancy Schwartz; Alan Secrest; John Seigenthaler; Jim Sensenbrenner; Joanne Sheehan; Jeff Shesol; Doug Shipman; Norman Siegel; Steve Slotin; Frank Smith; Debbie Spielberg; Nancy Stearns; Ron Sullivan; Marge Tabankin; Doug Tanner; Nick Taylor; Hank Thomas; Sue Thrasher; Muriel Tillinghast; Jeffrey Toobin; Faya Ora Rose (Sanders) Touré; Kathleen Kennedy Townsend; Calvin Trillin; Cynthia Tucker; Anne Tumlinson; Maria Varela; Lyn Vaughn; Kim Walker; Ruth Wall; Gale Walldorff; James Waller; Keith Washington; J. C. Watts; Cora Weiss; Peter Weiss; Burton Wides; Robert Wilkins; Gary Williams; James Williams; Mignon Morman Willis; Alan Wolfe; Sean Wilentz; Andrew Young; LaRochelle Murray Young; Jeff Zeleny; Bob Zellner; Dorothy Zellner; Ron Zirpoli; Jim Zwerg.

BOOKS

Adams, Frank. *Unearthing Seeds of Fire: The Idea of Highlander*. Winston-Salem, NC: John F. Blair, 1986.

Ahmann, Mathew, ed. *The New Negro*. Notre Dame, IN: Fides, 1961.

Allen, Frederick. *Atlanta Rising: The Invention of an International City, 1946–1996*. Atlanta: Longstreet Press, 1996.

Allen, James, ed. *Without Sanctuary: Lynching Photography in America*. Santa Fe: Twin Palms, 2000.

Anderson, Carol. *One Person, No Vote: How Voter Suppression Is Destroying Our Democracy*. New York: Bloomsbury, 2018.

Anderson, Jervis. *A. Philip Randolph: A Biographical Portrait*. Berkeley: University of California Press, 1986.

———. *Bayard Rustin: Troubles I've Seen: A Biography*. New York: HarperCollins, 1997.

Applebome, Peter. *Dixie Rising: How the South Is Shaping American Values, Politics and Culture*. New York: Times Books, 1996.

Arsenault, Raymond. *Freedom Riders: 1961 and the Struggle for Racial Justice*. New York: Oxford University Press, 2006.

Asim, Jabari, and Earl B. Lewis. *Preaching to the Chickens: The Story of Young John Lewis*. New York: Nancy Paulsen Books, 2016.

Baer, Kenneth S. *Reinventing Democrats: The Politics of Liberalism from Reagan to Clinton*. Lawrence: University Press of Kansas, 2000.

Ball, Molly. *Pelosi*. New York: Henry Holt, 2020.

Ball, Thomas E. *Julian Bond vs. John Lewis*. Roswell, GA: W. H. Wolfe Associates, 1988.

Barnouw, Erik. *Tube of Plenty: The Evolution of American Television*. New York: Oxford University Press, 1990.

Bayor, Ronald H. *Race and the Shaping of Twentieth-Century Atlanta*. Chapel Hill: University of North Carolina Press, 2000.

Beardslee, William R. *The Way Out Must Lead In: Life Histories in the Civil Rights Movement*. Westport, CT: L. Hill, 1983.

Behnken, Brian D., Gregory D. Smithers, and Simon Wendt, eds. *Black Intellectual Thought in Modern America: A Historical Perspective*. Jackson: University Press of Mississippi, 2017.

Belafonte, Harry, and Michael Shnayerson. *My Song: A Memoir of Art, Race, and Defiance*. New York: Alfred A. Knopf, 2011.

Belfrage, Sally. *Freedom Summer*. Charlottesville: University Press of Virginia, 1965.

Berman, Ari. *Give Us the Ballot: The Modern Struggle for Voting Rights in America*. New York: Farrar, Straus and Giroux, 2015.

Bernstein, Barton J., and Allen J. Matusow. *Twentieth-Century America: Recent Interpretations*. New York: Harcourt Brace Jovanovich, 1972.

Bird, Kai. *The Outlier: The Unfinished Presidency of Jimmy Carter*. New York: Crown, 2021.

Blake, John. *Children of the Movement*. Chicago: Lawrence Hill Books, 2007.

Bodroghkozy, Aniko. *Equal Time: Television and the Civil Rights Movement*. Urbana: University of Illinois Press, 2013.

Bond, Julian. *A Time to Speak, a Time to Act: The Movement in Politics*. New York: Simon & Schuster, 1972.

Bond, Julian, and Michael G. Long, eds. *Race Man: The Collected Works of Julian Bond*. San Francisco: City Lights Books, 2020.

Boomhower, Ray E. *Robert F. Kennedy and the 1968 Indiana Primary*. Bloomington: Indiana University Press, 2008.

Bourne, Peter G. *Jimmy Carter: A Comprehensive Biography from Plains to Post-Presidency*. New York: Scribner, 1997.

Branch, Taylor. *At Canaan's Edge: America in the King Years, 1965–68*. New York: Simon & Schuster, 2006.

——. *Parting the Waters: America in the King Years, 1954–63*. New York: Simon & Schuster, 1988.

——. *Pillar of Fire: America in the King Years, 1963–65*. New York: Simon & Schuster, 1998.

Brauer, Carl M. *John F. Kennedy and the Second Reconstruction*. New York: Columbia University Press, 1977.

Broderick, Francis L., and August Meier. *Negro Protest Thought in the Twentieth Century*. Indianapolis: Bobbs-Merrill, 1966.

Brown-Nagin, Tomiko. *Courage to Dissent: Atlanta and the Long History of the Civil Rights Movement*. New York: Oxford University Press, 2011.

Bruce, Preston. *From the Door of the White House*. New York: Lothrop, Lee & Shepard, 1984.

Bruner, Richard. *Black Politicians*. New York: David McKay, 1971.

Bryant, Nick. *The Bystander: John F. Kennedy and the Struggle for Black Equality*. New York: Basic Books, 2006.

Bunch, Lonnie G. *A Fool's Errand: Creating the National Museum of African American History and Culture in the Age of Bush, Obama, and Trump*. Washington, DC: Smithsonian Books, 2019.

Burner, Eric. *And Gently He Shall Lead Them: Robert Parris Moses and Civil Rights in Mississippi*. New York: New York University Press, 1994.

Cagin, Seth, and Philip Dray. *We Are Not Afraid: The Story of Goodman, Schwerner, and Chaney and the Civil Rights Campaign for Mississippi*. New York: Macmillan, 1988.

Canon, David T. *Race, Redistricting, and Representation: The Unintended Consequences of Black Majority Districts*. Chicago: University of Chicago Press, 1999.

Carawan, Guy, and Candie Carawan, eds. *Sing for Freedom: The Story of the Civil Rights Movement Through Its Songs*. Bethlehem, PA: Sing Out Corp., 1990.

Carmichael, Stokely, with Ekwueme Michael Thelwell. *Ready for Revolution: The Life and Struggles of Stokely Carmichael*. New York: Scribner, 2003.

Carroll, Fred. *Race News: Black Journalists and the Fight for Racial Justice in the Twentieth Century*. Urbana: University of Illinois Press, 2017.

Carson, Clayborne. *In Struggle: SNCC and the Black Awakening of the 1960s*. Cambridge, MA: Harvard University Press, 1981.

——, ed. *The Student Voice, 1960–1965: Periodical of the Student Nonviolent Coordinating Committee*. Westport, CT: Meckler, 1990.

Carter, Dan T. *The Politics of Rage: George Wallace, the Origins of the New Conservatism, and the Transformation of American Politics*. Baton Rouge: Louisiana State University Press, 2000.

Carter, Daryl A. *Brother Bill: President Clinton and the Politics of Race and Class*. Fayetteville: University of Arkansas Press, 2016.

Carter, David C. *The Music Has Gone out of the Movement: Civil Rights and the Johnson Administration, 1965–1968*. Chapel Hill: University of North Carolina Press, 2014.

Catsam, Derek. *Freedom's Main Line: The Journey of Reconciliation and the Freedom Rides*. Lexington: University Press of Kentucky, 2009.

Chafe, William H. *Civilities and Civil Rights: Greensboro, North Carolina, and the Black Struggle for Freedom*. New York: Oxford University Press, 1980.

Chappell, David L. *A Stone of Hope: Prophetic Religion and the Death of Jim Crow*. Chapel Hill: University of North Carolina Press, 2004.

———. *Waking from the Dream: The Struggle for Civil Rights in the Shadow of Martin Luther King, Jr.* New York: Random House, 2014.

Clarke, Thurston. *The Last Campaign: Robert F. Kennedy and 82 Days That Inspired America*. New York: Henry Holt, 2008.

Cobb, Charles E. *On the Road to Freedom: A Guided Tour of the Civil Rights Trail*. Chapel Hill, NC: Algonquin Books of Chapel Hill, 2008.

Cole, Eddie Rice. *The Campus Color Line: College Presidents and the Struggle for Black Freedom*. Princeton, NJ: Princeton University Press, 2022.

Colley, Zoe A. *Ain't Scared of Your Jail: Arrest, Imprisonment, and the Civil Rights Movement*. Gainesville: University Press of Florida, 2014.

Colton, Elizabeth O. *The Jackson Phenomenon: The Man, the Power, the Message*. New York: Doubleday, 1989.

Conkin, Paul Keith, Henry Lee Swint, and Patricia S. Miletich. *Gone with the Ivy: A Biography of Vanderbilt University*. Knoxville: University of Tennessee Press, 1985.

Coski, John M. *The Confederate Battle Flag: America's Most Embattled Emblem*. Cambridge, MA: Harvard University Press, 2006.

Cunningham, Megan. *The Art of the Documentary: Ten Conversations with Leading Directors, Cinematographers, Editors, and Producers*. Berkeley, CA: New Riders, 2005.

Curry, Constance, et al., eds. *Deep in Our Hearts: Nine White Women in the Freedom Movement*. Athens: University of Georgia Press, 2002.

Daniels, Maurice Charles. *Saving the Soul of Georgia: Donald L. Hollowell and the Struggle for Civil Rights*. Athens: University of Georgia Press, 2013.

Delmez, Kathryn E., John Lewis, Linda T. Wynn, and Susan H. Edwards, eds. *We Shall Overcome: Press Photographs of Nashville During the Civil Rights Era*. Nashville: Vanderbilt University Press, 2018.

D'Emilio, John. *Lost Prophet: The Life and Times of Bayard Rustin*. Chicago: University of Chicago Press, 2003.

Deutsch, Stephanie. *You Need a Schoolhouse: Booker T. Washington, Julius Rosenwald, and the Building of Schools for the Segregated South*. Evanston, IL: Northwestern University Press, 2015.

Dittmer, John. *Local People: The Struggle for Civil Rights in Mississippi*. Urbana: University of Illinois Press, 1994.

Divine, Robert A. *The Johnson Years, Vol. 3: LBJ at Home and Abroad.* Lawrence: University Press of Kansas, 1994.

Donaldson, Gary A. *Liberalism's Last Hurrah: The Presidential Campaign of 1964.* New York: Skyhorse, 2016.

Dowd, Douglas F., and Mary D. Nichols, eds. *Step by Step: Evolution and Operation of the Cornell Students' Civil-Rights Project in Tennessee, Summer, 1964.* New York: W. W. Norton, 1965.

Doyle, Don H. *Nashville Since the 1920s.* Knoxville: University of Tennessee Press, 1985.

Duberman, Martin. *Howard Zinn: A Life on the Left.* New York: New Press, 2013.

Dudziak, Mary L. *Cold War Civil Rights: Race and the Image of American Democracy.* Princeton, NJ: Princeton University Press, 2000.

Dunbar, Tony. *Leslie W. Dunbar: Reflections by Friends.* Montgomery, AL: New South Books, 2016.

Egerton, John. *A Mind to Stay Here: Profiles from the South.* New York: Macmillan, 1970.

Eig, Jonathan. *King: A Life.* New York: Farrar, Straus and Giroux, 2023.

Etheridge, Eric. *Breach of Peace: Portraits of the 1961 Mississippi Freedom Riders.* New York: Atlas, 2008.

Euchner, Charles C. *Nobody Turn Me Around: A People's History of the 1963 March on Washington.* Boston: Beacon Press, 2010.

Evans, Sara M. *Personal Politics: The Roots of Women's Liberation in the Civil Rights Movement and the New Left.* New York: Alfred A. Knopf, 1979.

Fager, Charles. *Selma, 1965.* New York: Scribner, 1974.

Fairclough, Adam. *To Redeem the Soul of America: The Southern Christian Leadership Conference and Martin Luther King, Jr.* Athens: University of Georgia Press, 2001.

Farmer, James. *Lay Bare the Heart: An Autobiography of the Civil Rights Movement.* Fort Worth: Texas Christian University Press, 1985.

Faulkenbury, Evan. *Poll Power: The Voter Education Project and the Movement for the Ballot in the American South.* Chapel Hill: University of North Carolina Press, 2019.

Fenno, Richard F. *Going Home: Black Representatives and Their Constituents.* Chicago: University of Chicago Press, 2003.

Fischbach, Michael R. *Black Power and Palestine: Transnational Countries of Color.* Stanford, CA: Stanford University Press, 2019.

Fitzgerald, Michael W. *Reconstruction in Alabama: From Civil War to Redemption in the Cotton South.* Baton Rouge: Louisiana State University Press, 2017.

Flamm, Michael W. *In the Heat of the Summer: The New York Riots of 1964 and the War on Crime.* Philadelphia: University of Pennsylvania Press, 2017.

Fleming, Cynthia Griggs. *Soon We Will Not Cry: The Liberation of Ruby Doris Smith Robinson.* Lanham, MD: Rowman & Littlefield, 2000.

Forman, James. *Sammy Younge, Jr.: The First Black College Student to Die in the Black Liberation Movement.* New York: Grove Press, 1968.

———. *The Making of Black Revolutionaries: A Personal Account.* New York: Macmillan, 1972.

Frady, Marshall. *Jesse: The Life and Pilgrimage of Jesse Jackson.* New York: Simon & Schuster, 2006.

From, Al, and Alice McKeon. *The New Democrats and the Return to Power.* New York: Palgrave Macmillan, 2013.

Gaillard, Frye. *Cradle of Freedom: Alabama and the Movement That Changed America*. Tuscaloosa: University of Alabama Press, 2015.

Garrow, David J. *Bearing the Cross: Martin Luther King, Jr., and the Southern Christian Leadership Conference*. New York: William Morrow, 1986.

———. *Protest at Selma: Martin Luther King, Jr., and the Voting Rights Act of 1965*. New Haven, CT: Yale University Press, 1978.

———, ed. *We Shall Overcome: The Civil Rights Movement in the United States in the 1950's and 1960's: Martin Luther King, Jr. and the Civil Rights Movement*, vols. 4–6. Brooklyn, NY: Carlson, 1989.

Gelbman, Shamira Michal. *The Civil Rights Lobby: The Leadership Conference on Civil Rights and the Second Reconstruction*. Philadelphia: Temple University Press, 2021.

Gentile, Thomas. *March on Washington, August 28, 1963*. Washington, DC: New Day, 1983.

Gillespie, Andra. *Whose Black Politics? Cases in Post-Racial Black Leadership*. New York: Routledge, 2010.

Gillette, Howard. *Class Divide: Yale '64 and the Conflicted Legacy of the Sixties*. Ithaca, NY: Cornell University Press, 2015.

Gillon, Steven M. *The Democrats' Dilemma: Walter F. Mondale and the Liberal Legacy*. New York: Columbia University Press, 1992.

Gilpin, Patrick J., and Marybeth Gasman. *Charles S. Johnson: Leadership Beyond the Veil in the Age of Jim Crow*. Albany: State University of New York Press, 2003.

Glen, John M. *Highlander: No Ordinary School 1932–1962*. Lexington: University Press of Kentucky, 2015.

Goudsouzian, Aram. *Down to the Crossroads: Civil Rights, Black Power, and the Meredith March Against Fear*. New York: Farrar, Straus and Giroux, 2014.

Grant, Joanne. *Ella Baker: Freedom Bound*. New York: Wiley, 1998.

Gray, Fred D. *Bus Ride to Justice: Changing the System by the System: The Life and Works of Fred Gray, Preacher, Attorney, Politician*. Montgomery, AL: New South Books, 2013.

Greenberg, Cheryl Lynn, ed. *A Circle of Trust: Remembering SNCC*. New Brunswick, NJ: Rutgers University Press, 1998.

———. *Troubling the Waters: Black-Jewish Relations in the American Century*. Princeton, NJ: Princeton University Press, 2006.

Greene, Melissa Fay. *The Temple Bombing*. Cambridge, MA: Da Capo Press, 2006.

Grose, Christian R. *Congress in Black and White: Race and Representation in Washington and at Home*. New York: Cambridge University Press, 2011.

Halberstam, David. *The Children*. New York: Random House, 1998.

Hamburger, Robert. *Our Portion of Hell: Fayette County, Tennessee: An Oral History of the Struggle for Civil Rights*. New York: Links, 1973.

Hamer, Fannie Lou. *To Praise Our Bridges: An Autobiography*. Jackson, MS: Kipco, 1967.

Hampton, Henry, and Steve Fayer, eds. *Voices of Freedom: An Oral History of the Civil Rights Movement from the 1950s Through the 1980s*. New York: Bantam Books, 1990.

Hansen, Drew D. *The Dream: Martin Luther King, Jr., and the Speech That Inspired a Nation*. New York: Ecco, 2003.

Harmon, David Andrew. *Beneath the Image of the Civil Rights Movement and Race Relations: Atlanta, Georgia, 1946–1981*. New York: Garland, 1996.

Hastert, Dennis. *Speaker: Lessons from Forty Years in Coaching and Politics*. Washington, DC: Regnery, 2004.

Hedgeman, Anna Arnold. *The Trumpet Sounds: A Memoir of Negro Leadership*. New York: Holt, Rinehart and Winston, 1964.

Hedin, Benjamin. *In Search of the Movement: The Struggle for Civil Rights Then and Now*. San Francisco: City Lights Books, 2015.

Height, Dorothy I. *Open Wide the Freedom Gates: A Memoir*. New York: Public Affairs, 2009.

Hendershot, Heather. *When the News Broke: Chicago 1968 and the Polarizing of America*. Chicago: University of Chicago Press, 2022.

Himmelfarb, Gertrude. *The People of the Book: Philosemitism in England, from Cromwell to Churchill*. New York: Encounter Books, 2011.

Hogan, Wesley C. *Many Minds, One Heart: SNCC's Dream for a New America*. Chapel Hill: University of North Carolina Press, 2007.

Holloway, Jonathan Scott. *Confronting the Veil: Abram Harris, Jr., E. Franklin Frazier, and Ralph Bunche, 1919–1941*. Chapel Hill: University of North Carolina Press, 2002.

Holsaert, Faith S., et al., eds. *Hands on the Freedom Plow: Personal Accounts by Women in SNCC*. Urbana: University of Illinois Press, 2010.

Hornsby, Alton. *Black Power in Dixie: A Political History of African Americans in Atlanta*. Gainesville: University Press of Florida, 2016.

Houston, Benjamin. *The Nashville Way: Racial Etiquette and the Struggle for Social Justice in a Southern City*. Athens: University of Georgia Press, 2012.

Howard, John, ed. *Carryin' On in the Lesbian and Gay South*. New York: New York University Press, 1997.

Hyatt, Richard. *Zell: The Governor Who Gave Georgia Hope*. Macon, GA: Mercer University Press, 1997.

Jackson, James E. *Three Brave Men Tell How Freedom Comes to an Old South City, Nashville, Tenn*. New York: Publisher's New Press, 1963.

Jackson, Richie Jean Sherrod. *The House by the Side of the Road: The Selma Civil Rights Movement*. Tuscaloosa: University of Alabama Press, 2011.

Jacobs, Paul, and Saul Landau. *The New Radicals: A Report with Documents*. New York: Random House, 1966.

Jacoby, Tamar. *Someone Else's House: America's Unfinished Struggle for Integration*. New York: Basic Books, 1998.

Jeffries, Hasan Kwame. *Bloody Lowndes: Civil Rights and Black Power in Alabama's Black Belt*. New York: New York University Press, 2009.

Johnson, Robert David. *All the Way with LBJ: The 1964 Presidential Election*. New York: Cambridge University Press, 2009.

Jones, Bartlett C. *Flawed Triumphs: Andy Young at the United Nations*. Lanham, MD: University Press of America, 1996.

Jones, Doug. *Bending Towards Justice: The Birmingham Church Bombing That Changed the Course of Civil Rights*. New York: All Points Books, 2019.

Jones, William Powell. *March on Washington: Jobs, Freedom, and the Forgotten History of Civil Rights*. New York: W. W. Norton, 2013.

Jordan, Vernon E., and Annette Gordon-Reed. *Vernon Can Read!: A Memoir*. New York: Public Affairs, 2001.

Joseph, Peniel E. *Stokely: A Life*. New York: Basic Civitas, 2014.

———. *Waiting 'til the Midnight Hour: A Narrative History of Black Power in America*. New York: Henry Holt, 2006.

Kapur, Sudarshan. *Raising Up a Prophet: The African-American Encounter with Gandhi*. Boston: Beacon Press, 1992.

Katznelson, Ira. *When Affirmative Action Was White: An Untold History of Racial Inequality in Twentieth-Century America*. New York: W. W. Norton, 2005.

Kennedy, Caroline, ed. *Profiles in Courage for Our Time*. New York: Hyperion, 2002.

Kennedy, Kerry, and Thurston Clarke. *Robert F. Kennedy: Ripples of Hope*. New York: Center Street, 2018.

Kennedy, Peggy Wallace, and H. Mark Kennedy. *The Broken Road*. New York: Bloomsbury, 2019.

Kilpatrick, Judith. *There When We Needed Him: Wiley Austin Branton, Civil Rights Warrior*. Fayetteville: University of Arkansas Press, 2007.

Kimball, Penn. *Keep Hope Alive!: Super Tuesday and Jesse Jackson's 1988 Campaign for the Presidency*. Lanham, MD: Joint Center for Political and Economic Studies Press, 1992.

King, Martin Luther. *Stride Toward Freedom*. New York: Harper, 1958.

King, Mary. *Freedom Song: A Personal Story of the 1960s Civil Rights Movement*. New York: Morrow, 1987.

Klehr, Harvey. *Far Left of Center: The American Radical Left Today*. New Brunswick, NJ: Transaction Books, 1988.

Kolchin, Peter. *First Freedom: The Responses of Alabama's Blacks to Emancipation and Reconstruction*. Westport, CT: Greenwood Press, 1972.

Kotz, Nick. *Judgment Days: Lyndon Baines Johnson, Martin Luther King, Jr., and the Laws That Changed America*. Boston: Houghton Mifflin, 2005.

Kruse, Kevin. *White Flight: Atlanta and the Making of Modern Conservatism*. Princeton, NJ: Princeton University Press, 2007.

LaFayette, Bernard, and Kathryn Lee Johnson. *In Peace and Freedom: My Journey in Selma*. Lexington: University Press of Kentucky, 2013.

Larson, Kate Clifford. *Walk with Me: A Biography of Fannie Lou Hamer*. New York: Oxford University Press, 2021.

Laue, James H. *Direct Action and Desegregation, 1960–1962: Toward a Theory of the Rationalization of Protest*. Brooklyn, NY: Carlson, 1989.

Lawson, Steven F. *Black Ballots: Voting Rights in the South, 1944–1969*. New York: Columbia University Press, 1976.

———. *Civil Rights Crossroads: Nation, Community, and the Black Freedom Struggle*. Lexington: University Press of Kentucky, 2003.

———. *In Pursuit of Power: Southern Blacks and Electoral Politics, 1965–1982*. New York: Columbia University Press, 1985.

———. *Running for Freedom: Civil Rights and Black Politics in America Since 1941*. New York: McGraw-Hill, 1997.

Leahy, Patrick J. *The Road Taken: A Memoir*. New York: Simon & Schuster, 2022.

Lee, Chana Kai. *For Freedom's Sake: The Life of Fannie Lou Hamer*. Urbana: University of Illinois Press, 1999.

Lemann, Nicholas. *The Promised Land: The Great Black Migration and How It Changed America*. New York: Alfred A. Knopf, 1991.

Lesher, Stephan. *George Wallace: American Populist*. Cambridge, MA: DaCapo Press, 1994.

Lewis, Andrew B. *The Shadows of Youth: The Remarkable Journey of the Civil Rights Generation*. New York: Hill and Wang, 2009.

Lewis, David L. *King: A Biography*. Urbana: University of Illinois Press, 1978.

Lewis, David L., and Charles W. Eagles, eds. *The Civil Rights Movement in America: Essays*. Jackson: University Press of Mississippi, 1986.

Lewis, Finlay. *Mondale: Portrait of an American Politician*. New York: Harper & Row, 1980.

Lewis, John. *Across That Bridge: Life Lessons and a Vision for Change*. New York: Hyperion, 2012.

Lewis, John, Andrew Aydin, and Nate Powell. *March*. Three-volume collected slipcase edition. Marietta, GA: Top Shelf Productions, 2016.

Lewis, John, Andrew Aydin, Nate Powell, and L. Fury. *Run*. New York: Abrams Comicarts, 2021.

Lewis, John, with Michael D'Orso. *Walking with the Wind: A Memoir of the Movement*. New York: Simon & Schuster, 1998.

Lewis, John, with Kabir Sehgal. *Carry On*. New York: Grand Central, 2021.

Lincoln, C. Eric, and Lawrence H. Mamiya. *The Black Church in the African-American Experience*. Durham, NC: Duke University Press, 1990.

Litwack, Leon F. *Been in the Storm So Long: The Aftermath of Slavery*. New York: Random House, 1979.

Lomax, Louis E. *The Negro Revolt*. New York: Harper & Brothers, 1962.

Long, Michael G. *Martin Luther King, Jr., Homosexuality, and the Early Gay Rights Movement: Keeping the Dream Straight?* New York: Palgrave Macmillan, 2012.

Lovett, Bobby L. *The Civil Rights Movement in Tennessee: A Narrative History*. Knoxville: University of Tennessee Press, 2005.

Lubell, Samuel. *White and Black: Test of a Nation*. New York: Harper & Row, 1964.

Lublin, David. *The Paradox of Representation: Racial Gerrymandering and Minority Interests in Congress*. Princeton, NJ: Princeton University Press, 1997.

Lukas, J. Anthony. *Don't Shoot—We Are Your Children!* New York: Random House, 1971.

Lyman, Princeton. *Partner to History: The U.S. Role in South Africa's Transition to Democracy*. Washington, DC: U.S. Institute of Peace Press, 2002.

Lynd, Alice, and Staughton Lynd. *Stepping Stones: Memoir of a Life Together*. Lanham, MD: Lexington Books, 2009.

Lyon, Danny. *Memories of the Southern Civil Rights Movement*. The Lyndhurst Series on the South. Chapel Hill: University of North Carolina Press, 1992.

MacLaine, Shirley. *Don't Fall Off the Mountain*. New York: W. W. Norton, 1970.

Manis, Andrew Michael. *A Fire You Can't Put Out: The Civil Rights Life of Birmingham's Reverend Fred Shuttlesworth*. Tuscaloosa: University of Alabama Press, 1999.

Margolick, David. *Promise and the Dream: The Untold Story of Martin Luther King, Jr. and Robert F. Kennedy*. New York: Rosetta Books, 2018.

May, Gary. *Bending Toward Justice: The Voting Rights Act and the Transformation of American Democracy*. New York: Basic Books, 2013.

_____. *The Informant: The FBI, the Ku Klux Klan, and the Murder of Viola Liuzzo.* New Haven, CT: Yale University Press, 2005.

McAdam, Doug. *Freedom Summer.* New York: Oxford University Press, 1990.

McCain, John, and Mark Salter. *Why Courage Matters: The Way to a Braver Life.* New York: Random House, 2004.

McDew, Charles, and Beryl Gilfix. *Tell the Story: A Memoir of the Civil Rights Movement.* Published independently, 2020.

McGuire, Danielle L. *At the Dark End of the Street: Black Women, Rape, and Resistance.* New York: Alfred A. Knopf, 2010.

McGuire, Danielle L., and John Dittmer, eds. *Freedom Rights: New Perspectives on the Civil Rights Movement.* Lexington: University Press of Kentucky, 2011.

McPherson, Harry. *A Political Education: A Washington Memoir.* Austin: University of Texas Press, 1995.

McWhorter, Diane. *Carry Me Home: Birmingham, Alabama: The Climactic Battle of the Civil Rights Revolution.* New York: Simon & Schuster, 2001.

Meacham, Jon. *His Truth Is Marching On: John Lewis and the Power of Hope.* New York: Random House, 2020.

Meier, August. *The Transformation of Activism.* Chicago: Aldine, 1970.

Meier, August, and Francis L. Broderick. *Negro Protest Thought in the Twentieth Century.* Indianapolis: Bobbs-Merrill, 1966.

Meier, August, and Elliott M. Rudwick. *CORE: A Study in the Civil Rights Movement, 1942–1968.* New York: Oxford University Press, 1973.

Mfume, Kweisi, and Ron Stodghill. *No Free Ride: From the Mean Streets to the Mainstream.* New York: One World, 1996.

Michel, Gregg L. *Struggle for a Better South: The Southern Student Organizing Committee, 1964–1969.* New York: Palgrave Macmillan, 2004.

Mills, Nicolaus. *Like a Holy Crusade: Mississippi 1964.* Chicago: Ivan R. Dee, 1992.

Minchin, Timothy J., and John A. Salmond. *After the Dream: Black and White Southerners Since 1965.* Lexington: University Press of Kentucky, 2011.

Minta, Michael D. *Oversight: Representing the Interests of Blacks and Latinos in Congress.* Princeton, NJ: Princeton University Press, 2011.

Mixner, David B. *Stranger Among Friends.* New York: Bantam Books, 1996.

Monteith, Sharon. *SNCC's Stories: The African American Freedom Movement in the Civil Rights South.* Print Culture in the South. Athens: University of Georgia Press, 2020.

Morgan, Charles. *A Time to Speak.* New York: Holt, Rinehart and Winston, 1979.

Morris, Aldon D. *The Origins of the Civil Rights Movement: Black Communities Organizing for Change.* New York: Free Press, 1984.

Morrison, Joan, and Robert K. Morrison, eds. *From Camelot to Kent State: The Sixties Experience in the Words of Those Who Lived It.* New York: Oxford University Press, 2001.

Mullins, Lisa. *Diane Nash: The Fire of the Civil Rights Movement: A Biography.* Miami: Barnhardt & Ashe, 2007.

Murphree, Vanessa. *The Selling of Civil Rights: The Student Nonviolent Coordinating Committee and the Use of Public Relations.* New York: Routledge, 2006.

Neary, John. *Julian Bond: Black Rebel.* New York: William Morrow, 1971.

Newfield, Jack. *A Prophetic Minority.* New York: New American Library, 1966.

Niven, David. *The Politics of Injustice: The Kennedys, the Freedom Rides, and the Electoral Consequences of a Moral Compromise*. Knoxville: University of Tennessee Press, 2003.

Norrander, Barbara. *Super Tuesday: Regional Politics & Presidential Primaries*. Lexington: University Press of Kentucky, 1992.

Norwood, Stephen H. *Antisemitism and the American Far Left*. New York: Cambridge University Press, 2013.

Nussbaum, Jeff. *Undelivered: The Unseen Speeches That Would Have Rewritten History*. New York: Flatiron Books, 2022.

Obama, Barack. *A Promised Land*. New York: Crown, 2020.

Olson, Lynne. *Freedom's Daughters: The Unsung Heroines of the Civil Rights Movement from 1830 to 1970*. New York: Scribner, 2001.

O'Reilly, Kenneth. *Racial Matters: The FBI's Secret File on Black America, 1960–1972*. New York: Free Press, 1991.

Pace, Courtney. *Freedom Faith: The Womanist Vision of Prathia Hall*. Athens: University of Georgia Press, 2019.

Padgett, Marty. *A Night at the Sweet Gum Head: Drag, Drugs, Disco, and Atlanta's Gay Revolution*. New York: W. W. Norton, 2021.

Page, Susan. *Madam Speaker: Nancy Pelosi and the Lessons of Power*. New York: Twelve, 2021.

Parker, Frank R. *Black Votes Count: Political Empowerment in Mississippi After 1965*. Chapel Hill: University of North Carolina Press, 1990.

Patterson, James T. *Freedom Is Not Enough: The Moynihan Report and America's Struggle over Black Family Life*. New York: Basic Books, 2010.

Payne, Charles M. *I've Got the Light of Freedom: The Organizing Tradition and the Mississippi Freedom Struggle*. Berkeley: University of California Press, 1995.

Payne, Les, and Tamara Payne. *The Dead Are Arising: The Life of Malcolm X*. New York: Liveright, 2020.

Peck, James. *Freedom Ride*. New York: Simon & Schuster, 1962.

Petrus, Stephen, and Ronald D. Cohen. *Folk City: New York and the American Folk Music Revival*. New York: Oxford University Press, 2015.

Phillips, Betsy. *Dynamite Nashville: The FBI, the KKK, and the Bombers Beyond Their Control*. Nashville, TN: Third Man Books, 2024.

Pimblott, Kerry. *Faith in Black Power: Religion, Race, and Resistance in Cairo, Illinois*. Lexington: University Press of Kentucky, 2017.

Pineda, Erin R. *Seeing Like an Activist: Civil Disobedience and the Civil Rights Movement*. New York: Oxford University Press, 2021.

Podesta, John, and John Halpin. *The Power of Progress: How America's Progressives Can (Once Again) Save Our Economy, Our Climate, and Our Country*. New York: Crown, 2008.

Polletta, Francesca. *Freedom Is an Endless Meeting: Democracy in American Social Movements*. Chicago: University of Chicago Press, 2004.

Pomerantz, Gary. *Where Peachtree Meets Sweet Auburn: The Saga of Two Families and the Making of Atlanta*. New York: Penguin Books, 2009.

Powledge, Fred. *Free at Last?: The Civil Rights Movement and the People Who Made It*. Boston: Little, Brown, 1991.

Prasad, Devi. *War Is a Crime Against Humanity: The Story of War Resisters' International*. London: War Resisters International, 2005.

Pratt, Robert A. *Selma's Bloody Sunday: Protest, Voting Rights, and the Struggle for Racial Equality*. Baltimore: Johns Hopkins University Press, 2017.

Pride, Richard A., and J. David Woodard. *The Burden of Busing: The Politics of Desegregation in Nashville, Tennessee*. Knoxville: University of Tennessee Press, 1985.

Purdum, Todd S. *An Idea Whose Time Has Come: Two Presidents, Two Parties, and the Battle for the Civil Rights Act of 1964*. New York: Henry Holt, 2014.

Raboteau, Albert J. *Slave Religion: The Invisible Institution in the Antebellum South*. New York: Oxford University Press, 2004.

Raines, Howell. *My Soul Is Rested: Movement Days in the Deep South Remembered*. New York: Penguin Books, 1983.

Ransby, Barbara. *Ella Baker and the Black Freedom Movement: A Radical Democratic Vision*. Chapel Hill: University of North Carolina Press, 2007.

Reeves, Richard. *President Kennedy: Profile of Power*. New York: Simon & Schuster, 1993.

Remnick, David. *The Bridge: The Life and Rise of Barack Obama*. New York: Alfred A. Knopf, 2010.

Risen, Clay. *The Bill of the Century: The Epic Battle for the Civil Rights Act*. New York: Bloomsbury, 2014.

Roberts, Gene, and Hank Klibanoff. *The Race Beat: The Press, the Civil Rights Struggle, and the Awakening of a Nation*. New York: Alfred A. Knopf, 2006.

Robnett, Belinda. *How Long? How Long? African American Women in the Struggle for Civil Rights*. New York: Oxford University Press, 1999.

Rohler, Lloyd Earl. *George Wallace: Conservative Populist*. Westport, CT: Praeger, 2004.

Romano, Renee Christine, and Leigh Raiford, eds. *The Civil Rights Movement in American Memory*. Athens: University of Georgia Press, 2006.

Rorabaugh, W. J. *The Real Making of the President: Kennedy, Nixon, and the 1960 Election*. Lawrence: University Press of Kansas, 2012.

Rothschild, Mary Aickin. *A Case of Black and White: Northern Volunteers and the Southern Freedom Summers, 1964–1965*. Westport, CT: Greenwood Press, 1982.

Salzman, Jack, Adina Back, and Gretchen Sullivan Sorin, eds. *Bridges and Boundaries: African Americans and American Jews*. New York: George Braziller, 1992.

Scanlon, Jennifer. *Until There Is Justice: The Life of Anna Arnold Hedgeman*. New York: Oxford University Press, 2016.

Schlesinger, Arthur M. *A Thousand Days: John F. Kennedy in the White House*. Boston: Houghton Mifflin, 1983.

———. *Robert Kennedy and His Times*. Boston: Houghton Mifflin, 1978.

Schroeder, Pat. *24 Years of House Work—and the Place Is Still a Mess*. Kansas City, MO: Andrews McMeel, 1999.

Schultz, Debra L. *Going South: Jewish Women in the Civil Rights Movement*. New York: New York University Press, 2001.

Sellers, Cleveland. *The River of No Return: The Autobiography of a Black Militant and the Life and Death of SNCC*. New York: William Morrow, 1973.

Silver, Carol Ruth. *Freedom Rider Diary: Smuggled Notes from Parchman Prison*. Jackson: University Press of Mississippi, 2014.

Singh, Robert. *The Congressional Black Caucus: Racial Politics in the U.S. Congress*. Thousand Oaks, CA: Sage, 1998.

Siracusa, Anthony C. *Nonviolence Before King: The Politics of Being and the Black Freedom Struggle*. Chapel Hill: University of North Carolina Press, 2021.

Sitkoff, Harvard. *A New Deal for Blacks: The Emergence of Civil Rights as a National Issue: The Depression Decade*. New York: Oxford University Press, 1978.

Skipper, John C. *Showdown at the 1964 Democratic Convention: Lyndon Johnson, Mississippi and Civil Rights*. Jefferson, NC: McFarland, 2012.

Slate, Nico. *Colored Cosmopolitanism: The Shared Struggle for Freedom in the United States and India*. Cambridge, MA: Harvard University Press, 2017.

Smith, Stephen, Catherine Ellis, and Robert Penn Warren, eds. *Free All Along: The Robert Penn Warren Civil Rights Interviews*. New York: New Press, 2019.

Sokol, Jason. *The Heavens Might Crack: The Death and Legacy of Martin Luther King, Jr.* New York: Basic Books, 2018.

Stern, Mark. *Calculating Visions: Kennedy, Johnson, and Civil Rights*. Perspectives on the Sixties. New Brunswick, NJ: Rutgers University Press, 1992.

Stoper, Emily. *The Student Nonviolent Coordinating Committee: The Growth of Radicalism in a Civil Rights Organization*. Brooklyn, NY: Carlson, 1989.

Sugarman, Tracy. *Stranger at the Gates: A Summer in Mississippi*. 1965; Westport, CT: Prospecta Press, 2014.

Sugrue, Thomas J. *Sweet Land of Liberty: The Forgotten Struggle for Civil Rights in the North*. New York: Random House, 2008.

Sutherland, Elizabeth. *Letters from Mississippi*. New York: McGraw-Hill, 1965.

Swain, Carol M. *Black Faces, Black Interests: The Representation of African Americans in Congress*. Lanham, MD: University Press of America, 2006.

Tate, Gayle T., and Lewis A. Randolph, eds. *The Black Urban Community: From Dusk Till Dawn*. New York: Palgrave Macmillan, 2006.

Tate, Katherine. *Concordance: Black Lawmaking in the U.S. Congress from Carter to Obama*. Ann Arbor: University of Michigan Press, 2013.

Taylor, Cynthia. *A. Philip Randolph: The Religious Journey of an African American Labor Leader*. New York: New York University Press, 2006.

The Presidential Nominating Conventions, 1968. Washington, DC: Congressional Quarterly Service, 1968.

Theoharis, Jeanne. *A More Beautiful and Terrible History: The Uses and Misuses of Civil Rights History*. Boston: Beacon Press, 2018.

Thernstrom, Stephan, and Abigail M. Thernstrom. *America in Black and White: One Nation, Indivisible*. New York: Simon & Schuster, 1997.

Thurman, Howard. *With Head and Heart: The Autobiography of Howard Thurman*. San Diego: Harcourt Brace Jovanovich, 1981.

Todd, Lisa Anderson. *For a Voice and the Vote: My Journey with the Mississippi Freedom Democratic Party*. Lexington: University Press of Kentucky, 2014.

Torres, Sasha. *Black, White, and in Color: Television and Black Civil Rights*. Princeton, NJ: Princeton University Press, 2003.

Troy, Gil. *Moynihan's Moment: America's Fight Against Zionism as Racism*. New York: Oxford University Press, 2013.

Tuck, Stephen G. N. *Beyond Atlanta: The Struggle for Racial Equality in Georgia, 1940–1980*. Athens: University of Georgia Press, 2003.

Vanden Heuvel, William, and Milton Gwirtzman. *On His Own: Robert F. Kennedy, 1964–1968*. Garden City, NY: Doubleday, 1970.

Viorst, Milton. *Fire in the Streets: America in the 1960s*. New York: Simon & Schuster, 1981.

Visser-Maessen, Laura. *Robert Parris Moses: A Life in Civil Rights and Leadership at the Grassroots*. Chapel Hill: University of North Carolina Press, 2016.

Vivian, C. T., with Steve Fiffer. *It's in the Action: Memories of a Nonviolent Warrior*. Montgomery, AL: New South Books, 2021.

Walker, Lydia. *Challenge and Change: The Story of Civil Rights Activist C. T. Vivian*. Alpharetta, GA: W. H. Wolfe, 1993.

Walters, Ronald W. *Black Presidential Politics in America: A Strategic Approach*. SUNY Series in Afro-American Studies. Albany: State University of New York Press, 1988.

Warren, Robert Penn. *Who Speaks for the Negro?* New York: Random House, 1965.

Washington, Booker T. *Up from Slavery*. New York: Penguin Books, 1986.

Watson, Bruce. *Freedom Summer: The Savage Season That Made Mississippi Burn and Made America a Democracy*. New York: Viking, 2010.

Watters, Pat. *Down to Now: Reflections on the Southern Civil Rights Movement*. New York: Pantheon Books, 1971.

Watters, Pat, and Reese Cleghorn. *Climbing Jacob's Ladder: The Arrival of Negroes in Southern Politics*. New York: Harcourt, Brace & World, 1967.

Webb, Sheyann, and Rachel West Nelson. *Selma, Lord, Selma: Girlhood Memories of the Civil-Rights Days*. Tuscaloosa: University of Alabama Press, 1980.

Weisbrot, Robert. *Freedom Bound: A History of America's Civil Rights Movement*. New York: Plume, 1990.

Whitaker, Mark. *Saying It Loud: 1966—The Year Black Power Challenged the Civil Rights Movement*. New York: Simon & Schuster, 2023.

Whitby, Kenny J. *The Color of Representation: Congressional Behavior and Black Interests*. Ann Arbor: University of Michigan Press, 1997.

Wilkins, Robert Leon. *Long Road to Hard Truth: The 100-Year Mission to Create the National Museum of African American History and Culture*. Washington, DC: Proud Legacy, 2016.

Wilkins, Roy, with Tom Mathews. *Standing Fast: The Autobiography of Roy Wilkins*. New York: Viking Press, 1982.

Wilson, William Julius. *The Declining Significance of Race: Blacks and Changing American Institutions*. Chicago: University of Chicago Press, 1978.

Wofford, Harris. *Of Kennedys and Kings: Making Sense of the Sixties*. Pittsburgh: University of Pittsburgh Press, 1992.

Wright, Gavin. *Sharing the Prize: The Economics of the Civil Rights Revolution in the American South*. Cambridge, MA: Harvard University Press, 2013.

Young, Andrew. *A Way Out of No Way: The Spiritual Memoirs of Andrew Young*. Nashville: Thomas Nelson, 1994.

———. *An Easy Burden: The Civil Rights Movement and the Transformation of America*. Waco, TX: Baylor University Press, 2008.

Young, Andrew. *The Politician: An Insider's Account of John Edwards's Pursuit of the Presidency and the Scandal That Brought Him Down*. New York: St. Martin's Griffin, 2010.

Zellner, Bob, and Constance Curry. *The Wrong Side of Murder Creek: A White Southerner in the Freedom Movement*. Montgomery, AL: New South Books, 2008.

Zinn, Howard. *SNCC: The New Abolitionists*. Boston: Beacon Press, 1964.

DISSERTATIONS AND OTHER UNPUBLISHED THESES

Anderson, Judy Kay. "Nashville's Contribution: The Original Leadership of SNCC." Undergraduate paper, university unknown, 1965.

Goodwin, Sage. "Making the News: The Development of Network Television News and the Struggle for Black Freedom in the 1950s and 1960s." Ph.D., Oxford University, 2021.

Gore, Shannon. "Civil Rights Television Documentaries in the United States: 1960–1966." Ph.D., Northwestern University, 2009.

Koen, Charles E. "My Story of the Cairo Struggle." Ph.D., Union Graduate School, 1980.

Kurhajec, Anna Lillian. "Impossible Allies: SNCC, Black Freedom, and the Civil Rights Liberal Alliance." Ph.D., University of Illinois at Urbana-Champaign, 2015.

Lee, Barry E. "The Nashville Civil Rights Movement: A Study of the Phenomenon of Intentional Leadership Development and Its Consequences." Ph.D., Georgia State University, 2010.

McNealey, Tonya Powell. "Organizing for Civil Rights: A History of the Voter Education Project, Inc." M.A., University of West Georgia, 2016.

Pope, Andrew. "Living in the Struggle: Black Power, Gay Liberation, and Women's Liberation Movements in Atlanta, 1964–1996." Ph.D., Harvard University, 2018.

Riley, Andrew. "C.A.U.T.I.O.N., Inc.: The Fight for Atlanta's Olmsted Parks and Historic Neighborhood, Druid Hills, 1982–1992." Unpublished research paper, 2017.

Rudnick, Howard. "A Coincidental Cup of Kenyan Coffee: SNCC and Malcolm X Recast the Struggle in Nairobi." Undergraduate paper, Washington University, 2011.

Slate, Nico. "A Dangerous Idea: Nonviolence as Tactic and Philosophy," September 2019.

Sumner, David E. "The Local Press and the Nashville Student Movement, 1960." Ph.D., University of Tennessee, 1989.

JOURNAL ARTICLES

Allen, Archie E. "John Lewis: Keeper of the Dream." *New South* 26:2 (Spring 1971): 15–25.

Alridge, Derrick P. "From Civil Rights to Hip Hop: Toward a Nexus of Ideas." *Journal of African American History* 90:3 (Summer 2005): 226–52.

Arnesen, Eric. "Civil Rights and the Cold War at Home: Postwar Activism, Anticommunism, and the Decline of the Left." *American Communist History* 11:1 (Apr. 2012): 5–44.

———. "No Graver Danger: Black Anticommunism, the Communist Party, and the Race Question." *Labor: Studies in Working-Class History of the Americas* 3:4 (Dec. 2006): 13–52.

———. "The Final Conflict? On the Scholarship of Civil Rights, the Left and the Cold War." *American Communist History* 11:1 (Apr. 2012): 63–80.

Bond, Julian. "SNCC: What We Did." *Monthly Review* 52:5 (Oct. 2000): 14–28.

Boots, Cheryl, and Julia Katzman. "Civil Rights Activism, Singing, and the Beloved Community: An Interview with Representative John Lewis." *Impact: The Journal of the Center for Interdisciplinary Teaching and Learning* 4:1 (Winter 2015). Online.

Bullock, Charles S. "The History of Redistricting in Georgia." *Georgia Law Review* 52:4 (2018): 1057–104.

Carter, Wesley. "C. T. Vivian: Baptist Champion of Civil Rights." *Baptist History and Heritage* 50:3 (2015): 43–53.

Cha-Jua, Sundiata Keita, and Clarence Lang. "The Long Movement as Vampire: Temporal and Spatial Fallacies in Recent Black Freedom Studies." *Journal of African American History* 92:2 (2007): 265–88.

Cobb, Charlie. "Revolution: From Stokely Carmichael to Kwame Ture." *Black Scholar* 27:3/4 (Fall/Winter 1997): 32.

"Congressman John Lewis: An American Saint." *Journal of Blacks in Higher Education* 21 (Autumn 1998): 42–43.

Crosby, Emilye. "I Just Had a Fire!: An Interview with Dorie Ann Ladner." *Southern Quarterly* 52:1 (Fall 2014): 79–110.

"Don't Believe the Hype: Chronicle of a Mugging by the Media." *Black Scholar* 19:6 (1988): 27–43.

Dunne, Matthew. "Next Steps: Charles S. Johnson and Southern Liberalism." *Journal of Negro History* 83:1 (Jan. 1998): 1–34.

Eskew, Glenn T. "Barack Obama, John Lewis, and the Legacy of the Civil Rights Struggle." *American Studies Journal* 56:4 (2012). Online.

———. "The State in Recent Civil Rights Scholarship." *Alabama Review* 72:2 (2019): 79–98.

Fairclough, Adam. "Civil Rights and the Lincoln Memorial: The Censored Speeches of Robert R. Moton and John Lewis." *Journal of Negro History* 82:4 (Autumn 1997): 408–16.

Faulkenbury, Evan. "An Uncommon Meeting of Minds: The Council for United Civil Rights Leadership in the Black Freedom Struggle, 1963–1967." *Journal of African American History* 104:3 (June 2019): 392–414.

Frank, Sherry Z. "Bridge to the Beloved Community: John Lewis's Interracial and Jewish Community Outreach." *Journal of Law and Religion* 37:1 (2022): 46–49.

Franklin, Robert M. "Justice and Good Trouble." *Journal of Law and Religion* 37:1 (Jan. 2022): 27–32.

Gillespie, Andra. "John Lewis and the Durability of Transcendent Race Politics." *Journal of Law and Religion* 37:1 (Jan. 2022): 55–62.

Good, Paul. "The Meredith March." *New South* 21:1 (Summer 1966): 2–21.

Gritter, Elizabeth, and Julian Bond. "Interview with Julian Bond." *Southern Cultures* 12:1 (2006): 76–91.

Halberstam, David. "The Children: How the Unique Courage and Faith of Ordinary People Changed America." *Idaho Law Review* 36:1 (1999): 1–7.

Hale, Jon F. "The Making of the New Democrats." *Political Science Quarterly* 110:2 (Summer 1995): 207.

Hall, Jacquelyn Dowd. "The Long Civil Rights Movement and the Political Uses of the Past." *Journal of American History* 91:4 (Mar. 2005): 1233–63.

Hill, George H., and Raymond Trent. "The Congressional Black Caucus: A Bibliography." *Bulletin of Bibliography* 42:2 (Mar. 1985): 67–79.

Horowitz, Rachelle. "Tom Kahn and the Fight for Democracy: A Political Portrait and Personal Recollection." *Democratiya* 11 (Winter 2007): 204–51.

Isaac, Larry W., Jonathan S. Coley, Daniel B. Cornfield, and Dennis C. Dickerson.

"Preparation Pathways and Movement Participation: Insurgent Schooling and Non-violent Direct Action in the Nashville Civil Rights Movement." *Mobilization: An International Quarterly* 21:2 (June 2016): 155–76.

Isaac, Larry W., Daniel B. Cornfield, Dennis C. Dickerson, James M. Lawson Jr., and Jonathan S. Coley. "Movement Schools and Dialogical Diffusion of Nonviolent Praxis: Nashville Workshops in the Southern Civil Rights Movement." *Research in Social Movements, Conflicts and Change* 34:1 (Nov. 2012): 155–184.

Jeffries, Hasan Kwame. "SNCC, Black Power, and Independent Political Party Organizing in Alabama, 1964–1966." *Journal of African American History* 91:2 (Spring 2006): 171–93.

Jensen, Kipton. "The Growing Edges of Beloved Community: From Royce to Thurman and King." *Transactions of the Charles S. Peirce Society* 52:2 (2016): 239–58.

Johnson, Terrence L. "Moral Faith and the Legacy of John Lewis's Political Vision of 'Good Trouble.'" *Journal of Law and Religion* 37:1 (Jan. 2022): 37–45.

Kilson, Martin. "From Civil Rights to Party Politics: The Black Political Tradition." *Current History* 67:399 (November 1, 1974): 193–99.

Kuhn, Clifford. "There's a Footnote to History: Memory and the History of Martin Luther King's October 1960 Arrest and Its Aftermath." *Journal of American History*, 84:2 (Sept. 1997): 583–95.

Lawson, Steven F. "Freedom Then, Freedom Now: The Historiography of the Civil Rights Movement." *American Historical Review* 96:2 (Apr. 1991): 456–71.

———. "The Outsider." *Journal of Civil and Human Rights* 1:1 (Spring/Summer 2015): 121–26.

Lewis, John. "Reflections on Judge Frank M. Johnson, Jr." *Yale Law Journal* 109:6 (Apr. 2000): 1253–56.

Lewis, John, and Archie E. Allen. "Black Voter Registration Efforts in the South." *Notre Dame Law Review* 48:1 (Oct. 1972): 105–32.

Lewis, John Robert. "The King Legacy: Dr. Martin Luther King Jr. Celebration Lecture." *Vermont Law Review* 30:2 (2006): 349–60.

Lichtman, Allan. "The Federal Assault Against Voting Discrimination in the Deep South, 1957–1967." *Journal of Negro History* 54:4 (1969): 346–67.

Lucks, Daniel S. "Martin Luther King, Jr.'s Riverside Speech and Cold War Civil Rights." *Peace & Change* 40:3 (July 2015): 395–422.

Mabee, Carleton. "The Crisis in Negro Leadership." *Antioch Review* 24:3 (Fall 1964): 365–78.

McWhorter, Diane. "The Enduring Courage of the Freedom Riders." *Journal of Blacks in Higher Education* 61 (Autumn 2008): 66–73.

Meier, August. "The Successful Sit-Ins in a Border City: A Study in Social Causation." *Journal of Intergroup Relations* II (Summer 1961): 230–37.

Miller, Mike. "SNCC, the Student Nonviolent Coordinating Committee, Gathers 50 Years After It Started: A Report on the Reunion." *Poverty & Race* (Aug. 2010): 3–5.

Miller, Steven P. "Whither Southern Liberalism in the Post-Civil Rights Era? The Southern Regional Council and Its Peers, 1965–1972." *Georgia Historical Quarterly* 90:4 (Winter 2006): 547–68.

Morris, Aldon. "Black Southern Student Sit-in Movement: An Analysis of Internal Organization." *American Sociological Review* 46:6 (Dec. 1981): 744–67.

Murphree, Vanessa D. "The Selling of Civil Rights: The Communication Section of the Student Nonviolent Coordinating Committee." *Journalism History* 29:1 (Spring 2003): 21–31.

Nasstrom, Kathryn L. "Between Memory and History: Autobiographies of the Civil Rights Movement and the Writing of Civil Rights History." *Journal of Southern History* 74:2 (May 2008): 325–64.

Parry-Giles, Shawn J., and Trevor Parry-Giles. "Collective Memory, Political Nostalgia, and the Rhetorical Presidency: Bill Clinton's Commemoration of the March on Washington, August 28, 1998." *Quarterly Journal of Speech* 86:4 (Nov. 2000): 417–37.

Pauley, Garth E. "John Lewis, Speech at the March on Washington." *Voices of Democracy* 5 (2010): 18–36.

———. "John Lewis's 'Serious Revolution': Rhetoric, Resistance, and Revision at the March on Washington." *Quarterly Journal of Speech* 84:3 (Aug. 1998): 320–40.

Rice, Bradley R. "The Battle of Buckhead: The Plan of Improvement and Atlanta's Last Big Annexation." *Atlanta Historical Journal* 25 (Winter 1981): 6–22.

Richardson, Judy. "Womanpower and SNCC." *Massachusetts Review* 52:2 (Summer 2011): 179–88.

Rosenfeld, Sam, and Nancy Schwartz. "A Mix of Motives: The Georgia Delegate Challenge to the 1968 Democratic Convention and the Dynamics of Intraparty Conflict." *American Review of Politics* 37:2 (2020): 48–70.

Sarvis, Will. "Leaders in the Court and Community: Z. Alexander Looby, Avon N. Williams, Jr., and the Legal Fight for Civil Rights in Tennessee, 1940–1970." *Journal of African American History* 88:1 (Winter 2003): 42–58.

Schmidt, Christopher W. "Divided by Law: The Sit-Ins and the Role of the Courts in the Civil Rights Movement." *Law and History Review* 33:1 (Feb. 2015): 93–149.

———. "The Sit-In Cases: Explaining the Great Aberration of the Warren Court." *Journal of Supreme Court History* 43 (Nov. 2018): 294–320.

Schmidt, John R., and Wayne W. Whalen. "Credentials Contests at the 1968—and 1972—Democratic National Conventions." *Harvard Law Review* 82:7 (1969): 1438–70.

Seymour, Tom. "Danny Lyon, Soul of a Radical." *British Journal of Photography* (Nov. 2014): 42–48.

Shor, Francis. "Utopian Aspirations in the Black Freedom Movement: SNCC and the Struggle for Civil Rights, 1960–1965." *Utopian Studies* 15:2 (Winter 2004): 173–89.

Smith, Charles U. "The Sit-Ins and the New Negro Student." *Journal of Intergroup Relations* 2:3 (Summer 1961): 223–29.

Stone, Chuck. "Black Political Power in the Carter Era." *Black Scholar* 8:4 (1977): 6–15.

Stoper, Emily. "The Student Nonviolent Coordinating Committee: Rise and Fall of a Redemptive Organization." *Journal of Black Studies* 8:1 (Sept. 1977): 13–34.

Summerlin, Donnie. "We Represented the Best of Georgia in Chicago: The Georgia Loyalist Delegate Challenge at the 1968 Democratic National Convention." *Georgia Historical Quarterly* 103:3 (2019): 57–99.

Sumner, David E. "A Clash Over Race: Tennessee Governor Ellington Versus CBS, 1960." *Journalism Quarterly* 68:3 (Fall 1991): 541–47.

Taylor, Michael Ray. "Drawing *March*: A Conversation with Nate Powell." *Arkansas Review* 47:1 (Apr. 2016): 3–14.

Thelwell, Ekwueme Michael. "SNCC, the Struggle, and the W. E. B. Du Bois Department: An Introduction for Charles E. Cobb, Jr., and Judy Richardson." *Massachusetts Review* 52:2 (2011): 163–73.

Tucker, James. "The Politics of Persuasion: Passage of the Voting Rights Act Reauthorization Act of 2006." *Journal of Legislation* 33:2 (May 1, 2007): 205.

Walmsley, Mark Joseph. "Tell It Like It Isn't: SNCC and the Media, 1960–1965." *Journal of American Studies* 48:1 (Feb. 2014): 291–308.

Walton, Hanes, Jr. "Public Policy Responses to the Million Man March." *Black Scholar* 25:4 (Fall 1995): 17–22.

Wilkins, Fanon Che. "The Making of Black Internationalists: SNCC and Africa before the Launching of Black Power, 1960–1965." *Journal of African American History* 92:4 (2007): 467–90.

Wittner, Lawrence S. "The National Negro Congress: A Reassessment." *American Quarterly* 22:4 (Winter 1970): 883–901.

Wynn, Linda. "The Dawning of a New Day: The Nashville Sit-Ins, February 13, 1960–May 10, 1960." *Tennessee Historical Quarterly* 50:1 (1991): 42–54.

Young, Robert M. "Nothing but a Man: Filmmaker's Perspective." *Black Camera* 3:2 (Spring 2012): 91–100.

Yuill, Kevin L. "The 1966 White House Conference on Civil Rights." *Historical Journal* 41:1 (Mar. 1998): 259–82.

FILMS AND TELEVISION DOCUMENTARIES

Bagwell, Orlando, et al., dirs. *Eyes on the Prize*. Blackside, 1987.

Cohen, Helen, and Marc Lipman, dirs. *Arc of Justice*. Open Studio Productions, 2016.

Dowdey, Kathleen, dir. *John Lewis: Get in the Way*. PBS, 2017.

DuVernay, Ava, dir. *Selma*. Paramount Pictures, 2014.

Gorsuch, Joe, dir. *Selma: The City and the Symbol*. CBS, 1965.

Inaba, Ian, dir. *American Blackout*. Guerrilla News Network, 2006.

Kelly, Bill, dir. *'68: The Year Nebraska Mattered*. NET Television, 2008.

Lichtenstein, Brad, and Yoruba Richen, dirs. *American Reckoning*. Frontline, 2022.

Lyon, Danny, dir. *SNCC*. Danny Lyon, 2020.

Nelson, Stanley, dir. *Freedom Riders*. Firelight Films, 2011.

———, dir. *Freedom Summer*. Firelight Films, 2014.

Pelosi, Alexandra, dir. *Pelosi in the House*. HBO Documentary Films, 2022.

Porter, Dawn, dir. *Bobby Kennedy for President*. RadicalMedia, 2018.

———, dir. *Good Trouble*. Magnolia Pictures, 2020.

Rogers, Shari, dir. *Shared Legacies*. Menemsha Films, 2020.

Smith, Robin, dir. *Come Walk in My Shoes*. American Public Television, 2007.

Terry, Joe, dir. *George Wallace: A Politician's Legacy*. Alabama Public Television, 1988.

York, Steve, dir. *A Force More Powerful*. Zimmerman, Inc., 1999.

Young, Robert, dir. *NBC White Paper: Sit-In*. NBC, 1960.

IMAGE CREDITS

INDEX

Page numbers beginning with 571 refer to endnotes

satyagraha, 26, 31, 38, 39, 77
  see also nonviolent resistance
Savage, Gus, 399, 459, 464
Sawyers, Marcus, 545
Scalia, Antonin, 471, 504
Schardt, Arlie, 225, 226, 251
Schechter, Phil, 57
Scheer, Robert, 432–33
Schmoke, Kurt, 385
Schrag, Oswald, 260
Schroeder, Patricia, 386, 411, 412, 413
Schulberg, Budd, 276
Schumer, Chuck, 393
Schwartz, Peter, 100
Schwerner, Michael, "Mickey," 174–76,
  182, 184, 189, 426
Schwerner, Rita, 187
Sciolino, Elaine, 453
SCLC (Southern Christian Leadership
  Conference), 26, 40–41, 60, 98,
  102–3, 105, 113, 125, 153, 207–8,
  210, 259–60, 262–63, 264, 273,
  274, 289, 311, 508
  Jackson and, 353–54
  March on Washington and, 127, 133
  on Meredith March, 253
  Raleigh conference of, 58–61
  scholarship given to Lewis by, 97
  Selma-to-Montgomery March and,
    215–32
  SNCC, tension with, 87, 207, 215–17,
    226, 229, 247–48, 584–85
Seay, Solomon "S.S.," 85
segregation, 17, 21, 22, 69–70, 96, 111,
  113–14, 117–19, 155, 162–63,
  166, 168, 170, 335, 343
  in churches, 236
  in Democratic Party, 189
  in Lewis's youth, 10, 14, 16
  lunch counter sit-ins to stop, 30–36,
    37–54, 63–68
  stand-ins against, 66–68
  at Troy State, 28–30
Seigenthaler, John, 77, 81, 83, 84, 137,
  278

Sellers, Cleveland, 162, 229, 235, 248–50,
  253, 260–61, 289, 610
Selma, Ala., 154–57, 207–32
Selma (film), 510
Selma Times-Journal, 155
Selma-to-Montgomery Marches, 215–32
  anniversaries of, 352
  designated as historic trail, 433
  idea for, 215
  Jackson and, 353
  thirty-fifth anniversary of, 509
  Turnaround Tuesday, 225–26
  see also Bloody Sunday
Senate, U.S., 173, 307, 326
  Appropriations Committee, 462, 463
  Civil Rights Act passed by, 173
  Judiciary Committee, 396, 472,
    474–75
  and National Museum of African
    American History and Culture,
    459, 464, 466
  Roberts confirmation hearing, 472–73
  Thomas confirmation hearings,
    394–97
  Voting Rights Acts passed by, 235, 477
  see also Congress, U.S.
Senegal, 193
Sensenbrenner, Jim, 474–75, 504
"separate but equal," 16, 49
September 11th attacks, 455–58
Serbia, 458
Seven Storey Mountain, The (Merton),
  218, 560–61
sexual harassment, 202, 396–97, 602–3
Shanor, Charles, 395
sharecropping, 7, 8, 96, 145, 146, 155–56,
  183, 186, 266, 302, 315, 359, 448,
  469, 471
Sharpton, Al, 427–28, 546
Shelby County v. Holder, 503–4, 510, 512,
  562
Shelton, Robert, 81
Sheridan, Walter, 270–71
Sherrod, Charles, 123, 203, 249, 257,
  266–67